AF330079

MUNICIPAL MANAGEMENT SERIES

Local Government
Personnel Administration

THE MUNICIPAL MANAGEMENT SERIES

Winston W. Crouch

EDITOR

University of California, Los Angeles

Local Government Personnel Administration

Published for the

Institute for Training in Municipal Administration

by the

International City Management Association

MUNICIPAL MANAGEMENT SERIES

David S. Arnold
EDITOR

Managing the Modern City

Principles and Practice of Urban Planning

Management Policies in Local
   Government Finance

Local Government Personnel Administration

Municipal Police Administration

Municipal Fire Administration

Urban Public Works Administration

Community Health Services

Effective Supervisory Practices

Public Relations in Local Government

Policy Analysis in Local Government

Developing the Municipal Organization

Managing Municipal Leisure Services

Small Cities Management Training Program

Library of Congress Cataloging in Publication Data

Main entry under title:

Local government personnel administration.

   (Municipal management series)
   Bibliography: p.
   Includes index.
   1. Local officials and employees—United States.
2. Personnel management—United States. 3. Local
government—United States. I. Crouch, Winston
Winford, 1907–   II. Institute for Training in
Municipal Administration. III. Series.
JS358.L62   352′.005′10973   76–4817
ISBN 0–87326–014–7

Copyright © 1976 by the International City Management
Association, 1140 Connecticut Avenue, N.W.,
Washington, D.C. 20036. All rights reserved, including
rights of reproduction and use in any form or by any
means, including the making of copies by any photo-
graphic process, or by any electronic or mechanical
device, printed or written or oral, or recording for
sound or visual reproduction, or for use in any
knowledge or retrieval system or device, unless permission in writing is obtained from the copyright
proprietor.

Printed in the United States of America.

THE INTERNATIONAL CITY
MANAGEMENT ASSOCIATION

The International City Management Association is the professional and educational
organization for chief appointed management
executives in local government. The purposes
of ICMA are to strengthen the quality of
urban government through professional
management and to develop and disseminate
new approaches to management through training programs, information services, and
publications.

Managers, carrying a wide range of titles,
serve cities, towns, counties, and councils of
governments in all parts of the United States
and Canada. These managers serve at the
direction of elected councils and governing
boards. ICMA serves these managers and local
governments through many programs that
aim at improving the manager's professional
competence and strengthening the quality of
all local governments.

The International City Management Association was founded in 1914; adopted its
City Management Code of Ethics in 1924 (the
first local government professional group to do
so) ; and established its Institute for Training in Municipal Administration in 1934. The
institute, in turn, provided the basis for the
Municipal Management Series, generally
termed the "ICMA Green Books." ICMA's
interests and activities include public management education; standards of ethics for
members; the *Municipal Year Book* and other
data services; urban research; and newsletters,
a monthly magazine, *Public Management,*
and other publications. ICMA's efforts for the
improvement of local government management—as represented by this book—are
offered for all local governments and educational institutions.

Foreword

The International City Management Association has published *Local Government Personnel Administration* to provide a better understanding of the all-important human relations dimension that the word "personnel" implies as it helps shape the structure of contemporary local government. The personnel factor, in this context, has particular significance when—to borrow a phrase from the Preface to this book —those concerned with, or responsible for, urban management find themselves increasingly preoccupied with "the administrative processes involved in selecting, training, motivating, and compensating the people who comprise the urban government's work force." In the 1970s, as every local government manager is well aware, new concerns—equal opportunity, affirmative action, collective bargaining, and many more—have changed the traditional perceptions of personnel administration in one of the fastest growing categories of national employment.

This book contains a thorough treatment of all aspects of local government personnel administration—from historical development to manpower planning, from work force structuring to recruitment and staffing, from the selection process to employee training and development, from compensation and labor relations to motivation and personnel unit management. We feel that the book will be of practical use to local government managers and their support staffs, to elected officials, and to the wide range of teachers and students whose courses touch upon personnel and personnel-related matters. We feel that all these groups of read-

ers will find this to be a readable, up-to-date, and authoritative managerial text.

Local Government Personnel Administration replaces *Municipal Personnel Administration*, a predecessor volume in the well-known Municipal Management (Green Book) Series, which last appeared in its sixth edition in 1960. Our new volume has been prepared under the editorial supervision of Winston W. Crouch, until his recent retirement a distinguished member and former chairman of the political science department at the University of California, Los Angeles. Professor Crouch brings an unrivalled perspective to bear on a complex subject and has gathered together a distinguished group of authors.

Like other books in the Municipal Management Series, the present volume allows full scope to individual authors in presenting their approaches to complex areas of subject matter. Nevertheless, an overall managerial perspective has, we feel, been fully maintained. Like others in the series, this book has been prepared for the Institute for Training in Municipal Administration. The institute offers in-service training specifically designed for local government officials whose jobs are to plan, direct, and coordinate the work of others. The institute has been sponsored by ICMA since 1934.

We are grateful for the help provided by the then Public Personnel Association (since 1973 consolidated with the Society for Personnel Administration in the International Personnel Management Association), and especially to their then executive director, Kenneth O. Warner, during the important early planning stages of this volume. We are also grateful to the numerous practitioners and teachers who have helped us at various stages of manuscript preparation with their advice and comments.

Three staff members of ICMA's Publications Center worked with Professor Crouch and the authors during the development of this book. David S. Arnold, the center's director, assumed primary responsibility during the planning and author selection stages; Richard Herbert, senior editor, handled manuscript review and editing; and Dorothy Caeser, editorial assistant, worked on illustration selection and research. Final editing and preparation of the entire manuscript for the printer was done by Carla Lofberg Valenta. The Index was prepared by Emily Evershed.

MARK E. KEANE
Executive Director

International City
Management Association

Washington, D.C.
March 1976

Preface

This book is about the administrative processes involved in selecting, training, motivating, and compensating the people who comprise the urban government's work force. Like most employers, the urban government must compete with others to obtain qualified personnel who will perform or provide services within its territorial jurisdiction. Understandably it seeks to employ a stable work force, with a large proportion of its employees remaining on its payroll for many years and with some pursuing a lifelong career. To achieve this desired end, compensation and the conditions of employment must be sufficiently attractive to draw and retain an adequate complement of qualified workers.

The modern urban government employs a variety of workers; hence the policies and procedures adopted must be comprehensive enough to apply to a variety of conditions while preserving the central policy goal—employment and retention of workers on the basis of individual merit.

Most urban governments are engaged mainly in performing services; they do not manufacture, process, or sell commodities in a competitive sales market. As entities within a state political and constitutional system, cities and counties perform the functions authorized by state law and approved by elected local officers.

Moreover, most local governments, cities and counties alike, perform a wide range of functions. Only districts and special authorities are confined to one or two functions, such as water supply, bus transportation, electric power generation and distribution, or education. Yet both multi- and single-function local governments employ persons representing a broad range of occupational skills and knowledge and holding both white-collar and blue-collar positions. They seek the skilled persons who are in heavy demand by private-sector employers, but they also recruit many others who specialize in activities unique to governmental programs.

Urban governments differ widely, of course, in the size of their work forces. Some employ thousands while many have a total payroll numbering one hundred or fewer persons. These differences derive principally from differences in population size of the constituency, the number of functions performed, and the particular allocation of activities among levels and units of government within a state. The differences are also related to the capacity of the local tax base to support governmental functions.

Predictably, practices and procedures of personnel administration in a large jurisdiction will differ from those in a small one. This book will discuss general concepts, procedures, and issues that are current in local governmental administration rather than dwell on the specific affairs of either the large or the small cities. Nevertheless, conscious effort has been made in several chapters to provide information about those cities employing 1,000 or fewer workers.

Local Government Personnel Administration has been written on the premise that personnel administration is an integral part of the management process. Personnel transactions traditionally have not been regarded as technical, separate transactions having their own special goals that satisfy only the technicians; on the contrary, personnel transactions are built into the total process by which the local government agency achieves its goals. A second premise of the book is that the implementation of employment policies is a collaborative effort involving employees at all levels as well as administrators and elected policy makers.

Contributors to this book present analyses and observations based on a variety of perspectives and backgrounds. Taken together, the selection of contributors exemplifies the close relationship between universities and public agencies that has characterized public administration in the United States since the mid-1930s. A few contributors are primarily university professors who have worked in government for comparatively short periods; others teach part-time while directing a local governmental agency. Most have served for several years as personnel administrators in city, state, or federal governments.

I wish to express thanks to each of the busy professionals who generously accepted invitations to contribute to this book and who responded so well. I owe a particular word of gratitude to my wife, Lois, who aided in numerous ways, particularly when illness interrupted the timetable for the book. It has been a pleasure to work with David S. Arnold, Richard Herbert, and Dorothy Caeser of the ICMA staff.

Winston W. Crouch

University of California,
Los Angeles

Los Angeles
March 1976

Table of Contents

Figures

Local Government
Personnel Administration

1

Local Government Personnel Administration: The Setting

*For forms of government let fools contest;
What'er is best administer'd is best.*

ALEXANDER POPE

PERSONNEL ADMINISTRATION RELATES to the people who constitute the work forces which perform all those tasks necessary to deliver governmental services and to exercise governmental functions. Consequently it is concerned with the human resources of the bureaucracies serving the cities and other units of local government.[1] In examining the subject, it is appropriate to consider first some of the quantitative dimensions of the human resources thus employed—the growth in the number of state and local government employees and the growth in the number and kinds of functions. Then, after a brief description of the professionalization of public personnel administration, the historical background and the conceptual development of the field will be discussed together in detail.

Quantitative Aspects of Local Personnel Administration

In the aggregate, local governments in the United States represent a major set of employers of the nation's manpower resources. As of October 1, 1972, the cities' payrolls numbered 2,348,000 full-time and part-time employees, or almost 17 percent of the total of persons who worked for governments in this country.[2] This figure was larger than the total of civilian employees working for the federal government and was only slightly smaller than that representing civilian employees working for the fifty states. Counties had 1,343,000 persons on their payrolls; townships employed another 363,000 and special districts, 303,000 more. School districts, with 3,513,000 on their payrolls, of course topped all categories of government employers. In all, a grand total of 10,808,000 Americans worked for state and local governments.

Not only are the state and local governments large-scale employers but, taken as a group, they have been for many years a major "growth industry" when measured by the number of functions performed, dollars spent, and number of persons employed (see Figure 1-1). Their work force expansion has been particularly notable since the close of World War II. The Census Bureau reports that

total government employment in the United States has risen each year since 1953, with State and local governments accounting for most of the changes in this 19-year period. . . . During the 21-year period [beginning with 1951 and] ending with October, 1972, the full-time equivalent number of State and local government employees rose 141 percent, and October payrolls of these governments went up 596 percent.[3]

The phenomenal growth of the municipal governments' work forces during the cited period has been attributed to the increase in the size of urban populations, a result of both the postwar rise in births and the movement of people from the rural and small-town areas to the metropolitan central cities and their surrounding suburbs. Many other factors also account for this rise in the number of local government employees, not the least of them being greater expectations among citizens of what government should do for urban populations. Local citizens generally have demanded that more extensive police and fire protection be provided, more and better public recreational facilities be offered, and health care services be expanded, to name a few new expectations of traditional functions. Moreover, numerous federally financed programs depend on the local governments to implement national goals and policies for health, welfare, and safety. All of these factors require that more workers be recruited and supervised locally.

Growth has been influenced in another way by new technologies, such as those involving the use of electronics. As a result of these developments, the administrative systems are able to perform many new tasks while also being forced to make drastic revisions in many older ones. In some instances, the new technologies make it possible to reduce the number of persons employed in certain types of clerical activities, but they also generate other record-keeping and information-processing activities which require the employment of numerous persons possessing skills not previously sought or available.

Public concern expressed over new policy issues also has brought growth as well as change to the local governments' work forces. Water pollution control, housing, urban renewal, development planning and zoning, to mention a few, have become pressing matters requiring policy decisions in local governments. They cause large expenditures of public funds and additional staff. For example, in 1975 nationwide unemployment produced new pressures on local governments, requiring the establishment of public service work programs in response to federally financed plans in which new sets of workers were recruited and managed on short-term assignments. All these factors that have influenced the growth of local government work forces have made their impact on local personnel policies and procedures as well as on their staffs.

It is probably correct to claim that most local governments are among the largest employers in their respective communities, although data about employment in specific areas usually are in constant flux. The personnel policies and procedures that community-level governments adopt will not only be subject to considerable local scrutiny and discussion but predictably will influence significantly the economy and general welfare of their respective jurisdictions. Nevertheless, in most areas, no one local government stands alone as the all-inclusive public employer. In addition to the city, there is the county and one or more school authorities and special districts—all of whom hire personnel, meet payrolls, and spend tax revenues derived from similar economic bases. Each jurisdiction's personnel transactions are influenced by, and have an effect on, the activities of each of the others. Salary and benefit policies of one jurisdiction are watched by the employees of other jurisdictions; and hiring programs, particularly those aiming to recruit specially skilled workers, feel the effects of other agencies' recruiting. In short, local government personnel programs are not administered in social and economic vacuums.

The Development of Public Personnel Administration as a Profession

Knowledge of how a set of policies or a group of procedures developed over time may not necessarily enable an administrator to analyze and resolve all problems encountered in the daily schedule, but it is likely to provide perspectives that enable one to better interpret and implement the policy goals of one's organization. One may not actually ask the specific questions, Why are we doing what we are doing? or, Why are we doing this task in the way we are doing it?, but the general thrust of

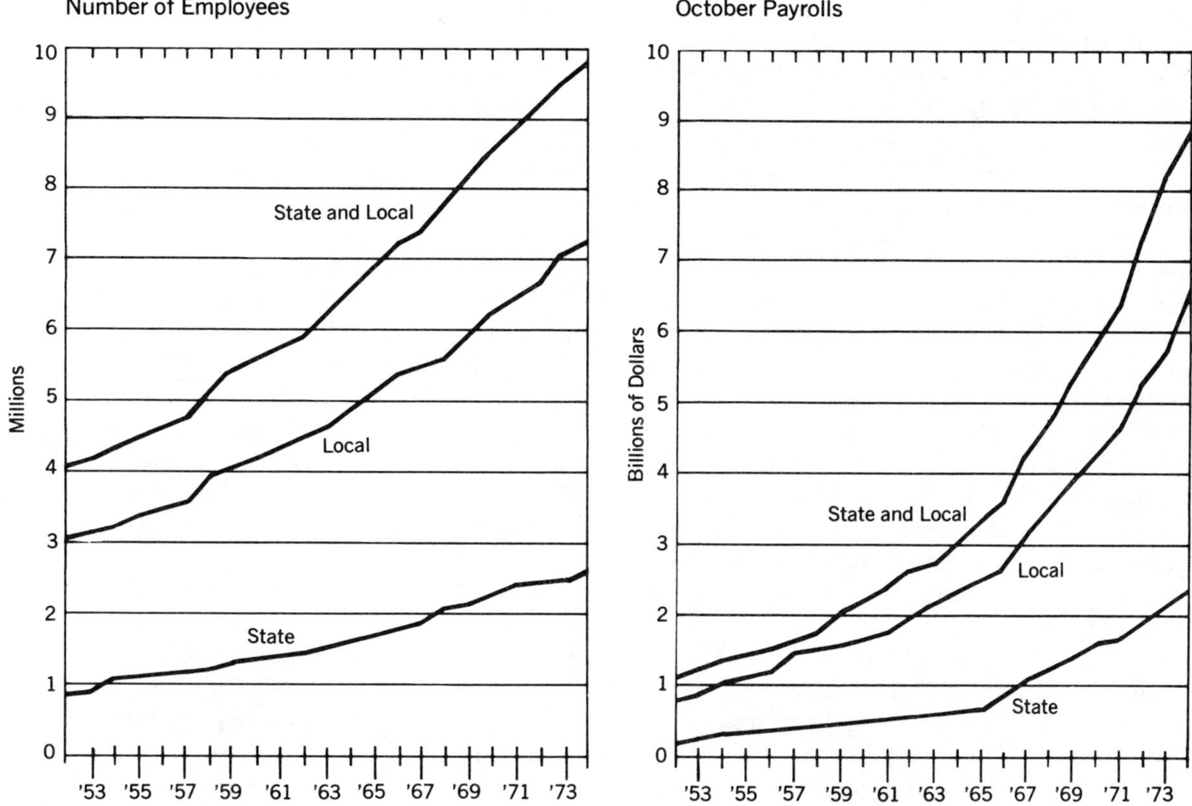

FIGURE 1–1. *Growth of employment and payrolls of state and local governments, 1952–74. (Source: Based on U.S., Department of Commerce, Bureau of the Census, PUBLIC EMPLOYMENT IN 1974, SERIES GE 74, no. 1, Washington, D.C., Government Printing Office, 1975, p. 8.)*

such an inquiry is basic to the performance of professional-level administration in accordance with modern concepts.

Wallace Sayre, writing in 1948 from his long experience as a personnel officer in the federal civil service, as a civil service commissioner of New York City, and as a professor of government at Cornell University, observed that public personnel administration was involved too much with technique and was not sufficiently sensitive to the purposes to which the techniques were being applied.[4]

At the time Sayre wrote his critical essay, the study of organization theory and of the decision-making process in organizations was just beginning to receive attention. Although many individual administrators practiced analytical

methods that they had devised for themselves or that were based on experience learned under supervision, it was not customary to commence the planning of a task by consciously specifying the goals associated with either the entire organization or the specific subunit responsible for the task. Nor was it usual in the rather generally worded statute or administrative directive that initiated the action to spell out a series of alternative means or techniques that might be selected to achieve the goal. Procedures and techniques that had been learned tended to be repeated without further evaluation.

During World War II many intellectually creative persons were thrust into newly formed civilian and military jobs which necessitated the application of personnel policies to large numbers of persons working to achieve a national goal—victory over an enemy force. They often protested the procedures they were required to use in selecting, managing, and rewarding persons under their supervision. Above all, they were impatient with delays caused by procedures which had been developed under very different conditions.

Personnel administrators in the United States first developed a body of information and sets of procedures when they had to implement statements of public policy such as "hire on the basis of merit," "keep political patronage out of hiring and promotion," and "give equal pay for like work." These broadly stated, even simplistically worded, policy goals needed to be implemented by specifically devised procedures and techniques, but frequently the broad statements were also augmented by detailed statutory language, commission rules, or, in the case of local governments, charter provisions intended to limit the administrators' authority.

Nevertheless, personnel administration, like other areas of the administrative discipline, has sought to establish rational methods to perform activities that previously had been based on intuition, "hunch," limited information, and personal relationships. For example, Tom L. Johnson, a much praised mayor of Cleveland, Ohio, who held office in the early 1900s after making a fortune in street railway development, was fond of saying that he made up his mind quickly and trusted that he would be right 50 percent of the time when making official appointments, authorizing expenditures of public funds, or giving operating instructions. By contrast, professional career administrators find it necessary to formulate methods that will permit them to obey the legal requirements yet get the job performed smoothly with a minimum of resulting criticism when they implement city charter or statutory provisions relating to examining candidates, determining eligibility for promotion, or working out pay rates for classes of jobs.

Procedures and techniques also have an element of the routine about them. Administrators faced with large work loads cannot afford the luxury of treating each case, problem, or item as a unique situation to be subjected to a full-blown process in which all relevant information is gathered and a large number of alternative solutions is explored before a decision is made. Personnel administrators have developed their share of techniques about how to do certain types of transactions. Rules, procedural guides, and instructions from supervising officers seek to routinize the work for less experienced staff members.

Since Sayre stated his views in 1948, there has been no dearth of other views expressing varying concepts about what public personnel administration is or what it ought to be. For example, the annual conferences of the International City Management Association and the International Personnel Management Association are forums at which contending views are voiced, policies examined, and techniques argued. Diverse viewpoints are also expressed by persons engaged in administering training programs and in formulating graduate study curricula used by candidates preparing for administrative careers. Numerous other persons engaged in the more general academic curricula also contribute to knowledge, attitudes, and methods which tend to influence the thinking of those concerned with the scope and content of public personnel administration, both as a subject of instruction and as a practice.

The training and educational programs depend on the research and writing produced by several scholarly disciplines such as psychology, political science, public administration, sociology, and management. Since 1948 the so-called "knowledge explosion" in general has contributed enormously to public personnel administration as well as to other fields. The behavioral sciences and the managerial disciplines have evolved out of several other traditional fields of study.[5] They have produced volumes of analyses, research, experimentation, and discussion. Some of their research efforts have been purposive and problem-solving in intent; many others have been pursued by individuals and teams of researchers seeking answers to questions of interest to scholars but not related immediately to the working world. The outcome of these efforts has been a large body of literature which is organized around several themes, approaches, and paradigms.

An elemental part of any profession is the existence of a body of knowledge and a supporting literature which provides a basis for the performance of those who are considered legitimate members of the particular profession. Professional administrators involved with the personnel process can call on a large literature. Personnel practices and procedures show the influence of concepts disseminated by the literature and the published results of research, although direct contact between research specialists and public personnel programs is still less frequent than is desirable.

Nevertheless, public personnel administration is not shaped wholly by the experience and knowledge of those who practice it nor is it based entirely on analyses and research conclusions provided by scholars in the numerous relevant fields. Many of the policies which give public personnel administration its shape and substance are the product of the political process in which professional administrators are only one, and sometimes a minor, element. Personnel administration, like every other aspect of public affairs, is governed by statutes and rules which result from the interplay between interest groups and ideologies, on the one hand, and political institutions such as legislatures, executives, courts, and administrative commissions, on the other. Policies like those which insist that selection be made in accordance with a rule of three (requiring consideration for employment from among the three highest ranked available candidates) or that hiring preference be given to military veterans are widely established examples of the impact on public personnel policy made by the demands of interest groups despite alternative views expressed by some professionals or researchers.

Recent federal court decisions which require that job relatedness rather than general personal aptitude be the primary criterion of tests illustrate another type of influence, one which has resulted from the application of judicial concepts of fairness to a specific problem even though previous research and practice may have been moving in different directions. Like-

wise, federal legislation adopted in response to political interest group demands on the Congress, such as the laws that established nationwide standards for hours of employment and set compensation norms for work performed in excess of a standard number of hours, is another example showing how the interrelationships in a federal political system affect local personnel administration.

Historical and Conceptual Aspects of Public Personnel Administration

The theoretical and policy underpinnings on which the performance of public personnel administration rests have undergone numerous changes over several decades. They grew first out of broad political attitudes and concerns. In the twentieth century they have been influenced by concepts in the political, administrative, and academic worlds relating to theories of organization, management, and the role of the federal, state, or local executive in a democratic form of government.

The first deliberate consideration of public policies concerning federal government personnel took place in the United States during the Reconstruction era following the Civil War. Civil service reform agitation led to the adoption by Congress of the pioneering Pendleton Act in 1883.[6] Urban and local governments did not establish personnel policies by statute or charter until shortly before 1900. Until then, the practice of patronage almost completely dominated their affairs.

THE PATRONAGE SYSTEM

The Jacksonian or populist justification for patronage in government employment rested on the notion that the tasks of government did not require education, training, or experience, and consequently any citizen could perform them. Exponents of this view professed a belief in the equality of citizens that extended beyond political rights to include equal ability to perform the tasks of government. From this premise the argument followed that the public interest could not be harmed if those who performed government work were replaced frequently by others. This unsophisticated theory was challenged first by the civil service reform movement and later by the scientific management theories of administration.

The patronage issue in relation to public personnel administration has been discussed and written about extensively. The many books and journals of political and administrative reform tell the story both in general terms and with specific case examples. The writings of Lincoln Steffens and Ida Tarbell, published between 1900 and 1910, are generally credited with stirring most of the public interest in municipal reform, including the development of formal personnel policies.[7] Of more recent vintage is Robert Caro's *The Power Broker,* which gives an interesting and insightful analysis of the activities of Henry Bruere, Frederick A. Cleveland, Robert Moses, and the New York Bureau of Municipal Research in the civil service movement in New York City.[8]

The beginnings of formally expressed public policy toward the subject of patronage were rooted in a determination to eliminate or reduce the use of favoritism, which was elemental to patronage. The determination to replace patronage with objective, analytical methods as the basis for selection and promotion rested on the concept that the primary emphasis in selection should be on skills, knowledge, and experience required to do the job rather than on previous service to a political candidate, faction, or party.

The use of patronage in American governments historically had resulted in gross instability of the public services, most positions turning over with each change in the appointing authorities. Payrolls were also frequently padded, the number of employees hired having no relationship to the program needs.

During the period when patronage became an issue of controversy, patronage-based appointments were regarded as being linked with the desire by political organizations to construct a power base on which to win elections. Many who were preoccupied with the effort to remove patronage attacked the particular types of political organizations that historically had depended heavily on this practice. They were, at the same time, seeking to create other bases for election politics.

Even today the patronage issue cannot be treated as a settled matter. Although the main thrust of today's highly organized election campaigns no longer focuses on promises of patronage but rather on fund-raising efforts and mass media advertising, patronage has not been eliminated. The ability to determine who gets government jobs and the authority to fix the criteria for job selection continue to be two of the most significant points at issue in public affairs. Even nonpartisan election of officers, specified for local governments by law in many parts of the nation, has not eliminated the operation of patronage but has merely changed some of the methods used.

Moreover, political interest groups are often vigorously active in demanding the appointment of certain persons in preference to others for routine as well as policy-making jobs. The alleged basis of these group demands is not desire to win future elections but to influence the scope or direction of administrative programs. These interest groups range from those who are concerned mainly with programs and who desire to see persons who are trained in favored methods or indoctrinated in preferred attitudes appointed to key positions, to ethnic and national-origin groups who want to obtain employment for larger numbers of their constituents.

THE CIVIL SERVICE MOVEMENT

Historically the civil service movement in local governments was based on efforts to curb those uses of political favoritism considered most injurious to the public interest. Its objective was to achieve what Frederick C. Mosher has called "government by the good."[9] It intended to remove the coercive pressures that caused public employees to contribute money and time to partisan political candidates, to the detriment of their performance in the work for which they were being paid.

In general, civil service procedures, policies, and organizations first employed in local and municipal government were copies of those developed by the Pendleton Act and other statutes for the national government. These policies emphasized competitive examinations in the selection of entry-level employees and generally supported promotion on a personal merit basis.

The theory of the separation of powers served as the basis for establishing appointive commissions which were to operate independent of elected officials and top appointive administrators and which would exercise the rule-making, administrative, and semijudicial responsibilities required to conduct the personnel program. Civil service statutes and city charter sections were written on the premise that a semi-independent body charged with responsibility for spelling out the details of policy, administering the personnel activities, and hearing appeals from aggrieved employees was the appropriate organization to prevent patronage politics from interfering with the administration of local government. Civil service became noted for its concern with procedures which were based on the conviction that administrators and supervisors, as well as politicians, were likely to encroach on the rights and interests of the employees. Accordingly, the commissions were cast in the role of interpreters and guardians of employees' rights.

Those who wrote the basic civil service legislation did not conceive that public employees might organize themselves as interest groups who would lobby on behalf of their membership and serve as champions of employee interests and rights. When employees did form organizations, civil service commissions and their staffs frequently adjusted to the fact. But, essentially, civil service procedures are based on the idea that an official body will examine the issues and formulate and administer rules to guide the conduct of all parties involved in the personnel administration process. The procedures are based on law and not on contracts or agreements reached through negotiation with groups or individuals.

Because they operate in accordance with rules which they have made under legal authorization delegated to them by statutes or local charters, civil service commissions are subject to review in many of their transactions by the courts.[10] While commissions retain their own supervisory officers to ensure compliance with concepts of administrative due process in relation to employee interests, commissions themselves have been subjected to judicial review to ensure that they observe those elements of due process that the courts have been traditionally sworn to protect. Consequently, municipal personnel administration frequently has been encumbered with legalisms that frustrate and dismay administrators and some citizen interest groups.[11]

The theory on which the civil service system was originally based did not envision that public policy could be the product of a consensus or amalgam of group interests. Commissioners were expected to identify the public interest and arrive at policies which would advance that interest. However, the process by which commissioners are selected often confirms an informal recognition of certain group interests or attitudes toward public policies. For example, some cities attempt to maintain a balance between the business community and organized labor in making commission appointments; others include a representative of city employees on the commission as well. Still other kinds of interests are often acknowledged when commission appointments are under consideration. In no instance, however, can a commission of three or five members "represent" the spectrum of interests that exist in a community.[12]

In essence, civil service commissions have not had a specific constituency to respond to or to look to for support when under attack. Theoretically their constituency is the public at large, although in the earlier years there were in many communities civic reform groups that attempted to perform the constituency role with respect to civil service commissions. Whether the employees regard themselves as part of the commission's constituency depends largely on the relationships that have developed between the commission, the line administrators, and the employee organizations in a particular city. Unionized employees frequently allege that civil service commissions are part of the management apparatus and are not the neutral parties the employees demand should serve as arbitrators of employer-employee disputes.

THE MERIT SYSTEM CONCEPT

Reaction to the rigid formalism often associated with civil service agencies led to the advocacy of a new overarching concept—the merit system—to epitomize public personnel policy and guide its implementation. This change was more than a change of name. The newer concept stresses the processes of personnel administration and gives less attention than the traditional civil service gave to structure. It places positive emphasis on selection, advancement, and retention of employees on the basis of demonstrated individual merit. In its theoretical outline, the merit system offers a series of rewards to those employees who demonstrate industriousness and competence. It stresses selection and reward over disciplinary action. Accordingly, this approach to personnel administration might possibly be called "the restricted front door–open back door" system, in contrast to the civil service plan which was often referred to as "the restricted front door–closed back door" system. Like many characterizations, these contain some general truths and several distortions.

The merit system concept, as it is widely applied, often has an orientation toward the viewpoint and values of managers. Its literature tends to focus attention on the responsibility of managers and supervisors to select, retain, and reward those employees most able to perform particular jobs. The merit concept, however, like that underlying the civil service system, does not explicitly depend on the existence of groups, either in management or as organized employees, to make it function.

When the merit principle is discussed with reference to organization and structure, considerable diversity is evident in practice. Many merit system programs are actually civil service organizations, inasmuch as they operate under semi-independent commissions which exercise their responsibilities in accordance with authority delegated them by statutes or charter sections. But a considerable number of other merit system programs are structured in a way that permits the general legislative body, such as the city council or board, to promulgate the basic personnel policies for the work force. They also make use of a part-time board or commission composed of persons from the community to advise on policies and recommend solutions to disciplinary actions after an aggrieved employee appeals for a hearing by this board. Responsibility for the ultimate decision is placed with the central administration, subject to approval by the elected body. This type of framework has been widely advocated in the 1970s.[13]

A slightly different model places responsibility for personnel administration entirely with the organization's management and provides no formal advisory board. The chief administrative officer is responsible not only for developing and submitting to the governing body proposed regulations but also for implementing those policies.[14] This model depends largely on trust in the ability and integrity of the chief administrator to preserve a fine balance between the general public interest and the interests of the employees—a trust the original civil service concept did not assume. When public confidence in truly professional administrators is established and supported, the perceived need for independent commissions or formally structured advisory agencies tends to diminish.

A guide prepared by the New Jersey State Department of Civil Service aptly summarizes the objectives of the merit system and modern personnel management:

Regardless of the form of government, the personnel officer should be professionally competent, with free access to the appointing official, and placed high enough in the organization to be able to deal authoritatively with top managers of the jurisdiction. Personnel must be hired and advanced in accordance with merit. What they know and can do is important, not who they are or who they know.

The most important objectives of personnel management are:

- To maintain a public service of high competence and character;
- To foster in managers, supervisors, and employees an attitude of responsive service to the public;
- To carry out pertinent public policy as expressed in law, executive orders, regulations or otherwise;

- To utilize manpower resources wisely and economically;
- To provide a work environment which stimulates initiative, imagination, productivity, personal development, and cost consciousness;
- To treat employees, individually and in groups, equitably and fairly; to help them to achieve personal satisfaction and pride in their work; and to enhance their opportunities for career advancement through training and the utilization of their abilities;
- To establish and maintain a career system which will provide opportunities for advancement through training, education, development, and utilization. The system should foster skill development and advancement in accordance with employee interest and abilities;
- To recognize and deal with employee representatives in accordance with law or policy; to promote relationships with these representatives that are constructive and beneficial to the collective interests of the employees and the accomplishment of the mission;
- To maintain the high reputation of the government as an employer and to contribute to constructive community relations;
- To preserve and nourish the traditional values of government, including integrity, continuity, nonpartisanship, and the principles of merit which are essential to the mutual confidence that exists between government and the public it serves.[15]

THEORIES OF MANAGEMENT

Management theories have influenced the thinking in the field of public personnel administration, because the two subjects interrelate in the administrative process. One of the first breakthroughs reached in the effort to create a conceptual basis for management and administration in the United States was that achieved by those working in what is commonly referred to as the scientific management movement, which developed a set of concepts and values which Frederick C. Mosher has called "government by the efficient."[16] The concepts and methods identified with this movement are those associated chiefly with the name of Frederick W. Taylor, although many others active then and since have also contributed. His experiments involved the isolation and measurement of all possible variables associated with human physical effort and the tools employed in turning out productive work. He sought to discover the "one best way" to accomplish production tasks. Taylor studied industrial production primarily, but his method and the spirit associated with it spread to group enterprises generally, including those in public administration.

The influence exerted by the spirit of Taylorism on public administration thought appeared first in the official study commission reports and academic literature that set the principles of efficiency and economy as the primary goals of administration. One of the first expressions of this mode of thought was the report by the Taft Commission on Efficiency and Economy which was presented to the President and Congress in 1912. Staff work for the commission had been directed by Frederick A. Cleveland, who previously had headed the New York Bureau of Municipal Research. Much of the management theory that went into the report was based on work done earlier in city government.

Other highly influential national commission reports that reflected somewhat similar philosophies and methodologies were those made by the President's Committee on Administrative Management (Brownlow Committee) to President Franklin D. Roosevelt in 1937, and by the U.S. Commission on the Organization of the Executive Branch of the Government (Hoover Commission) in 1955. Each of these was based on the concept that getting well-trained persons into government positions was not sufficient in itself but that government should also be conducted economically and efficiently.

The Brownlow Committee was particularly concerned with accomplishing administrative reorganization in order to focus authority in the chief executive, who then would direct administrative operations. To achieve this overarching objective, the committee recommended that the personnel function be placed under the chief executive, who then would become fully involved in the development of the government's personnel policies. Thus the Brownlow report was the first major official study to break away sharply from the thought patterns affirmed by the classical civil service reform movement and advocate an executive-centered merit system.

The Brownlow and Hoover reports, although concerned solely with national administration, had considerable influence on those persons addressing themselves to local government issues. (During the 1950s and early 1960s, "Little Hoover" commissions were set up to study the organization and operation of states and cities.) Both of these prestigious study commissions based their investigations on the premise that the objectives of efficiency and economy could be achieved only through the empirical study of data and the development and application of the principles of administration. The theory of public administration advanced by some considered it necessary to separate the study of administration from that of politics: The proper sphere of administration was to be one in which only analytical methods were employed.[17]

One effect of the approach taken by those who were influenced by the efficiency and economy school of thought was that it resulted in organization of the factual data about public administration into several distinct categories. Consequently, the literature about public administration as well as the content of university classes preparing students for administrative careers came to be structured according to conceptual terms such as organization, management, personnel administration, planning, and budgeting.

One of the major books that appeared in the 1930s and which influenced public administration thought for two decades was prepared for use by the Brownlow Committee. It was *Papers on the Science of Administration,* by Luther Gulick and Lyndall Urwick.[18] The first author was one of the three members of the Committee on Administrative Management; the second had extensive experience with industrial organization and as a consultant to manufacturing and service enterprises in England. Gulick's essay, "The Theory of Organization," introduced the acronym so often associated with his work thereafter—POSDCORB—which called attention to planning, organizing, staffing, directing, coordinating, reporting, and budgeting as the major functional elements of the chief executive's work.

While personnel administration was considered primarily a "staff" function in organization by Gulick and Urwick in other portions of the book, in this essay Gulick wrote that

the necessity for central purchase, for personnel administration, for budgeting and fiscal control rests on other considerations and not on the philosophy of the general staff.[19]

Moreover, he emphasized that "coordination by ideas" was more important than organization for the proper functioning of the executive, noting:

The most difficult task of the chief executive is not to command, it is leadership, that is, the development of the desire and will to work together for a purpose in the minds of those who are associated in any activity. Human beings are compounded of cogitation and emotion and do not function well when treated as though they were merely cogs in motion. . . .

Personnel administration becomes of extraordinary significance, not merely from the standpoint of finding qualified appointees for the various positions, but even more from the standpoint of assisting in the selection of individuals and in the maintenance of conditions which will serve to create a foundation of loyalty and enthusiasm. The new drive for career government service and for in-service training derives its significance not so much from the fact that better persons will enter the service when the chance for promotion is held out to them, but from the fact that a career service is a growing and learning service, one that believes in the work and in the future of the enterprise.[20]

In emphasizing the executive's responsibility to develop the desire and will to work together with staff and to create a foundation of enthusiasm and loyalty, Gulick prefigured the work of those like industrial executive Chester Barnard whose writings about the role of the executive were widely read during the 1940s and 1950s. Nevertheless, Gulick's preoccupation with principles of organization and POSDCORB caused most later readers to associate his writings with the "principles" approach to public administration and to the efficiency and economy school of thought. Barnard, on the other hand, has been remembered more for his analyses of the management process and for perceptions of the human relationships between managers and other participants in the organization.[21]

BEGINNINGS IN INSTRUCTION

Programs for teaching personnel administration began in the United States about the same time that the scientific management and the efficiency and economy movements began producing literature. One of the first programs to give instruction and therefore to conceptualize about public personnel administration was the New York Bureau of Municipal Research, founded in 1907. Its training program, an adjunct of its research, consultation, and advocacy projects, was led by Charles A. Beard, who is better remembered for his later work as an American historian. Beard, however, had a great deal to do with the formulation of ideas about public personnel administration during the period from 1911 to 1925. Trainees were given some group instruction and were assigned to work with staff members on field research and consultation projects in city government while also participating in staff discussions. Instruction was mainly by what is now known as internship experience. Initially the bureau had no academic connection, although it later was affiliated with Columbia University.

Numerous other bureaus of municipal research patterned on the New York institution were soon organized in other large cities. Not all conducted training programs, but one of the best known for this phase of work was the Detroit bureau, headed by Lent D. Upson, which ultimately affiliated with Wayne State University. Most of these early bureaus were financed by public interest donors and were dedicated to municipal reform. Most were active supporters of municipal civil service programs, although many soon expressed a preference for executive leadership in personnel programs. The Institute of Public Administration, the successor to the New York bureau, became an influential national voice in this matter under the leadership of Luther Gulick.

During the decade of the 1920s many universities established bureaus of municipal research on their campuses as a community service arm. In most instances, the director of the bureau held a faculty appointment in the political science department, taught classes in public administration, and directed a service and information program which reached city officials in the neighboring areas or the state at large. Major examples were the bureaus at the state universities of Illinois, Minnesota, Kansas, and Texas. Somewhat later, bureaus of public administration were formed at the state universities of California (Berkeley), Michigan, Alabama, and Oregon providing similar but expanded programs. By 1950 numerous state, municipal, and endowed universities had established bureaus of government or administration with programs similar to those of the prototypes.

Establishment of university instruction in public personnel administration was closely associated with the political science departments when the latter separated from political economy, history, and public law faculties. Frank Goodnow at Columbia University and John A. Fairlie at the University of Illinois were among the first to offer courses in public administration and also to devote attention to the subject of personnel. These beginnings date between 1908 and 1915. Somewhat later William Bennett Munro created a municipal administration course at Harvard. Leonard D. White at the University of Chicago was the first both to make public personnel administration a specialized subject of university research and teaching and to become a nationally recognized scholar. He had been recruited and encouraged by his chairman, Charles E. Merriam, one of the major academic statesmen of the era as well as a civic reform activist in Chicago. From 1930 on, most political science departments having sufficiently large staffs to permit specialization could offer at least an undergraduate course in public personnel administration. Those sponsoring master's programs in public administration also often gave graduate courses in the subject.

The Role of Textbooks. The initial university efforts to offer courses in this subject were stimulated and their content shaped by textbooks that were then just appearing. Much of the early instruction had depended on official reports and advocacy literature prepared by persons involved in the civil service reform movement. The first college-level textbook to give systematic treatment to the subject of public personnel was Leonard D. White's *Introduction to the Study of Public Administration,* published in 1926.[22] This was followed by William E. Mosher and J. Donald Kingsley's *Public Personnel Administration,* the first book devoted exclusively to the subject.

Mosher, who was then director of the Maxwell Graduate School of Citizenship and Public Affairs at Syracuse University, had been associated with Charles Beard at the New York Bureau of Municipal Research. Mosher disclosed that *Public Personnel Administration* had been outlined as early as 1921, but that prior to its publication in the early 1930s its authors were influenced by the work of Henry C. Metcalf and Orway Tead who had just published their *Personnel Administration* for business and industry. According to Mosher:

The basic philosophy of personnel administration as an integral part of administration as well as the factors entering into it, are to be credited to Metcalf and Tead. . . .

A major premise associated with this philosophy was expressed by Mosher as follows:

Thoroughgoing reform of personnel administration is long overdue. In view of the recent extension of governmental activities on every level from the local to the federal units, such a reform is required today as never before. Efficiency, economy, justice, self-interest, all point to the necessity of working out and adopting a positive personnel policy. It is the purpose of this work to describe such a policy.[23]

The Mosher/Kingsley book continues to be a dominating college text for public personnel administration. O. Glenn Stahl, who undertook the revision of later editions, is now the sole author. Another pioneer textbook writer who exercised a forceful influence over the conceptualization of public personnel administration was John M. Pfiffner of the University of Southern California.[24] Each edition of his public administration text contained extensive discussion of this subject. Unlike White, whose experience was mainly with the federal government, Pfiffner was primarily associated with local government programs.

The International City Management Association served the municipal administration field when in 1935 (as the International City Management Association) it published its first edition of *Municipal Personnel Administration* as part of what became known as its Municipal Management Series. Revised editions of this book have enjoyed wide use in training courses and university classes as well as in city offices where they are used as a reference source. Its *Municipal Year Book,* another important reference source, contains data relating to city personnel practices.

In 1940 the Committee on Public Administration of the Social Science Research Council published a series of case reports that stimulated the use of the case method for instruction of persons entering public employment. The first set of public administration cases contained four devoted to personnel: guidance to an employee offered transfer; readjustment of a dissatisfied employee; grievance handling; and employee relations and race discrimination.[25]

Authors who published texts devoted principally to public personnel administration after those by Mosher and Pfiffner focused their attention more exclusively on issues and data pertaining to federal civilian employment. They did, however, make reference to special issues in local affairs.[26]

The Role of Industrial Psychology. Meanwhile, with the publication in 1913 of Hugo Munsterberg's *Psychology and Industrial Efficiency,* industrial psychology emerged as a specialized area of study within the broader field of general psychology. American adherents of this specialty tended to concentrate more heavily at first on problems of personnel selection and placement.[27] This emphasis was boosted by the experience of psychological testing in the army during World War I and by the establishment of the Psychological Corporation in 1921 for the production of test materials. Public agency examiners frequently called in as consultants university faculty members teaching testing and measurements. Industrial psychology courses soon explored a wide range of topics, such as job analysis, motivation and morale, training, counseling, and grievance resolution in work groups—part of the training ground of persons who sought careers in personnel administration in either the public or private sectors.

Psychologists traditionally used laboratory

methods but many struck out to conduct field studies, surveys, and controlled experiments, with the consent of industrial and commercial firms' management, to gather empirical data about human behavior in work situations. They implemented their findings in training programs sponsored by firms and some governmental agencies as well as in their own universities and adult extension classes.

Human Relations in Management

Chester Barnard, Mary Parker Follett, Fritz Roethlisberger, and Elton Mayo usually are considered the founding figures in the human relations approach to management. They developed a "process approach" to administration which emphasized basic subjects such as communications and decision making. Mary Follett recognized the psychological aspects of administration and stressed the significance of interactions between managers and workers, stating, for example, that a business should be "so organized that a workman has an opportunity of influencing you as you have an opportunity of influencing him."[28] She also contributed significantly to the idea of management as a profession.

Roethlisberger's findings based on empirical research conducted at the Western Electric Company became a landmark in administrative thought. His discoveries fueled an interest in the human relations approach and provided an incentive for many others to conduct studies in plants and offices.[29] Mayo's major contribution was emphasizing the usefulness of studying workers' behavior in all its complexity, including the physical, economic, physiological, and psychological elements.[30]

Initial Impetus. The human relations school of thought and investigation greatly stimulated the developing field of personnel administration. First, it gave impetus to those who wished to improve working conditions, health and welfare benefits, recreational programs, and similar activities that increased the attractiveness of work and the environment in which it was performed. Second, it encouraged thinking about employee morale, the nature of supervision and leadership, communications within the work organization, and employer–employee relations. Supervisor training and executive development programs stem from much of the pioneering work of Barnard, Roethlisberger, and Mayo. One of the interesting features of this school's literature is that writers using this approach cut across several established fields of knowledge, drawing from several specialties.

Social psychology also contributed to a broadened understanding of administration and management in general. Among the concepts it introduced are those relating to social norms, status, social role, perception, and communication. A subgroup in this field, deriving from the innovative work of Kurt Lewin, examines the behavior of small groups in large-scale organizations.[31] Group dynamics has figured centrally in training, supervision, and executive development programs conducted in government and industrial agencies.

Schools of business also exercised a major influence on the personnel aspects of management, although for many years they devoted themselves exclusively to the study of management in the market economy. Beginning with the Harvard School of Business, numerous universities and a few colleges established schools devoted to educating potential managers, accountants, and investment analysts for the business community. Many of the more prestigious universities recruited faculties from the older fields of economics, psychology, and sociology, as well as from the applied discipline of business. Instruction in management contributed to the concept of the manager's role as a motivator of employees in a work organization to accomplish organizational goals. At the time, it was the practice of business firms to give the officer responsible for the personnel function the title of "employment manager." The term and the resulting organization tended to reflect a centralization of responsibility at headquarters and a reduction in the role of the line supervisors.[32]

Rejection of this centralization theme in the 1940s led to the focusing of attention on the roles of the several levels of supervisors. Passage of legislation in the 1930s recognizing unions and establishing processes and institutions dealing with employer–employee relations had its impact on the business community's conception of personnel administration and the business schools' teaching programs.

Increasingly, firms' employment managers became industrial relations managers, and business schools responded by developing courses in industrial relations.

The Lessons of World War II. Experiences during World War II and immediately afterward with recruiting, assigning, training, and managing large numbers of persons both for civilian and military operations produced new perceptions regarding people in work organizations. Moreover, these experiences triggered the beginnings of a new wave of investigation, experimentation, and application of knowledge. Among the results were new techniques in the assessment of individual capabilities to perform in stress situations, conceptions of leadership requirements, application of classification techniques to the military organizations, training for all types of jobs and classifications, and group motivation and morale. The human relations approach, initiated some years earlier, received added impetus from research studies such as Alexander H. Leighton's *The Governing of Men,*[33] based on a civilian internment camp situation, which yielded important insights into the behavior and management of people in organizations.

Psychology, sociology, public administration, business administration, and interdisciplinary combinations generated new fields of inquiry. One such example is the work of Herbert Simon, a political scientist and public administration scholar who taught in schools of industrial management. His challenge to Gulick's POSDCORB and principles approach and his enthusiastic advocacy of Barnard's perception of the management process sparked considerable research and teaching in public and industrial management.[34] Much of his work concentrated on the decision-making process, but his book, *Organizations,* was a systematic study of the behavior of individuals and groups in organizations. All of his studies drew heavily from the discipline of psychology.

The subjects of decision theory, communications, and organization theory were engaging the attention of numerous other researchers working in disciplines such as mathematics and sociology as well as economics.[35] They not only influenced thinking on the functions and behavior of management but they also broadened the concepts about the organization as a whole and the people who constituted it.

Sociologists, beginning with the German scholar Max Weber, have made rich contributions to the understanding of human organizations, including work units.[36] Weber's term, *bureaucracy,* has imbedded itself in the language of administrators, writers, and political officers alike to describe tightly controlled, hierarchically structured organizations. Managers use the formal distribution of authority and the allocation of responsibility as important guidelines in choosing one or another form of structure—centralized, decentralized, functional, hierarchical, or "flat."[37] Studies of formal organization produced volumes of literature dealing with the concepts of role and role perception relating to managers, supervisors, and workers.[38]

Others approached the subject from the standpoint of managing change in organizations. Chris Argyris, for example, took the position that there is inevitable conflict between formal organizations and the individual; consequently, he stressed the need to replace large-scale organizations with groups oriented to individual need which would lessen the dependence of the subordinate on the hierarchy and encourage the growth of so-called "democratic conditions."[39]

Sociotechnical Contributions. Another approach, the sociotechnical systems approach, focused on technology as a major variable affecting interaction and activity. It has been described as follows:

The view that individual behavior is a dependent variable affected by the structure of the organization, especially by technology, has stimulated research into the relationship among activities, interactions, and sentiments and such organizational characteristics as the physical and spacial arrangements of work and the formal organizations as it establishes the lines of communication and interaction. These researchers seek to develop methods of changing the technology and organization to influence interaction patterns. . . .[40]

The merging of research and investigation by many established disciplines and the advance of the proposition that management and administration were forms of human activity that cut across many fields of study produced several results in educational programs. Schools of public administration, as well as the programs in business administration, assembled teaching staffs trained in a variety of disciplines, with the result that their students received varying blends of interdisciplinary training prior to their entry into the public services. In fact, in the 1950s the proposition was made that administration was a field in its own right.[41]

Some schools, such as Cornell University, combined business and public administration. Schools of business in many universities reorganized as graduate schools of administration, on the premise that their curricula were devoted to the study of management of large-scale organizations—public, private-profit, and nonprofit alike. While some schools retained courses which presented the established concepts of personnel administration, others reconstituted their offerings to incorporate a human behavior approach.

The Role of Industrial Relations. Preceding these changes was the development from 1948 onward of institutes of industrial relations and labor-management in numerous universities. The experience with labor–management relations during World War II, the growth of unionism in industry, and organized labor's increased interest in educational programs provided the impetus for creating these institutes. Their research and teaching staffs were drawn from several academic disciplines, including law, but the directing personnel usually had had experience with the operations of the War Labor Board between 1941 and 1946. The orientation of the research, teaching, and external training programs was toward the labor aspects of the subject. Although these programs were often separate from the business or public administration programs, their presence in the universities made available an alternate instructional approach.

During the first twenty years of their existence, those institutes and schools concentrated on industrial labor–management relations, but when unions began to roll up impressive numbers of members among public employees, they turned active attention to the public sector. The New York State School of Industrial and Labor Relations, established at Cornell University, is one of several major examples.[42] Graduates of these programs have been employed not only as analysts and negotiators for public employee unions but also as government labor relations specialists and as personnel administrators. Some of these same programs train arbitrators for service as third-party neutrals in public sector employer–employee disputes, a developing phenomenon in the public employment field in the 1960s and 1970s.

In traditional public personnel administration, manpower analysis and planning was seldom considered. To the extent that it was, the subject was assumed to be part of the recruitment and selection process. As the labor market became tight in the 1950s and 1960s and the scarcity of talent in many specialized fields became more and more evident, recruitment took on some planning dimensions. But as O. Glenn Stahl wrote, "Manpower analysis is less a settled discipline than it is a philosophy and technique in the process of development."[43]

At the same time, most local governments gave relatively little attention to developing potential labor resources in the local labor market. From 1966 on, the national government implemented a variety of programs, both action- and planning-oriented, seeking to make possible the entry of disadvantaged people into the labor market and to achieve full employment. In response to these programs, many university schools of management and institutes of industrial relations began to offer courses in manpower planning and analysis and to produce new sets of graduates equipped with the skills appropriate to the new specialization.

Manpower analysis and planning came to mean much more than training and placing disadvantaged persons and members of minority groups, important as that is in itself. Garth Mangum and David Snedecker offered the following definition of manpower:

We reserve the term 'manpower' for the labor market and relate it to employment; i.e. work that is employed human effort that results in income. Therefore human resource developments would include all aspects of health, education, and employability development . . . , even such diverse social and economic functions as housing and transportation, insofar as they affect the social and personal as well as the economic productivity of people.[44]

The thrust of federal manpower policy from 1966 on was toward local labor market manpower planning, and the Comprehensive Employment and Training Act (CETA) of 1973 brought local governments directly into this activity. Personnel programs and staffs were involved in the planning and implementation of recruitment, placement, training, and supervision of personnel financed in accordance with the act.

In a slightly different sense, some other national policies and legislation since the 1960s activated still other concepts concerning the employment of the national and local labor markets' human resources. Fair employment statutes and affirmative action programs required state and local governments to employ larger percentages than had been hired previously of women, minority-group applicants, and persons who have suffered social and educational disadvantages. While these programs forced the development of new techniques and procedures, particularly those in examining and selection, an equally large impact was felt on human attitudes, relationships, and behavior in the work organization. This development placed new demands on managerial perceptions, skills, and roles. It also drew upon the skills of personnel specialists in ways that had not been fully used before. In essence, it represented a new application of certain aspects of the human relations approach which had been established many years earlier.

CURRENT TRENDS

If human generations are measured by thirty-year intervals, it could be said that public personnel administration by the late 1970s was a third-generation system of knowledge, concepts, and skills. It had undergone numerous changes in each category. The subjects it encompassed by that time had increased many times over. Its definition of purpose and its generic title continued to be reexamined; proposals for restatement came in from many sources. Public personnel administration in 1975 was very different from what it was in 1883, 1907, or even 1960 (the latter date being the year when ICMA published *Municipal Personnel Administration,* the predecessor of the present volume).

Public personnel policy stems basically from statutes, charters, ordinances, and rules which reflect an amalgam of ideologies and interests championed by interest groups. At the same time, much of local government personnel policy is the product of negotiations between officers representing the public as the employer and representatives for organized public employees. This product materializes as written contracts, memoranda, or as formal policies.

More than any previous development, the establishment of employee organizations has influenced the shifting of personnel administration more decidedly toward the executive-centered model of organization. The resulting pressures cause those officers and employees who perform various management roles on behalf of the public employer to be mindful of all aspects of the personnel process. A nationwide study published in 1972 stated:

Even where unionism has caused no organizational change, there has been a shift in tone or atmosphere of the employment relationship. This new relationship reflects a transaction between relatively equal parties, each with strengths, each with limitations resulting from the other's strengths. . . . Thus there has been a weakening of what might be called 'management-by-itself.'[45]

This same study also noted:

The continued sharpening of the distinction between management and employees has been urged here. This is a logical result of the bilateralism fostered by effective unionism. Such a two-party approach also leads to clearer understanding, more specific accountability, and thus more effective administration.[46]

To perform effectively in this bilateral situation, those occupying managerial roles need both a clear knowledge of public personnel administration goals and skills and a willingness to draw upon the specialized knowledge and skills of associates and assistants.

Summary

This chapter has outlined the general setting of local personnel administration, beginning with a statistical survey of the local and state government work force and its functions. Both work force and functions have grown in response to the growth in technology and in urban populations. Discussion moved on to the shaping of public personnel administration as a profession by describing the internal evolution from hunch to the analytical formulation of policy and procedure and the external influence of the political process. And, finally, the chapter presented a full discussion of the historical development of public personnel administration—the patronage system and the civil service movement—and its conceptual framework—the merit system concept, theories of management, concepts of instruction, and human relations in public personnel management.

[1] O. Glenn Stahl, PUBLIC PERSONNEL ADMINISTRATION, 6th ed. (New York: Harper & Row Publishers, Inc., 1971).

[2] U.S., Department of Commerce, Bureau of the Census, PUBLIC EMPLOYMENT IN 1972, GE 72, no. 1 (Washington, D.C.: Government Printing Office, 1973), pp. 1–3.

[3] Ibid.

[4] Wallace S. Sayre, "The Triumph of Techniques Over Purpose," PUBLIC ADMINISTRATION REVIEW 8 (Spring 1948): 134–137.

[5] One of the early analyses of this development is by Morton Grodzins, "Public Administration and the Science of Human Relations," PUBLIC ADMINISTRATION REVIEW 11 (Spring 1951): 88–102.

[6] Paul Van Riper, HISTORY OF THE UNITED STATES CIVIL SERVICE (New York: Harper & Row Publishers, Inc., 1958). Another interesting reference source for the early history of national governmental personnel policies is the series of administrative histories written by Leonard D. White, beginning with THE FEDERALISTS (1948).

[7] Ibid.

[8] Robert A. Caro, THE POWER BROKER: ROBERT MOSES AND THE FALL OF NEW YORK (New York: Alfred A. Knopf, Inc., 1974), chapters 4 and 5.

[9] Frederick C. Mosher, DEMOCRACY AND THE PUBLIC SERVICE (New York: Oxford University Press, 1968), pp. 64–70.

[10] H. Eliot Kaplan, THE LAW OF CIVIL SERVICE (New York: Matthew Bender and Co., Inc., 1958), chap. 9.

[11] Felix A. Nigro, PUBLIC PERSONNEL ADMINISTRATION (New York: Holt, Rinehart and Winston, Inc., 1959), pp. 354–356; Kaplan, THE LAW OF CIVIL SERVICE.

[12] Winston W. Crouch, GUIDE FOR MODERN PERSONNEL COMMISSIONS (Chicago: International Personnel Management Association, 1973).

[13] National Civil Service League, A MODEL PUBLIC PERSONNEL ADMINISTRATION LAW, reprinted in GOOD GOVERNMENT (Fall 1974); Nigro, PUBLIC PERSONNEL ADMINISTRATION, chapter 2.

[14] Nigro, PUBLIC PERSONNEL ADMINISTRATION, pp. 48–51.

[15] State of New Jersey, Department of Civil Service, A MODEL PERSONNEL SYSTEM FOR NEW JERSEY COUNTY AND MUNICIPAL GOVERNMENTS (Trenton, 1974), pp. 5–6.

[16] Mosher, DEMOCRACY AND THE PUBLIC SERVICE, pp. 70–79.

[17] Bertram M. Gross, THE MANAGING OF ORGANIZATIONS, vol. 1 (New York: The Free Press of Glencoe, 1964), chap. 6; Dwight Waldo, THE STUDY OF PUBLIC ADMINISTRATION (New York: Random House, 1955).

[18] Luther Gulick and Lyndall Urwick, eds., PAPERS ON THE SCIENCE OF ADMINISTRATION (New York: Institute of Public Administration, 1937).

[19] Ibid., p. 31.

[20] Ibid., p. 37.

[21] Chester I. Barnard, THE FUNCTIONS OF THE EXECUTIVE (Cambridge, Mass.: Harvard University Press, 1938).

[22] Leonard D. White, INTRODUCTION TO THE STUDY OF PUBLIC ADMINISTRATION (New York: The Macmillan Company, 1926).

[23] William E. Mosher and J. Donald Kingsley, PUBLIC PERSONNEL ADMINISTRATION (New York: Harper & Row Publishers, Inc., 1936), foreword and p. xiii.

[24] John M. Pfiffner, PUBLIC ADMINISTRATION (New York: Ronald Press, 1935). Later editions of this book were coauthored with Robert Presthus. Pfiffner also wrote MUNICIPAL ADMINISTRATION (Ronald Press, 1940) and THE SUPERVISION OF PERSONNEL (Prentice-Hall, Inc., 1951).

[25] Committee on Public Administration, CASE REPORTS IN PUBLIC ADMINISTRATION (Chicago: Public Administration Service, 1940).

[26] Nigro, PUBLIC PERSONNEL ADMINISTRATION; Robert T. Golembiewski and Michael Cohen, PEOPLE IN GOVERNMENT (Itasca, Ill.: F. E. Peacock Publishing Co., 1970); William G. Torpey, PUBLIC PERSONNEL ADMINISTRATION (New York: Van Nostrand Rheinhold Company, 1953); and N. Joseph Cayer, PUBLIC PERSONNEL ADMINISTRATION IN THE UNITED STATES (New York: St. Martin's Press, 1975).

[27] Laurence Siegel, INDUSTRIAL PSYCHOLOGY (Homewood, Ill.: Richard D. Irwin, Inc., 1969).

[28] Mary Parker Follett, DYNAMIC ADMINISTRATION: THE COLLECTED PAPERS OF MARY PARKER FOLLETT, eds. Henry C. Metcalf and Lyndall Urwick (New York: Harper & Row Publishers, Inc., 1940). She expressed the same idea in "The Process of Control," in Gulick and Urwick, PAPERS ON THE SCIENCE OF ADMINISTRATION.

29 Fritz Roethlisberger and W. J. Dickson, MANAGE-MENT AND THE WORKER (Cambridge, Mass.: Harvard University Press, 1939); Roethlisberger, TRAINING FOR HUMAN RELATIONS (Boston: Harvard University Graduate School of Business Administration, Division of Research, 1954).

30 Elton Mayo, THE HUMAN PROBLEMS OF AN INDUSTRIAL CIVILIZATION (New York: The Macmillan Company, 1933).

31 Mason Haire, ed., MODERN ORGANIZATION THEORY (New York: John Wiley & Sons, Inc., 1959).

32 Richard P. Calhoon, PERSONNEL MANAGEMENT AND SUPERVISION (New York: Appleton-Century-Crofts, 1967), p. 6.

33 Alexander H. Leighton, THE GOVERNING OF MEN (Princeton, N.J.: Princeton University Press, 1945).

34 Herbert A. Simon, ADMINISTRATIVE BEHAVIOR (New York: Macmillan Publishing Co., Inc., 1958); Herbert A. Simon, Donald W. Smithburg, and Victor A. Thompson, PUBLIC ADMINISTRATION (New York: Alfred A. Knopf, Inc., 1950), chapters 15–17 which deal specifically with public personnel; James G. March and Herbert A. Simon, ORGANIZATIONS (New York: John Wiley & Sons, Inc., 1958).

35 Haire, ed., MODERN ORGANIZATION THEORY; Barry E. Collins and Harold Guetzkow, A SOCIAL PSYCHOLOGY OF PROCESSES FOR DECISION-MAKING (New York: John Wiley & Sons, Inc., 1964); Roland N. McKean, EFFICIENCY IN GOVERNMENT THROUGH SYSTEMS ANALYSIS (New York: John Wiley & Sons, Inc., 1958); Norbert Wiener, THE HUMAN USE OF HUMAN BEINGS (Boston: Houghton Mifflin Company, 1954); Richard A. Johnson, Fremont E. Kast, and James E. Rosenzweig, THE THEORY AND MANAGEMENT OF SYSTEMS (New York: McGraw-Hill Book Company, 1963).

36 Max Weber, THE THEORY OF SOCIAL AND ECONOMIC ORGANIZATION, trans. Talcott Parsons (New York: Oxford University Press, 1947).

37 Abraham Zaleznik and Anne Jardim, "Management," in THE USES OF SOCIOLOGY, eds. Paul F. Lazarsfeld, William H. Sewell, and Harold L. Wilensky (New York: Basic Books, Inc., 1967).

38 Peter M. Blau and W. Richard Scott, FORMAL ORGANIZATIONS (San Francisco: Chandler & Sharp Publishers, Inc., 1962); P. M. Blau, THE DYNAMICS OF BUREAUCRACY (Chicago: University of Chicago Press, 1955); M. Dalton, MEN WHO MANAGE (New York: John Wiley & Sons, Inc., 1959).

39 Zaleznik and Jardim, "Management," in PERSONALITY AND ORGANIZATION, ed. Chris Argyris (New York: Harper & Row, Publishers, Inc., 1957), pp. 205–306; Chris Argyris, INTERPERSONAL COMPETENCE AND ORGANIZATIONAL EFFECTIVENESS (Homewood, Ill.: Richard D. Irwin, Inc., 1962).

40 Zaleznik and Jardim, "Management," in PERSONALITY AND ORGANIZATION, p. 207; W. F. Whyte, MAN AND ORGANIZATION: THREE PROBLEMS IN HUMAN RELATIONS IN INDUSTRY (Homewood, Ill.: Richard D. Irwin, Inc., 1959).

41 Stephen B. Sweeney and Thomas J. Davy, eds., EDUCATION FOR ADMINISTRATIVE CAREERS IN GOVERNMENT SERVICE (Philadelphia: University of Pennsylvania Press, 1958); Martin Landau, "The Concept of Decision Making in the Field of Public Administration," in CONCEPTS AND ISSUES IN ADMINISTRATIVE BEHAVIOR, eds. Sidney Mailick and Edward H. Van Ness (Englewood Cliffs, N. J.: Prentice-Hall, Inc., 1962).

42 Both its INDUSTRIAL AND LABOR RELATIONS REVIEW, a quarterly journal, and its research publications list reflect a sharp swing since 1970 toward interest in the government sector.

43 Stahl, PUBLIC PERSONNEL ADMINISTRATION, pp. 97–104.

44 Garth Mangum and David Snedecker, MANPOWER PLANNING FOR LOCAL LABOR MARKETS (Salt Lake City: Olympus Publishing Company, 1974).

45 David T. Stanley, MANAGING LOCAL GOVERNMENT UNDER UNION PRESSURE (Washington, D.C.: The Brookings Institution, 1972), pp. 30–31.

46 Ibid., p. 151.

2

Administering the Personnel Function

All the problems of personnel administration today, whether in the public or the private sphere, are conditioned by the fact of bureaucratic organization. Given that fact, the task of the executive and more specifically of the personnel administrator becomes one of stimulating flexibility and adjustment to changing conditions.

WILLIAM E. MOSHER

J. DONALD KINGSLEY

IF WE ACCEPT O. Glenn Stahl's general statement that personnel administration refers to the "totality of concern with the human resources of organization,"[1] then it follows that we cannot exclude any element of personnel management from our study. Accordingly, in discussing the administration of the personnel function, this chapter will examine and evaluate the various types of personnel departments, the broad range of personnel functions, the organization of the personnel department, and, finally, the two principal challenges facing personnel professionals in the 1970s—public employee unionism and the concept and implementation of affirmative action.

Personnel responsibilities are shared throughout an organization. The governing board sets policy in line with prevailing law and ordinances. The chief executive implements these policies and, in most instances, has authority to formulate policies of his or her own. Department heads and subordinate managers, in the daily supervision of employees, interpret policies and make personnel decisions. Even rank-and-file employees themselves get into personnel administration. Organized employees typically do so through the process of collective bargaining. Unorganized and organized employees alike affect personnel decision making through their participation in suggestion systems, attitude surveys, the organization's channels of communication—in short, by registering directly or indirectly their approval or disapproval of what management does.

While each echelon of an organization may have various personnel *responsibilities,* personnel *administration* most likely will be assigned to a specific unit established for this single purpose. The division of functions between this central personnel department and management's line departments will be studied in detail following a discussion of organizational alternatives to the central personnel department.

The authority, functions, and even the structure of central personnel departments most likely are determined by law or ordinance. These laws represent the judgment of legislative bodies as to the best system of personnel administration in a given environment. Legislatures engaging in rational deliberation will consider the following elements in such a law:

1. In a given environment, what degree of independence from management does the cen-

tral personnel agency need in order to assure the integrity and operation of the merit principle within the organization? Initially, the civil service movement was essentially a reform movement dedicated to suppressing the practice of patronage. Inasmuch as the administrators themselves were largely responsible for patronage offenses, it was only logical to place many personnel decisions—an area much abused—beyond their authority. Hence, the independence of the typical civil service commission. Currently, legislative bodies generally have more confidence in administrators. In fact, legislative bodies appoint the chief executives in council–manager cities and remove them if public confidence in them wanes. Thus more recent laws are more likely to place the bulk of authority in the hands of chief executives with a proportionate decrease in the need for independent commissions.

2. In a given environment, what laws, if any, impose restrictions on the role assigned to central personnel departments? For example, if a city has the statutory right to determine its own personnel organization structure yet must conform to specific state mandates, these mandates must be followed.

3. In a given environment, what functions can be performed more efficiently if assigned to a central personnel department? Efficiency in this sense relates not only to the needs of the line departments but also to the needs of the public, particularly applicants for employment. For example, is the organization so large that each of its line departments could handle its own recruiting, or would the interests of applicants and departments alike be served better by referring all applicants to a central personnel unit? Is each line department large enough to justify forming its own testing staff, or should the testing function be centralized to meet the needs of all departments?

4. In a given environment, what is the need for uniformity in the development and application of personnel policy? Uniformity is possible at least theoretically, since most policy formulation is reserved to top management or delegated to a central personnel unit. It

is difficult to conceive of a situation in which some degree of uniformity is not important, particularly since the advent of public employee collective bargaining. Unions who represent different groups of workers in the same jurisdiction always will seek the optimum from among the various packages of employment conditions. Even unorganized employees are quick to point out other departments which apparently treat their employees better. Therefore, some centralization of policy formulation is necessary, although the urgency of this need does vary from jurisdiction to jurisdiction.

Types of Personnel Organization

THE INDEPENDENT CIVIL SERVICE COMMISSION

For decades the independent civil service commission, with administrative authority over certain personnel functions, was the model for personnel management in most progressive local governments. According to this model, an independent commission composed of three or five members was created. Usually the commissioners were appointed by the mayor or some other chief executive. However, various procedures evolved which served to minimize mayoral control over the commission. Most common of these procedures was the long-term appointment (usually six years) of commissioners in order to span the term of most mayors. Another protection was the prohibition against dismissal of a commissioner except for just cause, which was aired at a public hearing. This prevented mayors from creating vacancies which they could then fill with their partisans. Other variations of checks included appointment of each commissioner by a different appointing authority and appointment by the mayor from a list compiled by a distinguished panel established solely for the purpose of making nominations.

Basic Assumptions. The basic assumption underlying the concept of assigning personnel authority to an independent agency was that it was the public administrators who needed policing. These officials were perceived as rascals who, in the absence of any regulation or external controls, would instinctively revert to the spoils system. Hence, the authority given to the independent commission, especially in the early reform period, often focused on those functions most frequently abused. Most common was the testing and certification function. If public administrators were suspected of appointing political allies, the independent commission would then hold examinations and certify not more than three or five candidates for consideration for appointment. If the administration was accused of promoting only its political friends, the law empowered the commission to give promotional tests and in some cases certify only the name of the top-scoring candidate.

The foundation of the independent commission's authority lay in its power to establish the position or job classification plan, which would ensure that all employees be treated equally. The classification plan helped determine who was eligible to compete for appointment or promotion. Administrators thus were prevented from favoring friends with excessive pay raises while withholding raises from political opponents. Enforcement powers were given to the commission, usually through the requirement of payroll certification. The jurisdiction's disbursing officer was enjoined from making any salary payment without civil service commission certification that each appointment had been made in accordance with law.

Civil service commissioners, like many members of other public boards, could be characterized as amateurs. It was purely coincidental if a commissioner had any competence in personnel matters. They also could be characterized as politically motivated. Laws frequently specified that not more than two out of three or three out of five commissioners be of the same political party. According to this logic, bipartisanship was equated with nonpartisanship.

As amateurs, commissioners were generally not compensated, or they might receive a token salary. It was assumed they would function part-time, meeting once a month or, in exceptional situations, once a week. Given these conditions, clearly they needed authority to hire staff. Usually the top-ranking staff member was referred to as the secretary and chief examiner of the commission. The size of the remaining staff depended on the size of the commission and the scope of authority granted to the commissioners. All detailed work was performed by the staff. The extent of commission review depended upon circumstance. Generally the commission adopted and modified its rules, regulations, and policies upon recommendation by the staff.

The principal function reserved for the commission itself, as distinguished from its staff, was hearing employee appeals. Civil service employees, after completing a probationary period, were given the statutory right to appeal dismissals, demotions, and in some instances, suspensions. Except in the largest jurisdictions, such appeals were always heard by the commission itself sitting as a court. Depending on the law, the commission's decision—which could uphold, reverse, or modify the particular action—might be final, could be appealed to a court, or might only be advisory to the appointing authority.

Limitation of Commission Authority. The extent of the authority of the independent commission, in addition to being influenced by the political climate of the state or local jurisdiction, was also influenced by the particular stage of personnel administration development prevailing when the law mandating the commission was passed. Laws enacted before the 1930s came when personnel administration was in a rather primitive stage. Beginning in the 1930s the scope of personnel administration broadened. Legislation then began reflecting this change, while some older laws were updated. As personnel administration matured as a profession, enterprising civil service staffs saw opportunities for contributions to their jurisdictions more useful than mere policing of wrongdoing. Thus, while not legally authorized to do so, some staffs developed programs considered quite comprehensive and forward-looking for their time. Staffs of cities such as Los Angeles, Milwaukee, and Detroit continue to enjoy excellent reputations for professionalism in both procedure and program.

By contrast, other commission staffs were content either to continue in their legally-mandated policing role, or else they were legally constrained from expansion of function on the reasoning that additional power by the independent commission was assumed to erode the power granted to the organization's administration. Some commissions still are more comfortable with a limited role and distrust management to the point that policing, rather than cooperating, is the animating activity. This attitude has its merits, as partisan politics is not dead in all local governments.

An Evaluation. Unquestionably, the concept of the independent civil service commission was right for its time. For half a century, beginning in 1883 with the Pendleton Act, civil service commissions served as the guardians of the merit principle. Their stewardship of that principle was one of the forces which produced effective and positive change in many local governments.

It should be recognized, however, that the independence of civil service commissions is further evidence of American faith in structure —a faith which of course can be discerned in areas other than personnel. Theoretically, patronage was an evil which could be eliminated simply by erecting an independent structure housing the guardians of merit. As it has actually turned out, this structural independence has remained in effect in many jurisdictions even after the commissions learned they could retain their integrity while still cooperating with the administrators whose actions they were established to police. To the extent, then, that cooperation is proper and mutually useful, independence becomes less compelling. It is for this reason that many cities have developed staff personnel departments as an alternative organization model to the independent commission.

THE STAFF PERSONNEL DEPARTMENT

The principal alternative model to the independent civil service commission is the staff personnel department. (The basic guidelines for this model are set forth in the model city charter of the National Municipal League.[2]) In this type of organization, the chief executive —the mayor or city manager—appoints the personnel director who in turn appoints the personnel staff. The personnel director is a member of the executive staff and participates in management along with the department managers.

Obviously, this type of organization must be specified or at least generally authorized by law. Frequently it is accompanied by legal authorization for the personnel director, or the city manager on recommendation of the personnel director, to make rules and regulations governing personnel matters, which may or may not require approval of the city council.

Very often an independent board exists as an adjunct to the staff personnel department for the purpose of hearing employee appeals, and in some instances it also serves an advisory function. The appellate function is comparable to grievance arbitration under union contracts. While 95 percent of union contracts in private industry contain a binding arbitration clause ensuring the arbitrator's right to review and adjust disciplinary actions, this type of clause is still rare in government organization. Instead, the civil service commission or some other appeals board established by law performs this function. In an informal survey of 66 cities with over 100,000 population, this writer found that 60 percent of the cities responding had a central personnel department under the chief executive, of which over 75 percent had independent appeals and advisory boards.

The rationale for the development of the personnel department as staff arm to the chief executive rests primarily on the need to give the chief executive authority commensurate with his or her accountability. With as much as 70 percent of municipal expenditures going for payroll and employee benefits, there are those who contend that the chief executive is handicapped by too narrow a scope of authority over personnel matters.

Challenges of the 1970s. Discussion of this matter of accountability can be approached best by examining two of the most challenging personnel problems of the 1970s—public employee collective bargaining and affirmative action. In both instances the chief executive is responsible for results, but the ability to achieve them may be limited by the existence and operation of an independent commission. For example, an employee organization might be negotiating with the chief executive or his or her representatives over a variety of terms and conditions of employment. If some of these matters are beyond the authority of the chief executive and fall instead within the bailiwick of the independent commission, the chief executive is powerless to reach a full settlement. To make matters worse, from the standpoint of the chief administrator, the union in some instances may arrive at a deal with management and then go to the independent civil service commission to get additional benefits which properly should have been considered in a one-package settlement.

Affirmative action likewise is problematic, and even more so when authority is divided. Being a single-purpose body, a civil service commission may regard its procedures as institutionalized and unchanging. When the chief executive asks for change in order to comply with the city's affirmative action plan, thereby guaranteeing the city's right to continue receiving federal funds, the commission, with no financial responsibility for city operations, can and has refused to change.

This certainly is not to say that all civil service commissions react in this manner. Some have enviable records of cooperation with management. Some have excellent staffs, performing a broad range of personnel functions and participating as members of the chief executive's cabinet. In fact, some play a prominent and valuable role in collective bargaining. The problem seems to be that the success of these independent commissions depends more on the personalities involved than on structure. The departure of key individuals can, and has, meant substantially less satisfactory results.

In response to the many transformations in the concept and practice of personnel administration, particularly since 1955, the National Civil Service League in 1970 published a revised edition of its *Model Public Personnel Administration Law*,[3] recommending that personnel responsibility be centered in the chief executive supported by a personnel department. In place of the independent civil service commission with administrative powers, the league proposed the substitution of a citizen personnel advisory board. According to league commentary: "The board, although devoid of any legislative, judicial or administrative functions connected with the jurisdiction's personnel administration, can still serve a valuable purpose as a communication link between the community and its elected representatives." In the league's model, the citizen board would not act as an appeals board; this function would be handled by a hearing officer appointed by the board itself rather than by the chief executive.

The league's proposal would place in the hands of the personnel director and the chief executive the responsibility for promulgating rules (called "policies" in the league statement). These rules, which would be adopted only after public hearing, would apply to all the usual personnel functions and would be effective in lieu of prescriptive legislation.

Variations in Practices. As indicated earlier, most medium-sized cities have adopted the model of a central personnel department as staff to the chief executive. However, there are many variations of the National Civil Service League's model ordinance, some of which are the result of the peculiar susceptibility of personnel management to abuse—the very susceptibility which caused the rise of the independent commission model decades ago.

For example, some cities limit the choice of the chief executive in appointing a personnel director by requiring another agency to conduct examinations and then to furnish the chief executive with a list of three names from which the appointment can be made. Some cities provide the personnel director with some form of protection, either the usual civil service right of appeal or the right to demand a public hearing. Some cities limit the authority of the chief executive to promulgate personnel rules by requiring that such rules be approved by the city council; in other cities, the council can only approve or disapprove, and cannot modify, personnel rules.

The provisions for personnel of the 1973 charter adopted by the city of Detroit are of particular interest because Detroit's civil service commission has established a reputation for competence and integrity. While the commission under the previous charter had a range of authority wider than that of many other commissions, it did not have responsibility for labor relations. A separate department under the mayor assumed this responsibility and the commission's staff cooperated with the labor relations director. The 1973 charter retained the commission for purposes of appeals and review of rules, but the responsibility for initiation of rules and policies as well as for all administration was shifted to the personnel director. The director was appointed by the commission, with the approval of the mayor, for a four-year term. Labor relations was made a division of the personnel department, with the division head appointed by the mayor although reporting to the personnel director. Wide latitude was given the personnel director in the formulation of rules and policies.

An Evaluation. The staff personnel department is the approximate equivalent of a personnel department in private industry, where competent personnel administration is considered essential by top management. Many industrial personnel departments are headed by officers of vice-presidential rank. Likewise, from the viewpoint of the chief executive in government, the staff personnel department is crucial. But success in achieving results can be frustrated by the chief executive's lack of authority over the very personnel decisions which produce good results.

The performance of personnel administration under independent commissions varies widely. It has been observed that "personnel administration is the triumph of technique over purpose." While such a commentary perhaps is less pertinent in the 1970s than in previous decades, unfortunately there are still too many examples to which it applies.

Accordingly, the Municipal Manpower Commission in 1962 published a report[4] advocating the abolition of the independent civil service commission and its replacement with a staff personnel department. In the commission's assessment, the independent civil service commission was not coping adequately with the needs of municipalities for professional, technical, and administrative personnel. This report anticipated the concern from the late 1960s on with the problems of affirmative action and employee organizations.

A good reason for changing from the independent commission model to the staff personnel department model exists where the independent commission is denied authority over a sufficiently broad range of personnel matters. For example, cities operating under Ohio law have civil service commissions with authority over position classification but not pay, and authority over determining entry requirements but not training. In some instances this artificial dichotomy has necessitated the formation of a staff personnel department along with the independent commission in order to provide leadership in those matters over which the independent commission has no control. The results usually are not satisfactory. The two entities spend too much time either striving for cooperation or fighting each other, which makes the operation both less efficient and less effective.

Stahl outlines an important point about the independence of the personnel function:

A distinction must be made between doing and auditing. An auditor must have detachment and independence, and for this purpose there is need in public personnel administration for some authority to review what is going on, to report on it, to try to achieve correction of what it deems to be flaws, and, when all else fails, to expose its findings to public view and the potentiality of legislative or judicial correction. But such functions as ongoing recruitment, examination, selection, position classification, training, and all that go with them, are 'doing' functions—that is, they are essentially executive in character. It is idle to pretend that they can operate properly without close association with and indeed without the participation of the agencies that are performing government services and exercising its controls.[5]

The difference in attitudes toward management problems held by staff members of independent commissions compared to those in a staff personnel department is illustrated in a 1974 study of the administration of discipline in municipal work forces.[6] This study included data from 66 large and medium-sized cities— 26 with independent civil service commissions and 40 with staff personnel departments. Staff personnel departments were more influential than independent civil service commissions (81 percent vs. 68 percent) in determining disciplinary policy. While 85 percent of staff departments furnished consultation services to line managers having disciplinary problems, only 69 percent of independent commissions were found to do so. Handling of disciplinary problems was included in managerial training programs in 58 percent of cities with staff personnel departments but in only 38 percent of cities with independent commissions. While 49 percent of managers in cities with staff personnel departments felt restricted by regulations governing disciplinary cases, 62 percent of managers felt such restrictions in cities with independent commissions. Fifty-five percent of cities with staff personnel departments were satisfied that they had effective disciplinary procedures, while only 44 percent of those with independent commissions expressed the same satisfaction. Admittedly, these data were based on perceptions of persons actively engaged in the administering of discipline and, therefore, may have included some bias. But the differences in these percentages are sufficient to conclude that a staff personnel department is more closely identified than the independent commission with top management.

It is worth repeating that structure in itself does not solve problems. Some independent commissions with authority over a broad range of personnel matters and with a tradition of cooperation have proved quite effective. Therefore, it is necessary to consider the climate of each community in determining what system functions best in a given environment.

VARIATIONS OF THE TWO MODELS

The foregoing discussion elaborated on the two polar models of personnel administration —one completely independent of administration, the other completely subservient. In addition, there are various combinations and permutations which have arisen in different environments which deserve consideration.

Semi-independent Agencies.   Some independent civil service commissions are tied more closely to the administration by a variety of devices. For example, Cincinnati has an independent civil service commission that is powerful in terms of its legal authority over examinations, classifications, appeals, and a few

lesser matters. But it cannot even appoint its own secretary. A special charter provision permits the city manager to appoint the commission secretary, who automatically then is city personnel officer. The commission secretary has rule-making power in those areas of personnel management which are forbidden the commission by state law. There is only one personnel department. For approval of policy, the personnel officer must turn to the commission; on other matters the personnel officer acts independently or with city manager approval.

Kentucky state law provides a different method of tying the commission and the administration together in cities of the first class such as Louisville. There the mayor is a member of the commission. While this arrangement poses some problems when the mayor is required, as in an appeal hearing, to vote on an action of his or her own administration, it is at least a recognition of the interlocking aspects of the relationship between management and personnel administration.

Specialized Personnel Agencies.   In some instances, personnel engaged in specific services —most commonly police and fire—have been placed under a separate personnel commission. Both Detroit, under its former charter, and Milwaukee have police–fire personnel commissions independent of both the administration and the independent civil service commission responsible for other city employees. This arrangement permits a concentration of attention on a narrow range of functions, but it does little to solve or simplify the problem of managerial accountability.

Personnel Administration in Single-Purpose Agencies.   American government is replete with single-purpose public agencies, many of which employ thousands of workers. The most common examples are school systems; others include public utility districts, park districts, public housing districts, sanitary districts—the list continues *ad infinitum*. When these entities are truly independent—that is, when they have independent taxing authority as well as the authority to set terms and conditions of employment for their workers—a personnel department based on either the independent civil service commission model or the staff personnel department model is essential. Whether the jurisdiction is single-purpose or, as in the case of municipalities, multi-purpose, the problems and principles of personnel administration remain the same.

Problems are likely to arise if the special district is dependent upon a multi-purpose district for final determination of employee decisions such as salary levels. This dependence may be a matter of legal authority or of budgetary approval. For example, a city council is placed in a difficult position if it is required to approve a budget for a semiautonomous agency that provides higher salary ranges for its employees than are paid the balance of city workers. In such cases, some type of centralization of personnel management seems desirable in order to minimize policy differences.

Another problem, which is most likely to arise within school districts, stems from the dichotomous condition created by two personnel units within the same district—one for professional personnel and one for all other workers. This is not unlike the example given earlier of the specially-created police–fire personnel commissions. Whenever there are two sets of actors, there are two different decisions possible, even given the same set of facts. In developing its personnel structure, a jurisdiction, single- or multi-purpose, must consider the structure's impact on personnel policy formulation and must be prepared to cope with inevitable policy disparities resulting from division of this responsibility.

Personnel Functions

In order to determine the type and size of organization required for personnel management, it is necessary first to consider the functions to be performed. Then it is necessary to consider whether those functions can and should be performed in a central department or in line departments.

There are several general factors which must be considered in making the latter decision:

1. Legal requirements for centralization: Those jurisdictions with independent civil service commissions may find that the basic laws establishing the commission assign specific functions to it.
2. Size of jurisdiction and size of departments: Relatively small jurisdictions are likely to centralize personnel operations in order to achieve economy of scale. On the other hand, larger jurisdictions with large departments may find it expeditious to decentralize some personnel operations.
3. Existence of qualified operating department personnel offices: This factor is closely related to jurisdictional size. It is very unlikely that small jurisdictions can afford a departmental personnel office. Where they do exist, however, they can be delegated a number of functions which otherwise might be centralized.
4. Tradition: Some agencies have operated traditionally on a centralized or a decentralized basis. The original reasons for the tradition may no longer be recalled; nevertheless, the tradition should at least be considered. However, it need not be a controlling factor in the decision.

Because of these variables, the following description of possible personnel functions will include those which are most commonly performed in operating (or line) departments but which will be found in central personnel departments when, for whatever reason, the operating departments cannot perform them. (Functions which preferably are performed in operating departments are identified by the abbreviation OD).

1. Policy formulation and control
   a. Develop and implement policies in all aspects of personnel administration; secure administrative and legislative approval as required; issue in practicable form to operating managers and employees.
   b. Interpret policy statements as they apply to new or unusual situations.
   c. Audit personnel transactions, using the authority of payroll certification requirements when they exist, to assure conformance with law and organization rules and policies.
2. Job analysis and salary administration
   a. Assemble detailed descriptions on new or changed positions, with the aid of operating managers.

b. Evaluate such positions in relation to existing class specifications.

c. Develop new or interpret existing class specifications in light of changing conditions, in cooperation with operating managers.

d. Use job analysis techniques to discern organizational problems; consult operating managers for solutions to problems.

e. Develop lines of promotion based on job qualifications and relate results to studies of training needs and resources.

f. Study wage factors recognized by organization policy, and make recommendations for salary adjustments based upon these factors.

g. Recommend pay scales other than the usual scales for new appointees when justified (OD).

h. Recommend special pay scales in accordance with policy when justified for employees in special conditions such as hazardous assignments, shift differentials, meritorious service, etc. (OD).

i. Maintain information on wages, salaries, and benefits necessary for union negotiations.

j. Administer provisions of wage and hour laws relevant to jurisdiction.

k. Evaluate the jurisdiction's total compensation package, including such forms of nonmonetary compensation as leave, insurance, retirement benefits, and medical services.

3. Staffing

a. Develop and administer the jurisdiction's affirmative action program, with operating department support.

b. Identify "problem areas" (areas where women and minority groups are under- or overrepresented) and then ascertain staffing needs.

c. Develop aggressive recruitment techniques.

d. Compile comprehensive directories giving sources of supply of qualified applicants.

e. Improve the quality of applicants when necessary by conducting pre-examination training programs.

f. Develop, administer, grade, rank, and validate examinations for entry into the service and for promotion where promotions are based on examination; obtain assistance of operating managers as required.

g. Requisition lists of eligible applicants; conduct interviews; select appointees from the list (OD).

h. Conduct background investigation of eligible candidates or delegate this task to operating managers, depending on organization resources and the nature of the position.

i. Maintain qualifications file on current employees, in cooperation with operating departments, and refer to it when considering promotions, training, and special assignments.

j. Check new appointments for adherence to law, organization policy, and the rules governing selection.

k. Evaluate placements through follow-up inquiry with managers.

4. Performance standards and evaluation

a. Develop a system for rating and for recording ratings of employees throughout jurisdiction.

b. Set up performance standards (OD).

c. Make appraisals of performance in accordance with performance standards and record appraisals using the rating system (OD).

d. Provide guidance to operating managers developing and improving employee performance.

e. Develop and encourage the use of various forms of employee recognition aimed at improving performance.

f. Develop a disciplinary action policy and cooperate with operating managers in its administration, with the positive objective of improving employee performance.

5. Training and development

a. Develop training policy which identifies the roles of the central personnel department, operating departments, managers or supervisors, and employees in providing employee training which meets the organization's affirmative action requirements.

b. Make continuing analyses of training needs, in cooperation with operating departments.

c. Set up training programs in accordance with policy, or assist operating departments in establishing their own training programs.

d. Prepare training materials.

e. Educate managers in on-the-job training techniques.

f. Serve as liaison with outside training resources such as universities, vocational schools, and professional organizations.

g. Develop, with the cooperation of operating departments, an adequate safety education program.

h. Check periodically on the adequacy of working conditions in all departments and make recommendations for changes or modifications.

i. Administer provisions of the Occupational Safety and Health Act or any equivalent state law.

6. Employee relations

a. Advise management at all levels on all matters affecting employee morale and motivation.

b. Represent the jurisdiction in all relationships with employee unions.

c. Prepare for and represent the jurisdiction in negotiations with employee unions leading to agreements on terms and conditions of employment.

    d. Establish and administer a grievance procedure.

    e. Process grievances in accordance with the established procedure (OD).

    f. Counsel employees and supervisors on any on-the-job problems.

    g. Develop and administer a service award program, in cooperation with operating departments, designed to improve employee morale and productivity.

    h. Arrange for the provision of adequate employee health services, including special services attendant to job hazards.

    i. Make arrangements for employee recreation services.

7. Administrative and employee communication

    a. Develop and practice a policy of open communication with employees.

    b. Establish a house publication oriented toward employee needs.

    c. Keep employees well-informed of their rights and responsibilities through an employee manual and occasional supplementary publications.

    d. Organize a personnel advisory committee or similar mechanism for regular communication with line managers.

    e. Develop and implement a suggestion system and other means for maintaining the flow of communications upward.

8. Separations

    a. Develop a system for conducting exit interviews and instruct operating managers in interview techniques.

    b. Process retirements and advise retirees on their benefits (OD).

    c. Establish policies governing reductions in force and apply policies as required; anticipate reduction or any other change as far in advance as possible, and arrange for transfers, retraining, etc., to minimize the hardship of layoffs felt by both the employees and the jurisdiction.

9. Records and reports

    a. Maintain files in conjunction with operating departments on employee work histories.

    b. Maintain and analyze statistics on turnover, employee demography, and other related information useful in personnel administration and in negotiation with employee unions.

    c. Develop forms and procedures for use in the management of personnel matters on the departmental level.

    d. Process appointments, separations, and other personnel transactions in accordance with law and organization policy.

    e. Keep records of accidents and injuries, and process workmen's compensation claims, in cooperation with operating departments.

10. Personnel research

    a. Conduct attitude surveys when appropriate.

    b. Study testing, interviewing, and rating processes.

    c. Make analyses of employee absence rates, turnover rates, and other matters which might affect efficiency and incentive; determine causes of problems and suggest alternative solutions.

Organizing the Personnel Department

The foregoing list of functions illustrates the range of possible personnel activities, to be performed either centrally or by delegation to operating departments. There is no standard by which to determine what combination of functions is "right" or "wrong." Law, custom, and size of jurisdiction are the controlling factors. However, some generalizations can be made. Discussion of several of the factors to be considered in organizing any personnel department follows. (See Figure 2–1 for an illustration of the relationships of these elements to one another.)

Size of Staff. Staff size of personnel departments varies according to the number of employees of the jurisdiction, the scope of their missions, and the proportion of personnel functions performed centrally. Because of wide variations in staff size, averages are not much more than general indicators of conditions and practices throughout the nation. Typically, a personnel department will employ one staff member for every 200–250 employees—a ratio of .4 to .5 per 100 employees of the jurisdiction.

Large jurisdictions tend to have fewer personnel employees in relation to the number of the jurisdiction's employees. This is partly due to economy of scale and partly due to the fact that the organization is large enough to justify decentralization of many personnel functions to the departments. Generally, large jurisdictions—those with 1,000 or more employees—are likely to have a personnel staff in the range of .2 to .4 per 100 employees. Smaller jurisdictions tend to have more employees—from .5 to .7 per 100 employees—in their personnel departments, particularly if no operating department is large enough to justify a departmental personnel officer.[7]

Size of the Personnel Budget. In addition to reflecting the size and other particulars of the personnel staff, the budget in some instances includes information on employee benefits administered by the central personnel department. Thus the figures on total personnel expenditures are not readily comparable from one city to another without detailed information on the items included.

Budgetary figures normally are presented on the basis of the total number of dollars per employee of the jurisdiction. However, in order to eliminate the influence of the cost of employee benefits which might be included in the budget of some cities' personnel departments, it is more useful to compare the salary budget of the personnel department with the total salary budget of the jurisdiction and then establish a ratio. If comparisons are desired, this procedure is generally more reliable.

The typical personnel salary budget per covered employee in large cities as of 1972 was in the range of $20 to $50 a year. Figures for smaller cities tended to be higher. The budget figures reflected average pay levels, which vary from city to city. In general, West Coast cities paid higher rates to all types of public employees; therefore, their average personnel allotments per employee were generally higher. It was not unusual to find cities whose personnel salaries averaged over $100 per covered employee.

These variations indicate that comparisons must be made with extreme caution. They rarely can be used to successfully determine the "proper" budget for a given city's personnel operation.

The Specialist vs. the Generalist Model. There are two basic models for organizing a personnel staff. One allows for the specialization of each personnel employee, the other provides for a group of generalists.

According to the first model, the department is organized around the following principal personnel functions: position classification and pay, recruitment and testing, employee development, affirmative action, employee and union relations, to name the most important.

The number of specialized sections of the department is dependent on the variety of functions performed and the size of the staff. The larger the staff, the greater the need for the tendency toward specialization.

Organizing by specialization theoretically ensures the greatest range of expertise. By concentrating on one aspect of personnel administration, a technician can develop a high level of competence in less time than if he or she were responsible for a wider range of activities.

The second organization model assigns to one or more personnel generalists all types of personnel problems emanating from an assigned operating department. The generalist may be required to classify staff positions, recruit and examine applicants for employment, develop training programs, and serve in various ways as a link between the central personnel department and the assigned operating department (s). Depending on the size of the jurisdiction and the range of central personnel department activities, there may be more than one generalist assigned to one department; or one generalist may be responsible for the personnel activities of several departments. With this organization model, the personnel technician develops expertise in the functioning of the line departments. Such an organization structure is used when a major objective is the improvement of relationships between the central personnel department and the line departments.

Obviously, the advantages of one organization model become the disadvantages of the other. As a result, some personnel departments attempt to combine the two. They may develop small specialist staffs, each staff member dealing with a major personnel function. The balance of the staff might be generalists responsible for the liaison function just described. This combination can work well in medium-sized or large departments where the staff is large enough to permit division. Such a mix retains the advantage of the specialist model—the expertise developed through extensive, concentrated experience—while also maintaining uniform application of personnel procedures among the various departments. Specialized staffs are more likely than staffs of generalists assigned to individual departments to concern themselves with departmental interaction. At the same time, the combination staff does include some generalists who perform the liaison role with individual departments.

It should be noted that large jurisdictions, which have personnel officers in most operating departments, find the generalist approach less advantageous. Here each operating department's personnel officer is able to perform the liaison role and thus does not need an opposite number within the personnel department but indeed may need the level of expertise required in a given situation that comes from specialized experience.

Staff Direction and the Role of the Commission. Regardless of the size of the personnel staff or the type of personnel organization structure, some type of pyramidal hierarchy is necessary in order to assign accountability for performance. The apex of the personnel pyramid should be the personnel director, not an entire commission. Whether intermediate supervisory positions are required depends essentially on the size of staff. If the staff is sufficiently large to justify specialization, very likely then it is large enough to justify one or more levels of intermediate responsibility. Each personnel department is unique; each needs to develop its own particular hierarchy.

The personnel director should have complete control over the staff and be accountable for results. If there exists a civil service commission or its equivalent, it should be limited to an advisory role, to appeals, and, if the law so requires, to the approval of policy, but it should not enter into day-to-day personnel decision making.

The role of the personnel director in relation to the commission therefore is a sensitive one. If the commission is legally accountable for operation of the merit system, the personnel director must develop harmonious relations with the commission that still permit him or her to maintain administrative control over the personnel staff. How can this be done? Essentially it is a matter of accommodating the personality of each commissioner. As a general rule, personnel directors will succeed in this relationship if they are open in their relations with the commission; if they come to meetings with recommendations on each problem which they present for commission decision; and if they can demonstrate to the commission's satisfaction that they can be relied upon to handle daily operations without commission intervention.

Legally there is nothing a personnel director can do to stop a commission from interfering with personnel administration. On the practical level, however, there is much that can be done if necessary. For example, the personnel director could meet with new commissioners upon their appointment and describe his or her ideas of how the commission could be more effective. The personnel director also should refrain from dumping any "hot potatoes" in the commission's lap. If the commission must become involved in some administrative matter, it should be deflected from getting involved with other problems which are comparatively minor in nature.

Most civil service commissions are responsible for hearing appeals to various personnel decisions, primarily disciplinary action. The director's relationship with the commission is different when it is exercising its appellate function. Here, recommendations from the director ordinarily are not in order, for the director may well have made, or been a party to the making of, the decision being appealed. If the credibility of the commission as a neutral hearing body is to be preserved, the director must avoid any suggestion of influence over its decisions. If, for example, the commission meets in executive session to consider the testimony and evidence of an appeal, the director should not even be present unless specifically requested. If the director's advice is sought—for example, on the advisability of a transfer instead of a dismissal—he or she should respond only to the specific request and not take advantage of being present in an executive session to influence the commission's decision.

On the other hand, if the commission is responsible for making policy on any aspect of personnel management, the director has a responsibility for submitting formal recommendations and for explaining and defending them before the commission. Only in this way can top management formulate a set of regulations governing personnel that embodies a consistent philosophy.

There may be times when the commission is called upon to investigate its own director and staff. Since the typical commission is composed of amateurs in public administration who have neither the expertise nor the time to conduct a thorough inquiry when the integrity or neutrality of their staff is in question, the commission generally is not capable of making such an investigation. Accordingly, it is advisable that the commission retain a consultant to conduct such inquiries. A consultant would not only save time but would bring to the investigation the talents for which, in other situations, the director and his or her staff are employed.

The Role of the Department Personnel Officer.   Large operating departments may well be justified in having their own personnel officers and in some cases a complete personnel staff, even though a central personnel department may exist to serve the entire jurisdiction. Department personnel officers work for the department which employs them, not for the central personnel department. Nevertheless, their presence affects the role of the central department and may affect the size of its staff.

Where they exist, department personnel officers normally serve as a link with the central

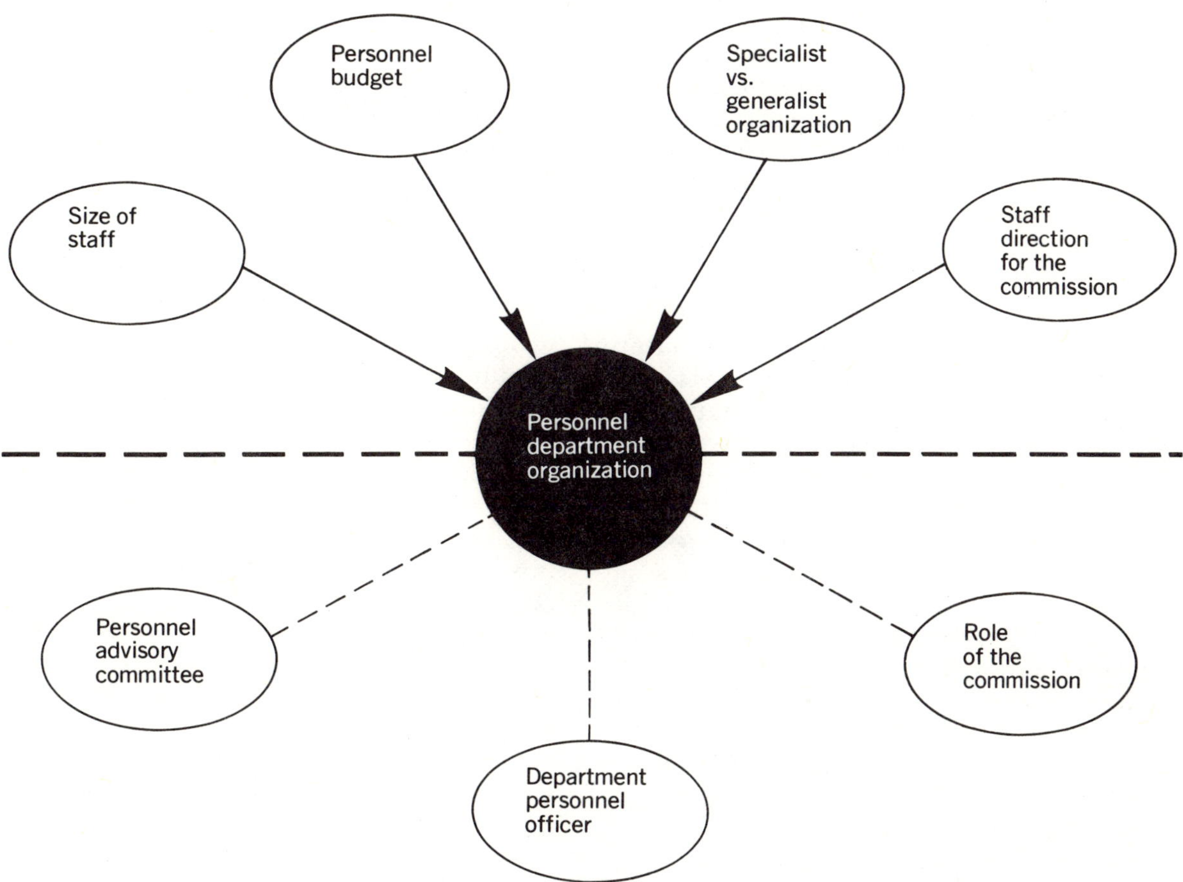

FIGURE 2–1. *Direct and indirect elements of personnel department organization. See text for further discussion.*

personnel unit. Depending upon law and local practice, the department personnel officer is likely to be responsible for functions such as selection, employee development, internal communications, relations with labor organizations which represent department employees, specialized recruitment, classification and ranking of positions, and department personnel records —all of which obviously overlap those of the central department. As a result, close cooperation is necessary to avoid duplication.

The Personnel Advisory Committee. One way to minimize such unnecessary duplication and at the same time assure uniformity of action and policy among the various operating departments is through the formation and operation of a personnel advisory committee. This is usually an informal group assembled by the personnel director for the purpose of discussing personnel problems, policy, and practices. This committee coordinates policy among the various units, advises the personnel director on the impact of present policy, and obtains commitment to proposed change. When committee members are part of the process of policy development, they are more likely to feel that they have a stake in the successful implementation of the resulting policy. Furthermore, the committee is a good coordinating mechanism. It facilitates agreement, for example, on the roles of the personnel department and the line management in recruiting efforts which may require resources beyond those of the central department.

When such a committee is formed, it is only natural that departments which have personnel officers be represented by their officers on the committee. Other departments may be represented by those officials who are assigned the personnel function in addition to their other responsibilities. If each operating unit is represented by a staff member who is actively concerned with personnel matters, then there will be strong commitment to committee activities.

As important as such a committee may be to any personnel director, it is especially valuable if the central personnel department functions as an independent commission, because here the committee can serve as an effective link with the administrators who are responsible for the overall operation of the jurisdiction.

Organizing for Collective Bargaining

The rise of public employee unionism (see Chapter 10) has made a forceful impact on public personnel administration. In the past, civil service commissions often adopted a paternalistic posture toward employees. Commissions may have been powerless to prescribe competitive pay rates, but they could be influential in the provision of benefits (in the form of vacations, sick leave, paid holidays, and compensation for other nonproductive time) which often were handed down in a benevolent manner. Employee morale was important, but unfortunately public employers seldom met with employees to discuss work conditions, benefits, or problems of morale.

Public employee unionism, characterized by the collective negotiation of terms and conditions of employment, was the result of a number of causative forces: paternalism; the success of private unions in getting higher pay; rising expectations among employees of sharing the American dream; and the labor movement's shift from indifference to concern with public sector employees. As a result of all these conditions, by the late 1960s public employee unionism was "the growth sector" of the union movement.

While union membership in the private sector remained stable (and actually declined as a proportion of the total labor force), two public employee unions showed the fastest growth in the entire labor movement. The American Federation of Government Employees (AFGE), representing primarily federal employees, demonstrated the greatest percentage increase in membership of any labor union in the late 1960s. The American Federation of States, County, and Municipal Employees (AFSCME), representing generally the public, nonfederal sector, showed the largest numerical increase—525,000 members by 1970 —making it one of the largest unions in the AFL–CIO. In the early 1970s AFSCME continued to grow at the rate of about 1,000 new members every week. A 1971 survey[8] published by the Bureau of Labor Statistics found that in 87 percent of the cities surveyed, over 50,000 public employers dealt with one or more employee organizations, representing 74 percent of these cities' aggregate work force.

Many state legislatures have enacted legislation guaranteeing public employees the right of organization and representation. Although these laws vary widely, basically they all assure public employees the right of collective negotiation, mandate grievance procedures, prescribe some form of resolution in interest disputes in the event of an impasse, and set guidelines for determining the composition of the bargaining unit and the means of bargaining. (Chapter 10 deals with these elements at greater length.) Simply stated, by the late 1960s one could claim with confidence that public employee unions were here to stay.

Decision Making under Collective Bargaining. The primary point about a collective relationship is that the decision-making process is changed. When unions are recognized, paternalism or any other form of unilateral decision making disappears and is replaced by bilateral decision making—here, agreement reached between management and the employee organization on terms and conditions of employment. The right to agree carries with it the corollary right to withhold agreement, and both unions and public management have exercised this right. Clearly, bilateral decision making is not a process of first consulting with employee representatives and then going ahead with initial plans. Rather, it is a process of presenting proposals, persuading, arguing, presenting counterproposals, compromising, and, finally and ideally, reaching agreement.

Impact on Management. Collective bargaining forces a change in the decision-making style of the public administrator and, consequently, requires new skills. Management must have these skills if relations with unions are to be harmonious. Management's representatives must be capable of persuading others rather than merely ordering a course of action or policy. The authoritarian administrator will be unable to implement his or her ideas, no matter how sound, since employees will be denied the very thing they seek through collective action—participation in the decision-making process.

Another requirement of management is the need for information usable in collective bargaining. The entire range of information needs cannot be described here; it depends on the scope of issues to be bargained and the sophistication of management and union representatives. However, some general types of information are essential regardless of the bargaining context. For example, management needs to know the cost of a given wage increase, regardless of who initiates the increase. Unions commonly seek more paid nonproductive time, so management needs to know the cost of an additional holiday or an extra week's vacation after ten years of service. Since collective bargaining adds a new dimension to the decision-making process, management needs information which enables it to respond to union needs and to sell its position to union negotiators (and vice versa). For example, if other cities' wage rates are a matter of union concern, management may need to study salary levels of other similar cities, even though its basic salary decisions will be influenced more by the local labor market.

Unions generally bring many issues to the bargaining table. The number, which itself affects the range of information needs, depends on circumstances, including the method the union uses to construct its negotiating proposals. The range of information needs is also affected by the framework of bargaining as specified by statute, if one exists; by the state labor relations board, if one exists with power to prevent unfair practices by either party; by custom; or by management's willingness to negotiate only tangential aspects of the standard terms and conditions of employment. The broad scope of bargaining permitted in some agencies means that in some instances negotiations will involve administrators other than personnel and finance types. For example, when a teachers' organization attempts to bargain class size or education policy, the determination of management's approach to the bargaining may involve curriculum experts as well as personnel and budget analysts.

Significance of Impact. The impact of collective bargaining points to one clear conclusion: that any public jurisdiction which bargains with employee unions must have a competent labor relations unit, capable of gathering the information needed for bargaining. The unit must have a close enough relationship organizationally to the chief executive, to whom bargaining responsibility is normally delegated, to have his or her confidence. This means that the labor relations unit should be a staff department to the chief executive.

The unit should be headed of course by a director skilled in labor relations. In any but the smallest of units, the chief executive is well advised to remain outside the actual bargaining, since the skills of even a good executive do not necessarily include the ability to negotiate with unions. The many responsibilities of a chief executive usually leave little time for bargaining, which often requires large blocks of time. Many jurisdictions have several bargaining units, each with its own time demands. Most important, management negotiators may overcommit themselves at one session, but when the principal negotiator is the chief executive, he or she cannot back down at a future session on a statement or commitment once made, whereas a labor relations director can arrive at a session and report that he or she was unable to get confirmation of a proposed position. Similarly, at the end of negotiations a union might refuse to ratify an agreement recommended by its negotiators.

The duties of the labor relations unit vary according to the size of the jurisdiction, the number of bargaining units, the number of unionized employees, the scope of bargaining permitted under law or policy, and the placement of the unit in the management hierarchy. Generally, labor relations units have the following duties:

1. Representing management in formal negotiations.
2. Representing management at both the final internal step of the grievance procedure and then in arbitration if it is authorized and negotiated.
3. Assembling all necessary information for bargaining purposes, including areas such as labor market information, consumer price information and other indexes, turnover rates, grievances, results of employee attitude surveys, organization personnel policy, and all other information anticipated in the process of negotiations.
4. Representing management in the day-to-day dealings with employee representatives. This function cannot be overemphasized, for the climate for formal negotiations is often determined by these informal contacts. An openness in furnishing information, for example, will very likely produce a much more cooperative attitude on the part of union leaders which may carry over into the bargaining session. Willingness to explain nonnegotiable policies—disciplinary standards, for instance—can make such policies seem far more tolerable to employees because, if they are clearly understood, they are less likely to arouse union hostility.
5. Determining management's position in bargaining. The chief negotiator (usually the labor relations director) needs to present management's position and management's response to union demands. This requires close cooperation with all line managers who supervise members of a bargaining unit. All these people need to be able to assess the effects on their operations if management does agree with a given union demand. Likewise, and very important, they should inform the labor relations director of any sections of the prevailing union agreement which make current operations more difficult, more costly, or less effective.
6. Training managers and supervisors in labor relations. Relationships with unions and union members form on the job. The immediate supervisor of a union member may have to handle a grievance and make a decision requiring the interpretation and application of clauses of a union agreement. How judiciously this is handled in part determines the number of grievance appeals and the general climate of labor–management relations, which in turn will very likely affect the next bargaining session.

Supervisors must have training in handling employees in general and organized employees in particular. They need to interpret existing union contracts and keep abreast of changes as they are negotiated if they are to implement the changes in the manner intended by the parties. All too frequently, supervisors learn of contract terms from their union counterparts, the stewards.

Relations with Personnel Department. The foregoing discussion established that a qualified labor relations unit is essential and is responsible to the chief executive. How, then, should this unit relate to the personnel department?

It is clear from the requirements of the labor relations unit that there is substantial overlap in duties with the personnel department. The labor relations unit must have on hand information on employee status—salary, age, seniority, marital status, retirement status, etc.—as such items affect the cost of various employee benefits subject to negotiation. Employee records, then, must be made available to the labor relations unit; duplication of records should be avoided to cut costs.

The labor relations unit also is likely to be the point of contact between union officials and the jurisdiction. But many union questions will arise over matters falling directly within the authority of the personnel department—questions relating to the status of individual applicants on eligibility lists; recent appointees, especially in a union shop; employees eligible for promotion; benefits tied to seniority, and other matters. Conceivably, the union could go directly to the personnel department, but such circumvention of the established chain of command should be avoided. Regular contact with the union negotiators enhances the labor relations director's understanding of the personalities involved, which can be important to the director when he or she approaches the bargaining table.

Training programs, very often conducted by the personnel department for managers and supervisors, should include classes in labor relations. This kind of training experience becomes particularly valuable when a new contract comes into force. Depending upon circumstances and atmospherics, it may or may not be good timing for the personnel department to conduct a training class at the time when a contract is being negotiated or enacted.

These examples of overlapping interests emphasize the need for close liaison between labor relations and personnel units. This interface is complete when both units are under the same head, e.g., the personnel director who serves also as the labor relations director. This is a common arrangement, but succeeds only when the personnel function is handled by a staff department under the chief executive, because the latter is so intimately connected and preoccupied with the union relations process that it would be inefficient to assign this function to an independent commission—even assuming that the chief executive had the power to make such an assignment. The combination works especially well in many medium-sized cities, but has also proved equally effective in large cities such as Philadelphia.

When the personnel function is legally assigned to an independent commission, the labor relations function still is likely to remain under the chief executive, thereby involving two offices which, of course, can cooperate effectively as they do in Milwaukee and Cincinnati. In these cities the personnel staff makes accessible all information necessary in collective bargaining. The personnel director's stake in the outcome of the bargaining process is higher by having him or her serve as a member of the management team. This arrangement, workable in some settings, may resist institutionalization, precisely because its viability depends heavily on the mutual cooperation of management officials.

ORGANIZING FOR LABOR RELATIONS

The Integrated Agency. When both labor relations and personnel functions are placed in the same department, labor relations usually is handled in either of two ways: (a) as a division of the department, headed by a director who ordinarily handles the negotiations, or (b), particularly in small and medium-sized cities, as an added duty of the personnel director, who personally handles negotiations. In either case, the person in charge of labor relations needs the authority to command staff time both before and during negotiations. First call on computer operations is also essential, even if these operations are the responsibility of another agency of the government. Authority of this nature is crucial, because there are many urgent situations during bargaining. For example, if a union presents a counterproposal, it must be "costed" before management can respond; yet there is little enough time, especially if the expiration of the current contract is imminent, in which to prepare a response, much less conduct a cost analysis. Once again, instant command of both staff and computer time is vital.

Whether the labor relations official needs staff assistance on a continuing basis depends largely on the size of the organization and the number of unions and unionized employees. Large cities with multiple bargaining units such as New York and Detroit need staffs of negotiators in addition to analysts. Smaller cities, especially those with fewer bargaining units, may need only one negotiator, with the necessary research done by other personnel technicians.

The Separate Agency. When a separate agency handles labor relations, it is most likely headed by a director appointed by the chief executive. As with an integrated agency, the size and nature of the staff depends on the availability of services from the personnel department and, to a limited extent, from the finance department.

It should be kept in mind, however, that when the personnel department offers staff assistance to the labor relations director, thus keeping the latter's staff small, there are inevitable heavy demands on the personnel staff which are not limited simply to furnishing statistical information. For example, the union may wish to negotiate what it calls "inequity adjustments"—special increases for specific classes—usually over and above whatever it negotiates on an across-the-board basis. Consequently, a series of classification studies must be conducted, and it may be the personnel technicians who must examine the duties of these classes to determine if special treatment is in order.

In short, the advent of collective bargaining has made and will continue to make its influence felt by the staff of the personnel department, even though this unit is not directly involved in bargaining. If experience shows that the personnel staff cannot react to demands within the time limits imposed by the bargaining process, the labor relations director can be expected to develop a self-sufficient staff of his or her own, a development which, among other things, will incur duplication of effort.

The Union View. Union leaders generally request one place within management to which they can go for authoritative answers to their questions. They need information on a variety of member concerns, and they generally seek a direct and ready line of communication.

However, they are not in agreement on the degree of control management should exercise over the personnel function. The AFSCME usually supports the merit principle but not the merit system. This organization, as protector of its members' rights, views typical civil service protection as undercutting the services that the union can provide its members. Furthermore, this union seeks to win seniority clauses governing promotion, an objective incompatible with the conventional civil service system. As the AFSCME perceives it, the civil service is a means of selection—and nothing more—of new employees on the basis of merit.

Police and fire organizations, on the other hand, usually are more supportive of the civil service system. They generally endorse the examination system, both for entry and for promotion. Both professions have frequently supported legislation which would restrict management's control over hiring and promotion decisions—the rule-of-one requiring promotion of the highest-ranked candidate, prohibition against lateral entry, and the like.

Civil service employee associations, assuming in the 1970s bargaining postures typical of trade unions, along with the uniformed services tend to support the more traditional civil service operations. Other employee organizations form alliances according to local experience. An effective independent civil service commission may find employee organizations among their strongest supporters.

SUMMARY

Public employee unionism is a permanent feature of working America of the mid-1970s. Most medium-sized and large cities by the early 1970s were dealing with employee unions, whose rates of growth showed no signs of slackening.

The unions' principal impact on top management is manifested in a radical change in the style of decision making. The change from unilateral to bilateral decision making, allowing less time for arriving at decisions, is traumatic for some managers. Personnel departments also feel the force of employee unions. The rise of unionism is accompanied by closer scrutiny of all personnel decisions affecting the employee/member. Unions demand employee information, often from personnel department records. The number of registered grievances increases, promulgated and supported by the employee organization, although it must be noted that many of the conditions breeding grievances probably predate the appearance of these organizations.

Unions, particularly those in a position to maintain a paid staff, have developed impressive expertise in union–management relations that management must match. For this reason, qualified labor relations personnel must be recruited. Whether they are on the staff of the personnel department or in a separate unit is less important than their ability to represent management with the competence that unions represent employees.

Organizing for Affirmative Action

Federal and state legislation, institutional policy, and the traditional merit principle guarantee equal employment opportunity for all U.S. citizens. However, experience and studies since the late 1960s have revealed that, even in jurisdictions which have established excellent reputations for adherence to the merit principle, women and minorities typically are underrepresented in the nation's work force. Even where there is equitable numerical representation, these "affected groups" are likely to be underrepresented in the higher-paying positions.

Explanations and interpretations abound to account for this inconsistency—the inability of women and minorities to obtain qualifying experience, the lower average educational level of minorities, the reluctance of some women and minorities to apply for positions if they think they might be rebuffed, and various forms of unconscious bias that can permeate the best merit system.

National policy has been adopted by Congress with the specific purpose of eliminating all bias in employment. The Equal Pay Act of 1963 ensures equal pay for equal work. More broadly-based policy is contained in Title VII of the 1964 Civil Rights Act, and state and local employment practices are covered by the 1972 amendents to the act. Specifically, Title VII bars *all* discrimination in employment and the conditions of employment that is based on race, color, creed, national origin, or sex. The act provides for its enforcement through the Equal Employment Opportunity Commission, which until 1972 simply conciliated with disputing parties but which since 1972, when it received the mandate to litigate, prosecutes employment discrimination cases.

Affirmative action means, in effect, that despite the nominal institutionalization of a merit system, the fact that women and minorities have not fared well in terms of both salary and job status requires special measures to assure them of better opportunities. In short, an employer who does not have women and minorities on the staff in numbers roughly in proportion to their numbers in the metropolitan population and distributed equitably among occupational classes and pay grades must, in accordance with law and federal executive order, affirmatively seek to redress the balance. If an employer is found in noncompliance with the affirmative action plan, then the employer's compliance agency within the federal government may cut off or delay the employer's federal funding.

Affirmative Action Plans.   Employers are expected to draw up their own affirmative action plans to reflect local resources and needs. Obviously, such plans vary widely, but there are several common elements:

1. An officer must be placed in charge. Usually this responsibility falls to the personnel department. In medium-sized and large jurisdictions, it is usually necessary to employ someone full-time as an affirmative action officer.
2. A grievance procedure should be developed through which employees may file complaints alleging discrimination in promotion, transfer, assignment, or discipline. This procedure may be separate from, or incorporated with, a standard grievance procedure or civil service appeal process.
3. The affirmative action officer and his or her staff must maintain records on placement of women and minorities and make periodic reports showing "good faith efforts" and progress in meeting goals and timetables set for the hiring and promotion of these groups.
4. The affirmative action officer participates in the organization's recruitment program and its employee development program to assure against any continuing discrimination.

Impact of Affirmative Action.   Many objections have been raised to the concept of affirmative action. Some critics object in principle: They favor equal employment opportunity —simply, nondiscrimination—rather than an outreach program on behalf of any segment of society. Others believe that affirmative action will result in lowered employment standards and performance. (Affirmative action prompts re-evaluation of job criteria and standards, and consequently the courts have abolished standards such as minimum height and weight requirements, because they work a "disparate effect" against an entire class, in this case, women or certain minority groups.)

The impact of affirmative action is likely to be less disruptive if recruitment and testing are handled competently. (These topics will be the subject of thorough consideration in Chapter 5.) Here it suffices to point out that standards and procedures will be preserved *if* they pass a validation test based solely on job-related criteria—a requirement set forth in the Supreme Court decision in *Griggs v. Duke Power Co.* (1971). In the event that a discrimination charge is filed, the burden of proof now is on management and not the applicant to show that the employer did not in any way discriminate against an applicant or an employee.

Affirmative action does indeed have its dollar and time costs. For example, elimination of invalidated "screening-out" procedures which once were easy crutches for overburdened personnel staffs requires added personnel manpower. Additional personnel is also needed to administer the various tests (written, oral, psychological, agility, etc.) to applicants attempting to qualify for positions. Moreover, changing old habits has its psychological costs. As of 1976 the resulting impact of these costs and changes remained to be seen. But proponents of affirmative action continued to believe that it would ultimately result in greater equity, greater efficiency (because once neglected resources would be utilized), and, generally, greater professionalism.

Summary

The purpose of this chapter was to show that in order to maximize the potential of the human resources of a public agency, it is essential that an effective personnel department be developed. Inasmuch as it is top management's responsibility to utilize these human resources, management should retain control over the personnel function. When this responsibility has been delegated by law to an independent commission, the personnel director should make every effort to develop good communications and cooperation between the commission and management.

The structure and size of the personnel department depends on the functions to be performed. A wide range of possible functions exists, and it may be desirable in some instances that some of these functions be performed within operating departments rather than in a central department. Because the functions range so widely, there are no standards which are particularly useful in determining the size of the personnel staff and its budget.

As pointed out in the chapter, the two major problems facing public personnel administrators in the 1970s were relations with public employee unions and the implementation of affirmative action plans—both phenomena arising out of the late 1960s. Both concerns require the attention of executive officers; they cannot properly be delegated to line departments. And even if the primary responsibility for their administration were lodged in a separate department, the personnel department must remain directly and actively concerned.

---

[1] O. Glenn Stahl, PUBLIC PERSONNEL ADMINISTRATION, 6th ed. (New York: Harper & Row Publishers, Inc., 1971), p. 16.

[2] National Municipal League, MODEL CITY CHARTER, 6th ed. (New York: National Municipal League, 1964), pp. 26–28.

[3] National Civil Service League, MODEL PUBLIC PERSONNEL ADMINISTRATION LAW (Washington, D.C.: National Civil Service League, 1970).

[4] Municipal Manpower Commission, GOVERNMENTAL MANPOWER FOR TOMORROW'S CITIES (New York: McGraw-Hill Book Company, 1962).

[5] Stahl, PUBLIC PERSONNEL ADMINISTRATION, p. 362.

[6] Paul O. Popp, James Belohlav, and George Mongon, STUDY OF DISCIPLINARY ACTION PRACTICES IN MUNICIPAL GOVERNMENT (Cincinnati: University of Cincinnati College of Business Administration, 1974).

[7] Figures presented in this section are based on information contained in BUDGETS, STAFFS, AND PAY RATES OF PUBLIC PERSONNEL AGENCIES, 1972, published by the International Personnel Management Association. This publication, normally updated every two years, is available only to agency members of the association.

[8] U.S., Department of Labor, Bureau of Labor Statistics, Division of Industrial Relations, Office of Wages and Industrial Relations, MUNICIPAL PUBLIC EMPLOYEE ASSOCIATIONS, Bulletin No. 1702 (Washington, D.C.: Government Printing Office, 1971).

3

Manpower Planning

There is surely no greater wisdom, than well to time the beginnings, and onsets, of things. . . . The ripeness, or unripeness, of the occasion . . . must ever be well weighed.

FRANCIS BACON

PUBLIC PERSONNEL MANAGEMENT, generally believed to be scientifically-oriented, actually involves much decision making that is based on information far from complete or perfect. It would be difficult to find an example more apt than the field of manpower planning to illustrate the unscientific aspects of public administration.

Background

The concept and term "manpower planning" itself entered into the operations of personnel specialists only since the late 1960s. Before World War II the public generally regarded with suspicion any kind of planning. For its part, management viewed planning as little more than a crisis technique. Only gradually, as the public grew increasingly receptive to planning, did public administrators begin to include planning as an integral component in jurisdictional structures and recognize its importance to effective and rational decision making. As a consequence of this and another attitudinal change—the public's acceptance of a broader scope of governmental activity—planning burgeoned during the 1960s in a variety of functional areas. Inasmuch as this broadened scope required the recruitment into public service of persons possessing new knowledge and technical skills, management had to direct its attention to anticipating and meeting future personnel needs. Hence, manpower planning itself became a recognized field.

No observer or practitioner, however, would deny the difficulties inherent in manpower planning. Great progress indeed has been made in developing methods to compensate for the highly uncertain variables with which the manpower planner must deal; nevertheless, manpower planning at best is a problematic undertaking. And yet there is widespread conviction that, despite all the complications, some kind of systematic attention to a jurisdiction's future manpower needs is better than their complete disregard. William R. Monat, representative of this basic sentiment, goes on in reference to the entire scope of manpower policy to state that it ". . . has a strong and comprehensive aura about it. The reality . . . has been and is likely to remain somewhat less cohesive, productive, and dramatic than the term insinuates."[1] Similarly, O. Glenn Stahl likens manpower analysis to ballet as an art finely balanced on top of a science.[2]

THE SCOPE OF CONCERN

It is useful, then, to attempt to define the scope of concern. Frederick Harbison sees manpower policy as broadly "concerned with the *development, maintenance,* and *utilization* of actual and potential members of the labor force."[3] Consensus does exist for the need of manpower planning to take into account both current and future needs in human resources. However, the primary focus of a planner, by definition, is the future. Stated simply, the manpower planner's chief function is to forecast future needs for human resources, evaluate the adequacy of manpower supply to meet those needs, and develop strategies for adjustment when demand exceeds supply. By contrast, when the labor supply exceeds its demand, manpower planning has only marginal utility as a management skill, although even when this condition prevails, it still has relevance as a social skill.

In the United States manpower planning is applied to several areas in the public sector:

1. National macro-manpower planning to determine the levels of economic growth necessary to achieve employment targets or to fill the human resource needs for meeting national goals;
2. National manpower program planning for administration of programs designed to remedy the problems of special groups of persons;
3. Micro-manpower planning for the specialized needs of private business firms, employer associations, and public agencies.[4]

State and local governments may be involved operationally in all three of these areas, to be elaborated later in this chapter. Another useful distinction in the application of manpower planning is that to be made between "client-oriented" programs (whether in the public or private sector) and those programs designed to facilitate performance in the labor market in general, without reference to specific clients.[5] Manpower planning in local governments focuses principally on the former type of program. In short, the diversity in the overall scope of manpower planning is indicated in its concerns ranging from ways and means of attracting qualified employees, retaining them, and better fitting them into the needs of the organization or jurisdiction.

Limitations. If manpower planning were to deal satisfactorily with these concerns, then its value to management would be proved. In actuality, however, manpower planning has not established a history of accomplishment. Even

as of the mid-1970s some important contextual difficulties existed which militated against further achievement of planning's potential.

First, there remained a widespread commitment to the idea that the free market was capable of adjusting whatever disparities arose between supply and demand. Adam Smith's legacy of a self-regulatory market (regulated, that is, by an "invisible hand") was still powerful. Indeed, many economists still strongly defended the capacity of the market to regulate adequately the labor supply, but also there grew a general awareness that in some circumstances the market responded too slowly.

Second, delegation of responsibility for manpower planning was highly fragmented. The federal government by the 1970s had assumed some overall manpower planning responsibilities beyond those which certain federal agencies had assumed for their own purposes. At the same time several agencies such as the Bureau of Labor Statistics, the Bureau of the Census, and the U.S. Civil Service Commission had increased their general involvement in manpower planning and forecasting. However, by far the major portion of responsibility for the development of manpower-related programs in the public sector still rested with state and local governments.

Third, aside from the fragmentation of the manpower planning function within the federal system, there remained the question of where to vest this function within the jurisdictions. Should there be an organizational unit with comprehensive manpower planning authority for the entire jurisdiction? Or should manpower planning be conducted piecemeal by each agency possessing program responsibilities? Compelling arguments could be advanced for each side of the question.[6]

The Manpower Planner. Another issue in manpower planning still unresolved by the mid-1970s was the determination of standard (and ideal) qualifications in education and experience of manpower planners. In order to be sufficiently familiar with all the dimensions of manpower planning, manpower planners at a minimum ought to have studied business or public administration, psychology, economics, education, and statistics.

The lack in state and local jurisdictions of sufficient numbers of people with the desired background had forced greater federal attention to and involvement with manpower problems, and as of the mid-1970s it was certainly reasonable to expect that the federal role in manpower planning would continue to grow.

The Intergovernmental Personnel Act of 1970 in its provision for a grants program devoted to the improvement of personnel management at the state and local level made funding available for some manpower planning activities and programs. More directly, the Emergency Employment Act of 1971, administered by the Department of Labor, gave the federal government a stake in manpower planning by funding programs to provide public sector jobs for the unemployed. Its broadened successor, the Comprehensive Employment and Training Act, passed in 1973 and assigned again to the Department of Labor for implementation, could be expected to result in even greater federal initiative in manpower planning. The debate about the appropriate degree of federal responsibility for assisting state and local governments in solving their manpower problems—an important issue both in its practical and its ideological aspects—continued throughout the 1970s.

In fact, at the state and local levels of government, manpower planning has assumed increasingly greater salience. The trend in the states and in the larger urban jurisdictions during the 1960s and 1970s was to establish separate agencies to administer manpower programs, resulting in varying degrees of centralization of a function which otherwise had been shared among personnel departments, budget offices, and general planning agencies.

Not unexpectedly, the policy product derived from this highly fragmented structure had been lacking in consistency. It is useful at this juncture to recall Monat's comments about the nature of manpower policy: Manpower legislation at the national level, he writes, illustrates how policy seldom can be described as "a single, isolated, and original accomplishment, but rather represents a cumulative process of many and often overtly unrelated precedents."[7] The same observation applies as well

to manpower policy making at the state and local levels.

ORIGINS OF MANPOWER POLICY

In the United States the origins of anything worthy of being called "manpower policy" date from the Full Employment Act of 1946, which committed the federal government to an active role in the labor market—a commitment representing emphatic rejection of the theory of the self-correcting market. That particular theory had been weakening throughout the New Deal years, as evidenced by the high priority given unemployment as a target for remedial legislation. The Full Employment Act of 1946 became law, however, when the process of recovery had already proceeded a long way; hence its real significance may be more symbolic than real.

The second major landmark in the development of manpower policy in post-World War II America was the passage in 1962 of the Manpower Development Training Act.[8] A shift in emphasis had occurred: Since the depression years the government's chief objective had been to create new jobs; since the 1960s the focus had changed to the maximizing of skills. In the early 1960s there were many jobs available, yet there was an insufficient number of qualified persons to fill them. At the same time increased political attention was being directed to leaders of the civil rights movement who pointed out, among other things, the higher rates of unemployment among black Americans. To many policy makers this appeared to be a concrete problem that federal efforts might go a long way toward correcting. The Economic Opportunity Act of 1964, part of the program known as the "War on Poverty," was the means chosen by Congress, under the urgent prodding of the Johnson administration, to approach the problem.

By the mid-1960s the federal government had been sponsoring programs with direct and major manpower implications for both the public and private sectors. Likewise, fiscal policy had been having its direct manpower consequences. Indeed, a convincing case could be made that indirect stimulation of the economy through fiscal policy in the form of higher taxes creates a greater demand for jobs than the direct stimulation produced by manpower programs, as illustrated by various experiences during the War on Poverty. Even after the demise of that program, enactment of manpower policies continued to be easier than legislative proposals involving fiscal policy, because manpower programs enjoyed greater general support. Yet the United States has never established a comprehensive manpower policy, and for reasons already noted such an enactment would be unlikely, although certain events in the 1970s pointed toward that eventual possibility. In elaborating on the importance of manpower programs to metropolitan growth, Monat also characterizes the comprehensive manpower policy:

[T]ransportation policies, land-use and planning policies, metropolitan tax policies, housing policy, policies conductive to the growth of producer service industries, educational policies, other public service policies, as well as the more familiar and traditional employment policies, are all linked together. While the linking processes may be crude and imperfect, and numerous interstices may exist, it is the effort to deal systematically with all important related sectors and events that distinguishes a *comprehensive* manpower policy from an array of programs all of which are concerned with employment issues but are otherwise not conceptually, programmatically, or structurally related.[9]

Indeed, the absence of basic coordination and design in our approach to manpower policy is a serious weakness, and it exacts a heavy social cost during periods of high unemployment. Garth Mangum has noted the tendency of federal programs to compete with one another "for the privilege of serving the unemployed" rather than being "a carefully honed and polished set of tools available to the social and economic mechanics for application in the appropriate combination"; moreover, "each tool tends to belong to a separate mechanic who has only that tool and insists on applying it regardless of fit."[10] Local jurisdictions in need of manpower assistance often become frustrated just in trying to identify those points in the federal government where such assistance may be obtained (although there are indications that federal officials have became increasingly aware of this problem).

Application.   The principal local problem which requires manpower assistance is unemployment, although it must be recalled that manpower policy has far greater potential than simply serving to remedy unemployment. Under some circumstances, alarming levels of unemployment may persist despite the existence of manpower programs. Mangum makes an apt illustration of this paradox when commenting on the limits of educational programs as remedies for unemployment: "Education as a major answer to general unemployment . . . ," he observes, "can guarantee only better educated unemployed."[11] In fact, in the mid-1970s there was a surplus of college educated persons and a scarcity of those with technical competence. Other manpower strategies to reduce unemployment range from wide-scale job restructuring to worker-relocation programs that compensate workers for expenses incurred in moving to an area where demand for manpower is greater or equal to its supply. (In the United States, such programs have not been very successful or politically popular.)

Economic Constraints.   Manpower planning of course depends heavily on economic conditions. The National Urban Coalition has noted the close relationship between the general level of demand for goods and unemployment. The relationship of both factors to each other also produces variations in price levels. In the United States the historical tendency has been to place a higher priority on the achievement of price stability (with uneven success) than on the maintenance of high levels of demand, even if higher levels of unemployment result from reducing demand through monetary or fiscal policy.

This contrasts with the pattern of policies in most other developed countries which try to keep unemployment at manageable levels while avoiding excessive price instability. Rather than pursuing a policy of decreasing aggregate demand, these countries follow multiple strategies, including efforts to expand employment in the public sector; acceptance of higher levels of inflation in order to keep unemployment under control; the institution of limited guidelines or controls on wages and prices to keep unemployment relatively low and prices relatively stable; or some combination of the three.[12]

The National Urban Coalition concluded that the United States ought to be willing to accept a higher rate of inflation (i.e., higher than 3 percent) in the interests of reducing unemployment (i.e., below 4 percent). It must be emphasized, however, that the relationship between inflation and unemployment is far from precise. The coalition's argument and conclusion clearly lose their persuasiveness if, for example, the economy at a given period is characterized both by inflation substantially greater than 3 percent and by unemployment significantly higher than 4 percent.

In order to determine an appropriate manpower strategy, hard choices must be made as to the priority of goals: maintaining high demand to encourage growth, holding down inflation, or holding down employment. There are also limits on the capacity of fiscal policy to manipulate the economy, notwithstanding the possibility of reaching a consensus on the order of priorities, because of the number of various competing interests having substantial stake in the policy decision. For example, it is not realistic to expect labor to determine reasonable priorities for its membership when both unemployment and inflation are alarmingly high.

THE ROLE OF ORGANIZED LABOR

Organized labor has presumed a role in determining manpower policy at the national level and, frequently, at the state and local levels as well where programs developed at the national level are implemented. In general, however, organized labor has failed to achieve its full potential in manpower planning. Although labor has frequently influenced manpower programs, often making them more "humanistic" and welfare-oriented, it has never developed its own coherent and comprehensive manpower policy.[13]

Given the diversity and fragmentation of the American labor movement, the lack of a systematic manpower policy is certainly understandable. Organized labor would be an unlikely pacesetter in objective manpower policy making when its own nature is so partisan, its

stake in the outcome is so great, and when the public interest itself is so elusive. Richard A. Lester raises the question of whether it is possible to reconcile "rational planning for use of the nation's labor resources" with "two-sided, decentralized negotiations based on bargaining power and protection of sectional interests."[14]

In certain respects, however, labor has proved to be a constructive force in manpower policy formulation. The collective bargaining process has made its own contribution to some elements of planning. Other labor practices incorporated in manpower policy are advance notification of layoffs, hiring pools for the reemployment in one corporation plant of workers laid off in another plant, and employer-sponsored job retraining programs—all products of labor union insistence. Directly related to manpower policy are humanistic labor achievements such as severance pay, unemployment benefits, and early retirement programs.[15] Even the seniority system, which some critics declare is a discriminatory and unfair basis for promotion and other work opportunities, has been effectively defended as a positive contribution to manpower policy.

Labor's comparatively weak role in shaping overall manpower policy stands in sharp contrast to the situation in Sweden where organized labor operates much closer to the centers of decision making. In the United States labor has had to withstand opposition from management and even from government itself, which often seems to prefer that labor keep its distance. Nevertheless, given the fragmented character of manpower policy in this country, labor has often prevailed. The Emergency Employment Act of 1971, which created over 300,000 jobs in the public sector during its first years and which the Nixon Administration had opposed, helped reduce unemployment and enabled many persons variously categorized as "disadvantaged" to secure governmental employment with the possibility of advancement. In 1973 the act was recast and expanded to become the Comprehensive Employment and Training Act.

Organized labor vigorously and successfully opposed efforts by the Nixon administration to "decategorize" all federal manpower programs and combine them into a special manpower revenue-sharing program with a budget significantly smaller than the budget for the combined categorical programs. The administration attempted to apply the principles of its "new federalism," arguing the importance of decentralization in bringing about greater efficiency.

Labor, however, looked on the proposal as an abdication of executive responsibility and publicized tne large number of job-creating programs that would have been either terminated or else submerged in the special revenue-sharing program. If the latter were to have actualized, the power of Congress to set standards and the capacity of the federal government to monitor the programs would have been undercut.[16] Evaluation of labor's overall role in manpower program development in turn requires evaluation of any preconceived notions that critics or observers may have about organized labor. On balance, given the natural difficulty for any group to transcend its own interests beyond a certain point, labor's contributions to manpower planning may be judged positive.

ATTITUDES: THE SUBJECTIVE COMPONENT

An understanding of economic conditions and labor interests, and the bearing of both on the manpower planning process, goes far but not all the way in determining the final policy product. Attitudes, too, are crucial. David McClelland in *The Achieving Society*[17] develops a convincing relationship between achievement motivation and economic growth, demonstrating that variations in the former helped explain differences in the latter. According to Harold Sheppard, various "subjective variables" must be taken into account in research on manpower problems:

Attitudes, the definition of situations, motives, and frames of reference are not identical for different individuals, groups, or societies, nor are they constant in time. Furthermore, while they may often be correctly viewed as *effects* . . . of external conditions, they may also possess or acquire a functional autonomy and act as *causes* . . . in the economic realm. Contemporary research in the area of unemployment problems rarely is carried out with this possibility in mind. More frequently, social and . . . psychological concomitants are studied only as possible results of such problems.[18]

To illustrate his point about attitudes, particularly as it relates to unemployment, Sheppard goes on to note the general acceptance of the idea that the remedy for extensive unemployment in one area is extensive migration to other areas where economic opportunity is greater. He questions the validity of this strategy by calling attention to the absence of evidence indicating any favorable effect of such movement on the unemployment rate in the areas of out-migration. Migration, he argues, might well be a solution to the problems of the individual but not to the problems of the area. Indeed, there is no real guarantee that significant numbers of the unemployed will move to areas of ostensibly greater employment opportunity instead of trying to make the best of remaining where there is high unemployment. On the other hand, there is also the real possibility of a "stampede effect" in which job openings once publicized attract an oversupply of workers.

Sheppard lists the conditions—objective and subjective—which must exist before mobility becomes possible:

1. Legal exit and entry rights from and to areas;
2. Universal awareness of opportunities elsewhere;
3. A desire to improve employment and income status, even at the cost of leaving family, friends, and property, if any;
4. Absence of discrimination and prejudice in the new area;
5. Willingness to move to, and live in, a new social environment;
6. Means of transportation to the new area;
7. Occupational interchangeability.[19]

The list indicates some of the subtler complexities of the manpower planner's task. Attitudinal factors such as the degree to which an individual is future-oriented and willing to plan, the level of anxiety over job interviews, and an individual's job expectations and approach (active or indifferent) to job hunting all have implications for the efforts to mesh supply with demand in the labor market and for the role of state employment services as well. Sheppard cites evidence suggesting that an intermediary agency like a state employment service is more likely to be used by persons with certain attitudinal characteristics, such as high job interview anxiety and low achievement motivation, whereas persons possessing a positive attitude toward seeking employment may compensate substantially for difficulties which stem from the general economic level.[20]

Policy Goals

The foregoing discussion suggests the value of manpower planning as a social skill in implementing public policy. Specifically, the three major policy issues addressed by manpower planning are: 1) how to upgrade the work force, 2) how to develop and maintain a balanced work force profile, and 3) how to implement equal employment opportunity programs.

Upgrading the Work Force. As to the first goal of raising the general level of competence of the work force, it is necessary to examine the relationship between the educational system and the job market. With allowance for local variations, some overall observations may be made. First of all, the average educational level of the American work force continues to rise. Second, the work force is becoming more equalized in educational preparation. If nearly every worker has a high school diploma, then a high school diploma will mean very little as a job requirement, although the *quality* of that education, insofar as it can be evaluated, may well assume greater importance.

Third, education and training have not always been associated with employability. Indeed, the general perception of a direct association between education and employability is largely a development dating only from World War II.[21] Moreover, it is not really clear whether that association does indeed obtain. Does the demand for trained employees antedate the supply, or vice versa? In other words, does the nature of the work force change in such a way as to make it necessary to hire persons with more education than formerly, or does the larger pool of educated persons in the potential work force induce a preference on the part of employers to hire such persons rather

than those with fewer years of formal education?

Fourth, a direct correlation between education and productivity is alleged, although the relationship is very difficult to confirm. There is, to be sure, a direct correlation between educational level and lifetime earnings. As educational level rises, the likelihood of unemployment diminishes.[22] Of course, there are special circumstances making for exceptions. For example, the post-World War II baby boom produced an explosive rise in school enrollments in the 1950s and 1960s, with a corresponding demand for teachers; in the 1970s, with the boom off the rise, there materialized a glut of teachers. Similarly, as the space race, which had high political priority during the 1960s, began being challenged during the 1970s by other priorities, substantial personnel cutbacks in the space program were made, with the effect on the employment market of an overload of physicists, astronomers, and other scientists specializing in related areas. As a general rule, however, the greater the education, the greater the likelihood of finding a job. Again, a strict correlation between education and productivity is unverified.

Developing and Maintaining a Balanced Work Force Profile. The second policy issue relating to manpower planning as a social skill is how manpower planning can contribute to developing and maintaining a balanced work force profile. Essentially, this profile is achieved when the pool of available manpower roughly matches the needs of the system for certain educational requirements and special skills. A work force profile is not balanced when there are large numbers of persons in the pool who are either overqualified or underprepared in relation to job specifications. But as the goals of the system change, the needs for skills and knowledge also change. For example, the goal of self-sufficiency in energy production which the nation set for itself in the mid-1970s is bound to alter radically its employment needs. Geologists and mining engineers conceivably will be sought at a premium.

Ordinarily, change in general categories of employment (e.g., professional, clerical, laborer, service, etc.) tend to be incremental.

Trends since World War II have been fairly consistent, with the greatest expansion occurring in the general category of professional and technical workers. The only category that experienced substantial contraction was that relating to farm occupations.[23] The growth in the number of governmental employees and academics during the post-World War II period accounts for a larger portion of the increase in the size of the professional and technical categories. For example, during the decade 1955–1965 the number of state and local governmental employees rose from 4.7 million to 7.7 million, an increase of 63 percent.

The incremental nature of change in employment patterns points to another difficulty encountered in manpower planning. Accurate forecasting is essential, and yet precision in planning is almost impossible. The market is self-correcting up to a point; manpower policy seeks to reduce the gap between market imbalances and the goal of a balanced work force. Leonard A. Lecht of the National Planning Association puts it thus:

As we use the economy's growth in resources . . . to transform more of the country's aspirations into reality, our manpower problems are likely to concern ways and means of improving education and training, of utilizing more effectively the existing manpower potentials, and of increasing mobility, rather than the issues posed by the presence of a large mass of unskilled, poorly educated, and unemployed Americans.[24]

The basic question, then, concerns the means of attaining these goals. An awareness of the interdependence of the various aspects of manpower policy is of course essential. The most direct way of adjusting for those aspects would be to assign the planning function entirely to the federal government. If it were to marshal all its resources, presumably the federal government could hammer out a program or set of programs which could bring about a balanced work force profile. But the social cost might be too great for the public to bear, for while it is important that the political system make maximum utilization of the manpower resources it has at its disposal, maximization of individual freedom of choice is even more important.

Ideally, according to Levitan, Mangum, and Marshall, "only the lack of potential competence should restrain preparation and access to individual occupation choice."[25] Accordingly, to facilitate the maximization of individual choice, these writers emphasize the need for maintaining both lateral and upward mobility and the need for providing government assistance to individuals in adjusting to changes produced by both the economic cycle and technological advance.[26] These are enormous tasks which would seem to call for a comprehensive policy promulgated from a central source. Levitan and his associates conclude that quite possibly "trial-and-error" policies, however fragmented, may be "more compatible with a pluralistic society such as ours."[27] A balanced work force profile definitely is a desirable goal, but not if the means necessary to achieve it are too dear.

Implementing Equal Employment Opportunity Programs. Finally, as its third major policy goal, manpower planning must address itself to the implementation of equal opportunity and fair employment programs which the system has instituted since the 1960s. This may very well be the goal which manpower planning can serve most effectively, although that is not to minimize the complexities involved in its implementation.

The principle of equal employment opportunity for all persons, some of whom belong to groups suffering a history of job discrimination (and other forms as well) is now accepted by all but a small minority of Americans. Again, it is determining the means of achieving that objective which becomes the focus of controversy. The federal government itself has taken the initiative in shifting the approach from a negative to a positive one. The obligation to take "affirmative action" to redress continuing job discrimination is based on the experience that a policy of "nondiscrimination" was simply inadequate. Daniel Seligman has identified four discrete positions characterized by varying degrees of vigor with which disadvantaged groups are sought out:

1. *Passive nondiscrimination,* which treats the races and sexes alike but which largely ignores the

consequences of past discriminatory treatment of certain classes and groups and makes little effort to advertise job openings.

2. *Pure affirmative action,* by which greater effort is made to increase the pool from which persons are hired or promoted, the specific criterion for which is strictly individual qualifications without reference to race or sex.

3. *Affirmative action with preferential hiring,* which systematically favors minorities and women in employment decisions in order to compensate for past abuses and which has been referred to as a "soft quota system" because its targets are not inflexible.

4. *Hard quotas,* which requires the hiring of firmly set proportions of applicants from the targeted groups.[28]

While some federal agencies during the early 1970s appeared to be promoting hard quotas, the number of state and local jurisdictions adopting such a policy was relatively small. By the mid-1970s the real (and heated) debate was whether affirmative action involved preferential hiring. The Equal Employment Opportunity Commission, the compliance offices within various federal agencies, and state affirmative action offices often do call for the establishment of goals and timetables aimed at increasing the number of women and minorities in the work force of the organization or jurisdiction in question, but the Equal Employment Opportunity Commission itself has cautioned against "discrimination in reverse" and has emphatically rejected the concept of hard quotas.

In a recessionary economy with unemployment rising, affirmative action and the intense competition for few jobs work against each other to create a volatile situation.[29] Nevertheless, because of the increased entry into the work force of minority groups and women, and because of their militancy, it has become imperative to develop strategies to improve their opportunities for recruitment and promotion on a scale significantly greater than that for the remainder of the labor force. High priority has been assigned to redressing the underrepresentation of these "affected groups" in professional, technical, and management positions.

Effective implementation of equal employment opportunity programs at the state and local level involves a fine degree of coordination of all personnel practices. According to

guidelines issued by the Equal Employment Opportunity Commission, most affirmative action programs in the public sector (and in the private sector as well) consist of eight major steps:

1. The issuance in writing of a policy statement, signed by the chief executive officer, committing the jurisdiction to the goals of the program.

2. The appointment of an official with responsibility and authority to direct and implement the program, with the responsibilities of that official and of other supervisory personnel, along with their accountability, clearly defined.

3. The communication of the policy both within the jurisdiction and outside it to potential sources of recruitment in particular and to the community in general.

4. The survey of current jurisdictional employment of minorities and women by department and job classification, with particular attention to determining areas of "concentration" (more of a particular group than is in proportion to their presence in the work force) and "underutilization."

5. The development of goals and timetables to correct for deficiencies found in item 4.

6. The development and implementation of specific programs as needed, including procedures for recruitment, selection, upward mobility, wages and salaries, benefits and conditions of employment, policies relating to layoffs, terminations, and discipline, and including union contract provisions which affect personnel procedures.

7. The establishment of auditing and reporting procedures enumerating management's "good faith efforts" made toward achievement of equal employment opportunity goals, enabling proper evaluation by the jurisdiction's compliance agency of each phase of the program.

8. The development of internal and community programs supporting the policy and its goals.[30]

The chief obstacle to the implementation of affirmative action programs most likely is the inertia which too often characterizes bureaucratic organizations both in public and private sectors. It should be kept in mind also that both open and covert resistance may be found among personnel of many jurisdictions as well as within communities and organizations, and consequently the specific form of any given plan may have to be reshaped in light of that resistance. Union agreements, too, may surface as an obstacle to full implementation of affirmative action plans. As is true of the planning process in general, it is no less true of planning for affirmative action specifically, that both goals and the strategies adopted to achieve them are subject to review and modification as circumstances dictate. If targets are not met, perhaps they were set at unreasonably high levels or perhaps the programs or officers were inadequate to the task of implementation. In either case, alteration is indicated.

There are no universal formulas for implementing equal employment opportunity programs or for reducing large-scale unemployment. Since rates of unemployment run relatively higher among minority groups, and since the majority of members of minority groups live in the cities, unemployment and its effects in many respects are a special problem of urban areas. Accordingly, the Committee for Economic Development examined the problem of how to provide greater employment opportunities for disadvantaged groups in American cities. Its program, while undramatic and incremental, represents a sound and reasoned effort to come to terms with a difficult and potentially explosive situation. The following are a few of the recommendations the committee published in 1970:

1. Greater attention to worker motivation and to work as a source of psychic satisfaction. This may be encouraged by broadening the conventional approach to training from a "one-shot" effort aimed only at placement in entry-level jobs to a more comprehensive effort emphasizing continuing education and thus making for greater vocational adaptability and cultural enrichment. Specifically, training programs outside the "regular" educational system are recommended, precisely because it is the failures of that system which have necessitated remedial programs.
2. Continued financial support to businesses which offer special training and employment programs, with such support preferably in the form of special contracts rather than tax incentives. Recommendation was made that the contract process itself be simplified.
3. Continued responsibility by the federal government for funding manpower programs generally, with the states designing and carrying out these programs. When the states and local governments lack the technical competence to implement their own manpower development programs, the federal government should initiate the programs and in all cases should retain the role of monitor. Specifically, recommendation was made that the states could profitably assign more manpower program responsibilities to their respective employment security agencies, even though this may call for reorganizing these agencies. There ought to be state manpower plans and frameworks organized to activate the plans; state inaction should not be allowed to delay implementation of manpower programs in urban areas.
4. Promotion of educational and research programs in manpower-related subjects in institutions of higher education.
5. Rethinking the question of whether raising the minimum work age contributes to the goal of eliminating poverty. The committee suggested that such action actually may have the effect of restricting rather than expanding the number of jobs. One possible remedy is differential wage rates applied to the below-20 age group, the aged, and the partially disabled, which may reduce the reluctance of employers to hire inexperienced workers at wages comparable to those of persons who offer greater productive potential because of experience and ability. However, it was noted that a possible "displacement effect" may be created—that is, an employer may find it profitable to continually hire young persons and then dismiss them when they reach the age of 20. Consequently, some economists favor the complete elimination of the minimum age.
6. Comprehensive job restructuring, particularly for low-grade jobs. The most important element of such efforts relates to the elimination of artificial barriers, notably the assumption that certain positions be reserved for certain classes of persons. If job qualifications which fail to pass the test of job relatedness are removed from job specifications, then of course more opportunities are opened up to the disadvantaged. As a result, paraprofessionals could assume positions once held exclusively by professionals.
7. Greater accessibility of information to the available labor pool about openings in the job market. The special isolation attendant to poverty makes it essential to broaden access to job opportunities at wages commensurate with

productivity, even though implementation of this recommendation may be difficult. Both public and private employment agencies need to augment their efforts to inform the urban poor of job openings both in the city and in the suburbs. This in turn indicates a high priority for improving urban transportation systems and achieving open housing.

8. Modifications in public welfare programs so that incentives to take jobs are provided recipients by enabling them to keep a graduated proportion up to a cutoff point of their welfare support.

9. Establishment of a nonprofit corporation charged with training and with providing jobs for marginal employees. The committee recommended focusing on "regular," emergency, and "peak-season" jobs in both public and private sectors, as well as public service work which though desirable might otherwise be neglected. Initially, such "job corporations" would operate on an experimental basis in selected communities. The chief advantage of such a corporation, in the view of the committee, would be greater management flexibility and freedom from restrictive regulations that characterize a more traditional governmental agency.[31]

Even though the program summarized here dates from 1970 and is the product of a group with a decided business orientation, albeit modulated by the participation of representatives from the academic community, it is nevertheless one serious attempt to devise a comprehensive strategy to deal with some of the nation's manpower problems while at the same time recognizing the difficulties involved in achieving full potential of manpower planning as a social skill.

Progress actually was made during the 1970s toward the fulfillment of parts of the committee's program. For example, a greater role for many institutions of higher education in manpower research had developed. The public increasingly favored altering the welfare system so as to provide more work incentives; similarly, management in both the public and private sectors grew increasingly aware of the benefit to itself in restructuring jobs to bring about greater worker enrichment. However, even given a consensus among political decision makers as to the value and relevance of such a program, it would be far from self-executing.

Process

The practice of manpower planning was still in its infancy in the 1970s; a knowledge base for policy decisions was materializing only gradually. Nevertheless it was clear that manpower planning, however imperfect, was—and continues to be—a valuable aid and that potentially it had even greater value.

MANPOWER PLANNING AS A MANAGEMENT SKILL

While manpower planning plays its role at the federal level (macro-planning, as it were), it is also a management skill which has wide applicability within an agency or jurisdiction. The pitfalls of estimating manpower needs notwithstanding, planning has become unquestionably a major management function. Herbert Simon has commented on the inadvisability of any organization's chief executive to become preoccupied with routine operations, for organizations should be able to routinize most activities so that regular involvement by top management is unnecessary. Rather, top management's responsibility is to "meet changing demands and opportunities in its environment."[32] This in itself presents a basic rationale for planning. If an organization is to be able to meet and respond to these demands and opportunities, the likelihood of its successfully doing so is greater if it seeks to anticipate and plan for them.

No suggestion is made that manpower planning is a substitute for decision making. However, it does provide an important basis for the decision-making process. The various solutions and approaches that are products of the manpower planning process must be evaluated by management with the greatest scrutiny. For example, suppose management discovers the possibility of a serious gap in its technical manpower needs over its next five-year period. Manpower planning offers many solutions, but it is management that must decide whether to prepare for the prospective problem by diverting its resources principally into greater automation *or* into developing technical training programs for present employees *or* into job restructuring to take advantage of its present manpower base *or* into upgrading salaries and working conditions in order to improve its recruiting and its operating program, *or* some combination of these alternatives.

It should be clear that manpower planning presupposes accurate position classification. To cite this relationship seems to be restating the obvious, as it is difficult to envision an organization engaging in manpower planning if it is lacking so elemental a property of modern personnel systems as job classification. This simply is to stress the importance of a sound and current position classification plan with built-in procedures for regular review, because it bears a basic relationship to both the recruiting process and the evaluation of training needs.

Before elaborating some of the means by which manpower planning can become a management skill, one further observation seems appropriate. In a perceptive article written in 1962, Edward Banfield remarked on the infrequency with which the planning process conforms to a rational decision-making model. Such a model calls for identifying the possible options available as well as the likely consequences following adoption of any option. Armed with this information base the decision maker can then choose the policy alternative which would yield at least cost the desired outcome.

However, in reality, Banfield continued, while rational planning presumes "a clear and consistent set of ends,"[33] these often are nonexistent. This situation obtains not only because predicting the future is so difficult (because of the unpredictability of chance and accident), but also because the ends themselves change. What may seem during a period of full employment a farsighted and worthy program for enriching jobs to ensure greater job satisfaction in the future may be subordinated under less favorable economic circumstances to the higher priority of simple job creation. "Organizations," Banfield noted, "have a decided preference for present rather than future effects,"[34] although it might be expected that public jurisdictions are in a better position than private organizations to "postpone satisfactions."

The frequent reference to the difficulties accompanying the planning process is not meant to disparage but to underscore the genuine usefulness and worth of manpower planning. An awareness of where manpower planning can go wrong is a prerequisite to deriving any payoff from planning; otherwise, manpower planning cannot be an effective management skill.

As a management skill, manpower planning has applicability to personnel concerns such as recruitment and selection processes; internal adjustments such as reductions in force, reemployment programs, and improvement of employee utilization by transfer or job restructuring; alterations in the structure of the jurisdiction's work force (for example, a change in the ratio of clerical to professional staff); employee development; and the jurisdiction's procedures in record keeping and data gathering. Each of these relationships will be examined at appropriate points. Some of these are illustrated in Figure 3–1.

Broadly speaking, manpower planning relates to both the skills and numbers of persons comprising the work force. Indeed, the objective of manpower planning is the relatively simple one of attempting to match job needs with the best qualified persons or, in other words, "to ensure that the right number and the right kind of people are in the right place at the right time."[35] It follows that the jurisdiction must identify its manpower needs and then address itself to how best these needs may be met.

Determining manpower needs involves both an analysis of employee turnover and the specific program requirements of the jurisdiction. Analysis of employee turnover begins with gathering data about position titles and job classifications for all present employees in the jurisdiction. Accurate record keeping of course makes it easier to compute the average term of employment and the average annual loss rate from both separations and reassignments. Actual analyzing of the accumulated data may be somewhat more difficult. Complicating variables themselves must be analyzed; for example, fluctuations in the number and kind of vacancies filled each year may themselves have future

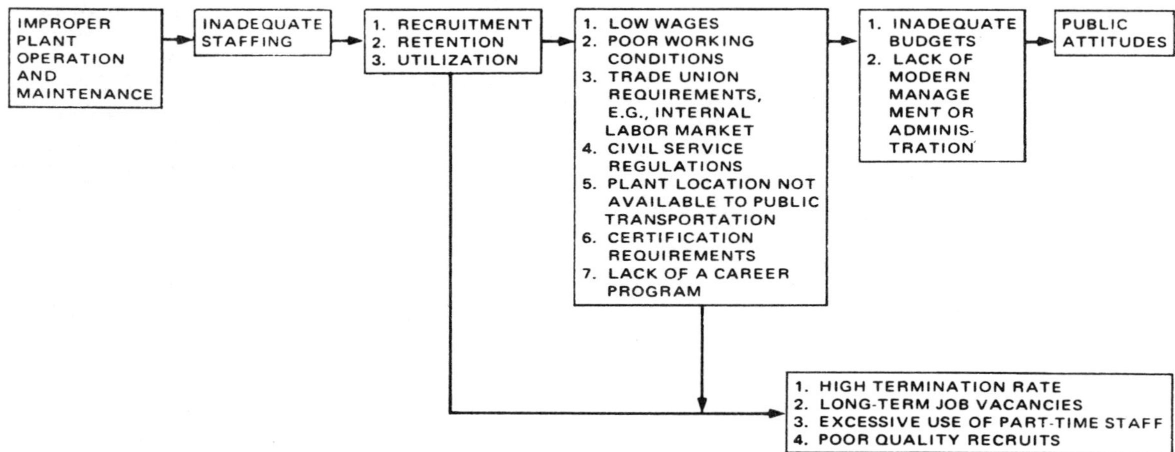

FIGURE 3–1. *A possible sequence of manpower problems in a wastewater treatment plant. This diagram illustrates the complex interaction of many recruitment, employment, and working condition variables in manpower planning. (Source: Based on U.S., Environmental Protection Agency, Office of Water Programs,* MANPOWER PLANNING FOR WASTEWATER TREATMENT PLANTS, *report prepared by Olympus Research Corporation, Washington, D.C., Government Printing Office, 1972, p. 116.)*

consequences in that turnover rates tend to be higher among new employees than among long-time employees. Experienced personnel managers will be able to estimate probable future turnover rates in the jurisdiction.

Projection and Forecasting. At this juncture it is important to emphasize that projection is to be clearly distinguished from forecasting. The former involves the mere extension of a past trend into the future, without taking into account variables which might alter that trend. Projecting involves an element of prediction only if events expected to occur in the future are predicted to be basically like those in the past. On the other hand, forecasting is essentially predictive. In the context of manpower planning, forecasting is the process of anticipating both labor supply and demand for the future. Forecasting must consider possible future circumstances which may differ from those in the past. Its purpose is to establish an information base, using the best available data, from which can be developed strategies for eliminating disparities between the supply and demand of manpower.

Naturally, the more accurate the forecast, the more valuable forecasting is as a management tool. If it is to be accurate, forecasting must be monitored constantly. As more data (data that are reliable, it is to be hoped) come to the manpower planner, the forecast must be adjusted accordingly. Indeed, it is possible to make a forecast that is accurate for the wrong reasons. For example, perhaps the forecaster overestimated both supply and demand, in which case he or she is simply lucky if the future actually brings bigger needs for both. However, rather than allowing for a constant error between forecast and eventuality, the forecaster must ask why earlier forecasts were in error.

In general, it is advisable to forecast for relatively short periods. There are few circumstances permitting management to project more than five years in advance. However, manpower planning must be individualized, because each jurisdiction is different from all others; accordingly, the planning process in each jurisdiction will have some unique features of its own. Quantitative techniques are being increasingly refined to make possible more reliable forecasting; manpower planning does not thereby cease, however, to have its qualitative aspect as well. Even the most sophisticated forecasts need to be tested, both during and after formulation, against the perceptions of those line managers most strategically placed to make their own kind of forecasts of staffing needs.

Estimating the Supply of Manpower. Beyond the consideration of employee turnover as it relates to the determination of future staffing needs, manpower planning also may be affected by the nature of specific program requirements. When new programs arise, when old programs are terminated, or when existing programs are altered, staffing needs may be directly affected. Unless such program changes are reactions to emergency situations, they can be anticipated in the budget. The manpower planner must stay in close touch with the budget process in all its stages.

A related element to be considered by the manpower planner is productivity, which may affect the decision of whether to fund various staffing requests. At this point recruiting decisions also may be affected by the attitude of labor unions, which sometimes seem suspicious of efforts by management to improve productivity, on the grounds that productivity may be improved at the unions' expense. However, there is growing recognition within the labor movement of the direct relationship between productivity and wages. Higher wages in the public sector, of course, depend largely on higher taxes. At the same time, there is the possibility that the forces motivating increased productivity will be superseded by those which actually compel lower productivity, since more Americans could thereby be given work.[36]

The validity of such an argument is primarily a question of macro-policy, relating to manpower planning as a social skill, but it also has growing importance to management and to local policy makers as an approach to the general problems of local unemployment. A very general question for the future that planners must consider now is whether technology will lead to a day when leisure rather than work is the norm. If so, there may follow a diminished commitment to the work ethic.

The nature and breadth of these concerns is indicative of how the manpower planning process cuts across the entire range of public personnel management. For example, the formulation of action programs in local jurisdictions to correct disparities between manpower needs and manpower supply must recognize traditional and legal constraints on recruitment such as residence requirements, age limits, and veterans' preference rules. In the 1970s such restrictions were being carefully scrutinized for validity and fairness, but by no means were they being eliminated altogether. Heated debates were taking place on what should take top priority in selection and promotion—affirmative action or the seniority system, veterans' preference, the tenure system, etc.

The task of balancing manpower needs with supply presents management with a large number of policy options, singly or in combination: For example, should the main efforts to identify manpower supply be directed toward sources outside the organization or those inside? Should the chief approach in making appointments be based on competitive procedures established by the merit system or on noncompetitive procedures? Even when a choice among these alternatives has been made, further questions and options must be addressed by management: Should attention be directed toward persons whose qualifications relate to other positions within the jurisdiction, to those who may be dissatisfied because career advancement opportunities seem limited, or to those who are overqualified for the positions they presently occupy? Management must also determine the emphasis to be placed on training (and retraining) programs: Should such programs be established in order to encourage movement? Still another consideration is job restructuring: To what extent may a jurisdiction's future manpower needs be met by a basic restructuring of positions?

Job Restructuring. Job restructuring has been receiving increasingly serious attention in the 1970s. A 1973 report to the Secretary of Health, Education, and Welfare revealed widespread worker dissatisfaction. Only 43 percent of a cross section of white-collar workers responded affirmatively when asked whether, if given the chance, they would choose similar work again; the figure drops as low as 24 percent for blue-collar workers.[37] It is assumed that the degree of dissatisfaction varies depending on whether reference is made to the public or private sector and depending on the kind of work involved (i.e., services, manufacturing, etc.). One of the chief causes of worker discontent, as revealed in the report, is the persistence of "Taylorism," a product of the scientific management movement which developed in the early years of this century. Management's chief objective in incorporating Taylorism was to improve efficiency by increasing output and decreasing unit costs, made possible by the mechanical examination of work flow.

The report disclosed that job discontent is also the result of diminishing opportunities to be one's own boss. The decline in individual autonomy is almost implicit in the documented trend toward larger and more pervasive organizations. Between 1950 and 1960, for example, wage and salary workers even on farms increased from 61 percent to 80 percent, suggesting a corresponding decline in self-employment. Similar trends are apparent even among occupations traditionally regarded as self-employed, such as writers and lawyers.[38] The human relations school of management, beginning with the Hawthorne experiment (see Chapter 12) arose largely as a reaction to Taylorism. Likewise, prospects for job restructuring seemed to serve well both as a viable alternative to the generally declining prospects for self-employment and as an imaginative, individualized response to worker dissatisfaction.

The manpower planner must understand the pervasiveness of this discontent to properly deal with it. Admittedly, the actual restructuring of jobs is the general responsibility of management, but manpower planners, in fulfilling their responsibility for devising strategies to fill the gap between demand and supply, do a disservice to management if they ignore the problem of employee morale. Finally, even though attention to national and regional norms and trends is essential, the manpower planner's primary attention will be directed to the situation in the local jurisdiction.

Aids for the Planner. It must be clear by now that the many variables involved greatly complicate the manpower planning process and are responsible for manpower planning's un-

scientific aspect referred to in the introduction to this chapter. There are, however, some important materials which, properly used, can increase the reliability of manpower supply forecasts, particularly if the planner has little forecasting experience.

The annual *Manpower Report of the President* and the periodic reports of state employment security commissions are invaluable. *Survey of Current Business,* issued by the U.S. Department of Commerce, and reports by the two Congressional appropriations committees are helpful in keeping abreast of general economic trends. In determining manpower supply, special focus should be directed to population trends (notably, a higher birth rate among blacks than among whites), trends in manpower shortages in various occupations, and enrollment trends for both high schools and colleges. Even an awareness of curriculum developments may prove useful to the projection of manpower trends. Furthermore, the manpower planner must keep current with developments in a variety of areas which at first glance may seem to be of only marginal relevance to the projection of manpower trends. A case in point is the impact of new transportation systems. The opening of rapid transit lines in metropolitan areas can be expected to alter both the character and the magnitude of elements of the labor supply.

Of major relevance to the projection of manpower trends is affirmative action—both its successful implementation and adverse reaction to it. Affirmative action forces a reevaluation of the role women and minority groups play in the work force. Historical work trends for women show they have sought employment in large numbers immediately following the school years, thus creating a bulge in their employment figures from age 18 into the early 20s. During the child-bearing years they become a far less important element in the market. However, around the age of 40 they reenter the labor market in great numbers. Factors such as low turnover, seriousness of purpose, and high productivity among these women workers make them highly attractive to employers. Since the 1960s, however, the number of career-oriented women has been increasing. As a consequence, the future availability of women to the labor market may show a closer correlation with their numbers in the various age groups.

Estimating the Demand for Manpower. As to estimating demand, there are generally fewer materials to utilize directly. One federal agency recommends conducting a survey of the twenty or thirty largest employers in the manpower planner's local labor market on the ground that in most cases this sample will represent more than half the market. Smaller employers have greater difficulty estimating their demand, since it tends to be closely tied to the general business climate.

Management may choose to meet its demand for manpower by technological means. Modifications in production techniques may offer the most effective and efficient way of solving problems of labor supply. Public employers, however, may encounter formidable political constraints in adopting such a course of action, particularly during periods of relatively high unemployment. This alternative is cited only to indicate the range of options available to management. Again, imaginative manpower planners do not confine their attention only to the influence of economic conditions.

Doing the Estimating. At this point some of the methods used for projection and forecasting should be noted. The basic method is that of proportionality as applied to time-series data. What is the relationship between the optimum employment level indicated by budget requests and the amounts actually appropriated? A variant calculation entails establishing the relationship between budget requests and prevailing employment levels. Either method could be used to forecast for individual occupations as well as for all occupations collectively. Planners who find direct and consistent relationships between these and related variables—budget requests, budget appropriations, employment levels—are, of course, in a good position to help develop sound manpower policies.

Obviously, the more similarities there are in such relationships, the more reliable is the method of proportionality, based as it is on the idea that the budget-making process is characterized by incrementalism. For example, if

the ratio of actual employment to optimum employment for four successive years is .90, .88, .86, and .84, what ratio can be forecast for the fifth year? A trend appears, and simple projection alone points to the next time-series figure of .82. Averaging the figures actually may be more appropriate for forecasting. The longer adequate records have been kept, the more a forecast may be made with confidence, but needless to say, manpower planners should not rely strictly on projections alone.

Another important element of forecasting involves data on terminations whether due to death, retirement, resignation, discharge, or reduction in force. If records have been kept complete, the manpower planner is able to make reasonably sound forecasts on death and retirement rates. As for resignations and discharges, forecasting is riskier because of the absence of a relationship to age, but even here the method of proportionality ought to yield forecasts with a high probability of accuracy. However, judgment must be made whether to base a forecast on a trend determined by past data or whether to average the data in the absence of a clear trend.

Having established the turnover rate, regardless of method, it is then desirable to forecast the source of replacements, an essential step in making adequate plans for training programs. Again the basis must be data derived from the recent past. Replacement may be made by promotions, from new appointments, or from horizontal movement. The relative numbers from these various sources will determine the kinds of training programs which the jurisdiction must institute.

While the manpower planner inevitably will rely primarily on variations of the method of proportionality, greater sophistication may be introduced in several different ways. The most obvious of these is regression analysis, which presupposes a fairly advanced understanding of statistics. Treatment of its applications is beyond the province of this chapter. (See appropriate listings in the bibliography.)

Basically, regression analysis relies heavily on comprehensive historical data or at least data based on fairly large samples. When these prerequisites are missing, the manpower planner may find it useful to consider the method known as decision analysis forecasting. Sometimes confused with the Delphi process, regression analysis nevertheless is significantly different.[39] The Delphi method involves a group of knowledgeable authorities who exchange information with each other anonymously for the purpose of reaching a consensus about, for example, future trends. Based on several discrete steps, the Delphi method depends on systematic communication and assumes that aggregate opinion at each step will induce each individual to consider carefully his or her estimates and so modify them to accord with the opinions of most members of the panel. The Delphi method has applications for manpower planning, especially in its effort to discern long-term trends. Although it is a complex method to administer, there is evidence to suggest that it yields a notable degree of accuracy.

Decision analysis forecasting (DAF), on the other hand, while also involving ideally a group of experts, does not depend on an exchange of opinion among those experts and may even, when necessary, be utilized by only one. A study of DAF published in 1974 emphasized that in order to keep current, it uses "the most expensive original input"—namely, the time and considered judgments of top management. Through the "prediction adjustment capability," which is built into DAF largely by probability theory, DAF can remain flexible and absorb additional information, and thereby modify its forecasts. By contrast, regression analysis often becomes quickly dated unless considerable cost and effort are expended to keep data current.

Decision analysis forecasting entails arraying probable outcomes in a table, accompanied by a statistical index of their relative probabilities. Most commonly a diagram is set up resembling the branches of a tree, which reflect the several combinations of possible contingencies.[40] Figure 3-2 illustrates such a simplified branch diagram. In the example shown in Figure 3-2 the likelihood of having to recruit for a new management position is conditioned by the likelihood of a budget increase. The sum of the probabilities of the separate outcomes is always equal to unity. To illustrate, the proba-

bilities of the four possible outcomes in Figure 3-2 are computed by multiplying the respective conditional probabilities as follows:

Obtaining a new management position on the basis of a sizeable budget increase	.14
Not obtaining a new management position on the basis of a sizeable budget increase	.06
Obtaining a new management position on the basis of only a moderate budget increase	.08
Not obtaining a new management position on the basis of only a moderate budget increase	.72
	1.00

Thus, the probability of securing the new position is .22, obtained by adding .14 (assuming a sizeable budget increase) to .08 (assuming only a moderate increase). The most complex step in decision analysis forecasting is assigning relative weights to the various outcomes which represent likelihood (or, in some cases, preferences). The risks of miscalculating relative weights, however, appear to be no greater than the risks taken with many other forecasting methods which rapidly become obsolete as new data become available. The abundance of variables which must be reckoned and the ready availability of statistical data which bear on manpower decisions make it highly desirable to build flexibility into whatever forecasting method is being used, thus achieving "adaptive" or "feedback" forecasting. Finally, it is appropriate to restate the need for imposing reasonable limits on the forecast period. As noted earlier, in most cases forecasting at the level of the local jurisdiction for periods of more than five years in advance has little or no utility.

Considering all the contingencies (e.g., budgets, alterations in missions, the state of the economy, high-level decisions, etc.), it is understandable that one might dismiss altogether the possibility of estimating manpower needs. But increasingly planning is recognized as a basic management responsibility and, however problematic, it seems increasingly necessary.

After all, there are few if any answers about which specialists in any field would be in universal agreement.

Asking the Right Questions. What has been stated so often with regard to academia and research generally also pertains to manpower planning: Asking the right question often is as important as getting the right answer. Indeed, the exercise of identifying the right question itself frequently exhausts the entire range of possibilities. The following representative list of some of those general questions preoccupying manpower planners again reveals the need for planners with generalized backgrounds.

1. How ought manpower planners coordinate their projecting and forecasting techniques with the position classification process? Should some measure of manpower planning occur prior to classification?
2. Given the context and functions, what is the model supervisory structure? What is the optimum number of supervisory levels? The question recalls the literature of public administration concerning "span of control," i.e., the number of persons that a manager can supervise effectively. The conventional answer ranges generally between three and fifteen persons. Since the 1960s greater attention has been given to the frequency and intensity of the supervisor/employee relationship, with less attention to the number of persons involved. Equally important is the question of the manager's time. How much and what kind of supervisory authority can be delegated to employees? How much training is required for effective delegating? How much face-to-face contact between supervisor and employee is necessary or desirable? The same questions must be asked in establishing a viable working relationship between professional and clerical personnel. As organizational purposes and conditions vary, so will these relationships.[41]

It is tautological to point out that the smaller the number of persons to be supervised, the greater the possibility for intense supervision. However, this truism is variously affected by different supervisory structures, requiring that the manpower planner be flexible even when dealing with a tautology. Management and manpower planners

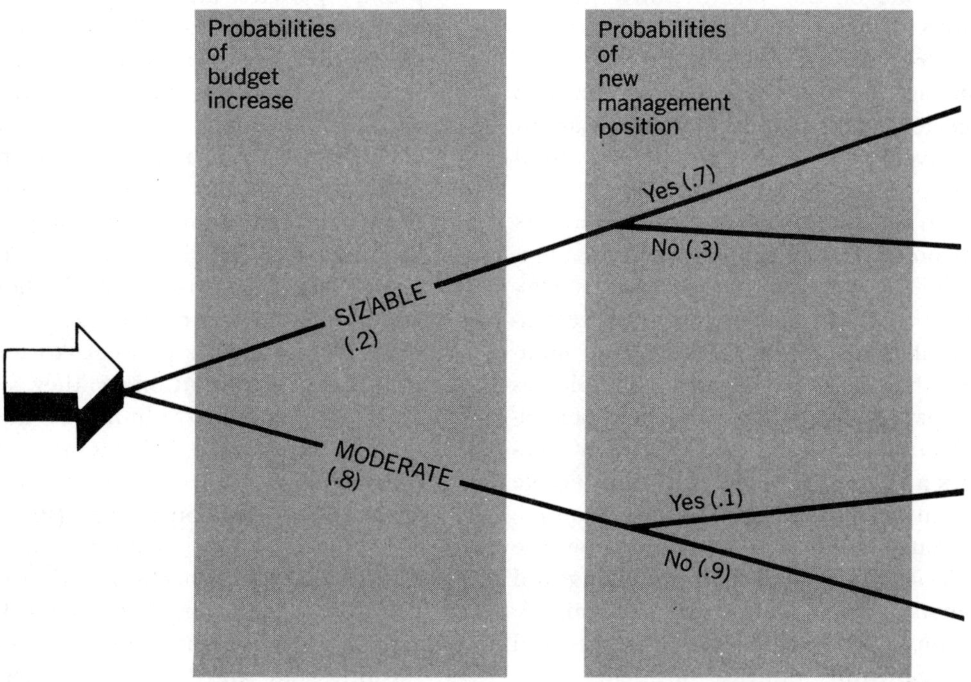

FIGURE 3–2. *Simplified branch diagram illustrating decision analysis forecasting procedure. See text for further discussion.*

need to ask whether too narrow a span of control, which necessitates an increase in the number of levels within the hierarchy and, correspondingly, a more pointed organizational structure, actually results in increased costs, diminished morale, excessive time lost between decision and action, or excessive involvement of management in matters which properly could be handled at lower levels. On the other hand, too broad a span of control could produce an uncontrollable situation. In either case, the quality of supervision is crucial to control—another general consideration for the manpower planner.

3. What is the optimum relationship between manpower planning and training programs? What should be the role of staff development and training in the manpower planner's efforts to provide a steady supply of personnel—either from recruitment outside or from promotion within—so that the jurisdiction's requirements for efficiency and for affirmative action can be met? It may be necessary at an early stage of the manpower planning process to take inventory of the qualifications of the jurisdiction's present employees in order to determine their need and capacity for training. With this information base the manpower planner can help management make sounder judgments about the relative weight in the jurisdiction's total training program given to entry-level training and training to upgrade and update. As already noted, competitive demand for manpower or a shortage in its supply may prompt the manpower planner to recommend that management remedy these manpower imbalances through new technologies rather than through recruiting new personnel. The trade-off, however, is that new technologies may require their own considerable investment in retraining present personnel, even though ultimately they may be the most efficient way of both economizing and compensating for a manpower problem.

4. As to employee development programs and equal opportunity policies, how does management make certain that procedures for selecting employees for training and development are free of bias and consistent with fair employment practices?

5. What is the probable impact of a change in certification requirements on the supply and demand of labor? Ordinarily the consequence of upgrading certification requirements is a decrease in the supply of qualified manpower and an attendant rise in its cost. The same consequence also may be expected of increased unionization.

6. How may the manpower planner best orchestrate manpower decisions with the jurisdiction's personnel policy? If employee morale is low or if the grievance procedure is inadequate (possibly indicating defects in personnel administration), then securing a sufficient supply of new recruits may be an especially troublesome problem. It follows that whatever personnel policies affect the rate of turnover also concern the manpower planner. Fine points of personnel policy that the manpower planner must understand include basic wage and salary structure, fringe benefits, working conditions, the nature of motivations utilized, disciplinary policies, and, in particular, promotion policy (i.e., do sufficient opportunities exist within for advancement and self-actualization, or does the jurisdiction tend to fill vacancies through new hirings?) In short, if those aspects of a jurisdiction's personnel policy apparently responsible for an abnormally high number of resignations can be pinpointed and eliminated, the manpower planner's task is made both easier and ultimately more useful.

7. How are manpower planners to follow new trends and information as they surface in their own field, an admittedly diffuse and largely unscientific field? One particularly comprehensive source is the Personnel Management Information Service (PMIS) of the U.S. Civil Service Commission, a service established in connection with the administration of the Intergovernmental Personnel Act of 1970 for the stated purpose of informing state and local governments of developments in the personnel field. However,

since the manpower planning function is so broadly dispersed among the various agencies of the federal government, there is no single adequate source of information on the state of the profession.

8. When and to what degree may management and manpower planners at the local level rely on federal assistance in solving manpower problems? The improbability of developing a comprehensive national manpower policy was noted earlier; indeed, some critics question whether a comprehensive policy would even be desirable. The needs of each jurisdiction are only one part of a multitude of considerations that impinge on national manpower programs as they develop piecemeal. For example, periodically the federal government launches programs aimed at creating jobs in order to cure economic ills or training the disadvantaged in order to compensate for past inequities. The problem, as some jurisdictions have learned through experience, is that although federal assistance may appear very attractive, given the short-term and usually qualified nature of much of that assistance, the jurisdiction may be left without adequate resources of its own, in the event of a cutoff or reduction of federal funding, to carry out the obligations undertaken. Hence, there is the obvious need for the manpower planner to be well-acquainted with the details of federal programs.

These questions are such that they cannot be answered easily or without qualification. Manpower planners must be content with trends and tendencies, and sometimes with even less. For example, research conducted in the private sector indicates conflicting evidence about a positive correlation between the size of a firm and the proportion of employees who are "non-operatives" or part of the "supportive component" (administrative, technical, and clerical employees) and who do not, unlike blue-collar workers, contribute directly to the firm's primary output.[42] If there is uncertainty about even a descriptive question of this part, there should be little wonder why there are no hard prescriptive answers as to the "best" ratio between blue-collar and white-collar workers or between professional and clerical personnel within a jurisdiction.

PLANNING IN CONTEXT

One final concern deserves attention: the locus of the manpower planning function within the jurisdiction. Restated, this concern is a question of whether to delegate all or part of the manpower planning function to the operative agencies within a jurisdiction or to centralize that function at a point organizationally close to the chief executive. In smaller jurisdictions the problem usually is resolved by assigning all manpower planning responsibilities to the persons who have assumed the personnel function.

The larger the jurisdiction, however, the more crucial the issue of where manpower planning takes place. On the one hand, it is obviously advantageous to management to assign manpower planning responsibilities to one agency, whether that unit be the personnel or the general planning agency. In addition, centralizing the manpower planning function presents a context more favorable for the implementation of more refined and sophisticated techniques of projection and forecasting. On the other hand, if the planning responsibility is broken down by function and distributed among the working parts of the organization, then there usually is greater exposure and access for individual users to current and accurate data essential for manpower decision making.

Perhaps more important than the determination of where the planning responsibility lies is the development of strategies for ensuring coordination between the various departments within the jurisdiction and the planning staff when it is to prepare its recommendations to top management for manpower decisions. In most cases the data-analyzing units are not the data-generating units. The locus of the planning function is heavily dependent on how that gap between the gathering of data and its interpretation is bridged.

Manpower planning represents a good illustration of how sharp distinctions perceived at one time between line and staff can become blurred. Historically, planning has been perceived as a staff function. It is indeed a staff function insofar as it extends advice and makes recommendations to management about policy matters, but at the same time it is a line activity, since planners must work directly with the operating departments if the plan is to be properly implemented. Again, in most cases the structural arrangement is less important than good interaction among the principals.

As a staff function, manpower planning inevitably poses some problems for management. Leonard Sayles has identified certain difficulties common to most advisory relationships, of which the planning/management relationship is an example. For one, rather than wait for management to request advice, the adviser may be anxious to take the initiative. On the other hand, fearful that management's responsibility might be infringed, the adviser might avoid taking responsibility for a problem. Still another difficulty arises when the adviser, or planner, becomes more sympathetic to subordinates, i.e., the operating departments, than to management itself, or vice versa. It is presumed that the manpower planning staff will not interfere in the relationship between the jurisdiction's top management personnel and its department heads. That potential does exist, and structural distinctions are by no means a guarantee of noninterference. According to Sayles:

In the modern organization, expertise is distributed among many specialized groups and a given problem can call for engineering, standards, methods, personnel, and many other types of knowledge. The boundary lines are never clear. . . .[43]

Sayles suggests the existence of inherent conflict between persons oriented toward ideas and those who emphasize action.[44] He describes the successful advisory relationship as that in which the adviser responds to discrete distress signals from management and demands no credit later for problem solving. Sayles possibly expects greater sacrifice in ego gratification on the part of the adviser than is realistic. For its part, management must be alert to any psychological barriers developing between it and the advisory staff and between the advisory staff and the operating departments. The adviser's, or planner's, effectiveness is seriously jeopardized if he or she is perceived as anything other than a source of guidance and cooperation.[45]

Intimately related to the concern about the locus of the manpower planning function is general accessibility to personnel records. If manpower planning is centralized with the personnel staff, then personnel records can be utilized more readily in the projection and forecasting process. And if personnel records are decentralized, there may still be the opportunity for the manpower planning staff to offer technical assistance on the gathering and maintenance of personnel data. Records must be retained and kept up to date on items such as occupational assignments within the jurisdiction; educational and work qualifications as well as aptitudes and interests of individual employees; on-the-job training; detailed budget information, including shortfalls and vacancies by occupation; and terminations and promotions by occupation. A form which includes a number of elements on which manpower projections are based is reproduced as Figure 3-3.

Summary

Manpower planning is an increasingly useful tool for public management. While it is an enterprise in which interpretive skills are still primary, the statistical processes which back it up have become sufficiently accurate that its potential purpose of ensuring that the right person be placed in the right job at the right time is imminent. As a social skill it may be said to have been born with the passage of the Full Employment Act of 1946, and it came of age during the War on Poverty during the Johnson years. There has never been a truly comprehensive national manpower policy, largely because interest groups having a stake in the outcome of planning tend to keep it fragmented. At the same time, manpower policy has been used to facilitate recovery from recession and to equalize opportunities for disadvantaged groups—albeit with an uneven record of achievement for both. A future concern may be the relationship between manpower policy and leisure.

As a management skill, manpower planning

Characteristic	1971	1972	1973	1974	1975	1976
Recommended total						
Recommended full-time						
Recommended full-time equivalents						
Budgeted total						
Budgeted full-time						
Budgeted full-time equivalents						
Actual employment						
Actual full-time						
Actual full-time equivalents						
Actual full-time employment equivalents						
Actual/recommended employment						
Budget shortfall						
Budget shortfall rate						
Vacancy						
Vacancy rate						
Employment shortfall						
Employment shortfall rate						
Total terminations						
Separations						
Quits						
Discharges						
Death and retirement						
Transfers out						
Accessions						
New hires						
Transfers into						
Upgrade						
Horizontal						
Termination rate						
Separation rate						
Quit rate						
Discharge rate						
Death/retirement rate						
Transfer out rate						
Accession rate						
New hire rate						
Transfers into rate						
Upgrade rate						
Horizontal rate						
Number trained						
Number that require training						
Total number certified						
Number certified this year						

FIGURE 3–3. *Summary data matrix of employment characteristics for Operator I. (Source: Based on U.S., Environmental Protection Agency, Office of Water Programs,* MANPOWER PLANNING FOR WASTEWATER TREATMENT PLANTS, *p. 171.)*

is closely linked to many aspects of the personnel function. While the direct interests of manpower planning lie in the areas of recruiting, turnover, and employee utilization, indirectly manpower planning concerns itself with anything which may create a gap between labor supply and demand, including the apparently disparate work elements of morale, grievance procedures, certification, and unionization, as well as salaries and fringe benefits. The manpower planner also must recommend to management those policies which are consistent with the objectives of equal employment opportunity. With such a broad field of activity, manpower planning, once clearly a staff function, has also become operational as a line function as well. Manpower planners are most useful as advisers to the jurisdiction's top management when they can present the most up-to-date and accurate information that can be acquired from the working departments, which in itself assumes a mutually supportive relationship between the manpower planning office and the line departments.

In sum, manpower planning as of the 1970s had not reached its full potential, but it had achieved, despite its natural conditions of contingency and change, remarkable sophistication during its short history.

---

[1] William R. Monat, "The Once and Future Revolution: Manpower Policy in the United States," PUBLIC ADMINISTRATION REVIEW 20 (January/February 1970): 69.

[2] O. Glenn Stahl, PUBLIC PERSONNEL ADMINISTRATION, 6th ed. (New York: Harper & Row Publishers, 1971), p. 98.

[3] Quoted in "Introduction" in Robert A. Gordon, ed., TOWARD A MANPOWER POLICY (New York: John Wiley & Sons, Inc., 1967), p. 3.

[4] U.S., Environmental Protection Agency, MANPOWER PLANNING FOR WASTEWATER TREATMENT PLANTS, prepared for the Office of Water Programs by Olympus Research Corporation, 1972, p. 5.

[5] Quoted in Gordon, TOWARD A MANPOWER POLICY, p. 3.

[6] A. Lee Fritschler, Andrew W. Boesel, and Ernest A. Englebert, "Public Sector Manpower Planning in the United States," paper presented at triannual meeting of the International Institute of Administrative Sciences, Mexico City, 22–26 July 1974.

[7] Monat, "The Once and Future Revolution," p. 73.

[8] For a brief historical background, see Garth L. Mangum, "The Emergence of a National Manpower Program," in Gordon, TOWARD A MANPOWER POLICY.

[9] Monat, "The Once and Future Revolution," p. 77.

[10] Mangum, "The Emergence of a National Manpower Program," p. 28.

[11] Ibid., p. 31.

[12] National Urban Coalition, COUNTERBUDGET: A BLUEPRINT FOR CHANGING NATIONAL PRIORITIES, 1971–1976 (New York: Praeger Publishers, Inc., 1971), p. 29.

[13] For a general discussion of labor participation in manpower planning, see Richard A. Lester, "The Role of Organized Labor," pp. 317–332, and accompanying discussion by Nat Weinberg, pp. 333–349, in Gordon, TOWARD A MANPOWER POLICY.

[14] Ibid., p. 321.

[15] Ibid., p. 337.

[16] See American Federation of Labor–Congress of Industrial Organizations, LABOR LOOKS AT CONGRESS, 1973 (Washington, D.C.: American Federation of Labor–Congress of Industrial Organizations, 1974).

[17] David McClelland, THE ACHIEVING SOCIETY (New York: Van Nostrand Reinhold Company, 1961).

[18] Harold L. Sheppard, "An Integrated Approach to Manpower and Economic Development," in DIMENSIONS OF MANPOWER POLICY: PROGRAMS AND RESEARCH, eds. Sar A. Levitan and Irving H. Siegel (Baltimore: The Johns Hopkins University Press, 1966), p. 260.

[19] Ibid., pp. 262–263.

[20] However, there also is the possibility that members of minority groups make regular use of public employment services because they lack the contacts—friends and relatives—who are able to help them find work. See Sar A. Levitan, Garth L. Mangum, and Ray Marshall, HUMAN RESOURCES AND LABOR MARKETS (New York: Harper & Row Publishers, 1972), p. 101.

[21] Ibid., p. 92.

[22] Ibid., p. 98.

[23] Statistical elaboration of these trends is found in the annual MANPOWER REPORT OF THE PRESIDENT, prepared by the U.S. Department of Labor.

[24] Leonard A. Lecht, MANPOWER NEEDS FOR NATIONAL GOALS IN THE 1970's (New York: Praeger Publishers, Inc., 1969), p. 40.

[25] Sar A. Levitan et al., HUMAN RESOURCES AND LABOR MARKETS, p. 579.

[26] Ibid.

[27] Ibid., p. 580.

[28] Daniel Seligman, "How 'Equal Opportunity' Turned into Employment Quotas," FORTUNE 87 (March 1973): 161.

[29] For a discussion of some applications of the equal employment opportunity program which seem to have overtones of reverse discrimination, see James G. Driscoll, "Scram, White Man," THE NATIONAL OBSERVER, 13 July 1974, p. 1.

[30] U.S., Equal Employment Opportunity Commission, AFFIRMATIVE ACTION AND EQUAL EMPLOYMENT: A GUIDEBOOK FOR EMPLOYERS, vol. 1 (Washington, D.C.: U.S. Equal Employment Opportunity Commission, 1974), pp. 16–17.

[31] Committee for Economic Development, TRAINING AND JOBS FOR THE URBAN POOR (New York: Committee for Economic Development, 1970).

[32] Herbert A. Simon, "The Decision Maker as Innovator," in CONCEPTS AND ISSUES IN ADMINISTRATIVE BEHAVIOR, eds. Sidney Mailick and Edward H. Van Ness,

(Englewood Cliffs, N.J.: Prentice–Hall, Inc., 1962), p. 66.

[33] Edward C. Banfield, "Ends and Means in Planning," in Mailick and Van Ness, CONCEPTS AND ISSUES IN ADMINISTRATIVE BEHAVIOR, p. 75.

[34] Ibid., p. 77.

[35] Environmental Protection Agency, MANPOWER PLANNING FOR WASTEWATER TREATMENT PLANTS, p. 95.

[36] For an elaboration of some of the implications of increased productivity, see National Commission on Productivity and Work Quality in cooperation with the Ford Foundation, SO, MR. MAYOR, YOU WANT TO IMPROVE PRODUCTIVITY (Washington, D.C.: Government Printing Office, 1974).

[37] Special Task Force to the Secretary of Health, Education, and Welfare, WORK IN AMERICA (Cambridge, Mass.: MIT Press, 1973), p. 15.

[38] Ibid., pp. 17–23.

[39] For a thorough discussion of decision analysis forecasting, see U.S. Civil Service Commission, Bureau of Executive Manpower, DECISION ANALYSIS FORECASTING FOR EXECUTIVE MANPOWER PLANNING, Executive Manpower Management Technical Assistance Paper No. 3 (Washington, D.C.: Government Printing Office, 1974). Its comparison with the Delphi approach begins on p. 3.

[40] For a discussion of diagramming the options by "branches," see Civil Service Commission, DECISION ANALYSIS FORECASTING FOR EXECUTIVE MANPOWER PLANNING, pp. 13–16.

[41] For a discussion of social science research on the proper balance between management and staff, see Harold Koontz, "Making Theory Operational: The Span of Management," JOURNAL OF MANAGEMENT STUDIES 3 (October 1966) : 229–243.

[42] For a summary of current literature on the relationship between the "supportive component" and the workers who contribute directly to the primary output of an administrative unit, see James L. Price, HANDBOOK OF ORGANIZATIONAL MEASUREMENT (Lexington, Mass.: D. C. Heath & Company, 1972), pp. 19–26.

[43] Leonard Sayles, MANAGERIAL BEHAVIOR (New York: McGraw–Hill Book Company, 1964), p. 89.

[44] Ibid., p. 90.

[45] Some remarks relevant to manpower planning are contained in James H. Pickford, "The Local Planning Agency: Organization and Structure," in PRINCIPLES AND PRACTICE OF URBAN PLANNING, ed. William I. Goodman (Washington, D.C.: International City Management Association, 1968), pp. 540–545.

4

Structuring the
Work Force

When you are studying any matter or consider-ing any philosophy, ask yourself only what are the facts and—the truth that the facts bear out. Never let yourself be directed either by what you would wish to believe, or by what you think would have beneficial social effects if it were believed. But look only at—the facts.

BERTRAND RUSSELL

ORGANIZATIONS REACT to both internal and external change, and change, whatever the source, has a pronounced effect on the structure of the work force. Inside the organization, program objectives and specific job elements will affect the work force structure; outside the organization, broad as well as specific socioeconomic influences and controls likewise will be influential. The purpose of this chapter is to place and analyze traditional and modern organizational concepts and management styles in a context of change. Accordingly, organizational as well as societal concerns will be related to the structural aspects of the work force. The classification system will be reviewed, for it is through it that the work force is structured.

Overview

The best structure of an organization is the simplest one that will achieve the organization's objectives. Beyond this observation, there is no model organizational structure, nor is there a standard classification or evaluation system. Structure and system are only means to an end, rather than ends in themselves. What determines the shape, character, and structure of an organization's work force are the jurisdiction's needs, objectives, values, and resources —all of which are constantly changing.

TRADITIONAL ORGANIZATIONAL STRUCTURE

Theory of Bureaucracy. Around the turn of the century the German sociologist Max Weber developed the theory of bureaucracy that would result in the "ideal" organization. Organizational problems such as capricious judgment, abuse, nepotism, and favoritism would be overcome by following his proposed principles that required precise rules and procedures. According to Weber, the most effective and most efficient organizational model was based on the following principles:

1. The structure of the organization is hierarchical, with each individual responsible to one person for his actions and for those of subordinates.
2. Position descriptions and organization charts spell out who has what responsibility in the division of labor, which is to be based on functional specialization.
3. Specific rules and procedures ensure optimum performance, uniformity, and proper coordination in the execution of all organizational tasks. Assignments to the various

jobs and offices are based on technical competence as determined by objective criteria, such as examinations.

4. Emphasis is placed on job security; accordingly, lifetime tenure, formalized promotion procedures, regular salary increases, and guaranteed pension rights are basic to the model.
5. "Social distance" should be maintained between managers and subordinates: Interpersonnel relations should be impersonal. Rules establish the rights of employees.

The classical concept of bureaucracy relied exclusively on the power to influence through rules and procedures, reason, and the law. The bureaucratic model has been used relatively successfully in achieving its goals; many of its basic features are found in most organizations today. Some aspects of the bureaucratic model have proved inefficient, counterproductive, or outmoded, especially if applied in excess or in the wrong work setting. Experience has shown that rules can be arbitrary and irrational; confusion and conflict in roles or job assignments can occur; and informal organizations can replace if not subvert the objectives of formal organizational structures.

Scientific Management. Scientific management, based on the work of Frederick Taylor and his associates, was another important organization concept which advocated the following principles to achieve the "one best method," namely, the most efficient organization:

1. Break the job down into its smallest component set of tasks.
2. Study each task to determine the one best method of its performance.
3. Place persons in the job who have the requisite aptitudes and attributes, and train them to perform according to the one best method.
4. Control the manner in which the job is performed; establish a time limit for completion of the job; pay according to output through a piece-rate system; and closely supervise performance of the job.[1]

Classical organizational theory was epitomized in Luther Gulick's essay, "Notes on the Theory of Organization,"[2] written in 1937. It was in this essay that the mnemonic device POSDCORB (planning, organizing, staffing, directing, coordinating, reporting, and budgeting) was popularized to indicate the real work concerns of the executive that in general still pertain today.

Modern Organizational Structure

Questioning of the traditional organizational structures began as a result of the Hawthorne studies conducted in the 1920s and described in the writings of Elton Mayo and Chester I. Barnard in which the terms "human relations" and "modern management" were coined. As early as 1938 studies were undertaken of the informal group or organization within the formal organization. Barnard claimed that the formal organization could not exist very long without the informal organization.[3] The formal organization provides the skeletal, impersonal structure; the informal organization, in contrast, is personal and provides the driving force. Since 1950 a tremendous amount of research has been developed on important organizational concerns such as leadership, job satisfaction, motivation, communications, work incentives, and personal and organizational development. Much of this research has questioned and reevaluated traditional assumptions about organizations and the people in them.

A major questioner has been the behavioral scientist. The continuing debate over managerial methods and styles has created a jungle of theory and a profusion of so-called "best" methods that tend to discourage anybody seeking assistance. Any discussion of organizational theory also should recognize Parkinson's Law as well as the Peter Principle and the implications they have for the organizational and the job structure.

According to Parkinson's Law, "work expands so as to fill the time available for its completion." Parkinson also believed that the number of staff members in the organization was bound to increase regardless of the amount of work to be performed and even if the work load were declining. The Peter Principle declares that "in a hierarchy every employee tends to rise to the level of incompetence."[4] In other words, a substantial proportion of those in middle- and top-management positions have been advanced to their first, and even second, levels of incompetence after having been judged competent in the performance of a lower-level position.

The industrial psychologist Abraham Korman has outlined some factors that should be reviewed in organizational restructuring. He finds continuing value in the classical organizational model, notably for its emphasis on order and predictability, for its clarity of the rules of behavior, and its provision for rational and quick decisions. However, he deplores the constraints to creativity and productivity caused by overdependent relationships and organizational inflexibility. In sum, Korman proposes the following:

1. "Idea" people should be hired to overcome the effects of dependency and to promote creativity. This is a primary and not a secondary objective.
2. Persons who are significantly different from those traditionally employed should be hired to insure that fresh ideas are brought into the work force.
3. Increased job rotations and personal and job development should be encouraged in order to develop self-confidence and a sense of self-growth as well as to stimulate creativity.
4. Management controls should be results-oriented rather than oriented to the approach or the process by which the work is performed. Such orientation increases the employee's sense of competence and also reduces overdependency.
5. Greater employee participation in decision making should be encouraged. Employees should be involved in the planning of work and in making decisions on how to carry it out.
6. Employees should be encouraged to identify with their profession and with outside interest groups, thereby lessening their dependency on the organization.
7. Suggestions for change from "below"—the staff of the organization—should be encouraged to overcome any dependency relationships, to facilitate better communications, and to promote new ideas.
8. Ad hoc task forces or project teams should be appointed whenever feasible. For example, set up temporary teams to handle special problems or specific projects. These project teams may be composed of organizational representatives performing functions relevant to the problem assigned.
9. Decrease the number of supervisory levels in the organization in order to encourage in-dependence and to remove or lessen some of the traditional bureaucratic inhibitions to organizational change.
10. Broaden the performance appraisal process beyond the traditional manager-worker interchange to include self-appraisals and peer appraisals.[5]

Management Styles. Perhaps the most important management style introduced since the 1960s is Management by Objectives (MBO). MBO deals with two major organizational concerns: motivation and appraisal. Motivation involves the stimulation of employees to achieve high quality as well as quantity in productivity; appraisal is the assessment of productivity achieved.

MBO's three basic principles of goal setting are as follows:

1. The manager assumes responsibility for identifying the organizational goals and objectives shared by management with subordinates, the achievement on which is focused their combined talents and efforts.
2. Each person must understand the organizational goals to be achieved and must be able to state in advance his or her area of responsibility.
3. All persons must have worked out a plan for achieving the goals which pertain to their particular areas of responsibility and must be prepared to have their performance objectively measured by results, insofar as the results can be attributed to conditions under their effective control.

The dominant concept underlying the MBO approach is simply that people are more likely to accomplish something if they know clearly what they are trying to accomplish. In requiring a definite commitment by people, MBO makes some fundamental assumptions about human behavior. (It should be noted that the assumptions which managers make about human behavior have an important bearing on the work force structure.) Stated simply, MBO makes the optimistic assumption that people not only do not need to be coerced to work but actually can learn actively to seek greater responsibility. (See Chapter 12 for a discussion of Douglas McGregor's "Theory X" and "Theory Y" about worker motivation.)

MBO also seeks to personalize the process of setting objectives: "If a man's most powerful driving force is comprised of his needs, wishes, and personal aspirations, combined with the compelling wish to look good in his own eyes for meeting those deeply held personal goals, the management by objectives should begin with *his* objectives."[6] MBO, like most schemes, does not provide an automatic solution to managerial problems, but the judicious and selective use of MBO elements can "become a powerful managerial tool for managers who apply it with judgment."[7]

Management Principles. Over the years various criteria have been developed that should prove useful in making decisions relating to the structure of the work force.[8] Some of these principles are summarized here:

1. Authority and responsibility: The responsibility exacted for actions taken should balance the authority delegated for such actions. (According to Barnard, "You can't operate a large organization unless you delegate responsibility, not authority but responsibility. Authority comes second."[9] Authority is intended to furnish managers with a tool which, properly used, contributes to the achievement of organizational objectives.

2. Division of work: The better an organization structure reflects the systematic classification of its tasks, the more it assists in their coordination by creating a system of interrelated roles, and the more these roles are designed to fit the capabilities and motivations of its employees, then the more effective and efficient an organization structure will be.

3. Definition of functions: When an individual has a clear definition of the results expected, the activities undertaken, the authority delegated, and when the control and information relationships with other positions are understood, then the more fully the individual can contribute toward accomplishing organizational objectives.

4. Learning from others: In order to avoid reinventing the wheel, organizations and individuals should build on the experience of others. A better wheel can be built by utilizing accumulated knowledge.

5. Responsibility: Managers should expect to be held accountable for the activities of their subordinates within the organization.

6. Lines of authority: The clearer the lines of authority extending throughout the entire organization, the more effective the decision making and the communication within the organization.

7. Separation of responsibility: Individuals who are responsible for checking on the activities of another department cannot discharge their responsibility adequately if they are required to report to the department whose activity they are expected to evaluate.

8. Span of management: There is a limit to the number of people that can be supervised effectively by one manager. The limit to the span of management cannot be specified numerically but, rather, is contingent upon such factors as the type and character of the work activities being supervised, the frequency of the supervisor's contacts with subordinates, the training and capacity of both supervisor and subordinates, and the extent to which a particular supervisor is able to delegate authority. Usually the span of management or control is greater for managers at the lower levels than those at the upper levels of the organization.

It should be emphasized that no concept, style, or principle, no matter how old or how recent, can be applied with assurance of success. They are merely tools to achieve better understanding and, depending on the circumstances, may require adaptation.

Management Philosophy. Consideration should be given to developing a management philosophy which will fit what are termed the "felt" needs of the organization. These needs consist of the perceived value judgments held by all the people who constitute the organization. They vary from one organization to another, since the political and social environment, which greatly influences what we perceive and feel, varies among jurisdictions. A statement or a restatement of management philosophy is especially useful when a new and significant organizational concern has arisen. For example, collective bargaining in the public sector or an affirmative action program for minorities and women may require a reevaluation of an organization's philosophy. The so-called "good faith" approach on the part of management to both these concerns is recommended.

Structuring the Work Force

THE JOB:
THE BASIC BUILDING BLOCK

The basic building block and key element in the structure of the organization is the job. (Many public personnel administrators prefer the term "position.") The commonly accepted definition of a job is a group of duties and responsibilities assigned or delegated, requiring the full-time or part-time employment of one person. How the job is designated and designed affects the way in which the organization will function.

Consequently, increasing attention has been given to the well-designed job, which entails consideration of job restructuring, redesign, enlargement, and enrichment. The job that is well-designed is (a) a complete job; (b) a job where the maximum amount of job control and decision making rests in the hands of the incumbent; and (c) where the incumbent receives good feedback on job performance from the job itself.

Changes in job design will affect other formal and informal organizational and management variables, and in turn will be affected by them. Moreover, according to O. Glenn Stahl, "Most managers can accommodate . . . both external and internal conditions beyond their direct control by the simple expedient of re-examining the manner in which duties and tasks have been combined for the attention of individual workers."[10]

When analyzing a job for purposes of redesign, the structure of the job has significance. Work content, duties and responsibilities, and the major or critical tasks are basic elements in the job structure. Briefly, each job is made up of a cluster of major and minor tasks, and each task has its task elements or operations. Each duty and responsibility is made up of one or more tasks, with the number and kind varying from job to job. Each duty and responsibility, in order to be performed at an acceptable standard level, requires the possession of knowledge, skills, and aptitudes that either must be brought to the job or can be acquired on the job.

The work change cycle, the relationship of work to the jobs, and the job information and evaluation systems in the organization are summarized in Figure 4-1. Management specialist Peter Drucker has made the apt observation that there is a difference between "doing the right job and doing the job right." "Doing the right job" involves the appropriateness of the work content as it relates to the organization and its goals and objectives. "Doing the job right" requires that the job be well-designed, which includes as a beginning a clear and accurate job description. A good job description also facilitates employee selection as well as orientation, training, and work performance evaluation.

In any organization a reasonably up-to-date job description should be available for every position. The job applicant or incumbent also should understand that the job description is an item having equal or greater importance than the original employment application form. The quality of the personnel program and the success of any job evaluation system is keyed to the job description. A good job description describes what is expected of the employee. If all job descriptions are well written and specify precisely the objectives of a particular job, then it follows that the organizational objectives more likely will be accomplished. Inadequate or nonexistent job descriptions usually result in misunderstanding or irresponsible behavior.

The job description should not be viewed as an instrument to restrict incumbents but to facilitate and encourage full utilization of their talent and imagination. The degree of detail in the job description should be sufficient to assure that the major or critical tasks are covered. The minor or incidental tasks need not be covered, unless there is a special problem which requires a full indepth job

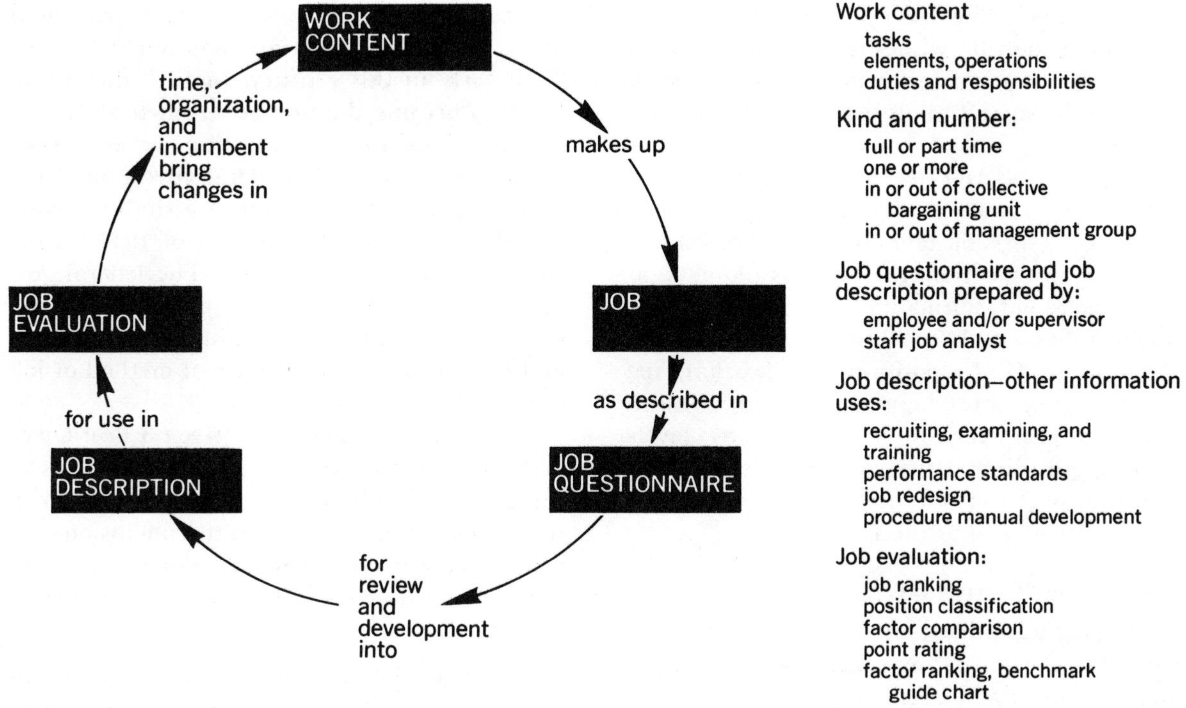

FIGURE 4–1. *Components of the work change cycle. See text for further discussion.*

study. (See Chapter 9 for a more detailed discussion of this topic.)

A well-designed position questionnaire also should be constructed in such a manner that it will produce responses sufficiently specific to be quantified. In large organizations staff analysts may be used to prepare job questionnaires and job descriptions, resulting in standardized forms. The analyst should not dictate job or work content but should bring to light and resolve questions about work overlap and duplication. It is desirable that the job information system correspond with the Dictionary of Occupational Titles' system of titles, codes, and other references.

THE DICTIONARY OF OCCUPATIONAL TITLES (DOT)

The DOT represents the most comprehensive compilation of community employment standards and categories in use throughout the United States at the present time. The information in the third edition of the Dictionary (issued in 1965), which includes some 35,550 occupational entries, was the result of more than 75,000 job analyses conducted in thousands of work establishments. The 1965 edition includes 6,432 more jobs than earlier editions. A fourth edition, planned for early 1977, will present additional data and changes. Major revisions are expected in Volume 2, related to worker traits.

The DOT was developed for use in job placement and counseling, but it is also helpful in recruitment, job analysis, and other related activities. The other major occupational classification system available in the United States is that of the Bureau of the Census developed expressly for census-related purposes. Efforts are being made to establish a standard occupational classification system.[11]

The DOT is valuable to the personnel analyst in identifying tasks, standardizing jobs, and in creating career ladders and lattices. The DOT contains information about job titles, job descriptions, examples of work performed, worker requirements, guides for matching applicants with requirements and for matching training with methods of entry, as well as job classifications. The DOT also can serve as an aid to anyone who wishes to develop a custom-made reference guide or job analysis manual to meet the special needs of a particular organization.

Some of the DOT's basic terminology and methodology can be adapted to fit various sizes and types of organizations. For precise position classification, the DOT is too general, as it does not normally distinguish between various class levels such as Accountant I and Accountant II. In position classification, special attention must be given to distinguishing the job characteristics between class levels. EEOC guidelines issued in 1974 for content validity procedures require a listing of the DOT title as well as the DOT code.

THE CLASSIFICATION SYSTEM

The classification system (also known as a job evaluation or job rating system) adopted by an organization is, in effect, a position inventory or an information and grading system. The system may be quantified, based on factor comparison or ranking, or it may be nonquantified, based on job ranking or position classification. Briefly, the classification system is an organized procedure whereby all positions are grouped in broad occupational categories and then subdivided according to levels of difficulty and responsibility. The process is one of aggregating and analyzing the work of the organization. The type of system employed and the methodologies used in applying it of course should fit the needs of the particular organization. The principles and standards that are part of any job evaluation system should be viewed as guides to making good decisions and not as substitutes for reasoning.

The procedure known as job evaluation (or job analysis), originated by Frederick W. Taylor in 1881, led analysts to break each job into its constituent parts, known as operations and elements. Job evaluation, as developed by Taylor, became the basis for time studies which have been used to establish performance standards and set piece rates for compensation. It has also enabled analysts to determine the unnecessary activities and motions that cause loss of time, energy, and wages.

Modern position classification, a particular method of job evaluation, was not developed until early in this century. In 1912 the city of Chicago became the first governmental unit to install a position classification system. After considerable study the federal government undertook partial installation of a similar system in 1923. The Classification Act of 1949 revised the 1923 system considerably. The federal government's implementation of the position classification method has influenced most state and local governments' choice of method of job evaluation.

In 1967 the House Committee on Post Office and Civil Service conducted a comprehensive review[12] of all job classification systems then in use in the federal service. In its conclusions the committee was critical of the systems used, citing among its major findings the following points:

1. Although job evaluation and ranking in theory should provide the basis for good personnel management, it was not seen as doing so in practice.
2. Classification and ranking systems have not been maintained, administered, or adapted to meet the rapidly changing needs of the federal government.
3. Classification as a management tool was not found in general use. Many officials commented that the only function of classification in their organization was to serve as a basis for fixing pay.

The findings of this report led to further legislation, and early in 1972 a report was released by the Job Evaluation and Pay Review Task Force, directed by Philip M. Oliver. The report, known as the Oliver Report, recommended a new, comprehensive job evaluation and pay plan for the federal government. Some of its findings indicated that line management was not involved sufficiently in the job evaluation process, and that job evaluation was not being used as a broad-gauged management tool.

Inasmuch as it appeared in the mid-1970s that a number of federal departments and agencies would implement the plan of job evaluation recommended by the Oliver task force, attention here will be directed to that plan, the so-called "factor ranking-benchmark-guide chart system," following a discussion of the more commonly used position classification method of job evaluation. Other traditional methods of job evaluation include (a) job ranking; (b) point rating; and (c) factor comparison.

Job Ranking. Job ranking is the simplest and perhaps oldest method of job evaluation: Jobs are ranked on the basis of their relative worth. In one such technique, the job analyst or rater ranks the job descriptions or job cards according to their specifications. Where several raters are used, differences in the rankings must be reconciled. This method may be suitable in organizations where there are relatively few jobs and where it is reasonable to expect one or several raters to have a thorough knowledge of all jobs.

The basic weakness of the job ranking method is that it does not provide a refined measure of each job's worth. As the number of positions increases, this weakness grows more noticeable. Attention to existing wage rates and titles in ranking often means insufficient attention given to the differences between jobs. In contrast, position classification requires that the analyst refer to a predetermined class specification or scale when evaluating jobs.

Point Rating. The point rating method of job evaluation was initially developed by the Western Electric Company and has been used by many private sector organizations such as General Electric Company and the U.S. Steel Corporation. Jobs are evaluated quantitatively on the basis of the elements—the responsibilities, skills, efforts, and working conditions—that comprise the demands of the job. Like position classification, the point rating method requires the use of a manual or scale that describes the job factors and assigns varying weights to them. Point manuals have been developed by corporations and trade associations as well as management consultants.

In developing a manual that fits the specific needs of a given organization, these basic steps ought to be followed:

1. Analyze the jobs to be evaluated and determine which factors or characteristics are to be measured in quantifying job worth.
2. Set a standard of measurement appropriate to each factor of the various jobs.
3. Define both factors and standards.
4. Assign weights to the factors in proportion to their relative importance in the organization.[13]

Factor Comparison. The factor comparison method of job evaluation was developed by Eugene Benge in the late 1920s. As is the case with the point rating method, this technique analyzes one factor at a time. It differs from the point and the position classification method in that the specifications of the job to be evaluated are compared to specifications related to key or benchmark jobs in the organization. These specifications serve as the job evaluation scale or reference. Thus, a factor comparison scale develops as part of the job evaluation process rather than proceeding from an established scale or specification.

Responsibility, skill, mental effort, and working conditions are typical elements that comprise the factor comparison scale. The basic steps of this method of job evaluation are as follows:

1. Select the key or benchmark jobs.
2. Rank the key or benchmark jobs by their factors.
3. Rank and apportion wage rates of key or benchmark jobs among the factors.
4. Compare factor ranking of jobs with wage apportionment rankings.
5. Construct a factor comparison scale using key or benchmark jobs.
6. Analyze, relate, and evaluate the remaining jobs according to the scale.

In determining the key or benchmark positions, noncontroversial jobs located on varying levels of difficulty should be selected. These jobs should have complete and accurate job descriptions whose specifications have been developed by thorough job analysis. The key or benchmark job also should have a wage rate that is both externally and internally consistent, and the job should not be under any dispute or pending grievance action. The primary disadvantage of the factor comparison method is that it usually proves to be too complicated for employees to understand. This result often occurs when an organization does not have a sufficient number of positions that are genuine key or benchmark jobs.

Position Classification. The position classification method of job evaluation classifies positions in various kinds (classes) and degrees (grade levels) of groupings according to a predetermined standard—the classification plan. Any given position specification (job description) is determined by the parameters set forth in the more general class specification.

Position classification is based on the concept that the position and not the incumbent is the object to be classified. Classification standards (class specifications) are the tools for evaluating the job, not the person holding the job. This does not necessarily mean that the incumbent cannot affect the classification of the job. Positions are classified on the basis of current duties and responsibilities of the job. When assignments are not narrowly structured, it is possible for the incumbent to so change the work content that a change in classification is required. Moreover, when training and experience are closely related to the character and quality of the work to be performed, the incumbent's qualities may well affect the job and the classification level. Sometimes the relationship of incumbent to position should be adjusted up or down after the position becomes vacant. If this adjustment is not made, problems involving relationships of other positions may arise.

The type of organization structure adopted will affect the relationship between the worker and the job. In a closed or highly structured organization, the job is almost the only element that determines the classification level. In a more open and less structured organization, the classification plan is more responsive to the worker than to the job.

Whatever particular classification plan is selected, it is the final product of the process of identifying and describing the different kinds and levels of work in an organization. The objective of the classification plan is to produce important information about the similarities and differences between classes of positions on which personnel decisions are based. A viable classification plan does the following:

1. The classification plan provides a uniform and meaningful title structure and terminology for use in preparing payrolls, budgets, official ordinances, etc. The common title language enables various persons such as employees, union representatives, arbitrators, taxpayers, public managers, and legislators to communicate more easily. However, an established plan should not prevent the use of administratively approved working titles for public discussion or legal purposes.

2. Employees and their representatives are assured that the jobs have been objectively analyzed and that uniform treatment will be accorded to salary and other related matters where positions having similar duties are involved.

3. New positions can be established more readily in relation to positions already classified. Likewise, the pay level for new positions can be related more accurately to established positions.

4. A viable classification plan gives employees an understanding of the lines of promotion and can help prepare them for promotion.

5. It provides a general basis for advertising job opportunities and for providing answers to applicants' questions about the requirements of the job.

6. It provides basic information with which to develop training programs.

7. It is an important reference used in manpower planning, programming, funding, and review. Emergency drafting of manpower proposals is not uncommon. A classification plan with a common title structure enables faster and more accurate preparation.

8. It serves as a specific reference point for use in collective bargaining. It should be noted that any third-party interpreter, such as an arbitrator, will probably interpret the language of the contract both literally and with a bias favoring employees. For example, if a benefit provision is so worded that it can be interpreted as applying to survey engineers but was intended to apply only to Civil Engineer I, the classes of Civil Engineer II and Civil Engineer III may receive an unintended benefit.

9. A good plan facilitates greater efficiency in

the personnel function by expediting personnel transactions and reducing confusion in job information, thereby reducing the probability of error both in decision making as well as in the processing of personnel records.

Many unions view job evaluation as a threat to the free collective bargaining process, claiming that it tends to limit bargaining and freeze the wage structure. Indications are that these views may be moderating somewhat.[14] Most plans were basically designed by management but have been modified by union input through bargaining. Feelings of dissatisfaction among blue-collar workers often stem from the fact that plans have not been kept up to date or that employees did not understand the plan in the first place. Dissatisfaction with a plan may also arise if the plan gives inadequate recognition to employee intellectual contributions, is used as the sole criterion for establishing wages, or is suspected of being used to downgrade jobs.

To reduce the likelihood of adverse employee reaction and increase the likelihood of successful use of a classification plan, an advisory committee may be appointed to participate in installing and maintaining the plan.[15] Such an advisory committee should represent management, the appropriate supervisors, the union, and the employees whose positions are being classified. Training and orientation of the committee is recommended. A committee functions best when it is charged with studying a full occupational group of a plan rather than a single position.

COLLECTING POSITION INFORMATION

To classify positions correctly it is necessary to secure complete information about the current duties and responsibilities involved in each position. This information is obtained in several ways.[16] One way is to ask employees to complete a position classification questionnaire in their own words. These statements are then reviewed by departmental supervisors who can indicate whether the employee's memorandum is complete and accurate, add information omitted by the employee, and comment further about currently assigned work.

The original employee statements or questionnaires are submitted, unchanged by the supervisors, to the classification analyst who reviews them and notes subjects for further inquiry. The degree and type of follow-up performed depends on variable factors such as the number of positions being studied and analyzed; the type of job being studied; constraints placed on the study in terms of time and total study needs; and the degree and nature of the collective bargaining relationship, if any, as it relates to the positions being studied.

In the first major follow-up study to a survey, consideration should be given not only to known or suspected problem areas but also to key or benchmark positions. Additional interviews with individual employees and supervisors also are advised. Employees selected for interviews should be those who are sufficiently knowledgeable about the work and who represent a fair sample of the work being performed by several persons. The individual interview at times can be supplemented by observing the employee perform certain key tasks of the position; administering a follow-up questionnaire in the form of a task statement checklist; and asking the employees to maintain a work log of all tasks or duties over a specific period of time.

In securing position information, all written statements and other results of contact with employees should emphasize that the classification study pertains only to the duties and responsibilities of the job, not how well the job is being performed. It also should be emphasized that the study is concerned with the officially assigned work of the employee, not with the employee's qualifications for such work.

In addition to contacting employees and supervisors, the job analyst who is studying the position for the first time should also use other data to obtain job and work information. A current organizational chart is most useful to a classification study, particularly a study which involves analysis of all positions in an organizational unit. Every organization, even a poorly designed one, can be charted. The chart indicates how various positions are related along principal lines of decision-making authority. Sometimes the mere charting of an organization will show clearly the inconsistencies or undue complexity which then can be corrected. Earlier as well as current organization charts can give the analyst important insights into position relationships. Nevertheless, the analyst who makes or participates in decisions concerning class title and class levels will find these charts to be limited but helpful tools, because the organization's chart normally shows only formal authority relationships.

A chart's major weaknesses are that it omits significant informal relationships between positions; it can easily become outdated because it indicates what was intended at some past time but does not indicate current intent; and, finally, in the absence of positive top leadership, it can act as a negative force restricting organizational change that otherwise may be desirable.

Other data instrumental to job analysis are basic statutes, the city charter, local ordinances and resolutions, training manuals, and bargaining unit certifications where formal collective bargaining exists. Moreover, even out-of-date data such as old job descriptions and class specifications can help the job analyst develop a picture of the various positions as they have developed over time.

While the job is the basic building block in the position classification process, the class is a key reference point. Determining the class to which a specific position belongs is a very important decision. For each position, the analyst considers the following:

1. The general nature of the work, occupation, or profession.
2. Difficulty and complexity of assigned work:
   a. Supervisory responsibility: How much responsibility is delegated in planning, organizing, staffing, directing, disciplining, coordinating, and reviewing the work of others?
   b. Decision making: How much actual responsibility is authorized for making final commitments? What is the consequence of an error?
   c. Personal relationships: Will the employee be required to resolve the problems of other people, either inside or outside the organization? Will the employee be required to persuade the public to conform to a standard or to some course of action?
   d. Creativity: Does the work require the employee to develop new programs or approaches and solve new problems?
   e. Supervision received: Is the employee's work closely inspected or is the job so highly structured that there is little need for supervision?
   f. Variety and degree of knowledge and skill: What special knowledge, skills, or training must the employee have acquired prior to assuming the position and what can be acquired by on-the-job training?
   g. Working conditions: Does the work involve hazardous duties, physical strain, unusual hours, or other such conditions that are an unavoidable part of the job?

When making a decision about a job class, the analyst first sorts the questionnaires and job description data into occupational groups, such as engineering, typing, or planning, and then into occupational subgroups according to levels of responsibility and difficulty. These subgroups serve as tentative classes. Every job assigned to a particular class must be sufficiently similar to the others to justify being given the same official title, the same pay range, and the same general conditions of employment.

It is advisable that classes be broad or expanded when setting up a new classification plan. The procedure is much like buying shoes for a child: The shoes should be as large as possible, yet still fit properly. Too narrow a concept of class necessitates too many position classification decisions. At any rate, the pressure of events will cause the size and scope of the class to narrow to some degree.

WRITING CLASS SPECIFICATIONS

The class specification is a written description that must accurately reflect the specific type, level, and complexity of work performed. The format for class specifications may differ somewhat from agency to agency, but the following items generally are included:

1. Title: The class title should be a brief and descriptive designation of the type of work performed. When a class contains a series, numerical suffixes as in Clerk Typist I and Clerk Typist II usually are used to designate the level within the class, with the Roman numeral I representing the lowest class in the series.
2. Definition: This is a brief statement describing the work performed in the class.
3. Nature of work: This section emphasizes those basic characteristics which distinguish the class from others and clarifies its size and scope. This section also may describe the supervisory arrangement; the reporting relationship within the organization; the number and type of subordinate classes; and the size and scope of authority and program responsibility. Because this section specifies the relative difficulty and responsibility of the class, thereby establishing its level within the organization, it is the section of the class specification which is most important when determining the class to which a specific position is to be allocated.
4. Examples of work: This section gives typical examples of work performed. The listing of examples is intended to be descriptive, not restrictive. It is not intended to describe all the work performed in all positions in the class. In heavily populated classes, such as police patrol officer, only one portion of one work sample may apply to a given position. The performance of one or more duties listed should not be considered conclusive evidence that a particular position belongs in a particular class. A position properly belongs in a class only when it meets the full set of criteria defined by the class specification as a whole.
5. Minimum educational and experience requirements: This section presents a statement in quantitative and qualitative terms of the background of training and experience which is expected to provide a person with the knowledge, skills, and aptitudes considered necessary for the successful performance of the work represented by the class.
6. Essential occupational traits: This portion details the specific knowledge, aptitudes, and skills required to perform successfully the work assignments within the class. Increasingly, greater emphasis has been placed on the minimum essentials required for entrance to the job rather than on desirable requirements or those requirements that can be satisfied on the job.
7. Special requirements: This section specifies legal or other special requirements to qualify for a position in the class. Examples are a medical license, driver's license, architect's registration, or a swimming certificate. Special physical requirements that have been validated as necessary for job performance also are presented here. Some class specifications also include information on lines of promotion. Frequent reference should be made to the Dictionary of Occupational Titles for uniformity in terminology.

After a tentative decision on class allocations has been made, it is normal procedure to consult the operating department, which then has an opportunity to review the classification plan for errors or oversights. This review also serves to increase the legitimacy of the classification process.

STRUCTURING FOR FLEXIBILITY IN THE CLASSIFICATION PLAN

It is advisable that the classification plan allow for flexibility in the way in which positions are filled so that persons may be recruited at levels lower than the journeyman or experienced professional level. When experienced persons are in short supply, or when, for affirmative action purposes, it is desirable to employ qualified but inexperienced persons, an entry-level position should be established, if possible. Many agencies permit the use of a controlled "under-fill" arrangement which provides some flexibility in the position level. When a vacancy occurs, the most suitable class level can be determined after reviewing appropriate eligibility lists and affirmative action goals. When a position is filled at the lower level, the incumbent can be promoted to higher levels as qualification standards for the higher level are met.

The procedure authorized for filling positions at particular class and grade levels may influence considerably the flexibility enjoyed by the appointing authority. Provisions of collective bargaining agreements also may freeze certain position or grade levels, which reduces the flexibility of a classification plan. In Milwaukee, Wisconsin, the Position Ordinance of the city is the official document that mandates staffing authority, and all appointments must be consistent with that instrument. However, to provide flexibility, after listing all authorized position titles and the number of the positions in each department, the ordinance also states that whenever a vacancy arises in any position named in the ordinance, the position may be filled by the appointing officer's appointment of an eligible person to a position of a lower grade to perform the duties assigned.

The fully effective analyst's concerns extend beyond the classification plan. The quality of the whole organization can be improved if recognition is given to the concept of position management. The North Carolina State Department of Personnel, in its *Personnel Manual,* defines position management in the following manner:

Position management involves design and control of individual positions to achieve a proper balance of values among the following management considerations: number of positions; total cost of services; maximum use of scarce or costly manpower skills; maximum attraction, retention and motivation of competent personnel; provision for maximum development opportunities; effective use of work processes, equipment and techniques; and clear delineation of duties and responsibilities. Position management is inherently the responsibility of managers and supervisors. Staff assistance in this area is available to management from the State Personnel Department.

The Factor Ranking-Benchmark-Guide Chart Evaluation System

This is the job evaluation system that was devised for the federal government and included in the Oliver Report early in 1972. As noted before, the objective was to provide a modernized approach to classification of federal government positions. The Task Force on Job Evaluation and Pay Review spent two years and $700,000 studying the classification systems then in use by the United States and Canadian national governments, as well as other systems in both the public and private sectors. The task force devised different job evaluation systems for the four major groups comprising the federal service: trades and labor positions; clerical and technical positions; administrative, professional, and technological positions; and supervisory and management positions.

Upon release of the Oliver Report, the U.S. Civil Service Commission set up a test and implementation group to validate the systems and then implement their installation if they proved workable. This review group studied approximately 366,000 positions as a part of the validation effort. Implementation of the systems, except for the trades and labor positions, has started. The system for supervisory and management positions has begun and a combined system covering the administrative, professional, and technological positions group and the clerical and technical positions group was scheduled to begin in 1976.

The factor ranking-benchmark-guide chart system developed by the task force can be established in a manner that provides some flexibility in that the factors used in evaluating positions can be modified to fit a variety of conditions. Another positive feature of this system is that the active participation of operating management in the installation phase not only is encouraged but is essential. The fact that the various factors are in themselves objective does not eliminate the necessity for subjective judgment in their application.

Explanation of this method of job evaluation is best begun with the following brief definitions:

- Factor: One of four or five key job elements individually examined in the evaluation process.
- Ranking: Arranging in order from lowest to highest.
- Benchmark: An agreed upon permanent point within a ranking or a specific position at a specific point within an array of evaluations.
- Guide chart: Controlling with a matrix that portrays sub-elements of factors used with numeric values assigned to interest points.

Factors. While there are many factors that can be listed, they are all placed in one of the following five categories:

Factor I: Requirements. The knowledge and abilities needed to perform the work of a specific factor.

Factor II: Difficulty of work. The complexity or intricacy of work and the mental demands required to perform the work of a specific position.

Factor III: Responsibility. The degree of freedom to act and the impact of work performed on the objectives and mission of the organization.

Factor IV: Personal relationships. The nature of interpersonal relationships and its importance to the ability to get the work accomplished.

Factor V: Other. Other specific job-oriented elements which also should be considered in the job evaluation process. Such elements, for example, for supervisory positions include accountability and number of workers supervised; for manual labor, physical demands and working conditions.

Ranking. Ranking is achieved by a process that makes subjective value judgments concerning the relationship of two positions to each other. There are only three possibilities in ranking: Either Position A is higher than Position B, or Position A is lower than Position B, or Position A is equal to Position B. Positions are ranked by the use of factors, each factor in turn comparing position A to position B in terms of the factor definition, with one of the three possible rankings (higher, lower, or equal) assigned for each of the four or five factors used. These rankings are then combined to form an overall ranking.

Benchmark. The benchmark position is the key to this particular system of job evaluation. Each series of choices based on factor ranking results in a composite total of choices. When these are assigned numerical values, they yield a total score which assigns positions A and B to specific points within an array of evaluations. Each time these decisions are made, they add to the array and therefore increase the number of benchmark positions. Each addition to the number of benchmark positions makes it easier to arrive at the factor ranking choices for positions not yet evaluated. Finally, when all positions to be evaluated within the organization are studied, they are all considered benchmark positions. The total evaluated structure is therefore built from the many specific decisions, each of which involves the selection of higher, lower, or equal ranking.

Guide Chart. The guide charts are matrix reference measuring devices or yardsticks used in the factor ranking process to select one of the three choices (higher, lower, or equal) required for each of the four or five factors used. A separate and specific guide chart must be developed for each of the factors used. (After the guide charts were developed for the federal service, they were validated.)

The guide chart concept recognizes that the charts developed for the federal service can be modified or expanded. The particular guide chart used by an organization should comply, whenever possible, with the specific values and concerns of the organization. The guide charts form an integral part of an operational factor-ranking benchmark system of job evaluation. The guide charts are the basic tools to be used, along with the benchmark job description, for determining the grade level of jobs outside the criteria sample of jobs.

The factor ranking-benchmark-guide chart system, as noted from its description, incorporates many of the common features of the other traditional job evaluation systems such as job ranking, point rating, factor comparison, and position classification.

Summary

The work force structure is better understood when it is described by means of a classification system. Ideally, this system is sufficiently flexible to adapt to the changing needs of the organization. In contrast to the more traditional model, organizations increasingly are becoming more open and therefore less structured.

A classification system is simply an organized means of structuring the work force by grouping all jobs into occupational categories and then subdividing them into their appropriate levels of difficulty and responsibility. An organization's classification system depends on accurate and up-to-date data gathered internally and externally in order to develop rational job descriptions and carry out other important activities of job analysis.

The outlook as of the mid-1970s was that greater attention would be directed to the uniqueness of different kinds of work. The state of the economy, particularly the high rate of unemployment, and a rethinking of the work ethic and leisure time has prompted management of various organizations to consider flexible work schedules and shared work arrangements. This of course would affect the work force structure and the classification system. On this point Levinson notes that "different kinds of work require different patterns of formal relationships and duties, different patterns of formal rules and procedures and control and measurement of systems, and different time dimensions and different goals."[17] The more flexible the system, the easier the adaptation to these changes.

[1] Frederick W. Taylor, THE PRINCIPLES OF SCIENTIFIC MANAGEMENT (New York: Harper & Row, Brothers, 1911).

[2] Luther Gulick and Lyndall Urwick, eds., PAPERS ON THE SCIENCE OF ADMINISTRATION (New York: Institute of Public Administration, 1937).

[3] Chester I. Barnard, THE FUNCTIONS OF THE EXECUTIVE, 30th anniv. ed. (Cambridge, Mass.: Harvard University Press, 1968), p. 122.

[4] Laurence J. Peter and Raymond Hull, THE PETER PRINCIPLE (New York: Bantam Books, 1969), p. 7.

[5] Abraham K. Korman, INDUSTRIAL AND ORGANIZATIONAL PSYCHOLOGY (Englewood Cliffs, N.J.: Prentice-Hall, Inc., 1971).

[6] Harry Levinson, THE GREAT JACKASS FALLACY (Cambridge, Mass.: Harvard Business School, Division of Research, 1973), p. 95.

[7] James Owens, "The Values and Pitfalls of MBO," MICHIGAN BUSINESS REVIEW 26 (July 1974): 14.

[8] Harold Koontz and Cyril O'Donnell, PRINCIPLES OF MANAGEMENT, 4th ed. (New York: McGraw-Hill Book Publishers, 1968), p. 423.

[9] William B. Wolf, CONVERSATIONS WITH CHESTER I. BARNARD (Ithaca, N.Y.: Cornell University, New York State School of Industrial and Labor Relations, 1973), p. 35.

[10] O. Glenn Stahl, THE PERSONNEL JOB OF GOVERNMENT MANAGERS (Chicago: International Personnel Management Association, 1971), p. 36.

[11] In 1966 the Interagency Committee of Occupational Classification was organized under the aegis of the Office of Management and Budget to attempt to develop a standard occupational classification system (SOC). The enactment of manpower and educational legislation and the need to deal with developing problem areas had placed increased demands on the Department of Labor and other federal agencies to furnish labor force, employment, income, and other data needed to appraise the occupational structure and requirements of the work force. This in turn created a real need for a common terminology and a coded system of occupations. The objective of SOC is to develop a system precise enough to describe occupational characteristics in sufficient detail to be useful in determining if a worker will be able to do a specific job while being flexible enough to permit groupings of occupations into distinct categories for purposes of long-range analysis. The guiding principle of the system is "work performed." Its coding system and nomenclature used to identify, classify, and codify occupations can be applied to a broad framework and can be adjusted to meet the specific needs of various agencies. Plans for SOC call for an occupational codifying system constituted of fifteen to nineteen major groups, compared to twelve for the census system and nine for the current DOT system.

[12] This 467-page report, titled REPORT OF JOB EVALUATION AND RANKING, was based on the written views of (a) all federal department and agency heads, (b) all heads of employee organizations, and (c) all federal executive boards, associations, and field personnel councils. Also, interviews were conducted with 283 operating officials and personnel officers.

[13] John A. Patton, C. L. Littlefield, and Stanley Allen Self, JOB EVALUATION (Homewood, Ill.: Richard D. Irwin Co., 1964), p. 136.

[14] Harold James, "Issues on Job Evaluation: The Union View," PERSONNEL JOURNAL 51 (September 1972): 675–679.

[15] Herbert Zollitsch and Adolph Langsner, WAGE AND SALARY ADMINISTRATION, 2nd ed. (Cincinnati: South-Western Publishing Company, 1970), p. 160.

[16] A structured procedure for obtaining and recording job analysis data is presented in the HANDBOOK FOR ANALYZING JOBS, prepared by the Manpower Division of the U.S. Department of Labor (Washington, D.C.: Government Printing Office, 1972). This handbook provides the analyst with comprehensive information about job and worker requirements. The basic techniques discussed are flexible and thus adaptable to local situations. Another helpful reference for job analysis is the guidebook for state and local governments titled JOB ANALYSIS: DEVELOPING AND DOCUMENTING DATA, prepared by the Bureau of Intergovernmental Personnel Programs of the U.S. Civil Service Commission (Washington, D.C.: Government Printing Office, 1973). See pages 9–11 for a checklist for the job audit.

[17] Levinson, THE GREAT JACKASS FALLACY, p. 31.

5

Recruitment and Staffing

To be a Seeker is to be of the best sect next to a Finder, and such a one shall every faithful, humble Seeker be at the end.

OLIVER CROMWELL

Cᴵᵀᴵᴱˢ ɪɴ ᴛʜᴇ ᴍɪᴅ-1970s and the 1980s will find one of their greatest challenges to be the recruitment of capable personnel for public service. The ultimate success or failure of government programs depends on men and women who are highly qualified, motivated, skilled, and dedicated to their careers in local government. The attraction of the best people will require that public personnel systems develop "positive recruitment—imaginative, well planned searches for qualified job applicants."[1] The Advisory Council on Intergovernmental Personnel Policy in its first report (issued in March 1974) to the President and the Congress recommended this principle:

Every effort should be made to make public employment as attractive as possible to those most likely to make their greatest contribution through public service. Personnel systems which discourage potentially high caliber public servants through unnecessary administrative procedures are not operating in harmony with this principle.[2]

The Challenge

Staffing government positions in a wide variety of administrative, professional, and technical (APT) fields will require imagination, determination, and enthusiastic involvement of key people in personnel agencies. In developing its *Model Public Personnel Administration Law,* the National Civil Service League reinforced this need when it stated:

The jurisdiction must develop a system of recruitment that interests the most capable persons in public service and a selection system that insures the highest caliber employee. The work to be performed in the public service challenges the best ability in the country. Governments must seek out ability and persuade the able to serve the public.[3]

In 1962 the Municipal Manpower Commission prepared a comprehensive survey of the problems and challenges facing local government in attracting APT people into urban government.[4] The study focused on the growing number of requirements for specialized talents as the rapid increase in the demand for local government services intensified a demand for engineers, accountants, chemists, biologists, sanitarians, public safety experts, computer programmers, personnel experts, planners, psychiatrists, and attorneys.

The capacity of cities to solve their problems depends on effective recruitment programs that will attract people who are skillful at planning, directing, and delivering government programs efficiently and economically as well as providing opportunities for citizen participation in decision making. The challenge in finding talented persons was highlighted in a special report released by the National League of Cities in June 1973.[5] This study noted that by 1975 approximately three million professionals would need to be recruited, replaced, and trained in state and local public service to meet growing demands. In a comprehensive survey of current personnel systems in state and local governments conducted by the National Civil Service League, it was reported in the spring of 1971 that more than three-quarters of a million state and local government job opportunities (exclusive of positions in educational institutions) would develop within a year and that at any given time nearly 360,000 state and local government jobs were vacant.[6]

The National League of Cities and the U.S. Conference of Mayors in a study issued in March 1973 titled *Local Government Approaches to Capacity-Building* reported that in well over half of the jurisdictions surveyed the majority of key department heads were either within ten years of retirement or were close to it.[7] This points to the need for effective recruitment of qualified replacements for public service positions. The study projected that the greatest rate of growth during the coming five to ten years would occur in administration and management; social services; planning; law enforcement; mass transportation; ecology; and housing and urban renewal.[8] The study also pinpointed particular skills which were difficult for local governments to meet:

Registered nurses
Traffic engineers
Plumbing and gas inspectors
Civil engineers
Administrative personnel
Landscape architects
Data processing/computer personnel
Accountants and finance analysts
Administrative managers
Labor relations specialists
City planners
Electrical engineers
Museum curators
Social services specialists
Doctors and medical personnel
Legal personnel
Tax collectors
Environmental sanitation personnel
Economic development specialists
Library administrators
Research personnel
Engineering specialists[9]

It is clear, then, that the challenges facing local governments are great, and success in meeting those challenges depends largely on the recruitment of competent, dedicated people. The purpose of this chapter is to examine the principal elements of the recruitment effort —its problems, costs, sources of qualified manpower, and the actual recruiting process itself. Attention also is directed to equal employment opportunity and its central importance to the overall recruitment program.

PROBLEMS OF RECRUITMENT

While it is obvious that there is a need for creative and effective recruitment by local governments to meet the needs for the skilled manpower noted above, it is important to recognize a series of problems which have hampered past efforts of personnel agencies to mount successful recruitment programs. By identifying and analyzing these difficulties it is hoped that local jurisdictions will be more effective in their future recruitment programs. The most significant of these problems to be discussed here includes the low prestige of public service; salary and fringe benefits; a shortage of selected skills; lack of a career system; barriers to minorities; fragmentation of jurisdictions; complicated administrative procedures; and residence requirements.

Low Prestige of Public Service. Studies have shown that the public has a higher regard for private employment than for public sector work; moreover, local government employment has been rated behind both the state and the federal government as desirable places to work.[10]

There are a number of reasons why local government is held in low esteem. Many people believe that government workers are parasites—inefficient and performing far below their capabilities. Others argue that corruption and bureaucratic red tape prevent public servants from effective performance. Through the educational process and the free market business environment, many young people are encouraged to go into private business instead of considering government careers. Some citizens resent the intrusion of government regulation into the areas of water and air pollution control, environmental planning, and community development programs for the poor, and this resentment naturally extends to government personnel. Richard L. Chapman and Frederic N. Cleaveland likewise note the decline in the public service ethic and the mounting pressure directed at public administrators to produce results in the face of rapid change and increasingly complex problems.[11] Somehow the prestige of working for cities, school districts, and counties must be enhanced if high calibre men and women are to be attracted to public sector employment.

Salary and Fringe Benefits. Low salaries and inadequate fringe benefits have been forceful deterrents preventing local governments and federal recruiters from competing with private employers in attracting highly skilled manpower. This problem as well as the problem of limited recruiting staffs are typical of many of the nation's 18,516 incorporated cities and 3,044 counties.[12] In the study *Local Government Approaches to Capacity-Building* already noted, the National League of Cities found that low salaries, a national shortage of selected skills, and competition were the three most significant factors accounting for recruitment difficulties.[13] Cities will have to mount a concerted effort in the immediate future to improve both the salary levels and the fringe benefits if they are to compete with the private sector in attracting men and women with professional education and training.

Shortage of Selected Skills. As of the mid-1970s it was becoming increasingly difficult for cities to recruit individuals with special skills such as traffic engineers, planners, administrative assistants, and community development specialists.[14] During the Depression it was relatively easy to recruit professional personnel because government at all levels provided security and thus was a more attractive employer than the private market. It was also a time of declining birth rates. In the 1970s, however, many experienced officials in public service were retiring, and it was anticipated that there would be a relatively smaller pool of talented individuals in the 25–44 age bracket for cities to draw upon for administrative, professional, and technical personnel.[15] Chapman and

Cleaveland advance some timely recommendations that, if adopted, would strengthen the relationships among governments at all levels as well as universities and the personnel administration profession itself in helping provide the skilled manpower to overcome shortages in the public sector.[16] Finally, institutions of higher learning need to develop realistic educational programs to meet the critical shortage of skills in government.

Lack of a Career System. Considerable strides have been made to develop comprehensive career systems among local governments in the United States. About eight out of every ten public service employees of cities, counties, and states are covered by merit systems which provide for nonpolitical, objective methods of selection and which guarantee against removal on political or other subjective grounds.[17] Nevertheless, not only is a systematic career system lacking for two out of every ten public service employees, but rarely do career systems provide the flexibility and continuity that allow for regular progression or for systematic improvement of individual skills that make effective use of university programs, or that involve adequate recognition and support of employee performance from senior officials of city governments.[18]

Barriers to Minorities. In the past there existed discrimination based on religion, race, sex, and physical handicaps which worked against attracting the best qualified individuals to consider local government employment. The courts have recognized that through the years various governmental recruitment systems have often followed discriminary hiring practices.[19] In the 1960s and 1970s efforts were made to overcome the effects of past discrimination. Later in this chapter some effective steps initiated in the 1970s by progressive local governments for recruiting minorities will be discussed.

Fragmentation of Jurisdictions. Another limitation in recruiting capable persons for public service is the great number and the variety of local jurisdictions. The fragmented nature of the job market with many local governments, school districts, townships, counties, and special districts competing with each other hampers efforts to recruit competent employees and frustrates and confuses the applicant.[20] Positions and responsibilities in government may overlap, and the friction and conflict that may arise among governmental leaders may also serve to deter individuals of high quality from entering public service.

Complicated Administrative Procedures. One of the problems that face many merit systems is the need to streamline procedures in recruiting, selecting, and staffing to meet manpower needs while at the same time maintaining the necessary forms and procedures to ensure that only the most qualified men and women are considered for employment. These procedures reduce as far as possible the exercise for political influence over the selection process. Long waiting periods for civil service certification and the fees charged for tests make for complicated procedures that discourage potential employees.

In a study conducted by the National Civil Service League in 1970, it was found that 94 percent of all jurisdictions required a high school education, 88 percent gave written tests, and in hiring for entry-level APT personnel 92 percent of the jurisdictions required a college degree, with 65 percent giving a written test. Yet only 54 percent of the jurisdictions surveyed had ever validated any tests to be certain that they were job-related.[21] Reducing the time in processing job applications, in taking tests, and in selecting for the position will go a long way to encourage greater numbers of qualified individuals to apply. In addition, the elimination of unnecessary testing and the use of job-related criteria and validated tests will enhance the creditability of local governments in the community.

Residence Requirements. Some governments restrict their recruitment pool by placing arbitrary residence requirements upon potential employees. In another 1970 study conducted by the National Civil Service League, it was disclosed that about one out of every four local jurisdictions had some kind of residence requirement for entry-level APT positions.[22] Even in those jurisdictions imposing a residence requirement, this requirement was waived in periods of shortages.

There is some evidence that more and more jurisdictions are requiring their employees to live within their city limits. In a study conducted by the National League of Cities and the U.S. Conference of Mayors, it was found that slightly more than one-third of the jurisdictions reporting stated that residence requirements were not enforced for any public professional.[23] However, there appears to be a strong tendency to hire professionals from within city or county limits, since this study showed that less than 10 percent of the then current professionals came from outside. There is growing feeling among some public officials that requiring public servants to live in the local jurisdiction contributes both to the tax base and to an improved attitude on the part of the professional working for the local government. Unquestionably, the effort to enforce residence requirements will reduce the available manpower to fill local government positions in fields where manpower skills are scarce. The Advisory Council on Intergovernmental Personnel Policy in its report to the President and Congress cited earlier stated that it was inappropriate for jurisdictions to require that new employees be selected only from among current residents if such policy prevented the jurisdiction from hiring highly qualified personnel.[24]

THE ATTRACTIONS OF LOCAL GOVERNMENT EMPLOYMENT

While it is instructive to identify the problems facing recruitment in the public sector, it is also important to focus on the factors that encourage individuals to seek employment in government.[25] These include establishment of the following: a healthful, creative environment; positions providing opportunities for development; teamwork; and a mission communicated to employees.

Environment. A healthful, creative environment that promotes mutually beneficial interpersonal relationships will attract persons of high calibre to government. In its *Municipal Manpower Project Report for Dover, New Hampshire,* the New England Municipal Center highlighted the role of the personnel director in this effort when it noted that he or she should work to assure a work environment that attracts qualified employees with adequate and properly administered personnel regulations and promotional and developmental opportunities.[26]

A healthy ethical climate not only facilitates decision making and group solidarity but also helps accomplish local government's goals and objectives. If current employees enjoy a stimulating environment, they will encourage their friends and neighbors to seek employment in the public sector.

Opportunities for Development. One of the most important elements in developing a strong recruitment program is the availability of positions that provide opportunities for professional development and growth. All city governments should examine existing positions for their measure of job satisfaction and challenge to the employee as well as for their appeal to prospective applicants. A useful way to encourage potential recruits is to establish clear and widely publicized career patterns for advancement that enable individuals to move from position to position and assume more challenging assignments as they master lower-level ones. If local governments are to attract the qualified individuals they need, the personnel function will have to become a central feature of the overall planning process and mission of the city. As of the mid-1970s there was little evidence of long-range manpower planning being undertaken at the local level.[27]

Personnel directors will have to be kept informed of the long-term professional needs of the various departments of city government, which implies close working relationships among the top elected officials and all department heads, including personnel.[28] Chief executives will have to play a more active role in determining the types of skills required to operate and support local government programs. Thus, a detailed and realistic career system in keeping with the needs of local government should be developed and continually revised.

Teamwork. If a public agency is characterized by a strong team approach to solving problems and to delivering government services, the excitement generated by such teamwork may easily be communicated to potential employees.

Just as successful sports teams build on the mix of skills of all team players, so public agencies should draw on a variety of skills among their employees to meet the many daily challenges facing local government. Both the Peace Corps and VISTA are excellent examples of how dedicated leaders have inspired their members to perform effectively, whether it be in helping to build roads in Colombia or assisting ghetto children to read in New York City. Of course, clearly defined objectives are a necessary preliminary to developing teamwork.

Mission. Finally, the mission of local public service should be communicated to every employee as well as to all citizens living in the community. In defining a city's mission, the refined skills of goal setting, long-range strategy planning, and citizen communication are required.[29] Most cities have a variety of missions, and sometimes recruiters as well as top managers have been remiss in not communicating clearly to employees, potential applicants, and the general public the range of local government goals and objectives. Action and social value are found in many municipal jobs, and personnel directors and recruiters should capitalize on this by informing the public of the many worthwhile features of working for the city government. The emphasis on service would have particular appeal to many college graduates who have a strong desire to serve their communities. (Witness the thousands of volunteers who joined the Peace Corps and VISTA.)

COSTS OF RECRUITMENT

In addition to understanding the vital factors that affect recruitment, one should also carefully examine the outstanding costs that municipalities face in implementing an effective and comprehensive recruitment program.

Personnel directors as well as others involved in the recruiting process should identify and understand these recruitment costs. Matthew Jackson has focused on the actual costs, potential costs, and hidden costs that must be considered in any recruitment program.[30] Some of these include the costs of the recruiting personnel, the costs of advertising and brochures, medical expenses for pre-employment medical examinations, the costs of tests, overhead costs, administrative costs of hiring new employees, training costs, the costs incurred in hiring a candidate who eventually fails, the costs of rejecting a candidate who would have been successful in the job, and, also to be considered, the costs of failure to the candidate.

The prestige and efficiency of management and government suffer a hidden cost when programs and activities fail because persons lacking required job qualifications were hired to perform responsible positions in municipalities.[31] When personnel managers and executives better understand the ramifications of these actual, potential, and hidden costs of recruitment, greater attention will be given to the development of sound, imaginative, and effective recruitment programs that will actively search out the best possible candidates.

The Method

SOURCES OF RECRUITMENT

In developing a sound recruitment program, personnel managers must recognize there is a variety of labor market sources to consider when recruiting for the public service. Traditionally, except for top-level professional positions such as department heads or city managers, most local governments have relied on the local labor market for their supply of professional personnel.[32]

Current Employees. Employees working in local government may be one of the prime sources of manpower from which to fill openings.[33] These individuals usually are knowledgeable about the requirements and responsibilities of public service and thus may be able to assume a new position with a minimum of training and orientation. In any large jurisdiction there are bound to be employees whose skills are not being fully used.[34] Progressive governments will take action to identify and use the skills of all their personnel and will transfer persons with requisite skills to new openings. The use of skill banks, personnel records, and job postings facilitates this purpose.

A study conducted by the public jurisdictions in the North Central Texas Council of Governments noted that intradepartmental preference systems hinder transfers and lateral entry, discouraging alternative career progress by limiting opportunities for advancement and promotion from within the ranks.[35] Imaginative use of lateral transfers will generate and encourage more broadly trained persons for public service and will help fill recruitment needs as well. In Simi Valley, California, the city manager found that rotating department heads for three-month periods and establishing management research teams which provided for easy flow of personnel from department to department to meet specific needs were innovations that improved performance.[36]

Former Employees. The morale of the public agency may often be raised by hiring former employees who have been laid off when openings develop for which they are qualified. Training and orientation costs are often reduced and the start-up time is lowered when former employees are rehired.[37]

Employee Referrals. Employee referrals may also be an excellent source of recruitment.[38] Since persons generally associate with individuals who have similar backgrounds, friends and acquaintances of government employees may make good recruits for public service. The success of this effort ultimately depends on the morale of present employees and their attitude toward working for government and for their supervisors. Use of referrals is much less costly than most other means by which recruiters seek applicants from the general labor market.

Walk-ins and Write-ins. Personnel departments can realize great savings in recruitment efforts by carefully evaluating walk-ins and write-ins (persons who seek employment of their own initiative), although they are not a major source of manpower.[39] Even during the widespread unemployment of the mid-1970s, the number of walk-ins and write-ins employed in government at all levels was quite large. The letters and resumés submitted by walk-ins and write-ins may form the foundation of a skill bank that can be referred to from time to time as vacancies arise. In any event every applicant —walk-in, write-in, or whatever—should receive prompt attention and, if qualified, should be granted a personal interview as soon as possible. Such treatment is positive public relations for government. Of course, for highly skilled personnel in short supply such as the professionals in the medical and health services, finance and management, and in engineering and allied technical fields, it may not be possible to recruit from among walk-ins or write-ins.[40]

Educational Institutions. One of the most bountiful sources of manpower for clerical and administrative personnel is high schools.[41] Most of the larger high schools provide training in shorthand, bookkeeping, and typing as well as industrial arts, machine shop, and electricity. Local government recruiters should provide school administrators and counselors with adequate information on the working conditions, environment, salary, and fringe benefits of employment in local government, thus encouraging students to consider careers in public service. Just as the military services have found an attractive market for recruits among high school graduates, local governments should use a variety of methods that will be discussed later in this chapter to reach the high school student.

Business schools and technical institutes provide courses in office machine operation, computer programming, accounting, and many other similar skills. Graduates of these institutions are usually more mature and experienced than high school graduates.

College and university recruiting, though highly competitive, offers a rich resource of manpower for local governments. The focal point for recruitment at most institutions of higher learning is the college placement office. Personnel recruiters would be especially well-advised to study the chapter titled "How the College Placement Office Operates in Campus Recruiting" in *Effective College Recruiting* by George S. Odiorne and Arthur S. Hann,[42] in which is provided valuable ideas about preparation for recruitment, interview techniques, standards used by recruiters in judging candidates—and also how students rate recruiters.[43]

New ways of conveying to college students the opportunities in government service should be explored by local recruiters.[44] One way is to establish contact with professors of political science and public administration; visits between professors and personnel officers should be encouraged. Students may gain a better appreciation of the benefits of working in local government through exchange visits to municipalities or by having government leaders speak to student clubs, classes, and campus organizations. Honor societies, management clubs, political science associations, and other groups can serve as the forum for panels, films, and discussions on public service careers. Peace Corps returnees often have done an effective job of relating their experiences to college students and encouraging applicants to seek government employment. In many areas of the country students may be generally uninformed about local government, as was reported in a survey conducted in the North Central Texas area in 1970.[45] Many steps such as cooperative work programs, internships, and other innovative recruitment methods can be taken by local governments to reach college youth. Two-year colleges also are a good area for recruitment, where training in nursing, mechanical technology, electrical technology, and a variety of other semiprofessional skills is common and often results in associate degrees.

Employment Services. The U.S. Employment Service within the Department of Labor not only aids and encourages state employment services which assist in finding jobs for the unemployed but often may be a source of manpower for local governments.[46] Although state employment services have not been particularly instrumental in filling high-level professional positions, it may be quite useful in blue-collar placement. While there are an estimated 8,000 privately owned employment agencies, these organizations generally recruit technical, professional, managerial, and administrative positions for the private rather than for the public sector.[47]

Consultants and Executive Recruiters. Consultants and recruiters specializing in recruitment of executives have refined a professional approach that has been very effective in recruiting top-level management talent for positions of responsibility in the private sector since the end of World War II.[48] This means of recruiting is seldom used by local governments because of its high costs and because of the requirement in the public sector for wide advertising of openings. However, it is an option that should be considered carefully when a scarce skill is needed or when a particular consultant or executive recruiter has screened and produced with speed, economy, and care a highly selective list of well-qualified candidates for final selection by top government executives.

RECRUITMENT TECHNIQUES

This brief review of the diverse sources of labor supply has shown the variety of possible options and sources of supply open to progressive governments in their efforts to recruit talented men and women for public service. One of the most widely used methods of recruiting is advertising.

Advertising. The success of any recruitment program depends in large part on advertising, and the success of advertising in turn depends on the quality of the service being advertised. Local governments which have employees with high morale and which demonstrate effective delivery of government services with proper consideration for citizen participation and their involvement in decision making will find imaginative advertising an effective method for recruitment.

The standard principles of advertising include attention, interest, desire, and action.[49] This four-point guide may be used in analyzing whether one's advertising program will succeed in drawing interested applicants. Since each advertisement is in competition with others, the ones that stand out will be most effective. While want ads do not allow for much originality in format, display ads making use of a variety of type faces, logos, photographs, drawings, or borders will attract attention.[50]

The challenge of the job, special privileges, salary, and fringe benefits can be used to direct the reader's attention to the position in particular and to government employment in general. The "you" approach which concentrates on awakening a response in the reader emphasizes job satisfaction and personal values and also may appeal to family needs such as insur-

ance, nearby school facilities, or tuition refund for schools. Finally, response needs to be activated by asking the potential applicant to phone, write, or visit the local government offices. Including a name, phone number, and a time for calling will encourage action on the part of the reader. However, it is important that the advertisement specify the position's requirements and qualifications in order to restrict applicants to those most qualified. (See "Writing Employment Advertising" in *Recruiting and Selecting Personnel* and appropriate sections in *Recruiting, Interviewing, and Selecting: A Manual for Line Managers* for important suggestions and examples for conducting an effective advertising campaign.[51])

The form and location of the advertisement will depend largely on the prestige of the job advertised, the budget allocated for advertising, the size of the qualified labor pool, and the location of the job.[52] In recruiting for key APT positions in local government it will often be necessary to recruit nationally or at least regionally. The Municipal Manpower Commission in 1962 noted that personnel practices of local governments at that time were unequal to the task of attracting the number and calibre of APT personnel needed; moreover, the quality of APT personnel employed at the time was inadequate to cope with current or emerging metropolitan problems.[53]

Over a decade later many local governments still showed a preference for the traditional hiring processes and red-tape procedures, making it difficult for public officials to select candidates outside the prescribed personnel network[54] and likewise making it difficult for interested candidates to connect with the personnel system of the local government. Many jurisdictions were authorized to advertise nationally or regionally only when local requirement efforts resulted in few qualified applicants being placed on civil service lists.[55] The ideal in recruiting is to encourage advertising in as broad a market as possible to attract a wide selection of candidates so that managers will have a choice.

The Examination Announcement. One of the first pieces of literature that the personnel office prepares when seeking applicants for employment is the examination announcement. In every announcement certain information should be included. Announcements of vacancies should be as uniform as possible and include the title of the position, description of the position, typical duties and responsibilities, minimum acceptable qualifications, essential skills and abilities, concluding with a statement confirming equal employment opportunity.[56]

It is also essential that information be provided about how to make an application. In addition, the complete announcement indicates both the evaluation methods to be used in assessing applicants and whether or not the position has promotion possibilities. Information regarding employee benefits such as retirement, group insurance, hospitalization, and holidays also should be stated. The appropriate use of cartoons, photographs, and color will brighten examination announcements and will distinguish them from other advertising. Both the ditto and mimeograph process may be used.[57] An announcement which meets these criteria is reproduced in Figure 5-1.

It must be kept in mind that the purpose of the announcement is to attract attention. Accordingly, the principles of advertising noted earlier including attention, interest, desire, and action should be followed in designing these announcements. The key is to use attention-getting words and phrases, keep the message simple, and use pictures and drawings that will catch the eye.[58] Once the announcement has been prepared, the next consideration is where to post it.

Posting of Job Vacancies. Imagination is required in placing examination notices so that as many individuals as possible in the community will learn of the openings. Post offices, libraries, recreation centers, barber shops, restaurants, churches, community action agencies, community centers, filling stations, high schools, colleges, universities, business schools, YMCAs and YWCAs, Chamber of Commerce offices, athletic clubs, departments of employment security, and national guard or reserve training centers usually prove good outlets for informing the public about jobs in the public service.[59]

There are a variety of methods by which ag-

gressive personnel offices can communicate with the community the need for skilled and unskilled manpower in city government. A brief look at some of these methods will be instructive to recruiters. In the planning of a sound, imaginative recruitment program it is advisable to build around a theme, such as "Building for the Future," that may be incorporated in a number of ways in the release of recruitment materials. Applicants then will be able to identify easily with the theme, which helps in recruiting. The U.S. Navy uses effective themes such as "The New Navy of the Exciting '70s—What's in It for You," "Something Special. The Navy Life," and "Want to Go Places Fast? Go Navy," and the other services have used similar appeals which have stimulated increased interest in military careers. Local governments perform interesting and valuable functions, so it should not be difficult to develop appealing themes for their recruitment programs. The variety of methods for reaching the public will now be explored.

Newspapers. The daily newspapers are important media for bringing job openings to the attention of readers through want ads and display advertising. Neighborhood and community papers also are excellent means for reaching the public. For example, in the Atlanta, Georgia, metropolitan area there are about thirty neighborhood newspapers that serve different segments of the Atlanta community. In most urban areas there are a number of weeklies and other community papers that can be useful outlets for information on career openings.

In addition, occasional news stories highlighting the accomplishments of a local government employee coupled with information about job openings is another good means of attracting thoughtful attention. A concerted effort to issue news releases on outstanding local employees, whether they be in the police, fire, or sanitation department, will create over time a favorable impression in the community regarding work in local government, while also contributing to the improvement of employee morale.

Television and Radio. News releases announced on television and radio, along with

FIGURE 5–1. *Job announcement for position of firefighter, city of Sacramento, California.*

The City of Sacramento Offers:

. . . Able and ambitious men and women a real chance for a career of service. Recruit Firefighters receive training in fire-fighting methods, modern fire prevention practices, salvage operations and related activities.

HOW TO APPLY

If you meet the following requirements submit an application by 5:00 p.m., November 28, 1975.

Submit Application to:

City of Sacramento
Personnel Department
801 9th Street, Room 101
Sacramento, CA 95814

EXPERIENCE: None required.

AGE: Must be at least 21 and not over 35 years of age on the last day applications are accepted. Any successful candidate reaching age 36 before appointment will be removed from the eligible register.

EDUCATION: High school graduation or other educational equivalent is required.

HEIGHT AND WEIGHT: There is no height requirement, but weight must be proportional to height and age.

VISION: Not less than 20/40 in either eye uncorrected; and corrected to 20/20 in the better eye and not less than 20/25 in the lesser eye. Contact lenses are not permitted. Color blindness is disqualifying. Color perception will be tested on American Optical HRR Plates 12-16. Failure on any one of these plates is disqualifying.

MEDICAL: Applicants are required to take a thorough medical examination given by the City physician. This examination will include a hearing test, eye test and low back X-ray. The decision of the City physician shall be final.

RESIDENCE: A Firefighter must move within a 25 air-mile radius of the center of the City of Sacramento within one year following appointment.

OTHER: Applicants must, by date of application, possess a valid California Motor Vehicle Operator's license and have a good driving record. Prior to appointment, each successful candidate will be fingerprinted and a thorough character investigation will be conducted.

VETERAN'S PREFERENCE: To claim veteran's preference (10 points), a copy of the military discharge form DD-214 must be **presented at the time the application is filed.**

FIGURE 5–1. *(continued.)*

THE EXAMINATION

The examination consists of three parts weighted as follows:

Physical Agility	Pass/Fail
Written Test	Pass/Fail
Interview	100%

Candidates must successfully complete each part of the examination. Those candidates who successfully complete the physical agility test will be notified of the time and place of the written test. Interviews will be scheduled for candidates who successfully complete both the physical agility test and the written test. A minimum rating of 70% is required to achieve a place on the eligible register.

WORKING CONDITIONS

CURRENT HOURS ON DUTY: A Firefighter reports for duty at 8:00 A.M. and goes off duty at 8:00 A.M. the following morning. Firefighters are on call at all times, at the fire house, during the 24-hour duty period to respond to fire alarms, rescue and emergency calls, and various citizen requests for assistance.

Scheduled activities during a firefighter's 24-hour duty period average about eight hours, including drills, planned study, equipment maintenance, prefire planning, inspection and related duties. The remainder of the 24-hour on-call standby time at the firehouse is generally used at the employee's option; this includes eating, sleeping and leisure time activities.

A Sacramento Firefighter is on duty four 24-hour periods and is off eight 24-hour periods in every 12-day cycle. For example, in November, 1975, the "C" platoon is on duty for the ten 24-hour periods indicated in red.

"C" PLATOON* NOVEMBER 1975

Sun	Mon	Tues	Wed	Thurs	Fri	Sat
2	3	4	5		7	
9	10		12		14	15
16	17		19		21	22
	24		26	27	28	29

*Each 24-hour period begins and ends at 8:00 A.M.

CURRENT SALARY RANGE

$482.91 bi-weekly starting salary with regular increases to $586.73 bi-weekly. This is approximately $1046.00 to $1271.00 per month.

FIGURE 5–1. (*continued.*)

CURRENT EMPLOYEE BENEFITS

PAID VACATIONS: During the first four calendar years of service an employee receives 10 days of vacation per year. From the 5th year through the 14th year an employee receives 15 days of vacation; after 15 years a employee receives 20 days. The value of a Firefighter's vacation day is equivalent to 1/5 of a duty week.

SICK LEAVE: A Firefighter earns sick leave at a rate of 1 day per month. The value of a Firefighters sick leave is equivalent to 1/5 of a duty week. After five years eligible Firefighters may be reimbursed once a year for part of their unused sick leave.

INJURY LEAVE: Firefighters injured in the line of duty receive full pay for up to one year or until they receive a disability settlement.

PAID HOLIDAYS: Firefighters receive the equivalent of eleven and one half holidays per year. The fire duty schedule is, in addition to holiday credit, designed to include time off for eleven and one half holidays. The value of a Firefighters holiday is equivalent to 1/5 of a duty week.

HEALTH PLAN: The City of Sacramento contributes up to $82.13 per month toward medical and dental insurance for Firefighters and their dependents. Firefighters have a choice of group insurance plans.

CREDIT UNION: Facilities and services are readily available to City employees.

LONGEVITY PAY: After 20 years of service Firefighters receive a $100 bonus per year. After 25 years, Firefighters receive a $300 bonus per year.

EDUCATION: Tuition fees, up to $30, will be paid per semester for Firefighters enrolled in an approved school.

DISABILITY & DEATH: Liberal disability and death benefits are available to protect Firefighters and their families.

RETIREMENT SYSTEM: Firefighters may retire as early as age 50, and retirement is mandatory at age 60. Firefighters may earn up to 75% of the average of the three highest consecutive years of salary.

UNIFORM ALLOWANCE: Firefighters are paid a uniform allowance of $125 once a year.

The information contained herein does not constitute either an expressed or implied contract and these provisions are subject to change.

AN EQUAL OPPORTUNITY EMPLOYER

EXAMINATION #1416   OCTOBER 7, 1975

FIGURE 5–1. (*continued.*)

interviews with experts on topics such as pollution control and crime control, innovative educational programs, as well as short, eye-catching vacancy announcements may arouse response among a broad audience. Public service announcements may be used both to advertise openings in government and to inform the public of the activities and services of local government.

Talk shows or panel discussions in which the mayor or other local public officials answer questions and discuss problems can stimulate public interest in government and also highlight career opportunities. Featuring women and members of minority groups who are prominent government employees on these programs as well as in newspaper stories will work to encourage applications from women and minorities. Some communities televise or broadcast regular weekly feature shows focusing on significant activities of local government. Thirty-second radio and TV spot announcements have proved to be an especially effective means of communicating job openings. Some educational television stations such as Channel 8 in Atlanta, Georgia, provide coverage of the meetings of the city council or board of education, during which job vacancies or other opportunities may be brought to the attention of the viewing audience.

Mailing Lists. If complete and up-to-date files on qualified applicants are maintained by recruitment offices, information can be sent to these applicants as vacancies occur. While this procedure requires some recordkeeping, overall recruitment costs can be reduced considerably if placements are made this way.

An active personnel office will maintain contact with major community training and employment agencies and inform them about job openings. For example, in its recruitment efforts the city of Fort Lauderdale, Florida, seeks assistance from the Broward County Adult Vocational Center, the Broward County Opportunity Center, the Community Action Migrant Program, the Economic Opportunity Coordinating Group, the Manpower Development Training Agency, the Opportunities Industrial Center as well as the Florida State Employment Service.[60]

The numerous local community action groups present in almost all urban areas may be helpful sources in informing individuals about vacancies. To cite Fort Lauderdale again, the city works closely with important community action groups such as the Broward County Community Relations Commission, the Broward Manpower Planning Council, the Economic Opportunity Coordinating Group, the National Alliance of Businessmen, the federal Work Incentive Program (WIN), the Youth Employment Program, as well as a variety of women's organizations including the Business and Professional Women's Association, the Soroptimist Club, the Quota Club, the Zonta Club, the Council of Women's Clubs, and the American Businesswomen's Association.[61] Finally, university placement officers and professors of public administration can be requested to post notices on bulletin boards and bring job information to the attention of students.[62]

The Recruiters. Personal contact with high schools, institutions of higher learning, as well as community and professional associations contribute to building good rapport among all segments of the community. Recruiters—both whites and members of minority groups—need to communicate with community leaders and representatives of various organizations on a regular basis to encourage their members to consider careers in local government. Minority and disadvantaged individuals may be inspired to apply for work in local government if recruiters use outreach techniques such as visiting local hangouts (drugstores, taverns, and poolrooms) and urging probation officers and welfare and religious workers to refer to them individuals who may qualify for local government jobs.[63] The effective recruiter is one who has developed a "feel" for the problems and challenges in recruiting and thus can determine which types of recruiting methods will succeed given a certain vacancy and given a certain locale and its labor pool.

Speakers Bureaus. Cities often find that a well-organized government speakers bureau is an excellent way of reaching and informing diverse audiences about job opportunities and careers. Visits by recruiters, police, firefighters, and local government department heads made to high school and college classes, civic clubs, community organizations, and professional associations provide not only an information channel about government activities and jobs but also the physical presence that is missing in most advertising.

Visits, Displays, and Open Houses. Local governments would be well-advised to initiate more visits, displays, and open houses to encourage people to consider careers in government.[64] The armed forces have developed well-planned programs for open houses, enabling the public to learn more of their activities and programs. Professors, high school teachers, and counselors should be invited to bring their classes to see how some department of local government operates, such as a fire station, a police station, or a public works department. Through experiences like these young people begin to develop an affinity for the work of municipalities. Information on careers in government also may be distributed by the community's tourist bureau or the Chamber of Commerce. Shopping centers and airport terminals also are good outlets for public information.

Work Study Programs and Internships. Two of the most effective means of recruiting young people for local government employment are cooperative work study programs and internships. Approximately 300 four-year colleges, including about 40 colleges that are predominately black, have cooperative education programs which provide for varying periods of study and study-related work.[65] Many two-year colleges have begun similar training programs in the fields of law enforcement, nursing, and firefighting. Recruiters should welcome and encourage the development of these programs.

While cooperative work study programs provide the opportunity for students to learn about careers in municipalities while also obtaining a college education, a cautionary note is in order. If the program is to be effective, it will require the time, patience, and understanding of the supervisors and the active support of top management to develop and operate a program that includes a variety of challenging assignments and that will really

help train the student in the workings of local government.[66]

The intern program and its significance for municipalities was noted in a study of the results of the Georgia intern program, a statewide year-round program which placed qualified students in short-term, full-time, agency-defined internships in state, local, and public service agencies. The study showed that 51 percent of responding interns stated that their vocational goals had been significantly strengthened by participation in the program, while 20 percent stated that their vocational goals had been substantially changed by their intern experience.[67] Forty-nine percent of those responding went on to work in government at some level.

The "service-learning" intern program model developed by the Southern Regional Education Board provides increased manpower for short-term research assistance, combining formal education with opportunities in which students initiate practical activities and assume responsibilities.[68] It can be an exciting way to attract top-ranking students to careers in government and public affairs.

With assistance from funds provided by the Intergovernmental Personnel Act of 1970, the League of California Cities during 1974 placed twenty-one administrative aides, recruited from academic institutions, in various California cities needing additional manpower.[69] This demonstration project involved twelve students working full-time for three months and nine students working part-time for six months. An evaluation was made at the end of the project period. The Intergovernmental Personnel Act also has funded a project providing graduate students from universities in Connecticut with public personnel administration experience in both state and city agencies.[70] It is anticipated that upon completion of the internship projects the interns will be able to be recruited into public service.

Interest in internships continues to grow; several national associations such as the Society for Field Experience Education, the National Center for Public Service Internships, and the Cooperative Education Association encourage and promote experiential education.[71] The experience of New York City's internship program represents a model for other local governments. Success of the New York program in the judgment of the interns depended on the following conditions:

1. A distinct and respectable position within the office organization.
2. Maximum support in carrying out research.
3. Minimum day-to-day supervision.
4. Freedom to make mistakes and learn from them.
5. Serious discussion of project results.
6. Frequent contact with and access to the office supervisors.
7. A wide choice of interesting topics.[72]

In short, well-developed internship and cooperative work study programs are excellent means for stimulating this interest and developing closer ties between educational institutions and municipalities.

Professional Associations. In the search for individuals to fill high-level APT positions in city governments, there are many professional associations that can be consulted for their availability data and other services. For example, the *Nation's Cities 1974–75 Annual Directory* published in *Nation's Cities* magazine provides useful information about major national associations such as the American Society of Public Administration, the International Personnel Management Association, the National Civil Service League, the American Society for Planning Officials, and the National League of Cities which issue their own publications and provide assistance in advertising for positions.[73]

There are a variety of other professional channels to refer to in recruitment. For example, the Urban Technical Services Program of the National League of Cities–U.S. Conference of Mayors makes use of outlets such as the National Registry of Engineers and *Engineering News Record* to recruit engineers for local government; contacts TACTICS (a minority professional association) which sends mailings to about 110 presidents of black colleges; distributes notices to 116 National Urban League job bank programs; and contacts 110 college and university placement offices.[74] One of its most effective channels for recruitment is the ACTION hotline newsletter. In addition, notices are sent from the Department of Housing and Urban Development to cities across the country.

With financial support from funds provided by the U.S. Civil Service Commission under the Intergovernmental Personnel Act, the Pennsylvania State Civil Service Commission's Division of Research and Special Projects, Bureau of Examination, has established *SWAP,* a publication released periodically that contains information on the latest personnel developments, including job vacancies in the personnel field that should interest local governments.

Other Methods. Other methods exist to which recruiters may resort in filling local government positions. For example, it is productive to distribute in different sections of the community action-oriented employment posters featuring photos of women and minority employees.[75] Mobile trailers that visit different parts of the city and adequate supplies of application blanks placed at various points are recommended outreach efforts. It also is advisable to arrange that some recruiting offices remain open during some weekday evenings and on the weekends to allow employed persons to inquire or apply without inconvenience to them.[76]

Recruitment Literature. While it is important to know about and use the described sources of recruitment, attention must be focused as well on the preparation of brochures and other materials advertising career opportunities in local government. If at all possible, information for each major occupation in local government should be prepared in handout form.[77] Odiorne and Hann, in a chapter titled "Recruiting Brochure and the Company Image," discuss the contents of such a brochure that applies to government employment as well as to the private market.[78] At the least, brochures should include a table of contents, an index of job opportunities, and descriptions of the government and its positions, compensation policy, and application procedures.

Publications of the U.S. Civil Service Commission such as the following may serve as guides: *Trends in Federal Hiring,* a newsletter for college placement directors; *Government '75,* a booklet describing the general kinds of jobs filled and majors sought by the federal government; *Federal Career Directory* (BRE–39), a reference source providing extended treatment of agencies, occupations, and programs; *Federal Recruiting* (BRE–50), an index of the organization and structure of agency recruitment programs directed mainly at college placement directors; and other brochures on specific occupations.[79]

Finally, two particularly attractive brochures published by the U.S. Civil Service Commission, *The Human Equation: Working in Personnel for the Federal Government* and *Key People: Careers in Education with Your Federal Government* can serve as models for the preparation of brochures as well as useful references for local government. A broader appreciation of the variety of recruitment literature can be gained from *Guide to Federal Career Literature,* a directory of about 250 publications from 46 federal departments and agencies that applies to nationwide recruiting.[80]

The Application. While aggressive and imaginative recruitment is vital to the selection process, the application form also plays its own significant role in recruitment. To be most effective, the application should be used systematically.[81]

The comprehensive application form records basic information about the applicant such as personal data, educational background, and work history with dates, positions, and brief descriptions of duties and responsibilities.[82] Very often applicants reduce their chances of being hired by submitting incomplete application forms. As a means of encouraging applicants to fill out the application blank carefully and to the best of their ability, local governments might consider distributing a brochure modeled after one prepared by the Selection Resource Center of the Arizona State Personnel Commission titled *Selling Yourself with the Application Form.*[83]

Application forms should be constructed carefully, and personnel officers should recognize that minority groups may view the application form in ways different from the interviewer who refers to the application during the interview. Frequently, and with some justification, blacks, Puerto Ricans, and Mexican-Americans have perceived the application form as a useless tool, feeling that the information requested has little to do with the individual's ability to work.[84]

During the 1970s considerable research in applied psychology was conducted and findings published regarding the use of weighted application blanks, of specially scored interest inventories, and of specially scored biographical antecedent inventories toward prediction of criteria. Warren S. Blumenfeld has studied the successful administration of the weighted application and has provided a wealth of references that local government leaders might consider in systematically developing weighted application blanks.[85]

Information requested on employment applications should be strictly job-related; information regarding years at given addresses, marital status, date of marriage, and spouse's employment are irrelevant and should not be requested. Requests for race or recent photographs are interpreted by some applicants as an attempt to fill positions on the basis of sex, race, or age; therefore, such requests should not be made. Information regarding arrest records also must be deleted from the application form.[86] Finally, information requested on salary history should be examined carefully for possible past discrimination in pay. The two sample applications reproduced in Figures 5-2 and 5-3 exhibit the results of the thoughtful preparation necessary in designing a useful and nondiscriminatory application form.

In using the application blank, interviewers should separate the applications into three groups: the "invite" group (those applicants invited for interviews); the "hold" group (those applicants who missed only on some nonessential points and whose application thus are to be held in abeyance pending a decision on the "invite" group); and the "reject" group (those individuals obviously not suited for employment).[87]

Some jurisdictions may find it useful to send

MONTGOMERY COUNTY MARYLAND

Employment Application

COUNTY OFFICE BUILDING, ROOM 330
ROCKVILLE, MARYLAND 20850
PHONE: (301) 279-1271

Please type or print all answers in ink.

Personnel Use Only	
CMU	COF

PERSONAL DATA

POSITION DESIRED: _______________________________ SALARY DESIRED $ __________

DATE AVAILABLE: ______________________ Available for: ☐ Full Time ☐ Part Time ☐ Temp. Employment

1. NAME: ____ Social Security No. ____|___|____
    LAST   FIRST   MIDDLE   OTHER

2. ADDRESS: ____
    NUMBER & STREET   CITY   STATE   ZIP CODE

3. DATE OF BIRTH ____________|________|__________
    MONTH   DAY   YEAR

4. PHONE: Area Code/Number   HOME: ____|_______________   OFFICE: ____|_______________

5.

> *To be completed by Public Safety Applicants Only - (Police, Fire, Corrections, Sheriff)*
>
> U.S. CITIZEN ☐ Yes ☐ No HEIGHT: __ Ft.__ In. WEIGHT:____ Lbs.

6.

EDUCATION AND TRAINING

Circle Highest Grade Completed: seven or less 8 9 10 11 12

Did you Graduate: No ☐ Yes ☐ Year ______

High School Equivalency Test: Date Passed: State Awarded:

TYPE OF SCHOOL	SCHOOL NAME CITY & STATE	TYPE OF DIPLOMA OR DEGREE AWARDED	MAJOR FIELD	GRADE AVER-AGE	DATES ATTENDED FROM MO.	YR.	TO MO.	YR.
LAST HIGH SCHOOL ATTENDED								
COLLEGES ATTENDED								
OTHER (Military, Trade, Business, Secretarial, etc.)								

SPECIAL QUALIFICATIONS (include active technical/professional licenses and numbers, academic or professional awards, Bar Membership, State/Date of Membership, etc.)

FOREIGN LANGUAGES SPOKEN OR READ:

SKILLS: Typing ______ W.P.M. Shorthand ______ W.P.M. Other __________

AN EQUAL OPPORTUNITY EMPLOYER
M/F

3/74

FIGURE 5–2. *Employment application form, Montgomery County, Maryland.*

7.   <u>EMPLOYMENT HISTORY</u>   Page 2.

IN THE SPACE PROVIDED BELOW, GIVE YOUR EMPLOYMENT HISTORY, BEGINNING WITH YOUR PRESENT OR MOST RECENT EMPLOYER AND LIST ALL POSITIONS HELD, INCLUDING MILITARY, PART-TIME, SUMMER, VOLUNTEER WORK, AND ANY PERIODS OF UNEMPLOYMENT. AN EXPLANATION OF ANY PERIOD OF UNEMPLOYMENT SHOULD BE INCLUDED UNDER ITEM 15 PAGE 4.

a. NAME OF EMPLOYER: _______________________   FROM: ____|____   TO ____|____
   ADDRESS: _________________________________   MO.   YR.   MO.   YR.
   ____   SALARY BEGINNING: ______________ PER ANNUM
   PHONE: ___________________________________   PRESENT: ______________ PER ANNUM
             AREA CODE   NUMBER   NAME & TITLE OF SUPERVISOR: ______________
   JOB TITLE: _______________________________   _______________________________________
   REASON FOR LEAVING: ______________________
   ____   MAY WE CONTACT: ☐ Yes   ☐ No

              BRIEFLY DESCRIBE THE NATURE AND DUTIES OF YOUR POSITION

____
____
____

b. NAME OF EMPLOYER: _______________________   FROM ____|____   TO: ____|____
   ADDRESS: _________________________________   MO.   YR.   MO.   YR.
   ____   SALARY BEGINNING: ______________ PER ANNUM
   PHONE: ___________________________________   FINAL: ______________ PER ANNUM
             AREA CODE   NUMBER   NAME & TITLE OF SUPERVISOR: ______________
   JOB TITLE: _______________________________   _______________________________________
   REASON FOR LEAVING: ______________________   _______________________________________

              BRIEFLY DESCRIBE THE NATURE AND DUTIES OF YOUR POSITION

____
____
____

c. NAME OF EMPLOYER: _______________________   FROM: ____|____   TO: ____|____
   ADDRESS: _________________________________   MO.   YR.   MO.   YR.
   ____   SALARY BEGINNING: ______________ PER ANNUM
   PHONE: ___________________________________   FINAL: ______________ PER ANNUM
             AREA CODE   NUMBER   NAME & TITLE OF SUPERVISOR ______________
   JOB TITLE: _______________________________   _______________________________________
   REASON FOR LEAVING: ______________________   _______________________________________

              BRIEFLY DESCRIBE THE NATURE AND DUTIES OF YOUR POSITION

____
____
____

d. NAME OF EMPLOYER: _______________________   FROM ____|____   TO: ____|____
   ADDRESS: _________________________________   MO.   YR.   MO.   YR.
   ____   SALARY BEGINNING: ______________ PER ANNUM
   PHONE: ___________________________________   FINAL: ______________ PER ANNUM
             AREA CODE   NUMBER   NAME & TITLE OF SUPERVISOR: ______________
   JOB TITLE: _______________________________   _______________________________________
   REASON FOR LEAVING: ______________________   _______________________________________

              BRIEFLY DESCRIBE THE NATURE AND DUTIES OF YOUR POSITION

____
____
____

IF ADDITIONAL SPACE IS REQUIRED, PLEASE ATTACH AN ADDITIONAL SHEET UTILIZING THE SAME FORMAT OR USE SUPPLEMENTAL EMPLOYMENT HISTORY SHEET.

FIGURE 5–2. (*continued.*)

8. <u>REFERENCES</u> Page 3

LIST THREE PERSONS WHO ARE NOT RELATED TO YOU BY BLOOD OR MARRIAGE WHO HAVE NOT ALREADY BEEN LISTED IN ITEM NO. 7 WHO CAN COMMENT ON YOUR EDUCATION AND/OR WORK EXPERIENCE.			
FULL NAME	COMPLETE HOME ADDRESS	OCCUPATION	PHONE: OFFICE HOME
			O: ______ H:
			O: ______ H:
			O: ______ H:

9. DISMISSALS AND/OR FORCED RESIGNATIONS: Have you ever been dismissed from any position? ______________ Have you ever been forced to resign from any position? ____(If answer is Yes to either or both of these questions, give complete details under Item No. 15 page 4)

10. CRIMINAL TRAFFIC, AND/OR CIVIL COURT RECORD: Have you ever been convicted of an offense in an adult court? _______ (If answer is YES, give complete details under Item No. 15 page 4. A conviction will not automatically exclude you from employment consideration.)

11. CONDITION OF HEALTH: Have you had any serious illness, operations, or accident in the past 5 years? ______________ If yes, please explain in Item No. 15 page 4. Do you now or have you ever been awarded disability payments of any kind? _______ If yes, please explain under Item 15, page 4.

12. HAVE YOU EVER BEEN AN APPLICANT OR EMPLOYEE OF THE MONTGOMERY COUNTY GOVERNMENT?_____
If Applicant   Date of Application: _________________   If Employee   Position Title: ________________
                Position Applied For: ________________   Employment Dates: ________________

13. PLEASE INDICATE SOURCE FROM WHICH YOU LEARNED OF THIS POSITION: ______________________

<u>GENERAL INFORMATION</u>

In order to prevent a delay in the processing of your application, please be sure you have signed and dated this form on page 4 and answered every question clearly and completely.

Each applicant appointed to a County position must meet all merit system requirements of the position, including the successful completion of a verbal/written entrance examination, medical examination and a confidential investigation, and each appointee must submit all requested documents.

----

14. <u>OPTIONAL</u>

The following information is requested for Personnel Office Use Only in order to assist us in complying with EEO reporting guidelines. Since this information will *not* be considered for employment purposes, you may elect not to furnish this information until an employment offer is confirmed.

1. RACE: American Indian _____ Black _____ White _____ Hispanic Heritage _____

Asian American _____   Other _________________________________

2. SEX: Male _____   Female _____

AN EQUAL OPPORTUNITY EMPLOYER
M/F

FIGURE 5–2. (*continued*.)

EQUAL EMPLOYMENT OPPORTUNITY INFORMATION

(Personnel Office Use Only)

The individual identified on the other side has been appointed as follows:

NAME: ____

POSITION: ____

DEPARTMENT: ____

DIVISION: ____

DATE: _______________________________

15. SPACE FOR DETAILED ANSWERS TO OTHER QUESTIONS	
ITEM NUMBER	WRITE IN LEFT COLUMN NUMBER TO WHICH ANSWERS APPLY.

I, the undersigned, certify that I have read and fully comprehend this form in its entirety and that the information herein provided is true and complete to the best of my knowledge. I understand that should any statement I have made prove false, misleading or erroneous, it may result in the rejection of my application or discharge from the County service. In submitting this application, I further understand that it becomes the property of the Montgomery County Government and will not be returned.

____   ____

Signature of Applicant   Date Signed

We thank you for making application for employment with the Montgomery County Government.

AN EQUAL OPPORTUNITY EMPLOYER
M/F

FIGURE 5–2. *(continued.)*

out questionnaires to job applicants to determine their attitudes concerning the employment process. King County, Washington, found there was considerable support, based on the results of the returned questionnaires, for their recruitment system. Small "interest cards" are completed by applicants for retention by the employment division in the King County office of personnel and then mailed out to applicants when exams are announced.[88] The use of these questionnaires and cards are excellent means by which local personnel of-

---

OFFICE OF PERSONNEL
COUNTY OF FAIRFAX
10409 MAIN STREET
FAIRFAX, VA. 22030
(703) 691-2591

Please read the instructions before completing the application:

- Your application will be processed by the Office of Personnel for Merit System positions only. The Office of Personnel has no jurisdiction over exempt positions as defined by the Merit System Ordinance.

- Your entire application must be completed. Incomplete applications can not be considered.

- Print or type clearly.

- Mail or bring your application to the Office of Personnel at the address listed above. The Office of Personnel can not be responsible for applications sent directly to other agencies.

- Applications are maintained in the active file for one year.

- If you feel that you have not been treated fairly or in a courteous manner, you should report the incident to the Personnel Director or to the Fairfax County Civil Service Commission (in writing, preferably).

- Comments or complaints about the employment procedure will be answered, in writing, as soon as possible. Comments or complaints will not affect this or future applications for employment.

- The U.S. Equal Employment Opportunity Commission also investigates discriminatory practices alleged by an applicant or employee. It is suggested that you first file your complaint at the local level.

You may detach this page for your records.

FIGURE 5–3. *Employment application form, Fairfax County, Virginia.*

An Equal Opportunity/Affirmative Action Employer

PRINT IN INK

Mail To: FAIRFAX COUNTY PERSONNEL OFFICE 4100 CHAIN BRIDGE ROAD, FAIRFAX, VIRGINIA 22030

Mr.
Ms.   (Last)   (First)   (Int.)   Social Security Number

Present Address   (Street)   (City)   (State)   (Zip)   Telephone
Home   (   )
Office   (   )

Have you ever worked for Fairfax County?   When?   Where?
YES ☐   NO ☐

Do you have a driver's license?   YES ☐   NO ☐   Chauffeurs license?   YES ☐   NO ☐

Type of position desired?   Lowest acceptable salary for which you will be considered:

Other positions for which you wish to be considered:

Education: Circle the highest grade completed 1 2 3 4 5 6 7 8 9 10 11 12   Did you graduate?   YES ☐   NO ☐

	School Name and Location	Dates To	Dates From	Date Graduated	Degree	Major Area of Study
High School or GED						
College or University						
Trade						
Other Education BA+ ___ hrs. ☐ Masters ☐ PhD ☐						

Scholastic Honors—Honorary Societies

Have you ever been discharged or forced to resign from any position?   YES ☐   NO ☐

Were you ever in the U.S. Military Service?   YES ☐   NO ☐

Were all discharges granted under honorable conditions?   YES ☐   NO ☐

Are you a U.S. Citizen?   YES ☐   NO ☐

List past or present chronic ailments

Have you ever made a claim for disability before a workman's compensation commission resulting from a job incurred accident or illness?   YES ☐   NO ☐

A) State nature of injury and part of body affected:

B) State amount compensated $ _______________

THE INFORMATION BELOW IS FOR STATISTICAL PURPOSES ONLY AND DOES NOT REMAIN WITH YOUR APPLICATION.

Birth Date	Place of Birth	Hgt.	Wgt.	Race	Eye Color	Hair Color

Have you ever been convicted for or presently charged with violation of laws other than minor traffic violations? Include conviction under court martial while in U.S. Military Service. A YES reply does not disqualify the application.   YES ☐   NO ☐

If Yes, give date, place, charge and disposition.

FIGURE 5–3. *(continued.)*

EMPLOYMENT●Begin with your present or most recent employment; list number and positions of people you supervised in each position under ''Description of your work''. Include Military Service.
You may attach a separate resume as long as ALL information requested is included.

Present or last employer	Description of your work
Address	

Starting salary	Present salary	Position Title		Dates From: To:
Supervisor's name and title			Reason for leaving, if not presently employed	

Employer	Description of your work
Address	

Starting salary	Final salary	Position Title		Dates From: To:
Supervisor's name and title			Reason for leaving	

Employer	Description of your work
Address	

Starting salary	Final salary	Position Title		Dates From: To:
Supervisor's name and title			Reason for leaving	

Employer	Description of your work
Address	

Starting salary	Final salary	Position Title		Dates From: To:
Supervisor's name and title			Reason for leaving	

How did you learn about the position for which you applied?

I **HEREBY AUTHORIZE** Fairfax County to obtain from my present and past employers all data needed to support this application. I hereby certify that the foregoing statements are to the best of my knowledge true and correct and I agree that any misstatement or omission as to material fact will constitute grounds for disqualification of my application or dismissal from the employ of Fairfax County.

I **UNDERSTAND** I am required to pass the County's physical examination and that all new employees are fingerprinted and verified through the Federal Bureau of Investigation.

_______________________________________   ___________________
Applicant's Signature   Date

Name   Last   First   Middle   Date

This is a valid Certification of
statistical information
____
Signature

FIGURE 5-3. *(continued.)*

fices can gauge the effectiveness of their recruitment system and application form, making changes when necessary.

Cooperative Recruiting Efforts. Section 204 of the Intergovernmental Personnel Act of 1970 provides among other things for the U.S. Civil Service Commission to join, on a shared-cost basis, with state and local governments in cooperative recruiting and examining activities in accordance to jointly agreed procedures and regulations.[89] Likewise, some local jurisdictions cooperating with other jurisdictions find they are able to save limited resources and often reach and interest a broader public.

As of 1974 fourteen intergovernmental job information centers had been established involving the U.S. Civil Service Commission, while eighteen state and local jurisdiction joint centers were set up.[90] These centers involve joint manning of information facilities by clerks who remain employed by their respective public agencies but are crosstrained to provide information on employment opportunities and hiring procedures in all the participating governments. For example, in Florida, intergovernmental job information centers have been established in Jacksonville, Orlando, Tampa, and Pensacola. The center in Pensacola combines the recruiting efforts of the city of Pensacola, Escambia County, the state of Florida, and the U.S. Civil Service Commission. The result in all participating jurisdictions has been a larger number of qualified applicants.[91]

One of the most successful forms of intergovernmental cooperation in personnel recruitment and selection is seen in the Utah Intergovernmental Personnel Agency, established December 1972. This agency serves as a one-stop center for applicants seeking clerical jobs with the state of Utah, Salt Lake City County, Utah State University, the University of Utah, and nearby counties. Information about public employment is obtained at one location instead of at a dozen or more locations in and around Salt Lake City.[92] Clients need fill out only one application and take only one test or a series of tests in order to be considered for employment by all participating jurisdictions. Governments participating in the center's activities are spared the interruptions caused by walk-in applicants, and thus both the applicant and the agency are saved time, money, and inconvience. Through this system both the employer and the applicant have access to a wider base of information about the availability of prospective jobs and employees.[93]

Other cooperative recruiting programs involve sharing of costs of preparation, publication, and distribution of recruitment materials; joint paid advertising; and intergovernmental recruiting activities at educational institutions or other sources of manpower.[94]

Joint recruiting teams may encourage careers in government. As an illustration, on January 22, 1975, a government employment information seminar was held at Georgia State University to acquaint students with the purposes and benefits of a career with federal, state, or local government. Representatives of the U.S. Civil Service Commission, the State of Georgia merit system, the Fulton County personnel board, the DeKalb County merit system, and the city of Atlanta personnel department discussed the recruiting and examination process of their respective jurisdictions.

Finally, Intergovernmental Personnel Act funds were used in 1974–1975 to develop intergovernmental personnel service centers in Denver, Seattle, and Milwaukee to provide job information and recruitment materials. These centers are expected to be of great benefit to their respective jurisdictions.[95]

Selection Criteria and Recruitment Procedures. The development of any sound recruitment program must be accompanied by a thoroughgoing job analysis, which gives attention not only to the frequency of tasks but also to their relative importance.[96] In the past there has been a tendency to place such a high premium on educational requirements and professional certification that the number of candidates for job openings was unfairly restricted.[97] According to Mortimer M. Caplin, president of the National Civil Service League, out of an estimated 500,000 new jobs created each year in state and local government, a minimum of 100,000 could go to the poor if existing barriers were removed. Moreover, an additional 100,000 job vacancies could be claimed for disadvantaged, well-motivated workers through positive changes in existing systems.[98]

Decision after decision rendered by the courts has made clear that qualifications and requirements established for positions within government—local or otherwise—must be job-related. There has been a tendency to screen out minority candidates through restricted recruitment and arbitrary qualification requirements. Again, requirements for appointment or promotion unrelated to performance should be eliminated, including requirements of age, sex, height, weight, residence, voting or arrest record, irrelevant convictions, and degrees or years of education.[99] In many cases certificates of proficiency could be accepted in lieu of performance tests for skills such as typing or stenography if received from fully accredited and recognized business schools and other preparatory institutes.[100] State license requirements may be another barrier preventing employment, particularly in some engineering or other technical positions.[101]

In short, every effort should be made by the local government to see that license requirements are valid and essential to job performance and are not merely requirements that have been carried over from past conditions and circumstances.

Equal Employment Opportunity

The Equal Employment Opportunity Act of 1972 extended coverage of Title VII of the Civil Rights Act of 1964 to include state and local governments. This law requires all cities to extend to all individuals equal employment opportunity in hiring, training, compensation, promotion, and other conditions of employment without regard to race, color, religion, age, sex, politics, or national origin. Cities are taking positive steps to promote equal opportunity for all their employees by developing innovative and systematic affirmative action plans.[102]

Recruitment is the first significant phase in establishing a fair employment system. Beginning with a clear-cut affirmative action policy that designates some high-level official such as the equal employment officer or the labor relations officer responsible for administering the program, affirmative action plans call for specific recruitment programs and activities to encourage more women and minorities to seek city employment. It is vital that unequivocal commitment by top-level management be restated from time to time to ensure the success of the affirmative action program.[103]

While many of the recruitment methods discussed in this chapter also apply in the recruiting of women, members of minority groups, and disadvantaged persons, a few additional points might be noted briefly because they are elemental to the overall recruitment program.

Obtain and train recruiters who relate well with the minority community, who understand how to relate with women's groups and organizations, and who can stimulate interest in government jobs. Develop strong, imaginative outreach campaigns that seek out women, minority groups, and the poor and that work in cooperation with community agencies in recruiting.[104] Prepare selected employee case histories, brochures with employees' photos, news stories, and alumni career directories as a follow-up on successful minority employees and women, and distribute these materials to all major recruitment sources.

Keep all recruitment literature and vacancy notices readable and understandable for the disadvantaged. Simplify the application form and provide assistance for application completion wherever appropriate. Insert recruitment literature in correspondence with citizens, such as bills or receipts for rent in public housing, tax forms, application forms for licenses, calls to jury duty, and welfare checks.[105] Explore with community sources the feasibility of establishing day care centers; provide information in personnel offices and notify employees regarding the location of such facilities.[106] This will be particularly helpful for potential female recruits to city government. See that all advertisements and all city stationery include the notice "An Equal Opportunity Employer" to reconfirm with employer and applicant alike this important government policy.[107]

Establish progressive maternity leave policies that are consistent with Equal Employment Opportunity Commission guidelines.[108] Such policies permit maternity leave to be taken much the same as sick leave, with the length of leave determined by the employee and her doctor. The employee would return to work with all employment rights and benefits intact.

Finally, recruiters should be reminded that in all dealings (including interviewing) with women and members of minority groups, a professional, courteous, common-sense approach is expected and does work best.[109]

Summary

The recruitment and staffing process is a fundamental activity of personnel administration. It is hoped that this chapter, in discussing recruitment problems, costs, sources, and the actual process of recruiting in accordance with the requirements of equal employment opportunity, will prove useful to local governments in developing and implementing sound and mutually beneficial programs that will bring the most talented and motivated individuals into government work. Ultimately, of course, the success of any recruitment program and, in particular, the principles of equal employment opportunity, depends on the continuing commitment and effort of top management, departmental directors, personnel administrators, and on the employees themselves.

[1] International City Managers' Association, MUNICIPAL PERSONNEL ADMINISTRATION, 6th ed. (Chicago: International City Managers' Association, 1960), p. 73.

[2] Advisory Council on Intergovernmental Personnel Policy, MORE EFFECTIVE PUBLIC SERVICE (Washington, D.C.: Government Printing Office, 1974), p. 16.

[3] National Civil Service League, A MODEL PUBLIC PERSONNEL ADMINISTRATION LAW (Washington, D.C.: National Civil Service League, 1971), p. 7.

[4] Municipal Manpower Commission, GOVERNMENTAL MANPOWER FOR TOMORROW'S CITIES (New York: McGraw-Hill Book Company, 1962), p. 2.

[5] Michael A. DiNunzio and Nancy Hall, "Manning Tomorrow's Cities: In Search of Professionals," NATION'S CITIES 11 (June 1973): 26.

[6] Jacob J. Rutstein, "Survey of Current Personnel Systems in State and Local Governments," GOOD GOVERNMENT 87 (Spring 1971): 6.

[7] National League of Cities–U.S. Conference of Mayors, LOCAL GOVERNMENT APPROACHES TO CAPACITY-BUILDING (Washington, D.C.: National League of Cities–U.S. Conference of Mayors, 1973), p. 22.

[8] Ibid., p. 27.

[9] Ibid., p. 18.

[10] Felix A. Nigro, MODERN PUBLIC ADMINISTRATION, 2nd ed. (New York: Harper & Row, Publishers, 1970), p. 16.

[11] Richard L. Chapman and Frederic N. Cleaveland, eds., MEETING THE NEEDS OF TOMORROW'S PUBLIC SERVICE: GUIDELINES FOR PROFESSIONAL EDUCATION IN PUBLIC ADMINISTRATION (Washington, D.C.: National Academy of Public Administration, 1973), p. 18.

[12] DiNunzio and Hall, "Manning Tomorrow's Cities," p. 10. See also Institute of Urban Studies, University of Texas at Arlington, EXECUTIVE MANPOWER FOR URBAN GOVERNMENT, vol. 2: EDUCATION FOR CAREER SERVICE (Arlington, Tex.: University of Texas, 1970).

[13] National League of Cities–U.S. Conference of Mayors, LOCAL GOVERNMENT APPROACHES TO CAPACITY-BUILDING, p. 16.

[14] National League of Cities–U.S. Conference of Mayors, AN EVALUATION OF THE NATIONAL URBAN TECHNICAL SERVICES RESEARCH AND DEMONSTRATION PROGRAM (Washington, D.C.: National League of Cities–U.S. Conference of Mayors, 1973), p. 20.

[15] Nigro, MODERN PUBLIC ADMINISTRATION, p. 16.

[16] Chapman and Cleaveland, MEETING THE NEEDS OF TOMORROW'S PUBLIC SERVICE, p. 52.

[17] Rutstein, "Survey of Current Personnel Systems in State and Local Governments," p. 3.

[18] Chapman and Cleaveland, MEETING THE NEEDS OF TOMORROW'S PUBLIC SERVICE, p. 54.

[19] William H. Brown III, "Moving Against Job Bias in State and Local Governments," GOOD GOVERNMENT 89 (Winter 1972): 15.

[20] Chapman and Cleaveland, MEETING THE NEEDS OF TOMORROW'S PUBLIC SERVICE, p. 41.

[21] Barry S. Bader, "Opening Public Jobs to the Disadvantaged," in NATIONAL CIVIL SERVICE LEAGUE LEADS THE WAY IN PUBLIC PERSONNEL MODERNIZATION, ed. National Civil Service League (Washington, D.C.: National Civil Service League, 1972), pp. 3–4.

[22] National Civil Service League, "Survey of Current Personnel Systems in State and Local Governments," p. 17.

[23] National League of Cities–U.S. Conference of Mayors, LOCAL GOVERNMENT APPROACHES TO CAPACITY-BUILDING, p. 23.

[24] Advisory Council on Intergovernmental Personnel Policy, MORE EFFECTIVF PUBLIC SERVICE, p. 11.

[25] See John D. Palmer, "Finding the Best Brains: Recruitment of Quality Personnel for Public Service in Georgia," ATLANTA ECONOMIC REVIEW 19 (July 1969): 22–24.

[26] New England Municipal Center, MUNICIPAL MANPOWER PROJECT REPORT FOR DOVER, NEW HAMPSHIRE (Durham, N.H.: New England Municipal Center, 1973) p. 6.

[27] DiNunzio and Hall, "Manning Tomorrow's Cities," p. 35.

[28] Ibid.

[29] Ibid.

[30] Matthew Jackson, RECRUITING, INTERVIEWING, AND SELECTING: A MANUAL FOR LINE MANAGERS (London: McGraw–Hill Book Company, 1972), pp. 4–5.

[31] Ibid., p. 6.

[32] National League of Cities–U.S. Conference of Mayors, LOCAL GOVERNMENT APPROACHES TO CAPACITY BUILDING, pp. 21, 23.

33 Jackson, Recruiting, Interviewing, and Selecting, p. 28.

34 Arthur R. Pell, Recruiting and Selecting Personnel (New York: Simon & Schuster, Inc., 1969), pp. 10–11.

35 Institute of Urban Studies, University of Texas at Arlington, Executive Manpower for Urban Government, vol. 1: A Regional Manpower Profile (Arlington, Tex.: University of Texas, 1970), p. 13.

36 DiNunzio and Hall, "Manning Tomorrow's Cities," p. 37.

37 Laurence Lipsett, Frank P. Rodgers, and Harold M. Kentner, Personnel Selection and Recruitment (Boston: Allyn & Bacon, 1964), p. 18.

38 Pell, Recruiting and Selecting Personnel, pp. 12–13; Jackson, Recruiting, Interviewing, and Selecting, p. 28.

39 Pell, Recruiting and Selecting Personnel, p. 14.

40 National League of Cities–U.S. Conference of Mayors, Local Government Approaches to Capacity-Building, p. 17.

41 Lipsett et al., Personnel Selection and Recruitment, pp. 23–24.

42 George S. Odiorne and Arthur S. Hann, Effective College Recruiting (Ann Arbor, Mich.: Bureau of Industrial Relations, University of Michigan, 1961), pp. 45–105.

43 Ibid.

44 See Palmer, "Finding the Best Brains."

45 Institute of Urban Studies, A Regional Manpower Profile, p. 9.

46 Pell, Recruiting and Selecting Personnel, p. 34.

47 Ibid., p. 35.

48 Ibid., p. 43; Jackson, Recruiting, Interviewing, and Selecting, p. 20.

49 Pell, Recruiting and Selecting Personnel, pp. 19–20.

50 Ibid.

51 Pell, Recruiting and Selecting Personnel, pp. 19–20; Jackson, Recruiting, Interviewing, and Selecting, pp. 30–39.

52 Jackson, Recruiting, Interviewing, and Selecting, p. 31.

53 Municipal Manpower Commission, Governmental Manpower for Tomorrow's Cities, pp. 53–54.

54 National League of Cities–U.S. Conference of Mayors, An Evaluation of the National Urban Technical Services Research and Demonstration Program, p. viii.

55 National League of Cities–U.S. Conference of Mayors, Local Government Approaches to Capacity-Building, p. 21.

56 U.S., Civil Service Commission, Intergovernmental Personnel Programs Division, Atlanta Region, A Personnel Management System for Shelby County, Tennessee (Washington, D.C.: U.S. Civil Service Commission, April 1974).

57 International City Managers' Association, Municipal Personnel Administration, p. 73.

58 Robert W. Coppock and Barbara Brattin Coppock, How to Recruit and Select Policemen and Firemen (Chicago: Public Personnel Association, 1958), p. 7.

59 Coppock and Coppock, How to Recruit and Select Policemen and Firemen, p. 8; U.S., Department of Housing and Urban Development, Personnel Management in Local Model Cities Programs, Model Cities Management Series, bulletin 2 (Washington, D.C.: Government Printing Office, 1971), pp. 5–6.

60 R. H. Bubier, "Affirmative Action Plan for the City of Fort Lauderdale," memorandum 166–74 (Fort Lauderdale, October 30, 1974), p. 8.

61 Ibid.

62 Palmer, "Finding the Best Brains," p. 23.

63 Floyd A. Decker, Andrew B. Horgan III, and Lawrence A. Williams, Municipal Government Efforts to Provide Career Employment Opportunities for the Disadvantaged (Washington, D.C.: National League of Cities, 1969), pp. 22–23.

64 Palmer, "Finding the Best Brains," p. 23.

65 U.S., Civil Service Commission, Achieving Job-Related Selection for Entry-Level Police Officers and Firefighters (Washington, D.C.: U.S. Civil Service Commission, 1973), p. 11.

66 See Harlan T. Cooper, "Internships in State and Local Governments in the South," paper delivered at the Southern Political Science Association annual meeting, New Orleans, Louisiana, November 7–9, 1974, for a discussion of the development of internships in Southern states.

67 Christopher P. Seale, "Impact of the Georgia Intern Program on Participants' Vocational Goals," paper delivered at the Southern Political Science Association annual meeting in New Orleans, Louisiana, November 7–9, 1974, pages 7–8.

68 Harlan T. Cooper, "Internships in State and Local Governments in the South," p. 4.

69 U.S., Civil Service Commission, Summary of Selected FY 1973 IPA Grant Projects (Washington, D.C.: U.S. Civil Service Commission, May 1974), p. 70.

70 Civil Service Commission, Summary of Selected FY 1973 IPA Grant Projects, p. 89.

71 Cooper, "Internships in State and Local Governments in the South," p. 39.

72 Sigmund G. Ginsburg, "New York City's 1968 Summer Intern Program," Public Personnel Review 30 (July 1969): 145–148.

73 Nation's Cities 1974–75 Annual Directory, comp. Catherine Satterlee, Nation's Cities 12 (July 1974): pp. 14–15 and 33–35.

74 National League of Cities–U.S. Conference of Mayors, An Evaluation of the National Urban Technical Services Research and Demonstration Program, pp. 12–15.

75 Civil Service Commission, A Personnel Management System for Shelby County, Tennessee, p. 11.

76 Department of Housing and Urban Development, Personnel Management in Local Model Cities Programs, p. 6.

77 O. Glenn Stahl, Public Personnel Administration, 6th ed. (New York: Harper & Row, Publishers, 1971), p. 110.

78 Odiorne and Hann, Effective College Recruiting.

79 Allan W. Howerton, "Recruiters' Forum," Civil Service Journal 15 (October/December 1974): 19.

80 U.S., Civil Service Commission, Guide to Federal Career Literature (Washington, D.C.: Government Printing Office, 1969).

81 Warren S. Blumenfeld, "Application, Application," Atlanta Economic Review 23 (May/June 1973): 8.

82 Arthur R. Pell, Recruiting and Selecting Personnel, pp. 91–101.

83 The brochure is reproduced and discussed in Wayne

R. Porter and Edward L. Levine, "Improving Applicants' Performance in the Completion of Applications," PUBLIC PERSONNEL MANAGEMENT (July/August 1974): 314–317. The brochure may be obtained on request from the Selection Resource Center, Arizona State Personnel Commission, 831 W. Jefferson St., Phoenix, Ariz. 85007.

84 Jackson, RECRUITING, INTERVIEWING, AND SELECTING, p. 60.

85 Blumenfeld, "Application, Application," pp. 10–13.

86 Jackson, RECRUITING, INTERVIEWING, AND SELECTING, p. 60.

87 Civil Service Commission, A PERSONNEL MANAGEMENT SYSTEM FOR SHELBY COUNTY, TENNESSEE.

88 J. L. Stone, "The Use of an Applicant Service Questionnaire," PUBLIC PERSONNEL MANAGEMENT (March/April 1974): 155–157.

89 U.S., Civil Service Commission, Bureau of Recruiting and Examining, INTERGOVERNMENTAL COOPERATION IN RECRUITING AND EXAMINING (Washington, D.C.: U.S. Civil Service Commission, August 1973), p. 3.

90 U.S., Civil Service Commission, Bureau of Intergovernmental Personnel Programs, INTERGOVERNMENTAL PERSONNEL NOTES (Washington, D.C.: U.S. Civil Service Commission, April 1974).

91 Ibid.

92 Lyman F. Smart and Jack E. McIntosh, "An Interim Report on the Utah Intergovernmental Personnel Agency," paper presented at International Personnel Management Association international conference, Miami Beach, Florida, November 1973.

93 Smart and McIntosh, "An Interim Report on the Utah Intergovernmental Personnel Agency"; William M. Timmins, "Intergovernmental Cooperation in Personnel Recruitment and Selection," STATE GOVERNMENT ADMINISTRATION (May 1974): 8–10.

94 Civil Service Commission, INTERGOVERNMENTAL COOPERATION IN RECRUITING AND EXAMINING.

95 Civil Service Commission, SUMMARY OF SELECTED FY 1973 IPA GRANT PROJECTS, pp. 82, 546, and 568.

96 Harry Kranz, "Are Merit and Equity Compatible?" PUBLIC ADMINISTRATION REVIEW 34 (July/August 1974): 437–438.

97 Mortimer M. Caplin, "Let's Revamp Merit Systems for Today's Needs," in NATIONAL CIVIL SERVICE LEAGUE LEADS THE WAY IN PUBLIC PERSONNEL ADMINISTRATION, p. 17.

98 Ibid., p. 18.

99 Jean J. Couturier, "Governments Can Be the 'Employers of First Resort,'" NATIONAL CIVIL SERVICE LEAGUE LEADS THE WAY IN PUBLIC PERSONNEL ADMINISTRATION, pp. 24–26.

100 Civil Service Commission, A PERSONNEL MANAGEMENT SYSTEM FOR SHELBY COUNTY, TENNESSEE.

101 National League of Cities–U.S. Conference of Mayors, LOCAL GOVERNMENT APPROACHES TO CAPACITY-BUILDING, p. 55.

102 See Bubier, "Affirmative Action Plan for City of Fort Lauderdale."

103 U.S., Civil Service Commission, Bureau of Intergovernmental Personnel Programs, AN EQUAL OPPORTUNITY PROGRAM FOR STATE AND LOCAL GOVERNMENT EMPLOYMENT (Washington, D.C.: U.S. Civil Service Commission, 1970), p. 1.

104 Caplin, "Let's Revamp Merit Systems for Today's Needs," pp. 25–26.

105 Civil Service Commission, AN EQUAL OPPORTUNITY PROGRAM FOR STATE AND LOCAL GOVERNMENT EMPLOYMENT, p. 6.

106 Caplin, "Let's Revamp Merit Systems for Today's Needs," p. 19.

107 Civil Service Commission, AN EQUAL OPPORTUNITY PROGRAM FOR STATE AND LOCAL GOVERNMENT EMPLOYMENT, p. 6.

108 See U.S., Civil Service Commission, EQUAL EMPLOYMENT OPPORTUNITY COURT CASES (Washington, D.C.: U.S. Civil Service Commission, 1974), pp. 48–51, for cases dealing with this issue.

109 "Recruiters Forum," CIVIL SERVICE JOURNAL (October/December 1973): 3–4.

6

The Selection Process

. . . to train communities through all their grades, beginning with individuals and ending there again, to rule themselves.

WALT WHITMAN

TRADITIONAL PERSONNEL SELECTION PROCESSES are based on management, work, and merit concepts that reflect neither the realities of contemporary organization life nor the present state of learning in the areas to which these processes apply. They are firmly established, however, in most public personnel agencies, particularly those that operate under a civil service law. There is scant evidence to show that such agencies are predisposed to change. Old processes—like habits—have been perpetuated rather than probed, despite the extent to which new pressures have increased in number rather than declined. As John W. Macy, Jr., notes:

Today's job is made more difficult by the fact that someone in an earlier time cast his thoughts in concrete when they should have been written in wet sand.[1]

Introduction: The Practitioner's Dilemma

The personnel practitioner involved in the selection process sits on the horns of a dilemma, the elements of which produce both challenges

---

Portions of the material in this chapter are adapted from Nesta M. Gallas, PUBLIC PERSONNEL SELECTION: A BEHAVIORAL ANALYSIS OF CURRENT PRACTICES (Ann Arbor, Mich.: University Microfilm, 1968).

and risks. The challenges lie in considering what can be done to update the process and make it both representative of and responsive to the diversity of the clienteles and the publics it serves.[2] The risks lie in upsetting the status quo and in opening the system to pressures and ways of learning to which it may be neither receptive nor exposed.

Although the practitioner's predicament is perplexing, the situation is not intractable. The climate for change is improving. The focus of any real push for planned change (whether desired or not) is bound to be on the practitioner and personnel agency served.[3] The practitioner and the public personnel agency that fail to react to the pressing needs for change contribute to the maintenance of a selection process that is irrelevant and dysfunctional for the public service and the profession.[4]

THE QUESTION OF PROFESSIONALISM[5]

The field of public personnel selection has borne the brunt of criticism directed toward both individual and occupational levels of professionalism and the lack of empirical research to support existing selection processes. Since what is done is organizationally based, the selection process varies from public agency to public agency, although a common pattern does prevail. The concerned personnel administrator will incur considerable stress from the conflicts that arise in trying (1) to balance the external demands for change in the selection process with internal and union resistance to change; (2) to achieve peer or supervisor consensus on what parts of the selection process to restructure and how to go about it; (3) to support the selection process with a viable body of knowledge and theory; (4) to decide from what disciplines or theories the process should derive; and (5) to find ways to translate into actuality the results of research. As the backgrounds of those doing public personnel selection vary significantly, so do their attitudes and perceptions about these questions. Accordingly, so vary the problems and the needs for and the value of change. The nature of the selection function and the way it is performed in the public sector render the personnel process an "occupation in conflict."[6]

The problem of professionalism in this field can be defined in precise terms by asking how adequate the state of knowledge in personnel selection is, how pertinent it is, how accepted it is, and how it actually relates to the selection process as performed in a public personnel agency. To answer these questions requires that each agency reevaluate its selection process and the assumptions on which it is based in relation to the following:

1. The position of administration in terms of the political, social, economic, technological, and judicial systems and forces that surround the public personnel agency and condition its existence and development.
2. Changing concepts of merit and of career development that are evolving from the influence on public personnel selection programs of collective bargaining, equal employment policies, court decisions, civil rights legislation, federal mandates, affirmative action, the women's movement, and other movements, trends, and events.
3. Theoretical and conceptual advancements in the study of complex organizations and their application to personnel selection systems and processes in various public organizations and at various organizational levels.
4. The current state of knowledge in the sociology of work as evidenced in the changing world of work, workers, and work relationships.
5. Current behavioral science concepts about the competencies involved in the work and work behavior of individuals as present or prospective organization members.

The Need for Reappraisal

The most compelling reason for a reappraisal of the selection process is that human resources are our resources that are the most valuable and the most costly. The effectiveness of human resources in an organization depends on individual competencies and limitations, management policies affecting work and workers, and environmental influences both external and internal. Personnel selection, as that phase of personnel management which deals with people as human resources, must undergo changes if it is to reflect the changing world of work, the changing concepts of merit and career development, and the changing ways of thinking about individuals doing work in the public sector.[7]

The personnel process, as but one of many systems within a total management system, helps shape a social system that is involved in accomplishing organization goals.[8] Traditional ways of selecting individuals as human resources for this social system have been found lacking or even counterproductive as knowledge about individuals, work, work groups, organizations, and human organization behavior has grown. Consequently, as a key area of personnel, selection programs need to be carefully scrutinized. If traditional assumptions on which the selection process is based clash with sound concepts about the work behavior of individuals as organization participants, major changes in the process should be contemplated and encouraged.

Efforts are constantly directed to the selection of persons to enter and advance in both public and private employment. Neither crystal balls nor psychological tests have proved adequate in predicting work effectiveness. The selection process continues to pose problems not answerable in terms of the techniques and tools used. Each new technique or tool gains its share of advocates and critics. The extent to which a new concept is accepted and applied appears at times to be related more to personal preference, publicity, or salesmanship than to evidence supporting the claims of its advocates or the challenges of its critics.

The task of selecting competent personnel, while common to all organizations, is fraught with special problems in public service careers.

Interpersonal relationships between career administrators and governing bodies—elected or appointed—are always affected by personnel choices. Administrative influences wax or wane with the quality of career personnel. Sensitivity to diverse personnel policy issues is needed, plus a special brand of toughness to combat unexpected attack and nullification efforts. Changing shades and mixtures of political opinion and pressure complicate the ability of career systems to cope with the diverse elements of the power system within which they work. Selecting talented personnel strains any administrator working in any framework, whatever the tools employed. In a public setting, where selection is done at the expense of taxpayers who hold all sorts of opinions about whom they expect to serve their public needs, the timeliness of selection practices is of compelling importance.

The selection process needs to keep questioning how it does things as well as why it does things a particular way. In short, continuous evaluation is required. If verified conceptualization supports a current practice, continuation of the practice is warranted. If support is lacking, rejection or revision may be necessary. A selection process based on assumptions which no longer can predict or explain individual performance hampers organizational effectiveness.[9] To withstand scrutiny by interested publics, including the academic community, the selection process needs to relate realistically to current concepts and conditions. Indications are that it does not.

A Conceptual Framework for the Selection Process

In this chapter some key terms are used and related in particular ways. Since these terms are not yet part of the public personnel vocabulary, their definition as used in this chapter is presented in the following short glossary. Selection concepts discussed in this chapter are oriented toward the behavioral sciences.

Selection. "Selection implies preference and choice tied to a set of values. 'Public personnel selection' means preferential choosing of human talent for public service in accordance with the values attached to the personnel system. Although careers and merit immediately come to mind as values inherent in a public system, these are just words. Their meaning rests on what is done and why it is done in a specific system as perceived by those concerned."[10]

Human Resources. Human resources refers to the work competencies and limitations of individuals as organization members. Specifically, it refers to their achievements, intelligence, creativity, personality, perceptions, interests, values, motivation, and leadership as related to the job and its context.

Process. Process refers to the action, way, or method of doing whatever it is that is being done. It does not in itself indicate whether the action, way, or method is right or wrong, good or bad.

Current Selection Process. Current selection process refers to the usual or most common way, method, or action followed in the preferential choosing of human resources for public service. In this chapter it is termed the traditional model since it is well-established and observable, having been handed down from one generation of practitioners to another. Although it includes recruitment, examination, certification, and placement, examination is emphasized since this is the traditional point of emphasis. (Other parts of the cycle also will be discussed in this chapter.)

The Selection Cycle. The selection cycle includes (1) projecting both short- and long-range human talent needs of public programs; (2) searching out human resources to fill projected needs; (3) making these resources available on a continuing basis with competencies identified and behavior predicted; and (4) determining work performance of human resources provided. It represents a continuing cycle which revolves around human talent needs, human resources, and work performance.[11]

The Merit Tradition

In its historical sense the merit tradition is the conceptual framework for most public personnel selection programs. The philosophy and principles of this framework have provided a reference point for the drafting and passage of civil service, merit system, and career service laws and have served as a model for structuring selection programs, as a popular yardstick for measuring the degree of merit in selections made, and as a guiding, if sometimes invisible, hand in the practice and politics of selection.

The merit tradition, as it relates to the selection process, has several key principles: The best shall serve the state, and all citizens will be afforded equal opportunity to compete for the privilege of public service. These principles, when expressed in legal provisions, usually require the following:

1. That all appointments and promotions be made solely on the basis of merit and fitness to be determined by competitive examinations which are practical in character;
2. That open competitive examinations be used to test the relative fitness of applicants for entry in the public service;
3. That public announcement of examinations be made sufficiently in advance to inform all interested citizens of the opportunities for public employment;
4. That the names of candidates eligible for appointment and promotion be listed in order of their relative excellence in competitive examinations;
5. That the persons standing highest on the eligibility lists receive appointments.[12]

As with many traditions, different interpretations and applications of these requirements have evolved. The original elements have been broadened, embellished, and modernized. A sorting out of the concepts related to selection shows the complexities and contradictions involved. The traditional ideas can be categorized as follows: the criteria of competence; the emphasis on equalitarianism; the creed of competition; the principle of practical tests; the objective of objectivity; the necessity for neutrality; the privilege of participation; the concept of closed careers; and the insistence on impartiality.

These ideas and the tradition from which they emerged now are seen as somewhat questionable for the 1970s. As society's needs and values change, there is a need to redefine merit as it applies to the selection process. Such redefinition appeared, for example, in the 1970 edition of *A Model Public Personnel Administration Law,* published by the National Civil Service League. Proposed provisions on selection called for policies that provide "for recruitment of capable persons and for administering culture fair open evaluations, to determine the relative fitness of applicants for positions in the public service" and "for the certification to the appointing authority of the names of persons who are categorized as qualified to fill a vacancy."[13] The redefined provisions continue:

Effective recruiting demands more than the passive approach involved in announcing vacancies in public service in obscure places, and examining those who present themselves as a result of such stereotyped announcement. The jurisdiction must develop a system of recruitment that interests the most capable persons in public service and a selection system that insures the highest caliber employee. The work to be performed in the public service challenges the best ability in the country. Governments must seek out ability and persuade the able to serve the public. In his quest for persons who are qualified for particular positions in the public service, the director should be free to utilize any combination of selection criteria, e.g., education and experience, and any written, oral, or performance test of capacity, knowledge, manual skills or physical fitness. The director must take special precautions, however, to ascertain that whatever tests he uses are, as nearly as possible, culture fair and that such tests are validated. A test can be judged valid if a direct relationship can be shown between test results and job performance. . . .

Many jurisdictions currently require the director of personnel to certify to the appointing officer three individuals who received the highest scores on the public service examination. The appointing authority is then required to appoint from those three names. The 'rule of three' has been criticized for the lack of flexibility that it affords the appointing authority. Further, many examination results often reveal that the margin between the highest score and, for instance, the tenth highest score is only a fraction of a percentage point. In order to give the operating agencies and departments maximum flexibility in the selection of personnel, yet at the same time assure that the public servant will be chosen from persons who are qualified, this draft provides that the director of personnel, using objective criteria, shall categorize those persons eligible for a position as being qualified. The appointing officers shall then make their selection from such persons. If the list of qualified persons is excessively long, the jurisdiction may consider only certifying a workable number of persons to the appointing authority.[14]

The merit principles drafted in 1973 by the President's Advisory Council on Intergovernmental Personnel Policy also reflected some changes in emphasis. One of the six merit principles endorsed as a basic personnel management requirement for federal grants-in-aid recommended "recruiting, selecting, and advancing employees on the basis of their relative knowledge and skills, including open consideration of qualified applicants for initial appointment."[15]

The council issued several specific caveats in regard to this principle:

1. It should not apply to all positions.
2. Since authority for the employment, advancement, development and direction of each public employee rests with the chief executive, civil service commissions with total responsibility for the personnel process and completely independent of the chief executive are not compatible with this principle.
3. The observance of a rigid "rule of one" or "rule of three" or other very restricted number of highly qualified persons can be an inappropriate restriction on the latitude of an appointing authority.
4. Seniority as a primary criterion for promotion is not in accord with this principle since selection techniques should encourage infusion of new blood at higher levels and mobility between jurisdictions.[16]

In its generalized comments on the principle, the council stated that

All parts of a selection system, including the exercise of supervisory judgment, must be job-related. The system should provide an assessment of applicants' relative skills, knowledges, past and prospective performance, abilities and potential. . . . The use of tests which are non-job-related is an example of a selection practice which would be inconsistent with this merit principle. Also inappropriate are selection techniques which result in the selection of the most highly educated applicants when the job concerned does not require a high degree of education.[17]

MERIT SELECTION,
EQUAL EMPLOYMENT OPPORTUNITY,
AND DISCRIMINATION

In a supplementary report the council, in commenting on failures to assure "equal employment access to all members of the community," stated that

Part of the problem is that we have tolerated, at least to some degree, blatant discrimination in public employment. The 1972 amendments to the Civil Rights Act are specifically directed to putting an end to such practices. A much larger part of the problem, however, is complacency—the presumption that passive non-discrimination is equivalent to the assurance of equal employment opportunity.[18]

To counteract this state of things the council prescribed the following features for a successful selection program:

All selection procedures (including written, performance or oral tests, education and experience ratings, structured interviews, reference vouchers and application forms) must be designed to assure nondiscrimination and equal opportunity. An essential step in achieving this is to see that selection devices of all kinds measure relevant job requirements and are reliable and valid.
• Where tests are used they should be professionally developed, be based on careful job analyses and validated by appropriate methods. They should be administered under standardized or uniform conditions with uncomplicated instructions.
• All selection devices should be reviewed and updated under a systematic plan to assure current relevance and adequacy.
• In evaluating candidates for management positions, especially high level management positions, evidence of the candidates' commitment to equal employment opportunity should be required.[19]

The existence of discrimination in the selection process is not readily recognized by many public employers.

Many employers, perhaps most public employers, have felt that they have not been discriminating in the past and think that they are somehow immune from Title VII litigation, because they do not intend to discriminate. Discrimination in most jurisdictions is a thing of the past according to many personnel directors. However, the volume of suits being filed in federal district courts against public jurisdictions suggests that public jurisdictions are still discriminating *and most frequently unknowingly*.[20]

Traditionalists in what might be called the classical school of merit selection maintain that the current versions of merit do not change the basic truths. Avant-garde personnel specialists of the let's-shake-up-the-selection-system school see nothing valid in the merit tradition. Truth means validity and validity means proof. No systematic research has been conducted to determine that the traditional concepts are essential for effective personnel selection. As a result, what is done and how merit is interpreted has come under increasing challenge. Whether the traditional concepts and process represent the idealism of professional public personnel officers or merely a clinging to clichés to justify an established way of life is a question frequently being raised.

At times 'personnel' has been referred to as a field of endeavor engaged in by a coterie of myopic technicians. Not only are they myopic according to some critics, but they also wear blinders which narrow their already dim view.[21]

As one study proposed,

civil service should be put on a sound evolutionary footing. . . . It should give men, who are not created equal, an equal opportunity to apply their particular talents in the service of their fellows.[22]

The merit tradition is elemental to the study of the selection process, because it relates to the shift from defensive tactics to the selection of the person most fit for public office and, since the early 1970s, to the need for representativeness and responsiveness. Despite the ubiquity of slogans about the best serving the state that appear on letterheads, publications, posters, etc., a report to the 86th Congress observed that

the reputation of the public service generally . . . is not high enough so that it serves as a positive attraction to people. Any picture of civil service examining procedures as a means of choosing a few of the best from clamoring hordes of office seekers is as old-fashioned as the roll-top desk and the frock-coated dispenser of patronage.[23]

MYTHS OF THE MERIT TRADITION

Study of the selection process also requires a look at the myths which surround the merit tradition. That there are myths is readily demonstrated. Any practitioner drawn into a lay discussion of selection for the public service will hear a few examples, since they are bound to be mentioned whenever the civil service is mentioned.

The following folk tale is an example:

[The civil service is] a unique system under which it is assumed that people are simply organic compounds, subject to laboratory methods. Examinations are given to these specimens, and on the basis of results, they are neatly catalogued and filed until needed. Orders are filled on the general understanding that short of an Act of God, there will be no returns or exchanges. The finished product is a pale, quiet individual, faithful in a dim sort of way, disinclined to originality, but capable within a limited field of an insolence that makes one wonder why it is called 'civil.'[24]

History will record the early 1960s as an era of aggressive action taken by some groups directly concerned with the conduct of public personnel selection programs to combat this myth.[25] The late 1960s and early 1970s will be seen as a period of discovery of the potency of minority, disadvantaged, and women's groups that added new dimensions and demands to both the reality and the myth. The influence of these groups has led to a flood of pronouncements and regulations:

Whether by design or by chance, personnel selection has become one of the most over-regulated areas in American life, with the U.S. Constitution; state constitutions; federal, state, and local laws; federal, state, and local executive orders; federal, state, and local court decisions and hearing decisions; and federal, state and local regulations and guidelines. Not surprisingly, conflicts and inconsistencies—not to mention confusion—in the legal structure are inevitable outcomes of these circumstances, which makes organization of the field difficult and somewhat arbitrary (and, more importantly, probably also serves as an impediment to justice) .[26]

The merit tradition of selection, the folklore, the public image, and the forces for change converge in a seesaw of confusion. At one end sits the merit tradition expressed in high ideals; in the middle, the public image, reportedly dull and unimaginative; and at the other end, the current clamor for representativeness and responsiveness—all of which are affected by conflicting controls. The resulting imbalance, when all these elements are active, is likely to continue as long as the traditional model of selection prevails.

[E]ven if there were an organized and consistent legal framework, conflicts are bound to exist between legal standards and professional or scientific standards in a technical area, such as personnel selection, because (1) the lawmakers intended to supersede scientific standards for other considerations (e.g., political), (2) the lawmakers were unaware of the scientific standards, (3) the laws had unintended and unforeseen effects, or (4) the scientific standards changed, as a result of new technology and research, at a faster rate than the laws could be changed.[27]

The Traditional Model and Its Characteristics

A generalized picture of the selection process as traditionally performed, detailing its characteristics, assumptions, and dynamics, is presented in the following discussion. A review of selection practices in 1964 confirmed that the model was still an accurate reflection of reality. The process was the same, although hardware instead of people was being used for some of the tasks. The use of machines and computers was the main change. Another review of the 1945 outline in 1974 prompted one reviewer to state "it is remarkably up to date—and this suggests there hasn't been much change in the last 30 years."[28] The stability of this traditional model is also supported by correspondence, reports, field visits, discussions with agency staffs, meetings of professional associations, and the professional literature.

The traditional model can best be characterized as a task/trait/test-oriented model for filling vacant positions. The process starts with the determination that a vacancy exists or may occur for which no eligibility list is available; the process ends when an eligible candidate is appointed to fill the vacancy.[29] It is a lengthy process, considering the number of steps required from start to finish and the time consumed. Although the span of work represents a continuum from vacant position to filled position, the process may be analyzed in four distinct phases: recruitment, examination, certification, and placement.

The first three phases of the model—recruitment, examination, and certification—generally are performed by one or more specialist or functional units of a central personnel agency. The bulk of time taken in the operation of the model is spent on the first two phases, with examination being the most time-consuming and the most technical phase. Certification and placement require less time and receive less emphasis and attention.[30] Placement is usually conducted by the agency in which the vacancy exists, with the appointment or placement subject to review for legality by the personnel agency, followed by a probationary period.

The information base of the model is the position classification plan and documents related to it. Key characteristics of the model are standardization, practicality, and objectivity of the tasks of positions that are or may become vacant as well as the tests taken to determine eligibility. A standard approach is used in all phases, usually spelled out in detail in procedural manuals. Permissible variations in the approach occur when pressured by a labor shortage or affirmative action. Some variations are allowed for differences in the kind and level of the occupations in which vacancies exist, but when these occur they are work-oriented rather than people-oriented.

Examination of applicants is the core concept of the traditional model. Examination requires the construction and administration of tests.[31] EEOC guidelines define a test as

any paper-and-pencil or performance measure used as a basis for any employment decision. The guidelines apply to ability tests which are designed to measure eligibility for hire, transfer, promotion, membership, training, referral or retention. This definition includes, but is not restricted to, measures of general intelligence, mental ability and learning ability; specific intellectual abilities; mechanical, clerical and other aptitudes; dexterity and coordination; knowledge and proficiency; occupational and other interests; and attitudes, personality or treatment. The term 'test' includes all formal, scored, quantified or standardized techniques of assessing job suitability including, in addition to the above, specific qualifying or disqualifying personal history or background requirements, specific educational or work history requirements, scored interviews, biographical information blanks, interviewers' rating scales, scored application forms, etc.[32]

In the traditional model the tests most commonly used are written tests, performance (work sample) tests, oral (interview) tests, and physical fitness and agility tests. Written tests, primarily objective, are used to test for position-related subject matter, knowledge, aptitudes, and intelligence factors.

The desired end result of these paper-and-pencil tests is to fairly rate candidates by a practical written instrument in modern, short answer, multiple choice form covering the knowledges and skills needed to perform the duties involved in the position.[33]

Oral (interview) tests are used primarily to evaluate personality, training, and experience. The usual form of the oral test is an individual in session with an interview board. Performance (work sample) tests are used primarily to fill clerical, unskilled, and semi-skilled labor and trades positions. Physical fitness and agility tests are used primarily for entry-level law enforcement and fire service positions. Throughout the testing, applicants use identification numbers, not names. Anonymity is maintained to assure objectivity in the testing process.

Objectivity, particularly in written tests, is the principal requirement in the examination phase. Written tests have the unqualified and enthusiastic support of a large number of practitioners engaged in the selection process, particularly those whose academic interest and degree prior to entering the public personnel field was in psychometrics. The dedicated test technician with this credential takes pride in writing a test that is deemed practical for any occupational field or level. Such a technician will express doubts about the competence of test developers and administrators not so trained and can be expected to advocate the requirement of a psychometrics background as a cure for incompetence. This faith in tests as the gospel of selection is characteristic of the model.[34]

The goal of examination, as expressed in correspondence with some practitioners, includes the following:

1. The identification and hiring of those applicants who are most likely to possess to the highest degree the traits deemed necessary or valuable in achieving success on a particular job;
2. The scientific measurement of those individual differences which relate to job requirements;
3. Group testing of job applicants to ascertain the degree to which they possess knowledge, skills, and abilities needed to meet job requirements;
4. The breakdown of the job to accurately define the duties and human qualifications needed to achieve the necessary degree of proficiency in each type of work assignment for testing purposes and to test for these duties and qualifications.

Decisions in the examination phase of the traditional model are based on the functions itemized in the following revised version of the 1945 outline.

OUTLINE OF FUNCTIONS
PERFORMED IN THE SELECTION PROCESS:
THE TRADITIONAL MODEL

   I. Receiving assignment to hold an examination for a specified class.
     A. Checks with certification office to obtain information about latest eligibility list for the class:
       1. Date when list was established;
       2. Date list does or did expire;
       3. Number of persons available on list;
       4. Number of temporary or provisional appointments made to positions and when they expire.
     B. Contacts operating units concerned as to urgency.
     C. Sets, recommends, or obtains deadline when examination should be completed.
     D. Determines whether examination can be held concurrently with other assigned examinations in the same or a similar field.
     E. Establishes a time frame for recording progress or meeting an established control system for completion of the examination.
  II. Obtaining, preparing, and reviewing job descriptions or specifications for the class and

supplementing them with an independent job analysis as a basis for documenting the content validity of the selection devices to be used. (This procedure varies among public personnel agencies according to size, legal restrictions, organizational setup, and age of the agency. In a large agency, part of this work ordinarily will have been performed by a classification technician. In a small agency, one staff member may do all or part of the work.)

A. Pulls pertinent job and class specification material from files if available:
1. Questionnaires from classification surveys;
2. Class definitions;
3. Job analysis sheets.

B. Contacts operating unit or units in which positions in the class occur for information about the salient features of the work and factors to be emphasized in the examining process:
1. Studies departmental organization and procedures;
2. Interviews employees directly supervising the work;
3. Observes employees in the classification under actual working conditions when desirable or feasible;
4. Peruses material prepared within operating unit for employees' information or guidance.

C. Reviews any available research in the occupational field to determine worker characteristics, job standards, and other significant factors.

D. Sets up minimum and desirable qualifications for success in the work:
1. Education;
2. Experience;
3. Knowledge, skills, abilities, and aptitudes;
4. Personal characteristics.

E. Submits specifications to operating unit or units for suggested changes, omissions, or additions.

F. Prepares final draft of specifications for approval.

G. Supervises clerical work involved in preparing copies of specifications for adoption by governing board or commission.

III. Outlining the examination.

A. Analyzes minimum and desirable job-related qualifications for success in the work and lists various components to be examined (see II–D: Sets up minimum and desirable qualifications).

B. Determines the nature of the examination:
1. Written or technical oral;

2. Performance or practical, including in-basket tests;
3. Physical (such as strength tests for laborers);
4. General qualifications evaluation:
    a. Training and experience;
    b. Personal or interpersonal skills and characteristics (in some agencies this is combined with training and experience);
5. Seniority (promotional examinations only);
6. Performance or promotability rating (promotional examinations only).

C. Assigns weights to examination parts based on job analysis conducted.

D. Recommends dates when and places where examination should be held:
1. Opening and closing filing;
2. Date written test will be given or note to effect that date will be announced;
3. Geographical designation of places where written test and oral interviews will be given, indicating civil service agency or other authority in another city, county, or state to be contacted regarding arrangements for holding examinations if necessary.

E. Indicates tentative plans for administration of the examination:
1. Help needed:
    a. Monitors;
    b. Technical assistance:
        (1) Staff members;
        (2) Special examiners;
    c. Oral committees:
        (1) Composition;
        (2) Number;
2. Physical facilities and material requested:
    a. Rooms:
        (1) Estimated number of applicants on basis of previous examinations;
        (2) Size of available rooms;
        (3) Facilities available in other localities;
    b. Equipment: tools of the trade used or being tested;
    c. Supplies.

F. Discusses features of outline with operating units.

G. Obtains approval of outline.

IV. Publicizing the examination.

A. Prepares bulletin of examination:
1. Contacts operating unit involved if additional information is needed to supplement that already on hand;
2. Obtains earlier bulletins to use as guide in preparing current bulletin;

3. Consolidates and summarizes job descriptions, specifications, and outline of examination material into bulletin form;
4. Sets up format:
   a. Type of heading to be used;
   b. Style type, if it is to be printed;
   c. Color paper;
   d. Special pictorial or illustrative material to be included;
   e. Arrangement of material;
5. Has rough draft of bulletin typed and edits rough draft;
6. Obtains approval of bulletin;
7. Supervises clerical work involved in preparing bulletins for distribution.
B. Disseminates bulletin:
  1. Indicates mailing lists to be used;
  2. Specifies what special mailing lists should be compiled;
  3. Lists other sources to be notified.
C. Determines other publicity media to be utilized:
  1. Radio announcements;
  2. News releases:
   a. Metropolitan and local newspapers;
   b. Professional and trade journals;
  3. Classified advertisements (if law of agency permits).
D. Contacts labor sources in person, by telephone, or by mail:
  1. Labor unions;
  2. Professional organizations;
  3. Civic groups;
  4. United States Employment Service;
  5. Minority and women's groups and agencies.
V. Developing the examination from approved outline.
A. Gathers additional examination data (see II: Obtaining, preparing, reviewing, and supplementing job descriptions or specifications for the class):
  1. Obtains specimen examination folder containing previous examinations;
  2. Obtains pertinent data from operating unit, including examples of work or materials used;
  3. Assembles other reference materials:
   a. Examinations from other agencies;
   b. Standardized tests;
   c. Books, pamphlets, and periodicals;
   d. Laws relating to the work;
  4. Revises or supplements outline of examination if necessary.
B. Constructs tests to be used:
  1. Written test:
   a. Determines tests to be included:
    (1) Number;
    (2) Subject or topic;
    (3) Length;
    (4) Percentage of items to be included in each test;
    (5) Type of items best suited for each test:
     (a) Multiple choice;
     (b) True–false;
     (c) Matching;
     (d) Free answer or essay;
     (e) Comparison;
     (f) Completion;
     (g) Special types.
    Note: Multiple choice is the most frequently used type; the other types are seldom used.
   b. Selects old tests or test items from files:
    (1) Studies results of old tests and test items used previously from recording of statistical analysis and eliminates the old tests and test items which have proved too easy, too difficult, or too ambiguous, or which have a low discrimination index;
    (2) Revises old tests or test items to fit examination requirements and checks that questions are properly keyed and reference is indicated;
   c. Drafts new tests or test items:
    (1) Documents source and references for each new test item;
    (2) Indicates correct answer;
   d. Has tests and test items checked and edited:
    (1) By supervisors;
    (2) By authorities in the field;
    (3) By senior staff members;
   e. Rates items for difficulty and appropriateness and clarifies words and phrases;
   f. Compiles items into test form:
    (1) Spiral omnibus;
    (2) Power test;
   g. Tries out tests, whenever possible;
   h. Revises tests on basis of tryout:
    (1) Rearranges order of items;
    (2) Adds, eliminates, or revises items;
   i. Prepares cover sheet indicating:
    (1) Weights assigned to each part of the written test;
    (2) Scoring method;
    (3) Time limits;
   j. Prepares instructions:

(1) For administering test;
(2) For taking test;
k. Prepares key copy;
l. Sets up rules for scoring and indicates scoring factors;
m. Submits test for approval;
n. Makes any changes necessary;
2. Technical oral test (this type of test can be used when there are only a few candidates and when required knowledge lends itself to discussion questions) :
 a. Determines subject matter of field to be covered;
 b. Determines approximate number of questions to be used;
 c. Draws up tentative questions, model answers, and reference notes;
 d. Has questions and answers checked by competent authorities;
 e. Revises test and puts questions in final form;
 f. Determines time to be allotted to each applicant;
 g. Devises rating sheet and scoring method;
 h. Submits test for approval;
3. Performance or practical test:
 a. Investigates type of equipment or machines that can be used in testing:
   (1) Determines primary pieces of equipment or machines that are basic to the job;
   (2) Determines equipment or machines which could be eliminated (In some cases skills in the operation of one machine will indicate proficiency or transferability of skill, i.e., key punch and verifier, different types of punch presses, etc.) ;
 b. Pulls old performance tests from files;
 c. Contacts experts in the field such as company representatives or employees supervising the work, depending on type of equipment and policy, and solicits suggestions as to the best procedure to follow in setting up test:
   (a) Basic skills to be tested;
   (b) Best equipment to use for test;
 d. Drafts preliminary test;
 e. Has test checked and tried out by expert;
 f. Revises test in final form;

g. Sets maximum time allowance;
h. Prepares instructions:
   (1) For administering test;
   (2) For taking test;
 i. Designs rating sheet and scoring method;
 j. Makes preliminary arrangements for using equipment and machines;
 k. Submits test for approval;
4. Physical test:
 a. Determines physical capacities to be tested;
 b. Determines what job-related equipment should be used for testing purposes such as dynamometer, chest squeeze, knee squeeze, or back lift (although anthropometric instruments are available, job-related requirements may disqualify their use) ;
 c. Prepares instructions:
   (1) For administering tests;
   (2) For taking tests;
 d. Sets up rating sheet;
 e. Determines standards to be used in scoring;
 f. Determines conversion methods to be used in scoring;
 g. Submits test for approval.
C. Constructs rating scales for general qualifications evaluation (standard rating scales are used extensively; however, for highly technical and professional positions, specialized rating scales are frequently designed) :
1. Training and experience:
 a. Determines basis on which education and experience is to be evaluated:
   (1) Quantity: number of points to be assigned for each appropriate time period, e.g., months, years, etc.;
   (2) Quality: additions and deductions should be made;
   (3) Continuity and progressiveness: additions or deductions should be made;
   (4) Related types of education and experience for which credit should be given in addition to specific types designated in minimum qualifications;
 b. Determines point system to be used in arriving at final rating;
2. Personal and interpersonal skills and characteristics:
 a. Determines the appropriate ap-

praisal format and structure, e.g., individual or group interview;

    b. Determines what behaviors or characteristics are job-related and can be observed and evaluated, such as:

        (1) Appearance;

        (2) Voice, speech, language;

        (3) Poise, manner, bearing;

        (4) Organization and presentation of ideas;

        (5) Judgment and decision making capacity, including receptivity to others' ideas and positions;

        (6) Alertness and comprehension;

        (7) Frankness;

        (8) Friendliness, openness, and sensitivity to others;

        (9) Self-confidence;

        (10) Overall personal suitability;

    c. Determines which factors or variables should be given most consideration;

    d. Determines point system to be used in rating;

    e. Designs rating form.

D. Supervises the clerical work involved in preparing and assembling examination material:

    1. Duplicating material;

    2. Assembling test pamphlets;

    3. Packaging materials.

E. Makes final arrangements for holding the tests and the qualifications appraisal interviews:

    1. Date, place, and time of examination: Instructs clerical staff to arrange necessary details such as obtaining permission to use schools and other public buildings, sending notices, arranging for monitors, and other details;

    2. Special examiners:

        a. Selects panel of examiners from professionals in the field;

        b. Obtains approval of examiners selected;

        c. Contacts examiners and arranges all details with them.

VI. Processing applications.

A. Establishes general policy to be followed by subprofessionals in interpreting minimum qualifications.

B. Supervises or reviews acceptance of applications:

    1. Personally reviews borderline or questionable cases;

    2. Talks with persons being rejected in potentially controversial cases.

C. Reviews applications and indicates what verifications should be conducted and when.

D. If temporary vacancies exist, interviews and approves applicants for temporary appointment.

E. Approves or denies requests for late filing.

VII. Administering the examination.

A. Written examination (in most instances written examinations are administered by high-grade clerical employees in accordance with instructions prepared by the examiner):

    1. Assembles candidates in examination room;

    2. Establishes rapport;

    3. Distributes examination materials;

    4. Supervises filling out of necessary forms;

    5. Explains and illustrates use of IBM answer sheet, when used;

    6. Reads directions for taking test;

    7. Announces maximum time allowance and times the test;

    8. Walks around examination room and observes candidates to see that instructions are being properly carried out;

    9. Collects test material at end of maximum time allowance;

    10. Makes any announcements relating to the remaining parts of examination yet to be taken.

B. Technical oral examination:

    1. Determines how examination will be recorded (by use of electronic or other recording equipment);

    2. Explains briefly to staff member or assisting special examiners the procedures to be followed:

        a. Uniform method of asking questions;

        b. Standards to be used in rating answers:

            (1) Use of model answers as a guide;

            (2) Leeway allowed in answers;

    3. Questions each applicant individually;

    4. Rates applicants on basis of answers to questions and records ratings;

    5. Collects completed examinations and forwards them for scoring.

C. Performance or practical test:

    1. Supervises setting up of equipment and machines to be used;

    2. Distributes materials;

    3. Works with expert in administering test if not thoroughly acquainted with

equipment and machines and instructs candidates what to do, when, and how;

4. Checks constantly to see that all candidates are being tested under the same conditions:
   a. Uniformity of tools used;
   b. Condition of equipment or machines;
5. Keeps track of maximum time allowance;
6. Collects completed specimens of work when available from the printer, key punch operator, machinist, tool-sharpener, etc.

D. Physical test:
   1. Sets up job-related equipment to be used;
   2. Explains equipment to be used to assistants:
      a. Method of making readings from equipment for rating purposes;
      b. Instructions to be given applicants;
      c. Method of demonstrating use of equipment;
   3. If required, requests applicants to sign waiver releasing jurisdiction from responsibility in case of injury;
   4. Demonstrates use of equipment to applicants;
   5. Watches carefully to see that applicants do not overexert themselves;
   6. Records readings from equipment.

VIII. Conducting evaluation interviews.
   A. Designates rating form to be used or designs new rating form (See V–C: Construct rating scales) .
   B. Determines general policy to be followed in interviewing:
      1. Prepares sample or situational questions that might be used;
      2. Outlines standards or yardsticks to be followed in rating candidates.
   C. Sets up interview schedule:
      1. Determines approximate length of time to be allowed each interview;
      2. Indicates room arrangements to be made.
   D. Determines who will do the interviewing:
      1. Examiner and additional member of examining staff;
      2. Examiner and outside specialist or committee of outside specialists:
         a. Requests operating units and other designated sources for suggestions as to possible interviewers;
         b. Obtains approval of persons suggested;

c. Contacts persons to serve;
d. Forwards sample rating sheets and instructions for use to committee members;
e. Coaches committee members on procedures to be followed;
f. Supervises interviewing to assure the maintenance of adequate standards.

E. Interviews candidates:
   1. Peruses candidates' applications, references, and other available data;
   2. Calls candidates into the interview room individually;
   3. Introduces candidate to interviewers;
   4. Establishes rapport, putting candidate at ease and ready to talk;
   5. Asks pertinent questions in order to obtain information from the candidate regarding abilities, interests, and personality traits which may predict success;
   6. Fills out rating form recording essential facts;
   7. Evaluates data and information and gives candidate a final numerical rating.

F. Devises statistical methods to be used when more than one committee is used in order to adjust for discrepancies in ratings.
G. Writes letters of appreciation to committee members for their services.

IX. Preparing the eligibility list.
   A. Sets up procedures and systems for making use of tabulating equipment, if available, for appropriate phases of this work.
   B. Supervises clerical work involved in scoring objective tests in accordance with instructions.
   C. Scores essay or free answer tests with assistance of another staff member or special examiners:
      1. Scores answers of all applicants to one question before proceeding to the next question and indicates score on separate scoring sheet;
      2. Has another staff member or special examiner rescore questions without reference to other examiner's scoring.
   D. Examines results of item analysis (see XI: Conducting statistical studies) :
      1. Reviews statistics of written examination which have been prepared:
         a. Notes difficulty of each test, distribution of scores, behavior on individual items as to difficulty and discriminating value, including discriminating value for the majority and the minority groups;

b. Rechecks answers and wording of items when necessary:
  (1) High percentage of error;
  (2) Minus discriminating values;
  (3) Minority discrimination evidenced;
2. Indicates any changes to be made in the written test as a result of review:
  a. Items to be eliminated;
  b. Multiple answer to be allowed;
  c. Answers to be changed;
3. Obtains approval of changes to be made;
4. Posts changes to master copy of test and item cards.

E. Supervises weighting of test parts, combining of test scores, and computing of final averages.

F. Supervises computing of seniority and service ratings.

G. Recommends cutoffs on the basis of:
1. Frequency distribution;
2. Number of anticipated vacancies and length of list required;
3. Calibre of candidates;
4. Critical scores previously established;
5. Majority/minority mix.

H. Presents final eligibility list for adoption and promulgation.

X. Reviewing examination results and handling appeals.

A. Reviews papers with candidates when requested:
1. Interviews candidates to discover particular information desired or nature of complaint;
2. Informs candidates of rating received on the various parts of the examination:
  a. Explains to each candidate where ratings placed him or her in relation to other candidates, showing frequency of distribution if available;
  b. Answers questions regarding ratings if information is not of a confidential nature (references or a particular interviewer's rating are confidential);
  c. Furnishes any additional information which will help clarify the rating;
3. Allows candidates to compare written test with a master copy;
4. If a candidate wishes to present formal appeal, explains the procedure which must be followed.

B. Receives written appeals and makes recommendation to superior as to action to be taken:

1. Analyzes appeals:
  a. Reads appeal carefully, noting each contention made by the appellant;
  b. If appeal is over the written test, reviews appellant's paper and rechecks marking of items and flags disputed items for further study;
  c. If appeal is over the oral test, reviews application, rating sheets, and references to determine if appellant has been rated fairly in accordance with standards used at time of interview;
2. If papers were marked by or oral ratings were given by special examiner, makes arrangements for sending each appeal and all related papers to the examiner;
3. Determines recommendations to be made for disposition of appeal:
  a. Receives recommendations made by special examiner who has analyzed appeal;
  b. Prepares memo stating basis of appeal and presenting facts which justify a "change" or "no change" decision;
4. Testifies, when necessary, if formal hearing is held;
5. Makes notations of disposition of case for future reference in order to avoid recurrence of cause for appeal.

XI. Conducting statistical studies of examination results.

A. Supervises the making of item analyses:
1. Determines method to be used, selecting from a number of different methods, of which the following two listed are most commonly used:
  a. High-low-third, or other high-low system;
  b. Bi-serial R;
2. Interprets results:
  a. Eliminates faulty items;
  b. Changes answers or allows a multiple answer;
  c. Indicates test items to be reworded before being reused.

B. Determines statistical methods for combining scores of different tests or other selection devices:
1. By percentiles;
2. By conversion.

C. Outlines studies for determining reliability:
1. By self-correlation:
  a. Effect of lengthening a test;
  b. Correlation with a repetition of test;

2. By computing index of reliability;
3. By computing standard and probable error of measurement.
D. Outlines procedures for documenting content validity of the total selection process and, where feasible, for undertaking studies of construct- and criterion-related validity if the research capabilities and policies of the agency permit.[35]

ASSUMPTIONS OF THE TRADITIONAL MODEL

Since a set of assumptions can be considered rudimentary theory, the assumptions which underlie the traditional model as outlined above need to be identified and analyzed. The assumptions of the model can be grouped in two categories: (1) assumptions about organizations, and (2) assumptions about individuals.

The assumptions about organizations are rooted in reform for the purpose of eliminating spoils as well as improving management systems. The reform movement to eliminate spoils led to establishment of the merit tradition. The assumptions of the merit tradition, presented earlier, served to safeguard the integrity of the selection process. They led to the following series of subordinate but related assumptions:

1. Equal opportunity means treating people alike.
2. Treating people alike means standardizing procedures.
3. Standardized procedures make for objectivity.
4. Objectivity is needed to determine relative merit and fitness.
5. Relative merit and fitness means measuring how people differ.
6. How people differ relatively means ranking objective measurements from high to low.
7. The highest measurement indicates the most merit; the lowest measurement, the least.

These assumptions led to further assumptions about measurement—specifically, what to measure and how to measure it. The advent of position classification plans resolved the question of what to measure and gave the model its task orientation. Position classification meets all key requirements of the traditional model:

standardization, objectivity, and practicality. It is the result of an impersonal process which focuses on duties and responsibilities determined by a logical division of the work to be done to perform functions essential to accomplishing organizational objectives.

The requirement of standardization is satisfied, since the position classification plan specifies either directly or indirectly the standards for (1) the language and format in announcing examinations; (2) education, experience, and other minimum or desirable requirements for admission to announced examinations; (3) knowledge, skill, and ability areas to be tested in examinations; and (4) possible positions to be filled by those on the eligibility lists resulting from examinations. Objectivity is likewise obtained, since written data about positions rather than persons are recorded in advance of a vacancy and become the basis for selection. By eliminating or limiting the opportunity for personal contact with appointing officials to gain information about tasks assigned to a position, the risk of personnel agency staff being subject to undue influence from outside sources is reduced. Finally, practicality is achieved: What could be more practical than tying in selection processes with the tasks assigned to the vacant positions?

Position classification also is the link to the other element of the reform movement—scientific management and related concepts of efficiency.

The 'scientific management' movement, beginning around the turn of the century, introduced a much-needed emphasis upon the 'efficiency at the workplace' into business management thinking. Typical modern personnel programs have their roots in this movement. . . . Techniques for work measurement . . . made it possible systematically (rationally) to analyze, classify, and evaluate jobs. Such job study provided objective standards. . . .[36]

Organizations in the traditional model are viewed as functional hierarchies in which structure is all-important.[37] The employee is regarded more as an instrument than as an individual. Attention is directed to structuring an organization on the basis of recognized principles of administration such as POSDCORB.[38]

The assumption is that structuring the organization so as to scientifically utilize the worker as a mechanism leads to efficiency. Although the organization is visualized as a unified entity—a collective whole—actual attention in selection concentrates on tasks performed by positions rather than on position content as related to work situations and to the goals of the organization as a whole. The assumptions about how an organization operates and how to achieve merit result in an approach isolated both in regard to the selection process and to the analysis of the positions for which selection is to be made. The unit of selection in the traditional model is the task assigned to vacant positions as described in the position classification plan.

The trait and test orientation of the traditional model is derived from assumptions about individuals and individual differences that arise in response to the question of how to measure. Stated simply, what to measure leads to the position classification plan; how to measure leads to psychological tests and trait measurements. Psychological exploration of individual differences introduced the science of psychometry to personnel selection. Based on assumptions from early psychometric research, identification and appraisal of individual characteristics and capabilities are believed to assure competent employees and, in turn, competent employees assure effective organization. It is considered both realistic and essential that a continuing effort be made to refine techniques for identifying and appraising task-related traits, thereby making for better selection decisions.

Such efforts can be based upon psychometrics, defined as the application of mathematics and statistics to psychological data. . . . The psychometrist is the specialist in scientific psychology who works on problems of measurement; most of his work is done with psychological tests. The test specialist is a research worker; he uses available tests and develops other measures as he needs them. He uses, and in some situations develops, mathematical principles and procedures for making predictions of future behavior from measures available at the time of employment.

The job of the test specialist is to provide a scientific basis for selection and placement. This he does through psychometric analyses, by determining the validity of generalizations about relationships between characteristics of job applicants and their subsequent behavior at work. These generalizations, stated mathematically, enable prediction within known limits of error. Prediction of future behavior, whether mathematical or merely implicit and subjective, forms the basis on which the employment interviewer or supervisor makes a decision about an individual applicant: to reject him for one job but consider him further for another, or to place his name on a waiting list.[39]

The traditional model assumes that variations in work performance occur because people differ in their traits. A "main strategy for imposing order upon individual differences was to study traits, one at a time and in combination with another."[40] Personnel selection has as its basis the demonstrable fact that people are different.

All this implies measurement. . . . Test specialists think of personal attributes as the dimension along which people differ. Psychometric descriptions of less obvious differences between people require (1) identification and definition of the dimension to be measured, and (2) an appropriate scale of measurement.[41]

The tools of psychometry are psychological tests and other measurements. These tools are used to identify differences in knowledge, skills, abilities, aptitudes, interests, and personality traits. Emphasis is placed on individual scores as they relate to summarized group scores. This approach fulfills the requirements of standardization and objectivity of the traditional model. Particular emphasis is placed on objective written tests, on the assumption that they are scientific.

[A] science of testing is possible because a way has been found to ask questions so that the responses made to them can be expressed by a number. . . . The outstanding characteristic . . . is that the number that is the score . . . is a stable number. . . .[42]

The basic methodology of scientific selection has been laid down; the way to ask questions so that scores will be reliable and stable has been discovered; the way to write questions so they will be revealing has been established; statistical methods for the evaluation of tests and questions have been developed.[43]

Some differences among individuals, such as differences in physical build and appearance, can be measured by simple observation. Measuring height and weight, however, will not indicate whether one has good eye-hand coordination or good hearing or if one is color-blind. These psychomotor and sensory acuities have a bearing on individual differences in performing certain job tasks.

Individuals also differ in emotional stability, ability to understand, and ability to deal effectively with other persons. They differ in their training, acquired knowledge, and occupational skills. Individual differences are not reduced or eliminated by training; to the contrary, practice in a particular task is more likely to accent the differences of individuals in their performance.

All these assumptions point to differential psychology, i.e., the psychology of individual differences that provides the basis for measuring differences in traits. It is the field which claims to have developed psychometric instruments for measuring individual characteristics objectively and for providing the norms from which predictions can be made with stated degrees of reliability and validity. The key question of how to correlate individual trait differences and fitness for the performance of tasks assigned to positions can be answered by using psychological tests.

This statement is made, however, with one reservation, and that relates to the question of practicality. A civil service test is perceived as practical only if it looks practical to the lay person and especially to the competitor.

Rigorous application of this standard of practicality requires not only careful scrutiny of the broad areas of knowledge and aptitudes sampled in the test as a whole, and of the general area covered in each item, but also attention to the several individual concepts and even the separate words in each item. In a test composed of multiple-choice items, for example, the competitor may not recall merely the question or just the question and the best answer—obviously, he may not know which answer is intended to be best. But he may remember and criticize some of the answers intended to be 'distracters,' 'decoys,' or 'confusions,' as they are variously termed. If an item constructor innocently includes Socrates in a distracter, he should not be surprised if the examination is later published as

absurdly impractical because it inquires into the competitor's knowledge of Greek philosophy. Particularly in the case of examining bodies not far removed from the publics they serve, every examination item should be reviewed from the standpoint of how it might look in the public press.[44]

Many practitioners assume, with supporting evidence from examination appeals, from commission reactions, and increasingly from regulatory agency court decisions, that neither the public regulatory agencies nor the courts will accept the use of tests which appear unrelated to job content and requirements.[45] Such tests lack what used to be called face validity and what is now known by a more sophisticated term—content or rational validity.

Face validity implies an apparent relationship between a description of work contained in an examination announcement and expectations of administrators and the lay public about a particular kind of work. Face validity was thought to convey the impression of validity and reliability in predicting job performance, whether or not the test was in fact valid for this purpose or whether any attempt had been made to determine its validity. Face validity involved "rapport" and public relations. For example, items used in civil service examinations

should look practical to the competitors and appear reasonable in view of job duties and responsibilities. They should contain no features likely to arouse emotional antagonism on the part of the public, any professional groups concerned, or the competitor.[46]

Content validity, the current term, means that all steps taken in the selection process, including all selection devices, can be documented as clearly job-related. It is now a central concept in the selection process.

The need for content validity, practicality, and a limited approach to standardization are key differences between civil service tests and psychological tests (particularly those used in clinical settings). These requirements consequently preclude the use of published tests to any appreciable extent by public personnel agencies. Many civil service tests are specially developed by the public personnel agency. Unlike tests prepared by a reputable test publisher, they usually are not subjected to approved methods of standardization, which includes establishing norms and determining reliability and validity. Not all commercially available tests, however, undergo rigorous item analysis or norm, reliability, and validity studies. Ultimately, of course, they cannot withstand scrutiny by the courts, the EEOC, or the Office of Federal Contract Compliance. Even if they can, "the recency of the study and the population on which it is based" becomes critical. "In almost all court cases, the age of a test and its supportive validation are considered in determining the usefulness of a test for selecting current applicants."[47]

DYNAMICS OF THE TRADITIONAL MODEL

The dynamics of the traditional model can be described as a transactional affair in which action is likened to a game.[48] The goal of the game is to fill vacancies—known or anticipated, but usually known. The more vacancies filled and the faster they are filled, the more successful the players. The overall plan to reach the final move—filling a vacancy—is conditioned at each step by what happens as a result of the previous step. It is difficult for any of those playing the game to plan moves in advance because of the unpredictables involved in each step, e.g., number of applicants, the scores they achieve, etc. The rules of the game are rigid, being rooted in laws and regulations. The interpretations of the rules set important procedural precedents loaded with historical and environmental influences.

Each game involves three teams: (1) the personnel agency staff; (2) officials of operating departments in which a vacancy exists or is expected to occur; and (3) the applicants. The number of players on each team depends on the particular setting in which the game is played. Their skill depends on how much practice they have had in playing the game in that setting. Regular spectators to the game, in addition to the general public, include employee unions or associations, representatives of minority and women's groups, and exempt officials of the jurisdiction where the play takes place. There are three leagues recognized in which the game is played: large agencies, medium-sized agencies, and small agencies.[49] The particular league in which an agency plays and reports that it does is based on the number of budgeted positions in the jurisdiction.

The personnel agency team considers its position an offensive one, although it frequently finds itself on the defensive. This team concentrates its strategy on erecting a series of hurdles which only the most fit will be able to clear. These hurdles are set up as education and experience rating standards (both minimum and desirable), critical scores in written and performance tests, oral interview boards, and other fixed regulations about moral and physical fitness. The operating department concentrates its strategy on finding ways to remove, reduce, or bypass the hurdles to be cleared, to change the standards they find unrealistic, or to shorten the time limits allowed to complete the process. Those applicants who are not disqualified or who do not withdraw from competition at any stage of play concentrate on how to clear each hurdle by using whatever means or support available to them.[50]

Since players on each team tend toward strong convictions about their own skill and how the game should be played, stalemates are not uncommon. These may stop all action for prolonged periods of time until agreement on the point in question is reached or resolved by official referees such as a civil service commission, advisory council or personnel board, regulatory agency, or the courts. It is rare when all three teams and the players on each are satisfied with the game's outcome. Postmortems are common, some of which necessitate prolonged processing by the courts before there is a final disposition.

The traditional model as described in its characteristics, assumptions, and dynamics is typical of well-established public personnel agencies created by a civil service or merit system. The effectiveness of the model is discussed in the following section.

EFFECTIVENESS OF THE TRADITIONAL MODEL

The effectiveness of the selection process as developed by the traditional model can be gauged from reports of empirical research, standards of test development and test use, approaches to program evaluation, and views of the critics.

Reports of Empirical Research. Reports of empirical research on the effectiveness of the traditional model as a whole or in its totality are conspicuous by their absence. Some research on specific parts or phases (primarily the examination phase) of the model can be found. Except for data on beliefs about selection concepts and practices collected by the Municipal Manpower Commission for its 1962 report, *Governmental Manpower for Tomorrow's Cities,* no published reports of empirical research appear to exist as of the mid-1970s.

The dearth of reports of empirical research is particularly noticeable in the professional journals. Both historically and currently the bulk of this material consists of descriptions of and opinions about the practices used by various public personnel agencies.

The status of personnel research as it relates to the selection process has been documented by a number of writers.[51] Again, a paucity of pertinent research is revealed. The lack of research and the absence of any integration of research efforts and findings widens rather than narrows the gap in knowledge of the selection process and its effectiveness. The pressure for greater research has increased since passage in the latter part of the 1960s of civil rights legislation for fair employment and related personnel practices. Serious questions have been raised about the adequacy of the research strategies generally used in the field of personnel selection.

The demand for unbiased selection methods focused on testing and consequently placed personnel psychologists in an unaccustomed limelight. Such attention proved to be embarrassing, not only because testers had ignored minority groups but, as importantly, because the quality of research done even on the majority group left much to be desired.[52]

The extent to which the selection process enables a "full utilization of the disadvantaged, blacks, women, the elderly and other special groups"[53] is now a major concern. Response to this concern—and the challenges it precipitated —generally is regarded as disappointing.

STANDARDS OF TEST DEVELOPMENT AND USE

The development and use of tests to measure traits that serve as the basis for predicting task performance are the principal components of the traditional model. Consequently, comparing the practices in test development and use of the traditional model with recommended practices for psychological test development and use is one measure of effectiveness. Guides for evaluating psychological tests range from the detailed procedural steps recommended by the American Psychological Association to the general recommendations and standards of test development and use reported in personnel management, psychological testing, and industrial psychology journals and textbooks.[54]

Current material in each of these categories illustrates how the field of psychological assessment and the standards it prescribes is changing. New techniques are being developed, older ones are being rejected, and new conceptual outlooks are being created. Regardless of which reference is cited, there is consensus that classic psychometric theory with its assumptions about how to match positions and people is too mechanistic and ignores situational and social factors. There is a recognized need to broaden the traditional model to include these elements in describing and analyzing job content. To ignore such factors contributes to the probability of faulty selection and placement.

A number of methodological advances are reported in the literature of the 1970s which emphasize that "personnel selection does not take place in a neat unidimensional world and that ultimate job performance is the product of many interacting variables."[55] "Cross domain studies" which include individual, job, and organizational variables and other systems-oriented approaches are recommended. These approaches stress the need to measure noncognitive attributes as well as individual characteristics in an organizational context.[56]

Terms such as reliability and validity, as traditionally used, are being replaced by more precise terms that attempt to reflect the imprecision of measuring individual differences. Although the uniqueness of individuals is still the foundation of test development and use, approaches to measuring human individuality are being broadened and placed in a social and situational perspective. "The science of human differences has reached a transitional state. . . . The search for grand universal principles has been abandoned. What is now sought are limited contingent conclusions about specific populations in particular situations"[57] that include a concern for the lack of permanence of characteristics measured. Concepts of "behavioral consistency" and "individual strategies for dealing with situations" are being found more advantageous and useful than the trait concepts of the past.[58]

Reasoning of the 1970s contends that the traditional model reflected many myths, which can be stated as follows: Doing tasks well requires traits in which individuals differ. By testing for traits you can identify the individuals who will do tasks well. Organizations made up of positions which are made up of tasks that are alike will be efficient if they select as employees those individuals who have been tested for the traits tasks take. To test for the traits tasks take, you treat all individuals alike to see how they differ. Individuals whose test scores show that they have traits which are alike are matched to jobs which have tasks that are alike—provided matching is made in the order that the individuals differ. The individuals with the most square traits best fit jobs with square tasks. The individuals with the most round traits best fit jobs with round tasks, and so on.

The trait theory and the myths on which it was based failed to consider (1) an individual as a totality—a unique total system; (2) individual behavior as a social and situational function; (3) work as the interaction of a human group; and (4) failed to consider an organization as a goals-oriented social system. The influence of situational factors and work groups on individual workers, how individuals adjust their responses to the social milieu, and other evidence of how organizational behavior is shaped into a social system by groups large and small all are overlooked by trait theory. An expectation that is hoped will become reality is that

the emphasis on simple selection models [will] decrease in favor of a systems approach which will include, on a conceptual level at least, not only the subject's aptitudes, but his motivation, the training afforded him, the nature of the organization's reward system, quality of supervision, etc. Such a model has clear relevance to the question of fair employment, but is, of course, not at all limited to that special problem.[59]

Some specific steps to be followed in the initial development of tests for use in the selection process are summarized here:

1. A thorough job analysis to systematically collect data for and formulate job requirements;
2. A systematic analysis of the nature of job requirements formulated in the first step in terms of specific behaviors that make the difference between success and failure in the job, from which to draw a series of inferences and hypotheses about such personal characteristics as aptitudes, abilities, and proficiencies, and the experience and training which effective job performance requires;
3. Development of a set of specifications for specific test items and other selection requirements and procedures based on the analysis of the preceding step in the form of inferences and hypotheses regarding the way in which aptitudes, abilities, and other requirements for successful job performance might be evaluated effectively through job related selection devices;
4. Development of specific test items and other evaluation procedures following recommended steps for item construction;
5. Follow-up research to check the correctness of the various analyses, inferences, and judgments which produced the selection devices used.[60]

Two caveats to note are that useful prediction requires that the data from each of these steps be placed in a situational and organizational context and that the strategies developed for assessing individual differences must relate to the kind of work situation in which the behavior is to occur. This is not done in the traditional model. As the model has been operationalized in many agencies, there is limited application of the first four steps, rare application of the fifth, and no concern for situational and organizational variables. The process as typically applied is not research, situation, or organization based in the sense that these terms are now used in differential and organizational psychology. (The latter field is now making important contributions to personnel selection.)

Other questions to be posed in evaluating a specific selection device bear on the extent to which the following requirements are met:

1. Are these provisions for uniformity of procedure in administering and scoring?
2. Were norms (including differential norms) for interpreting results established by empirical testing?
3. Were objective, empirical procedures followed in determining appropriate difficulty levels for different applicant groups?
4. Were empirical trials used to determine reliability and validity of selection devices in specified work and organizational situations prior to actual use?

Considerable emphasis is placed in public agencies on assuring that all selection devices are administered to all applicants in the same way, at the same time, and under the same conditions. Such devices, for the most part, are designed for groups. Both oral and written instructions are prepared in considerable detail in advance. It is necessary for monitors to follow the instructions to the letter. Practice periods, special instructions, and time allowances are uniform. Uniform scoring instructions and objective scoring are standard operating procedure. Indications are that this process meets the conditions set forth except for unresolved questions of fairness to members of disadvantaged groups.

No evidence exists to show that norms for interpreting results are generally available in public agencies. The selection process usually does not include establishing norms in advance of administering tests to an applicant group. Where norms for tests are available, such norms usually have been established after administering the test to an applicant group and not by pretesting a criteria group or groups. Thus they are norms for groups of applicants

rather than norms based on a pretest of a representative sample of employees doing the kind of work for which a test is developed. Empirically established norms based on either a standardized or a differentiated sample are the exception rather than the rule.

Although the accepted methodology for analyzing levels of difficulty includes test tryouts and defining the sample for analyzing difficulty, determinations of difficulty levels in public agencies are usually a matter of judgment rather than the result of research. Again, the objective measurement of the difficulty level of civil service tests and test items, when done at all, usually takes place after administering a test rather than before the test is used for predictive purposes. Analysis to determine item difficulty is based on actual test responses of applicants rather than on testing a defined sample. The traditional model generally did not include procedures for establishing an empirical order of difficulty for test times, test segments, or tests as a whole.

As understood in psychometrics, reliability means stability or consistency. Reliability concerns the extent to which a test consistently measures whatever it purports to measure. It represents the consistency of scores obtained by the same persons when retested with the identical test or with an alternate or equivalent form of the test. Recommended standards of test development require a thorough objective testing of reliability before a test is administered. In the public personnel field, measures of reliability are not regularly made either before or after a test is used or reused on a group of applicants. Recommended standards are not met in regard to reliability.

The most important factor in evaluating psychological tests is test validity. Validity as a generic term refers to the degree to which a test actually measures what it purports to measure. Various types of validity are recognized. The American Psychological Association in its *Standards for Educational and Psychological Tests and Manuals* describes three validity systems:

1. Content validity is demonstrated by showing how well the content of the test samples the class

situations or subject matter about which conclusions are to be drawn. . . .

2. Criterion-related validity is demonstrated by comparing the test scores with one or more external variables considered to provide a direct measure of the characteristics or behavior in question. . . .

3. Construct validity is evaluated by investigating what qualities a test measures, that is, by determining the degree to which certain explanatory concepts or constructs account for performance on the test.[61]

According to the APA standards:

Validity information indicates the degree to which the test is capable of achieving certain aims. Tests are used for several types of judgment, and for each type of judgment, a different type of investigation is required to establish validity.[62]

The differences between and methods for determining various types of validity are discussed at length in a number of reference tools available to the professional.[63] Although there is voluminous historical and contemporary literature on test validation, there are few points of unanimity on the proper way to validate a test. The criterion problem is still at issue.[64]

Validity concepts have become increasingly important in the selection process as a result of civil rights legislation and its relation to fair employment practices and equal employment opportunity.

[The] key issue for federal and state agencies as well as the federal courts and the unions is job-relatedness or, as psychologists would say, test validity, whether the test, or other assessment procedure, measures what it purports to measure for minority and nonminority applicants, and for men and women. EEOC and OFCC maintain that, wherever technically feasible, criterion-related validity must be established before a test or other objectively scored selection device can be used. Also, when tests are used to determine applicants' qualifications for a particular job, there must be data to show that the test standard is related to the job standard, that applicants who score at or above the test standard will work at or above the job standard, and that applicants who score below the test standard will work below the job standard.[65]

Questions about whether criterion or predictive validity procedures are possible or practical in a civil service setting appear to have been resolved: Indications are these procedures are not the answer. Recognition of this has relieved the tension created by prior assumptions that these were the procedures that should be used. Increasing attention is now being paid to content or rational validity as the most viable procedure for the public setting. Content or rational validity represents a logical relation between test and position rather than a quantitative relation.

Federal courts have indicated willingness to accept both rational validity and criterion-related validity as acceptable evidence to justify the use of tests. The definition of rational validity as it is emerging from the court decisions seems to be based on common-sense judgments of the reasonableness of the test or other procedures, on scientific data available on the test, and on the professional judgments of expert witnesses. The courts have made their findings on the basis of the answers to the following questions. Is the test professionally developed? up to date? skill-related (the test provides an indication of skills that are needed on the job but that are not necessarily empirically related to the job)? based on business necessity (essential for safe and efficient business operation)? based on a reasonable business motive or purpose? necessary for efficiency and morale?[66]

Common points raised when technical issues are brought out in court cases that involve testing are:

1. The EEOC testing guidelines are impossible to satisfy if taken literally. The EEOC recognizes this, but local fair employment practices commissions and most judges probably do not. Therefore, an expert witness from the EEOC may actually be helpful to employers who have made good faith efforts to satisfy the testing guidelines.

2. Witnesses may not quote from the technical literature (e.g., Boehm, 1972) unless the authors are available in court for cross-examination. Therefore, plan your testimony accordingly, or try to get the authors into court if their research is that vital to your case.

3. The APA testing standards were intended as guidelines for good testing practices, not minimum standards. Good practice varies with the varying conditions and purposes of each testing situation.

4. The value of a test to personnel selection varies in direct proportion to the validity coefficient

(Brogden, 1946, 1949; Jarrett, 1948). Introduce this concept into your testimony at an early stage before the judge is led to believe differently (e.g., that the value of a test is proportional to the square of the validity coefficient).[67]

Equal opportunity and affirmative action requirements have precipitated a concern for and controversy about differential validity. A failure to recognize either the possibility or the probability of differential validity within an applicant group impairs selection decisions.

To the extent that different behaviors or attributes lead to job success, test validation becomes more difficult. . . . If such differential validity exists but is not used in developing minimal hiring scores, accuracy of selection may be minimal. If it is recognized and used in the selection program, accuracy can be much improved. Thus it is always sound psychology and good business to conduct test-validation studies so that differential validity can be determined and its extent measured.[68]

The prediction is made that

the controversy centering on the possible differential validity of selection tests for majority and minority groups will abate. Several factors will cause that. More general utility considerations will come into play, and the question of test validity, in the narrow sense, will be put into perspective. Secondly, if governmental agencies and the courts continue to be very exacting in the evidence they will accept before allowing employment tests to be used, many organizations will give up testing due to an inability to perform the required research or an unwillingness to undertake it.[69]

A decision to give up tests, particularly paper-and-pencil tests, because of questions of validity is not only unwise but may impair effectiveness.

When public jurisdictions give up paper-and-pencil testing, they are giving up one kind of testing for now another kind, probably the interview. Public jurisdictions might find that paper-and-pencil testing, because of its objectivity, is easier to defend than a subjective, unstructured interview. Paper-and-pencil tests are subject to no more stringent legal standards under fair employment guidelines than any other selection device such as the oral interview. Many employers have acted hastily in giving up a valuable asset in employment.[70]

A paramount need in regard to validity as a measure of effectiveness is to recognize the specificity of any selection device. Namely, it should be

. . . specific to the test, the criterion, the job, the applicant group, and the company. Validity findings should not be generalized, nor should findings from one situation or from one ethnic group be applied to another. As circumstances change, tests need to be revalidated. If new job standards become important, the tests have to be evaluated against these new standards. Tests are useful tools to help select more accurately, but they are only tools. . . . [S]kill in using and interpreting these tools is crucial to maximizing their utility. . . . It is, after all, the person who makes the selection decision, not the tools.[71]

In addition, it is important to recognize the following exceptions and modify research findings accordingly:

1. Tests will differ in validity in different ethnic groups.
2. Tests can discriminate unfairly between different ethnic groups.
3. The validity of tests in ethnically heterogeneous samples may be improved by moderated projection techniques.
4. An effective index of cultural status relevant to test and job performance is not likely to be derived from standard biographical data.
5. Nonverbal tests may not necessarily be more accurate for use with minority groups.
6. Job training may improve scores on tests of types which might be used for selection.[72]

Possible outcomes of these research findings are that a selection device

1. may be valid for all ethnic groups and not discriminate unfairly among them;
2. may be valid for all ethnic groups but may discriminate unfairly among them;
3. may be valid for one ethnic group but not for another;
4. may be valid for no ethnic group.[73]

A number of issues are involved in using either different selection devices or different selection standards for different ethnic groups. The answers to these issues, however, do not reduce the need for separate validation and standardization for different ethnic groups.

[S]eparate validation and standardization for the different ethnic groups . . . retain all of the many advantages inherent in objective testing while at the same time avoiding the possibility of inadvertent discrimination that may occur when tests are given without regard to race or cultural status. It is true that a practical problem is raised, namely the question of developing tests for all of the many different ethnic groups, and some kind of cultural measure is necessary to eliminate the need to rely on racial classification and the problems raised thereby. Until such measures are developed, however, it is essential to proceed in the manner fairest to all job applicants. Validation irrespective of race may lead to discrimination; separate validation by ethnic group will not. In view of the extreme importance of fair employment for all ethnic groups, the choice of procedure is therefore an obvious one.[74]

QUALIFICATION STANDARDS OF THE TESTER

A different but related set of standards applies to the qualifications of persons developing tests or determining test use. Although these qualifications relate primarily to the procurement of test material from test publishers, they give an indication of what is considered appropriate background for those using tests in personnel selection. A basic requirement is membership in the American Psychological Association or a master's degree in psychology, with special training in the field of testing as applied to guidance or personnel. Three questions posed to determine who is competent to use tests in the selection process are:

1. Is the distinction between content, construct, concurrent, and predictive validity comprehended by the tester?
2. Is the tester familiar with sources of criterion bias?
3. Is the appropriateness of product moment, rank order, biserial, point biserial, and tetrachoric correlation understood?[75]

A tester who fails these qualifying questions will fail to distinguish good psychological testing from bad.

No organization should attempt a testing program without having it done under the supervision of someone who is specifically trained in the use of psychological tests. Several undesirable results can be expected when inadequately or improperly trained people handle testing programs. . . .[76]

APPROACHES TO PROGRAM EVALUATION

It is difficult to divorce an analysis of the approaches to evaluating selection programs that have a testing base from the question of validity. There is consensus that the effectiveness of personnel selection in which decisions are affected by test results depends in the first instance on test validity. The validity of tests is determinable by several approaches to validity, as previously discussed, only one of which—content validity—is within the technical competence of most public personnel agencies.

The evaluation of a system of selection is mainly a technical matter of validating the system as a whole and its component elements. It also involves, however, important administrative considerations. Foremost, of course, is the administrative routine of insisting on technical competence and completeness in actual validation. However, a practical evaluation must consider matters other than validity per se.[77]

A means of practical evaluation is determining whether the value derived from the use of any selection device exceeds the expense its use necessitates. Neither actual validation nor practical evaluation is a component function of the operation of the traditional model. Consequently, if the validity of tests or selection devices used is to be the measure of the model's effectiveness, effectiveness cannot be determined.

CRITICISMS OF THE TRADITIONAL MODEL

Views bearing on the effectiveness of the traditional model run the gamut from the narrative recounting by public administrators of their experiences, to professional and academic critiques based on formal studies and investigations. The narrative category, the most common form of criticism, includes armchair opinions defending or disapproving current practices. The target of most criticism is the use of objective or standardized written tests in the selection process.

The most frequently made points of criticism are summarized here. To the extent that each point represents an attack against the traditional model's emphasis on testing, the effectiveness of the model is challenged.

- Testing as "psychological espionage" is an invasion of privacy neither warranted nor justified.
- Psychological tests are not scientifically sound, being based on empiricism without the aid of theory.
- Psychological tests have no predictive significance for many work situations; what predictive validity exists is limited to learning or training situations.
- Testing results are conditioned by variables outside those being tested.
- Testing is used as a substitute for difficult selection decision making.
- Testing, which places a premium on conformity with set norms, brings into the organization more of what it already has, thus complicating the planning and accomplishment of change.
- Testing is not based on a good theory of behavior variables to be measured in the first instance nor on adequate criterion variables in the final analysis.
- Testing lends itself to coaching and cramming.
- Testing is too costly in relation to results.
- Testing deals with social and group measurement and prediction which is invalid when applied to individuals.
- Testing may have adverse and indeterminate societal consequences.
- Too much emphasis has been placed on test results and numerical test scores.
- Testing creates or reinforces an image of the organization as impersonal and callous; testing itself is an impersonal process.
- Valid criteria of job and occupational success and satisfaction are not available against which to check test results.
- Testing is based on abstract concepts of standardized performance by a standardized employee when, in reality, no such employee exists.
- Objective tests discriminate against the probing, subtle, and imaginative mind and favor the mundane, prosaic, and conformist thinker.

- The subject matter covered in many tests is unrelated to job content, is superficial, or could better be learned on the job.
- Personality tests are misused as selection instruments and, since they can be manipulated by the applicant, they encourage lying.
- Testing instruments designed for clinical use are administered in nonclinical situations.
- Tests frequently are poorly constructed, containing items that are trivial, absurd, and ambiguous.
- Objective short-answer tests overemphasize verbal factors.
- The middle-class language of tests amounts to a culture bias against deprived minority groups, the foreign-born, the older worker, and the slow starter.
- The predictive significance of tests is limited to specific tasks and questions found only in the test.
- Many tests used have not been validated and many are not valid for the purpose for which they are used.
- Many tests are used in situations for which they are inappropriate.

It is not possible to generalize about the extent to which those engaged in the selection process accept these objections. The main weakness of testing appears to stem from its dependence on classical psychometrics.

Influence of the Behavioral Sciences on the Selection Process

A pathology has developed from the adaptation of classical psychometric methods to public personnel selection which is revealed in a testing syndrome that affects all parts of the process. Practicing personnel administrators who recognize this condition face a dilemma. Much of the testing done is perceived both within and without the public sector as good. However, many testers admit to not knowing what many tests do, other than test for highly populated, routine white-collar and some blue-collar work, provided testees are products of an educational system in a typical middle-class environment. Written tests, individual interviews, and training and experience evaluations —the most common tests in the selection process—all are in need of a change.

These tests are assumed by psychometrists to measure different things, yet behavioral scientists claim "abilities are interrelated and continually affect one another."[78] If the labeling of tests is done only for reasons of face validity, then the results require reconsideration. No matter how skilled a practitioner may be, no selection device can be constructed that measures only one factor. The results are not signs but samples of behavior under certain conditions.[79] For example, high interest, which usually is not evaluated, may be a better measure than certain minimum requirements, since interest derives from motivation or desire to do a particular thing and do it well. "Interest measures are generally accepted today and can probably be worked into the selection pattern to a greater extent."[80]

Behavioral concepts point to an approach in which backgrounds are analyzed as they bear on occupational and career choices and in which behaviors are observed in interaction with either actual or simulated work situations and conditions. Backgrounds and behaviors objectively noted and analyzed in a psychological and sociological context become valuable data that could supplement or replace data from individual test or interview scores. In the behavioral approach there is less likelihood that assumptions or predictions will be made that do not stem directly from the data. Of significance here is a scholarly concern for what can be predicted from data derived from written tests and individual interviews. Continued use of individual interviews is particularly perplexing, since evidence of their ineffectiveness as a predictive selection device is growing.[81]

The foundation on which much of the original psychometric work in public personnel selection was based is crumbling. A redesigning of the process based on behavioral concepts is indicated, including those focusing on ethnic, economic, and cultural patterns and differences and the impact of social and situational circumstances on job performance. In short, there needs to be recognition that

different sets of behavior can lead to equivalent job success. . . . In addition, there is evidence not only that different people succeed on a particular job because of different behavior patterns but also that different attributes may account for the same behaviors. . . .

One of the many implications of these differences is the need to perform separate validity studies for different ethnic groups. The different cultural experience and exposure they have had may affect the relationship of tests to criteria. . . . Tests may underestimate the true ability of disadvantaged applicants and cause tests that are valid for the advantaged to be invalid for the disadvantaged. . . . Research to date has indicated that test-validity information derived from studies of the general population is not always appropriate for the disadvantaged. Some tests are valid if, and only if, interpreted differently for the disadvantaged.[82]

The idea of a double or different standard for different applicant groups does not mean either reverse discrimination or lowered selection standards.

The uneasy feeling arising from using a so-called double standard for minority groups appears to arise from a misunderstanding. The different standards are not used to give one group an advantage over the other. Rather, they are used to insure that people with equal probability of success will have an equal chance to be hired.

No one is suggesting that *job standards* be raised or lowered for different groups or that *selection standards* be manipulated to insure that the same proportion of applicants from different groups be hired. What is suggested is that selection standards be manipulated to *insure hiring the same proportion of potentially successful applicants from each ethnic group*. The difference between selection standards and job standards should be understood, and the concern should be to use selection standards most effectively to attain desired job standards. Certainly, it would be unwise for an organization to lower its job standards over a long period of time; yet it might be very advantageous to raise or lower selection standards differently as conditions warrant.[83]

The problem is complicated by the reality that

the background and experience of blacks and other ethnic groups are extremely varied, from complete isolation and lack of education to full participation in the cultural milieu of the country. Not all blacks or Spanish-speaking Americans are disadvantaged, and not all whites are advantaged. The problem becomes one of identifying and measuring the disadvantaging environmental variables. If an instrument measuring the extent of deprivation suffered by applicants could be constructed, it could be used in place of the ethnic group as a *moderator* between test scores and criterion measures. The moderator would be used to identify homogeneous subgroups of individuals drawn from various racial groups, and differential-validation studies would be performed on these subgroups.[84]

The variables of cultural deprivation among minority groups and women are particularly troublesome for a merit system. As yet no approaches have been developed in public service psychometrics to equitably mitigate the conditions in each category that have caused discrimination.

[M]ore work needs to be done to clarify the dimensions and to develop adequate measures of cultural disadvantage. . . . This is not easily accomplished, and requires going beyond using readily available biographical data. . . . There may well be culturally deprived majority group members whose test performance is affected in ways like that of the average minority group member, and culturally normal members of minority groups whose test performance is similar to that of the average majority group member. In short, race is a biological not a psychological characteristic, as is cultural deprivation. Thus a possible answer to the problems of fair employment which is basically psychological in nature would appear to lie in the direction of the measurement of the applicant's cultural status. Furthermore, such solutions would be more acceptable legally, and better understanding of the implications of cultural status would indicate ways in which members of culturally disparate groups behave differently at work. In turn, this should lead to investigation of the advantages of differential methods, not only of selection but also of training, motivation, supervision, and so forth.[85]

Moreover,

The specter of personnel selection by civil legislation has evoked considerable interest by parties both within and outside the profession. This in many ways has served as an impetus not only to discover new techniques but also to critically examine current practices concerning the full utilization of the disadvantaged, blacks, women, the elderly, and other special groups.

There is a heightened awareness that selection procedures do not operate in a vacuum but are part of a system. The appropriateness of a particular selection standard depends not only on the way the job is structured, but upon the type and duration of training, as well as other factors. A systems view of selection appears to be increasing in prominence. Perhaps we may one day see a cohesive theory of men and women at work.

While it seems clear that the classical selection model is giving way to a 'fairness' model, with specific attention to the selection of special groups, there seems to be little effort to associate selection systems with overall manpower requirements. It is quite possible that we will be faced with several manpower needs in years to come. . . . Obviously we need to look at mobility patterns as they affect employment practices. Most of all, there is a strong probability that we may move from selection systems per se to placement systems. To do so will require serious integration of existing systems, an area which is still in an embryonic stage.[86]

The influence of behavioral concepts on the selection process is pervasive, touching all traditional phases: recruitment, examination, certification, and placement. It presents important ideas for improving these functions, notably by emphasizing that factors outside the process have a bearing on results no matter how objective or refined the selection devices. The personnel practitioner, like it or not, is an applied social scientist.[87] A first principle of the behavioral approach is that how a person performs on a job is controlled as much by career choice, work group, and social, situational, and organizational factors as it is by individual characteristics. Consequently, the most successful process is one which combines behavioral concepts about individuals with concepts about occupations, work groups, and organizations. This calls for diversification, not standardization—a drastic departure for some agencies.

MAKING BEHAVIORAL CONCEPTS OPERATIONAL

If behavioral concepts are to be made operational in the selection process, efforts need to be directed to determine how techniques such as guided interviews, nondirective and depth interviews, self selections, interaction process analyses, biodata analyses, simulations, observations, and leaderless group discussions can be made job-related. These selection devices are a valuable means for obtaining information about and observing work behaviors. Role playing, sociometry, sociodrama, biodata patterns and responses, self-concepts, and peer and personal constructs are other approaches with predictive potential. All reveal aspects of work behavior that typically and traditionally are not sampled.

More situational testing; more measures of interests, creativity, motivation, interactions, perceptions, and values; more differential measures of intellect; more measures of organizational attractiveness; more critical analyses of biographical characteristics; more peer and self analyses and evaluations; less reliance on supervisory experience and prior education; less use of individual interviews for evaluation purposes; more attention to the distinction between job proficiency and job performance; more qualifying and less weighting and ranking of written tests—all of these modifications can be supported by behavioral research findings. Since career choices and occupational values differ, there is a need for tailor-made approaches for different career and occupational groups that take into account the values shared by such groups and, equally important, the values and characteristics of the agency in question.

The self selection that has taken place in occupational groupings could become a much more valuable sampling technique than it has been. Selection of a given occupation (when there has been a reasonable amount of free choice) offers an extraordinarily useful criteria for the study of individual differences.[88]

Selection in the public service must be done for a great variety of work and leadership roles. Frequently work is done by people interacting in their roles in many different bureaucratic organizations and in a variety of interpersonal situations. All individual, work, occupational, organizational, and environmental variables are not and cannot be known. No single approach developed from any one discipline exists which fits all variables for all acts of personnel selection. A many-sided model thus is required as a selection guide.

And it should be remembered that the model serves only as a guide and is not a guarantee of predictive validity in selection decisions. Important multidisciplinary breakthroughs are being made in behavioral science thinking and research from which a viable model of personnel selection can be built.

The overall impact of behavioral concepts on the selection process, especially in the degree of congruence between concepts and process, permits some general conclusions as well as some research hypotheses based on a synthesis of behavioral concepts.

General Conclusions

1. For effective human resources to meet the personnel needs of public programs, behavioral concepts about individuals plus job-related information and behavioral concepts about occupations, work groups, and organizations need to be synthesized toward development of a modern conceptual framework for the selection process. Realism in relating job content and the environment in which an agency operates is basic to operationalizing behavioral concepts.

2. The nature of work and the concepts of intelligence, personality, creativity, motivation, leadership, perceptions, interests, and values as they relate to selecting individuals for work are changing as a result of research and development in the behavioral sciences.

3. The traditional model of personnel selection fails to reflect the changing concepts of the behavioral sciences. Many assumptions from which the model was designed are tied to a state of knowledge belonging to the past.

4. Changing behavioral concepts relating to personnel selection create a theory-practice gap, the bridging of which requires that behavioral concepts be made operational through the redirection and redesign of the selection process described in the traditional model.

5. The redirection and redesign of the tradi-

tional model means discarding or revising those parts of the process based on old assumptions that have proved ineffective in favor of contemporary concepts that warrant special attention, particularly those concepts that pertain to the interaction and systems aspects of organization life.

6. The interaction and systems implications of behavioral concepts about individuals as organizational participants point to the need to develop a differentiated, job-related, and program-oriented selection model for predicting individual work effectiveness in human work groups in organizations.

7. Perceived weaknesses and dysfunctions of the traditional model appear to be directly related to the level and complexity of work. The model operates to overqualify for simple routine work at lower levels of occupational scales, to underqualify or become inoperative as work becomes increasingly technical and specialized and reaches higher professional, administrative and program levels, and to discriminate against women, minorities, and the disadvantaged.

8. The task/test/trait orientation of the traditional model needs to be replaced or conditioned where appropriate (depending on job, work, and program content) by a determination of occupational achievement levels of individuals or individual competency levels for contributing to work group accomplishment of program goals.

9. Increased emphasis on cultural and environmental factors, occupational data, differentials in the work ethic, and value systems in a merit context along with decreased concern with standardization, stability, and continuity in favor of diversification, innovation, and change are key requirements in developing an agency model for fitting human resources effectively to public programs.

10. There is a limit to what can be done by policy, procedural, and practice changes in recruitment, examination, certification, and placement, since work effectiveness comes from the constant interaction of individuals, work groups, and organizations. This interaction warrants increased atten-tion to situational, intergroup, and interindividual factors in these phases of the selection cycle.

A useful observation is that "we must so improve our methods of selection . . . that mediocrity will be detected before it is permitted to ripen into authority."[89] So comes the dilemma. Personnel selection was practiced long before the academics began to study, teach, research, and theorize about it. Although it is hoped that the period has passed when practitioners wanted little to do with academicians, there is still a long way to go if the gap between these two groups is to be bridged in order to work toward the mutual goal of finding a firm framework on which to structure a scientific selection process. A proper scientific approach to any subject requires

a happy marriage of theory and observation. The dangers of arm-chair speculation unsupported by empirical test are widely recognized; the perhaps more insidious danger of obsessive collection of 'facts' without the guide of significant hypotheses are less widely realized. What is certain is that neither observation nor theorizing can take place with any depth or precision until the necessary concepts—the necessary tools of thought—have been developed.[90]

Some research hypotheses based on a synthesis of pertinent behavioral concepts are presented here. Studies designed to draw out or test these assumptions might contribute to reducing the theory-practice gap as it exists in the selection process.

Some Research Hypotheses

1. Substitution of a situational approach to work and work behavior and an idiographic approach to individuality in work situations for the traditional task/trait/test approach will improve the effectiveness of the selection process.

2. The effectiveness of the selection process can be measured by its timeliness, that is, in its reflection of changes in the work ethic, work technology, worker availability, and occupational and organizational val-

ues; effectiveness also can be measured by the span of time necessary to adapt it to internalized changes in each of these areas.

3. The closer the match between the intellectual content of work (in both kind and level) and the intellect of those selected to do the work, the greater the work effectiveness of human resources.

4. Developing a typology of work situations within an organization will assist in identifying those factors most likely to produce an effective work force, e.g., interests, perceptions, values, behavior styles, career goals.

5. Certain white-collar and blue-collar organizational work of a routine, repetitive, unskilled, semi-skilled, and skilled nature lends itself to identification of work performance bands of minimum and maximum performance levels, the exceeding of which or failure to meet are disruptive to work group accomplishment of organization goals.

6. For those kinds of work—both occupational and organizational—in which differences in individual work performance beyond an established performance band do not affect work group accomplishment of organizational goals, the selection process should be designed to identify those individuals whose occupational achievement level will meet but not exceed the established performance band.

7. The effectiveness of a selection process to identify the creative individual depends on whether work situations exist that require and tolerate creativity and on how the creative individual is related to and utilized in work situations.

8. The identification of unique organizational characteristics and value systems is as significant to success of the selection process as the identification of individual characteristics, competencies, and value systems.

9. Predicting the work effectiveness of human resources is as dependent on determining the motivational capacities of individuals and the motivating conditions of work situations as it is on determining individual knowledges and abilities.

10. The contributions made by the selection process toward meeting organization goals depend on how realistically the intellectual, innovative, interpersonal, and motivational competencies of individuals are related to work situations and are introduced into interacting leadership and work roles in the organization as a social system.

11. Since work as reflected in both occupational and organizational hierarchies grows in complexity, individual development and growth as organization members assume a continuum from competence to incompetence. Consequently, the selection process should be designed to identify individual competency levels on a competency continuum and should be based on demands of work situations as related to potential intellectual, innovative, interpersonal, and motivational contributions to work group accomplishment of program goals.

---

[1] John W. Macy, Jr., PUBLIC SERVICE: THE HUMAN SIDE OF GOVERNMENT (New York: Harper and Row, Publishers, 1971), p. 19.

[2] At the opening session of the 1974 International Conference on Personnel Administration held in Montreal, Quebec, sponsored by the International Personnel Management Association (IPMA), John J. Carson in his keynote address emphasized the need to redefine merit in terms of representativeness and responsiveness. See also Harry Kranz, "Are Merit and Equity Compatible?" PUBLIC ADMINISTRATION REVIEW XXXIV (September/October 1974): 434–440.

[3] For discussions of planned change, see Warren G. Bennis, CHANGING ORGANIZATIONS (New York: McGraw-Hill Book Company, Inc., 1966); W. G. Bennis, K. D. Benne, and R. Chin, eds., THE PLANNING OF CHANGE (New York: Holt, Rinehart and Winston, Inc., 1961); Ronald Lippit, Jeanne Watson, and Bruce Westley, THE DYNAMICS OF PLANNED CHANGE (New York: Harcourt, Brace & World, 1958); Newton Marguiles and John Wallace, ORGANIZATIONAL CHOICE: TECHNIQUES AND APPLICATIONS (Glenview, Ill.: Scott Foresman and Co., Inc., 1973).

[4] A sampling of criticism documenting the needs for change can be found in the following: California Assembly Interim Committee on Industrial Relations, FINAL REPORT HOUSE RESOLUTION No. 500(K), Assembly Interim Committee Reports 1963–65, vol. 2, no. 9; LeRoy Collins, Orville L. Freeman, et al., THE MAZES OF MODERN GOVERNMENT: AN OCCASIONAL PAPER ON THE ROLES OF THE POLITICAL PROCESS IN THE FREE SOCIETY (Santa Barbara, Calif.: Center for the Study of Demo-

cratic Institutions, 1964) ; Nesta M. Gallas, "Personnel Selection," in A FRESH APPRAISAL OF BASIC PERSONNEL FUNCTIONS, personnel report no. 654 (Chicago: Public Personnel Association, n.d.) ; Griffenhagen-Kroeger, Inc., PERSONNEL CONCEPTS AND PRACTICES FOR MODERN URBAN GOVERNMENT, a report to the Municipal Manpower Commission, 1961; Franklin P. Kilpatrick, Milton C. Cummings, Jr., and M. Kent Jennings, THE IMAGE OF THE FEDERAL SERVICE (Washington, D.C.: The Brookings Institution, 1962) ; Macy, PUBLIC SERVICE; Municipal Manpower Commission, GOVERNMENTAL MANPOWER FOR TOMORROW'S CITIES (New York: McGraw-Hill Book Co., Inc., 1962) ; David T. Stanley, PROFESSIONAL PERSONNEL FOR THE CITY OF NEW YORK (Washington, D.C.: The Brookings Institution, 1963) ; Stephen B. Sweeney and James C. Charlesworth, eds., ACHIEVING EXCELLENCE IN THE PUBLIC SERVICE (Philadelphia: The American Academy of Political and Social Science, 1963) .

[5] For a discussion of professionalism and its application to the public personnel field, see Nesta M. Gallas and William H. T. Smith, "What It Takes to Make a Professional in the Public Service," in PUBLIC SERVICE PROFESSIONAL ASSOCIATIONS AND THE PUBLIC INTEREST, monograph 15 (Philadelphia: The American Academy of Political and Social Science, 1973) .

[6] The sense in which the phrase is used, as derived from a research study, is discussed in detail in George Ritzer and Harrison M. Trice, AN OCCUPATION IN CONFLICT: A STUDY OF THE PERSONNEL MANAGER (Ithaca, N.Y.: School of Labor and Industrial Relations, Cornell University, 1969) .

[7] Special Task Force to the Secretary of Health, Education, and Welfare, WORK IN AMERICA (Cambridge, Mass.: MIT Press, 1973) ; Jerome M. Rosow, ed., THE WORKER AND THE JOB: COPING WITH CHANGE (Englewood Cliffs, N.J.: Prentice-Hall, Inc., 1974) .

[8] Raymond A. Katzell, "Staffing and Developing the Organization," in BEHAVIORAL SCIENCE RESEARCH IN INDUSTRIAL RELATIONS, monograph 21 (New York: Industrial Relations Counselors, 1962) , p. 107.

[9] Edgar H. Shein noted that "attempts have been made to predict performance in all kinds of industrial jobs, in schools, and in colleges, in the military services, and even in private mental clinics. . . . Some success has been achieved, but the practical problems of developing scientifically sound selection procedures sometimes outweigh the ultimate gains achieved. . . . The whole procedure of selection may have organizational consequences not desired by the organization." Edgar H. Shein, ORGANIZATIONAL PSYCHOLOGY (Englewood Cliffs, N.J.: Prentice-Hall, Inc., 1965) , p. 22.

[10] For a discussion of these concepts, see Nesta M. Gallas, "Toward a Theory of Selection," in RECRUITMENT AND SELECTION IN THE PUBLIC SERVICE, ed. J. J. Donovan (Chicago: Public Personnel Association, 1968) .

[11] Ibid., p. 23.

[12] This particular wording is patterned after that in the 1953 MODEL CIVIL SERVICE LAW prepared by the National Civil Service League and the National Municipal League. The 1970 version, A MODEL PUBLIC PERSONNEL ADMINISTRATION LAW, presents a different picture with a positive rather than a negative philosophy.

[13] National Civil Service League, A MODEL PUBLIC PERSONNEL ADMINISTRATION LAW (Washington, D.C.: National Civil Service League, 1970) , p. 7.

[14] Ibid.

[15] Advisory Council on Intergovernmental Personnel Policy, MORE EFFECTIVE PUBLIC SERVICE: THE FIRST REPORT TO THE PRESIDENT AND THE CONGRESS (Washington, D.C.: Government Printing Office, March 1974) , p. 14.

[16] Ibid., pp. 14–16.

[17] Ibid., p. 11.

[18] Advisory Council on Intergovernmental Personnel Policy, MORE EFFECTIVE PUBLIC SERVICE: A SUPPLEMENTARY REPORT TO THE PRESIDENT AND THE CONGRESS (Washington, D.C.: Government Printing Office, October 1974) , p. 1.

[19] Ibid., p. 3.

[20] Richard E. Biddle, DISCRIMINATION—WHAT DOES IT MEAN? (Chicago: International Personnel Management Association, n. d.) . p. 1.

[21] Kenneth O. Warner, "Editorial Notes and Comments," PUBLIC PERSONNEL REVIEW XVII (October 1956) : 179.

[22] "To Restore Adventure to American Democracy," SATURDAY REVIEW (7 September 1963) : 42.

[23] U.S., Congress, House of Representatives, "A Report on How People are Recruited, Examined, and Appointed in the Competitive Civil Service," prepared by the U.S. Civil Service Commission for the Subcommittee on Civil Service, Committee on Post Office and Civil Service, April 1959 (Washington, D.C.: Government Printing Office, 1959) , p. 61.

[24] William Turn, "In Defense of Patronage," in "Improved Personnel in Government Service," ANNALS OF THE AMERICAN ACADEMY OF POLITICAL AND SOCIAL SCIENCE CLXXXIX (January 1937) : 22–28.

[25] For example, the "Quest for Quality" conferences of the American Society for Public Administration and the Public Personnel Association reported in the American Academy of Political and Social Science publication, ACHIEVING EXCELLENCE IN THE PUBLIC SERVICE, August 1963.

[26] L. W. Seberhagen, M. D. McCollum and C. D. Churchill, LEGAL ASPECTS OF PERSONNEL SELECTION IN THE PUBLIC SERVICE (Chicago: International Personnel Management Association, 1972) , p. 8.

[27] Ibid.

[28] Letter from Peter C. Giovannini, manager, Career Development Division, Personnel Department, The Port Authority of New York and New Jersey, September 4, 1974.

[29] The following definition of the selection process was included in the opening statement of a 1964 conference on public personnel selection: "The overall process of selection begins when the personnel office first becomes aware of the need to fill a vacancy and ends only when the employee has completed his probationary period successfully."

[30] Standard texts usually treat placement under appointments with the material on certification. It is not treated as such in this chapter.

[31] Dorothy C. Adkins, CONSTRUCTION AND ANALYSIS OF ACHIEVEMENT TESTS (Washington, D.C.: Government Printing Office, 1947) . A standard book used by practitioners in this field for many years.

[32] See sec. 1607 (2) of the 1970 EEOC GUIDELINES ON EMPLOYMENT SELECTION PROCEDURES.

[33] Statement of a leading consultant providing examination services to small agencies.

[34] Robert Ebel, Thelma Hunt, and Donald Harvey, IMPROVING PUBLIC PERSONNEL SELECTION, personnel report no. 635 (Chicago: Public Personnel Association, n. d.) . This publication includes three approaches

that point to the same conclusion, viz., that "there is a need for creating significant devices that will accurately measure task proficiency and trait strength." This commitment to testing is further evidenced by the increase in the use of tests. Lillian D. Long, in "Science Steps into Selection," a paper presented at the regional conference of the Eastern States Occupational Therapy Association (New York City, 27 April 1951), reported that sixty million standardized tests were given to about twenty million people in 1951. David A. Goslin in THE SEARCH FOR ABILITY (New York: Russell Sage Foundation, 1963) reported that between 150 million and a quarter of a billion standardized tests were being administered annually in the United States.

35 William E. Mosher, J. Donald Kingsley, and O. Glenn Stahl, PUBLIC PERSONNEL ADMINISTRATION, 3rd rev. ed. (New York: Harper & Bros., 1950), include in part II, "Staffing," a comprehensive account of the traditional model. They separate its operation into distinct stages. For example, "Recruitment ends with an application. The examining process begins with one" (p. 83). See also Felix Nigro, PUBLIC PERSONNEL ADMINISTRATION (New York: Henry Holt & Co., 1959), chapters 5 and 6, for another description of the model. Recent editions of these texts describe the process somewhat differently. Other versions and applications of the model can be found in various volumes of the ANNUAL REVIEW OF PSYCHOLOGY (Palo Alto, Calif.: Annual Reviews, Inc.) and in back issues of the journal of the International Personnel Management Association.

A capsule description follows of the examination phase of the model as it operates in the private sector:

Variables may be observed in the context of an interview or a standardized test situation, may be elicited in response to questions in an application blank, or may be observed in a job sample. . . . The kinds of variables . . . observed fall into the following general classes. The methods which have proved to be helpful are indicated in parentheses.

   a. Biographical information and work history (application blank, interview);
   b. Intellectual level and aptitude (tests, job samples);
   c. Specific areas of knowledges or specific skills (tests, job samples);
   d. Attitudes and interests (tests, application blank, interviews);
   e. Motivation, personality, temperament (tests, interview).

In general, tests have proved to be most valuable in those situations in which the job to be performed can be clearly described and in which a clear cut criterion of successful job performance exists. Thus clerks, machine operators, and pilots have been generally easier to select by means of tests than teachers, managers, or salesmen. (Schein, ORGANIZATIONAL PSYCHOLOGY, pp. 22–23).

36 Wilmar F. Bernthal, "Research Foundations for Modern Personnel Administration: A Review and Appraisal," THE PERSONNEL ADMINISTRATOR X (May/June 1965): 6.

37 Assumptions about organizations in the traditional model reflect the thinking of classical organizational theorists such as Max Weber, Henri Fayol, Luther Gulick, Mooney and Reilly, Lyndall Urwick, and Frederick W. Taylor. The most frequent conceptualization is the Weber model which represents the organization as functionally linked offices or positions arrayed in hierarchical order, bound together by rational laws, rules, and procedures which prescribe what is to be done and how it is to be done. This kind of organization is seen as an ideal framework within which specialized skills can be used to maximum effectiveness. The dysfunctions of this view are well documented in the current organizational theory literature.

38 A mnemonic device coined by Luther Gulick for a universal set of principles applicable to any kind of functional or organizational setting. These principles related to planning, organizing, staffing, directing, coordinating, reporting, and budgeting—or POSDCORB. It is now generally accepted that such principles do not exist and that the notion of a general set of principles applicable to an organization is fallible.

39 Robert Guion, PERSONNEL TESTING (New York: McGraw-Hill Book Co., 1965), p. 4.

40 Leona E. Tyler, THE PSYCHOLOGY OF HUMAN DIFFERENCES, 3rd rev. ed. (New York: Appleton-Century-Crofts, 1965), p. 7.

41 Guion, PERSONNEL TESTING, p. 6.

42 Long, "Science Steps into Selection," p. 1.

43 Ibid., p. 5.

44 Adkins, CONSTRUCTION AND ANALYSIS OF ACHIEVEMENT TESTS, pp. 11–12.

45 For a detailed discussion of legal aspects, see William C. Byham and E. Spitzer Morton, THE LAW AND PERSONNEL TESTING (New York: American Management Association, Inc., 1971), and Seberhagen, McCollum, and Churchill, LEGAL ASPECTS OF PERSONNEL SELECTION IN THE PUBLIC SERVICE.

46 Adkins, CONSTRUCTION AND ANALYSIS OF ACHIEVEMENT TESTS, p. 56.

47 Byham and Spitzer, THE LAW AND PERSONNEL TESTING, p. 85.

48 The importance of game theory in decision making is increasingly recognized in the study of organizations as evidenced by its inclusion in a number of texts, particularly texts in the decisional sciences.

49 The Public Personnel Association, now the International Personnel Management Association, at one time scheduled special sessions at its annual conferences on this basis.

50 THE PROMOTION OF LEM MERRILL, ICP Case Series, number 29 (University, Ala.: University of Alabama Press, 1954), gives a detailed account of the operation of the model and the moves by all three teams to win the game.

51 For example, see Bernthal, "Research Foundations for Modern Personnel Administration," p. 6; William C. Byham, THE USES OF PERSONNEL RESEARCH (New York: American Management Association, 1968); George W. England and D. W. Paterson, "Selection and Placement —The Past Ten Years," in EMPLOYMENT RELATIONS RESEARCH, eds. H. E. Heneman et al. (New York: Harper and Brothers, 1960); Cecil E. Goode, PERSONNEL RESEARCH FRONTIERS (Chicago: Public Personnel Association, 1958); Cecil E. Goode, ed., "Research and Results," PUBLIC PERSONNEL REVIEW XIX (October 1958); John W. Macy, Jr., "Psychological Testing and the Public Service," AMERICAN PSYCHOLOGIST XX (November 1965): 884; Anne Roe, THE PSYCHOLOGY OF OCCUPATIONS (New York: John Wiley & Sons, Inc., 1956), p. 314; Paul P. Van Riper, "Public Personnel Literature," PUBLIC REVIEW XXII (October 1961): 227–229.

[52] Douglas W. Bray and Joseph L. Moses, "Personnel Selection," ANNUAL REVIEW OF PSYCHOLOGY, 1972, p. 545.

[53] Ibid.

[54] Anne Anastasi, PSYCHOLOGICAL TESTING, 3rd rev. ed. (New York: Macmillan, Inc., 1968); Marvin D. Dunnette, PERSONNEL SELECTION AND PLACEMENT (Belmont, Calif.: Brooks/Cole Publishing Co., 1966); Guion, PERSONNEL TESTING; Edward F. Lindquist, ed., EDUCATIONAL MEASUREMENT (Washington, D.C.: American Council on Education, 1959); American Psychological Association, STANDARDS FOR EDUCATIONAL AND PSYCHOLOGICAL TESTS AND MEASUREMENTS (Washington, D.C.: American Psychological Association, 1966).

[55] Bray and Moses, "Personnel Selection," p. 555.

[56] Ibid., pp. 555–558.

[57] Tyler, THE PSYCHOLOGY OF HUMAN DIFFERENCES, pp. 500–501.

[58] Ibid., p. 502; Bray and Moses, "Personnel Selection."

[59] Bray and Moses, "Personnel Selection," p. 568.

[60] For a discussion of the application of these initial steps, see John C. Flanagan, "Improving Personnel Selection," PUBLIC PERSONNEL REVIEW XIV (July 1953): 107–112; "What They Say About Testing and What to Do About It," PUBLIC PERSONNEL REVIEW XXV (July 1964): 174–179.

[61] American Psychological Association, STANDARDS FOR EDUCATIONAL AND PSYCHOLOGICAL TESTS AND MEASUREMENTS, pp. 12–13.

[62] Ibid., p. 12.

[63] Stephen J. Musso and Mary K. Smith, CONTENT VALIDITY: A PROCEDURE MANUAL (Chicago: International Personnel Management Association, 1973); Dunnette, PERSONNEL SELECTION AND PLACEMENT, chap. 7; Vernon R. Taylor, TEST VALIDITY IN PERSONNEL SELECTION, Public Employment Practices bulletin no. 2, (Chicago: International Personnel Management Association, 1971).

[64] Bray and Moses, "Personnel Selection," p. 546.

[65] Bynham and Spitzer, THE LAW AND PERSONNEL TESTING, p. 105.

[66] Ibid.

[67] Seberhagen, McCollum, and Churchill, LEGAL ASPECTS OF PERSONNEL SELECTION IN THE PUBLIC SERVICE, p. 65.

[68] Bynham and Spitzer, THE LAW AND PERSONNEL TESTING, p. 128.

[69] Bray and Moses, "Personnel Selection," p. 568.

[70] Biddle, DISCRIMINATION—WHAT DOES IT MEAN?, p. 2, and John W. Gardner, EXCELLENCE: CAN WE BE EQUAL AND EXCELLENT TOO? (New York: Harper & Row, Publishers, 1961), who states that "Whatever their faults, the tests have proven fairer and more reliable than any other method when they are used cautiously within the limits for which they were designed" (p. 48).

[71] Bynham and Spitzer, THE LAW AND PERSONNEL TESTING, p. 145.

[72] James J. Kirkpatrick, Robert B. Ewen, Richard S. Barrett, and Raymond H. Katzell, TESTING AND FAIR EMPLOYMENT: FAIRNESS AND VALIDITY OF PERSONNEL TESTS FOR DIFFERENT ETHIC GROUPS (New York: New York University Press, 1968), pp. 30–33.

[73] Ibid., pp. 33–34.

[74] Ibid., p. 37.

[75] Richard S. Barrett, "Guide to Using Psychological Tests," HARVARD BUSINESS REVIEW XLI (September/October 1963): 146.

[76] Guion, PERSONNEL TESTING, p. 17.

[77] Ibid., p. 506.

[78] Chris Argyris, PERSONALITY AND ORGANIZATION (New York: Harper & Bros., 1957), p. 34.

[79] Ibid.

[80] John M. Stalnaker, "Educational Achievement and Career Potential," paper presented at the 1965 International Conference on Public Personnel Administration.

[81] See, for example, Kirkpatrick et al., TESTING AND FAIR EMPLOYMENT, p. 35; Guion, PERSONNEL TESTING, pp. 396–405; Dunnette, PERSONNEL SELECTION AND PLACEMENT, p. 65; Bray and Moses, "Personnel Selection," pp. 562–563; Bynham and Spitzer, THE LAW AND PERSONNEL TESTING, p. 63; and England and Paterson, "Selection and Placement," who have suggested a moratorium on literature on how to improve interviewing techniques until more evidence is gathered to vindicate interviewing as an assessment device.

[82] Bynham and Spitzer, THE LAW AND PERSONNEL TESTING, p. 128.

[83] Ibid., p. 142.

[84] Ibid., pp. 143–144.

[85] Kirkpatrick et al., TESTING AND FAIR EMPLOYMENT, pp. 38–39.

[86] Bray and Moses, "Personnel Selection," pp. 545–546.

[87] John M. Pfiffner, "The Metamorphosis of a Mind," James M. Pfiffner miscellaneous papers.

[88] Roe, THE PSYCHOLOGY OF OCCUPATIONS.

[89] Clarence B. Randall, quoted in PUBLIC ADMINISTRATION NEWS XII, section II (May 1963).

[90] A. D. Newman and R. W. Rowbottom, ORGANIZATION ANALYSIS: A GUIDE TO THE BETTER UNDERSTANDING OF THE STRUCTURAL PROBLEMS OF ORGANIZATION (London: Morrison and Gibb, Ltd., 1968), p. 475.

7

Employee Development
and Training

Let ignorance talk as it will, learning has its value.

JEAN DE LA FONTAINE

DEVELOPMENT AND TRAINING ACTIVITY in U.S. municipalities during the 1970s has been moving toward action training and research. Cities are beginning to consciously use it as a reeducative strategy of change. Training's "new look" has arisen in response not only to the general conditions of the times but also to the stimulus provided by the Intergovernmental Personnel Act and organizations such as the International City Management Association (ICMA), the International Personnel Management Association (IPMA), and the National Training and Development Service for State and Local Government (NTDS). In viewing the progress of training in the decade from 1965 to 1975, one could justifiably claim that remarkable advances had been made.

It is characteristic of the more effective training being undertaken in municipalities during the period 1965–1975 that it enters into and becomes part of most major organizational programs and activities. Increasingly training is being recognized as a strategy for achieving change, particularly as a means of obtaining acceptance and understanding of management's new policies and programs. Furthermore, employee development and training provide support for the vital personnel actions required in manpower planning, employer-employee relations, staff relations, productivity, and employee motivation. At the same time that the training process is gaining recognition as a valuable strategy of change, the more traditional concept of training continues to have its value in maintaining that the staffing process is neither complete nor successful unless employees become competent performers and experience psychological growth in the process of doing so.

In reviewing training discussions that took place in the early 1960s or before, one might wonder at the nature of terms such as pre-entry education, post-entry education, in-service training, and vestibule training. Much of the training performed then was narrowly focused, with orientation, job instruction, and supervisory training given the major emphasis in those enlightened jurisdictions which sponsored any training at all. Training has changed, particularly by making greater use of knowledge from the behavioral sciences and by broadening its scope of interest. The result is that training processes conducted in the 1970s lead to active engagement with the environment and to examination of a wide spectrum of substantive areas.[1]

The older, narrower definitions will not suffice within these new horizons, because training involves the *conscious* development and utilization of communication skills in the solution of major problems. This means giving greater attention to the various kinds of individual learning processes, which Frederick Fisher has classified as cognitive, affective, and psychomotor.[2] Cognitive objectives involve remembering or reproducing what has been learned, solving an intellective task by determining the essential problems, and reordering material to bring about a congruence of ideas, methods, or procedures previously learned. Affective learning objectives focus on attitudes, behavior, appreciation, values, and emotional threats and biases. Psychomotor objectives are concerned with muscular and motor skills involved in such tasks as typing, speech, or auto mechanics.

According to Fisher, training in all three kinds of learning should nourish the self and the self-structure of the individual as an employee or as a supervisor of the organization; they should enable the individual to influence and contribute to the organization; and they also should improve the ability of the individual and the organization to deal better with the external environment. In Fisher's opinion, the training and education of public administrators should take place in "massive continuing doses designed to mold new individuals, institutions, and total environments." These massive doses require that the administrator have an understanding of the concept of "self," a knowledge of new organizational forms geared to change, and up-to-date knowledge of cultural norms, interjurisdictional dilemmas, and potential intersystem linkages. "It also means the development of new skills in negotiation, consensus-building, intergroup problem solving, systems analysis (in the broadest sense), and the effective use of legitimate authority."

Society's preoccupation with change is not necessarily a matter of choice. Change is occurring, whether or not it is desired or desirable. Therefore, the question is not "Should we change?" but rather "How do we deal with change rationally and advantageously?" Managers desperately need a theory of change to govern their strategies for dealing with this phenomenon. Chin and Benne have constructed a framework for thinking about change which provides a useful starting point for those in search of a theory. According to them, change is dealt with in three different modes: (1) power-coercive, (2) rational-empirical, and (3) normative-reeducative.[3]

Power-coercive strategies are well-known in bureaucratic monocracies. The literature abounds with examples of the alienating effect that bureaucratic organizations have upon individuals, to the detriment of productivity. Robert Blauner's work on alienation, Robert K. Merton's study on the impact of bureaucracy, Philip Selznick's study of the mechanistic organization, and Chris Argyris' studies on the relationship of the individual to the organization all address the subject of the alienating and dissociative impact of bureaucratic structures.

The empirical-rational approach to change is illustrated by the activities of systems analysts who had as their direct forebears the management analysts who prospered during the post-World War II period and well into the 1960s. According to Chin and Benne, management analysis has been used largely for system maintenance rather than for system change. Focus on the individual role occupants has been a major deterrent to further development, because personnel selection and replacement strategies have not been sensitive to problems and difficulties in the social and cultural system. Because they work with blinders imposed by their limited definitions of problems, systems analysts need to ask themselves whether or not their work tends to perpetuate established ideology. Unless the ideas developed through research are diffused throughout the participant society, empirical-rational strategies are not effective in coping with change. Recognition of this limitation often leads to a reconsideration of training and education, which in turn leads to the third strategy—the normative-reeducative approaches.

Normative-reeducative strategies take note of the relation between individuals and their environment, and thus tend to be transactional. Humans do not simply wait for stimuli from their environment but interact with these stimuli to further their own goals. This suggests a close relationship between research, training, and action wherein humans can participate in their own reeducation.

Experimentation with development and training for action is compatible with the normative-reeducative mode. Action training and research strategy is problem-oriented by nature. Accordingly, ecological and environmental preservation, citizen participation, establishment and maintenance of law and order in both white-collar and inner-city areas, housing, transportation, labor relations, equal opportunity, government finance, and the various internal processes of government including budgeting and the delivery of services have come to be recognized as problems requiring action training.[4] Development and training, which some consider still to be in the developing stage, have not been confined to particular areas but have been introduced into many important operations. The nature of the training intervention is not so much to assist in solving actual technical problems as to help develop the skills of employees and citizens to solve problems and make choices. This technique involves discovering ways to communicate understanding and to achieve commitment.

With this introduction of training as an action-oriented strategy for change, the chapter proceeds with a detailed discussion of the various aspects of development and training. Attention is directed first to the range of training resources of which municipalities can avail themselves in developing their training programs. Next, the external, organizational, and personnel problems that determine training needs are outlined. Training policies and plans are briefly discussed and trends in training methodology are briefly listed. Finally, the chapter focuses on the evaluation of employee development and training.

Training Resources

The growing interest in action training has been accompanied by an increase in training resources. Although there are many new and promising training resources, the Intergovernmental Personnel Act must be seen as the one providing the principal stimulus.

INTERGOVERNMENTAL PERSONNEL ACT (IPA)

The Intergovernmental Personnel Act of 1970 has contributed significantly to employee de-

velopment and training in local government. The major purposes of the IPA are to strengthen management capabilities, contribute to problem solving through improved personnel processes, assist the process of decentralizing power whereby government can be brought closer to the people, and, through the achievement of these purposes, enhance front-line delivery for most public services.

In addition to providing funds to assist the total range of personnel activities, the act authorized the U.S. Civil Service Commission to help local government carry out training programs for employees; to award grants for graduate-level study by employees selected by the local governments; to provide for temporary assignments of personnel between federal agencies, local governments, and universities; and to offer individuals admission to federal agency training courses on a shared-cost basis.[5]

The admission of local government employees to federal courses provides many training opportunities which heretofore have been unavailable. Attendance was first authorized by the Intergovernmental Cooperation Act of 1968; passage of the Intergovernmental Training Act of 1971 opened the gates all the way for shared training opportunities.[6] The U.S. Civil Service Commission provides training through regional training centers in such fields as equal employment opportunity; supervision and management; personnel and labor relations; office skills and communications; bookkeeping, accounting and auditing; managerial sciences; and automatic data processing.[7] Seminars on these and similar subjects are designed to meet some of the out-service development and training needs of public leaders.[8]

The U.S. Civil Service Commission provides mid-level executive training in its executive seminar centers located at Berkeley, California; Kings Point, New York; and Oak Ridge, Tennessee. The Federal Executive Institute at Charlottesville, Virginia, provides by special arrangement for the participation of top municipal executives in its six-week seminars. If circumstances warrant, attendance is permitted without charge to the local government.[9]

Under the IPA, the U.S. Civil Service Commission also encourages the development of intergovernmental training centers. Examples of such centers are the University of Missouri's Suburban Network for Management Development and Training; California's state regional training centers; Virginia's Public Executive Institute, which provides training for state, county, and city employees; Tennessee's Center for Government Training; and the Kansas Center for Action Training.[10]

The U.S. Civil Service Commission publishes materials for training and development funding sources, including a valuable newsletter, *Intergovernmental Personnel Notes,* which provides information on training opportunities and activities. Other publications such as *Administration of Training,* a title in the Personnel Bibliography Series, and course manuals such as *Affirmative Action Planning for State and Local Government* are important training resources available to local governments.

Talent sharing is a method for sharing knowledge to solve mutual problems and provide development experience for participating employees.[11] To promote talent sharing, the Bureau of Intergovernmental Personnel Programs has established the Personnel Mobility Program, which is authorized by IPA to encourage the exchange of talent between local and federal units. In the early years of the program, more federal employees moved to take temporary positions in local government than local employees moved to federal positions. However, with the passage of each year, more local government personnel are accepting federal assignments. The mobility feature of IPA offers an easy opportunity to move the needed expertise between federal agencies and state and local governments for any period that does not exceed two years.[12]

Expenditure on IPA programs during the first few years were modest. About $5 million of the funds expended each year have been allocated to training; 62 percent of these funds have gone to meet local needs. Much that is useful has resulted from this small investment, and greater benefits could be expected if funding were to reach greater levels. There is little doubt that the IPA has stimulated much training and development activity in American municipalities and has contributed to an increase of training capabilities.

A government publication particularly instructive to jurisdictions seeking federal aid is the *Catalog of Federal Domestic Assistance,*[13] which provides information covering the following: federal agencies and the programs they administer; legal authorization for the programs; objectives of the programs; types of grants; uses and restrictions of the programs; eligibility requirements; application and award processes; assistance considerations; post-assistance requirements; financial information; program accomplishments; regulations, guidelines, and literature; information contacts; and related programs.

This catalog and the *Guide to Personnel Assistance for State and Local Government Institutions of Higher Education*[14] detail programs of the federal agencies which support training and manpower development. For example, the Department of Housing and Urban Development has financed programs that focus on a variety of urban issues, including the training of minority employees in local government management. The Economic Development Agency has funded a massive training and research effort to study worker motivation in state and local government.[15] Training funds have also been provided by the Economic Opportunity Act of 1964, Title I of the Higher Education Act of 1965, the Law Enforcement Assistance Act of 1968, Title IX of the Housing Act of 1964, the Emergency Employment Act of 1971, and the Environmental Protection Act of 1970.

NATIONAL TRAINING AND DEVELOPMENT SERVICE (NTDS)

With the establishment of a growing number of federally funded programs focusing on law enforcement training, environmental protection, health services, productivity improvement, and improved management, clearly the value of training to improve local government has been recognized. But until the 1970s the importance of training as a strategy in program implementation had not been fully appreciated. The creation of the National Training and Development Service (NTDS) and its availability to state and local governments had much to do with changing this attitude.

On May 1, 1972, the so-called "Big Six" of public interest groups, now expanded to the "Big Seven," activated the NTDS as a non-profit corporation. (The "Big Seven" is composed of the Council of State Governments, the International City Management Association, the National Association of Counties, the National Governors' Conference, the National League of Cities, the National Legislative Conference, and the U.S. Conference of Mayors.) From its inception, NTDS has been funded by the federal government through the Intergovernmental Personnel Act and by the Ford Foundation.

The concept of NTDS grew out of a 1970 conference sponsored by the "Big Six" organized to examine "the organizational development needs and the post-entry training needs of those involved in the policy and the management processes of state, county, and city governments." Participating in the conference were forty-six leading public administrators and scholars who produced an important report titled *Consensus at College Park*. The consensus is reflected in the following resolution approved by the conference participants:

Whereas, state and local governments have become in recent years a prime source of strength and hope to a nation threatened by social, economic, and environmental issues of great magnitude;

Whereas, our governing bodies at state and grass-roots levels have been challenged as never before by a unique mix of events—unparalleled growth, accelerating change, expanding technology, the concept of federalism and its opportunities to enhance state and local capability, and a broad spectrum of issues that tear at the fabric of democratic government;

Whereas, the Council of State Governments, the National Governors' Conference, the National Association of Counties, the National League of Cities, the U.S. Conference of Mayors, the International City Management Association, in recognizing the imperative of conditioning state and local governments to this expanding horizon of problems, has assembled a number of men and women concerned with these changes to seek new direction in the training and development of those who serve the governmental institutions of our nation's states, counties, and municipal governments;

Therefore, let it be resolved, that the executive directors of the public interest groups represented by the sponsoring associations move, with vigor, toward the establishment of an educational service dedicated to improving the competence of state and local government through in-service training programs of personal and organizational development to be operated and conducted for management and policy officials as a continuing education service to perform an outreach activity to support, complement, and stimulate state and local public and private efforts;

And be it further resolved, the continuing education service shall concentrate its efforts on coordinating interdependent program elements, including research and experimentation; the dissemination of training materials; serving as a clearinghouse of information and guidance; training trainers; offering technical assistance; developing a network of centers of institutional and organizational strength throughout the nation; maximizing public and private resources and capabilities to help meet the demands of the consumer training market; and presenting residential training programs for a very limited number of key executives, legislators, and specialists;

It is further resolved, that the six sponsoring organizations take initial steps at as early a date as feasible, to incorporate a continuing education service, constituting the governing board of itself plus others broadly representative of key interest groups, to be supplemented by strong advisory boards;

It is further resolved, that the six sponsoring organizations take all means possible to achieve the implementation of the symposium, and that an exhaustive effort be undertaken to seek out major commitments of resources to permit the achievement of the objectives of this consensus statement.[16]

In the first year of its existence, NTDS, the direct product of the conference, did much to justify the faith of its sponsors. Its staff went to the grass-roots level to gather information on the needs of local government officials. They conducted strategy workshops which involved more than 200 key state and local officials. They also carried their message to the annual conventions of the International City Management Association, the Public Personnel Association, the American Society for Public Administration, and other groups.

A major purpose specified in the consensus document was the training of trainers and development managers. Beginning in its first year, NTDS organized intensive four-week courses to develop the knowledge and skills required to apply normative-reeducative strategies to problems of change. Public organizations cooperated in this program by offering their agencies as laboratories where participants could learn to translate theory into action. The participating cities further benefited from this pragmatic approach from training groups that addressed such topics as community development, employer-employee relations, integration of work units, limits to community growth, and dating personnel systems.

Thomas W. Fletcher, former president of the NTDS, in an interview in *Nation's Cities* said that "Leadership at all levels of state and local government is up to their collective chins in a society with rapidly changing needs and values. They're being faced with brand new issues—issues for which they've often had no training, issues which require them to respond quickly and effectively, and that's in addition to the traditional problems which are assuming new twists and directions."[17] To cope with these conditions, Fletcher recommended that public agencies accept training as a basic strategy to help them move quickly and knowledgeably toward achieving new solutions to new problems. Accordingly, NTDS' most comprehensive seminar, based on the action training and research model, is structured to appeal to city managers and assistants, county commissioners, department heads, public interest group officials, personnel specialists, and university and institutional personnel. The seminars focus on management development, personnel growth, team building, organization development, communications, training designs, and other action-oriented processes.

In addition to numerous summer programs, NTDS activities include a five-day advanced management workshop titled "Building Open Systems" and a variety of prototype sessions focusing on problems such as policy development; citizen/local government understanding; cooperative and collaborative programs among mayors; the roles of city managers, council members, and school board officials; and productivity in local government. NTDS staff members also have worked with some cities to set up organization development sessions for team building and transactional analysis.

In addition, NTDS holds annual "Organization and Development Change" conferences prior to ICMA's annual conferences. Papers delivered at these meetings serve as case studies on organization development in the public sector. NTDS also has collaborated with the Menninger Foundation in sponsoring a managerial seminar titled "Toward Understanding Man." (A more inclusive title is suggested.) This service is planned to aid local officials; its agenda covers a mix of subjects, including human motivation, leadership, and behavioral understanding.[18] NTDS conducted a major study on worker motivation in state and local government and has also assisted the League of California Cities to assess municipal training needs in that state.[19]

An NTDS publications program has also been developed. Some monographs particularly useful to training and development managers are *Managing Change; Training for Action Research; Organization Development and Change; Management by Objectives for Public Administrators; Conference Planning; Building a Learning Community;* and *Group Leadership.* The NTDS quarterly, *Network News,* carries information on innovative programs and federal training activities available and useful to local governments as well as book reviews and discussions of issues and problems pertaining to training and development. The organization also publishes a series of paperbacks, including titles such as *Action Research for Training and Development, The Process of Program Evaluation,* and *Group Leadership.*

In short, the National Training and Development Service is proving to be a good means through which action-oriented training strategies based on reeducative approaches to change can be developed and tested to serve as models for managers in municipal governments. Its work supplements and enhances the established training programs of ICMA, the National League of Cities, and the U.S. Conference of Mayors.

INTERNATIONAL CITY MANAGEMENT
ASSOCIATION (ICMA)

ICMA's Institute for Training in Municipal Administration has provided training since

1935 for over 50,000 local government personnel. Much of the institute's efforts are geared to in-service training of line administrators. Its curriculum includes courses based on texts in the Municipal Management Series of which this book is a part.

In addition to courses offered through the institute, ICMA has undertaken a wide variety of training activities. Specific examples are workshops in the areas of collective bargaining; law enforcement leadership; small cities management training; productivity improvement; solid waste management; environmental management; growth management; integrated municipal information systems; minorities in municipal management; "show-and-tell" seminars; and technology field days (providing opportunities to see and discuss the operations of programs in various communities).

In writing about the ICMA program, Donald Borut noted that "as a membership association, the role of ICMA in training must be to respond to a variety of training needs and to recognize that individuals gain information and knowledge from a multitude of approaches."[20] The fact that municipalities continue to support ICMA training is sufficient evidence that the institute's programs are meeting important needs.

The Small Cities Management Training Program may serve as a case in point. With the assistance of an IPA grant, ICMA has developed a low-cost training course which enables managers to participate without leaving their cities. The main objectives of the course are (1) to provide managers and principal city officials with up-to-date information on management practices that currently are applied in smaller cities, and (2) to use modern group techniques that will both assist training participants to develop their communication skills and develop team work. A training guide developed originally for the Texas Municipal League served as the initial basis for preparing the small city manager to apply simple group techniques to encourage administrative cooperation in solving the problems which attend the management of a small municipality. Reaction of one participant to the program was that "for the first time the city has de-

partment heads working as a team, with basic knowledge of responsibilities of other departments."[21]

The Small Cities Management Training Program seems to hold considerable promise because of the form and economy of involvement and the practical action orientation. Development in 1975 of further written and multi-media materials suitable for use in the program's do-it-yourself, problem-solving sessions has resulted in an increase in the number of small cities participating, since in small jurisdictions time and money often prevent the development of action training and research capabilities.

STATE MUNICIPAL LEAGUES

State municipal leagues traditionally have engaged in programs to strengthen municipal management, primarily in training municipal officers. With passage of the Intergovernmental Personnel Act, the pace of their training activities has accelerated. In addition to the general objective of improving the level of expertise within their own organizations, many state leagues have developed expanded and innovative training programs.[22] In addition, state municipal leagues continually sponsor seminars on topics such as equal employment opportunity, occupational safety and health, and labor relations.

NATIONAL LEAGUE OF CITIES
AND THE U.S. CONFERENCE OF MAYORS

The National League of Cities and the U.S. Conference of Mayors, noting the growth of federally-sponsored programs, work jointly with receptive state municipal leagues to assist in implementing federally-funded programs in the cities. The rationale behind the effort is that the municipal leagues, by virtue of their continuous contact with the municipalities, can advise and encourage cities in the most efficient and imaginative provision of their social services, welfare practices, community development, community action, and equal employment hiring. In an example of coordinated action, the two bodies were designated contractors with the Office of Economic Opportunity to initiate action-oriented education programs intended to articulate an "intergovernmental human resources system." The program involved working with sixteen state leagues to distribute materials describing federal programs and their possible impact on local communities; develop and disseminate special reports on the "new federalism" to assist local government officials in understanding their new responsibilities; and bring groups together to decide upon the collaboration needed to implement these programs effectively.[23]

In reporting on the program, the National League of Cities noted that

> while each state league program is a distinct entity, and while the programs initially began with different emphases, the dictates of experience and circumstance seem to be pushing the projects in a common direction, that is, in the direction of analyzing state plans' processes, working with new regional planning entities, and building municipal capacities to deal effectively with social responsibilities which inhere in general and special revenue sharing. Such a program orientation is rooted in the understanding that these aspects of the effort are of the greatest advance to the central project's objective of insuring that social services are delivered effectively, and with an intelligent recognition of special local needs.[24]

The program has resulted in municipal leagues giving an understanding to the participating states of the benefits which accrue from human resources programs, as well as the impact such programs have on the future delivery of social services. This project is an example of training and development that has been used for purposes of program and policy implementation; it also is an example of the normative-reeducative change strategy in action.

INTERNATIONAL PERSONNEL MANAGEMENT ASSOCIATION (IPMA)

The International Personnel Management Association is yet another national organization which provides training assistance to municipal employees. It issues publications dealing with topics of current interest, offers on-the-spot consultations in labor-management matters, convenes national and regional conferences that act as educational forums, and

conducts seminars and workshops on timely subjects. For example, its direct training offerings have included four-day workshops on personnel selection and test validation; one-day briefings on the revised reporting requirements of the EEOC; workshops on public sector collective bargaining and strikes; three-day workshops on affirmative action program development; a ten-day basic course in personnel administration; and, of course, its annual conference.

In addition to the public interest organizations which contribute their resources to public employee training, there exist training-oriented associations, for example, the American Society for Training and Development. There also are a growing number of public and private organizations that offer courses that may be of interest to public sector employees.

INSTITUTIONS OF HIGHER EDUCATION

Institutions of higher education contribute both to pre-entry and post-entry education of the public employee. Since the 1960s it has become somewhat fashionable for universities to establish schools of public affairs. Universities generally have difficulty viewing the field of public administration as a subject sufficiently unique to be removed from the department of political science. Curriculum emphasis on "policy science" and the cachet of "public affairs," rather than public administration, apparently have brought these schools the academic respectability to justify the distinction in disciplines.

Another, but lesser, trend is combining the study of business and public administration to form schools of administration. The rationale behind this merger is that management is generic, and that good administrative practice ought to be applicable to public and private sectors alike. Although many argue that important differences do exist between the two sectors, proponents of the combination have persuaded some university administrations of the merit of such a plan. It remains to be seen whether schools of administration will acquiesce to the primary sources of support money and consequently emphasize the private sector to the detriment of the public sphere. At any rate, most university programs by whatever name are geared to pre-entry rather than post-entry education.

Except in a few noteworthy cases, universities have relegated the education of mid-career employees to university extension units. Most extension programs are entrepreneurial and self-supporting. On the other hand, most graduate and undergraduate education is an expensive enterprise in which the costs are greater than the tuition collected and, therefore, it is subsidized by other sources. By contrast, extension programs must proceed on a pay-as-you-go basis. Furthermore, most universities relegate extension credit to second-class status and do not allow it to be applied to regular degree programs. Universities thus imply that extension courses are not academically respectable. Rarely does a faculty member of national reputation teach an extension course. Moreover, extension faculty often are not included in the regular or tenured body of university faculty.

Nevertheless, in spite of these discouraging circumstances, some extension programs offer outstanding educational experiences and provide excellent opportunities for mid-career employees to develop. The merit of these programs is due mainly to the dedication of the faculty members and the capabilities and determination of the students who, at mid-career, perceive new educational needs and demonstrate a readiness to learn that is not evident in many college students.

In a study conducted in 1971, the Institute for Local Self-Government found that city and county officials were convinced that continuing education for public administrators was important. These officials felt universities should accept as students any individuals who are willing to learn and are capable of conducting inquiry. In their view, the university's involvement in the problems of urban culture should be central to university life:

It is the mission of a university to do the things that other institutions can't. It should be ready to move forward along new lines in continuing education—to experiment, to generate and try out original ideas and approaches in instruction, research, and public service. Through learning naturally resulting from a program of continuing education and public affairs, the university can introduce 'the innovative function' to urban affairs.[25]

Confining university activity to research and pre-service education poses particular problems, since public business is technical and professional as well as administrative. In most public jurisdictions are found lawyers, social workers, engineers, economists, public health personnel, park and recreation specialists, and many other professionals. Schools of administration and public affairs prepare a relatively small number of personnel who assume roles as administrative generalists. In large cities, the generalists rarely become heads of operating departments. Educational institutions thus provide pre-entry professional and technical education for one group and pre-entry administrative education for another.

But the real world demands the skills that are the product of a combined education. Only mid-career educational programs meet the broad educational needs of the public service. In-service training certainly can help upgrade employee knowledge and skill levels, but only universities have the intellectual resources to help embattled administrators keep up with the changing times. Public employees appear to want and need additional education in "theoretical and academic subjects which touch on community development, sociology and human relations."[26]

A few top-flight universities offer degree-granting programs to part-time, mid-career employees. A growing list of these includes American University, Columbia University, Boston University, Harvard University, University of Oklahoma, Syracuse University, University of Pittsburgh, Pennsylvania State University, George Washington University, New York University, and the University of Southern California.

The University of Oklahoma and the University of Southern California now offer degree courses on an "intensive semester" basis. Students enrolled in these courses do required reading in advance, attend classes for one intensive week, and undertake term papers or research projects, following which they frequently meet for a final one-day session to evaluate their work. The University of Southern California now has two major centers for graduate studies in public administration, one in Washington, D.C., and the other in Sacramento.

Several university centers work closely with municipalities in meeting research and training needs. Two research institutes, one at the University of California, Berkeley, and the other at the University of North Carolina, have been in operation for many years. The latter institute also provides a program of continuing education for local government officials. At the University of Texas, Arlington, the Institute of Urban Studies provides a wide variety of training for municipalities in that state. One of its most important programs is the training of trainers project, which is taken to the cities of Texas.

Other universities operate training centers in addition to regular academic programs. Some of the best known are the Center for Training and Career Development, University of Tennessee; the Institute of Public Service, University of Connecticut; the Georgia Municipal Association and Institute of Government, University of Georgia; the Institute of Public Administration, Indiana University; the Bureau of Public Administration, University of Maine, Orono; the Institute for Training and Development, University of Southern California; and the John Jay School for Criminal Justice, City College of New York.

The manifest value of the universities' contributions to municipal governments does not diminish the need for their even greater efforts in the future. It would be wrong, however, to expect the universities to carry the whole burden of continuing education. Indeed, community colleges, which have proliferated since World War II, constitute a rich source of training assistance. In contrast to the universities, community colleges tend to be very flexible and readily responsive to the educational needs of local government employees. Many such colleges attempt to provide a wide variety of needed courses, requiring only that these courses be attended by a sufficient number of public employees.

In most areas the community colleges appear eager to cooperate, especially if city officials work with them in pinpointing the areas of interest. Community colleges have been particularly helpful in training accountants, storekeepers, and computer personnel. Many offer a police science curriculum and, for mid-career employees, such courses as basic supervision, speed-reading, report writing, and public relations. Local jurisdictions may find that community colleges can provide much of the basic training for the lower-level employees, thereby freeing managers to use their talent and energy in more action-oriented types of training.[27]

Training Needs

With training resources available to both large and small municipal jurisdictions growing in number and kind, the necessity of determining how and to what degree to apply these resources arises. State leagues of cities have been particularly mindful of this, and those serving Arkansas, Kansas, Maine, Michigan, and California have conducted surveys to ascertain training needs.

Action-oriented training is one of the most pressing needs which municipalities are facing. A 1974 study of major training needs conducted by NTDS for the League of California Cities recognized three categories of problems: external, organizational, and personnel.[28] Seen from these perspectives, the organization's training needs transcend those for training people as managers, accountants, budget officers, or any other professional or technical position, since beyond these are action-oriented needs which relate to the problems plaguing most municipalities. An administrator needs to be trained not only to manage but also how to cope with various problems.

External Problems

External problems requiring special training that were identified by the NTDS study include the following:

Political and Intergovernmental Relations. Problems include overlapping governmental jurisdictions; federal, state, and general city law; and coordination and planning of redevelopment at all levels of government.

Finances. Problems involve problem-solving knowledge concerning scarce financial resources, inadequate tax bases, revenue sharing and other federal funding, and the problems attendant to financing projects mandated by outside agencies.

The Industrial Sector. Problems exist in obtaining acceptance of a downtown business area through public funding and raising income levels through provision of better employment opportunities.

Growth. Dealing with growth calls for education in planning and annexation, as well as study of the possible consequences of growth for the community's quality of life.

Community Relations. Approaching problems in this area requires an understanding of widespread public mistrust of government and officials. It also requires the education both of citizens in the role of local government and of officials in the ways in which they may become more responsive to citizens' needs and identify citizens' concerns. The media should be encouraged to cover the events and problems facing local government.

Minority Groups. Dealing with minority groups requires comprehensive understanding of cultural differences, militant groups, and interracial strife; gaining and maintaining support for improvements in minority sections of the city; improving communications between minority groups and other groups in the community; and changing employment laws which discriminate against these groups.

Demography. The needs of the community as determined by its demographic characteristics require of the administrator substantial knowledge of ways to increase employment opportunities and raise individual income levels; understanding the nature of the transient population and problems accompanying development and redevelopment, including excessive percentages in the school-age and welfare population, and other similar problems.

Housing. Many problems involving housing require increased awareness and exercise of new skills by municipal managers and employees. Principal housing issues involve senior citizen housing, zoning, low-cost housing, selection of contractors, declining neighborhoods, and building code enforcement.

Transportation. Managers and public works professionals need to be updated constantly on various transportation needs, including substandard streets; traffic control on incoming highways and arterial routes; mainlines, sidings, and the noise of railroads; priorities for state road and freeway development and their consequences; and traffic safety.

Parks. Issues involving public parks include determining the need for parks and open space and establishing beautification programs.

Industrial Base. Specialized information and funding know-how are needed to aid declining downtown business districts. Economic studies should be conducted to help cities deal with the problems of developing appropriate and desirable industry.

Social and Human Needs. Here the public official needs to deal with problems of inadequate services, high winter unemployment, the lack of training and vocational programs, integrating disparate groups into a harmonious community, and dealing with the special needs of senior citizens and youth.

Drug Abuse. It is becoming increasingly necessary for cities to develop effective drug abuse programs and to learn to experiment with preventive measures within the community.

ORGANIZATIONAL PROBLEMS

Organizational problems and the training required to deal with them include the following:

Labor Relations. The growing power of public service employee organizations suggests an obvious need for greater knowledge and skill on the part of city management in labor relations.

Police. In addition to concern over rising crime rates and the slow-moving criminal justice process, the work of the police should be coordinated with other city functions and with the needs of the community. Clashes between certain segments of the community and the police need to be examined and understood.

Water and Public Works. This field points

up the need for more knowledge of and skill in handling sewer plant operations and storm drainage; environmental agents; and funding for ecological problems. Attention also must be directed to safety and health standards.

PERSONNEL PROBLEMS

The wide range of municipal personnel problems identified in the NTDS study suggests a continuing need for training and problem solving. Areas in the greatest need of training are employee motivation; upgrading competence in semi-skilled positions; training in middle management; resolution of the union-civil service conflict; equal pay for equal work; recruitment of high-quality managers; salary upgrading in certain classes; personnel classification; orientation of new employees; retention of quality personnel in smaller cities; and interdepartmental cooperation.

Staff–Community Relations. Municipalities need to sensitize their employees to youth problems, marshal support from outside agencies, increase expertise in handling social problems, improve public relations, deal better with minority problems, and increase the opportunities for citizen participation.

Staff–Council Relations. Both the staff and the city council need to learn to communicate with each other, with particular attention paid to developing an understanding of each other's roles. New council members not only need to be oriented and trained in their jobs but they also need to learn more about municipal operations.

Communications. A perennial need in most organizations is the improvement of communications. Training in this art should be conducted on a continuing basis.

Work Operations. Municipal staff must have a means of keeping in touch with the needs of the community. Staff expertise in dealing with environmental problems such as noise and air pollution are also needed. There are many organizational problems which suggest the need for new and innovative methods. Each person should have training for his or her particular job, and municipal employees at every level should perform in accordance with a work-oriented training plan.

Decision Making and Policy Making. Managers and council members need assistance in dealing with council splits, legal constraints, and attempts to overregulate. And, of course, policy-making abilities can always be improved.

Training Policies and Plans

Some municipalities have found it useful to develop training policies which deal with matters such as agency responsibilities for training, release time, and tuition remission. When doing this a city council has an opportunity to set forth its expectations about the quality of performance and about the continuing obligation of department heads for the growth of employees.

Rarely do managers stop to compute the time taken to train employees. One can presume, however, that the less a particular training effort is planned, the more time that must be spent in training. If complex tasks are scheduled or if corrective action must be taken frequently because of unexpected happenings or inept execution, then training time will be indeed great. Managers who may not have actually designed or conducted a training program nevertheless will often spend hours issuing instructions and taking follow-up corrective action. This suggests that employers should understand that planned training usually saves more time than improvised training. Still, training does take time. Some jurisdictions have adopted a policy of setting aside as much as three percent or more of employee time for training and development.[29]

More and more cities are providing full-time tuition for after-hours schooling, and some are providing both time and tuition for course work performed in a master's program. Such policies recognize that training is valuable not only as a means of improving public services but also as an opportunity to further one's education. Such action-oriented training is a legitimate fringe benefit which encourages the employee to consider seriously a lifetime career in government. When action training becomes better understood for its wide application and variability, more administrators will recognize that such educational policies benefit not only the employee but the department and the community as well.

Although examination of the practices of municipalities in this country reveals a surprising lack of training plans, there are some general characteristics of the better plans that do exist which are worth noting. Here are some guidelines which may prove useful in developing a training plan:

1. The training plan should apply to both the individual and the organization.
2. The plan also should provide for the use of action training and research methods to study the environment, determine desirable new directions, and solve organizational and community problems.
3. Citizen participation in particular is amenable to normative-reeducative strategies of change, and therefore training plans should include contact and exchange with various segments of the community as much as possible.
4. The plan should include a statement outlining the range of skills and knowledge required for each level of every job category, coupled with suggestions of the training resources which will help employees gain those skills and knowledge.
5. Employees should develop individual training plans which compare their current skills and knowledge with that expected at the desired level. This plan also should list the steps necessary to close the skills-knowledge gap revealed by the analysis.
6. Employees should be given the opportunity to design learning plans to meet their own unique needs. Individual plans may exceed the type of development reflected in job-focused fact sheets. Employees should manage their own learning and even draw up a learning contract with their organization.
7. Similar plans should also be drawn for the continuing development of supervisors and managers. For example, most managers need indepth knowledge of the legal, political, economic, and technological processes related to the activities of municipal government. Accordingly, they need to understand the basics of budgeting, revenue and taxation, the consequences of growth, and motivation and organization theories, to name just a few areas. Here, too, the manager development plan should plot the difference between the manager's current level of knowledge and skills and the desired level.
8. The plan should specify the nature and scope of job training for basic operations which are routine.
9. The plan should list courses and programs arranged to meet the needs expressed in the plan.
10. Every program introduction, policy announcement, or organizational change should be accompanied by an action training plan which calls for communication with and feedback from those who will be affected; development of knowledge and skills required to implement the change; and sufficient departmental participation in developing the plan to permit those who must implement the change to become committed to it.

Of course, the training plan and the resultant training activities all should be based on the community's perceived needs and problems and on its concrete opportunities and resources.

Trends in Training Methodology

Out of the experience accumulated in training both civilians and members of the armed forces to meet the formidable challenges of World War II there emerged a wealth of "how-to-do-it" techniques that had proved highly effective in developing manual and clerical skills. One of the most useful of these techniques was "job instruction training," based on four steps: showing, telling, practicing, and evaluating. Standard practice manuals were devised to inform incumbents of the various requirements of each job and to instruct them in "how to do it." Job instruction training and standard practice manuals have continued to be useful to persons performing routine tasks.

Training first-line supervisors in supervisory practices has been conducted in many municipalities by an in-service training staff working with packaged programs or in cooperation with local community colleges. Since the end of World War II the nature of the work force has changed and the environment of the city has grown more complex, and consequently the need has arisen for training which reaches beyond the technical level found in universities, in on-the-job training, and in basic supervisory courses. Much of the emerging training methodology is oriented toward interpersonal relations. It is not suggested that these new methodologies supplant the established approaches to training and development but rather supplement basic training and instruction.

ACTION TRAINING AND RESEARCH

Traditional training attempts to convey general skills and knowledge that will help the participant become a better manager, a more knowledgeable budget officer, a faster reader, or an improved letter writer. The concept of action training is more specific: Action training is designed to develop within a given time period the particular skills and knowledge needed to execute a particular task or tasks. It is used when management needs to move new policies or programs from concept to reality. The action training process requires

(1) Focusing on objectives;
(2) Developing an understanding of the context in which the proposed action is to take place;
(3) Either overcoming the resistance to the proposed action by developing an understanding of the change itself and the reasons behind the change, or eliminating or modifying the proposed action;
(4) Helping persons who have implementation responsibility to acquire needed knowledge and skills to be effective in the implementation process.[30]

Action research is a procedure that is diagnostic and involves as participants those persons who will be affected by the outcome. It is occasionally, but not always, empirical; it is experimental, and, as a result of its conscious problem-solving purpose, it leads to commitment and responsible action. Essentially, action research is a method for determining the environment of an organization or community and then defining the problems and opportunities that exist. Action research is a normative-reeducative approach to change which operates on the theory that people learn and change by assisting in collecting data, defining a problem, and experimenting with possible solutions.

For example, if it is found that the level of tension in the organization is sufficient to cause management's notice, research is conducted to examine the restraining and the driving forces, and then action options are developed to reinforce the driving forces and mitigate the restraining ones. Furthermore, tentative actions for a limited time are taken to test possible solutions. If the experiments are successful, a program of change is designed to which the organization can commit itself. Participants acquire through training the knowledge and skills needed to carry out the change.

Action training is a necessary accompaniment to action research, because it is through training that participants gain acceptance and understanding. Action training is also an administrative strategy that, when competently applied, may be ranked in importance with the budgeting and personnel processes as an implementation strategy. Many of the training and data collection methods used in action training and research are used also in organization development.

Some specific examples of action training and research may assist in understanding the scope and power of this approach. Newark's mayor Kenneth Gibson, facing seemingly insurmountable problems in a strife-torn city in the late 1960s, authorized an action training and research effort known as "Mission Possible" to mobilize the support of employees for new efforts in implementing city programs. Subsequently, through the city's Policy and Development Office, action training and research methods were used in another project for developing urban homesteading as a means of improving community housing.

In Sioux Falls, South Dakota, the Center for Community Organization and Area Development continues to utilize the action training and research model to help the community cope with changes necessitated in dealing with such diverse problems as developing water systems, securing a new hospital, or providing housing for the aging. The work of the center has resulted in the construction of an effective community development network composed of 200 small communities comprising a total population of more than 250,000.

This model engages members of the communities to work as part-time enablers. "These are men and women living in the communities who devote eight hours a week *enabling* the community to identify its needs and to achieve them. Enablers are housewives, farmers, teachers, clergymen, retirees, social workers, bankers, etc."[31] The enablers engage the wider community. According to E. Delano Lind:

The people own what happens in the community, even when public agencies deliver services. When it's all done, citizens proudly declare, *This is our project.*

It increases willingness to take risks.

Action research organizes around tasks, not personalities.

It produces an openness to dialogue, enabling citizens to utilize individual differences instead of fearing and resisting them.

It moves the process away from the walling off of the expression of feelings toward making possible both appropriate expression and effective use of them.

It ensures that those affected by the decision will have a part in making it.

Team-building produces a new sense of cohesiveness among management, enablers, citizens, and agency personnel.

No longer is communication one-way; there is a horizontal flow of information among the various community segments and a sharing of community responsibility. The possibility of distorted communication is lowered. It does not avoid facing others with relevant data, but is open to appropriate confrontation.

Control passes from the few to the many. Emphasis shifts from competition toward collaboration.

Goal-setting is not seen as the sole responsibility of the management team, but as jointly planned effort giving citizens a major part in shaping their goals and evaluating results.

Action research takes seriously people's needs, the threats and rewards, the attitudes, values, responsibilities, and satisfactions in working toward shared goals. It is built upon and fanned by the idea that there is in any population a tremendous amount of undiscovered inventiveness and creative thinking. Action research brings out these hidden qualities.

Action research establishes an atmosphere of participant commitment and involvement, continuously drawn upon and further developed as the process proceeds.

Above all, action research and training ensures that changes will come not by default but by design.[32]

Grand Junction, Colorado, offered itself as an experimental city to two NTDS summer training and development seminars. The researchers and NTDS participants in training planned, prepared, and administered a survey which presented to the city a list of employee needs and desires along with a list of action options to help the city solve some of the problems identified. In the second seminar, the participants surveyed members of the community for their needs and desires. In both cases, the council listened, took action, and continues to communicate with both these groups.

The League of California Cities produced an "Action Plan for California Cities," a model of a well-designed action training and research plan. In the program, 411 California cities addressed themselves to the following purposes:

To direct attention to the most significant issues likely to face cities in the next 20 years,

To gain organizational consensus about the critical choices necessary to achieve a satisfactory future of the cities; to achieve spirited citizen participation and provide greater leadership possibilities,

To attract attention of the outside world to the priorities of the cities and,

To make the voice of the League more effective at the state capitol.[33]

In its action plan the California league asked mayors and council members, city managers, attorneys, planners, and other city officials to participate in action research processes directed toward making the critical choices necessary for shaping the future of local government. Clark Goeker, describing the process in a *Public Management* article, wrote:

Thousands of city officials, both elected and administrative, have spent innumerable hours, working on the Action Plan. Central to this approach has been the notion that people who are to take action must be involved in the research process from the very beginning. Not only will they more keenly realize the need for the particular action program finally decided upon, but their *ownership* of the plan is brought into the implementation phase.[34]

The action plan addressed four priority areas: environmental control and land use; social responsibilities of cities; achieving an adequate and reliable revenue base; and public service employer-employee relations. Consideration of governmental structure was a part of all four areas of inquiry. As a first educational step some of the participants prepared a handbook summarizing existing league policies relating to the four areas and prepared issue papers suggesting some possible alternatives to action. Then the League of California Cities' thirteen divisions and nine functional departments (representing mayors, city managers, city council members, attorneys, finance officials, city clerks, police chiefs, public works officers, and park and recreation officials) worked on the plan for a year. During that time the league worked diligently to broaden its leadership base and to support emerging leadership.

The league integrated the action training process in its regular meetings. For example, at a departmental meeting more than 300 city managers and assistants heard keynote speakers discuss the four priority subjects. Later they met in workshops to debate the issues and make specific recommendations as to approach and solution. The departmental meeting concluded with a business session during which the recommendations to the action plan were adopted. After that meeting the action plan was considered by the league's board. Then, along with the board's resolutions, the plan was submitted to all cities for review and comment. The league's general assembly adopted the action plan with only a few clarifying amendments.

As of early 1976, efforts are being made to implement the plan. A task force of mayors and council members is working to achieve legislative authorization of the plan. Other implementation strategies employed include consolidating the league's relationships with universities and expanding workshops and institutes. The league continues the search for solutions to the problems of environmental quality and land use authority and continues to give attention to subjects such as the social responsibilities of cities, public service employer-employee relations, and the achievement of an equitable revenue base. All these efforts foster participation, generate ideas, nourish a public conscience that supports action, and renew the feeling of commitment to an ever-evolving action plan.

With the aid of an IPA grant, the League of Kansas Municipalities, in conjunction with several private colleges, state universities, community colleges, and the state education commission, established its Action Training Center, whose program emphasizes training and development in internal management strategies. This unit's objectives are:

1. Building a continuing commitment to training and organization development by state and local governments;
2. Identifying and developing resources for public service training, particularly within higher education institutions;
3. Developing a public service training system which reflects overall needs combined with overall resources;
4. Marketing of 'package' training activities throughout the state and local governments.[35]

ORGANIZATION DEVELOPMENT

Organization development is "a complex educational strategy intended to change beliefs, attitudes, values, and structures so that they can better adapt to new technologies and challenges."[36] Although several intervention strategies are used by organization development practitioners, the most common one is a group approach. In this approach, a consultant, whether from inside or outside the organization, acts as facilitator for the group. The consultant/facilitator sets in motion a process intended to stimulate and bring about the changes which the group itself perceives sees to be desirable.

Many organizations use an approach called

"team building" in which the work team meets to examine and solve both work-oriented problems and personal problems arising within the work team. In addition to team building, organization development features processes that provide data feedback to the client group about their organizational performance. In these processes the participants are assisted in bringing to the surface and dealing with the conflicts that may be impeding team effort.

Organization development methods all involve intervention in the system in order to generate data relating to the problems under examination, to feed these data back to the relevant decision makers, and, finally, to aid in planning the actions to be taken. Organization development is a collaborative effort between the client group and a change agent. The normative goals usually sought are increased interpersonal competence, awareness and reduction of group tensions, better communication, a higher level of trust, and more effective team management.

Both the theory and practice of action training and research and of organization development have evolved along parallel lines. The sociotechnical systems approach to organization improvement and change uses many of the same training and development approaches employed by these two practices.

SOCIOTECHNICAL SYSTEMS

The sociotechnical systems approach employs action training and research as well as organization development strategies to produce an environment that is compatible with both the social and the technical needs of the organization's staff. The methodology of the approach is based on the premise that the following psychological requirements, present in most types of work, should serve as the basis from which jobs are developed out of tasks:

1. The content of the position's duties should be reasonably demanding of the employee's capabilities.
2. The job should allow the employee to learn and to continue learning on the job (but demanding neither too much or too little learning).
3. Some measure of decision making should attach to the employee.

4. The job should provide social support and recognition in the work place.
5. The employee should be able to relate what is done at work to the social processes of life.
6. The employee should feel that the particular job leads to a desirable future.[37]

Sociotechnical systems approaches are designed to help client institutions induce changes in their environment by their own efforts and become sensitive to those environmental changes which take place independent of their efforts.[38]

MANAGEMENT BY OBJECTIVES

Management by objectives, closely related to the sociotechnical systems approach, is chiefly thought of as a systems concept rather than as a training procedure. However, the method includes both a systems and an action training component. It seeks to elicit the participation of the employee in determining and accepting responsibility for his or her work unit within the legal constraints and objectives of the organization, while also receiving the rewards flowing from this participation.

The basic concepts embodied in management by objectives can be summarized as follows:

1. The objectives (explicit results expected to be accomplished) are diverse and multi-dimensional.
2. To be useful, the objectives must be understood by the persons designated to carry them out.
3. Objectives that are developed by persons who are to achieve them are likely to be more acceptable and have greater utility than those developed for them by management.
4. Organizations must take cognizance of an individual's goals and objectives so that *integration* of those goals and objectives supplants their *differentiation*.
5. Statements of objectives are of little use unless they enable the organization to determine whether or not the desired results have been achieved in the time specified. When objectives are so conceived, they may be considered to be operating objectives.
6. Operating objectives are inadequate if they do not include a means for measuring progress toward the achievement of results.
7. Objectives should meet the needs of individuals and organizations for both immediate and deferred gratification, if possible, but in any case, the former should not supersede the latter.

8. Individual responsibility for achievement of objectives should be a matter of specific understanding.[39]

Once the objectives have been accomplished, the organization's resources should be reoriented and regrouped toward achievement of other organizational and individual objectives which in turn express a desire for ethical, psychological, social, and material improvements.[40]

TRANSACTIONAL ANALYSIS AND GESTALT GROUP

Transactional analysis is another methodology which involves groups and the group process. It is a symbolic and abstract means of analyzing human behavior and interaction. Practitioners of transactional analysis, or T.A., have attempted to find a new language of psychology which in their view moves closer to the secret of human behavior. Transactional analysis is employed by a number of organizations as a development vehicle.

Another type of group training that has become more commonly used is Gestalt group. Frederick Perls, developer of this approach, was profoundly influenced by the German Gestalt school of psychology and thus chose the term for his groups. Gestalt groups are composed of five to eight participants who often meet weekly. Gestaltists point out that, although they are in firm control of procedure and interaction, their stance is not authoritarian, because they do not tell participants what to do.

The Gestaltist's basic concern is with the totality of human functioning. They are convinced that their taste is to make life livable. Their process entails recognition that one's finiteness leads to anxiety; their aim is not to eliminate anxiety but to accept it as part of the nature of things. The Gestalt approach is a "prepared quest for authenticity."[41] Gestalt groups are intensely personal, in contrast to the more impersonal development approach that characterizes instrumented learning.

INSTRUMENTED LEARNING

Instrumented learning is a term applied to a training and development process in which the trainers use carefully designed instruments to provide feedback to group participants and to generate data for discussions and growth. One of the best known of the instrumented approaches is the Managerial Grid. Robert Blake and Jane Mouton describe the grid as a process of self-assessment to reveal managerial aptitude. The grid touches on decisions, convictions, conflicts, emotions, efforts, and even humor. Participants complete an instrument which is scored according to concern for production or concern for people. From the data gathered, trainers provide a leadership profile which indicates each participant's management style.

GROUP LEADERSHIP METHODS

A wide variety of group leadership methods are used in staff meetings, action training and research projects, management by objectives training, and in the practice of organizational development. Some of the better known of these methods are discussed here.

Problem-Solving Sessions. The session leader provides the structural framework, the team members provide the input. This method involves gathering facts, developing action options, weighing alternatives, and making decisions. The problem-solving session is patterned on the scientific method; therefore, its effective use requires considerable training on the part of both the group and the leader.

Problem Census. This method elicits the ideas of group members and lists them without evaluation. Group members must make certain the ideas they suggest are recorded as they intended. When the list is complete, the ideas are reviewed briefly to clarify their meaning. If it is necessary to utilize the data for further action, the ideas may be assigned priorities by group members.

Brainstorming. This is a variation of the problem census but with a different purpose. Brainstorming focuses largely on innovative solutions rather than on delineating problems. In brainstorming, the group writes down the problems for which solutions are sought. Any idea is acceptable, even though it may sound silly. No evaluation of ideas is permitted, because the main goal is to generate them. Quality usually will improve after the first efforts.

FIGURE 7–1. *A relaxed, small group atmosphere is helpful to any training situation.*

Building on the contributions of others, referred to as "hitchhiking," is encouraged. Group members also are encouraged to think of "opposites" to the ideas that have already been suggested.

The Risk Technique. This approach is directed toward releasing the fears of group members. It is very useful when discussing subjects about which participants show hostility or a generally negative attitude. It is also helpful as a means of bringing out into the open latent objections to a program or policy. The approach is based on the assumption that open expression of fears is not defeating of the achievement of positive group goals, and that repression of feelings, fears, and resistance in a group acts as a barrier to effective group action.

In the risk approach, the problem is presented and the group is asked to identify the dangers or risks it involves. Each obstacle or risk is recorded, regardless of the group's feelings about it. When all fears have been expressed and examined, the group is asked: "Given the problems and objections to the program (or policy), what are possible ways in which it might be successfully introduced"?[42]

Subgrouping. The use of subgroups is particularly advantageous in large meetings where people either do not have sufficient opportunity to voice their views or are reluctant to speak out. Subgroups can be used as an icebreaker. A large group is divided into groups of two or three people to allow them to become acquainted with each other. Subgroups also are useful when it is appropriate to divide a large task into smaller tasks. Sometimes hostile or critical views are more freely expressed in subgroups. Sometimes the use of subgrouping breaks the monotony of lengthy meetings, permitting people to move around and interact with each other on a more familiar basis.

The Case Method. Christopher Langdell is credited as the innovator of the case method which was begun at the Harvard Law School in the 1880s. "This non-directive way of helping students to think for themselves slowly won acceptance in the study of law, medicine, business administration, and social work."[43]

Some cases used in training describe in complete detail a real situation and are based on long, careful research. The leader's role in this method is to assist students to sharpen their observation of the issues presented so as to better conceive possible solutions. On the other hand, cases may be only short vignettes which illustrate a point.

Simulations. Some simulations or games are very sophisticated and expensive. Others are simpler and may be devised to fit a unique training need. Some simulations are developed through extensive research. Many are computerized so that the person playing the game receives timely information on a developing situation and then can react to the information, feed the reaction back to the computer, and get results which indicate the degree of effectiveness of the decision taken. The advantage of computerized games over other methods is that they can incorporate operations research techniques. In the very near future computerized simulations will probably also incorporate predictive models, a development which should prove most helpful to the decision-making processes.

"In-basket" simulations, less sophisticated and less expensive than those described, are also useful. These consist of a series of documents that normally appear in the in-basket of a supervisor or manager. In a simulation exercise, participants are asked to act on these documents as if they actually were to materialize in their own in-baskets.

Role Playing. In the role playing situation participants are asked to assume the part of either real or imaginary persons and to carry on conversations and behave as if they were those individuals. Role playing provides an opportunity to learn by doing. In the process the individual learns, both intellectually and emotionally, about another's experience. Some trainers use videotape as a valuable adjunct to role playing enabling those engaged in the roles to get instant feedback on their performance.

Guided Discussion. The Socratic method of inquiry provides an excellent example of the possibilities of guided discussion. The task of the leader is to ask questions and to focus on issues in a manner that will lead to specific learning or conclusions. The method is best used when the leader is thoroughly familiar with the subject and when he or she has a mental plan of questioning which will help the student reach the desired goal.[44]

Free Discussion. In the free discussion, participants take the major responsibility for group action. An experienced group freely expresses attitudes and values; the role of the group leader is simply that of facilitator, who reduces his or her own psychological size to maintain a permissive climate while focusing the conflict, reflecting feeling, and clarifying the developing ideas.

Evaluation of Training Programs

Innovative and creative approaches to the conduct of training will continue to emerge. Obviously the method employed should be appropriate to the outcome desired. In evaluating training, it is necessary to determine whether the methods used have actually produced the desired learning. Although a great deal has been written about the evaluation of training, full and final evaluation cannot be made until operating units in public agencies are able to measure and evaluate their output in terms more explicit than is currently possible.

It is not reasonable to attempt to measure the impact of training on the operations of an organization that does not itself have measures of its output. The National Training and Development Service has made use of a case study approach which determines the "before and after" performance of training participants.

When participants demonstrate new skills and knowledge not previously employed, then it can be claimed that training has had an influence. Training programs that are based on the achievement of behavioral objectives can be evaluated in terms of the achievement or lack of achievement of those objectives. Achievement of training objectives may not be reflected immediately in the overall performance of the employing agency.

A common method of evaluation is to ask participants how they assess the usefulness of the programs to which they have been sent. A training office or training institute finds such data helpful, because a given program is not likely to prosper if the participants do not support it (even though a great deal can be learned from a training experience that was not enjoyable). An evaluation does not necessarily relate to the impact which training has on the performance of participants.

It seems likely that action training and research will be used increasingly in the future. Training as a strategy of program implementation appears to be gaining wider practice and acceptance. There is also some indication that universities will begin to accommodate the growing demand for mid-career training. Also, community colleges probably will play a major role in providing municipal employees with certain basic training. The major responsibility for training lies with the jurisdiction itself, however. It is local government management who must determine the need for training and then seek quality assistance from the available resources.

[1] National Training and Development Service, "Report to the Citizens of Park City." Washington, D.C., 1974. (Mimeographed.)

[2] Frederick W. Fisher, "Give a Damn about Continuing Adult Education," PUBLIC ADMINISTRATION REVIEW 33 (November/December 1973) : 496–497.

[3] Robert Chin and Kenneth D. Benne, "General Strategies for Effecting Changes in Human Systems," in TOMORROW'S ORGANIZATIONS: CHALLENGES AND STRATEGIES, eds. Jong S. Jung and William B. Storm (Glenview, Ill.: Scott, Foresman and Company, 1973) .

[4] Thomas W. Fletcher, "What is the Future for Our Cities and the City Manager?" PUBLIC ADMINISTRATION REVIEW 31 (January/February 1971) : 14–20.

[5] U.S., Civil Service Commission, "IPA Impact." Washington, D.C., 1974. (Mimeographed.)

[6] U.S., Civil Service Commission, Bureau of Intergovernmental Programs, INTERGOVERNMENTAL COOPERATION THROUGH IPA, report no. 152–12 (Washington, D.C.: U.S. Civil Service Commission, 1973) , p. 10.

[7] Ibid., p. 11.

[8] Ibid., pp. 24–25.

[9] Ibid., p. 10.

[10] Civil Service Commission, "IPA Impact," pp. 4–11.

[11] Civil Service Commission, INTERGOVERNMENTAL COOPERATION THROUGH IPA, p. 14.

[12] U.S., Civil Service Commission, THE IPA TITLE IV INTERGOVERNMENTAL ASSIGNMENT PROGRAM (Wash-

ington, D.C.: U.S. Civil Service Commission, 1973).

[13] U.S., Civil Service Commission, CATALOG OF FEDERAL DOMESTIC ASSISTANCE (Washington, D.C.: Government Printing Office).

[14] U.S., Civil Service Commission, Bureau of Intergovernmental Personnel Programs, Office of Technical Assistance, GUIDE TO PERSONNEL ASSISTANCE FOR STATE AND LOCAL GOVERNMENT INSTITUTIONS OF HIGHER EDUCATION (Washington, D.C.: Government Printing Office, 1972).

[15] National Training and Development Service, "Network News" (January 1974): 3.

[16] Council of State Governments, National Governors' Conference, National Association of Counties, National League of Cities, U.S. Conference of Mayors, International City Management Association, CONSENSUS AT COLLEGE PARK, report of a conference at the University of Maryland, College Park, Md., 20–22 May 1970.

[17] "Expanding Dimensions of Management Training," an interview with Thomas W. Fletcher, NATION'S CITIES 12 (January 1974): 35.

[18] National Training and Development Service, "NTDS and Municipal Government." Washington, D.C., 1974. (Mimeographed.)

[19] National Training and Development Service, REPORT AND RECOMMENDATIONS FOR THE CALIFORNIA MUNICIPAL TRAINING SERVICE (Washington, D.C.: National Training and Development Service, 1974).

[20] Donald J. Borut, "ICMA Training Programs," PUBLIC MANAGEMENT 56 (April 1974): 17–20.

[21] Quoted in Michael J. Murphy, "ICMA Small Cities Training Program," PUBLIC MANAGEMENT 56 (April 1974): 23.

[22] National League of Cities–U.S. Conference of Mayors, A PROFILE OF STATE MUNICIPAL LEAGUE PERSONNEL TECHNICAL ASSISTANCE PROGRAMS (Washington, D.C.: NLC–USCM, 1937).

[23] National League of Cities–U.S. Conference of Mayors, STATE MUNICIPAL LEAGUES IN THE INTERGOVERNMENTAL HUMAN RESOURCES SYSTEM (Washington, D.C.: NLC–USCM, 1973).

[24] Ibid., p. 50.

[25] Institute for Local Self-Government, CONTINUING EDUCATION FOR THE PUBLIC SERVICE (Berkeley, Calif.: Institute for Local Self-Government, 1971).

[26] Griffenhagen-Kroeger, Inc., "A Survey of In-Service Training Needs for California Local Government," in Institute for Local Self-Government, CONTINUING EDUCATION FOR THE PUBLIC SERVICE, p. 19.

[27] Institute for Local Self-Government, "Community College Programs for Public Service Occupations." Berkeley, Calif., n. d. (Mimeographed.)

[28] National Training and Development Service, REPORT AND RECOMMENDATIONS FOR THE CALIFORNIA MUNICIPAL TRAINING SERVICE.

[29] California State Personnel Board, "Annual Report of the Training Division." Sacramento, Calif., 1961. (Mimeographed).

[30] Neely Gardner, GROUP LEADERSHIP (Washington, D.C.: National Training and Development Service Press, 1974), p. 79.

[31] E. Delano Lind, "Building Community-wide Networks," PUBLIC MANAGEMENT 56 (April 1974): 15.

[32] Ibid., pp. 16.

[33] Clark Goeker, "Action Plan for the Future of California Cities," PUBLIC MANAGEMENT 56 (April 1974): 9.

[34] Ibid., p. 10.

[35] National League of Cities–U.S. Conference of Mayors, A PROFILE OF STATE MUNICIPAL LEAGUE PERSONNEL TECHNICAL ASSISTANCE PROGRAMS, pp. 27–28.

[36] Warren G. Bennis, ORGANIZATIONAL DEVELOPMENT: ITS NATURE, ORIGIN, AND PROSPECTS (Reading, Mass.: Addison-Wesley Publishing Co., 1969), p. 2.

[37] Emery and Einer Thorsrud, FORM AND CONTENT IN INDUSTRIAL DEMOCRACY (London: Tavestock Publications, Inc., 1969), p. 105.

[38] Eric Trist, "Systems Change," in DYNAMICS OF PLANNED CHANGE, eds. Warren G. Bennis, Kenneth Benne, and Robert Chin (New York: Holt, Rinehart and Winston, Inc., 1969).

[39] Peter Drucker, THE PRACTICE OF MANAGEMENT (New York: Harper and Row, Publishers, 1954) pp. 121–136.

[40] Neely Gardner, "Implementation: The Process of Change," paper presented at the Conference on Court Studies, Denver, Colorado, 9 May 1973.

[41] Abraham Levisky and James Simkin, "Gestalt Therapy," in NEW PERSPECTIVES ON ENCOUNTER GROUPS, eds. Lawrence M. Solomon and Betty Berzon (San Francisco: Jossey Bass, Inc., 1972), p. 15.

[42] R. F. Maier, PRINCIPLES OF HUMAN RELATIONS (New York: John Wiley & Sons, Inc., 1952), pp. 62–82.

[43] Paul Pigors, "The Case Method," in TRAINING AND DEVELOPMENT HANDBOOK, eds. Robert L. Craig and Lester Bitel (New York: McGraw-Hill Book Co., 1967), p. 174.

[44] Gardner, GROUP LEADERSHIP, p. 29.

8

Conditions of Employment

Of Equality . . . as if it harmed me, giving others the same chances and rights as myself . . . as if it were not indispensable to my own rights that others possess the same.

WALT WHITMAN

LEGISLATION GOVERNING public employment has become exceedingly complex and has been applied to a wide variety of terms and conditions of employment. Many directives exist to guide or limit administrators in their discretionary authority when making decisions bearing both on relations with their subordinates and on the selection of candidates for employment. Guidelines for employees likewise have been promulgated. Still other legislation pertains to the work environment and the conditions of health, safety, and welfare which government provides its employees in its various work locations and vehicles.

Implementation of these policies shapes the profile of a particular government as employer. It has much to do with determining how attractive government employment appears to potential candidates. It affects the degree of satisfaction that current employees derive from their work. It aids or frustrates management in its efforts to achieve the objectives of the organization. Whether at the national or local level, successful implementation of these employment policies in large part reflects and depends on the social and economic standards of the nation and the community.

Overview: Basic Influences

An essential part of any analysis of contemporary public employment policy is the identification of those constraints from outside as well as from within the organization that influence personnel decisions. Up until the mid-1970s, one scarcely needed to look further than the city's municipal code, management's policy memoranda, or possibly the rules and regulations of large departments such as public works and the police and fire departments to discover a city's policy governing most of the conditions of employment. Policy items were identified within the organization and policy statements were prepared in consultation with key administrators.

To a considerable degree, this process represented what organization theorists now characterize as a "closed decision-making system." By the decade of the 1970s, however, three influences arose that placed demands on the organization's decisions and actions regarding the conditions of employment. Two of these influences lie outside the organization, but all three influences interact and hence cannot be separated when discussing the personnel policy-making process.

FEDERAL AND STATE DIRECTIVES

Possibly the most complex influence is the web of national and state legislative and administrative directives that require the conformance of jurisdictions. Some of these directives are long-standing products of the traditional state-local relationship, and many have only slightly influenced local personnel policies and practices in the past. For example, state legislation providing for safety and health protection standards has been in force for several decades, but usually it applied to industrial plants rather than city governments. Local governments frequently were exempt and therefore permitted to determine their own standards. The general trend since the 1960s has been that the state will mandate policies and procedures to be observed by the local governments in areas such as employer-employee relations, employment practices, and conditions of employment.

Cities have long had to meet federal standards which were imposed as conditions for the receipt of categorical grants-in-aid, although most such standards related to expenditure procedures and program planning rather than to personnel policies. By contrast, Congressional legislation and presidential executive orders in the 1960s and 1970s have markedly expanded the federal influence over personnel matters at the local level. Federal legislation, together with supporting administrative directives and guidelines, is linked to federal grants applied through direct enforcement programs. Such legislation has had its impact on selection procedures, examinations, maximum hours, compensation, safety, and other personnel matters in local jurisdictions.

As part of the so-called "new federalism," states have been encouraged to adopt legislation paralleling the federal statutes, to establish enforcement mechanisms, and to assume responsibility in implementing both national and state policies with respect to both the public and private employment sectors. As a direct consequence of these developments, the number of federal and state agencies created to implement the policies has multiplied, producing an acute problem for local government administrators. Differences have arisen between federal agencies charged with implementing national policy, similar differences have appeared within state administrations, and complications have ensued in federal-state relations. All of these conditions, in addition to the growing demand for conformity with state and national programs, have introduced a large measure of uncertainty into local personnel administration.

COLLECTIVE BARGAINING

Collective bargaining, often mandated upon the local government by state legislation, introduces another influential constraint on local policy making governing the conditions of employment. Although public employee organizations tend to focus their efforts most heavily on bargaining about compensation, they attend also to other elements of the conditions of employment. For example, Jerry Wurf, president of the American Federation of State, County, and Municipal Employees (AFSCME), frequently has been quoted as saying that all subjects relating to public employment are bargainable.[1]

Whether or not public managers find this a realistic concept, many managers certainly recognize a need for consultation and the airing of views with employees prior to the establishment of standards and conditions of municipal employment. Regardless of the source of the demand or constraint, management needs to analyze clearly the local objectives underlying each policy or practice. In essence, the administrative function is a continuous process of negotiation, involving outside forces and groups as well as individuals and groups inside the organization.[2]

EMPLOYEE PARTICIPATION

The influence on personnel policy arising from within the organization lies in employee participation in the determination of a variety of conditions of employment. Responsive, responsible management will recognize this participation as an employee right and as valuable input that ultimately serves the interests of staff, management, and public alike. At the same time, management is reserved the right for sole determination of those conditions of employment the responsibility and implementation of which it believes cannot be formally shared. In this situation lies potential conflict, but potential also exists for an improved synthesis.

Traditional Conditions

The following is a discussion of the major conditions of employment and their establishment within the constantly changing context of these external and internal influences.

RESIDENCE REQUIREMENTS

Proponents of the merit principle long have contended with sound logic that a policy which limits employment solely to local residents restricts the number of qualified persons who could serve in government. Although the local labor market usually proves adequate in supplying unskilled workers and candidates for entry-level positions in many classes, a much larger market should be canvassed in the search for administrative, professional, and technical (APT) personnel. State and local laws imposing residence requirements are holdovers from an era when the level of skills required for most local government jobs was not high. As the percentage of positions requiring APT expertise has increased, many jurisdictions have rescinded or modified their earlier policies.[3]

However, some large jurisdictions have been put under continuous and formidable political pressure to confine their hiring to local residents and to promote to top administrative positions only from within the organization. Defense of this policy has been argued on the grounds that sufficient talent to fill all positions can be found within the metropolitan area and that local residents deserve and usually need the employment.

Critics contend that this parochial attitude is self-defeating. For example, in response to severe criticism of New York City's continuation of this practice, Mayor John Lindsay set the precedent of recruiting top budget and managerial personnel from the federal government and from other cities.[4]

Many cities which dropped their residence restrictions for entry-level slots or modified them for managerial and professional positions have established a different type of residence restriction on employees of certain classes, such as key executives and some public safety personnel. Employees holding these positions often are required to live sufficiently close to their places of employment so that they can respond to emergency calls within a reasonable period of time. The policy does not demand residence within the city limits or in a particular neighborhood.

Federal regulations implementing the Comprehensive Employment and Training Act (CETA) in 1973 have reintroduced local residence requirements for the employment of persons hired by local governments and compensated through that act's program. This particular policy has been defended on the basis that CETA was intended to provide emergency work relief for unemployed city residents. However, since federal aid is involved along with local funding, critics claim that the residence requirement unfairly protects a city's population from competition by newcomers to the city who seek employment.

Changing social attitudes and economic conditions have introduced new facets to the problem. Some cities have been accused of maintaining residence restrictions on municipal employment to prevent minorities from obtaining employment in the city work force. On the other hand, some cities which enjoy a high standard of living and have high property valuations are forced to recruit from neighboring areas in order to fill their work force requirements, notably for unskilled positions. Moreover, an increasing number of employees of central cities have relocated their residences in the suburbs in search of satisfactory living conditions for their families.

In reaction to this development, cities in several areas have been pressed politically to require newly hired employees to establish residence in the city within a specified time after they are placed on the payroll. Proponents of this policy support it on the grounds that municipal employees should identify with the city's political, social, and economic interests by participating in its affairs and paying a share of its taxes. Critics argue that this rule interferes with the employee's right to a preference in living environments and that the only requirements should be job-related, such as promptness in reporting for work and demonstration of competence on the job.

The California state supreme court in 1973 ruled that charter cities could establish this type of residence requirement, but the state's citizens later supported a constitutional amendment forbidding the practice. In 1975 the New York state legislature considered a law which would give cities the mandate to adopt the residence rule. While the policy does not prevent recruitment from an area greater than the metropolitan area, it does diminish the attraction of municipal employment for those persons who prefer to have some freedom of choice in selecting their place of residence.

CITIZENSHIP REQUIREMENT

From time to time some states have enacted legislation forbidding public agencies from employing aliens. Much of this legislation appears to have been in response to antipathies aroused during the period between the two major world wars and was initiated when the nation was sharply reducing the rate of immigration that earlier had populated the country. Some of the attitudes that motivated this legislation were similar to those which supported local residence requirements, i.e., the desire to reserve public jobs for local inhabitants.

Moreover, during the 1950s many individuals contended that employment of noncitizens in government positions constituted a threat to national security, although in actuality most jobs at the local level did not entail such risks. The time required for a bona fide resident alien to acquire full citizenship is a formidable barrier in seeking gainful, permanent employment. As manpower scarcities develop in certain occupations, such as hospital and health care work, legislation is revised in some cases to create exceptions.

In 1973 the U.S. Supreme Court ruled that a state law which flatly prohibited public agencies from employing aliens in the competitive civil service violated the first and the fourteenth amendments to the Constitution.[5] The Court considered such a statute to be overly broad, because it applied to all jobs, ranging from sanitation worker to the top administrator engaged in developing and implementing public policy. In the opinion of the Court, aliens could be barred from some jobs if doing so clearly was in the public interest; otherwise, a flat prohibition was unconstitutional.

VETERANS' PREFERENCE

The history of the veterans' preference policy in the United States is long and complicated. The policy varies in detail at the several levels of government as well as among jurisdictions. It was established after World War I, but many details were added during and after World War II. In general, its application to local government employment has been less complex and has extended less extreme forms of preference than its application to federal employment. Consequently, state legislation and city charter provisions establishing veterans' preference in local public employment have been less subject to controversy. Most discussions of the subject tend to deal with the principle of preference and center on the specifics of the Veterans' Preference Act of 1944, which applies to federal employment.

Two themes comprise the underlying philosophy on which most veterans' preference legislation has been based. First, public employment should be a continuing reward to those who served the country in the military during a war and, second, it should be used as well to help those returning from military service to adjust to civilian life. Those who challenge the policy find the first theme less convincing than the second, for a variety of reasons.

The reason most often cited relates to the great variance of hardship experienced by military personnel. For example, the person who served in a noncombat post, often alongside civilians, gains nearly the same preference rights as the person who experienced great hardship and danger in combat situations, and both gain preference rights over the person who served the nation in a civilian capacity. Others find the preference policy a gross discrimination against women and minorities, although considerable numbers of both categories have qualified since the 1960s. The U.S. Commission on Civil Rights pointed out the discriminatory aspects of the preference policy in its 1975 report to the President.

Many groups accept the second theme of the philosophy but advocate that a cutoff point be established in the application of preference. It has often been proposed that preference for appointment to government jobs be terminated five years after the veteran has returned to civilian life.[6] Other proposals go a step further and recommend that preference not be granted candidates for managerial or policy-setting positions, the rationale being that appointments to such key positions should be determined solely on the candidate's ability to perform the job well.

When competitive examinations are given, frequent practice is to add points to the veteran's earned score. In some instances, the law requires this bonus be added only if the veteran has attained an earned score above the cutoff set for a particular examination.

Equal Employment Opportunity (EEO)

Achieving fair treatment of members of minority groups by overcoming both discrimination in hiring as well as underutilization and discrimination on the job has been a major concern of many persons and groups since the 1930s. Beginning with the 1960s the same concern was activated regarding women in public employment. National policy now requires the implementation of affirmative action programs to change procedures and attitudes in order to redress the effects and patterns of past discrimination. The objective of these policies is to make the principle of equal opportunity in employment a reality. The focus of EEO legislation was originally directed solely toward the private sector but in 1972 was extended to include state and local governments as well.

Local government employers have operated for many years under statutory, constitutional, charter, and merit system directives that prohibit discrimination in employment on the basis of political views, race, national origin, or religious belief. Since the early 1960s, some of the merit system agencies themselves have been pressed to reexamine their procedures and practices to determine if they actually are meeting the spirit as well as the letter of these directives.[7] According to a summarization of the National Civil Service League:

It has become apparent to many government employers that merely enforcing a policy of 'nondiscrimination' does not result in instant equal job opportunity for all persons. Old attitudes and methods need review and revision. The effects of generations of discrimination and underutilization of minorities and women by many public and private employers still exist. Many minorities and women are locked in 'dead-end' jobs. Some minority group persons, disadvantaged by an inferior educational system in some sections of the country, lack the necessary skills and training to perform well paying public jobs. Many other minorities are fully qualified for public employment, but are blocked by artificial civil service barriers such as nonjob-related written tests, arbitrary educational requirements and unvalidated background examinations.[8]

States began passing EEO legislation for minorities in the 1950s, and at the same time state commissions on fair employment practices or human relations were created. The attention of these agencies was first directed toward industry and private contractors doing business with state and local governments, but later amendments to the legislation in many states brought local governments under their jurisdiction.

Federal Statutes

The federal government began legislating equal opportunity and affirmative action for local public housing and urban renewal agencies in 1950.[9] EEO requirements were included in federal contracts providing financial assistance administered by the Department of Housing and Urban Development. Most of the local agencies receiving such assistance were separate from city government and operated their own personnel programs.

Title VII of the Civil Rights Act. A number of local governments already had begun to review their records on the employment of women and minority groups even before Congress prohibited race or sex discrimination by private employers through enactment of Title VII of the Civil Rights Act of 1964. For example, the Berkeley, California, personnel department in 1961 conducted a study of the racial identity of its city employees, followed by a study of minority certification and appointment and a study of minority employment in its police and fire departments.[10] The department concluded that education and height and weight requirements constituted its most difficult set of problems in the recruitment of minorities for the police and fire departments; subsequently these criteria were revised.

In addition, the department initiated special recruitment efforts among minorities and analyzed the examinations given candidates for the fire department. Finally, personnel staff members surveyed the minority community and other groups for their perceptions of the city's employment of minorities in the fire and police departments. The findings of the survey then served as both a base for making policy decisions and a guide to communication efforts directed toward modifying these perceptions.

Shortly after passage of the Civil Rights Act, the U.S. Commission on Civil Rights studied the employment practices of the states and 628 local governments located in seven standard metropolitan statistical areas (SMSAs), namely, San Francisco-Oakland, Philadelphia, Detroit, Atlanta, Houston, Memphis, and Baton Rouge.[11] The commission found that members of minority groups were most likely to hold white-collar jobs in health and welfare—the so-called "traditional" job area for black Americans—and were least likely to hold such positions in financial administration and general control units. Indeed, new jobs carrying major responsibilites, high status, and good salaries had been developed and were held by minority group members, but these jobs were related exclusively to minority group problems.

Nevertheless, the commission found employment of blacks to be significantly higher in state and local governments than in private industry.[12] About 50 percent of the blacks working in these governments were employed by large central cities; another 25 percent were distributed among suburban cities and special districts. In each city surveyed, police and fire departments made the poorest showing of minority employment, with firefighting units having even fewer minorities in their ranks than

police units. The majority of black employees was found in the laborer and general service worker categories. As to Spanish-surnamed Americans, their employment patterns tend to vary between areas. The commission concluded that this minority group has more options available to them than blacks but substantially fewer than other whites.[13]

The commission concluded that the failure to hire minority workers stemmed from a variety of causes, such as lack of systematic recruiting efforts directed toward these groups, the use of long and needlessly difficult screening processes, and the minority communities' abiding distrust of government.[14] It had found that members of minority groups were less likely to succeed than other persons in the testing process. Many members of minority groups interviewed felt that widely used written tests had not been validated and did not measure job performance. Moreover, the reference to arrest and conviction records in public employment selection affects minority group members more adversely than it does others.

The survey data also showed that the proportion of promoted employees was about equal between the majority group and Asian-Americans, but that the number of Spanish-surnamed Americans promoted was considerably lower, and the number of blacks promoted was lowest of all. The commission concluded that:

Not only do state and local governments consciously and overtly discriminate in hiring and promoting minority group members, but they do not foster positive programs to deal with discriminatory treatment on the job. . . . Rarely do [they] perceive the need for affirmative programs to recruit and upgrade minority group members for jobs in which they are inadequately represented. . . . While civil service merit systems generally have broadened the opportunity for public service, they alone do not guarantee equal opportunity and equal treatment for minority group members.[15]

The Equal Opportunity Act. This 1972 amendment made Title VII of the Civil Rights Act of 1964 applicable to state and local governments. Affirmative action was declared a national goal, to be implemented according to guidelines and enforcement procedures established by the U.S. Equal Employment Opportunity Commission (EEOC) and the Department of Justice. Both bodies are authorized to act on employee complaints of sex or race discrimination and to initiate action to ensure compliance. The EEOC first seeks to secure voluntary settlement or compliance through conciliation and mediation procedures. If these procedures fail, the EEOC refers the case to the Attorney General who takes court against the state or local government employer.

The EEOC is authorized to review and act on a complaint made directly to it, although it is directed first to give the state or local agency an opportunity to handle a complaint filed under Title VII and falling within its jurisdiction. In an attempt to coordinate investigation and enforcement actions of federal and state agencies, the EEOC on July 1, 1974, published regulations in the Code of Federal Regulations and granted deferral status to certain state and local bodies to administer the federal law.[16] Moreover, the EEOC requires these bodies to submit copies of their rules and regulations so that it can determine if they are complying with all specifications of Title VII and have discontinued all prohibited practices.

Critics of this procedure point out that in a disproportionately large number of cases the state agencies pass the complaints back to the EEOC, thus further delaying corrective action. Consequently, there is a huge backlog of complaints filed with both state and local agencies and with the EEOC that has little chance of speedy resolution.

Grant Administration. Several statutes in addition to the Civil Rights Act and various executive orders require the U.S. Civil Service Commission and the Office of Federal Contract Compliance in the Department of Labor to work with state and local governments to obtain compliance with federal guidelines for personnel administration. Federal guidelines for the merit system of personnel administration were established originally in 1939 to cover five grant-in-aid programs administered by the Social Security Board and were extended subsequently by Congressional action to many other programs. It was estimated that in 1973 these standards applied to more than thirty grant programs involving approximately half the amount of the federal funds directed as aid to state and local governments.[17]

The Intergovernmental Personnel Act of 1970 (IPA) vested the administration of these standards in the U.S. Civil Service Commission. The advisory council established by the act recommended the application of six IPA merit principles to all federal grants which supported programs or projects of indefinite or long-term duration involving a substantial number of regular, permanent, paid employees.[18] In 1973 the commission, assisted by a task force composed of federal, state, and city personnel administrators, developed a set of guidelines for the evaluation of personnel operations.[19] In it was outlined a series of questions to be asked in evaluating the legal basis and policy commitment of local agencies to equal employment opportunity and affirmative action as well as to other aspects of personnel administration.

IMPLEMENTATION PROCEDURES
AND GUIDELINES

Differences in the interpretation of federal policy began occurring when the several agencies involved with protection of civil rights undertook the implementation of various directives issued to them. In March 1973 the EEOC, the departments of Justice and Labor, and the Civil Service Commission issued a joint statement declaring that the procedures they sought to apply in implementing affirmative action in employment entailed the setting of goals and timetables, which were to be used in measuring progress made by employing agencies in remedying past discrimination. In addition, the officials issuing the statement recommended that the federal courts be permitted to order an employer to make every "good faith effort" to meet specific goals and timetables if a pattern of discriminatory employment practices was found to exist.

Goals were to be defined in numerical terms and were determined with reference to both the expected number of vacancies and the number of qualified applicants available in the relevant job market. *No employer was to be required to employ a person who did not have the qualifications needed to perform the job successfully.* The only criteria to be used in judging an applicant's qualifications were those designed to measure his or her ability to do the job.

The memorandum concentrated on the validation of selection procedures, stating:

The selection procedure should be as objective and job related as possible, but until it has been shown to be valid for that specific purpose, it must be recognized that rank ordering does not necessarily indicate who will in fact do better on the job.

Five principles to guide action were specified and are summarized below:

1. Anticipated vacancies and availability of skills in the labor market are to be considered when setting goals and timetables.
2. Special recruiting and advertising should be directed toward those groups underrepresented in the work force, but selection should be from among those candidates who are qualified.
3. An employer is not to be asked to hire a specified number of persons, although a court should be asked to impose a numerical goal and timetable if it finds that an employer has engaged in racial or ethnic exclusion.
4. Persons who have been discriminated against should be restored to their positions, and applicants who have been excluded from consideration by discriminatory practices should be allowed to compete on the basis of standards no more difficult than those applied to advantaged groups.
5. Job related selection procedures are to be established and validated as rapidly as possible, recognizing that the procedures vary as to difficulty in achieving validation.[20]

The memorandum and guidelines elicited immediate response from a group of public associations which included the Council of State Governments, the International City Management Association (ICMA), the International Personnel Management Association, (IPMA), the National Association of Counties, the National Governors' Conference, the National League of Cities, the National Legislative Conference, and the U.S. Conference of Mayors.[21] This group affirmed its support of the concept that valid and job-related tests are fundamental to reaching fair hiring deci-

sions, but it protested that implementation of the guidelines would place an overly costly burden on local governments.

A central problem arose from the fact that the federal enforcement procedure recognized no distinction between merit system government agencies (many of which had initiated affirmative action plans) and those government units and private employers operating under non-merit systems. All employers alike were assigned the burden of proof of showing that their selection policies and procedures were fair and valid.

The public interest groups urged that jurisdictions operating under merit systems not be required to prove the validation of their tests until adverse impact had been demonstrated. Existing affirmative action plans should be recognized as commitment and as steps already taken toward achieving EEO goals. Furthermore, small jurisdictions also should be encouraged to develop and use employee selection systems through cooperation with other jurisdictions. The Civil Service Commission was urged to make its validated tests available for use by other agencies. Finally, the group claimed, content validity is the most practical and feasible validation method for use in the public sector and should be so acknowledged in the guidelines.

Further exchange of views took place between the task forces of the public interest associations and the federal agencies. For example, in 1974 in reaction to a federal staff draft of the uniform guidelines on employee selection procedures,[22] IPMA requested that federal agencies recognize the particular problems faced by and the limited resources available to small public jurisdictions in meeting the complex validation requirements proposed by the EEOC. Large cities also were confronted with the costly revision of procedures, and it was estimated that in several instances the average cost of a content validity study ranged between $4,000 and $6,000 per job class.[23] IPMA went on to request that a more objective definition be given to what is termed a "protected group" as it is used in the uniform guidelines. IPMA suggested that a more objective definition of minority status would reduce the potential for misapplication, evasion, or abuse of EEO practices and affirmative action goals.

The guidelines issued by the EEOC pertaining to the selection process hold that properly validated and standardized examinations are the proper means for arriving at selection decisions. Professionally developed tests are to be used in conjunction with other tools of personnel assessment, but they are complements to and must be based upon sound job design. The regulatory agency continues to maintain the position that the employer is obliged to demonstrate that the tests it uses are valid predictors of employee performance.[24] Moreover, a test which works a disparate effect against an entire class of persons protected by Title VII of the 1964 act will be considered discriminatory unless it has been validated or can be demonstrated to be a "bona fide occupational qualification" (BFOQ), such as restricting the job of wet nurse to women only. The guidelines establish several sets of minimum standards for validation.

The exchange between the Equal Employment Opportunity Coordinating Council and the public interest associations continues. The selection and use of specific enforcement actions and the precedents built up over time set by administrative and judicial decisions on employment discrimination cases will have great bearing on the success of EEO policy. Extensive work on the validation of professionally prepared tests has taken place, much of it assisted by funds provided under authority of the Intergovernmental Personnel Act. State leagues of cities, consortiums of small local governments, and state personnel agencies have done much to refine testing methods and standards and develop standardized test material.

Many agencies have reexamined their class descriptions to improve job design, eliminating those race or sex restrictions in class specifications which previously resulted in discrimination. Similarly, specifications in classification standards relating to promotion, as well as to the hierarchy of promotion classes, have been reviewed to determine their job-relatedness and reliability in predicting success on the job.

Much of the policy guiding government as well as private hiring and promotion practices in the 1970s has been shaped by the federal and state courts. Several significant cases were initiated by individuals or groups affected by discriminatory actions and were based on the civil rights acts of 1866 and 1871, with the Civil Rights Act of 1964 and the EEOC guidelines cited as background by the courts.

One of these cases, *Griggs v. Duke Power Company*, has had a significant impact on government practices.[25] In its decision the Supreme Court ruled that tests for employment must relate directly to job requirements. Although it recognized that tests are a legitimate part of the selection program, it held that educational requirements and educational diplomas and degrees which were not demonstrably related to the job could not be used as criteria of selection.

Another landmark case was *Carter v. Gallagher*, which dealt with hiring practices in a city fire department. The Court was presented statistical data which showed that over a 23-year period only six of twenty-four blacks who had taken the firefighter's examination had passed, and none of the six had received an appointment. The Court prohibited further use of the city's examination for fire personnel until it was validated in accordance with. EEOC standards and ordered the city to drop its requirement that applicants list their arrests. It did approve the requesting of information on convictions, but directed that the circumstances surrounding any conviction be considered carefully before the employment decision was made.

The Court also ordered the requirement of a high school diploma or GED certificate be discontinued as an entry-level firefighter qualification. Finally, the Court ordered the city to take affirmative action to remedy for past discrimination by setting a hiring quota in the recruitment of minorities.[26] An appellate court modified the last order, ruling that giving minority applicants an absolute preference in hiring was not legally warranted.

Nevertheless, the courts in a series of cases have recognized that the use of a mathemathical formula is a legitimate starting point for the shaping of a policy to overcome past discriminatory practices. In general, they have exercised wide discretion in fashioning a remedy for what they conclude to be a pattern of discriminatory actions.[27] One such pattern is the situation in which a police department assigns black officers only to black neighborhoods or to cases involving only blacks.[28]

Promotion practices also have been the subject of several suits. Promotion based primarily on seniority becomes a discriminatory policy when minorities have been hired so recently that none can qualify until several years have elapsed.[29] Some courts have ruled that a city could reduce seniority requirements for minorities if it were doing so to rectify a discriminatory situation, but they have frowned on the idea of a city creating additional promotional positions and reserving them solely for minority candidates.[30] On the other hand, another court has directed a city not to apply its affirmative action efforts toward promotion into the upper ranks of its fire department when doing so would result in giving minority candidates an absolute preference.[31]

Consent decrees entered into by a city and the Department of Justice under the jurisdiction of a federal district court have been used in several instances to initiate an affirmative action hiring program at the entry level in fire and police departments. These procedures have been negotiated usually after the court has ruled that the evidence, based on a statistical study of the numbers of minorities employed in the departments compared with their numbers in the city's population, indicated the existence of a pattern of discrimination.

As a result of these decrees city or departmental procedures are changed, usually according to a specific formula of preferential hiring enforced for a specific period of time for the purpose of correcting the documented imbalance. One example of this occurred in 1975 when Chicago agreed to hire 200 police officers, mostly minorities and women, to comply with a federal court order, the alternative being the withholding of revenue-sharing funds as a penalty for noncompliance. This action was based on requirements specified in federal legislation which provided aid for law enforcement programs.

Programs promoting equal employment opportunity for women in government have brought changes both in state legislation and in public personnel practices. Over the years states had passed legislation intended to protect women and juveniles in industry; many states also had introduced such protective legislation on behalf of women working in government. For example, women were not to be required to lift or carry objects exceeding certain weights as part of their job duties, nor were they to be required to work during certain hours or put in more than a specified number of hours per day or week. Some state regulations forbade a woman to return to work within a specified time after childbirth.

Opinion prevailing in the 1970s has held that protective laws, whether relating to employment or most other areas of life, in fact are discriminatory, because they apply to a general class of persons without regard to individual capabilities or preferences and because, in the final analysis, they may be more obstructive than protective.

EEOC guidelines, the regulations of state equal opportunity commissions, and court decisions have combined to bring about far-reaching changes in philosophy, policy, and practice, notably with respect to employment.[32] Differential treatment of employees based on sex is permissible only when a clearly sex-related distinction can be made, such as limiting the eligibility for the job of women's locker room attendant at a municipal swimming pool or other facility to female applicants. However, the same limitation cannot be supported in the case of the job of lifeguard.

In general, public merit system agencies have a better record than private sector employers in the establishment and implementation of formal policies relating to the employment of women. Classification and pay policies guarantee that men and women be paid equally for equal work in the same classification. Nevertheless, the equal opportunity component in personnel programs has made it necessary for merit system jurisdictions to review their class specifications for the artificial barriers of sex or race that have crept into them. For example, a classification still may be labeled "heavy duty," but women cannot be barred from applying for the jobs within that classification.

Police and fire department minimum requirements of height, weight, and strength have come under heavy challenge and most have been struck down on the grounds that they exceed realistic requirements for success on the job under modern conditions. Critics claim that these requirements work against most women and some minorities who otherwise might be well-qualified for jobs in these programs.

A principal theme appearing in many sex discrimination guidelines is that female applicants or employees must be regarded and treated as individuals rather than as members of a category or group. Traditional attitudes of society or the preferences of employees, supervisors, or clients are not acceptable bases for an employment policy that discriminates against women as a class.[33] Women are not to be denied employment on the basis of stereotyped comparative assumptions—whether favorable or unfavorable—long held about women as a class, such as their alleged greater capacity for assembling intricate equipment and performing detailed work or their supposedly higher rate of job turnover.

Several important changes have occurred in employment rules and practices with respect to pregnant women employees. Some public agencies at one time required pregnant female employees, particularly those in supervisory or executive positions, to resign rather than be granted maternity leave. The reasoning behind the policy was that this type of position required continuity of incumbency, and therefore the employee could not claim a right to return to her job after being absent for several months.

The EEOC statement that pregnancy shall be considered a condition comparable to illness and shall not necessitate loss of rights and benefits of the job has been resisted in some jurisdictions, with differences being resolved slowly. In the 1970s the trend in pregnancy policy was to permit women, with physician approval, to remain longer on the job before taking maternity leave and to return sooner after giving birth than previously was customary.

In general, the emerging principle being applied was that pregnancy leave and disability should be decided on an individual basis, taking into account medical counsel, job requirements, and individual personal preference. This policy has replaced regulations which compelled women to leave the job no later than the sixth month of pregnancy and forbade them to return to the job earlier than one full year after the birth of the child.

One of the most controversial areas of employment, and one which has seen numerous charges of sex discrimination filed with the EEOC and other agencies, is promotion or selection for supervisory and administrative positions. For many years most female professional or technical employees were found in welfare or health programs, and within these programs most were confined to jobs relating to women or children. The increase in the number of women educated and trained in a broad variety of fields has resulted in greater numbers employed in legal, law enforcement, engineering, and personnel programs at the local government level.

As the number of women in professional and technical positions has increased, the percentage of women in higher-salaried posts has risen. Despite these changes, however, the number and percentage of women appointed to supervisory positions remains small. Indeed, some women have become personnel directors and several hold executive positions in public health and hospital programs. In 1975 one California city chose a woman as its chief of police. But the numbers of such examples remain relatively small.

This state of things very likely will change in the near future. In short, as more women acquire the requisite education, training, and experience, management will come under ever growing pressure from women's organizations, staff groups, EEO commissions, and individual women themselves to promote qualified women to supervisory and administrative positions—positions of responsibility, higher pay, and power. The resulting keener competition among the best qualified of both sexes for top jobs will be in keeping with the principles of the merit system and is bound to improve the quality of public services.

Other Elements

LAYOFF AND REDUCTION IN FORCE

Over the span of an entire generation (1947–1974), local governments in the United States grew accustomed to dealing with expanding work forces. Reductions in force and, hence, layoffs were rare and generally were confined to a single department or program. The relatively few layoffs resulted mainly from changes or occasional reorganizations in programs, and, therefore, employees threatened with layoff often could be transferred across unit lines and be absorbed in the same classification elsewhere. Occasionally a reorganization required the retraining of a group of employees whose jobs had become redundant, enabling them to fit into other slots in the work structure. The merit system concept strongly implies that a satisfactory worker should be kept on in the work force whenever possible and should not be displaced by a new employee unless the quality of job performance has deteriorated to the point that dismissal is required.

In general, public employment policy is tending to be more responsive to employee preferences and attitudes. Strict interpretation of the merit system theory would dictate that in any layoff of employees made necessary because of lack of work or funds for a particular classification, the less meritorious performers should be separated out first. This application of the theory has seldom occurred because of the difficulties in constructing and administering objective ratings of performance.

Layoff customarily has been based on seniority in the affected class of positions—a policy generally advocated strongly by public employee unions. This practice also was acceptable to administrators, because it provided an objective method of deciding the layoff problem, although it did nothing to assure that the most dependable or competent employees in a class were to be retained. As a consequence, the policy resulted in the last person hired being the first laid off when a reduction in force became necessary.

Reinstatement or reemployment policies were designed to complement the layoff policy. Most merit system programs have established an order of reemployment that is inverse to layoffs—that is, as vacancies or new positions appear, the more senior workers are to be rehired prior to those more junior.

In the mid-1970s many municipalities faced substantial financial problems which necessitated drastic reductions in their work forces. National inflation, sharply rising costs of energy-dependent goods, taxpayer resistance to rate increases, and many other conditions produced budgetary problems which in turn led to the layoff of large percentages of city employees in an effort to balance the municipal budget. Layoff rules that had existed for many years were invoked, the major difference being that a larger number of employees were affected than in any previous year.

The complicating factor in this particular case stemmed from the fact that these relatively large layoffs followed closely upon the introduction of affirmative action programs which had resulted in the hiring of greater numbers of women and minority group members to remedy their past discrimination. In other words, a considerable portion of the employees laid off were members of minority groups and women, since these persons had been hired most recently and therefore ranked low in the seniority system.

Charges that the established layoff policies were discriminatory and in conflict with the newer EEO laws were countered by the argument that abandonment of the seniority principle would constitute discrimination against the longer-term, and possibly more competent, employee. As larger numbers of employees became subject to potential layoff, the matter became a major item in collective bargaining. Some unions sought to obtain "no layoff" provisions in employment contracts, a concept in sharp conflict with management's decision-making authority.

The controversy as it shaped up during the mid-1970s called attention again to the fact that both the seniority policy and the policy protective of the employment rights of newly hired groups ignores the need of the organization to retain the most competent and meritorious employees. Both policies place the concept of individual rights and needs above the organization's need to achieve its mission of service to the public. However, until more progress is made toward establishing objective and fully operational measures of job performance, concepts based on perceptions of individual benefits are likely to prevail.

Transfer and Reassignment

Transfer and reassignment—lateral shifts of employees between jobs in the same classification and level of compensation—are frequently used personnel practices. In many cases either action involves a change in work location or a move from one work unit to another.

Transfers may be used as an employee development and training technique to provide broader experience and exposure; transfers may also open promotional opportunities for the employee. Occasionally transfers are used as a means of finding the proper niche for a qualified employee whose personality clashes with that of the supervisor or other workers. Transfers frequently are sought by employees themselves for personal reasons, often for transportation purposes. Employee-initiated transfers usually must be approved by both the releasing and receiving supervisors.

Although similar to a transfer, a reassignment ordinarily is initiated by management and may be contrary to the wishes of the employee involved. In some jurisdictions, reassignment is limited to a shift within the employee's work organization where his or her status is established. A decision to reassign an employee may be based on any one of several objectives. One is the desire to strengthen the competence of workers in certain classifications by rotating personnel to develop a breadth of work experience. Another is the desire to meet the fluctuating work load needs of different administrative subunits.

Reassignment often occurs for disciplinary reasons or in an effort to resolve tensions arising either from employee-community, employee-staff, or employee-supervisor relations. The latter situation is publicized more often and thus has become the presumed reason for a reassignment. Basically, the authority to reassign employees within a classification and pay structure is fundamental to the exercise of management rights.

Hours of Work

Personnel administration is heavily involved with the matter of the hours public employees put into their jobs, although much of basic policy is determined by statutes, central administrative directives, and negotiated contracts. Inasmuch as a major local government function is the provision of services direct to citizens, the schedule of hours worked must be geared to the public's convenience as much as possible.

For example, city offices issuing licenses or permits must be staffed during hours when people can most easily reach city hall or its subcenters. The provision of police and fire protection or rescue and ambulance services at all hours of the day necessitates the maintenance of round-the-clock staffs. While some functions such as water supply and sewage disposal can operate mechanically and continuously, emergency crews must be available to make repairs or perform certain control tasks when the need arises.

Employees generally regard night work as less desirable than daytime work because it may be more dangerous and because it interferes with sleep, recreation patterns, and family life. Accordingly, it is common to pay a higher salary for regular work shifts during late night hours. In short, since a city government is a multi-function organization, it must administer several schedules of hours.

Because hours and schedules are closely related to compensation, the subjects figure prominently in collective bargaining. The development of formal contract negotiations in public employment has tended to produce differentials not previously recognized in the work schedules of some occupations. At one time management tended to favor a uniform policy, not only because it was easier to administer but also because such a procedure was thought to be equitable for all classifications and hence avoided friction between occupational groups.

Since World War II, the majority of public jurisdictions has operated on a standard 40-hour work week for most classifications except for the fire and police departments. About 25 percent of cities with a population of 10,000 or more have adopted a 35-hour week, and approximately 10 percent have held to a 44-hour week.[34] Typically, the bulk of any local government work force is on duty five days a week.

During the 1970s some governments have experimented with a four-day work week consisting of 10-hour days. The rationale for this change is that the longer daily schedule allows greater continuity of work, reduced transportation costs for the employees, and makes for better apportionment of employee time. Advocates of the plan also anticipated greater productivity and increased employee satisfaction. However, results of the experimental efforts have been mixed. Moreover, the need to keep public offices open at least five and sometimes six days a week requires a more complex scheduling of workers' assignments than was thought to be the case.

Another concept that has been attempted in some governments is permitting variable work schedules for employees whose primary duties do not require them to meet the public directly. This concept involves the setting of some measure of output for each employee and the fixing of the total amount of time to be worked during a measured period, such as a month. The employee then is permitted to work at varying blocs of time rather than be committed to report for work at a given time every day.[35]

While office employees of local governments ordinarily work a single shift during the daylight hours, police, fire, hospital, and custodial and cleaning personnel are faced with the need to maintain more than one shift to accomplish their particular missions. Fire departments are unique in that fire suppression crews or companies are required to be on duty at the firehouse for extended periods, ranging from 24 to 48 hours a shift and balanced by comparable periods of free time. Under these circumstances firefighters eat and sleep at the station during the duty period in order to be available for immediate call.

Moreover, the firefighter's standard work week of duty hours, which customarily has been longer than the work week of other local employees, is specified in city ordinances, charters, and state legislation. For several decades organized firefighters have campaigned to reduce the length of their average work week or total work year. By 1974 most cities having a population greater than 50,000 required a 56-hour work week of their fire departments.[36] A few cities reported having longer schedules, one city requiring as many as 84 hours, while a few reported a 40-hour week.

Police are not required to live at their stations during duty hours, but in many jurisdictions an individual officer's actual hours worked are extended because of the need to appear in court to testify on arrests made during the regular tour of duty. The standard work week for police in most cities is 40 hours.[37] A few cities report a schedule as short as 35 hours, and fewer still report a schedule longer than 40 hours.

Overtime has become an increasingly significant item in personnel administration and collective bargaining, one that is based on the policies defining the basic number of hours each employee is expected to work. The assignments which make up a job are organized so as to be accomplished in the basic number of hours, no matter how the time may be distributed over the day, week, or month. Moreover, compensation is based on the amount of time worked.

No matter how carefully work schedules may be planned, however, overtime is often made necessary by personnel shortages, peak work loads, and emergency situations. It is general practice to pay employees for overtime work either by allowing them compensatory time off or by giving them pay at a higher rate.[38] This practice does not apply to executive or key administrative positions, however, because the nature and demands of these positions are such that incumbents are expected to be available for duty without regard for hours. Many government employers authorize longer periods of annual leave for executives than for other employees as compensation in lieu of overtime payment.

First-line supervisors exercise a key role in determining the use of overtime, although their decisions are conditioned by general policy directives and budgetary restrictions. Unless managed equitably, distribution of overtime assignments can be a source of employee irritation and discontent. If assignments for overtime work are given frequently and compensated at premium rates, many employees understandably will consider overtime as a good means of supplementing their income and, therefore, they will resist efforts to reduce its use or to rotate assignments among other workers. Consequently, policies governing the use of overtime should be carefully drawn.

Fair employment legislation has mandated an application of policies of overtime work and its compensation that is stricter than most local policies. State laws frequently require that some form of compensation be given for all time worked by employees other than those in exempt classes, thereby eliminating the employee's option to volunteer short periods of help to complete a project. These directives cause supervisors and employees alike to become conscious of the clock. If an employee is permitted to work even a few minutes past closing time, the person is eligible to claim overtime compensation.

On this subject, Congress in 1974 amended the Fair Labor Standards Act to bring police and fire employees under its regulations. New maximum hour limits over a specific period of time were to be placed in effect, beginning in 1976. The maximum work period for firefighters stipulated in the amendment represented a considerable reduction from that in force in most cities. The nature of police and fire suppression work is such that these employees frequently may be called on to work long continuous periods to complete a task. At the same time, the need to maintain an adequate level of manpower may preclude the granting of large amounts of time off in recompense. Because the amended law placed a large financial burden on local governments and their tax resources, the National League of Cities challenged it in the Supreme Court.[39]

LEAVES

Leaves of absence from work are key conditions of employment. Leaves are interrelated with policies governing compensation; hence, their determination has become a subject for negotiation with employee organizations.

In modern personnel administration, several types of leave have come to be recognized as standard features of employment. The definition of terms and conditions under which leaves may be used is important for orderly administration. While some leaves, such as those relating to illness, may be taken when the employee needs them, most leaves depend on the mutual convenience of management and employee. It is fairly common practice for public jurisdictions to discharge an employee for abandonment of the position if he or she is absent from the job for three consecutive days without the supervisor's permission.

Policies covering illness leave vary considerably in detail. In general they grant a right to the employee to be absent because of personal illness; variations arise in the determination of compensation for the time missed. Some employers allow full pay for a specified number of days a year and partial compensation for an additional amount of time taken if the illness continues. Most employers set limits on the amount of leave that may be taken at one time without a medical examination being required to determine the employee's fitness to return to work. The supervisor is usually given discretionary authority to require verification of illness, regardless of the time taken. In many instances, the right to take leave has been given when a member of an employee's family is ill and the employee is exercising family responsibilities. Legislation in many states now authorizes local governments to make lump sum payments to employees for unused illness leave time accumulated over an extended period.

Certain holidays have traditionally been officially designated as such by federal and state law. Local government practice has been to grant compensation to employees for these days, although no work was required or performed. When the date of an official holiday falls on a weekend or other non-working day, this practice is frequently extended by granting a different working day off. Most government jurisdictions grant their workers a larger number of paid holidays than does the business community—a situation often considered in bargaining over public employee wages.

Annual leaves are based on the concept that employees need time away from the rigor of the job to rest and restore themselves mentally and physically. In practice, annual leave has come to be used for the transaction of personal business as well. Hence, this type of leave may be taken either in blocks of days or weeks or as portions of a day. The scheduling is dependent upon the mutual convenience of the employer and employee, and requires advance approval.

Eligibility for annual leave is usually one of the perquisites of permanent, full-time status and is not extended customarily to probationary, temporary, or provisional employees. Minimum annual leave usually is the equivalent of twelve working days, to be taken after the first year of service. As a reward for continuing good service, longer leaves frequently are granted those who have been employed ten years, and still longer amounts are granted for those completing twenty years. Furthermore, unused portions of annual leave may be accumulated and used during the ensuing year, although failure to use annual leave defeats its original purpose, namely rest and recreation.

Educational leave is another type of leave being recognized with increasing frequency. It is an added benefit intended to enable competent employees to further develop their abilities and thus find greater satisfaction in their work. Except in rare instances, this type of leave is given without pay. Such leave guaran-

tees the retention of employment rights for the worker while pursuing an educational or developmental program.

Frequently, short leaves are granted, either with or without pay, to those attending workshops or conferences whose programs are closely related to the employee's regular duties and are recognized as part of the employee development program. Another form of educational leave consists in the permission given employees to cut short some work days by a few hours to attend classes leading to a degree or certificate from local schools or universities. The benefits of release time, tuition assistance, or leaves of absence for educational purposes should be available to all employees and be included in established policies or guidelines applicable throughout the work force.

Occupational Health and Safety

The health and safety of employees understandably concerns any employer, public or private. Maintenance of worker health and prevention of accidents are conditions making possible the fullest utilization of the human resources employed in the production of goods and services. Public agencies responsible for the conduct of hospitals, schools, libraries, and other facilities serving large segments of the public have an additional concern lest unsafe buildings and poor health conditions among its employees jeopardize the public it is expected to serve. Health and safety standards and programs are the responsibility of top management; to a large extent, their implementation rests in the hands of first-line supervisors.

The safety movement, initiated and championed in the early years of this century by organized labor, forced states to pass workmen's injury compensation laws. In many states these laws apply to municipal employees, although the classifications of jobs covered vary widely.[40] Most commonly they cover hazardous occupational classes only; in a few instances they apply to nearly all classifications.

These laws in turn led to the retaining of doctors and nurses at work places to treat on-the-job injuries and illnesses and to assist in agencies' occupational health programs. Although many governmental agencies have been exempted from coverage of state industrial health and safety statutes, local government employers do call on the services of their public health and hospital staffs for assistance. However, the degree of attention city administrations have directed to occupational health and safety programs varies from jurisdiction to jurisdiction.

Concern over problems of compensating for job-related injuries, reducing health-connected absenteeism, and protecting retirement system funds has led many local governments to require appointees to pass physical examinations. Others require medical certification for employees as a condition for returning to work after illness or surgery. First-line supervisors generally carry the responsibility for determining if an employee at work is so ill as to be unfit to work and to pose a risk to other employees, and thus should be sent home.

Illness leave benefits and health insurance programs, paid wholly or in part by the public employer, have been established to protect employees and relieve them of some of the anxiety and hardship caused by sickness and injury. Compensation for the employee given early retirement because of a job-connected disability usually is financed from pension or retirement funds rather than directly from annual salary budget items.

Periodic reexamination of employees to determine physical fitness generally has not been required in public agencies unless the employee has suffered a major illness or injury that has caused a break in service. In part, this requirement has been avoided because of opposition from employees who fear reexamination might jeopardize their job and job rights. Some jurisdictions require periodic reexaminations of an employee who has undergone surgery or experienced an ailment that is either recurrent or has caused deterioration of ability to meet the demands of the job. This requirement often is coupled with reassignment to less demanding work.

Two other areas of employee health protection continue to demand study. The most difficult involves the health problems stemming from the employee's actions or associations after work hours and off the job. Illness or disability from these activities leads to absenteeism and reduced effectiveness on the job just as much as illness or disability occurring in the work environment. Barring the unfit employee from reporting for work may reduce the risk of accident or prevent the spread of contagious disease among other workers, but it does not maintain an even level of performance by the work force for the short run. Health education and, in some instances, early diagnosis are necessary preventive measures. Nevertheless, the employer has a limited opportunity to raise the level of consciousness and understanding of personal health practices among employees.

A more direct and tractable responsibility for the employer is preventing the work environment from becoming a threat to employees' health. Standards for occupational health protection are always subject to debate, but some matters previously not thought to be health-related have come under intense public scrutiny.

For example, the term pollution is now widely applied to things such as noise, radiation, gases and compounds in the atmosphere, and other noxious materials which affect the health of the community as well as workers on city jobs. These are not matters that can be treated by the physician or nurse staffing the ordinary industrial health office. Their control involves a range of functions—inspecting, monitoring of tests, and designing, planning, and constructing offices and plant facilities—which must be coordinated or combined. Also related to control are matters such as heating, ventilation, noise reduction, and sanitation. Here it can be seen how occupational health blends into the area of safety.

Most of these newer concerns and conditions were expressed in the Occupational Safety and Health Act of 1970 (often referred to as the Steiger Act), a comprehensive statute adopted by Congress and designed to be enforced by federal, state, and local action.[41] State and local governments were expressly exempt from its regulatory provisions in their capacity as employers, but Congress made financial assistance available to encourage the states to enact parallel legislation.

Congress also authorized state and local agencies to enforce national standards. State enforcement plans must be approved by the Assistant Secretary of Labor if they are to qualify for federal assistance and serve as the basis for enforcement of federal standards. Several states have adopted legislation in response to this program and many apply their regulations both to local governments and to private sector employers.[42]

The California Occupational Safety and Health Act of 1973 is a fairly good example of this type of legislation. Its stated purpose is

to assure safe and healthful working conditions for all California working men and women by authorizing enforcement of effective standards, encouraging employers to maintain safe and healthful working conditions, and providing for research and education in this field.[43]

The California act applies to all employees except those in domestic household service. Enforcement responsibility is vested in the Division of Industrial Safety in the Department of Industrial Relations. A state appeal board, whose members are appointed by the governor, has been created to hear appeals and requests for exceptions. Standards and definitions, although expressed in general terms in the statute, are to be developed and tested through research. After hearings and further study, administrative regulations are to be published in the state administrative code.

National OSHA standards are developed in a similar manner and are published in the *Federal Register*. Local governments in those states which have adopted legislation in response to the Steiger Act should continually reexamine their occupational health and safety programs. A report of the New Jersey Department of Civil Service recommends the following steps regarding safety:

1. A safety policy should be issued by each jurisdiction.
2. Safety should be included as a topic in top management meetings.
3. Safety rules and warnings should be conspicuously posted.
4. Safety should become a regular part of the training programs for supervisors and employees.
5. Administrators should take advantage of safety training and educational information available from the state department responsible for occupational health and safety work.[44]

EMPLOYEE POLITICAL ACTIVITIES

Merit system principles require that persons in career service jobs be dealt with equitably and without reference to their party affiliation or political attitudes. Political activity is related to the individual's basic rights protected by the Constitution. Nevertheless, individual rights, namely those relating to political activity while employed by a government, are not absolute or beyond limitation.

The government employer properly may be concerned with employees' political activity but not with their opinions or beliefs. Regulations limiting employee activities that are political in nature often distinguish between those activities which occur during working hours and those which take place after work. The first set of activities are most likely to affect or conflict with work performance and therefore directly concern the public employer. There appears to be general consensus that the public employer can and should forbid employees to engage in political activity during the hours of work and on city premises such as offices, warehouses, corporation yards, and police and fire stations. As to off-duty political activity, the employment relationship is less clear, of course, but personal behavior has to be considered.

Two questions arise immediately: Who should decide the restrictions to be imposed? What political activities may be defined as restricted or prohibited? In the past, it frequently was the department heads who made policy on the subject, with the result that regulations varied within the work force and appeared to relate more to the individual official's philosophy and preference than to community-supported public policy. In other cases, the manager or chief administrator issued an administrative directive setting forth uniform policy.

Actually, the subject of employee political activity is one that perhaps should be decided by elected representatives who consider the interests and wishes of the community and who are responsible to the electorate for the conditions laid down. In a very basic sense, the matter is something more than a condition of employment and has much to do with determining acceptable employee behavior. The matter is part of the legislative process and goes beyond the organization's management.

The question, in essence, is: Should the guiding philosophy behind a policy on employee political activity be one that requires public employees be entirely neutral and confine their political activity to voting and after-hour private discussions? Or is the policy to be based on a belief in the right of the employee to participate (or not participate) in political activity relating to any level of government, so long as it does not interfere with work performance?

Local government decisions on this matter, of course, must conform to state legislation and court decisions. States vary considerably in their reactions.[45] Case law interprets local statutes and policies with reference to state and federal constitutional standards. The California legislature, for example, enacted a statute in 1967 which established uniform policy applicable both to charter and general law cities on some aspects of employee political activity. Shortly thereafter the state supreme court ruled that if any public employer sought to restrict employee political activity, and if a public employee union brought suit, then the burden of proof would be on the employer to show that the restriction was necessary to protect the public interest and that no less restrictive rule would accomplish that purpose. By contrast, several states have little legislation at all on the subject.[46]

In 1939 Congress amended the Hatch Act to prohibit state and local employees whose salaries were supported by federal funds from engaging in partisan political activity. So long as federal money was distributed through contracts and grants-in-aid, city employees who were liable to the restrictions could be identified with some degree of accuracy.

Determination of proscribed activity rested mainly with the rulings of the U.S. Civil Service Commission and its interpretation of federal statutes. Any state or local public employer that permitted an employee to engage in the prohibited activity was subject to a penalty equivalent to the employee's salary. However, confusion arose when revenue sharing was launched. If the city applied these funds toward general programs or toward reducing local taxes, were all city employees then subject to the Hatch Act restrictions? The Treasury Department thought not, whereas the Civil Service Commission thought the restrictions should apply universally. The entire matter became moot late in 1974 when Congress recast federal policy with respect to state and local employees, nullifying most of the Hatch Act restrictions.

Historically, political activity has been thought to be synonymous with activity in a political party. Development of other forms of political activity render that conception too narrow. Removing party labels from city election ballots and requiring nonpartisan conduct of local government does not alter the fact that political activity, in some sense, takes place. Introduction of the initiative, referendum, and recall provides other opportunities for political activity that does not necessarily relate to parties. Likewise the requirement that proposals for city bond indebtedness be submitted to the voters (a requirement adopted in most states) provides still another chance for political activists to try to persuade citizens to adopt or reject a proposal.

Employee organizations engage in a variety of political activities to advance their cause. They lobby elected officials and state legislators, contribute funds to and support candidates for local and state office, and urge voters to go to the polls. Interest groups in general perform many activities traditionally considered typical of political parties. City employees who are officers or active participants in employee organizations, apart from paid organization representatives, frequently become involved in these activities.

Most regulations of political activity aim to eliminate coercion of public employees to contribute funds or take sides in politics. Candidates for office and their supporters are forbidden to enter places of public employment for the purpose of seeking contributions. Likewise, public employees and supervisors are prohibited from soliciting funds at any time from coworkers or subordinates. The use of a public position to advance a political view also is frowned on.

Distribution of campaign literature and the display of posters in places of work, and efforts by employees to persuade persons transacting business with the city to support or oppose a candidate or ballot proposition are prohibited. Display of campaign buttons on an employee's clothing or bumper stickers on a personally owned automobile is usually considered permissible. Buttonholing elected officials for the purpose of lobbying may be covered either in regulations pertaining to employee conduct or in a city's lobbyist ordinance. However, very few cities have enacted formal regulations controlling their employee or interest group representatives who regularly seek to influence city transactions.

The International Personnel Management Association offers a useful set of four alternative suggestions for possible regulation of public employee political activity. Each prohibits solicitation of assessments or contributions for political purposes and also directs that administrative action not be taken against public employees who refuse to contribute money or effort to aid political activities.

With reference to after-work activities, the IPMA guidelines offer several alternatives. One prohibits an employee from holding a political party office. Another declares that a government employee may not hold an office filled in a partisan election. A third requires the employee to take a leave of absence during his or her campaign and while holding a public office or party post. A fourth goes further and declares that a person holding a position in the classified service shall not (a) take an active part in a political campaign, (b) seek office in a political club or organization, (c) circulate or seek signatures to any nominating petition, or (d) act as a worker at the polls or distribute badges or other material favoring or opposing a candidate for any public office.[47]

Some cities—for example, San Diego, California—restrict employees from taking an active part in political campaigns which involve the employing government but do permit them to participate in school district, county, state, and national political activities on their own time. In other instances, the prevailing view is that city-county or city-school district relationships are so close that city employee involvement in the other unit's affairs would jeopardize intergovernmental relationships and produce a conflict of interest.

If a local employee is permitted to hold elective office in another government unit, conflict may arise if that person is in a class of position that makes decisions on contracts or similar matters involving the other government. Another test is whether the time requirements of the two positions produce a conflict. A city employee serving as a suburban school board member may experience no conflict if his or her employment calls for daytime duty and the board meets weekly or semimonthly at night.

One issue frequently raised concerning after-hour political activity has to do with the distinction between the performance of an employee's official duties and the exercise of his or her individual rights as a citizen. Consequently, regulations often prohibit police, firefighters, or any other uniformed employees from wearing their uniforms when they engage in political activity on their own time. Another approach is to require any employee who takes an active part in a political campaign to obtain a leave of absence. However, use of accumulated annual leave for this purpose often presents problems unless the employee is required to file notice of intent to use such leave prior to becoming involved in campaigning.

Conclusion

Local governments have found it increasingly necessary for effective administration to develop well-considered policies relating to a wide spectrum of conditions of employment, particularly regarding the principal conditions discussed in this chapter: residence and citizenship requirements; veterans' preference; equal employment opportunity; layoff and reduction in force; transfer and reassignment; hours and leaves; occupational health and safety; and, finally, employee political activity.

The need for a clarified municipal policy on the conditions of employment arises from several developments, including the growth of urban work forces, the rise of public employee unionism and the practice of collective bargaining, and the requirement to conform with federal and state statutes and guidelines. Furthermore, a clarified, rational policy not only helps to recruit high-calibre, motivated individuals to public service but also serves to guide and encourage government employees as they pursue their careers in government.

The conditions of employment come under constant review as new legislation is promulgated and as current legislation is amended, as unions grow in strength and refine their bargaining techniques, and as individual employees themselves press for their employment rights. Within this ever-changing context city management must define and assert its own rights in the determination of the conditions of employment.

---

1 Sterling D. Spero and John M. Capozzola, THE URBAN COMMUNITY AND ITS UNIONIZED BUREAUCRACIES (New York: Dunellen Publishing Co., Inc., 1973) , p. 189.

2 James G. March and Herbert A. Simon, ORGANIZATIONS (New York: John Wiley & Sons, Inc., 1963) , pp. 84–93, 131–135; Todd R. LaPorte, "The Study of Public Organization," and George Frederickson, "Organization Theory and New Public Administration," in TOWARD A NEW PUBLIC ADMINISTRATION, ed. Frank Marini (Scranton, Pa.: Chandler Publishing Company, 1971) .

3 O. Glenn Stahl, PUBLIC PERSONNEL ADMINISTRATION, 6th ed. (New York: Harper & Row Publishers, 1971) , p. 108; Municipal Manpower Commission, GOVERNMENTAL MANPOWER FOR TOMORROW'S CITIES (New York: McGraw–Hill Book Company, 1962) .

4 David T. Stanley, PROFESSIONAL MANPOWER FOR NEW YORK CITY (Washington, D.C.: The Brookings Institution, 1963) , pp. 85–134.

5 Sugarman v. Doyle, 413 U.S. 634, 5 FEPCases 1152 (1973) .

6 Commission on California State Government and Economy, MANAGEMENT MANPOWER REQUIREMENTS (1965) . The commission also recommended that the veteran be allowed to apply the preference credit once and should not be permitted to use it in candidacy for managerial or policy-level jobs.

7 Public Personnel Association, MINORITY GROUPS AND MERIT SYSTEM PRACTICE, Personnel Report no. 653 (Chicago: Public Personnel Association, n. d.) .

8 National Civil Service League, MODELS FOR AFFIRMATIVE ACTION (Washington, D.C.: National Civil Service League, 1973) .

9 U.S., Commission on Civil Rights, FOR ALL THE PEOPLE . . . BY ALL THE PEOPLE: A REPORT ON EQUAL OPPORTUNITY IN STATE AND LOCAL GOVERNMENT EMPLOYMENT (Washington, D.C.: Government Printing Office, 1969) , pp. 108–111.

10 Public Personnel Association, MINORITY GROUPS AND MERIT SYSTEM PRACTICE.

11 U.S., Commission on Civil Rights, FOR ALL THE PEOPLE . . . BY ALL THE PEOPLE.

12 Ibid., p. 5.

13 Ibid., p. 27.

14 Ibid., p. 31.

15 Ibid., pp. 131–132.

16 U.S. CODE, TITLE 29, chap. XIV, part 1601. (Washington, D.C.: Government Printing Office, 1974.) A good reference source is FAIR EMPLOYMENT PRACTICE MANUAL, a looseleaf publication updated periodically, published by the Bureau of National Affairs, Washington, D.C.

17 President's Advisory Council on Intergovernmental Personnel Policy, FIRST ANNUAL REPORT (Washington, D.C.: President's Advisory Council on Intergovernmental Personnel Policy, 1973) , p. 7.

18 Ibid., pp. 4–5.

19 U.S., Civil Service Commission, Bureau of Intergovernmental Personnel Programs, "Guidelines for Qualitative Evaluations of Personnel Operations in State and Local Governments." Washington, D.C., n. d. (Processed) .

20 "Federal Policy on Remedies Concerning Equal Employment Opportunity in State and Local Government Personnel Systems," memorandum issued 23 March 1973 over the signatures of Robert Hampton, chairman, U.S. Civil Service Commission; Stanley Pottinger, Assistant Attorney General; William Brown, chairman, U.S. Equal Employment Opportunity Commission; Philip Davis, Acting Director, Office of Federal Contract Compliance. Washington, D.C., 1973. (Processed.) The agencies represented by the signatories of this memorandum comprised the Equal Employment Opportunity Coordinating Council created by the Equal Employment Opportunity Act of 1972.

21 Memorandum from the Advisory State–Local Task Force on Uniform Employee Selection Guidelines, addressed to Joseph Robertson, director, Bureau of Intergovernmental Personnel Programs, U.S. Civil Service Commission. Washington, D.C., 5 November 1973. (Processed.)

22 Equal Employment Opportunity Coordinating Council, "Uniform Guidelines on Employee Selection Procedures." Washington, D.C., 24 June 1974. (Processed.)

23 International Personnel Management Association, IPMA SPECIAL BULLETIN, 4 September 1974.

24 U.S. CODE, Title 29, Part 1607.

25 Griggs v. Duke Power Co., 401 U.S. 424; 3 FEPCases 175 (1971) .

26 Carter v. Gallagher, 3 FEPCases 692 (U.S. District Court, 1971) ; 4 FEPCases 121 (U.S. Ct. App. 1972) .

27 Officers for Justice v. San Francisco Civil Service Commission, 371 F.Supp. 1328; 6 FEPCases 1283 (1973).

28 Allen v. City of Mobile, 331 F.Supp. 1134; 5 FEPCases 1226 (1971).

29 Ibid.

30 Fraternal Order of Police v. City of Dayton, 6 FEPCases 12 (1973). Decided by the Ohio Court of Appeals, 15 May 1973.

31 Hiatt v. City of Berkeley, 10 FEPCases 251 (1975). Decided by Superior Court, Alameda County, California. Cited by FAIR EMPLOYMENT PRACTICE CASES (Washington, D.C.: Bureau of National Affairs).

32 See, for example, "Guidelines on Discrimination Because of Sex," U.S. CODE, Title 29, Part 1604.

33 Ibid.

34 International City Managers' Association, MUNICIPAL YEAR BOOK, 1962 (Chicago: International City Managers' Association, 1962), pp. 192–194.

35 Robert J. Donahue, "Flex Time Systems in New York," and James Walker, Clive Fletcher, and Donald McLeod, "Flexible Working Hours in Two British Government Offices," PUBLIC PERSONNEL MANAGEMENT (July/August 1975).

36 International City Management Association, MUNICIPAL YEAR BOOK, 1974 (Washington, D.C.: International City Management Association, 1974), pp. 241–245.

37 Ibid., pp. 232–236.

38 International City Managers' Association, MUNICIPAL YEAR BOOK, 1962, p. 193.

39 The case of National League of Cities et al. v. Dunlop was heard by the Supreme Court during the October 1975 term.

40 U.S., Department of Labor, Bureau of Labor Standards, bulletin 210, "Workmen's Compensation Coverage of Public Employees" (Washington, D.C.: Government Printing Office, May, 1962). See also Clement Luepke, "City Employee Safety Programs," in MUNICIPAL YEAR BOOK, 1962, pp. 179–183.

41 THE WILLIAM STEIGER ACT, UNITED STATES CODE, title 29, chap. 15, secs. 651 et seq.

42 The state programs are described in the UNITED STATES CODE, title 29, ch. 7, part 1952.

43 California, LABOR CODE, part 1, div. 5, secs. 6300 et seq.

44 New Jersey, Department of Civil Service, A MODEL PERSONNEL SYSTEM FOR NEW JERSEY COUNTY AND MUNICIPAL OFFICIALS (Trenton, 1974), pp. 63–64.

45 Pamela S. Ford, POLITICAL ACTIVITIES AND THE PUBLIC SERVICE: A CONTINUING PROBLEM (Berkeley: University of California, Institute of Governmental Studies, 1963); REPORT OF THE COMMISSION ON POLITICAL ACTIVITIES OF GOVERNMENT PERSONNEL, vol. 2 (Washington, D.C.: Government Printing Office, 1968), pp. 91–107.

46 REPORT OF THE COMMISSION ON POLITICAL ACTIVITIES OF GOVERNMENT PERSONNEL, vol. 2, pp. 91–107.

47 International Personnel Management Association, GUIDELINES FOR DRAFTING A PUBLIC PERSONNEL ADMINISTRATION LAW (Chicago: International Personnel Management Association, 1973), pp. 44–46.

9

Compensation

RUDYARD KIPLING

THE YEAR 1976 IS AN OPPORTUNE TIME for a new book on local government personnel administration. Over thirty years have elapsed since the end of World War II and its lessons, and less than a decade remains before empirical validation can be attempted of George Orwell's prophecies for 1984. As for the 1970s, a growing number of strikes by city employees over pay and related matters took place. Although much has been said about the subject of compensation, most municipalities have done little except continue the basic routine of pay administration that has been followed since the days of their incorporation.

Background

Many important changes in public pay practice have occurred since *Municipal Personnel Administration,* the predecessor of this text, was published in 1960. For instance, on page 52 of that volume it was stated that "the bargaining power of government employees is weaker than that of private employees. There are limitations on the right to strike and to participate in politics." This statement may be still technically true in 1976, but certainly to a much lesser degree than in 1960. Another statement made on page 53 in the earlier book must be completely revised: "Governments are not covered by the Fair Labor Standards Act which sets a minimum wage for workers engaged in interstate commerce." The full impact of the 1974 FLSA amendments on municipal salary policy, especially fire and police pay, could not be assessed as of early 1976, but there could be no question that changes would be coming.

It is useful to emphasize that pay administration is an art, not a science. This is one of the few points of general agreement reached among compensation experts. A primary point to bear in mind about public pay administration is that there are some standard approaches but no single right way. There are almost as many interpretations as there are artists. Those looking for neat answers to complex questions are likely to be disappointed by any reference source they consult. By gaining an understanding of the principles and procedures which can be applied to public pay administration, one may create one's own answer.

This chapter will concentrate of the basics of the subject. The advent of collective bargaining will likely cause some rapid and widespread changes in public pay administration. Nevertheless, many practices of the past are still valid and will be continued. What needs to be learned, among other things, is how to conduct a salary survey, how to construct a salary schedule, and how to present salary recommendations in an intelligible manner.

The order of this chapter's discussion will be as follows: principles and assumptions of public compensation; statutory and constitutional limitations; the participating parties; historical perspective; the salary schedule; gathering the pay data; interpretation of the pay data; relationship between the classification plan and the salary plan; special problems in public pay administration; and, finally, a discussion of the outlook for the future.

Principles and Assumptions of Public Compensation

In developing a theory of public compensation, one proceeds from certain commonly accepted concepts, such as "a fair day's pay," "equal pay for equal work," "prevailing rates," and "compensation according to merit." In 1940 John W. Riegel, commenting on these familiar phrases, wrote that "the principles they suggest are generally approved by employers and employees. But these phrases do not connote acceptable procedures and standards of judgment by which salaries and wages can be determined. Accordingly, the rates which one party proposes as fair are often termed unreasonable by the other."[1] That observation pertains as much to the 1970s as when it was first made.

Before considering some proposed theories of public compensation, it is necessary to recall the objectives of the pay plan. Pay administration has been defined as "the art of paying the proper salary to an employee at the proper time."[2] The following guidelines should aid in achieving that goal:

1. The pay plan should provide salaries sufficient to recruit and retain competent employees for all positions. Assuming work conditions, benefits, and other aspects of the personnel program are basically comparable, one must offer salaries that are competitive with those offered by private industry and other public agencies. This is as true for higher-level classifications as for entry-level classes. Retaining employees whom the organization has trained as well as those it has recruited is very important. As of 1976, the federal government was experiencing extremely high turnover rates at the GS–15 and GS–18 levels because of the $37,800 ceiling on annual salaries.

2. The salary plan should provide incentives for employees to improve productivity. This actually may be the biggest problem facing public administrators at all levels. Considering some of the incentive approaches taken by industry may be impossible for at least two major reasons. First, the very nature of most public jobs does not foster a piece-rate approach. Second, employee groups have strongly resisted efforts to tie pay to productivity or performance evaluation.

3. An accepted principle of pay administration is that the salary level should be based on the relative difficulty and responsibility of the job. Study after study has shown employees to be concerned more about their salary in relation to others in the organization than about the absolute dollar amount they are paid. The relationship of the classification and the compensation plans will be discussed later in greater detail.

4. One of the essentials for a viable pay program is its acceptability to both management and employees. On this point some observers recommend the involvement in the process of a third party, be it a civil service commission or an outside fact-finder. Chances of acceptance are increased if the parties concerned have a full understanding of the procedures and standards applied, if they are allowed to participate in various stages of the pay-setting process, and if they have complete confidence in the technical accuracy of the staff involved in gathering and analyzing data.

5. The pay program must be flexible and reflect changes from both external and internal sources. The labor market, the classification structure, the organization of operating units, and various civil programs are in constant flux, and the pay plan must cope with all these changes.

Figure 9–1 illustrates the sequence of steps to be followed in developing a pay plan which meets these guidelines.

A large percentage of public employee organizations are clamoring for collective bargaining. Consequently, many states and municipalities have adopted employee relations ordinances incorporating collective bargaining. As far as can be determined, none of these ordinances spells out the specific goals of bargaining. Inevitably the question arises, Will the public employee's salary be set at the maximum rate that the employee representatives can extract from the city's negotiator?

It is doubtful that taxpayers would tolerate public employees' salaries exceeding those of their counterparts in industry. On the other hand, civil servants cannot be expected to subsidize public services by accepting lower rates of compensation than they could get elsewhere.

Many knowledgeable professionals contend that civil service and collective bargaining are incompatible. In particular they argue that "the prevailing wage clause is a restriction on the scope of bargaining, and its counterpart is unheard of in the private sector."[3] They recommend a collective bargaining system which approximates the system existing in the private sector, as free as possible from arbitrary restrictions on the scope of bargaining. (See "Labor Relations," Chapter 10 of this volume, for an in-depth treatment of this subject.)

It is not the purpose of this chapter to undertake a detailed analysis of the pros and cons of collective bargaining as the basis for salary setting in public agencies. (Ample evidence can be cited to show that the process does not expedite the settlement of wage disputes in public agencies.) Recommended for consideration here is an approach which appears most equitable for all parties: joint determination of the prevailing rate. By this approach both employer and employee representatives participate in the analysis and interpretation of the data, proceeding according to mutually acceptable techniques.

Before discussing what it is that is jointly determined, a clarification of terms is in order. Does the so-called "prevailing rate" mean a single rate of pay? Should the middle step of the salary range, the top step, or the actual average of the rates paid the city's employees be compared with the prevailing rate found by the salary survey?

The answers may lie in mechanics rather than semantics. Actually it is more precise to speak of a "prevailing salary range." Except when a single union rate prevails throughout a community, a surprisingly wide variety of rates generally is found in the typical salary survey. Regardless of how the data are collected, interpreted, discussed, or applied, public employee salaries should neither lead nor lag those paid their counterparts in the community.

Statutory and Constitutional Limitations

The legislative framework for setting municipal salaries is found in the city charter. The contents of these charter provisions vary greatly, ranging from a brief statement of general policy to a detailed guide for procedural compliance by the administrative staff. The

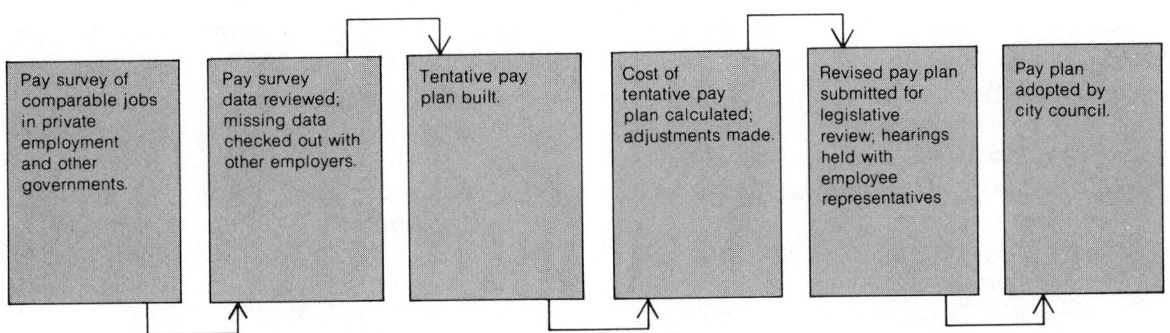

FIGURE 9–1. *Summary of steps in developing the pay plan.* (*Source: Unit 3, "Personnel Administration,"* SMALL CITIES MANAGEMENT TRAINING PROGRAM, *Washington, D.C., International City Management Association, 1975, p. 10.*)

clarity of intent also varies. Many jurisdictions have had to resort to charter amendment elections or to the courts to clear away the obfuscation of the original language.

With the advent of collective bargaining, it is essential to state clearly the statutory and constitutional limitations placed on the authority of the salary-setting body—assumed to be the legislative body—to adjust, amend, or ignore the salary data collected by the administrative staff.

An interesting example of a state legislature delineating the authority of local elected bodies is found in the California State Education Code. The authority of the elected boards of education to alter the salary recommendations submitted by the personnel commissions in those districts that have adopted provisions known as the merit system is expressed in Section 13719 as follows:

The commission shall recommend to the governing board salary schedules for the classified service. The governing board may approve, amend or reject these recommendations. No amendment shall be adopted until the commission is first given a reasonable opportunity to make a written statement of the effect the amendment will have upon the principle of like pay for like service. No changes shall operate to disturb the relationship which compensation schedules bear to one another, as the relationship has been established in the classification made by the commission.[4]

Obviously the exact wording of this section is not offered as a model of clarity. However, the passage has been consistently interpreted to mean that classification relationships cannot be altered by the salary-setting authority to the extent that an equal or lower class becomes a higher class, without presenting salary data to justify such adjustment. At least one legal adviser has held that any adjustment which amounts in effect to a bonus exceeding the data would have to be applied uniformly to all other classes.

A court decision regarding the prevailing wage clause in the Los Angeles city charter pertains to this particular problem. Section 425 of the charter reads as follows:

In fixing the compensation to be paid to persons in the city's employ, the Council and every other authority authorized to fix salaries and wages shall, in each instance, provide a salary or wage at least equal to the prevailing salary or wage for the same quality of service rendered to private persons, firms or corporations under similar employment, in case such prevailing salary or wage can be ascertained.[5]

The suit in question involved salary increases for the fiscal year 1971–72. Under what locally is known as the "Jacobs Plan," the uniformed personnel were entitled to receive a 7.837 percent increase in salaries that year. The city council voted an increase of only 3.75 percent, however, and the mayor vetoed the action. Subsequently the council approved increases amounting to 5.5 percent for all uniformed personnel except those in the higher ranks. This increase became effective November 15, 1971, after a wage-price freeze imposed by the federal government had expired.

The California State Court of Appeals held in a unanimous three-judge ruling that the employees were entitled to the full amount of the increase for the period extending from July 1 through November 14, 1971, and to the 2.3 percent difference (7.837 percent less 5.5) from November 15, 1971, to the time of granting the money.

The court's decision was based on the cited charter section which requires the city to pay prevailing wages. The so-called "Jacobs Plan" provides a formula which bases salary increases for sworn personnel on an index of wage increases for various other benchmarks that are used in an annual wage and salary survey. The city council had contended that there were no positions occupied by sworn personnel which involved the same quality of service as that rendered in private industry, and hence prevailing wages could not be determined for that group of employees.

Some of the parties who regularly participate in salary setting can be identified from the foregoing discussion. The next section will make positive identification.

The Participating Parties

No longer can public pay decisions be based on unilateral action. Organizations, groups, and individuals are involved. Although they may be similar in their views and desires, these parties are not identical. Consequently their various demands must be weighed separately.

Perhaps the greatest difference between pay determinations in the private and public sectors lies in the identity of the participating parties. Stated perhaps too simply, pay determination in the private sector can be categorized as a transaction which takes place between management who represents the ownership and employees who are represented by unions or organizations.

In the public sector, identifying who is management is a major problem. A common theme heard in most discussions about public sector collective bargaining is that only duly elected officials can serve as management, since it is they who have been entrusted by the citizen "owners" to run the government. Some critics contend that for truly effective bargaining, there should be a single spokesperson, i.e., the city manager or a designated negotiator.

Regardless of who makes the management decisions, the following parties all have a role in the salary-setting process for the public agencies:

1. The employee organization: The number of employee organizations depends on whether exclusive recognition is authorized. It is not uncommon to find three or more organizations claiming to represent employees in the same classification.
2. The individual employee: Although some agreements specifying exclusive recognition appear to preclude individuals from representing themselves, it is advised that under no circumstances should an individual with the courage and conviction to speak for his or her individual interest be denied the right to do so.
3. Special interest groups: Property owners associations are prominent among the special interest groups which frequently seek a voice in the salary determinations of local public agencies.
4. Civic groups: Groups such as the Chamber of Commerce are becoming increasingly active in shaping community policy in many jurisdictions.
5. The technical staff: The tasks of conducting the salary survey and recommending the pay rates for specific classes are technical functions which should be performed by a staff prepared to explain their actions to any or all of the listed parties. For reasons discussed more fully later, these tasks should be performed by the same group that is responsible for maintaining the classification plan.
6. The courts: The courts are a new party that has emerged on the scene and is exercising a forceful and definitive voice in the matter of public salary setting. With all due respect, it must be said that most judges are not likely to possess much expertise on the subject of salary administration. Therefore, it behooves all other participating parties to make the utmost effort to reach agreement rather than rely on the courts to resolve differences arising from varying interpretations of the salary provisions in city charters or state legislation.

An obvious question arises: Where does the public fit into this play of parties? Unfortunately only two answers present themselves. First, the public rarely gets into the process unless there is a need for drastic action such as a tax override election, which laws in some states authorize. Second, the public supposedly is represented by the elected legislative body. Certainly there is an obligation on those responsible for preparing and presenting salary recommendations to advise the public when and where discussions will be held about the various stages of the salary-setting process.

Historical Perspective

It is reasonable to assume that busy practitioners do not relish spending much time dwelling on a historical review of government pay processes. Also to be avoided are recitations of individual municipal experiences. Among the chief purposes of studying history is making use of what has proved successful and avoiding what has proved unsound. Citing a single case study should avoid much duplication.

One of the most comprehensive and highly

regarded studies of the pay policy problem for public employees was that conducted by Town Hall in Los Angeles. Town Hall is an organization of community leaders whose program focuses on problems of public importance. The organization's Municipal and County Government section published in May 1961 a report, *Pay Policies for Public Personnel,* that offered an impartial analysis of the subject and presented the various viewpoints which need to be considered in most jurisdictions.

The report's account of how the prevailing wage provision was incorporated into the city charter makes stimulating reading. For the purposes of this chapter, however, a review of the study's ten recommendations is more valuable. Since most of the recommendations were still being discussed as of this writing, a review of them presents an opportunity to analyze and discuss a variety of approaches to problems existing in the mid-1970s.

A brief background of the conditions which led to the study is in order. For the majority of public employees in the Los Angeles metropolitan area, the prevailing wage is determined by the annual wage and salary survey conducted in the Los Angeles County area. The survey, administered jointly by the City of Los Angeles, the County of Los Angeles, the Los Angeles city schools, and the City Housing Authority, was initiated during World War II and has been carried out each year since 1945.

Although conducting the survey is a jointly administered process, the analysis of data and the preparation of salary recommendations are done independently in each of the participating jurisdictions. The respective legislative bodies, which have the responsibility for levying the taxes from which the wages are paid, have final responsibility for adopting the salary schedules. Their discretion in doing so has been limited by court decisions. The courts have held in every case that inasmuch as the county and city charters provide that public employees shall be paid at least the same rate of wages as they would receive for like work in private employment under similar conditions, when a wage rate has been determined to be "prevailing," then public employees shall be paid that rate.

Both the survey and its application have been criticized by employee groups, elected and appointed government officials, and organizations representing taxpayers. The Town Hall study examined the history and the work of the salary-setting process. Special problems such as pay for fire and police, building trades workers, and executives were also considered. The report concluded in general that the existing wage-setting process should be refined and perfected rather than radically altered.

Summaries of the study's ten recommendations follow:

1. The provisions of the Charters of the City of Los Angeles and the County of Los Angeles which provide that employees should be paid at least the prevailing wage should be amended to provide that the employees should be paid the prevailing wage, as closely as it can be determined. The revised wording would give employees protection equal to that now intended. On the other hand, it would make clear that it is against public policy to pay wages higher than those prevailing in private industry. . . .

Among the developments that took place since the 1961 report was filed has been the enactment of the prevailing wage legislation which affects the Los Angeles city school districts, now separated into the Los Angeles Unified School District and the Los Angeles Community College District. The most recent development has been an attempt to submit a ballot proposal intended to remove the prevailing wage clause from the county charter. The main argument supporting the proposal is that under the collective bargaining ordinance, which the county adopted late in 1968, the employee representatives may use the data relative to prevailing rates as a base from which to bargain for still higher wages.[6]

2. Paying substandard wages is a self-defeating form of government economy. It results in lowered morale, a second-rate staff, and, in periods of normal employment, a lack of recruits to fill empty positions. If available revenues are inadequate to pay prevailing

wages to the existing number of employees, a government jurisdiction should, rather than pay substandard wages, postpone capital expenditures or curtail services, even if this involves a reduction in staff.

There are still many business leaders, elected officials, and even some government administrators who contend that public employees should be paid less than the prevailing rate in private industry because of compensating considerations such as greater security of employment, superior fringe benefits, and less demand for productivity.

Productivity has been the subject of intensified research in the 1970s. Escalating costs, increased demands for service, and growing resistance to increased taxes require that public administrators be able to demonstrate the full and effective utilization of manpower. The studies of the National Commission on Productivity should be followed by all government officials, particularly those who sit at the bargaining table or carry other responsibilities for pay administration. Hard data are available to counter the fables about lifelong sinecures and overgenerous benefits. The total compensation approach, discussed later, could put an effective end to the benefit controversy.

3. Wage changes should be made selectively by classes, and not as an across-the-board adjustment through which all employees in a jurisdiction receive the same percentage change in salary. The relationship among pay rates for different classes of jobs in private industry is constantly changing. The result of an across-the-board adjustment in public pay is that the salaries for some jobs are raised when they do not deserve to be. This is both unfair and unnecessarily expensive.

Increasing pressures very likely will cause even more confusion on this issue. The effects of the cost-of-living and the consumer price indexes on salaries will be treated separately. The idea that either index ought to be used as the sole basis for salary adjustment does not deserve serious consideration. However, as those who must make the final decisions on pay matters are subject to increasing harangues that the cost of a loaf of bread is the same for both the lowest-rank employee and the top executive, there will be a greater tendency for administrators to take the easy way out and grant everyone the same increase. (Rarely, if ever, will a uniform adjustment be shown for all classes.)

Demands were being voiced in the mid-1970s that the classes on the lower end of the salary schedules should receive a bonus or some benefit based on a more generous interpretation of salary data. These kinds of problems are best left to political decision makers. All that the pay administrator can do is present the data along with sound recommendations to the policy-making authorities.

4. In the present over-all five-step salary schedule, there is an approximate 5.5 percent differential between each step on any given schedule and the corresponding step on the schedules immediately above and below. This means that the salary for a particular job must usually be adjusted by at least 5.5 percent, or not at all, to overcome this and to permit salaries to be adjusted more closely to the results of the Joint Salary Survey. Intermediate schedules should be inserted half-way between the present schedules.

This recommendation was adopted in 1962 by the agencies participating in the survey and later by many others in the area. It has not proved a panacea, however, since the basic problem remains one of interpreting the salary survey data, especially on the point whether the particular index figure arrived at is closer to the next higher or next lower salary schedule.

A major dilemma caused by the creation of the 2.75 percent differential between succeeding salary schedules is the constant demand by employee representatives to have classifications established which recognize the same 2.75 percent differential. Again, more will be said later about the relationship between the classification and the compensation plans. At this point, a cautionary note should be made: There is no research evidence to show that, even with the use of point evaluation plans, classification distinctions of less than 15 percent intervals can be reliably made.

5. In the Joint Survey, efforts should be continued to improve the selection of benchmark jobs and to broaden the coverage of private employers surveyed.

Continuing attention has been focused and continuing criticism has been heard on this issue. In the 1970s the trend has been to increase the number of benchmark jobs used in the survey. This action has been in response to challenges raised by various groups about how salaries applying to 1,000 or more classifications can be set by reference to fewer than 50 benchmarks.

It is suggested here that it is far more important to strive to improve existing benchmarks and attempt to assure comparability than it is to dissipate efforts by introducing new and possibly confusing benchmarks. This is not to deny the need for new benchmarks that may arise because of new occupational fields or technological developments.

6. There should be created an Advisory Committee to the Steering Committee of the Joint Survey, composed of a representative of the interests of taxpayers, a representative of the interests of employees, and an impartial chairman representing the public interest, the last possibly a university or college official. The function of this committee should be to recommend improvements in the survey process and to call to public attention significant departures in any jurisdiction from the survey results.

This recommendation too was partially implemented. It actually represents a paradox, because while the intent clearly is to achieve uniformity among the survey participants, the fact is that one jurisdiction—the county—unilaterally heeded the recommendation but subsequently has become increasingly independent in its salary actions. The Los Angeles County

Citizens Economy and Efficiency Commission in July 1966 recommended a consolidation of all personnel functions, including the responsibility for salary and wage administration, and their assignment to one department. The position of director of personnel was established as a charter position and was given responsibility to administer all centralized personnel activities.

The concept of an advisory committee is essentially a sound one for whatever purpose. A fact-finding body is in reality an advisory committee. The major problem is to assure that all elements of the community are satisfactorily represented.

7. Either the Joint Survey Steering Committee, or an inter-jurisdictional committee created for the purpose, should meet at least annually to consider the possibilities (a) of greater job standardization or uniformity of job classes among the various jurisdictions and consequent uniformity of wage rates, and (b) of improved uniformity of fringe benefits and other conditions of employment among the various jurisdictions.

This is another partially implemented recommendation. The Survey Policy Committee holds one or more meetings before and after the Working Committee meetings to discuss improvements. Subsequent developments, however, particularly the development of separate organizational units for the purpose of negotiating with employee representatives in the City and the County of Los Angeles, have resulted in a greater tendency for each of the agencies to take unilateral action without consultation with the other members of the Survey Policy Committee.

8. The various jurisdictions should, individually or jointly, at least every five years, make a systematic comparison of the fringe benefits they are providing with fringe benefits provided by private employers. The objective should be to keep the level of aggregate fringe benefits provided to public employees up to, but not above, the level of such benefits in private employment. Al-

though it would, in principle, be desirable to evaluate such benefits annually and to adjust wage-survey rates upward or downward accordingly, the variety of fringe benefits (pensions, sick leave, vacations, health plans and others) is so great and the problem of computing their equivalent cash value is so complex that this is not a practical possibility.

This particular recommendation has been rendered groundless, not so much by the rapid advance of computer methods that handle calculations as by the prodding of the legislature and other groups. As mentioned earlier, various approaches to the determination of total equivalent compensation necessitates making an annual review of fringe benefits and their costs.

9. Employees and employee groups should be given a reasonable opportunity for advance consultation on the wage rate to be recommended. The procedures are not as important as the spirit in which this is done, but, in any event, consultation with employees through their representatives should be standard practice prior to the official transmission of the recommendation by the administrative officer to the legislative body.

In the estimation of some professionals, collective bargaining represents the ultimate in advance consultation with employee representatives. In those jurisdictions not under collective bargaining procedures, a series of meetings with administrators, employee representatives, and any other interested parties is held to discuss the interpretation of the data, benchmark by benchmark. A calendar of meetings at which preliminary salary recommendations, counterproposals, and, eventually, final salary recommendations are presented is published each year at the start of the salary survey season.

10. To secure the services of the most thoroughly competent executives in career positions, government must be prepared to pay compensation reasonably comparable to that paid by private business for the same skills and capacities. Salaries of career executives in public service should, therefore, be evaluated on the same basis as the salaries of other public employees, that of prevailing rates, and should not necessarily be limited by the salaries provided by charter or constitutional provision for elected officials.

Executive salaries have received considerable attention in the Los Angeles area, and some innovative approaches have been attempted. Parity with the private sector certainly has not been achieved. Nevertheless, a substantial number of public executives in the 1970s are earning more than $50,000 a year.

The Salary Schedule

The structure of the salary schedule is one of the fundamentals that must be completely rationalized in order to develop a comprehensive salary policy. The first step in the process of constructing a salary schedule is to determine the minimum and the maximum rates paid by the city. The answers to the questions, Who should set these limits? and How should they be set in the public service? are still to be found.

Current developments may soon render the concept of salary schedules obsolete. For example, union insistence on extracting the last dollar for an immediate adjustment has caused some jurisdictions to abandon or modify substantially the traditional type of salary schedule. This is not to suggest that there is something sacrosanct about the structure of the customary pay plans adopted by most jurisdictions. Actually, a strong case can be made for pay plans which do not exhibit the strict uniformity found in what are known as integrated pay schedules.

After determining the minimum and maximum rates to be included in the master salary schedule, the next step is to decide whether a single rate (flat rate) or a range of pay consisting of several pay rates (steps) shall apply to all classes. Most jurisdictions apply the step plan. Some of the reasons for doing so include the following:

1. A single rate provides no opportunity for granting increases based on seniority or merit. This denies the benefit of incentive to improve productivity and performance.
2. A single rate precludes flexibility in hiring rates for new employees. It assumes all new employees will be equally productive at the time of hiring. Further, it denies the opportunity to recognize past experience or exceptional training.
3. A single rate for all employees increases pressures for more frequent general wage increases and individual reclassifications.

The major use of the flat rate is in relation to classes that are so highly unionized that, in effect, a single rate of pay actually prevails in the community. One justification for the practice is that the policy of employing only those who qualify for journeyman status assures a standard level of proficiency; therefore, it is appropriate to pay all employees the same rate.

INTEGRATED AND NONINTEGRATED SCHEDULES

The terms "integrated" and "nonintegrated" pay schedule require explanation. In an integrated pay schedule, the rates are repeated several times. For each higher salary range, the bottom rate is eliminated and a higher rate is added as the maximum. Generally the rates assigned to a salary range remain constant and classifications are allocated to a higher range when a salary increase is granted.

In a nonintegrated schedule there may or may not be an overlapping of rates in succeeding salary ranges, and the same rate need not appear more than once. The amount of increase between rates and between ranges need not be uniform.

The integrated schedule is the more commonly used method. Advantages of this method are that it permits relatively fine distinctions to be made in allocating classes to salary ranges, and it makes payroll calculations much simpler. A problem with nonintegrated schedules is that typically they include rates which are so close to one another that the differences are

Salary Range	5 steps with 5% intervals				
	1	2	3	4	5
1	$500	$525	$551	$579	$608
2	525	551	579	608	638
3	551	579	608	638	670
4	579	608	638	670	704
5	608	638	670	704	739
6	638	670	704	739	776
7	670	704	739	776	815
8	704	739	776	815	856
9	739	776	815	856	899
10	776	815	856	899	944

FIGURE 9–2. *Sample integrated master salary schedule, showing five steps with 5 percent intervals. See text for further discussion.*

meaningless and therefore they provide no real incentive to employees. (See Figure 9–2 for an example of an integrated master salary schedule.)

SIZE OF STEPS

In an integrated pay schedule the difference between one step and the next higher step increases by a constant percentage. The increment most commonly employed is 5 percent. During the economic slowdown that took place in the late 1950s, considerable pressure was exerted to reduce the gap between pay ranges. One argument advanced was that employees preferred to receive annual increases of 2 or 3 percent rather than be forced to forgo an increase one year in order to receive a 5 or 6 percent increase the next year. In the Los Angeles area, where a 5.5 percent interval between pay ranges was applied, intermediate rates or half-steps were introduced in 1962. The percentage increment between succeeding ranges therefore was reduced to 2.75 percent.

It is true that this procedure permits a more precise application of the data, but equally true is the conclusion that it provides a basis for the application of increased pressure for a more liberal interpretation of the data when one of the indexes falls just short of the next higher salary range. Moreover, the accuracy of survey methods and data processing techniques has been subjected to sharper questioning.

There are no scientific research findings available which provide an answer to the question, How much of an increase is necessary to be meaningful and provide an incentive to the employee? A reasonable response is that the amount is likely to vary with each employee. In general, however, a percentage figure rather than a flat amount is the more appropriate basis for gauging the increment. It could be expected that a $50 a month increase would not mean the same thing to a senior administrator that it would to a typist, and almost certainly the administrator would receive a smaller net gain after taxes than would the typist.

Number of Steps

Common practice is to include five or six steps in a pay range. As indicated before, there is no scientific or even logical basis for this practice. A theoretically sound basis for determining the number of steps in a salary range would be the potential for increased productivity: How long does it take to master a position in the class? What opportunity for growth and development exists in the positions? Is the best employee's performance worth 25 percent more than the acceptable employee's effort?

Actually the latter possibility should be more bluntly and accurately stated as, Is the typical employee's performance worth 25 percent more after three and a half to four years on the job? The concept here is that those classes which are more complex or involve more responsibility and consequently take a longer period to attain top proficiency should have a wider range and greater number of pay steps than classes involving routine tasks that are quickly learned.

A number of other considerations affect the number of pay steps included in the salary range. Among these are adding longevity steps for dead-end classes; including shorter ranges for entry-level classes to stimulate employees to qualify for promotion; or varying the number of steps according to the range of data obtained in the community salary survey. The latter is considered a particularly valid approach when the agency has adopted a basic policy of a five-step range plan and the community data span only three or four steps of a range.

For any jurisdiction facing the need to construct a salary schedule, the "5–by–5" plan is suggested, which consists of salary ranges of five steps with a uniform increment of 5 percent between each step. This means that the spread between the minimum and maximum rate of the range is 25 percent. It is emphasized that this plan should be considered only as a starting point, with modifications to be made on the basis of community practice and the theoretical concepts outlined above.

The true test of a salary schedule is how well it accommodates the data, and a good reason for modifying a salary schedule is if it does not accommodate the data that have been gathered. However, before ascribing all ills to the structure of the salary schedule, it is in order to review basic procedures for conducting salary surveys to determine whether valid data have been gathered. The next section sets out some of the principal guidelines in gathering the pay data.

Gathering the Pay Data

Data are data, and thus it should be a relatively simple matter to collect and compile the salary data. Easier said than done. Salary surveys have been conducted for many years, and based on their experience a model salary survey could be developed. Before discussing the key factors in planning and conducting a salary survey, it is advisable to consider alternatives to the do-it-yourself approach.

A suggested first step is to review information resources already available. Is there a sound, reliable salary survey conducted by an organization, public or private, in your community? The United States Bureau of Labor Statistics covers 82 labor markets, and consultation with one of its regional directors is strongly recommended. Even if a cooperative effort with other agencies cannot be worked out, it is worth at least contacting these sources to avoid any duplication of effort in gathering pay data.

The American Management Association, the Administrative Management Society, the National Office Management Association, and the Merchants and Manufacturers Association are among the organizations that conduct highly respected surveys. Municipal leagues, associations of county governments, and state personnel agencies are other likely sources for salary survey data.

A growing trend is evident toward utilizing the interagency joint pay survey conducted by the several public agencies that operate in the same community. In addition to the obvious advantages of a joint survey, such as sharing the costs and avoiding duplication of effort, there are many valuable by-products, such as promoting an exchange of data on a variety of problems among the participating jurisdictions. It also produces an ecumenical effect by preventing the survey from being identified as the work of any one agency.

Funds have been allocated under the Intergovernmental Personnel Act of 1970 for projects to evaluate local agency compensation practices and to develop a salary and supplemental wage benefit information service. One of the criteria for such projects is that the study develop a transferable methodology or set of guidelines which can be used by other agencies. (Inasmuch as the results of the program had not been published as of this writing, readers are urged to refer to professional personnel journals such as *Public Personnel Management* for status reports of the program.)

There are drawbacks, of course, in using surveys prepared by others. The most obvious is the problem of assuring comparability. A most troublesome issue which is almost certain to arise relates to the time lag between the collection of the data and the implementation of the recommendations. Of growing concern also is the employee representative's insistence on knowing the sources of the data and participating in the collection of data. A sample page of a survey form found useful in the city of Los Angeles is reproduced as Figure 9–3.

If, after careful evaluation of the pros and cons, the organization decides to conduct its own salary survey, the two most important questions to consider in planning a survey are, What is to be surveyed? and What is the geographical area to be surveyed? These questions obviously are interdependent. The area to be surveyed must be manageable yet broad enough to yield a quantity and range of data sufficient for analysis.

Where: Defining the Survey Area

Usually the survey of clerical salaries will be limited to the immediate community. Employees generally are unwilling to travel long distances or relocate unless they are paid salaries significantly higher than those they could earn if employed closer to their homes. It would be difficult to justify such differentials for entry-level clerical classes unless highly unusual circumstances prevailed. On the other hand, if the agency is the only major employer of engineers in the community, then it is going to be forced to look elsewhere in order to obtain an adequate sample of salary data relating to that occupation.

There are also certain occupational areas such as police, fire protection, and recreation that are peculiar to government. Unless the organization is situated in a multigovernment metropolitan central area, the choice exists of either extending the area covered by the survey or else basing salaries on an internal alignment between classes within the organization itself. It is recommended that, unless there are legal restrictions confining an organization to a local survey, the area of the survey should be aligned with the area from which the organization recruits. A corollary is to relate the area of the survey to the area of competition for the particular classification being surveyed. On this point, data from national surveys may be taken into consideration.

What: Selecting Benchmark Classes

The decision about what to survey is likely to be the most controversial issue faced in planning the salary study. Increasingly employee representatives have contended that all classes not directly related to a benchmark class should receive an across-the-board raise so that everyone is treated alike. Some third party interests have criticized this position, saying that most surveys use too few benchmarks. They cannot comprehend how a survey using thirty, forty, or even sixty benchmarks can provide a sufficiently broad base on which to establish salaries for 1,000 or more classifications.

JOB DESCRIPTION	SUPPLEMENTARY NOTES	OTHER COMPENSATION	ACTUAL PAY RATES AND NUMBER OF EMPLOYEES DOING THIS KIND OF WORK
180. MACHINIST: Does journeyman work in cutting and shaping metal to precise dimensions within close tolerances, using precision machine and hand tools in the fabrication, assembly, installation, and repair of machinery, machinery parts, and machine equipment; working from blueprints and sketches, sets up and operates such machines as: lathes, shapers, planers, grinders, milling machines, and radial drill presses; makes bushings and bearings of brass, steel, copper, and babbit; turns, bores, shapes, drills and taps bases, frames, shafts, pulleys, gears, bearings, pins, bolts, and nuts; cuts grooves and slots; makes necessary calculations and uses calipers, micrometers, and gauges. Does not include machine operators.	Firm title: Reports to: Closest tolerance req. ______ Machines used ______ ______ ______ Works on ______ ______	Cash bonus— Explain: $ ____ per yr. Meals B | L | D 1 | 2 | 3 Value Per Mo. $______ Uniform Full | Partial Cleaning Value Per Mo. $______ Other: Value Per Mo. $______	Actual Pay Rates No. of Empl. Hrs. Per Week: **RATES ARE PER (Circle One)** Hour / Week / Every 2 Weeks / Year / Day / Month / Twice a Month / Other Do not Write in These Spaces
190. STATIONARY ENGINEER — HIGH PRESSURE (15 LBS. AND OVER): Operates and maintains high-pressure gas or oil fired boilers in supplying steam or high temperature high pressure water for other than power generating purposes; operates and maintains stationary air conditioning and refrigeration machinery; operates and maintains all auxiliaries associated with heating and cooling systems including pumps compressors, evaporators, condensers, and water softeners; makes minor emergency repairs on plumbing, piping, valves, electrical fixtures and other equipment; maintains a log of all operating conditions. An unrestricted Steam Engineer's License is required if working in the City of Los Angeles.	Firm title: Reports to: Use of steam ______ Major repair by: ______ Works on plant production machinery Yes___ No___ Employed in Los Angeles City Yes___ No___ License required Yes___ No___ Central Air Conditioning Yes___ No___	Cash bonus— Explain: $ ____ per yr. Meals B | L | D 1 | 2 | 3 Value Per Mo. $______ Uniform Full | Partial Cleaning Value Per Mo. $______ Other: Value Per Mo. $______	Actual Pay Rates No. of Empl. Hrs. Per Week: **RATES ARE PER (Circle One)** Hour / Week / Every 2 Weeks / Year / Day / Month / Twice a Month / Other Do not Write in These Spaces
200. GARAGE ATTENDANT: Performs manual tasks confined almost exclusively to the non-mechanical servicing of automotive equipment in shop, garage, and in the field, including the lubrications of automotive equipment; supplies automotive equipment with oil, water, air and gasoline; changes oil; changes tires and tubes; checks and replaces items such as batteries, spark plugs, and windshield wipers and oil filters; may wash and polish autos, busses, or trucks.	Firm title: Reports to: Duties include: Some lube work Yes___ No___ All lube work Yes___ No___	Cash bonus— Explain: $ ____ per yr. Meals B | L | D 1 | 2 | 3 Value Per Mo. $______ Uniform Full | Partial Cleaning Value Per Mo. $______ Other: Value Per Mo. $______	Actual Pay Rates No. of Empl. Hrs. Per Week: **RATES ARE PER (Circle One)** Hour / Week / Every 2 Weeks / Year / Day / Month / Twice a Month / Other Do not Write in These Spaces
210. Automotive Mechanic: Repairs a variety of gasoline and diesel-powered equipment such as passenger automobiles, trucks, busses and forklifts; diagnoses faulty engine operation; overhauls engines, manual and automatic transmissions, differentials, suspension systems, and manual and power assisted steering systems; replaces worn or broken parts; grinds valves; diagnoses malfunctions and repairs electrical systems, including generators, alternators, distributors, and ignition systems; repairs and overhauls hydraulic and air brake systems; diagnoses malfunctions and repairs auxiliary hydraulic systems; and may repair automotive air conditioning and refrigeration units.	Firm title: Reports to: Main work on: Bus ______ Truck ______ Pass. Auto ______ Others ______ Works on Diesel Yes___ No___ Commissions Yes___ No___	Cash bonus— Explain: $ ____ per yr. Meals B | L | D 1 | 2 | 3 Value Per Mo. $______ Uniform Full | Partial Cleaning Value Per Mo. $______ Other: Value Per Mo. $______	Actual Pay Rates No. of Empl. Hrs. Per Week: **RATES ARE PER (Circle One)** Hour / Week / Every 2 Weeks / Year / Day / Month / Twice a Month / Other Do not Write in These Spaces

FIGURE 9–3. *Sample job descriptions, supplementary notes, pay data, and other information for illustrative classes of municipal employees. See text for further discussion. (Source: Based on wage and salary survey form used by the city of Los Angeles.)*

It appeared in the mid-1970s that a major breakthrough in achieving greater comparability of the positions included in salary surveys was imminent. Both public and private employers, staffing fifteen or more employees, became subject to the provisions established by the U.S. Equal Employment Opportunity Commission. With growing attention directed to job analysis for selection purposes, a more comprehensive understanding of what the employee does and the critical knowledges, skills, and abilities required to perform the job would become available. With this information in hand, coupled with the removal of artificial barriers and specialized requirements, employers will find themselves competing in the same labor pool. The concomitant effect should be that wages will equalize.

A very important point should be made at this juncture: The technological advances achieved in the last two decades, particularly the capacity to amass, record, and tabulate huge amounts of data, provide the basis for making certain that equal pay is paid for equal work.

It is possible that some day there will be a uniform system of job coding, using perhaps the Dictionary of Occupational Titles as the foundation. If these codes were to be used on state or federal tax forms such as the W–2, it would then become a reasonably simple matter to program computers to extract the necessary data about specific benchmarks. Actually a prototype program, known as the Salary Information Retrieval System (SIRS), has already been developed by the System Development Corporation of Santa Monica, California.

Until prototype becomes functioning reality, the way to proceed in a survey is to collect data on a selected group of benchmark descriptions. In determining what to survey, the following considerations are offered:

1. There should be at least one benchmark for each occupational group. As discussed earlier, it may be necessary to survey outside the community to obtain an adequate sample.
2. Unless there are discrete factors, such as the distinction between stenographers and typists in the use of shorthand, it is unwise to select more than one benchmark for application to closely related classes in the same occupational group. The most perplexing question in salary administration is what to do when the survey data do not conform with differentials established under the classification plan. While there may be a genuine need to survey for a supervisory or management benchmark as a check on established differentials, there is no apparent need to collect data on succeeding levels in a hierarchy, such as Clerk-Typist A and Clerk-Typist B.
3. Some of the criteria for selecting a benchmark class are as follows:
   a. A benchmark class should involve jobs which can be defined clearly and concisely.
   b. It should involve jobs found in relatively large numbers in the survey area.
   c. It should involve jobs which are essentially the same in business and government.
   d. It should involve jobs for which standard titles are commonly used.
   e. Primarily, a benchmark class should involve entrance-level jobs. Some higher-level jobs should be included, but they must be jobs for which the skill and experience level can be clearly and easily defined. As desirable as it might be to have data on Senior Secretary, Chief Clerk, or Accounting Supervisor, other means of setting salaries for these classes of jobs must be used, because comparability cannot be assured in the usual salary survey.
   f. The number of benchmarks should be limited. Some occupational series will have several job classes that fit the preceding criteria. Ordinarily only one good benchmark is required to check the salaries for an entire series. Job relationships within a series which are already established and accepted should not be changed on the basis of a single survey.
4. The benchmark definitions are an elevated part of planning the survey. If the definitions are unsatisfactory, comparability will not be accurate and the survey results will

not be valid. If the definitions are good but too long, they will not be read through by many participants and, consequently, the results will have less validity. Some guidelines in preparing benchmark definitions follow:

a. They should be as concise as possible.
b. They must indicate the nature of the work. For jobs which have a common descriptive title, this part of the definition can be very brief.
c. The skill and experience level required to perform the job successfully should be spelled out clearly.
d. The extent of supervision exercised, if any, should be stated.
e. The definition should not be merely copied from an existing class description. This practice often results in the use of jargon peculiar to the organization conducting the survey, and this in turn may lead participants to make a premature judgment regarding noncomparability.
f. The definition should be incorporated with the title on the salary data sheet. If the definition is located in a separate section of the questionnaire, many participants will not bother to refer to it, with the possible result being a matching by title only, thus diminishing the likelihood of achieving real comparability of positions on which the data are being gathered.

How: Survey Methodology

Among the alternative methods of collecting salary survey data are mailed questionnaires, telephone or personal interviews with each participant, or, if only a few employers are involved, the conference method.

In the latter method the participants gather around a conference table and exchange data on the benchmarks in which they are interested. There are various advantages of the personal visit over the mail or telephone surveys. For instance, there is less chance of error in comparison of jobs. An experienced data collector can persuade the firm's representative to cooperate, explain the methodology, go over the benchmark descriptions and ask questions or offer explanations to minimize compara-

bility errors, record the data, thank the contact, and leave, thereby completing the contact in just one visit.

It is particularly important to provide the data collector with the information form and data of the previous year so that he or she can catch inconsistencies or errors before the new data are recorded. An additional benefit of the personal visit is the value derived from establishing a direct contact with the private firms in the community.

The two obvious drawbacks to the personal visit are time and money. Making appointments with the employers' representatives, working out an efficient schedule for the data collector, and completing all the visits within a limited time span can pose many problems. There is always the possibility that during the visit the employer's representative, a busy executive, may be interrupted with phone calls or decide the interview will take too much time and ask that the forms be left behind to be completed later. Or the employer's representative may either have to call upon or summon others in the company who know the job(s) well enough to help fill out the forms.

The mailed questionnaire method is considered the most practical by many survey experts. It generally requires longer time to complete than does the direct contact method. However, if one is faced with the task of either starting a new survey or greatly expanding one previously used, the mailed questionnaire is usually better received by participants because they can complete the forms at their convenience. Participants can refer the forms to a knowledgeable person who can check for comparability. Agencies using the mailed questionnaire claim they can achieve a 75 percent return if they also make appropriate follow-up efforts.

There appears to be a virtual consensus, particularly among smaller agencies, favoring a combination method—the mailed questionnaire followed by a personal visit to collect the completed form and resolve any problems relating to interpretation. The combination method does appear to offer most of the benefits achieved by both the other methods, although a cost-benefit analysis of the combination method remains to be conducted.

WHEN: TIMING OF THE SURVEY

The optimum time for a salary survey is salary adjustment time. For most jurisdictions operating on a July 1–June 30 fiscal year, this means an early spring survey, with the recommendations developed from it presented in late May or early June. This procedure can be criticized for its time lag. The problem is bad enough if it is simply a matter of data being collected in March and applied in July; it becomes more acute if the data collected in March actually represent an adjustment which private industry has granted its employees the preceding July.

An alternative would be to time the survey immediately after the majority of sources contacted have made their adjustments. However, analysis of the calendars of wage settlements reveals that salaries are adjusted throughout the year. Therefore, it is difficult to designate a time period when the greatest number of adjustments will be reported.

This particular fact has further complicated the controversy regarding the prevailing rate principle, since some contend that it is impossible to follow changes in the prevailing rates that take place on a monthly, weekly, or even daily basis. Those responsible for fiscal planning insist that prudent budgeting practice limits general salary adjustments to once a year. A reasonable compromise of the two views has been to conduct a semi-annual survey recheck on a basis more limited than the annual survey and then recommend adjustments for those classes which have fallen a set percentage behind the prevailing rate.

In periods of rapid, widespread salary escalation, pressures are exerted to consider adjustments even more frequently. Some groups have even renewed their proposals to tie salary adjustments to the Consumer Price Index to permit quarterly adjustments. The cost of living, as measured by the Consumer Price Index and as used or misused in salary adjustments, will be discussed later in this chapter.

WHO: DETERMINING THE SURVEY SAMPLE

Theoretically, a community salary survey should include data from every employer willing to participate. It is particularly important in large metropolitan areas that the survey sample reflect data from all types of employers in the community. A common criticism made of many existing surveys is that they overrepresent the large employers, i.e., firms with more than 200 employees.

It is obviously impractical to survey small employers who may have only one or two positions comparable to the survey benchmark descriptions. A notable exception is the need to contact smaller firms to get an adequate sample for specialized occupations such as architects and engineers. It is also suggested that conscious effort is made to include a representative sprinkling of small firms so that a test can be made of the hypothesis that they tend to pay either exceptionally high or exceptionally low rates.

It is extremely important that the makeup of the sample, measured by the industrial nature of firms contacted, be closely related to the industrial makeup of the community. Care should be exercised so that no one firm or industry completely dominates the survey. Dominance is possible, even in an area which has a widely diversified industrial base. For example, concern was widely expressed in the Los Angeles area in the past that the aerospace industries actually set the community rates because so much data derived from that source. Analysis showed that this concern generally was justified, even with respect to such unlikely benchmarks as clerk-typist and stenographer.

Organizations should consult the local Chamber of Commerce and the state employment service for readily available information about the community's industrial makeup. These bodies also are helpful in identifying firms which employ workers in particular occupations. Two additional sources of data not always included in salary surveys are unions and other public agencies. Even if the union data are used only to cross-check the data received from firms, the contact is valuable because it assures employees that all sources of data have been considered.

While there are those who criticize the practice of one public agency surveying other public agencies, claiming that it means chasing one another with the result that rates escalate, there are many public jobs which have no counterpart in industry and, thus, other public agencies are the only source of data on these jobs. Special-purpose public agencies which have independent governing boards should not be overlooked in such surveys. This category includes school districts, rapid transit districts, sanitation districts, irrigation districts, air pollution districts, and recreation and park boards.

Equally important as the coverage and content of the survey is the maintenance of the confidentiality of the data, that is, it should not be possible to identify any firm as the source of a specific rate or other data. This assurance usually is a necessary precondition to obtaining the participation of most firms. However, a growing number will permit their names to be included in a list of participants. Release of such a list encourages the participation of other firms and helps build confidence in the validity of the published survey data.

Emphasis has been made of the great care and diligence required in gathering the pay data. The next step is even more critical. Without accurate and objective analysis and interpretation of the pay data, all other efforts are nullified. It would have been reasonable to expect that by the mid-1970s a set of universally accepted standards would have been developed. Unfortunately that was not the case. Nevertheless, some suggestions regarding the interpretation of the data can be outlined.

Interpretation of the Pay Data

Interpretation of the data warrants more attention than it has received in the past. Depending on its interpretation, it is possible for the data to influence if not determine such things as the width of salary ranges, the number of pay grades, and the percentage interval between pay grades. It is necessary to advance beyond the traditional interpretation of the interquartile range, the median, and the weighted average.

Even a cursory inspection of the total range of data for each benchmark would be constructive. For example, a range of $348 to $1,080 per month for custodians could be expected to cause concern about the degree of editing the survey director has exercised. The actual configuration of the data also is instructive, as it facilitates a more accurate interpretation of the measures of central tendency. Is the distribution polymodal? Is it skewed? Are the rates paid by a single large employer influencing the entire community survey? Or does a single union rate dominate all other data?

Answers to these and many other perplexing problems can be found in the course of processing the data. A device known as an X–Y plotter attached to the tabulating equipment, or a simple prepackaged program for the computer can save countless staff hours of calculation and even more hours of wrangling about seemingly inexplicable quirks in the data.

Some critics are concerned that the provision of too much data, particularly if it must be shared in a collective bargaining session, will lead to prolonged debate over aberrations in the data, but this concern seems unfounded. The capability exists to determine with a high degree of accuracy various measures of central tendency of the data.

Whether it is advisable that all parties redefine the prevailing rate or substitute a concept of prevailing range, i.e., the weighted average plus or minus one standard deviation, is an appropriate subject for further study by academicians, practitioners, and negotiators. Suffice it here to say that it is time for an organization to review its procedures if, in correlating the first step of its salary range with the first quartile of the survey data, it finds its rate is exceeded by rates of a 75 percent margin of persons employed elsewhere performing similar work.

Steadfast adherence to a policy of starting all new employees at the first step of a set salary range means not only that the prevailing rate is not being offered but also that the organization is limiting its recruitment to those who are unemployed, those doing only lower-level work, or those in the bottom quartile of wage earners performing the work in question. The effects of this policy on an organization's work force, when there exists a real need to hire fully qualified journeymen for a class, should be self-evident.

On the other hand, many jurisdictions pay almost exclusive attention to the weighted average or median, matching the middle step of their salary range to that figure. The frequent result is that the top step of the range not only exceeds the third quartile but often may exceed the ninetieth percentile. This is not to suggest there is anything wrong in setting a maximum rate for a city employee that equals the maximum rate paid for the same work in the industrial community. It does raise a question, however, whether the city has the means of assuring itself that its top performers are matched in productivity and pay rates with their peers in industry.

Performance evaluation and productivity are the subjects of other chapters in this volume. As to the subject of public pay administration, it is advisable to use the third quartile resulting from the data as an effective limit for the normal maximum rates of the salary range for a benchmark class. Distortions caused by longevity steps or the possible introduction of incentive steps for outstanding performance of course should not be disregarded.

Relationship between the Classification Plan and the Salary Plan

There are two primary bases for setting salaries. These are: 1) comparison with wages paid by other employers, and 2) internal alignment —that is, establishing relationships among the various classifications in the organization, using one or more techniques of job evaluation. Actually all agencies with which this writer is familiar use a combination of the two.

Considering the diversification of work found in public agencies today, it is highly unlikely that the necessary time and money can be devoted to conduct a salary survey for each type of job. (This situation illustrates the point where the classification and salary processes are joined.) Although any of the techniques of job evaluation can be used to develop a relative ranking of jobs, the point evaluation technique is generally favored, probably because it has face validity and possesses apparent objectivity.

There are some who hold that position classification should be carried out separate from the determination of pay. Several jurisdictions still maintain a dichotomous practice whereby the civil service department is responsible for classification and the city manager's office makes the salary recommendations. A reason frequently advanced for this practice is that the classification plan is used for many purposes other than setting pay.

The job hierarchy established in the classification plan provides a foundation for most personnel activities. People are recruited for specific classifications, i.e., clerk, clerk-typist, clerk-stenographer. The same holds true for placement, training, job accounting, promotion, and layoff. Actually, most organization and management decisions—who does what, when, and how—are dependent on job analysis.

Unfortunately, the separation of classification from pay is based sometimes on the struggle for authority between the budgeting and the personnel units. If the budget agency has strong leadership, it likely will make the salary surveys and prepare the pay recommendations. Personnel administrators contend that recommending pay rates for individual classes requires a thorough knowledge of the classification plan. The compromise most often effected is that the budget officials make the pay recommendations on the basis of the classification plan established by the personnel staff. The desirable approach would be to regard the personnel and budget functions as phases of an integrated management process which produces a set of pay recommendations on which there is firm consensus. Anything less than that is apt to result in a weak position and hamper the administration's efforts in the bargaining process.

The first prerequisite for combining classification and pay data is a complete set of current class descriptions which accurately reflect the duties and responsibilities being carried out by incumbents and which also clearly delineate the degrees of difference between class concepts. Consideration of the classification policy to be adopted by the agency has been covered in Chapter 4. The point to be made here is that a policy of establishing "broad classes" enables the agency to either broaden the salary ranges and/or provide significant salary increments between levels of classes in the same occupational field. Conversely, if relatively minor differences result in many levels within a hierarchy or lead to the creation of many specialized classes, the differences in salary must be correspondingly smaller.

Despite some of the techniques or gadgetry which job analysts have developed, the degree of precision possible in classification judgments leaves much to be desired. It is doubtful if differences of less than 5 percent between classes could be scientifically validated. Some experts point out that it takes highly trained technicians to achieve reliable results using 15 percent intervals. Adopting a pragmatic approach, it is unlikely that any jurisdiction could financially support a salary structure which provides a 15 percent interval between each succeeding class level. This claim is reinforced when one considers today's conditions when employees or their representatives press for tangible recognition of every difference they can find.

It is suggested that we accept the definition of a pay plan as "the assignment of dollar values to job classes."[7] This is not to imply that there is anything mechanical about the process. It is essential before continuing this discussion of the pay plan, which is the essence of pay administration, that we carefully analyze the classification plan and recognize any weaknesses and aberrations which may have been introduced into it.

Perhaps the most perplexing problem in developing and maintaining the pay plan is how to reconcile the dilemma which arises when the salary survey data lead to conclusions directly contradictory to those produced by the classification analysis. Consider the case of the driver of the truck for the tree-trimming crew who might make more than the crew foreman. The problem is not really resolved by assigning the foreman to drive the truck, because that only leads to the equally knotty problem of how to price mixed-class positions, i.e., performing duties which are appropriately allocated to two or more classes.

Rather than create a series of special classes, it is usually preferable to give these classes special salary treatment. The most common approach is to base the salary on the preponderant duties. Others advocate paying according to the highest level of work involved. More sophisticated alternatives are to pay a differential over a base rate, or to maintain detailed time reports as to time spent in each class and pay accordingly.

A most useful visual aid when relating classification to pay is the levels chart. The variations of this device are practically unlimited. In its simplest form, it is a ranking of classes in a hierarchy according to the relative difficulty of duties and responsibilities. As a beginning it is suggested that the classes be plotted on a graph or grid in a manner that adequately reflects the differences in ranking between the classes in the occupational series. For example, does the class of secretary fit exactly halfway between the classes of administrative secretary and intermediate clerk-stenographer? Such comparisons are aided by point-rating plans, but it is not essential to have such a plan to prepare a levels chart.

It is strongly suggested that a second chart be prepared, listing the classes according to their current salary range. Even without resorting to transparency overlays (or other means of combining the two charts), visual comparison will readily confirm apparent misallocations which either can be explained in terms of labor market conditions or must be subjected to further study. It is desirable of course to have a master levels chart which shows at a glance the current classification and salary relationships of all classes. Many jurisdictions find it useful to purchase a magnetic display board for this purpose.

Several point evaluation plans are in existence which purportedly have been so carefully correlated with the pay plan that x difference in points can be translated into y difference in dollars. Whether or not these plans have been developed according to sound statistical and mathematical procedures is not the major question. If they have not been so developed in the past, certainly today's technology permits the necessary refinements.

Whether or not such refinement is needed in every jurisdiction is something to be decided according to local conditions. A general reminder is that however scientific the treatment of the classification data, the original base is a matter of judgment. While Bayesian statistics and other sociometric developments may justify a high degree of confidence in the results, the amount of credence given to educated guesses is dependent on who is doing the guessing.

As mentioned elsewhere, a breakthrough may be imminent. The dictates of the Equal Employment Opportunity Commission are demanding a more thorough type of job analysis than has been accepted in the past. The U.S. Civil Service Commission undertook a major research effort on the development of a framework for a factor-ranking benchmark system of job evaluation. As of 1976 no final report had yet been issued. A classification approach that will permit recognition and application of more precise differentials between levels of classes is most definitely needed.

Special Problems in Public Pay Administration

EXECUTIVE COMPENSATION

There is almost total agreement that the problems of public administration are growing ever more complex. A concomitant requirement is the need for the most able executive talent available to fill top-level government posts. Despite many important studies by groups such as the Citizens Advisory Panel on Federal Salary Systems chaired by Clarence Randall, McKinsey and Company in New York State, and various municipalities, including Hartford, Palo Alto, and Evanston, the vexing problem of the disparity between compensation of the higher-level employees in the public service and their counterparts in industry remains. At the lower end and through the middle levels of the salary hierarchy, government pay now compares reasonably with community rates. But, despite a sprinkling of $50,000 annual salaries for some public executives, many talented and experienced administrators feel compelled to leave the public service because of salary limitations or other deficiencies in their compensation.

To cope with the situation, one needs accurate facts, not just anecdotal data. True, it may be difficult to come up with salary survey data on industry executives which can be applied to the public sector, but it is not impossible. Among the kinds of executive positions in private industry which can be compared for salary purposes with positions in the government service are the following, with public service listed first, comparable private industry listed second:

Public Service
Chief administrative officer–city manager
Controller
Director of purchasing
Personnel director
Director of data processing
Director of stores

Private Industry
Vice president, operations
Controller
Purchasing director
Director of industrial relations
Data processing manager
Warehouse superintendent

The writer's experience in contacting private firms for data on administrative and executive positions indicates that the degree of comparability which can be established between executive jobs in industry and government is as great as that which can be established for many lower-level jobs.

Titles, size of units, and number of employees supervised may vary, but there are sufficient similarities between positions in industry and government to assume that both categories of employers may turn to the same labor market for recruitment. Evidence of the validity of this assumption is found in reviewing examinations authorized by jurisdictions using "dual certification" procedures which rank promotional and outside candidates in the same competition and in which candidates from private industry were chosen over those already in the public sector. Moreover, there is evidence to show that a number of mid-management employees have left local agencies to accept better positions in private industry.

A prerequisite to adequate public executive compensation is removal of any artificial ceilings imposed on salaries. Career government employees should receive compensation in keeping with their duties and responsibilities, irrespective of the comings and goings of elected officials and administrations.

The elected official usually seeks office for completely different reasons than does the career employee. The price of the job occupied by the career employee is determined for the most part by similar jobs in other public agencies or in private industry. The career employee's salary should not be compared to that of an elected official. Elected officials place their own sets of values on the job, whereas career employees are entitled to receive an adequate salary which is in keeping with their levels of responsibility as compared with their counterparts in the public service and in private industry. The one is determined by political forces and personal values; the other, by the forces of supply and demand and the fixing of pay commensurate with the work performed.

There are two distinct and separate procedures which can be used as the bases for determining executive compensation, even if direct comparability with positions in industry cannot be established. These are an executive trend survey and a pattern of established differentials.

The executive trend survey may be made up of several component surveys. The following are data sources which may be used:

1. *Private firms:* It is suggested that an attempt be made to gather data on executive salary adjustments from at least twenty-five private firms which are headquartered in one's community. Of course, if there are not twenty-five firms in the community, a lesser number will do, but a minimum of ten is suggested. The formula given for combining data from different surveys at the end of this section will allow one to substitute several small surveys for one large one.
2. *Public utilities:* Most states require public utilities to submit detailed reports of the total earnings of all their executives earning more than a set amount. Especially for those municipalities which operate their own utilities, a high degree of comparability with public utilities' executives can be determined.
3. *Other governmental agencies:* The percentage change in salaries for executives of the state, neighboring counties, and special districts is easily obtained by writing or calling the respective personnel offices.
4. *Other neighboring jurisdictions:* Data from neighboring jurisdictions and, in particular, at least five cities of about the same size and economic conditions should be collected.
5. *Other cities in the state:* Data from cities throughout the state of about the same size and economic conditions should be gathered.
6. *Other cities throughout the nation:* Data from cities throughout the nation of about the same size and economic conditions should be gathered.

It is essential to assure the reliability of the data in a trend survey of this type. A recommended technique is to verify that data are collected on the same individuals in the same positions from year to year. If there has been a replacement of if the incumbent has been appointed to another position, the data should show it.

Several major studies have been made on patterns of desirable and actual differentials. Studies by the American Management Association and the National Industrial Conference Board are primary examples. The one point of consensus is that compression, especially in middle management ranks, is almost unavoidable. The following guidelines are offered:

1. The differential between the top executive and the next closest executive level should approximate 30 percent. Stated another way, once the chief executive's salary is fixed, the closest subordinate should receive 70 percent of the chief executive's salary rate.
2. It would be desirable to continue the 30 percent differential through the executive levels. It is assumed, of course, that the criteria for designating executive positions have been fully met. Actual experience shows, however,

that few if any public agencies can apply the 30 percent differential policy to more than two levels of executive positions.

3. The difference between salaries of executives on any one classification level may vary within a range of 5 percent to 15 percent because of occupational differences, i.e., the chief fiscal officer is usually paid more than the chief purchasing officer, even though classification analysis may indicate the jobs are equal. It is emphasized that classes evaluated as equal should receive the same rate of compensation, unless there is clear evidence from survey data showing a basis for some difference.

A special policy is suggested regarding the interpretation of data for executive classes—namely, that the overall percentage movement indicated by the executive trend survey must equal or exceed a whole schedule increase before a salary adjustment will be recommended. The percentage amount which exceeds that necessary for the whole schedule increase is carried forward and added to the overall percentage figure computed for the following year. Statisticians will recognize that this chained index approach requires the establishment of a base year and that, if in any year an exception is made in the policy, a new base year must be established.

Faced with problems of compression on the one hand and reluctance to exceed preconceived limits for public salaries on the other, many jurisdictions have developed separate compensation plans for public executives. Some of the features incorporated in these plans have been: 1) pay schedules with smaller percentage differentials between steps within a range and between succeeding ranges; 2) peer ratings as the basis for individual adjustments; 3) ratings by the city manager or a council committee as the basis for individual adjustments; and 4) additional fringe benefits in lieu of additional salary compensation. One of the major disadvantages of a separate executive salary plan is that it singles out a small group for special treatment. Particularly in times of financial difficulties, it is popular to withhold increases from the top bureaucrats. Failure of executive salaries to keep pace also further compounds the problems of salary rate compression. For example, the federal government as of the mid-1970s has four executive levels —GS-15, 16, 17, and 18—but all have the same maximum attainable salary of $37,800.

<h3>THE COST OF LIVING AS MEASURED BY THE CONSUMER PRICE INDEX</h3>

The monthly report of the Consumer Price Index makes interesting and often humorous reading, but its use as a method of keeping salaries current must be seriously questioned. Reviewing the report for February 1974—to take a random month for purposes of illustration—can be seen that prices of food purchased for consumption at home rose 1.2 percent during January, while restaurant meals and snacks eaten away from home increased 0.1 percent. This would seem to lead to the conclusion, or at least establish the premise, that money could be saved by eating out.

If one reads further, one finds that "leading the food price increases were higher prices for cereals and bakery products, up 2.8 percent. Notably higher were prices of rice, cracker meal, and cinnamon rolls." What proportion of *your* budget was devoted to those items? Perhaps more of us were affected by this finding: "Prices of reading and recreation items rose 0.5 percent, with bowling fees and tricycles noted higher."

It is certainly not our purpose to discredit in any way the Consumer Price Index as a statistical concept representing the movement of prices for some 400 items of goods and services which wage earners may purchase. However, a common misconception about cost-of-living pay adjustments should be clarified. They are not designed to establish or set pay levels; instead, they are intended to compensate for changes in living costs. It is only by coincidence, and then only in rare instances, that cost-of-living adjustments result in meeting competitive rates in the community.

The only realistic approach to maintaining a pay plan that will support recruitment and retention of capable employees is one based on prevailing rates. Such a plan must be in existence prior to the addition of cost-of-living adjustments. In times of rapid, widespread increases in prices and wages in the community, consideration might be given to the use of periodic adjustments based on the Consumer Price Index. This should be regarded strictly as an interim measure, when time or other constraints would make a community wage and salary survey impractical.

Sam Zagoria, director of the Labor-Management Relations Service, speaking on the subject of "Cost of Living Clauses, Pro and Con" at the 1974 session of the U.S. Conference of Mayors, noted that "cost of living escalator clauses are increasingly taking center stage in both public and private sector negotiations." During the month of June 1974, political leaders on both sides of the party fence encouraged the enactment of cost-of-living escalator clauses. Senate majority leader Mike Mansfield, referring to the then prevailing 12 percent inflation rate, recommended the tying of all wages and salaries to the cost-of-living index. During the same week, Roy Ash, then director of the Office of Management and Budget and a former prominent industrialist, was quoted as urging unions to seek cost-of-living contract clauses to protect workers from inflation. Most economists subscribe to the view that such clauses, already in place for some 5 million industrial workers, are in themselves a cause of further inflation.[8]

Escalator clauses were reported to be in existence as of the mid-1970s in about fifty individual contracts in over a dozen large cities. They are being sought in other cities. Therefore, city pay administrators and elected officials should be familiar with the following pros and cons suggested by Zagoria:

A. Pros:
1. The employer can usually obtain a longer term contract by agreeing to such a clause.
2. The employer can thus defer some wage costs to the future.
3. The employer can obtain a lower general increase and, if the rise in the cost of living is halted, the total wage cost will be less.
4. In accepting a cost of living approach, the union or employee association would be accepting the principle that wages are to reflect cost-of-living adjustments only and would not involve annual improvement factors. The net result would be no real gain in wages.

B. Cons:
1. Uncertainty makes it difficult to budget ahead.
2. If the cost of living zooms upward, the city treasury will be in trouble.
3. The normal standards of comparability with private sector benchmark jobs or other governmental units will be lost; so will consideration of ability to pay.
4. If the clause is given to one group of employees and not to others, the city will be subjected to arguments about parity and traditional relationships and can expect some whip-sawing and leap-frogging.

Zagoria also suggests a series of questions which must be addressed and decided if a jurisdiction decides to adopt a cost-of-living clause. The most persuasive argument this writer is aware of can be illustrated by an excerpt from an item on page one of the previously quoted LMRS *Newsletter:* "Between 1958 and 1972 the Consumer Price Index rose 44.6 percent, the average annual municipal employee wage 110.3 percent. . . ." The statistics cited apply to the city of Detroit. This writer speculates that, no matter in what region your agency is located, the average salary of public employees in the area over the last ten or even five years has increased at a faster rate than the Consumer Price Index for that particular area. It must be kept in mind that the CPI was not designed to measure wage movement.

TOTAL EQUIVALENT COMPENSATION:
THE VALUE OF FRINGE BENEFITS

No discussion of wage and salary policy would be complete without a consideration of the value and effect of fringe benefits. Most surveys place the proportion of benefit costs in the total payroll package at more than 30 percent. An analysis of trends supports the prediction that benefits will soon represent more than one-third of the total personnel costs—a conservative estimate.

The first national survey of employee benefits for full-time personnel of U.S. municipalities, sponsored by the Labor-Management Relations Service and conducted in 1970, reported that "cities expend a higher percentage of working-time pay for fringe benefits on behalf of municipal workers than private industry pays on behalf of its workers." The U.S. Chamber of Commerce study, *Industry Employee Benefit Studies,* was the primary source of these data.

Despite much public discussion and despite the growth of a mythology, reference bases and guidelines are generally lacking by which to evaluate the effectiveness of the total compensation package provided employees, i.e., salary, wages, and benefits. This lack of reference bases, compounded by the misinterpretation of fragmented information, are the major reasons for the situation prevailing in the mid-1970s which was characterized by compaction of salaries, a pattern of benefits varying from inadequate to excessive, a piecemeal rather than an integrated consideration of compensation elements, a majority of employees not comprehending the value of the benefits provided them, and at least a small percentage of employees receiving benefits which they did not really want or were of little value to them.

The concept known as "Total Equivalent Compensation" (TEC) is an analytical tool that enables an employer to compare the total compensation that he or she pays with what other employers are paying for like work. It is hoped that this technique will help employers resolve most of the problems cited above. Simply defined, Total Equivalent Compensation is an integrated approach toward adjusting salaries and benefits for employees which supplements current practices for collecting data on the following: conducting an employee benefit survey; analyzing and costing the data on an actuarial basis to determine what the benefits would cost the agency; using any total dollar lag in benefits identified by the survey as the guideline with which adjustments to the benefit package are made; and recommending benefit changes only after considering the effect on the total benefit package.

TEC is necessary because, unlike salary or wage comparisons where "a dollar is a dollar," two employers can offer the same benefit programs and sustain different costs or offer different benefit programs and sustain equal costs. Unlike salaries, the costs of benefit programs

vary according to factors which are unique to each employer and employee group. Therefore, it is not valid to compare directly the benefits or their costs between employers. Adjustment must be made to reach a valid comparison for benefits and, hence, for total compensation. TEC is the proper tool to make this adjustment.

One further adjustment is needed to determine whether an agency lags or leads in total compensation. This adjustment relates to those benefits, primarily holidays, vacations, and sick leave, that are paid as a part of salaries. If two employers pay the same salary for similar work but one allows more vacation than the other, the employer allowing more vacation is also paying more in total compensation for the productive work time received. Since the cost of this difference is not identified in the TEC salary data, that data must be adjusted upward or downward, depending on the differences in holiday and vacation practices and sick leave usage existing between the surveyed employer and the agency.

In closing this discussion on TEC and the value of fringe benefits, attention must be called to the "shopping bag" approach to fringe benefits. With this approach, the agency provides a specified amount of benefits for each employee, and the employee is then free to choose from among a variety of benefit programs offered. The approach appears to have many advantages, a primary advantage being uniform cost. This approach permits better compliance with the principle of like pay for like work, since the unmarried employee would receive the same total gross compensation as one having several dependents. It would simplify and aid budgeting and other fiscal procedures. Most important, it should provide a significant boost to employee morale by allowing employees to select those fringe benefits which are of the greatest importance to themselves.

The Outlook

To forecast trends in public pay administration, we must forecast trends in government itself and in the national economy. How can one presume to offer predictions when even the top economists cannot agree on the ways to cope with inflation and unemployment occurring simultaneously? It is this very uncertainty which makes some things certain. Some predictions about the immediate future of public pay administration nevertheless can be made with a reasonable degree of conviction. Among the developments seen on the horizon are:

1. Increased unionization, or at least continuing growth of public employee organizations. It is virtually certain that there will be increased militancy on the part of those representing public employees. This will be particularly true as they face encroachment on their domain from two sides. There will be increased pressure on public agencies to contract out work which public employees could perform. Justification will be offered that the work can be done more efficiently and/or cheaply by the contractor's forces. It will also be claimed that the letting of government contracts will stimulate the economy. Programs for hiring the disadvantaged will limit the growth of those classes which have been the richest source of recruitment for the unions.

2. There will be tremendous membership drives, with strong competition developing even among different locals of the same parent union. One way to attract more members is to promise more benefits. This creates a corollary need to deliver more. A major problem already discernible is whether or not union leaders will be able to maintain control when the time comes to tell their members they have gotten all they can get. The strike of firefighters in Montreal, Canada, during November 1974 and the coal workers' reluctance to approve the initial settlement submitted to them in December 1974, are forerunners of this type of problem.

3. Public demand for increased services and new services probably not even contemplated today most assuredly will grow. This, in turn, means a need for new technology and job classifications which do not now exist.

4. Increasing public clamor for greater efficiency in governmental operations also is very likely. Productivity is a key word today and it will receive increasing attention as payroll costs soar. To achieve maximum productivity, governments must have the best management talent available. This need for top-level management may force a reconsideration of the limits now placed on public executives' salaries. Another certainty, however, is that it will be a long time, if ever, before parity in salary is achieved between the chief executive of a corporation and the top official of a city with comparable budget and staff.

5. It is also relatively certain that there will be an increase in innovations. Such innovations and new proposals should be examined carefully to determine if they have a solid research basis.

[1] John W. Riegel, SALARY DETERMINATION (Ann Arbor, Mich.: University of Michigan, Bureau of Industrial Relations, 1940), p. 34.

[2] R. Permin Everett, "The Pay Plan as a Part of Personnel Administration," in PRACTICAL GUIDELINES TO PUBLIC PAY ADMINISTRATION, eds. Kenneth O. Warner and J. J. Donovan, vol. 1 (Chicago: Public Personnel Association, 1963), p. 1.

[3] Los Angeles County Citizens Economy and Efficiency Committee, CIVIL SERVICE AND COLLECTIVE BARGAINING IN LOS ANGELES COUNTY GOVERNMENT: REPORT OF CIVIL SERVICE–EMPLOYEE RELATIONS TASK FORCE (Los Angeles: Los Angeles County Citizens Economy and Efficiency Committee, 1973), p. 40.

[4] California, EDUCATION CODE, div. 10, chap. 3, art. 5, sec. 13719 (Sacramento, 1973).

[5] "Recent Developments in California Public Jurisdictions," and "Documents," CALIFORNIA PUBLIC EMPLOYEE RELATIONS, no. 23 (Berkeley: University of California, 1974).

[6] Los Angeles County Citizens Economy and Efficiency Committee, CIVIL SERVICE AND COLLECTIVE BARGAINING IN LOS ANGELES COUNTY GOVERNMENT, pp. 39–45.

[7] Verlyn L. Fletcher, "Techniques in Pricing Jobs," in PRACTICAL GUIDELINES TO PUBLIC PAY ADMINISTRATION, p. 67.

[8] Sam Zagoria, "Cost of Living Clauses, Pro and Con," LABOR-MANAGEMENT RELATIONS SERVICE NEWSLETTER 5 (October 1974): 4.

10

Labor Relations

In the wide arena of the world, failure and success are not accidents as we so frequently suppose, but the strictest justice.

ALEXANDER SMITH

INDEPENDENT EMPLOYEE ASSOCIATIONS or affiliated labor organizations actively represent the interests of municipal employees in approximately forty states. As of the mid-1970s, over thirty-seven states and the District of Columbia have some kind of legislation regarding public employee relations that covers several classes or types of public employment. In at least seven states court decisions or directives issued by the attorney general regulate public employee relations. Over thirty-two state laws require parties to meet and confer, to negotiate, or to engage in collective bargaining. In the absence of specific legislation, some kind of bargaining nevertheless takes place.

Professional administrators recognize that the conduct of municipal personnel administration today must give special consideration to labor relations and collective bargaining of the various conditions of employment. This chapter is directed to a discussion of the concrete needs, problems, and responsibilities of local government managers confronted with the facts and realities of labor relations. While the experience and sophistication demonstrated in the labor relations field vary with the size and location of cities, there are some basic principles for the conduct of management-labor relations that are universally applicable.

Terminology

Before proceeding with the main discussion, it may be useful to review the basic terminology of labor relations.

A GLOSSARY OF SELECTED TERMS COMMONLY USED IN LABOR RELATIONS

Arbitration. Third-party settlement of disputes between individuals or parties outside a court of law. Labor arbitration most commonly is required to settle disputes of application or interpretation of a labor agreement between parties to the agreement. This is termed grievance arbitration.

Bargaining unit. The group of employees which a union or association seeks to represent as bargaining agent to negotiate wages, hours, and working conditions.

Certification. Official recognition by an impartial labor relations board that an employee organization is and shall remain the exclusive representative in collective bargaining for all employees in a given bargaining unit until it is replaced by another employee organization, is decertified, or dissolves.

Checkoff. Arrangement by which an employer deducts the amount of union dues and assessments from an employee's pay and turns over the proceeds to the treasurer of the union.

Collective bargaining. The performance of mutual obligations of the employer and the exclusive representative to meet at reasonable times, to confer and negotiate in good faith, and to execute a written agreement with respect to wages, hours, and other terms and conditions of employment. Neither party, however, shall be obliged to agree to a proposal or be required to make a concession.

Decertification. Withdrawal of a union's appointment as bargaining agent upon vote by employees in the unit that they no longer wish to be represented by that union.

Election. Process of determining the bargaining agent for a group of employees.

Exclusive representative. The employee organization that, as a result of certification by a state or local agency, has the right to be the sole collective bargaining agent for all employees in a given bargaining unit regardless of membership in the employee organization.

Federal Mediation and Conciliation Service. An independent government agency created under the Labor Management Relations Act of 1947 providing machinery for settlement of labor disputes. The American Arbitration Association provides similar types of services.

Impasse. Failure of an employer and an exclusive representative to reach agreement in negotiations.

Interest arbitration. The determination of the interests of the parties, as distinct from their rights, under an existing agreement. These interests are determined by an arbitrator or panel in light of the terms and conditions of a new or renegotiated labor agreement. This type of arbitration is recognized in this country as an alternative to the right to strike over a new agreement.

Management prerogatives. From management's viewpoint, "the right to manage," i.e., the right of management to make certain decisions and take certain actions without notifying, consulting, or negotiating with the union.

Multi-employer bargaining. In the private sector, collective bargaining involving more than one company in a given industry, region, or a metropolitan area.

Strike. An employee's refusal, in concerted action with others, to report for duty, to be willfully absent from work, to participate in a work stoppage, or to abstain in whole or in part from the full, faithful, and proper performance of the duties of employment, for the purpose of inducing, influencing, or coercing a change in the conditions, compensation, rights, privileges, or obligations of employment, or for the purpose of obtaining recognition as collective bargaining agent, or to bring attention to the failure to settle a grievance.

Overview

Labor relations in the context of local government has both its similarities and its differences with labor relations in the private sector. Basic to the study of labor relations in local government is an understanding of the powers and authority given to local jurisdictions by their respective states.

Within the American political and constitutional system, the powers of local government are limited by the terms of each state constitution. Each state legislature customarily prescribes their cities' organizational structure, powers, and responsibilities. Thus, cities are actually subject to the control of their respective state legislatures. Some modifications occur when states have provided for municipal home rule in their constitutions and when cities have availed themselves of such opportunities by local charter. However, home rule reduces state legislative control to only a slight extent.

Probably the power most significant to local government which is mandated to the states is the power to tax or to raise revenues. Unlike the corporation in private industry, the municipal organization can pass along to citizens using its services only the increases in the costs of providing such services, and these increases are delimited by the state taxing system. This situation becomes acute especially in periods of high inflation, because both the costs of providing services and the wage demands of employees rise while the community's demands for municipal services also rise or remain constant.

On the one hand, local government is the unit of government which is expected to be the most responsive to the needs of the community since it is closest to the people. On the other hand, the very nature of the collective bargaining process requires that elected officials also be responsive to the demands of local government employees for an improvement in wages, hours, and working conditions. To the extent that its resources are limited, this results in local government getting caught in a double bind. Local government officials thus are forced to look for alternative ways of providing municipal services, which includes consideration of contracting out services to other cities or private corporations. An alternative which has caused labor-management strife in the 1970s has been the layoff of employees to pay for increases in wages and benefits or to maintain services in an area other than that affecting the employees laid off.

Community residents are entitled to certain services, which include the protection of life and property, a clean and healthful environment, ease of movement within the community, and opportunities for leisure activities, all provided by credible administrators and elected officials. All these services must be delivered at costs manageable within the local government's debt limitations and its capacity to raise and receive revenues from the state, federal, and local sources. While employees are entitled to competitive wages and benefits, the public must pay for any increases in wages or changes in hours and working conditions for employees out of existing or newly created revenue sources. This works fine until the well runs dry, but cities are competing for limited financial resources.

In the private sector, survival of the corporation and its policy-making body is dependent on financial solvency. In the public sector, political survival often becomes of greater concern to members of a legislative body than the financial solvency of the government. Members of labor organizations and employee representatives have lobbied and pressured elected officials to take positions or make financial commitments before considering the impact upon community services. This is why professionals in labor relations advise elected officials to remove themselves from the collective bargaining process, in order that they can maintain the detachment and objectivity necessary to carry out effectively a policy-making role affecting many areas of local government responsibility.

One of the major differences between public and private sector negotiations is the composition of the bargaining team, which can lead to difficulties for a city. Elected officials of local government often are placed in the untenable position of needing organized labor's support and at the same time setting guidelines for the bargaining team representing the city management. This chapter later will explore the problem of the city's bargaining team facing an attempted "end run" on the part of the local union's bargaining team to make direct contact with elected officials. This maneuver occurs less frequently in the private sector.

Even though private corporations are profit-seeking entities and local governments are not, often the city or county is one of the largest employers in a given locale and, therefore, is in competition with private industry for employees with similar skills in the same labor market. Among other things this means that local government must keep up with private industry in its employment practices, particularly in regard to wages, hours, and benefits.

Historically, the American labor movement in both the public and private sectors has had few goals beyond higher wages, shorter hours, and better working conditions. By contrast, European unions in general are class-conscious and are closely linked to class-based political parties which pursue their announced objective of reorganizing the social order through nationalization of the means of production and exchange.[1]

The written labor agreement operative in the public and private sector is a peculiarly American phenomenon in force since the 1930s. Prior to that time American labor agreements were similar to the Western European idea of the collective agreement as a statement of general principles and purposes, to be implemented through the good faith of the parties or through job actions by workers rather than through invocation of their present status as legally enforceable documents.

ORGANIZING PUBLIC EMPLOYEES

Collective bargaining in the public sector at all levels of government has undergone radical transformation since 1962 when President John F. Kennedy issued Federal Executive Order 10988 encouraging management-employee cooperation in the federal service. Since that time the number of bargaining units representing federal employees has grown from twenty-nine to approximately 3,400 in 1974. The number of employees included in such bargaining units during the same period has increased from 19,000 to 1.1 million.[2] Although applicable only to the federal government, this order has had the same impact on public employment throughout the United States as the National Labor Relations Act had on private industry when it was passed in 1935.

Trends in union organizing at the local government level parallel those at the federal level: By 1974 union locals affiliated with national labor organizations had organized public employees in 83 percent of all cities over 25,000.[3] By 1967 at least ten states were engaged in practices of collective bargaining. That number grew to forty-four by 1975, involving both small and large local government employers in labor negotiations, meet and confer arrangements, or more informal bargaining over wages, hours, and conditions of employment.

This trend has important implications, especially since local government has become one of the most rapidly growing fields of employment in the United States. State and local government employment rose 65 percent from 1955 to 1965 alone, as compared with only 9 percent for the federal government and only 13 percent for the total civilian work force.[4]

Traditional Management View. It is useful to look at past attitudes and practices of management in public administration. To a certain extent the tradition was to ignore public employee demands for recognition, the rationale being that government is sovereign and its ultimate authority is not to be questioned. Furthermore, advancement in the public sector traditionally has been based on the merit system, while employee organizations and unions generally advocate an advancement system based on seniority. In theory these would seem to be incompatible principles, although in actuality they have worked together. Finally, by tradi-

tion, government employers were accustomed to unilateral decision making.

Changes in public employee attitudes demanded corresponding changes in public management's traditional reaction. As William Hazard wrote: "It is morally indefensible for the government to deny its employees the same privileges which it compels private employers to grant. . . . The government should be a model employer rather than lag behind industry in labor relations."[5]

Rising Expectations in Changing Times. The mood of social protest which swept the country in the mid-1960s expressed itself through public employee organizations. Accompanying various rising expectations was a sense of falling behind the private sector in wages and benefits while consumer prices were climbing fast.

The following data, as reported in the August 1968 issue of *Fortune,* helps illustrate the changing wage patterns in the private and public sectors up to the mid-1960s. State and local government workers in 1960 received average hourly wages of $2.13, compared with $2.68 for workers in private industry. By 1966 the difference was even greater: Public employees earned $2.77 an hour while private workers were earning an average of $3.35 an hour.[6] Understandably, public employees, growing greatly in number and in proportion to private employees, became less and less satisfied with their status.

Local Government Employee Militancy. Civil rights marches, open housing demonstrations, student sit-ins, and other forms of non-cooperation or civil disobedience apparently had their effect on government workers. Employee militancy has caused serious disturbances in ways other than walking off jobs. Some of the methods include refusal to work overtime, working much slower than usual, and staging mass resignations. In one city the majority of the members of the police department called in sick on the same day. In another city, police stopped writing and issuing traffic tickets. In still another, police began writing a flood of tickets.

In most cases public employees take such action for higher pay. Yet other reasons serve as catalysts, including concern over status, working conditions, unfair supervision, improper job assignments, unequal opportunity for advancement, inadequate training, unsafe work stations, inequitable disciplinary procedures and practices, and favoritism. The importance of and the relationship between such factors as they relate to employee satisfaction, motivation, and productivity cannot be stressed enough in analyzing employer–employee relations.

PUBLIC EMPLOYEE ORGANIZATIONS

Affiliated labor unions and independent employee associations, sensing the growing dissatisfaction in the public employee sector, have become increasingly involved in organizing local government employees for collective bargaining purposes. Occasionally both affiliated and independent organizations represent employees within the same city. Employees' demands and attitudes are many and varied, depending upon the union or associations involved as well as the individual officers of such organizations.

Probably the most common and important goals of labor are the "bread and butter" items of the agreement. Next, employees seek to be part of the decision-making process within the organization. Labor will want to claim and retain all rights and privileges it has enjoyed in the past while sharing some of the rights and prerogatives management still holds as "sacred."

In particular, management will seek

1. To conduct its affairs in all respects and in accordance with its responsibilities and powers;
2. To reserve to itself those rights concerned with the management and operation of the city, which include but are not limited to the following rights:
   a. To recruit, assign, transfer, and promote employees;
   b. To suspend, demote, discharge, or take disciplinary actions against employees for just cause;
   c. To determine methods, means, and personnel necessary for the operations of each department;
   d. To control each department budget;
   e. To take in emergencies whatever actions are necessary to assure the proper functioning of departments within the city.

For an examination of management and labor rights as they have developed in the public and private sector through collective bargaining and arbitration, it is useful for the local government manager to refer to specialized labor relations resource material.[7]

In the early 1970s approximately 1.5 million city workers were represented by labor organizations. Major public employee unions in this country include the following:

1. American Federation of State, County, and Municipal Employees (AFSCME): Represents public works and utilities employees, police personnel, and clerical, social service, and sanitation employees.
2. International Association of Fire Fighters (AFL-CIO): Represents firefighters almost exclusively.
3. International Brotherhood of Teamsters: Represents almost all types of local government employees.
4. Service Employees International Union (AFL-CIO): Represents almost all types of local government employees.
5. Professional and Technical Engineers: Represents public works, office, and professional employees such as building inspectors, urban planners, and office engineers.
6. Office and Professional Employees: Represents clerical and office employees and professional employees such as engineers; also represents police personnel through its Law and Justice Division.
7. International Brotherhood of Electrical Workers: Represents electrical utility employees almost exclusively.
8. Fraternal Order of Police: Represents law enforcement officers exclusively.

Other organizations represent transit workers and special groups. Overall, the American Federation of State, County, and Municipal Employees (AFL-CIO) and the International

Association of Fire Fighters (AFL-CIO) represent the largest number of workers.[8]

Independent employee associations represent almost every type of employee group imaginable in this country. Probably the most widespread development of independent associations is the example of police guilds or benefit associations. White-collar and professional workers have been organized in local government to a relatively small extent compared to such groups as police, firefighters, and trade and clerical workers. Moreover, white-collar workers and professional employees have been reluctant to join labor unions for the following reasons, among others:

1. Informal or formal associations of white-collar employees frequently have been influential enough to obtain reasonable benefits.[9]
2. White-collar workers, in contrast to blue-collar workers, have tended to identify with management in that both have minimal time-clock pressures, easier and more comfortable working conditions, a high degree of job security, and began receiving paid vacations before blue-collar workers did.[10]
3. Male white-collar workers tend to advance and achieve supervisory positions faster than blue-collar workers or uniformed personnel.
4. Many white-collar employees reportedly feel it is beneath their dignity to join a union. Evidently they perceive union tactics as crude and exploitative.
5. Many reportedly fear that joining a union would pit them against management and thus hurt their chances for advancement.
6. A generally higher level of job satisfaction prevails among white-collar workers than among blue-collar workers.[11]

However, management can be reasonably certain that separate bargaining units representing all kinds of white-collar workers will emerge on an increasing scale following the trend in the 1970s toward the greater organization of professional workers such as school teachers and principals, for example. Unionization of these professionals may contribute to the legitimacy of organizing white-collar workers in the public sector.

MANAGEMENT AND COLLECTIVE BARGAINING

Although by nature the collective bargaining process is an adversary one, it is also a process deriving from certain goals and objectives shared by management and employees. These mutual interests include the following:

1. Providing and sustaining high-quality services to the community and its citizens at a cost that will not jeopardize such services;
2. Encouraging a high level of productivity among employees and minimizing the waste of time and materials;
3. Promoting proper training and physical and mental fitness;
4. Maintaining adequate equipment so that personnel may perform their respective duties;
5. Retaining productive employees by providing adequate wages, hours, and working conditions;
6. Maintaining a relationship between employees and management characterized by good will and trust and by a constructive, open-minded approach to the resolution of departmental problems.

Most local government administrators recognize the reality of collective bargaining, meet and confer arrangements, and employer-employee discussions regarding wages, hours, and working conditions. Local government managers need not consider employee organization as a personal affront. Employees can hardly be blamed for exercising their rights under the law, nor can they be criticized for their preference for a bilateral rather than a unilateral process of setting wages and other conditions of employment.

Managers and department heads need to familiarize themselves with the applicable laws and the successful development of labor relations as they have evolved in other cities. They also need to maintain an atmosphere of openness and trust with employees. In negotiating with unions they should seek professional assistance from either the staff or outside consultants. If the bargaining process is conducted professionally, both employee interests will be served and management prerogatives will be protected, concessions will be made in appropriate areas, and the process will develop on an objective, issue-oriented basis rather than an emotional, personality-oriented basis. The collective bargaining process is an evolutionary one, and as such it should prevent management from giving too much too fast only to find itself in a position with nothing more to give.

Collective bargaining and meet and confer arrangements ordinarily are considered by both labor and management as the performance of the parties' mutual obligations to meet at reasonable times, to confer and negotiate in good faith, and to execute a written agreement with respect to grievance procedures and collective negotiations on personnel matters including wages, hours, and working conditions. Neither party shall be compelled to agree to a proposal or be required to make a concession by such obligation. Unilateral decision making regarding such matters has given way to a bilateral decision-making process. The process can be considered as an integrative whole as illustrated in the following summary, which outlines the roles of both labor and management during the various stages of the process.

THE COLLECTIVE BARGAINING PROCESS SUMMARIZED

I. The Organizing Stage
   (Note: Employee interest in organizing grows out of conditions such as inadequate or non-competitive wages and benefits; internal inequities; feeling a lack of on-the-job rights, security, and a voice regarding working conditions; poor job environment; and boring jobs. The union meets with employees, provides information, and solicits membership.)
   A. The responsibility of the union:
      1. The union must maintain good faith conduct and professional representation.
      2. It must respect the rights of management.
      3. At all times it must avoid interference with the normal operations of the organization.
   B. The responsibility of management:
      1. Management must understand employee rights, which include the right to join or not to join a union.
      2. Management must not interfere, restrain, coerce, or discriminate against employees in the exercise of their rights.
      3. Management should permit union representatives to have reasonable access to employees and should acknowledge the employees' right to gather information on unions.

      4. Management must remain neutral: It cannot favor or oppose organizing and it cannot favor one organization over another.
      5. Management should not interrogate employees.
      6. Management should not extend employee benefits during this period.

II. The Petition Stage
   A. The role of the union:
      1. The labor union submits a petition for recognition, accompanied by signature cards, to the pertinent state or local agency.
      2. The union makes a show of interest and presents a statement as to the proper bargaining unit, based on criteria such as common interests, similarity of duties, and common supervision.
   B. The role of management:
      1. Management reviews the appropriateness of the bargaining unit as stated in the petition, using the same criteria.
      2. It ensures the exclusion of supervisory, managerial, and confidential personnel from the bargaining unit being formed.
      3. Management brings together the appropriate managerial and supervisory personnel to raise their level of awareness about labor-management relations both in general and as it pertains to their particular organization.

III. The Election Stage
   A. The role of the union:
      1. The union obtains the order for election.
      2. The election campaign is conducted.
      3. The ground rules for election are established.
      4. The election is conducted by the appropriate state or local agency. It is union's responsibility to help get out the vote as well as to observe the election for propriety.
   B. The role of management:
      1. Management determines whether or not an election is necessary; if so, then it helps get out the vote so that all employees in the bargaining unit can express their views on the ballot.
      2. Management observes the election process for propriety.

IV. The Certification and Recognition Stage
   (Note: At this point, a single labor organization is certified for exclusive representation of all members in the bargaining unit whether each individual becomes a member of the union or not.)
   A. For the union, exclusive representation means that:

1. The union must represent all employees within the bargaining unit, whether or not they are members of the union.
2. The union has the right to process grievances.
3. All employees in the bargaining unit are bound by the terms of the agreement.
4. The union has the responsibility to inventory and respect the rights of management.

B. For management, exclusive representation means that:
1. Management negotiates with the labor organization on any matters within the scope of bargaining.
2. Management's right to deal with individual employees on such matters is limited.
3. The decision-making process on such matters becomes bilateral rather than unilateral.

V. Preparation for Negotiations

(Note: The purpose of negotiations is to permit employee participation in the establishment of working conditions and to resolve conflicts which arise between management and employees.)

A. Labor energies are put into:
1. Election of officers and subsequent selection of the negotiation committee;
2. Appropriate delegation of authority from the membership to negotiate and reach agreement;
3. Anticipation of management proposals;
4. Preparation of union proposals;
5. Establishment of a bargaining philosophy;
6. Making an inventory of problem areas regarding working conditions as articulated by the membership;
7. Conducting research into the developments of negotiations in similar organizations;
8. Reviewing management proposals;
9. Familiarization with collective bargaining legislation and the history of employer-employee relations in the organization;
10. Developing a positive attitude to the give-and-take of the collective bargaining process.

B. Management energies are put into:
1. Selection of the negotiation team;
2. Appropriate delegation of authority to negotiate and reach agreement;
3. Anticipation of union proposals;
4. Preparation of management proposals;
5. Establishment of a bargaining philosophy;
6. Making an inventory of internal operations to find potential problem areas that may become the subject of discussion at the bargaining table;
7. Conducting research into the developments of negotiations in similar organizations;
8. Reviewing union proposals;
9. Familiarization with collective bargaining legislation and the history of employer-employee relations in the organization;
10. Developing a positive attitude to the give-and-take of the collective bargaining process.

VI. The Negotiating Stage: The Preliminaries

A. The responsibility of the union:
1. Promoting teamwork among members of the negotiating committee;
2. Reviewing management proposals as they affect the interests and rights of the bargaining unit;
3. Making proposals;
4. Waiting for management's response.

B. The responsibility of management:
1. Promoting teamwork among members of the negotiating committee;
2. Analyzing the costs of union's proposals in light of the organization's ability to pay, its revenue estimates, salary and benefit studies, the cost-of-living index, and the appropriateness of the items presented;
3. Making proposals;
4. Waiting for union's response.

(Note: Both parties should draw up a checklist of *contract articles* to be negotiated in the contract. Such essential articles include:
1. Preamble
2. Definition of terms
3. Recognition of the union
4. Union membership
5. Check-off
6. Nondiscrimination
7. Seniority
8. Reduction in force and recall
9. Vacancies and promotions
10. Salaries
11. Overtime
12. Hours of work
13. Holidays
14. Vacation leave
15. Union official's time off
16. Training and development
17. Prevailing rights
18. Savings

19. Communications procedure
20. Performance of duty
21. Grievance procedure
22. Terms of agreement.)

VII. The Negotiating Stage: Initial Period
A. The role of the union:
1. Review past problems, practices, and procedures of employees and employer.
2. Meet with membership to formalize proposals.
3. Develop an outline of proposals.
B. The role of management:
1. Give initial consideration to union proposals and set the stage for management proposals.
2. Ask questions; clarify issues; sort out economic from noneconomic items.
3. Check effects of proposals with operating departments.
4. Assess the impact of proposals upon other employee groups.
5. Outline the first counterproposals.
C. The joint responsibility in establishing guidelines:
1. Avoid adversary relationships by focusing on issues rather than on personalities.
2. The right to caucus should be acknowledged.
3. Both sides must know collective bargaining laws and rules.
4. Establish timetables.
5. Develop a strategy before going into each session.
6. Keep good notes.
7. Tolerate open conflict.
8. Put proposals and counterproposals in writing.
9. Know the cost of proposals on the table.
10. Mutually agree on a meeting place.
11. Agree to discretion in dissemination of information exchanged during negotiations.
12. Keep a sense of humor.

VIII. The Negotiating Stage: Intermediate Period
A. The role of the union:
1. Identify areas of agreement.
2. Pass over and come back to areas of disagreement.
3. Reassess original positions, including financial condition.
4. Summarize the union's position.
5. Come to terms on all possible issues, both economic and noneconomic.
6. Put subsequent counterproposals in writing.
7. Check regularly with the membership.
8. Initiate steps to reach settlement and conclude bargaining.

9. Consider cooling off periods.
10. Make use of caucuses.
11. Keep in mind budgetary deadlines.
B. The role of management:
1. Identify the areas of agreement.
2. Pass over and come back to areas of disagreement.
3. Reassess original positions, including financial condition.
4. Summarize management's position.
5. Come to terms on all possible issues, both economic and noneconomic.
6. Put subsequent counterproposals in writing.
7. Check periodically with the organization's officers.
8. Initiate steps to reach settlement and conclude bargaining.
9. Consider cooling off periods.
10. Make use of caucuses.
11. Keep in mind budgetary deadlines.

IX. The Negotiating Stage: Final Period
A. The role of the union:
1. Maintain an open climate conducive to problem solving.
2. Know where the membership stands in its thinking regarding a settlement by making frequent use of the caucus.
3. Reevaluate union's unaltered positions on minor and major issues still on the table to test for reasonableness.
4. Give most serious consideration to trade-offs between salary, benefits, and other contract issues dealing with rights and security.
5. Check up on recent settlements to gauge their possible impact on final negotiations.
6. Keep discussion to major unsettled issues and do not introduce new issues or rehash issues already disposed.
7. Display a strong desire to settle while remaining firm on what the membership considers a final position, and reduce areas of agreement to writing.
8. Make efforts to convince management that the union's final position is reasonable and fact-oriented, while getting management's final position.
9. Go before the membership and recommend approval of the final form of the contract or declare an impasse.
B. The role of management:
1. Maintain an open climate conducive to problem solving.
2. Reevaluate management's unaltered positions on minor and major issues still on the table to test for reasonableness.
3. Give most serious consideration to

trade-offs between salary and contract issues, reducing areas of agreement immediately to writing.

4. Check up on recent settlements to gauge their possible impact upon final negotiations.

5. Keep discussion to major unsettled issues and do not introduce new issues or rehash issues already disposed.

6. Make final offer on unsettled items of concern to the union.

7. Display a strong desire to settle while remaining firm in what the mayor and council consider to be its final position, and reduce areas of agreement to writing.

8. Make efforts to convince the union that management's final position is reasonable and fact-oriented, while getting union's final position.

9. After union membership has voted on city's final offer, go before the mayor and council to recommend approval or declare an impasse.

10. Review and adopt the final budget.

(Note: Both labor and management bear responsibility in the final period to control information, particularly in regard to the press, so that rumors and exaggeration do not develop. Keeping the press out of negotiations is a good rule to follow.)

X. Resolution of Impasse

(Note: Either labor or management may declare that an impasse exists and call for mediation. On occasion, management and the union will file a joint request for mediation.)

A. Mediation:

1. Selection is made by mutual request or by the applicable state agency of a mediator such as the Federal Mediation and Conciliation Service or a public employee relations commission.

2. Both labor and management must be open and willing to discuss the specifics of their positions.

3. Mediator uses suggestion, feels out the two parties, and gives advice that is not binding.

B. Fact-finding:

1. Selection of fact-finder or fact-finding panel is made.

2. Investigation of the impasse is initiated by receiving facts from both parties, including items such as comparative data on wages, hours, and conditions of employment of similar personnel in public and private employment; the annual adjustment of the Consumer Price Index; and other factors normally considered in the determination of the conditions of employment.

3. Recommendations, usually advisory, are made to both parties for settlement.

4. Use of informed persuasion occurs, which may prevent a strike.

5. It is expected that both parties will make good faith efforts to consider and accept the results of the fact-finding procedure.

C. Arbitration:

1. Arbitrator is selected or arbitration panel is created.

2. Notice of hearings is given to the parties.

3. Record of the proceedings is taken.

4. Evidence, written and oral, is presented. Individuals may be called for their testimony.

5. Hearing must be concluded within a reasonable time.

6. Chairperson must make written findings and determine the dispute based upon the issues presented.

7. Decision is final and binding on both parties.

XI. Contract Administration

(Note: In this stage, which is crucial to good labor-management relations, both parties share a joint responsibility for the following:

1. Education of their respective constituencies in the provisions and changes in the contract and how to administer it;

2. Uniform interpretation and application of terms and provisions;

3. Good knowledge of grievance procedure;

4. Settlement of grievances informally before resorting to the grievance procedure;

5. Printing and distribution of the agreement;

6. Awareness of legislation affecting terms of the current contract and future contracts;

7. Training in negotiating;

8. Retaining records of personnel actions and grievances;

9. Seeking out professional advice when needed;

10. Awareness of labor relations in other jurisdictions.)

The collective bargaining process is schematized in Figure 10–1. In addition to basic labor–management roles, this figure also shows the parts played in various stages of the collective bargaining process by the city council and other local government officials in determining many policies; by the personnel and finance

Stages in the process	Participants in the process			
	Local government officials	Administration	Personnel agencies	Finance agencies
No organization	Unilateral decisions	Nonparticipatory management style		
Organization	Restraint	Restraint		
Petition	Review petition	Reviews petition	Review petitions; check lists	
Election	Call for election	Oversees election	Prepare voter list	
Certification and recognition	Formally recognize union as exclusive bargaining representative	Formal recognition of union	Begin authorization of payroll deductions	Payroll deductions
Preparation for negotiations	Determine extent of role in negotiating and establishing bargaining philosophy	Selection of negotiating team	Participate in negotiations	
Beginning phase of negotiations	Analyze labor proposals as a whole and establish guidelines	Analyzes labor proposals as a whole and establishes guidelines	Consider impact of labor proposals on personnel policies	Cost out labor proposals
Intermediate phase of negotiations	Review preliminary budget	Seeks areas of agreement and makes counterproposals	Disclosure of wage and benefit data	Prepare preliminary budget
Final phase of negotiations	Review final budget	Concludes agreement or reaches impasse	Planning and programming for contract changes	Final budget
Resolution of impasse—mediation	Present position to mediator	Presents history of negotiation and position to mediator	Part of negotiation team in mediation	Part of negotiation team in mediation
Resolution of impasse—fact-finding	Determine facts to be presented; may present facts	Selects management advocate; recommends third party; presents facts	Research	Research
Resolution of impasse—arbitration	Selection of arbitrator	Selects management advocate on arbitration panel	Research	Research
Administration of contract	Administer agreement	Educates supervisory personnel in provisions of agreement and labor relations practices	Print and distribute copies of agreement; record-keeping	Implementation of pay practices

FIGURE 10–1. *Schematic presentation of stages in the collective bargaining process by the principal participants in the process. The text primarily covers management and union roles at various stages, but this presentation shows that "management" may encompass local government officials, administration, personnel agencies, and other participants, depending on the stage in the process and the complexity and intensity of the issue. (Source: Cabot J. Dow, management representative, in cooperation with Ms. Pat Sisco, representative, American Federation of State, County, and Municipal Employees.)*

Stages in the process	Participants in the process			
	State legislature	Union	State mediation service	Electorate
No organization	Legislation sets salaries for state employees		Activity of wage and hour division	Taxation
Organization	Legislation	Meets with employees; provides information; solicits membership		Taxation
Petition	Legislation	Submits petition	Reviews petition	Taxation
Election	Legislation	Campaigns; oversees election	Conducts election	Taxation
Certification and recognition	Legislation	Becomes exclusive bargaining representative	Certifies union as exclusive bargaining representative	Taxation
Preparation for negotiations		Meets with membership; develops proposals; chooses negotiating team		Taxation
Beginning phase of negotiations		Receives management proposals; reviews past problems and procedures; establishes guidelines		Taxation
Intermediate phase of negotiations		Seeks areas of agreement; makes counterproposals		Taxation
Final phase of negotiations		Concludes agreement or reaches impasse	Notification of impasse if applicable	Taxation
Resolution of impasse—mediation	Legislation	Presents history of negotiation and position to mediator	Selects mediator; advises to reconcile parties to agreement: advisory authority	Taxation
Resolution of impasse—fact-finding	Legislation	Selects union advocate; recommends third party; presents facts	Selects third party; or labor advocate and management advocate select jointly	Taxation
Resolution of impasse—arbitration	Legislation	Selects labor advocate or arbitration panel	Provides arbitration services if requested; joint selection of third party	Taxation
Administration of contract		Educates officers in provisions of agreement and grievance procedures; on-going representation		Taxation

FIGURE 10–1. (*continued.*)

agencies in furnishing information and developing cost figures; by the state mediation service in helping provide third-party resources; and by the state legislature and electorate in providing alternate control.

MANAGEMENT'S RIGHTS AND OBLIGATIONS

In preparing both for contract determination or grievance resolution, it is imperative that management know and understand its rights.

Under common law, local government administrators possess a certain freedom of action which derives from their legal status and which is commonly called management rights or management prerogatives.

Advocates of strong management claim that under common law the employer, as the agent ultimately responsible for service to the public, may operate the business of the city as it chooses, except where its common law rights have been limited by Constitutional statute or by collective bargaining agreements. Management frequently takes the position that it need not look to the collective agreement to determine what rights it has reserved to itself but should look to it only when determining what rights it has given away or agreed to share with employees.

Thus one management representative has defined "the doctrine of reserved rights" as "the simple and understandable view that management, which must have the right to manage, has reserved its right to manage unless it has limited its right by some specific provision of the labor agreement."[12] Quite understandably, labor representatives deny that the rights of management are so broad. The rights of labor usually derive from past practice and from the labor agreement itself.[13] Since the 1960s there has been progressive invasion through legislation, collective bargaining, and arbitration into once exclusive and unchallenged areas of managerial decision making in local government.

SELECTING THE EMPLOYEE REPRESENTATIVE

Usually the employer has little to say about what organization the employees select to represent them in management-labor relations matters. Exceptions may occur from time to time when employees solicit the employer's advice or discuss the reputation of some union representative who is courting them for representation purposes. Such consultation usually will take place when employees are weighing the pros and cons of organizing an independent association or affiliating with a nationally recognized labor union.

The employee representative ordinarily is selected by means of signature cards. By signing the cards, employees are expressing an interest in joining a specific organization and giving that organization the authority to represent them in collective bargaining. They also agree to pay dues on a monthly basis to such organization. State agencies or any other agency set up by state law or local charter will check the cards for validity of the signatures before determining whether there is sufficient interest to certify an organization or whether there should be an election.

An election is held to determine the majority's preference as to what union will represent the employees in labor relations matters. The organization elected is then certified as the exclusive bargaining representative of the bargaining unit for purposes set forth in state law or local charter.

The organization certified will represent all employees in the bargaining unit regardless of whether they become members of the union or organization. Exclusive representation means that an organization has the sole and exclusive right and obligation to represent employees in the bargaining unit; no other organization can interfere and represent the employees while the agreement is in force. Procedures are set forth in most state statutes by which a group of employees can decertify an employee representative organization and petition to have another organization represent them, or they can decide against any representation at all.

Management and organized labor usually agree that there are both good and bad labor organizations, and that the characteristics of a good labor organization are as follows:

1. Represents all employees in the bargaining unit without discrimination;
2. Defends each employee's rights as set forth by the collective bargaining agreement;
3. Knows a valid grievance from a contrived one, and deflects the latter before it ever gets in writing or to the initial steps of the grievance procedure;
4. Acts aggressively on behalf of the bargaining unit but also is sensitive to the problems and needs of the employer;
5. Demonstrates stability and a good track record in developing trust and openness between employees and their employer.

Conversely, management and organized labor can agree that the characteristics of the bad labor organization are as follows:

1. Shows no sympathy or sensitivity for the employer's situation;
2. Wants to win all too quickly and will settle for short-term gains at the expense of long-term stability in labor-management relations;
3. Makes promises to employees which are unrealistic and which therefore the labor organization cannot deliver;
4. Looks continuously for grievances to process and pass through to the arbitration stage where decisions are binding;
5. Files unfair labor practices as a scare tactic;
6. Does not pay close attention to employee needs but simply collects dues;
7. Fails to keep its part of the agreement.

DETERMINING AND RECOGNIZING THE BARGAINING UNIT

Generally there is formal provision set forth by state law whereby a state agency will determine what is an appropriate bargaining unit in the event a dispute develops between a labor organization and the employer. It is only natural that disputes of this nature will arise from time to time, and it is of great importance to management interests that the question be properly settled.

It is up to management to define its community of interest, that is, who is a member of the management and supervisory team. State agencies may need to make the final determination, but the exclusion from the bargaining unit of supervisors and other personnel with different wages, hours, and working conditions is well-established and is in management's favor.

When an employee organization petitions for recognition—either directly to the employer or indirectly through a state administrative agency —such a petition should be in writing so the employer can formally respond. Before responding, the city manager and his or her bargaining representative should review the statutory authority of the employee organization seeking recognition and the positions and proposals which that organization is seeking to represent on behalf of the bargaining unit.

Determining whether a community of interests exists either among management or the bargaining unit requires the same test by both parties for similarities in the following items: duties (or an interchange of duties) ; skills and education; pay and pay systems; fringe benefits; hours of work; and supervision. In the case of the bargaining unit, a history of separate representation will also point to a community of interests.

In general, public works employees are not included in the same bargaining unit as clerical and secretarial employees, since their working conditions are different and thus they do not share a community of interests. On the other hand, in small cities there is an advantage to lumping together all employees except police and fire personnel, since management then can deal with fewer labor organizations. Ordinarily, cities with a population of less than 10,000 do not have more than four separate bargaining units.

STRENGTHENING MANAGEMENT'S POSITION

It goes without saying that it is important for the city manager to be continuously developing a strong management team. Members of such a team should be identified by their position as supervisors. Distinction usually is made between a "working supervisor" and an "executive or managerial" supervisor. Managerial employees, as opposed to supervisory employees, are those who formulate and implement policy. One means of determining if an employer has managerial status is whether he or she has the authority to make financial commitments on behalf of the employer.

Examples of municipal positions traditionally considered supervisory or managerial include the following:

1. All department heads such as police chief, fire chief, public works director, parks director, finance director, and other similar positions;
2. All division heads such as recreation superintendent, street superintendent, head librarian, and other similar positions;

3. All second-line supervisors such as accounting supervisors, street supervisors, police lieutenants, fire captains and battalion chiefs, and other similar positions.

Another major criterion is the confidentiality inherent in the position and also the authority to make financial commitments on behalf of the employer. Such positions include the city clerk, city treasurer, and administrative secretary to the city manager and/or department heads.

These supervisory, managerial, and confidential employees should not be in a general bargaining unit or in a separate unit of their own because of the possibility of a conflict of interest. Nevertheless, in the 1970s there was a trend toward organizing mid-level managerial and supervisory personnel into separate bargaining units.

The city manager then should develop a plan for treating managers and supervisors in special ways.[14] Some cities as well as private companies give their managers and supervisors increased opportunity to participate in discussing problems and making decisions. Developing for managers and supervisors special salary and benefit packages including special training programs involving travel, embellished life insurance protection, salary bonuses, and special annual leave is recommended. Attention should be given to the concerns of managers and supervisors to show them that executive management listens not just to the voices of labor organizations. Finally, including appropriate management personnel on the city's negotiating committee and giving them authority to formulate management positions and to represent the city at the bargaining table are advised as ways of building a strong and unified management team.

SELECTING MANAGEMENT'S
NEGOTIATIONS TEAM

There is no magic formula to determine the composition of the negotiations team. The indispensable prerequisite is that labor relations skills be present.

The supervisory and managerial personnel not on such a team will be part of the support and planning activity going into the collective bargaining process. This activity includes developing management requests and proposals to be presented to the union early in the negotiations process; reviewing and advising the bargaining team regarding union proposals and counterproposals; and taking responsibility for effective and uniform administration of the labor agreement. Maximum participation of such members should be encouraged. Members of the actual negotiations team will depend upon staff capabilities and the approach selected by the manager, mayor, or city council.

Typical composition of management's negotiations team includes the personnel director or labor relations adviser as chief spokesperson, the finance officer, and the city manager, if he or she so desires. Most professional administrators would prefer not to be present at the actual negotiations. However, it is more important that elected officials be removed from the process. The negotiations team representing the municipality should act as a buffer between elected officials and the employee organization and its interests. This maximizes the objectivity of the mayor and city council in making decisions affecting employees while also increasing their effectiveness in all other policy-making roles.

Often militant employees representing the local labor organization will make an "end run" around the negotiations team direct to the elected officials. Although there are circumstances when this may be allowed, in general it must be discouraged. Allowing such end runs will undermine chances of the city negotiations team to succeed in developing and executing its strategy during negotiations.

Before entering the negotiations process, management's negotiating team should solicit economic guidelines and policy direction from the mayor and city council. It should itself set some ground rules which will maximize the city's effectiveness at the bargaining table and encourage continued stability in the city's relationships with its employees. Such ground rules are as follows:

1. Avoid discussion of negotiations with the local press: Confidentiality is important.
2. Avoid discussion of negotiations or bargaining issues with individual employees.

3. The city's position should be stated through its chief spokesperson, who is to be supported by management personnel in technical areas such as department operations and finances.
4. Every effort should be made to keep the tone of negotiations at an objective and professional level in order to reach a reasonable settlement and maintain good rapport with employees.

In turn, the members of the city's negotiations team will need direction from the city council or mayor as to what it considers to be a reasonable wage increase for the duration of the agreement. Comparative data on wages and benefits, the expectations of employees, the financial condition of the city (commonly referred to as the "ability to pay"), and the weight the city feels should be given to increases in the Consumer Price Index (commonly referred to as the "cost of living") will have been taken into account.

A properly prepared spokesperson will have obtained some early suggestions on these matters. The negotiating team must also know if the elected officials are prepared to face a strike or accept the terms of compulsory binding arbitration if the negotiating team believes the demands and position of the labor organization have become unreasonable.

The Scope of Bargaining

The scope of bargaining is a problematic matter. Traditionally management prefers the scope to be as limited as possible while labor wants it to be as broad as possible. There is usually a middle ground. Part of the problem is that the term "working conditions" is imprecise as to scope and can be interpreted broadly or narrowly, depending on one's interests. One way to start defining the scope is to study the common law and see what kind of scope it has given to management's rights and those matters which traditionally have been subjects of the collective bargaining process in the public sector, specifically, local government.

Professionals in city management will readily agree that it is not advisable to negotiate away any rights and privileges of management not granted by the labor agreement to employees and their representatives. Furthermore, management should not relinquish the rights to establish methods of work; to establish staffing levels; to subcontract work out if it proves in the best interest of the public; to make appropriation of funds; and to hire, fire, suspend, discharge, lay off, or transfer employees for "just cause." Prevailing rights clauses and minimum manning clauses, for example, present formidable challenges to the rights of management and tend to place management at the receiving end of the negotiations process.

Matters which have normally and traditionally been subjects of the collective bargaining process in local government are listed in the summary of the collective bargaining process presented earlier in the chapter. Although the list is not exhaustive, it gives some idea of the distinction to be made between negotiable items and those which management generally considers non-negotiable.

When civil service rules and regulations conflict with the terms of a labor agreement, the civil service rules and regulations will prevail, since they are set forth by state or local charter. However, when the labor agreement is in conflict with city ordinances, the labor agreement customarily will govern.

Since the 1960s the trend in the private sector and in the public sector as well has been that the scope of bargaining has grown broader rather than narrower.

Other Conditions Affecting the Conduct of Bargaining

Most if not all states have passed legislation and many cities have provisions in their local charters that set up a timetable for budget preparation and for submission of the budget to elected officials for their consideration and adoption. These timetables should be taken into account when planning for negotiations. Ideally, all labor agreements should be settled prior to the submission of the budget to the elected officials. This will reduce the cost of wage and benefit adjustments to a known rather than an unknown factor, which is important to local program planning.

In order to meet budget deadlines, it is advisable for labor and management to exchange proposals and enter into negotiations at least five months prior to the submission of the budget. This leaves time for a full series of meetings to take place between labor and management; it also leaves some time for proceedings such as mediation, fact-finding, or arbitration to resolve an impasse, should it occur.

On the other hand, it is not uncommon for bargaining to continue beyond the end of the fiscal year. Management need not be overly concerned by this, since such delays are often unavoidable. Delays can work to the advantage of management if other agreements are settled and if the union's demands are unquestionably excessive. Likewise, the union may decide that if it cannot settle for more than management is willing to offer, then it would rather not settle at all and walk out. By and large, however, it is to neither party's advantage to unduly prolong negotiations.

Local Government Financing. The financing and revenue-producing capacity of local government frequently is limited. Most cities in most states receive revenues which are earmarked for certain purposes and, as such, they are not available for general wage increases. This is a particular problem when inflation is running at a double-digit pace. During a period of inflation the ability of local government to keep pace with the expectations or demands of employees often is contingent upon the cutting back of levels of service, i.e., police protection, street maintenance and repair, and park development, among other services. Self-funding services such as electric, water, and sewer utilities are a much different matter from the tax-supported local government services such as fire and police protection.

Political Pressures. Management cannot ignore the real or potential role of the political process in labor-management relations. The advantages of elected officials being on the firing line in negotiations usually are nil, as already pointed out. However, in large and "union" cities, labor support or lack of support often weighs heavy on the politician's mind.

In general, the degree of direct access that labor representatives or employees have with elected officials to lobby for increased wages and benefits is the degree to which there will be disruption in the collective bargaining process. Management cannot effectively and professionally represent local government interests at the bargaining table if concessions are being made on the street or in the corridors. Elected officials usually learn this lesson rather quickly and leave bargaining to duly appointed management representatives.

Union Access to the Budget. The local government budget is a public document open to the review and scrutiny of employees and their representatives. Thus, the employer can expect union representatives to attack various budgetary appropriations on the question of their value to the community. However, it is important that management not permit the union to decide what is a proper or improper expenditure. Debate on this question ultimately results in emotion-laden value judgments which usually prove counterproductive.

Control of Information. As much as possible, both labor and management should confine discussion and information regarding negotiations to the bargaining sessions rather than air the proceedings before their constituents or the general public. This is impossible, of course, in states with laws requiring that collective bargaining sessions be open to the public. Lack of control of information about the negotiations can hamper the flexibility of both sides in working toward settlement. Intentions stated at the bargaining table are easily distorted in their uncontrolled broadcasting. Finally, whatever gets into the newspapers often has a note of finality about it, which impairs ensuing sessions.

Single-Year vs. Multi-Year Contracts. There are advantages and disadvantages to both single-year and multi-year contracts. In the private sector both labor and management have observed that multi-year contracts encourage stability in labor-management relations. Otherwise, with single-year contracts the parties could be in perpetual negotiation. In the public sector, the two-year contract is probably the most common. Multi-year contracts are gaining greater acceptance by both labor and management as both parties have learned to live together and accommodate each other.

Adoption and Implementation of the Negotiated Agreement

An important principle in the adoption or ratification of any labor agreement that must be observed is that each side has the other party's word, orally but preferably in writing, that the package which both parties agreed on will be recommended by both parties' bargaining representatives to their respective constituencies. When labor representatives take a final offer to their membership, they must know for certain that if the membership adopts the package, then management representatives will recommend the package to the city council or the appropriate body.

As soon as the agreements are executed, copies should be made and distributed among the union membership and the appropriate management personnel. It is advisable then to conduct orientation sessions with supervisors who were not part of the negotiations but who will be affected by the provisions of the labor agreement. Training in the implementation of the agreement is necessary; the importance of uniform administration of the contract should be stressed. It should also be pointed out to supervisors that it is best to resolve grievances informally if possible and at the lowest possible level.

Impasse Resolution in Negotiations

Resolution of an impasse is accomplished through conciliation, mediation, fact-finding, or arbitration. (Reference is made here to impasses in contract negotiation as opposed to impasses over the interpretation or application of the labor agreement which may be the basis of a grievance.)

The distinction between collective bargaining, mediation, fact-finding, and arbitration can be seen more clearly if one considers each a stage in the relationship between labor and management, with collective bargaining seen as the first stage and arbitration the last. The intermediate stages are conciliation or mediation and fact-finding. Conciliation or mediation may be utilized as an aid to negotiation. The essence of mediation and conciliation is compromise. Neither the conciliation board nor the mediator makes a decision. Rather, the aim is to persuade the negotiators, by proposals or arguments, to come to voluntary agreement.[15]

Fact-finding is a quasi-formal process. The function of fact-finding is to investigate and assemble all facts surrounding an impasse. After the investigation, a panel or an individual fact-finder makes a report which may include recommendations and which, unlike the finding of an arbitrator, the parties have a choice of accepting or rejecting. This process is gaining greater acceptance all the time, particularly among the uniformed services in the states having collective bargaining statutes that affect local government.[16]

The agencies involved in these proceedings vary. Most states have an administrative agency or board that can be called upon to intervene in mediation, fact-finding, or arbitration. The American Arbitration Association, the National Center for Dispute Settlement, and the Federal Mediation and Conciliation Service have certified mediators and arbitrators available through their agencies.

Since the 1960s the process that has gained the most attention and controversy has been the compulsory binding arbitration of local government–labor disputes over provisions of an agreement. As of 1975 approximately thirteen states and the District of Columbia had compulsory binding arbitration. In addition, a considerable number of cities had also opted for such an alternative.[17] In most states, binding arbitration is not mandatory unless both parties agree to it. Increasingly, legislative bodies have turned to legislated interest arbitration, rarely used before the 1960s, as an alternative to the strike.

Experience has shown that binding arbitration may not eliminate all strikes, but the data also clearly show that it substantially reduces their frequency. For example, five strikes by firefighters took place in Michigan prior to the state's arbitration statute, but none has occurred since. One or two police strikes in that state occurred after the enactment of compulsory arbitration, but one of these happened because of a city's refusal to implement an award. None has taken place since. No strikes have been called by police or firefighters in Pennsylvania since that state began its use of arbitration in 1968. The experience in Minnesota, Nevada, and Wisconsin is similar.[18]

Management Strategies.   Fact-finding and compulsory arbitration are here to stay. Therefore, it is useful to discuss strategies that management might employ to use the processes to best advantage. Most professionals representing management in impasse proceedings would endorse these recommendations:

1. Stipulate the issues. Management should work with the union to stipulate precisely the unresolved issues for presentation before the fact-finding or arbitration panel. This document should contain all issues that are subject to the panel's recommendations or decision and should bear the signatures of both parties. Both the union and management should be discouraged from bringing up issues which were resolved earlier in negotiations.
2. Select a knowledgeable management representative for the panel. It is essential that management's representative understands the collective bargaining process so as to serve as a strong advocate for the city's position, particularly behind closed doors with the union representative and the neutral party. It is also advisable that the representative be knowledgeable about the history of the negotiations prior to impasse.
3. Select a mutually acceptable neutral representative on the panel. It is generally to the advantage of both parties to make every effort themselves to agree and choose the neutral third party. In this way the city and the union can maintain greater control over the process than if the neutral party is selected by a court or an agency of the state. The importance of the neutral party cannot be emphasized enough. Management should compile a list of recognized fact-finders or arbitrators and should know their track records of decisions and recommendations.
4. The city should present a well-prepared case before the panel. Some cities use legal counsel during the negotiations. A trial at-

torney would be especially suited to this role. A team of management personnel capable of financial analysis, operations review, and general personnel administration should support counsel. If the city so desires, professional assistance can be secured at relatively low cost to support the city's position. It is suggested that the city not try to stumble through the process the first time through. Specialized consultants or attorneys can be invaluable to management's case. It is always advisable to seek competent legal advice. Review laws and ordinances of the city to determine the constitutional and statutory authority of the city's legislative body.

Finally, it must be remembered that the objective of collective bargaining is to arrive at an agreement. The best agreements are those made by the two parties who will have to live by its provisions. Ultimately, fact-finding and arbitration are no substitutes for good faith collective bargaining.

RESOLUTION OF GRIEVANCES

Most labor agreements include provisions for a grievance procedure. It is becoming common practice in the public sector to specify binding arbitration as the final step in the settlement of a grievance, by which here is meant a dispute over the interpretation or application of the labor agreement in effect as opposed to a dispute or impasse over the negotiation of terms and conditions during bargaining.

From the viewpoint of management, it is preferable that grievances and any procedures for the settlement of disputes be restricted to the interpretation or application of the labor agreement as opposed to the interpretation of personnel rules and regulations, civil service procedures, or other practices outside the scope of the agreement itself. Otherwise, the union through the grievance procedure in effect can exercise veto power over the decisions and rights of management. The costs of arbitration usually are shared equally by the parties.

The arbitrator receives his or her authority from the labor agreement itself and from the submission agreement, if any, forwarded by the parties which establishes the issue(s) in dispute, the remedy sought, the undisputed facts, and the procedures to be followed. The arbitrator has the authority and jurisdiction to interpret and apply the provisions of the labor agreement insofar as it is necessary to settle the grievance, but the arbitrator has no jurisdiction or authority to alter or amend in any way the provisions of the agreement.

STRIKES AND WORK STOPPAGES

In the private sector in the United States the right to strike has been looked upon as "an essential economic freedom."[19] In the public sector, this conclusion is not so readily or simply stated because of the types of services performed by public employees, namely, police protection, fire protection, garbage collection and disposal, and emergency medical services. To strike would be to deprive the public of basic and often emergency services and thereby directly threaten life and property.

In general, labor agreements that specify arbitration as the final step in the grievance procedure, and state laws that specify arbitration as the final step in the collective bargaining procedure will prohibit strikes and work stoppages. This is not to say that strikes and work stoppages do not occur when these particular agreements or statutes are in force. Since 1965 it has been observed that in some cases an employee organization will strike anyway.

More strikes in cities have occurred as increasing numbers of workers have organized. In 1958 only 14 strikes occurred in local government; by 1970 approximately 200 local government jurisdictions were struck by their employees. These strikes have involved almost every segment of the work force, including police and firefighter personnel.

In Hawaii, Minnesota, Oregon, Pennsylvania, and Vermont, employees are permitted a limited right to strike. Most other state collective bargaining laws expressly prohibit employees from striking, while some states remain silent on the strike issue. Since 1970 enough evidence has been accumulated to permit one to conclude tentatively that fewer strikes tend

to occur in those jurisdictions granting a limited right to strike as opposed to those jurisdictions prohibiting outright the right to strike. However, this incidence of strikes could be due to the history of collective bargaining and labor relations in those particular areas.

From the point of view of labor, the right to strike is considered basic. Public willingness or unwillingness to tolerate strikes varies from city to city. Management is obliged to keep abreast of trends in public employee work stoppages or strikes and is advised to be prepared by developing a strike plan.

A satisfactory answer to the question of public employees' right to strike is yet to be found. The problem appears intractable, since there is merit to both sides of the question: The public welfare must continue to be served, but at the same time the rights of employees cannot be ignored.

INNOVATIVE APPROACHES TO LABOR RELATIONS

Since 1965 some innovative approaches have been employed in certain areas of the United States which represent positive contributions toward employer-employee relations in which collective bargaining is part of the setting.

Joint Labor-Management Relations Training. Since labor relations is a rather new field to both the employee and the manager in local government, the U.S. Civil Service Commission has funded several labor-management relations training programs at which representatives of both labor and management have participated in the same training sessions. Each training session is designed to include one representative of labor and one representative from management from a local government jurisdiction, with total representation usually limited between twelve and fifteen cities. Sessions focus upon individual participation in simulated negotiations and in mediation, fact-finding, and arbitration procedures.

Labor-Management Relations Service Network. Some local government associations have established the Labor-Management Relations Service network in response to the stated need of city and county officials. The purpose of such a network is to provide an up-to-date information service regarding contract negotiations, arbitration of police and fire disputes, and other matters bearing upon management's ability to respond effectively to the pressures of labor organizations in a given state or metropolitan area.

Multi-Employer Bargaining. The Vancouver area in the province of British Columbia, Canada, and municipalities in the Minneapolis-St. Paul area have made use of multi-employer bargaining, with varying success. Theoretically, the conditions of employment for the various types of public employees throughout a jurisdiction should tend to equalize following this kind of bargaining. Multi-employer bargaining has occurred within certain industries in private industry and has met with general success. Success of such bargaining in the public sector depends a great deal upon the negotiators and upon communication among participating employers.[20]

Final-Offer Arbitration. A new development in legislated interest arbitration is final-offer or forced-choice arbitration. Final-offer arbitration is quite simple. Both management and the union present their final best offer to the arbitrator. The arbitrator then selects the offer that appears most reasonable after hearing the presentations of both parties.

Theoretically, the procedure would force the parties, even at an impasse, to continue moving ever closer together in search of a position acceptable to both. In practice, the results have been less positive than anticipated. Judging from the experience of Michigan and Wisconsin and the cities of Indianapolis, Indiana, and Eugene, Oregon, with this process, the threat of final-offer arbitration does not appear to alter the negotiating stance of either party.

Application of Organization Development to Labor Relations. Separate and joint conferences have been held with management and labor representatives to explore approaches and purposeful action steps to bridge the gap between the existing relationship and the desired relationship between the parties. The parties are responsible for selecting the bargaining items, establishing priorities, assigning responsibility for follow-up, and checking periodically on progress. This approach is based on a model developed by the Federal Mediation and Conciliation Service.

Other Approaches. Although not so new, other basic approaches to collective bargaining are found to work effectively: package bargaining; management preparing its own set of proposals to present to the union rather than reacting to union proposals; refining the art of compromise; increasing the level of sophistication in discussions about performance and productivity; and replacing the seniority system with the merit system in labor agreements.

Finally, two other approaches gaining widespread acceptance are the combined use of mediation and arbitration ("med-arb") and the expedited, or "quickie," grievance arbitration resorted to in order to get a settlement without red tape or other complications.

Summary and Outlook

Labor relations and collective bargaining are well-established facts of life in the private sector. Increasingly, management in the public sector is learning to deal with the rise of organizing and unionism among its own employees. Effort has been made in this chapter to furnish government administrators with information and ideas on dealing with and improving labor-management relations. The chapter also intended to present an overview of the state of the art of collective bargaining as conducted in the 1970s. The chapter surveyed the existing public employee organizations, summarized the collective bargaining process, and described the procedures for settlement of disputes and impasses in bargaining.

To play an effective and intelligent role in labor relations, management must be well-informed of trends and legislation relating to the field. Its negotiating team must be open-minded and sensitive to the perspective of the employees and the proposals of their union; at the same time it must protect management's rights and prerogatives. The ideal final contract promotes the interests of management and employees alike.

The Outlook. In the mid-1970s when both employee expectations and the rate of inflation were rising fast, when traditional sources of revenue were dwindling or showing no growth, and when citizens demanded the delivery of existing levels of services without higher taxes, labor relations could be expected to become an ever more serious and central fact of management life, requiring not just concern but greater sophistication and imaginativeness in acting and reacting to the situation.

1 Paul Prasow and Edward Peters, LABOR ARBITRATION AND COLLECTIVE BARGAINING: CONFLICT RESOLUTION IN LABOR RELATIONS (New York: McGraw-Hill Book Company, 1970), pp. 4–5.

2 U.S., Civil Service Commission, Labor Relations Training Center, COLLECTIVE BARGAINING IN THE FEDERAL SECTOR (Washington, D.C.: Civil Service Commission, 1973).

3 International City Management Association, MUNICIPAL YEAR BOOK, 1974 (Washington, D.C.: International City Management Association, 1974).

4 Kenneth O. Warner, ed., COLLECTIVE BARGAINING IN THE PUBLIC SERVICE (Chicago: Public Personnel Administration, 1967), p. 21.

5 Frank P. Zeidler, "Impact of Collective Bargaining on Public Administration," in COLLECTIVE BARGAINING IN THE PUBLIC SERVICE, p. 151.

6 Kurt L. Hanslowe, THE EMERGING LAW OF LABOR RELATIONS IN PUBLIC EMPLOYMENT (Ithaca, N.Y.: 1967), p. 105.

7 Frank Elkouri and Edna A. Elkouri, HOW ARBITRATION WORKS (Washington, D.C.: Bureau of National Affairs, 1973), pp. 412–550. See also Prasow and Peters, LABOR ARBITRATION AND COLLECTIVE BARGAINING.

8 For a relatively current summary of organizations representing city employees and the numbers of employees they represent in different cities, see CITY EMPLOYEE REPRESENTATION AND BARGAINING POLICIES, GERR RF-56 (Washington, D.C.: Bureau of National Affairs, 1972).

9 W. D. Heisel and J. D. Hallihan, QUESTIONS AND ANSWERS ON PUBLIC EMPLOYEE NEGOTIATION (Chicago: Public Personnel Association, 1967), p. 3.

10 Arthur Thompson and Irwin Weinstock, "White-Collar Employees and the Unions at TVA," PERSONNEL JOURNAL 46 (January 1967): 15.

11 Ibid., p. 16.

12 Owen Fairweather, "American and Foreign Grievance Systems," in DEVELOPMENTS IN AMERICAN AND FOREIGN ARBITRATION (Washington, D.C.: Bureau of National Affairs, Inc., 1968).

13 For an excellent overview and treatment of this subject, see chapters 12 and 13 in Elkouri and Elkouri, HOW ARBITRATION WORKS.

14 For discussion of the importance of giving special treatment to supervisory and managerial personnel in a collective bargaining environment, see Roy Wesley, "Cities Reminded to Cherish Management," LABOR–MANAGEMENT RELATIONS SERVICE NEWSLETTER (October 1974).

15 Elkouri and Elkouri, HOW ARBITRATION WORKS.

16 For a discussion of the limitations of fact-finding, see William E. Simkin's article, "Fact-finding: Its Values and Limitations," in ARBITRATION AND THE EXPANDING ROLE OF NEUTRALS (Washington, D.C.: Bureau of National Affairs, Inc., 1970).

17 A complete listing and analysis of these statutes and ordinances through 1972 may be found in Joan Zeldon McAvoy, "Binding Arbitration of Contract Terms: A New Approach to the Resolution of Disputes in the Public Sector," 27 Col. Law. Rev. (1972).

18 For a review and evaluation of whether legislated interest arbitration serves the public interest, see Charles M. Rehmus, "Legislated Interest Arbitration," in PROCEEDINGS OF THE 27TH ANNUAL WINTER MEETING OF THE INDUSTRIAL RELATIONS RESEARCH ASSOCIATION, 1974.

19 Elkouri and Elkouri, HOW ARBITRATION WORKS, p. 6.

11

Staff Relations

Remember your humanity, and forget the rest . . .

BERTRAND RUSSELL

STAFF RELATIONS in the public sector has had a history of failure as well as success. The atmosphere surrounding staff relations is one of mistrust, and the basic reasons for this on both sides are lack of information, lack of training, and lack of experience. In dealing in staff, or in "people," relations, the professional in this field must develop the various skills of communications—not only verbal but also listening skills. And, of course, the ability to work within an adversary setting is a prerequisite for the parties of both sides.

Unions, where they figure in the picture, derive their strength from three main sources of power. The first source is the contract. This may or may not be a formal contract, because in some states a statutory recognition of labor organizations may not exist. In lieu of a contract, a working agreement or "memorandum of understanding" is prepared, and for all intents and purposes this document functions as a labor contract, differing from it in name and statutory authority only.

The second source of union power is its cohesive membership, which provides the union with a united front and sustains it in its dealings with management. A unique characteristic of unions in the public sector is that in those cities where unions exist, union membership is primarily voluntary. In the private sector, between 18 and 22 percent of the total work force are members of unions, and in most cases the membership is guaranteed through the instrument of union security agreements. In the public sector, with the membership being primarily voluntary, unions in the larger jurisdictions easily claim 65 percent of eligible employees. Conceivably, this could represent a circumstance favorable to management, because negotiation with a strong union, and particularly a strong voluntary union, generally is much easier than with a factionalized union that will not support a course of action democratically agreed to at the union meeting.

The Grievance and Union Power

The third source of power—and the one to which this chapter is devoted—is the grievance procedure. The grievance procedure is usually the least understood, least appreciated, but possibly the most subtle and powerful tool available to the union. How can this be? The simple answer is that a grievance procedure imaginatively used by the union in effect can be the vehicle by which the union can "share" the rights of management, whether or not those rights have been properly administered and whether or not management's attitude has been rational.

The delivery of improvements, whether they be higher wages, additional paid benefits, better working conditions, or resolved grievances, is the major goal of union officials. Their ability to use the grievance procedure is proportionate to the gains which they can deliver. For this reason the greater part of this discussion will center on grievance procedures. What are the various types of grievance procedures? In what settings are they used? The actual uses of the grievance procedure will be related to three types of union–management situations, the first being a situation where little or no union power exists, the second where there is recognized but limited union power, and the third being a bilateral, fully participative union–management relationship.

Discussion in this chapter will revolve around the three circumstances in which the grievance procedure is used. It is not the intention of this chapter to recommend any particular procedure; rather, the intent is to bring into focus the background of the grievance procedure so that management policy can be improved and preventive action can be taken in order to reduce the need for grievance activity.

Personnel policy provides the basis for management's actions. In most instances it also provides the rationale for union action, particularly if personnel regulations are vaguely written or arbitrarily enforced. The subject of personnel rules and regulations will be taken up in a separate section of this chapter. While the discussion in that section will not be as detailed as the discussion of grievances, personnel policy nevertheless is of tremendous importance in the administration of the grievance procedure. Throughout this chapter, observations and appraisals are offered during the discussion in order to provide a more practical approach to discussing the various facets of staff relations. A general summary concludes the chapter.

The Grievance Procedure

A grievance has been defined as any complaint —real, imagined, or contrived—on the part of an employee with regard to wages, hours, or any other terms and conditions of employment. This definition should be analyzed to fully comprehend the scope to which the grievance procedure applies. It is also useful to examine the origins of grievance procedures.

In the average contract, an employee organization wants three items. The first is the dues checkoff by which the employer upon request of the employee deducts union dues from the employee's pay check and forwards it to the union, thus providing the union with some economic stability. The second item is official recognition that the union is the only organization officially representing and negotiating employees' interests with management. The third item is the grievance procedure in one of the three versions that have evolved.

The first form of grievance procedure restricts the employee to taking issue only with the interpretation of the labor agreement. The second permits the employee to file a complaint only about an alleged instance of unfair treatment by a supervisor, such as not assigning overtime equally. The third and more comprehensive form permits complaining about any terms or circumstances of employment. This third version is by far the most interesting and potentially the most threatening to management because it requires the direct confrontation of union and management. Figure 11-1 represents a form provided by the American Federation of State, County, and Municipal Employees for use by its members in filing grievances in line with the first step of this version.

To refer to the first of the three types of labor–management situations mentioned—the situation where little or no union power exists —all too often management does little to hear, much less resolve, the grievance of the employee. Management exercises almost all initiative in developing personnel policies and procedures, and determines the climate in which staff relations are conducted as well. If by chance an employee's grievance is heard, it is usually within a paternalistic atmosphere.

A change in the attitude of management usually occurs at the first evidence of union activity. Supervisory personnel may appear more conciliatory, although some may become more overbearing. It is at this juncture that management either discourages further union activity by cooperating with union organizers or stimulates it by using or threatening to use repressive methods, sometimes even terminating activist employees. As might be expected

American Federation of State, County and Municipal Employees
Affiliated with the AFL-CIO

GRIEVANCE FORM
(STEP I)

Local Name and Number____Date________________

Employee's Name____

Present working title____Department__________________

Statement of grievance____

____

____

____

____

Action requested____

____

____

____

Signed:________________________________

Action taken____

____

____

Result____

____

____

F-29A

STEWARD'S COPY

FIGURE 11–1. *Grievance form used by the American Federation of State, County, and Municipal Employees (AFSCME). (Source: AFSCME.)*

with any repressive employer action, union activity quickly goes underground and bides its time while gaining membership and strength. Where management has instituted a fair and well-organized personnel program, unionization of employees may not be necessary.

The grievance procedure usually proves to be a highly responsive process. In an organization where no union exists, usually a two-step procedure is in place. The first step involves the immediate supervisor, who may or may not have authority to settle the grievance. If the immediate supervisor is restricted for some reason in solving the problem or decides against the complainant, generally the employee can take his or her complaint direct to a high-level authority who can resolve the grievance almost immediately. As the organization increases in size so does the number of steps in the grievance procedure, and there is a corresponding increase in time required for resolution.

In a nonunion or low-pressure employee situation, the same procedures used in union shops to forestall grievances should be established to ensure good staff relations. These include trained and perceptive supervisors who are on top of things, efficient and fair work practices, and good communications between management and employees. A large proportion of grievances are filed by employees who are uninformed and so file grievances in order to force communication.

Atmosphere

Whether or not an adversary relationship characterizes staff relations and is identified as such, the fact remains that management has something that is wanted by the other side—be it an unofficial staff group or an officially recognized union. A period of "push-pull" usually precedes the development of a harmonious union–management relationship in which both parties approach the bargaining process on equal footing. Through one means or another a concession is first won by the union, with the result that the balance of power appears to equalize.

In some cases the union may seem to have the upper hand, due to the fact that the union is able to muster its members for a concerted job action while management, convinced of the futility of negotiation and weary of pressure, may concede without a fight. However, in the ideal relationship both management and union have a forceful and imaginative attitude, with the union usually demanding and the management usually resisting, and with the recognition on both sides that gains and concessions will be made. Thus a kind of equilibrium, always in flux, can be achieved.

The corporate attitude is set at the top where the decision-making power resides. Recognizing this, the union may attempt to deal only with top management in order to get an immediate response to its proposals or demands. All too often management submits to this pattern, not realizing that this narrow relationship is unfavorable both to the union and to management mainly because it short-circuits the supervisor and does not permit problem solving at the lower level. At the lower level, problems can be identified and worked out to mutual satisfaction, which itself serves to foster respect between supervisor and union representative. When a problem that is bigger than both these parties does arise, then it is time to go up the ladder.

Periodic meetings between the upper echelons of union and management should be scheduled regularly as a means of facilitating communication, although this is not the entire agenda. It is advisable to publicize these meetings and use the minutes as a checklist to gauge how things are going. Of course this is not a substitute for either hard bargaining or grievance resolution. The possibility exists that, when presented with a problem, the supervisor may claim (incorrectly) that he or she has no authority to settle the grievance and immediately pass the buck up to top management. This is good reason for the union to harass management as well as the supervisor.

Within the framework of each organization's objectives and the union–management relationship, there is no reason why friendships cannot develop, nor is there any reason why members from both sides cannot have a business luncheon or occasionally socialize as long as neither party forgets its position and thus avoids compromise and loss of credibility with its own organization.

The ability to deliver is of paramount importance to union officials. It is advisable for management not only to recognize this obligation but to facilitate it to a degree, especially when doing so suits management's program strategy. Otherwise, management risks having a "reasonable" union representative lose his or her elected office and be replaced with a more aggressive and radical—"unreasonable"— representative.

TYPES OF
GRIEVANCE PROCEDURES

Four principal types of grievance procedures will be discussed and analyzed.

1. *One-Step Grievance Procedure.* This type of grievance procedure recognizes only a written grievance alleging incorrect or abusive management action which is filed by the employee with management. Response is due the employee within a short standard time limit. Unless an appeal can be filed with a higher-level authority such as a civil service commission or board of review, management's answer is final. This type of grievance procedure usually exists in those situations where there is little or no union organization, although occasionally in smaller jurisdictions where union power is established this grievance procedure works well because of the informality that generally prevails.

2. *Two-Step Grievance Procedure.* Generally this procedure is used in a work unit of moderate size, i.e., up to 250 employees. The first step involves the supervisor at the program level lying above the immediate supervisor of the employee but also below the highest-ranking authority capable of granting relief. Usually an informal verbal effort to resolve the grievance is required, but this usually proves ineffective.

The first step often is a matter of move and countermove in which the real objective is not grievance resolution but "sizing up": Management may be trying to size up the commitment and strength of the union, figuring that the degree of determination shown by the union

in the early stages of the grievance procedure is indicative of union staying power. On the other hand, the union itself may be testing management's initial reaction to union pressure, looking for signs of softening or retrenchment of attitude.

The second step in the procedure finds the grievance at the highest point of resolution authority. The first step allows both sides to weigh the other's willingness to move off or on a given position. The second step allows for negotiation to occur—negotiation that might be perceived by management as a trade-off. A union will agree to a trade-off if it feels the trade will set a precedent for a future proposal or program. Management may wish to obtain concessions of its own in the trade-off process.

As can be imagined, this two-step procedure can be successfully adapted for use in either the situation of limited union power or the situation of balanced union and management power.

3. *Four-Step Grievance Procedure.* Several levels within the organization are involved in this procedure. First, the grievance is filed or discussed verbally with the employee's immediate supervisor. Arbitrators and courts give considerable weight to efforts to verbally file the grievance. Where management or the unions have refused to undertake verbal discussion and thus possibly achieve early resolution of the grievance, hard decisions have had to be accepted.

The second step involves the division head; the third step, the department head; and the fourth step, the highest-ranking executive with resolution authority, who in a large jurisdiction is the personnel director and in a smaller jurisdiction is the city manager. The transmittal of the grievance through the various steps is usually automatic in that established time limits and required written responses reduce the chance of inordinate delay. Only at the last step is difficulty or delay likely to arise, for at this point both union and management have clarified (if not rigidified) their thinking and position.

A trade-off in grievance settlement is a problematic venture, since in most moderate to large organizations (250 or more employees) several other grievances may remain unresolved. Both management and union for strategic reasons like to have unresolved grievances with which to work. (See the next section on the uses of grievances.) From the union's standpoint, an unresolved grievance represents a potential means of wresting from management a right or a point which it was unable to win at the bargaining table. Therefore, it is important to develop a grievance procedure that specifies what can and what cannot be arbitrated, since theoretically any grievance can be arbitrated.

4. *Union–Management Grievance Board.* This procedure, the application of which became quite prevalent during the 1960s, makes new use of the four-step grievance procedure just described. After a grievance has been verbally discussed and has passed through steps one and two, it goes before a combined union–management board which hears the grievance, evaluates all data, and issues a finding. Both the employee and the supervisor may elect either to accept this finding or go on to step four of the procedure.

Even with union representatives sitting on the grievance board, there is no assurance that the employee will accept the board's finding, particularly if there are a number of opposing factions in the union. Unless the board can speak satisfactorily for both sides, no resolution will occur. Again, intra-union conditions as well as agreements for third-party intervention have a bearing on the effectiveness of the board.

The union–management grievance board seems to have greatest appeal in those government agencies where it is felt that the board's authority to issue findings on grievances is not enough to delimit management's authority. The authority to resolve grievances should never be underestimated. When the grievance procedure is being established, careful attention must be given to the dispersal of resolution authority and, thus, power.

In Kansas City where the four-step grievance procedure was instituted in the mid-1960s, most grievances did in fact reach the fourth step, chiefly because the inexperienced union was sizing up management. Since then, with training and mutual understanding, most griev-ances are resolved before the third step, which is as it should be. (See Figure 11-2 for a statement of the Kansas City procedure.)

USES OF THE GRIEVANCE

The grievance can be a valuable tool to both union and management. The following discussion will illustrate why.

In any relatively strong union–management relationship, a repertory of strategies has been developed which include union–management meetings, public relations, propaganda, threats and other forms of intimidation, and "banked grievances." Banked grievances are grievances which, in the interest of either union or management, have been left unresolved even though such grievances could have been settled earlier by some third-party action such as mediation or arbitration.

Banked grievances may be either legitimate or contrived. Legitimate grievances are less likely to backfire and cause undue strife than the contrived grievance. The contrived grievance could be misunderstood by even the grievant's associates or be pointed out as an example of unfinished business by an opposing faction in the union. Even the most experienced and astute union and management representatives might not recognize a cleverly contrived grievance. It is not uncommon for either side to believe a grievance has been resolved only to find the grievance surfaces later for bargaining purposes. Such situations are discussed next.

Union Demands and Management Counterproposals. Contract demands stipulated by a union usually include several items which fall within two general categories—noneconomic and economic issues. A noneconomic issue is one on which a price generally cannot be set. However, it should be noted that many seemingly innocuous noneconomic issues do in fact carry a price tag, albeit indirectly. Noneconomic issues include such items as time and place of meetings, stewards' rights, and grievance procedures. Economic issues may include wages, reduced hours, holidays, vacation, sick leave, and medical, dental, and other benefits.

Bargaining is a give-and-take process often characterized by periods of impasse. Usually

KANSAS CITY, MISSOURI
PERSONNEL RULES AND REGULATIONS

Rule XIII. APPEALS, GRIEVANCES, HEARINGS, AND INVESTIGATIONS

Section 13.1 APPEALS: Any permanent employee who is suspended, removed, or reduced in pay shall have the right to appeal this action to the Personnel Board. An appeal must be filed with the Personnel Director within ten (10) calendar days after the effective date of such disciplinary action. The appeal must be in writing and set forth the reasons why the disciplinary action is believed to be improper. (Charter, Article V, Sec. 125)

Section 13.2 GRIEVANCE POLICY: It shall be the policy of the city of Kansas City to give individual employees an opportunity to discuss their grievances with their supervisors in order to find mutually satisfactory solutions as rapidly as possible. In the presentation of grievances at any supervisory level, employees are assured of freedom from restraint, interference, discrimination, or reprisal.

a. REPRESENTATION: An employee may be represented by two (2) persons of his own choosing in the presentation of his grievance.

b. GRIEVANCE PROCEDURE:

1. ORAL REPORT: An employee who has a grievance shall first present his grievance to his immediate supervisor.

2. WRITTEN REPORT: If the oral grievance presentation fails to settle the grievance, the employee may within three (3) working days submit a written grievance report to his immediate supervisor. Within three (3) working days after receiving such grievance, the immediate supervisor shall furnish the employee with a written reply to the grievance.

3. APPEAL TO APPOINTING AUTHORITY: If the written reply to the grievance is not satisfactory to the employee, he may, within ten (10) working days after receiving the reply, submit an appeal in writing to his appointing authority. The appointing authority shall confer with the aggrieved employee and/or his authorized representative before rendering a decision. In all instances in which the appointing authority is not the department head, the decision of the appointing authority shall be endorsed by the department head. Such decision shall be reduced in writing and shall be delivered to the aggrieved employee within ten (10) working days of the date on which the appeal was received by the appointing authority.

4. APPEAL TO PERSONNEL DIRECTOR: If appeal to the appointing authority fails to resolve the grievance, the employee may, within five (5) days of receipt of the decision on the appeal, submit an appeal in writing to the Director. Within ten (10) working days of the receipt of such an appeal, the Director or his representative shall hear matters pertinent to the grievance. The decision of the Director shall be final and no further right of appeal shall be provided to employees. The Director shall forward one copy of the course of action he intends to follow to the employee concerned and to the appointing authority.

c. CLASSIFICATION GRIEVANCES: All grievances pertaining to the classification of an employee shall be made in writing to the Director. The decision of the Director shall be final in all matters of classification and the employee shall have no further right of administrative appeal.

d. RETROACTIVE ADJUSTMENT: All adjustments of grievances processed under this procedure shall be retroactive to the time the grievance is first submitted in writing by the aggrieved employee to his immediate supervisor.

e. PERSONNEL BOARD: This rule in no way supersedes or replaces a permanent employee's right to review by the Personnel Board in cases where the employee has been removed, suspended, or reduced in pay.

Section 13.3 CONDUCT OF INVESTIGATIONS: In connection with the review of a grievance, appeal, or for any other purpose necessary to determine the adherence to any provisions of these rules, the Director may conduct such investigation involving the production of records or reports by a municipal department which shall be conducted in such manner as to cause the least possible disruption or inconvenience to such department in the conduct of its regular work. (Charter, Article V, Sec. 118)

FIGURE 11–2. *Provisions for processing employee grievances in the personnel rules and regulations, Kansas City, Missouri.*

bargaining representatives manage to continue beyond the impasse because they understand that various trade-offs can be made. However, it is when a major impasse develops that the unresolved grievance presents itself as a bargaining issue. For example, if a work stoppage or slowdown is in effect and management wishes to return to full production, it might offer to settle certain banked grievances. On the other hand, the union will agree to resolution of these grievances only if it sees an advantage to doing so. Ordinarily there are always a few banked grievances available for such purposes.

For its part, the management team will use all available tools and strategies to counter union demands and reach a settlement that requires giving up as few economic and non-economic points as possible, particularly when management faces a strong union. In this situation an unresolved grievance may surface either by intention or by reference. Quite likely the management team is aware of those unresolved grievances that are most crucial to the union negotiating team. Key grievances may be alluded to as possible face-savers for both sides at a critical point when the bargaining has reached the "settle or strike" stage.

While no bargaining session can be portrayed as average, certain repetitious actions can be observed when there is no change in the composition of a given bargaining team. Such behavior may be challenged by the other side. Should this challenge be countered and the situation become inflexible, chips in the form of unresolved grievances may be played to forestall a walkout, a shutdown, or whatever. It can readily be seen how the unresolved grievance in this situation can provide forceful leverage for either side.

Extra Contract Demands. In the period preparatory to contract negotiation, the union usually plans alternative courses of action. These plans generally include a large number of demands, some of which the union is certain it cannot obtain in the negotiations. But these demands are important enough that the union may try to obtain them another way—through the grievance procedure.

Again, what the union could not get at the bargaining table, it may attempt to get through grievance "nibbling," which consists of raising a number of contrived grievances along with some legitimate grievances. It is not in the interest of the union to settle key grievances until it has a large enough backlog of unresolved grievances on which to trade. This accumulative process is time-consuming, and frequently management does not commit the necessary time, effort, and resources to counter or prepare for this process.

Safety Standards. In accordance with various state workmen's compensation laws, employers are required to provide a safe work place and safe working conditions. Most unions affiliated with the AFL–CIO have professionally-designed basic safety programs which have very high standards. These high-standard programs usually are more costly to establish and maintain than the minimum standards required by most state laws.

Often unions demand safety standards while not expecting they will be granted. Union shop committees will then determine the particular areas to be corrected and then file a grievance in an effort to gain this concession from management. Many such grievances are contrived. Unless management is aware of this approach, it may give away through the grievance procedure what it was able to keep at the bargaining table.

Of course there are legitimate safety hazards and there exist substandard working conditions and work places. The minimum safety standards established under most state workmen's compensation laws in many cases are not comparable to standards set up under the Occupational Safety and Health Act of 1970 (OSHA). This legislation is almost as important a piece of labor-related legislation as the Wagner Act (1935), the Taft-Hartley Act (1947), or the Landrum-Griffin Act (1959), because it is cross-jurisdictional—that is, it crosses state lines and supersedes state laws unless the state law meets or will be modified to meet the standards of OSHA. With this kind of tool, unions are able to proceed with either legitimate or contrived grievances designed to obtain desired ends. All too often management, under threat of penalty, rushes to comply with what it believed were standards only to find out later they were guidelines.

Harrassment of Supervisor or Organization. One historic method of gaining a point or removing an obstacle is harassment—here, harassment through use of the grievance procedure. As noted earlier, traditionally it has been the employee or the union which has resorted to the grievance to modify the policy or action of management, and not vice versa. Systematic and continuous misuse of that procedure constitutes a form of harassment.

Sometimes a supervisor is unrealistic in his or her demands or is actually abusive of subordinates, and the only way some employees know how to deal with the supervisor is to file a grievance. Since one grievance by itself will not cause the supervisor any consternation, grievances are filed in multiples and on a timetable. The amount of time management spends in investigating these grievances and the amount of time the supervisor spends on explanation can be considerable.

There are times when management will allow the supervisor to stand tough with employees or with the union, particularly when management perceives the union to be weak or when it feels it has made enough concessions at the bargaining table, for inevitably the point is reached when no further concessions can be made in the spirit of cooperation.

Management intransigence or refusal to negotiate may cause the union to harass the entire organization. This possibility pertains more to the private sector than to the public sector. But there are cases—New York City being a notable one—in which individual unions or associations of unions appear able to bring management to its knees through harassment and force it to concede to union demands which previously had been withheld at the bargaining table.

Occasionally accession by public management to the unions occurs because of a lack of direct support given management by elected officials. Without this support, managers, particularly those who have spent many years attaining their positions, become frustrated and give in.

Part of the problem lies with the legislative authorities in the jurisdiction. While they may pass generalized and sometimes specialized legislation, they may neglect or for some reason be unwilling to legislate the necessary enforcement machinery that would provide management not only with a program but also vital support. Another reason for lack of support of management is that many members of the legislature or city council are highly responsive to the demands of organized labor and are fearful of losing its political and financial backing in coming elections. While politics ideally should not enter into union–management relations, in reality government is a political organization first and a business organization second. The same applies to unions: It must be recognized that politics is the foundation of union strength.

Solving Grievances

Grievance resolution is the key to a successful day-to-day relationship between management and labor. Grievance resolution does not mean that one side must continually give in to the other, nor does it mean that the union is always ready and willing to file a grievance and follow it through to resolution. In many cases it is a minority of the union membership that files the majority of grievances, some of which may be contrived. This problem often is due to internal strife within the union. Of course, many grievances can be dismissed (and thus resolved) on technical grounds, such as improper jurisdiction or insufficient documentation.

It might be useful for management to consider a grievance procedure of its own. In the traditional labor–management relationship, it is presumed that only the union will make use of the grievance procedure to call management in its error. But there is no practice of the grievance procedure being used to take the union to task when it has transgressed. Granted, there is the disciplinary procedure, but it does not necessarily follow that discipline is the answer in all cases. What ensues is a discussion of the four major means of solving grievances when an impasse has been reached.

Mediation

Mediation is a form of third-party intervention. Unlike in the process of arbitration, the mediator or board of mediators is not intent upon making any particular settlement in favor of one side or the other. Mediation is unique in that the mediator is interested in bringing the parties together and facilitating a settlement which the parties themselves negotiate.

The procedure normally followed by a mediator takes place within a large room with two smaller rooms off to each side. The mediator is stationed in the large room and goes to speak with one of the parties in the smaller room to find out that party's perception of the issues at stake. The mediator also feels out each party for the possibility of a compromise settlement. If the versions of the issues strike the mediator as somewhat ludicrous or unrealistic, he or she will merely transmit the message to the other side. However, during the early phases the mediator will not speculate on the conditions for settlement. The mediator's role again is only to carry information and so arrive at final agreement.

After learning each party's views of the issues, the mediator will begin to evaluate their demands or counterdemands. At this point, the mediator will start asking leading questions designed to get across to each party the problems and obstacles to settlement as the other party sees them. At no time does the mediator make any recommendations, but he or she can suggest, "Now, if you were to give a little bit on this particular point, and if I were able to get the other side to give on this point, too, do you think there might be some possibility of a compromise here?"

At various junctures during the mediation process the mediator—and only the mediator—may make a statement to the public reporting on the issues and the progress, if any, of the mediation effort.

At the outset, of course, both parties are determined not to give in without a fight. In the mediation process they normally cannot be shamed into giving in, but instead they convince themselves through their own appraisal of each point that it is to their best interest that settlement be reached. Consequently, neither side loses face.

It should be recalled that mediation, oversimplified here, is a first step which, if unsuccessful, may lead to what might be characterized as second- and third-degree procedures—fact-finding and arbitration, respectively. When in the mediator's judgment both parties have moved close together on major issues, they are brought together in the large room to arrive at a settlement on those major issues and to trade on minor ones. If the first joint meeting does not work, the process is begun over again.

If the arbitration procedure is required, most arbitrators will take into consideration the fact that the parties have gone through the mediation process with no final settlement to show for it and thus open the proceedings by bringing some force to bear on one party or both parties to agree to something more or to something less than originally intended. In short, mediation should be viewed as the first step—and, it is to be hoped, the last step—in the process of solving either grievances or contract disputes.

Arbitration

Arbitration is another recurrent element in union–management relations. Briefly, arbitration is the process in which a third party, a referee as it were, hears a dispute or grievance, evaluates the various arguments forwarded, and then renders a decision. An arbitration case usually is a matter of winner take all, though some cases are decided in which both sides win a few points and lose a few when the arbitrator sees some merit in both positions.

Binding arbitration of course is the ultimate form of arbitration procedures. Binding arbitration may be interpreted as failure of the collective bargaining process to resolve a conflict. It is conducted by a single arbitrator or a multimember panel usually commissioned by both sides to the dispute with both sides sharing the costs. In some state labor relations legislation passed since the 1960s, arbitrators are automatically assigned by the administering state agency to settle disputes not resolved by a predetermined time limit.

Binding arbitration, as already noted, is a

fixture in labor–management relations, and those who use it with the greater resourcefulness are usually the unions. For instance, a union may follow a strategy of filing selective grievances with the predetermined plan of going to arbitration. Such action is designed to obtain key concessions which erode management's rights.

Advisory arbitration, on the other hand, as a procedure begins somewhat like mediation, fact-finding, and binding arbitration in that a panel is commissioned using the "striking" method (defined below) of selecting names for the panel. The actual hearing procedure differs from the more structured and trial-like procedure of arbitration in that the advisory arbitration panel utilizes several mediation procedures integrated into the fact-finding procedure while at the same time attempting to bring about a resolution of the impasse.

Only if the hearings begin to polarize will the panel resort to more formalized procedures. At this point the usual exchange of exhibits of evidence and the cross-examination will take place.

The findings of the panel are released in an "advisory manner," that is, the panel states its findings and recommendations to the parties but, unlike binding arbitration, neither party is legally bound to comply. This is also the case with the fact-finding procedure. Although the findings arrived at in the fact-finding procedure are released to the general public, usually the proceedings of advisory arbitration are kept confidential, although both sides may agree to publication if they feel it is in their best interests.

In short, advisory arbitration is effective only when both parties feel a moral obligation to accept and comply with recommendations that are but advisory and not binding. If either party feels its best interests are not being served by this procedure, it can reject the findings and recommendations and seek a more favorable or binding solution.

Fact-finding

Fact-finding, like arbitration, is the intervention of a third party to bring about a solution to an impasse. It differs, however, from arbitration in that it makes use of public pressure as a means of getting the parties together.

The procedure normally followed in fact-finding is very similar to that of arbitration. For instance, the fact-finding panel is usually selected by the striking method, that is, the alternate selection by the parties of those names on the fact-finding list as submitted by either a state agency, a federal agency, or any private organization.

When the fact-finders (usually three or five in number) have been chosen, a meeting is held to set up the ground rules for conducting the hearings. Such items settled in this meeting will include which party presents its case first, the type, number, and exchange of exhibits, the selection and swearing in of witnesses, as well as the number of caucuses allotted each party when the hearings are in progress.

Once the hearings begin, they must end by a specified date. The fact-finding panel then discloses, in confidence, its findings of fact and its recommendations to each party. Usually the two sides are given ten to fifteen days to evaluate the results and decide whether to accept, reject, or possibly modify the report.

Although the report of the fact-finding procedure is not binding on the parties, rejection by either party leads to further action on the part of the fact-finding panel, which includes publication of the report using all possible media so as to reach the broadest possible distribution. The assumption here is that large numbers of informed citizens or groups will literally force the recommendations on the parties. If the parties remain unmoved by public reaction to the report, the issue usually will be settled by the procedure of binding arbitration.

Final Best Offer

A relatively new approach to third-party intervention is what has become known as "final best offer." The unique quality of this approach is that each party to the dispute (and the dispute is usually about economic issues) must submit a final offer in writing to the arbitrator who in turn is required to choose the more reasonable offer of the two. In no way can the arbitrator change the offers submitted.

The compelling force in this process is that

each side knows that, should its offer be unreasonable, it will be turned down, and then that party could be saddled with the terms proposed by the other side. Accordingly, both sides on their own will moderate their approach, resulting in their final best offer.

Personnel Policy

The greatest asset any management organization can have is a sound and equitable personnel policy. These rules and regulations may be issued in the form of either general administrative directives or procedural manuals.

Personnel rules and regulations constitute for management what the union contract constitutes for its members—that is, clarification of the terms and conditions of employment, what is expected of both the employee and the employer, and, should problems arise, clarification of the means of settlement. Employees in the bargaining unit are subject both to the personnel rules and regulations of the organization and to the terms and conditions of the working agreement. Communication of the rules and regulations to employees is crucial if management is to accomplish the mission of the organization while also treating its employees equitably.

It is preferable, if financial circumstances permit, to have the rules and regulations printed in booklet form (just as a union contract is printed) and issue a copy to each employee, who will make acknowledgment by written receipt. This receipt is inserted in the employee's personnel file for future reference should questions ever arise. Likewise, management should require its own supervisors to understand the organization's personnel policy.

Management also must invest time and financial resources in the necessary in-depth training of its supervisory and management personnel as to the theory, structure, and actual implementation of all personnel rules and regulations. There should be a central coordinator or a coordinating group responsible for ascertaining that the various rules and regulations are internally consistent, job-related, conducive to the achievement of organizational objectives, and are in compliance with local ordinance, public law, and federal executive order.

Dealing with Infractions

Where there are rules, there will be infractions which must be met with some form of disciplinary action. In the disciplinary section of some contracts or working agreements there is provision for a multi-stage disciplinary procedure. This procedure may stipulate that the response to the first infraction be an oral warning; the second infraction, a written reprimand with a warning that a subsequent infraction will require dismissal; and the third infraction, dismissal. Where an active union exists, any management representative counseling an employee about infractions should have present a third person as witness and should provide the employee with a copy of the counseling proceedings, with a copy placed in the employee's file.

Naturally, there should be an appeals procedure instituted which the employee may use to have a fair hearing of what he or she may consider an unjust or excessive penalty. While individual jurisdictions vary as to what can be appealed, the issues usually appealed include service ratings, letters of reprimand, withholding of merit pay increases, suspensions, demotions, and dismissals. As in the case of the grievance, appeal usually goes first to a higher administrative authority and then to a quasi-judicial board such as the personnel board, the personnel review board, and the civil service commission. Such boards may uphold, modify, or set aside the action taken by management.

Occasionally further appeal can be made to the jurisdiction's chief executive, such as the mayor, the city manager, or the county manager. Some appellants may take additional avenues such as the local, state, or federal courts, particularly if charges of discrimination are involved.

It is clear then that special care must be given to any disciplinary matter. A well-prepared case will take considerable time and effort to document, but a case incompletely or improperly prepared may result in an appeal with its even greater costs in time and effort.

ADMINISTRATIVE REVIEW OF DISCIPLINARY ACTION

In a union–management contract there usually will be a clause regarding representation in the disciplinary procedure, which calls for the union representative to be notified in advance of contemplated disciplinary action against a union member. The clause will also stipulate that the union representative be present at the time formal action is taken against the employee.

There also should be provision for exceptions to this protocol, since there will be emergency situations, primarily in field operations such as police work and firefighting, when a supervisor has to take immediate action in the public interest. In other extraordinary situations, such as fights among employees or insubordination, the processes of notification and representation may have to be completed within twenty-four hours after occurrence. It goes without saying that the review procedures of disciplinary action should apply to *all* employees regardless of union affiliation.

It is now an accepted administrative practice that an agency, on request of the employee, will grant the employee a hearing. Laws providing for review of disciplinary action vary greatly among municipal jurisdictions, with some specifying review by the personnel agency and others by an independent administrative appeals board.

Due to the upsurge in the number of employees exercising their right to file grievances and appeals because of legal protection against reprisal, hearing officers have been appointed in some departments who review a proposed disciplinary action before they authorize its execution. However, one finds more frequently that the authority to review disciplinary action is still vested in the personnel agency itself, especially if there is the possibility of dismissal of the employee. Finally, wherever the authority of review lies, judgment must be made on whether the punishment fits the crime, or rather, whether the disciplinary action fits the infraction and its enforcement has been equitable.

Summary

There are many forms and aspects of staff relations, from the simple one-step grievance procedure to the more complex and costly arbitration procedure. Grievances will arise and must be dealt with; preferably, grievances should be discussed and resolved at the lowest level of management. The best overall approach is for the personnel department to practice and make known an "open door" policy and administer a fair and equitable program in order to avoid the filing of grievances, for it must be seen that grievances are symptomatic of a defective personnel system.

12

Motivation, Productivity, and Performance Appraisal

Without work all life goes rotten. But when work is soulless, life stifles and dies.

ALBERT CAMUS

WHEN THE CONCEPTS and techniques of personnel administration are brought together in one book, the two purposes most fundamental to it come to the forefront time and again: (1) the utilization of people as employees to accomplish the objectives—the work—of an organization, and (2) the utilization of an organization and its work to help employees as people meet their needs and goals. While the notion that organizations exist only to get work done was once dominant in some administrative approaches, today it is generally recognized that organizations must also serve the human needs of their employees. Otherwise, organizations cannot accomplish much of anything over the long run.

Other parts of this book have touched on these purposes underlying personnel administration, but in this chapter they are the principal subjects. Accordingly, the human dimension is discussed first. In the real world of government, the human factor in organizational management is as important as the second topic discussed—productivity or work objectives. Economic analysis generally places productivity first, of course, and often it stands as the sole consideration.

The emphasis of this chapter, as with the rest of this book, is on the "how" in personnel matters—how local government may be effective, efficient, and economical in producing results which meet citizen needs and objectives and at the same time how it may help employees fulfill their human needs. In personnel administration one practical dimension of these concerns traditionally has been employee performance appraisal. Here that important personnel function is treated as the third major topic related to individual and organizational evaluation and development.

Background: Changes in Basic Concepts

To be at all practical, how-to-do-it considerations require knowledge of research and of different concepts of human behavior. Because ideas which are considered basic in the field have changed so much over the years, questions of "how" presume an awareness of trends and varying current practices. This is particularly essential with respect to the first topic—how to meet employee needs and goals and how to tap their motivations to accomplish organizational objectives—but it also applies to the other two topics as well.

Because the basic concepts and practices in personnel administration have changed so markedly since the 1930s with respect to employee motivation, productivity management, and performance appraisal, the more significant trends are highlighted here before the chapter's main topics are examined in detail.

WORK-CENTERED MOTIVATION

Personnel administration's traditional concern with motivation is how to cause employees to produce desired organizational results. Conventional thinking in the 1970s is that *motivation must be work-centered.* Another generally accepted idea is that employees' differing needs and goals must be met to release their "will to work."

Early government and industrial management approaches to employee productivity emphasized force, control, and direction. During the first part of this century, scientific management advocates were preoccupied with the engineering of man/machine production lines. Job simplification and routinization were important personnel functions in private industry, where many personnel practices went under the impressive term of "industrial engineering."

Similar practices and reforms occurred at the same time in government administration in an effort to achieve "business-like efficiency" and "equal pay for equal work." As in the private sector, government at all levels assumed that, in general, employees would slough off or commit errors unless under constant supervision and coercion (economic or otherwise).

Research and experience since World War II has led to the conclusion prevailing in the 1970s that the achievement of organizational and personal goals lies with individual employee motivation. Motivation generally depends on satisfaction found in the work itself —the sense of achievement, responsibility, development, recognition, and advancement derived from the job.

At the same time there is wide acceptance of the idea that the employee's concept of self has a bearing on behavior and performance on the job, and that differing individual needs, perceptions, and goals must be satisfied on the job if employees are to be most productive. The motivation dimension makes "how-to" prescriptions difficult, because so much of it is situational and personalized. But experience reveals many common elements upon which government administrators may act. The basic job needs of most people have long been recognized: security, social and economic status, and self-respect or identity.

PRODUCTIVITY TECHNIQUES

Traditionally, administrators have equated productivity with the efficient and economical accomplishment of given objectives. As to techniques, the starting place was always assumed to be the development of the optimum ratio of total resource input to total output or, short of that, the optimum measures of output per labor hour. The basic ideas still pertain. But with the growing complexity and cost of government and its service functions, administrators are compelled not only to review the basic questions of efficiency and economy in productivity, but they are expected to deal also with the question of effectiveness and the question of techniques of program evaluation and of policy analysis as well.

To administer personnel functions, it is essential to understand current management approaches to effectiveness, efficiency, and economy as well as the background developments of current practices. In short, personnel administration's concern with improvement of productivity is intimately connected with the following related government management approaches to efficiency and effectiveness: performance budgeting; planning, programming, budgeting (PPB); social indicators aggregation and analysis; management by objectives (MBO); and program evaluation. Motivation and performance appraisal in particular are closely linked to the two techniques preferred in the 1970s—MBO and program evaluation.

Several aspects of productivity management merit the special attention of local government administrators. Because of the primacy of service functions in local government, effectiveness and efficiency measures for public service are in the greatest need of development, but few guidelines exist. Technological transfer holds the greatest promise of improvement in local government. Capital investment is the classic approach to improvement, but financial restrictions in government often rule it out. Employee incentives, related to motivation, are another principal means for improvement; in local government this may range from suggestion systems and achievement awards to incentive pay or other monetary compensation.

Of urgent importance in local government in the 1970s is the relationship between productivity improvement and collective bargaining. In some cases, governments, in aiming for productivity improvement, have made the mistake of negotiating work standards into labor–management agreements, thus freezing the standards so as to prevent desirable changes to meet technological or other developments. In these cases, productivity bargaining is required to alter past agreements. In other cases, labor representatives and managers consult regularly on ways to improve productivity and to meet employee needs and goals.

TRENDS IN PERFORMANCE APPRAISAL

Performance appraisal as practiced in government ranges from control-oriented supervisor evaluations of subordinates consistent with scientific management concepts, which were in vogue during the first third of this century, to in-depth dialogues and group analysis of the individual's work objectives and personal goals and perceptions.

In research and theory, if not in practice, it is possible to identify some relatively clear trends. These trends are: (1) from individual to group to management to organization appraisal; (2) from a control orientation to functional performance to total-factor productivity analysis to employee, productivity, and environmental appraisal; (3) from exclusion of employees to their participation in the appraisal process; (4) from periodic appraisals to more or less continuous evaluations; and (5) from performance appraisal to production and organization planning and review to a more or less different genre—program evaluation.

With performance appraisal placed in that challenging and changing context, it is still possible to point out several how-to-do-it dimensions of the topic. These depend first on an analysis of specific objectives; for example, providing feedback to employees, supervisors, or other managers; identifying people with the potential for promotion or special projects; establishing reference data for personnel decisions; or developing mutual goals, objectives, and evaluation criteria. Methods are numerous: use of production records; numerical, alphabetical, or graphic rating scales; field reviews or audits; critical incident appraisal; essay appraisal; self-evaluation; peer review; subordinate appraisal; and assessment centers, among others.

Trends in the 1970s were toward group processes, team building, and organizational change techniques and strategies of appraisal and planning. With the pressures of rising costs of government services and the increasing complexity of policy goals, management by objectives was becoming common in government, and techniques for setting objectives and evaluating results could be expected to emerge as important aspects of action research and organization development approaches.

Current Practice

With this overview of changing concepts and practices in each of the three main topics of this chapter, a more detailed analysis of each of them is now possible.

MOTIVATION

Ideas and practices of motivation in work organizations vary greatly within the United States and elsewhere in the world. Researchers and practitioners recognize two reasons for this diversity. First, great differences exist between cultures, subcultures, and life styles, yielding varying definitions of what constitutes a desirable quality of working life. In many respects these differences appear to be at least as persistent today among younger people who have lived all their lives in the United States as they were among early immigrants from other cultures.

Second, there is far greater recognition now of the complexities of human nature and behavior than was the case during the first third of this century when many of the foundations of public personnel administration were laid. Informed researchers and managers acknowledge the futility of discovering or practicing "the one best way" of motivation. There simply is no such formula, despite the occasional "expert" consultants who continue to peddle universal formulas.

The two key words which are fundamental to understanding current ideas of motivation are contingency and complexity. Approaches to motivation must be contingent on the persons and the work situations involved. And such approaches must recognize that human nature and behavior are complex and are not susceptible of single-theory (economic, spiritual, political, psychological, or social) interpretation.

Despite the contingency and diversity of real-life administrative situations and the complexities of human behavior, some practical guidelines to motivation have materialized out of a wealth of contributions from the behavioral sciences and other fields. As a beginning, the next section focuses on ideas and practices of motivation current in the 1970s by reviewing the philosophical and behavioral framework, some approaches to motivation, and various management concepts.

Philosophical and Behavioral Framework. In business administration and to a large extent in public administration, it was fashionable from the 1920s until the late 1960s to refer almost exclusively to psychology and related behavioral sciences as guides to motivation. Indeed before World War I and again since the mid-1960s, other sources have also been consulted. This is particularly the case with governments, where ideas from the reform eras of the 18th and 19th centuries still persist.

The basic ideas which define general expectations in government organizations and which, therefore, provide one practical framework for public administrators are those of constitutional democracy, its values of human dignity and rule of law, and its implementing principle of popular sovereignty and limited government.

It is important in personnel administration to understand that American political theory does not assert that these democratic values can be fully achieved, partly because it is understood that human beings are seldom satisfied long with what they attain. In effect, the democratic ideal presumes a continuing search for reasonableness in social relationships and a continuing reevaluation of the quality of life, with dreams always outdistancing prevailing reality. What this means for personnel administrators is that, if American democratic theory is sound, they never can expect to have "satisfied" employees or constituents so long as their government holds to democratic standards.

While public administration broke away from this classic view of human nature in the 1920s in the futile search for the "one best way," behavioral research since the mid-1960s has returned to precisely these same starting points: that it is in the nature of human beings to be generally dissatisfied; that human beings rarely find themselves in a stable state of utopian bliss but tend toward a continuing organismic valuing process; and that the "reasonableness" of institutions is measured by processes of change as much as by conditions of stability. According to democratic theory, reality lies in the creative tension between order and disorder. And according to the eminent behavioral scientist Carl Rogers, people develop dynamic self-concepts which in turn govern their behavior, and they are most likely to change when they search out the reasons and means for doing so.

Other than political theory and the behavioral sciences, the most influential ideas about motivation have come from the discipline of economics. When civil service merit systems were being established in the late 19th and early 20th centuries, conventional theory held that human motivation was essentially economic. Writing in 1960, Douglas McGregor, who developed one of the most convincing formulations of motivation theory, cited these early assumptions (which in fact he rejected) summarized here:

1. The average person dislikes and will avoid work.
2. People therefore must be forced, controlled, and directed to work.

3. People generally prefer to be directed, have little ambition, and above all they want security.[1]

This theory, labeled "Theory X" by McGregor, was an extremely pessimistic statement of "economic man" which prevailed in motivation theory in business until the late 1930s and early 1940s.

It would be most extraordinary if views about economic motivation which had held sway for so long were not founded on some observed manifestations of human behavior. Practical experience, backed by hard research, demonstrates that much human behavior is indeed oriented to economic considerations; but the economic dimension now is seen as only one of many components of motivation and is itself regarded as varying in importance from culture to culture.

A few economists, along with other social scientists, philosophers, religious leaders, and politicians, had challenged the preeminence of "economic man" all along. As early as the turn of the century, for example, the American economist Thorstein Veblen rejected the reigning view of his discipline in favor of a psychological conception of human nature. Although during the first several decades of the 1900s he was generally rejected by economists as a heretic, his early writing stressing the human elements of work were reread more sympathetically in the 1960s and 1970s.[2]

The most influential early challenge to the pessimistic view of human nature in motivation theory occurred in the late 1920s and 1930s. This was the result of research conducted at the Western Electric Company's Hawthorne plant. What started as a traditional industrial engineering study of the effect of proper lighting on work groups led to what business managers thought were revolutionary conclusions about human behavior.

The research showed that when lighting was intensified, productivity increased, but it also increased when lighting was dimmed to near-moonlight levels. This led the Harvard psychologists and engineers making the study to conclude that people's work may be affected more by their attitudes than by their physical surroundings. Years of research were devoted to further study, and the comprehensive conclusions were published in 1939.[3]

The influence of the Hawthorne studies was felt much earlier, however, with the 1933 publication of Elton Mayo's book, *The Human Problems of an Industrial Civilization*.[4] Mayo concluded that emotional factors were more important than logical ones in determining productivity. He stressed as most important those factors attendant to participation and involvement of workers in social groups. The force of this study was sufficient to establish the human relations movement in personnel management.

The number of studies of managerial and employee behavior and motivation in private business and government grew so prodigiously after the 1930s that it is not possible to review all their conclusions here. It is possible, however, to note a few other influential ideas about motivation which public personnel administrators need to know.

Probably the most widely accepted statement of the behavioral theory of motivation published in the 1950s and 1960s was the work of Douglas McGregor, then a professor of industrial management at MIT's Sloan School of Management. In one of his most influential articles, published in 1957, he urged practical application of behavioral science theory to the complicated process of performance appraisal.[5] He advocated an approach in which the individual employee establishes personal short-term objectives and evaluates his or her own performance in terms of meeting those objectives. He recommended that in appraisal reviews attention be directed to the employee's strengths.

McGregor's later restatement in 1960 of the positive view of human nature became virtual gospel in motivation research for over a decade, and it remains a useful summary of optimistic assumptions of employee motivation. McGregor's conclusions from behavioral science, labeled "Theory Y," were the following:

1. The expenditure of physical and mental effort in work is as natural as play or rest.
2. External control and the threat of punishment are not the only means for bringing about effort

toward organizational objectives. Man will exercise self-direction and self-control in the service of objectives to which he is committed.

3. Commitment to objectives is a function of the rewards associated with their achievements.
4. The average human being learns, under proper conditions, not only to accept but to seek responsibility.
5. The capacity to exercise a relatively high degree of imagination, ingenuity, and creativity in the solution of organizational problems is widely, not narrowly, distributed in the population.
6. Under the conditions of modern industrial life, the intellectual potentialities of the average human being are only partially utilized.[6]

It is not surprising that these views won quick and widespread acceptance in the United States, for they reflect the generally optimistic view of human nature basic to democratic political and legal theory. What is surprising is that so many business executives and even some public administrators in the 1960s found these ideas to be a novel revelation. Neither careful behavioral scientists like McGregor nor experienced political thinkers ever claimed that these optimistic assumptions about human nature were the entire truth. Nevertheless, in keeping with the preceding tendency to tout "the one best way," McGregor's views were quickly enshrined as infallible formula in business and government training courses throughout the 1960s.

Another figure having great influence on the development of motivation concepts during the 1960s was the psychologist Abraham Maslow.[7] Maslow stressed that each person has an "inner nature" in part unique and in part shared among people. As a foundation idea in motivation theory, his statement that individuals experience a hierarchy of different needs attracted the special consideration of managers. Maslow's concept of the "self-actualizing" person held that this characteristic emerged when general needs were met. Maslow generally accepted the traditional notion that needs at each level must be met before a person's behavior reflects much concern for satisfaction at higher levels. He also held that as lower-level needs are met, they are no longer motivators.

Even in the 1950s and 1960s the psycho-
logical concepts of human behavior which were based on motivation research tended to stress greater complexity and differences among people than were recognized by those who popularized McGregor and Maslow. And by the mid-1970s new and key words entered the vocabulary of personnel administration—expectations, differentiation, contingency, situational, complex human nature, and psychological contract.

The 1970s view is reflected in a critique by Harry Levinson which follows:

The hierarchy of needs model is valid, just as it is valid to say that a tree has a thin bark when it is young, a heavier bark when it is older, an even heavier bark in its old age, and that it needs more of certain kinds of nutrients at a certain point in its age than at another time. But that makes no differentiation among trees nor does it say whether the same processes occur to the same degree in oak trees, palm trees, or cypress trees. When it comes to the specifics of what one does (either as a manager or a psychologist) to influence motivation, such a conception, since it refers to such a broad class of activity, fails to help us understand enough about people to be able to predict behavior. However, if one thinks in terms of the conception of the ego ideal, he can come much closer to finding out what motivates individual people as well as groups of people, and act accordingly.[8]

Levinson himself stresses the individual's concept of self as an essential key to behavior. Understanding motivation depends, in his view, on specification of the kinds of needs which individual employees or groups of employees bring to the work situation and unconsciously assume the organization will fulfill —thus the term "psychological contract."

Kurt Lewin's studies in the 1950s advanced the related view that behavior is a function of the person with his individual differences and of his environment with its variables.[9] Carl Rogers' research of the 1950s reinforced Lewin's work, stressing the individual's concept of self.[10] These researchers laid much of the ground work for action training and research in the 1960s and for team building and organization development approaches of the 1960s and 1970s.

All of these efforts have contributed further support to the behavioral views about motivation prevailing in the late 1970s—that human nature is exceedingly complex and that situational and environmental variables render impossible universal prescriptions.

Approaches to Motivation. Since behavioral science indicates that motivation is contingent upon the self-concepts of complex individuals and their varied environments, what practical conclusions can personnel administrators act upon?

There are several guides, both general and specific. As to general approaches, first, administrators should not expect prescriptions developed for situations different from their own always to work out in their setting. It is sensible to borrow from the knowledge and experience of others, but adaptation to one's own situation and needs is usually required. Second, and extremely important, administrators must understand their own situations and have that knowledge widely shared in their organizations. Some approaches for achieving just that are reviewed later in this chapter.

As to specifics, there is wide agreement on two points stated earlier: (1) Motivation must be work-centered, and (2) employees' differing needs and goals must generally be met to release their will to work. In line with these specifics, a 1973 report of a special task force of the Secretary of Health, Education, and Welfare titled *Work in America*[11] identified the following factors as those which, "with high probability," are determinants of worker satisfaction and productivity:

1. Occupation and status. Major positive variables are: prestige; control over one's work conditions; cohesiveness of the work group; challenge; and variety.
2. Job content. Challenge, as perceived by the employee, appears to be the most important factor. Autonomy or self-determination is rated by workers in all occupations as the key element of an "ideal job." Variety in work content is the other factor rated highest.
3. Supervision. "Considerate and thoughtful behavior" of employers is rated high, along with supervision which shares decision making with subordinates. Participative management (delegated or shared authority and not the absence of authority) has a positive influence on productivity.
4. Peer relationships. Most people prefer to work as members of a group and not in isolation. Congenial peer relationships and interaction with fellow workers are valued factors in work.
5. Wages. "A level of wages that will support an adequate standard of living" in the perception of the employee is important to satisfaction. Equity—the employee's perception of the relationship of others' contribution and pay to his own—is the other key factor.
6. Job mobility and advancement. Seventy-five percent of workers surveyed said that it was important or somewhat important to them that their chances for promotion should be good. Large percentages also said they resent being trapped in a job.
7. Working conditions. Long hours, extreme temperatures, poor ventilation, and noise are key negative factors. Involuntary shift work is a major negative aspect of long hours because of its adverse impact on family life and other personal values associated with the quality of life.
8. Job security. Employment security is a prerequisite to job satisfaction, particularly for older workers.

The factors listed were distilled from a wide variety of applied research and practical experience in business and government organizations. In many cases, the conclusions were drawn from organizations which had attempted formula-type approaches to motivation. While such prescriptions almost always are subject to controversy and to stereotyped application that may be inappropriate in given situations, nevertheless they merit thoughtful consideration by personnel administrators. Two examples of such prescriptive approaches are those of Frederick Herzberg and the transactional analysis (TA) theories of the 1970s.

Herzberg's theory as reflected in two of his books published in 1966[12] and articles by Herzberg and others published in the *Harvard Business Review* and other management journals became the basis of extensive applied research in the 1960s. Herzberg observed that job factors related to worker motivation and satisfaction fall into two groups: motivators or satisfiers, and maintenance (hygiene) factors or dissatisfiers. His research revealed that motivating factors are those related to job content: achievement, recognition, responsibility, growth, and the work itself. Maintenance factors are those related to what Abraham Maslow described as lower-level human needs: organization policy and administration, technical supervision, pay, interpersonal relations, and working conditions.

It was Herzberg's contention that motivating or job factors are the sources of worker satisfaction and that the result of their absence is low productivity and no human satisfaction (as opposed to dissatisfaction). It was also his contention that maintenance or hygiene factors when not met are dissatisfiers and that at most their fulfillment results only in an absence of dissatisfaction.

This view of human nature as two-dimensional is easily subject to criticism. For example, the systems concept sees the nature of an individual as an integrated whole. As noted earlier, it is generally agreed that individual and environmental differences are too diverse to support without qualification a theory like Herzberg's.

Yet, despite valid bases for criticism, Herzberg's theory has been successfully employed in many organizations. One of the more impressive examples is its application at Texas Instruments, as reported by M. Scott Myers. Motivation research conducted at Texas Instruments over a six-year period beginning in 1960 led to these conclusions:

1. Employees are motivated by "a challenging job which allows a feeling of achievement, responsibility, growth, advancement, enjoyment of work itself, and earned recognition."
2. Employees become dissatisfied "when opportunities for meaningful achievement are eliminated and [when] they become sensitized to their environment and begin to find fault."
3. Factors which dissatisfy workers are mostly peripheral to their jobs: work rules, lighting, coffee breaks, titles, seniority rights, wages, fringe benefits, and the like.[13]

A quite different type of "formula approach" to motivation is one popularized in the late 1960s and 1970s in training programs for managers and rank-and-file employees, known as transactional analysis, or TA.[14] The ideas of TA were borrowed from practices in psychiatric therapy. At their simplest, the following are the major ideas of TA as ordinarily presented in training programs aimed at channeling employees' motivations into organizational outlets:

1. People require and respond to attention and recognition—"stroking," in TA language. Positive strokes, such as recognition for achievement, encourage growth and productivity; negative strokes, such as criticism of errors, are more supportive than no attention at all; absence of strokes, such as ignoring strengths and weaknesses, generally is crippling to an employee.
2. Individual personality is characterized by three ego states: (a) parent: the values, opinions, and procedures learned as a child from authority figures; (b) adult: the rational thinking and behaving person as a grown-up; and (c) child: the deep feeling, adaptation, rebellion, and affection of the person as a small child—the source of feeling OK or not-OK.
3. People engage in a variety of behaviors which provide ways of giving, getting, or avoiding strokes. These behaviors are work, withdrawal, rituals, pastimes, intimacy, and psychological games.

With respect to employee motivation, the conclusion of TA is that people work to get recognition. If they get positive recognition for accomplishment, they respond with personal satisfaction and productivity. If they do not get positive recognition, they invest their efforts to get negative recognition, and consequently their work suffers.

The underlying ideas of transactional analysis are subject to many of the criticisms of psychiatric therapy in general, such as the heavy emphasis on the supposed psychological impact of early childhood experiences. More critically, TA takes an exceptionally simple approach to complex human behavior. But it is precisely that which accounts for the popularity of the approach: It is comprehensible to many people.

Motivation and General Management Approaches. Applications of motivation concepts have been incorporated in a number of comprehensive approaches to management, such as management by objectives, the Managerial Grid of Robert Blake and Jane Mouton, and the contingency models of Paul Lawrence and Jay Lorsch. Each of these examples is briefly noted here.

There is no single reference source for the definition of management by objectives. At their simplest, the elements of MBO in actual practice are setting objectives, tracking progress, and evaluating results. Dimensions of this approach have been implemented in government and businesses in a variety of ways, ranging from rigid industrial engineering orientations, which ignore most of what is known about human motivation, to long-term organizational growth and effectiveness strategies based on contemporary behavioral science.

The latter approach as found in the city government of Barrington, Illinois (population 8,400), provides perhaps the best definition of MBO as a development strategy as implemented in the 1970s:

The goal of management by objectives is to train the organization to set objectives, to develop ways of meeting an objective, to schedule the resources needed to meet the objective by the specified accomplishment date, to analyze how the activity is being completed, and to evaluate whether the activity is meeting the objective.[15]

The MBO effort in Barrington included extensive training and application of team-building techniques for improvement of human interaction skills and problem solving. It also concentrated on communications, ranging from use of a detailed attitude survey to work group meetings aimed at exchanging information in order to implement changes.

The mechanics of MBO in government can be spelled out in some detail. But without some informed and strategic perspective such as that employed in the city of Barrington, these elements can degenerate into paperwork routine or can even defeat objectives. With that cautionary note, the following are the key elements of MBO in government administration:

1. Setting of goals, objectives, and priorities in terms of results to be accomplished in a given time;
2. Developing plans for accomplishment of results.
3. Allocating resources (manpower, money, plant and equipment, and information) in terms of established goals, objectives, and priorities;
4. Involving people in implementation of plans, with emphasis on communications for responsiveness and on broad sharing in authoritative goals and objectives;
5. Tracking or monitoring of progress toward goals and objectives, with specific intermediate milestones;
6. Evaluating results in terms of effectiveness (including quality), efficiency, and economy;
7. Generating and implementing improvements in objectives and results (increasing productivity through improved technology, better utilization of people, etc.).[16]

MBO became popular during the 1950s and 1960s in private business and in a few government organizations. The term was popularized by Peter Drucker's book, *The Practice of Management,* published in 1954.[17] In 1957 Douglas McGregor wrote the article mentioned earlier urging a new approach to performance appraisal—one oriented to employees setting their objectives and making a self-evaluation of accomplishment. This became one of the most influential articles ever published by the *Harvard Business Review* and was reprinted in 1972 as an *"HBR* Classic."

This article contributed significantly to the ideas of MBO while also revealing McGregor's ideas which were the basis of his later concepts of Theory X and Theory Y. McGregor stated that traditional performance appraisal failed because it put supervisors in the uncomfortable role of playing God in making judgments about the worth of individuals. He recommended a "sounder approach, which places the major responsibility on the subordinate for establishing performance goals and appraising progress toward them."[18] He thought that, in this objectives-oriented approach, performance appraisal sessions could serve also as counseling sessions.

While McGregor's views greatly influenced the human factors component of MBO approaches in the 1960s, they have come under challenge in the 1970s. Harry Levinson wrote an important article in 1970 in which he declared that management by objectives, in combination with performance appraisal, is self-defeating. The reason for this, Levinson claimed, is that "it misses the whole human point."[19] To Levinson, the objectives-setting and evaluation process by individual employees, which often is an aspect of MBO in private enterprise, differs little from Taylorism in that it is based essentially on an underlying reward/punishment psychology with the employee usually limited to adopting objectives within a narrow range of pre-set organizational goals.

For self-motivation of employees, Levinson held, it is first necessary for the organization to understand each person's needs and then to assess with the individual how those needs can be met in accomplishing the work of the organization. To implement MBO, then, Levinson advised that three steps be taken:

1. Assessment of the motivational base: whether the attitude toward people is that they are to be driven and manipulated or whether it is one of genuine partnership;
2. Group goal setting, task definition, and appraisal, along with shared compensation based on achievement;
3. Appraisal of appraisers: subordinate appraisal of managers and review of organizational objectives.[20]

Because of the importance of MBO to productivity improvement, other aspects of this approach will be examined later in this chapter in relation to dominant management concepts in government. At this point, however, two other examples of motivation related to general management models merit the attention of public personnel administrators.

One of these is the Managerial Grid of Robert R. Blake and Jane S. Mouton.[21] This team drew heavily on the conclusions of the behavioral sciences of the 1950s and early 1960s to formulate a grid that illustrates various leadership styles in terms of management's concern for production and for employees. Their theory was that the most desirable management approach is that which maximizes both concern for production and concern for people—that being a position of 9/9 on their grid which ranged from 1 (low) to 9 (high) for the two key management concerns.

The Blake-Mouton grid was developed as a vehicle for organization development, a strategy to be discussed briefly in the last section of this chapter. As such, one aspect of the grid concept has been extensively employed for team building in government and business. Drawing heavily on research oriented to the human relations school of motivation, the grid offers an instrumented framework for assessing individual and group behaviors. These behaviors are then categorized in terms of grid relationships and are assigned positions such as 9/9, 5/5, 1/9, or 9/1 to reveal styles.

In terms of motivation concepts based on the behavioral sciences of the 1970s, the Blake-Mouton grid may be criticized for failing to take sufficient account of situational and human variables. It makes universal generalizations, prescribes from relatively fixed formulas, and offers value judgments as to the most desirable management styles without much respect for differences among people and organizations. Despite the linearity of the grid back to the human relations school and its forerunner, scientific management, it has been broadly employed with satisfactory results. If balanced with the 1970s view of human and organizational behavior, it may serve as a preliminary model for assessment of alternative management styles.

A management model which stands in high contrast to the Blake-Mouton grid is the contingency model, whose organizational psychology is reflected in Harry Levinson's views summarized above. Influential researchers who have contributed extensive evidence in support of contingency theory are Paul R. Lawrence and Jay W. Lorsch of the Harvard Business School.[22] While they draw heavily on related literature of the behavioral sciences, Lawrence and Lorsch focus their research on how organizations function in distinctly different environments. They conclude that, rather than a "one best way," different requirements are placed on organizations in different environments, requiring varying degrees of differentiated thought patterns and behavior and of integration or collaboration. (Implications of the contingency model for organization development are treated in the last section of this chapter.) It may be enough here to say that, in contrast to the grid approach, the contingency model relies heavily on careful diagnosis of an organization and its environment as a prerequisite to action planning.

This review of motivation concepts and practices leads to the conclusion stated at the outset: General agreement exists that motivation must be work-centered and that employees' differing needs and goals generally must be met to release their will to work. But this review also reveals conflict between various theories and practices in human motivation and also, in some prescriptive approaches, reveals considerable lag of both behind current research.

PRODUCTIVITY

With this review of basic concepts of human behavior and motivation as background, it is now possible to examine actual practices employed by government to improve productivity. Although professional city and county administrators have worked to improve productivity ever since the inception of the council–manager form of government, they have devoted even greater attention to this responsibility since the early 1970s.

Massive expansion of government functions during the 1960s and 1970s, rapidly escalating costs during an era of long-term inflation, and the severe budget constraints that resulted account for the high priority placed on improving government productivity. Also, local government efforts have been facilitated during this period by supportive federal government action by the National Commission on Productivity and Work Quality, created in 1970, and by the experience derived from a productivity improvement project conducted within the federal government in the early 1970s.[23]

A definition of productivity is the natural starting point for analysis of the topic. But the practical meanings of the term are to be found in actual practices, and these are reviewed here under three subtopics which are of particular concern in public personnel administration: (1) employee incentives, (2) major government problems, and (3) related government management trends.

A useful preliminary definition of productivity is the ratio of total output to total resource input. The formula for expressing that is a simple one:

$$\text{output} \div \text{input} = \text{productivity}$$

In the actual management context, it is also useful to look at the inverse relationship:

$$\text{Input} \div \text{output} = \text{unit resource requirements}$$

While that simple formula is a useful point of departure, one must avoid narrow and confining definitions when seeking to improve productivity. Major productivity projects of the 1960s and early 1970s generally used the term "measurement" in identifying productivity changes. Unfortunately, usage of that term has resulted in a tendency to limit the scope of productivity. The term "productivity measurement" may suggest exclusive concern with efficiency and economy, when in practice, leaders in these efforts during the 1970s invariably stressed questions of policy and program effectiveness to be executed by government. That aspect is examined later in relation to government management trends.

Employee Incentives. In the effort to improve productivity and the quality of working life, local governments have instituted a wide range of monetary and other incentives, both positive and negative. These incentives have been carefully documented during the 1970s by research funded by the National Commission on Productivity and Work Quality with assistance from the International City Management Association.

The following descriptive list of types of state and local government employee incentives is taken from a 1975 report prepared by the Urban Institute based on the commission's research.

1. *Attendance incentives* involve monetary or non-monetary inducements to improve employee attendance. They can be used to encourage a reduction in sick leave use or lateness.
2. *Career development* involves the provision of well-defined promotional opportunities, such as career ladders, and their integration with training programs designed to qualify employees for the positions available.
3. *Competition and contests* usually involve monetary or nonmonetary rewards designed to encourage employees, individually or as groups, to improve performance in some facet of work (e.g., a prize for the fewest complaints received).
4. *Educational incentives* are official monetary or nonmonetary considerations given to encourage employees to continue their formal professional or technical education.
5. *Job enlargement* includes a variety of formal approaches designed to make the jobs of supervisory and nonsupervisory personnel more interesting or more responsible. For example:
   a. Job rotation: rotating an employee through several different assignments. Excluded here is rotation which is part of standard training programs for new employees.
   b. Team efforts: the grouping of employees into teams to encourage more cooperation and a broader and more varied view of the work process by the team members.
   c. Increased participation: the expansion of opportunities for employees to contribute to decision-making or problem-solving activities which are usually reserved for management and engineering personnel.
   d. Job redesign: a redefinition of work assignments to enrich and widen employee work efforts, perhaps incorporating all elements of job enlargement described above.
6. *Output-oriented merit increases* are permanent, nonpromotional increases in wages or salary given through the merit system on the basis of high-quality performance rather than, for example, for education.
7. *Performance bonuses* are financial rewards paid to individual employees specifically for high job performance. They do not result in permanent salary or wage increases.
8. *Performance targets* involve the identification of specific work-related targets. The degree of progress in meeting these targets may then be used as an important criterion in providing benefits or penalties. Such targets can be set by the employee (as in management by objectives) or by higher management.
9. *Piecework* is the practice of basing a worker's pay directly on the amount of output he produces. Variations of this practice include: payment of a specified amount of money for each unit of output produced; payment for each unit produced over a standard amount; or payment in terms of 'standard hours' earned for each unit produced.
10. *Productivity bargaining,* although not itself an incentive, is the formal process of using labor-management negotiations to link added employee rewards or benefits explicitly to productivity increases.
11. *Safety incentives* are monetary or nonmonetary awards designed to encourage employees to improve their safety records.
12. *Shared savings* is a financial reward distributed among employees of a department or of the entire organization. It is based upon the cost savings which the department or organization generates within a given period.
13. *Suggestion award programs* encourage employees to contribute ideas to decrease costs, increase the quality of service, or otherwise improve the operations of their organization. Either monetary or nonmonetary awards may be given for suggestions that are adopted.
14. *Task systems* involve paying a day's wages to employees who may leave work when they complete their assigned tasks, regardless of the length of time involved. For example, many sanitation workers are paid for eight hours, although they may leave work after completing their pickup route in less than eight hours.
15. *Variations in working hours,* such as staggered hours, the four-day work week, gliding hours, flexible hours, and similar programs can be viewed as nonmonetary incentives.
16. *Work standards* precisely specify the work to be accomplished by employees or groups of employees (e.g., maintenance or repair time for a specific activity, minutes to take a welfare application, etc.) .[24]

Public administrators who want to implement incentive systems of the sort listed need to keep in mind the necessity of adapting potential incentive programs to their own particular situations. They also should be aware of problems commonly associated with employee incentive programs.

Most important is consideration of unexpected adverse effects on employee satisfaction and productivity. For example, piecework incentive pay based on work standards may indeed generate an increased quantity of output, but at the expense of quality or of injury to employees. Sanitation employees may respond to fixed weight standards by watering down collected waste, for example, or, when assigned fixed routes without fixed hours, they may rush through work at the expense of quality service.

Job enlargement may provide greater satisfaction for some workers, but it may exclude other employees from performing the work. Job enlargement generally requires some training for incumbent employees and it may necessitate complex requirements for induction of new employees.

Conflict with other organizational needs may be difficult to resolve. For example, "flextime" requires special arrangements for covering all required hours of service, and thus may present supervision problems. Major obstacles may also arise from collective bargaining relationships, to be discussed later in this chapter.

But the many potential problems in implementing incentives should not deter public administrators from consideration of their use. These problems can be minimized by careful analysis of management and employee objectives, recognition of practical constraints, and formulation of a detailed design for implementation.

Major Government Problems. In addition to incentive programs, two problems of major importance in the improvement of government productivity warrant the special attention of public personnel administrators. These are (1) labor–management relations and (2) capital improvement and technological transfer.

Productivity bargaining is the primary question between management and labor in government productivity improvement efforts. But there are also other issues, such as implementation of incentive programs and determination of procedures to be followed in manpower adjustments for technological improvements.

Productivity bargaining is technically defined as the negotiation and implementation of formal collective bargaining agreements which stipulate changes in work rules and practices with the objective of achieving increased productivity and reciprocal worker gains.[25] Its applicability within a particular government or agency depends on whether there exist union rights in restrictive work rules subject to collective bargaining and on whether management has authority to negotiate on a *quid pro quo* basis bilateral changes in those rules which bar productivity improvement.

In many local governments, as in the federal government, restrictive work rules seldom are found to be the result of collective bargaining agreements. Also, many local government administrators who negotiate agreements often lack authority to negotiate reciprocal worker gains, such as higher pay. Given these common circumstances, there is little room for productivity bargaining in the technical sense of the term.

Negotiation of work rules such as manning levels, production standards, or classification levels that freeze existing criteria into labor–management contracts is a major error because of possible future adverse impact of those work rules on productivity. Some private labor–management contracts have included such specifications, with disastrous results for productivity. The best known example occurred in the railroad industry with the negotiation of manning levels for railroad engine firemen, which resulted in expensive featherbedding.

While it is common in private sector collective bargaining to negotiate personnel processes related to such rules, actual work standards generally are not negotiated into contracts. But in the public sector in the case of some local governments, the experience of private sector collective bargaining has been ignored, and manning levels have been negotiated for such employees as police, firefighters, and teachers. In these cases, the local governments will be forced to buy out these agreements in the future or they will have to sustain smaller savings from productivity increases that may result from technological, managerial, and other improvements in the production processes.

The experience of New York City is instructive. City officials there who already possessed legal authority to implement changes in work standards, such as manning levels, chose not to exercise that authority and allowed rigid standards to be frozen into contracts and practices. A careful researcher of that development concluded that "it appears that productivity bargaining, rather than being an inherently desirable maximizing strategy for management, is more akin to a necessary evil dictated by earlier dislocations of managerial power in the political and bargaining process."[26]

Aside from productivity bargaining, there are other approaches to bilateral labor–management action aimed at improved productivity and the enhanced quality of employee work life. Many examples exist in government of contract provisions for bilateral committees charged with the function of devising and implementing improvements in productivity. As another example, provision for the bilateral administration of contract terms of personnel processes such as grievances, civic affairs, or training and development can contribute to improved productivity and employee satisfaction.

Capital improvement and technological transfer also are primary questions associated with improvement in productivity and quality of work life in government. As a rule, the greatest gains toward improvement have resulted not from working "harder" but from working "smarter"—that is, productivity generally has been increased more by capital improvements, such as development and use of machines, than by increases in labor output achieved without such changes in production technology. Improved management and work processes also have resulted in major improvements in productivity, as discussed throughout this chapter, but these processes focus mainly on helping employees to work smarter and not on extracting "harder" effort from them.

In government, in contrast to most private organizations, funding of capital improvements is difficult. If capital improvements must be paid for from annual operating budgets, as in the federal government and in many state and local governments, very substantial capital improvements may result in politically unacceptable burdens on the citizenry. All too often government employees are expected to turn out products of high quantity and quality using out-of-date typewriters and calcula-

tors, restricted-use duplicators, old or heavy equipment, or unsafe vehicles. Sometimes unions pressure for improvements in union-organized functions at the expense of improvement in other functions. As an example, some firefighters have been successful in establishing expensive equipment and manning standards as alternatives to unacceptable insurance ratings and rates, with a resulting distortion of capital investment choices.

When technological change has been possible in government, as in the automation of routine billings and receipts, major personnel complications in making the changes often have arisen. Manpower planning for such conversions generally must provide for displaced employees, retraining of personnel for new work processes, and short-term utilization of transition staff. Where collective bargaining exists, bilateral cooperation is required to carry out such conversions.[27]

Productivity and Management Trends. Personnel administrators and managers of public employees must understand the general context of management's efforts to improve government productivity and the quality of work life if they are to contribute to and implement them. Several related basic public management approaches which have been developed since the late 1930s are reflected in some important trends in productivity improvement. These approaches include performance budgeting; planning, programming, budgeting (PPB); social indicators aggregation and analysis; management by objectives (MBO); and program evaluation.

These developments are most clearly seen in the federal government, and for that reason they are discussed here according to their chronological development at that level of government. Each of these practices, however, has been carried over to many state and local governments, and with the growing dominance of the federal government in public affairs, parallel approaches at the lower levels of government generally have become mandatory as conditions of federal program funding.

All of these management approaches are aimed at improved effectiveness, efficiency, and economy in government. That is, they are designed to help governments do the right things, do things right, and do so using resources economically. While all these objectives are essential, the key purpose of these efforts increasingly has become greater government effectiveness.

Performance budgeting efforts in the federal government can be traced back to 1939 with the assignment of the Bureau of the Budget to the Executive Office of the President. It is customary, however, to place the beginnings with the first Hoover Commission established in 1949 and the "little Hoover commissions" created in state and local governments.

As with all these management improvement efforts, it is impossible to identify exact dates of origin or termination. Instead, what is possible and needed is an understanding of the interrelationships of several efforts since the 1940s which are part of a continuing search for increased government effectiveness. Application of performance budgeting generally was at the operating unit level, such as in police departments and public works functions. The approach was management-oriented, and the key objective was work efficiency. The approach became practical in the 1950s because of the development of highly technical cost-benefit analysis capabilities.

During the period when performance budgeting was spreading to state and local government organizations and when PPB was being introduced into the Department of Defense in the 1960s, a major productivity measurement project was undertaken in the federal government. The project was based on an October 1962 memorandum issued by President John F. Kennedy, culminating in 1964 in the publication of a book consisting of five case studies designed to show federal managers how they might use productivity indexes "in determining courses of action in the operation of government agencies."[28] Unfortunately, when PPB became a fixed prescription in the federal government in 1965, program analysts who had worked on this productivity measurement project were shifted to the time-consuming requirements of that particular budgeting approach.

Planning, programming, budgeting (PPB)

was introduced into the Department of Defense in 1961. In contrast to performance budgeting, it was planning-oriented. PPB's principal objective was to rationalize policy making by providing objective information on costs and benefits of alternative ways of accomplishing proposed objectives and by providing measures of outputs in terms of effectiveness as defined by stated objectives. Unfortunately, when PPB was instituted throughout the government by President Lyndon B. Johnson in August 1965, it became associated with time-consuming, rigid, and uniform processes which were found to be inconsistent with workable management approaches in many federal agencies and state and local governments compelled to adopt the approaches.

Despite these shortcomings, program analysis was further refined in the PPB era, and productivity measurement efforts were continued under that umbrella. When the rigid PPB requirements were discontinued in the federal government in June 1971, the productivity measurement and program evaluation disciplines which had been developed during the period were well enough established to continue. Moreover, PPB set a continuing pattern of long-term planning in public administration.

The continuation of productivity improvement efforts was assured by two developments in 1970 and 1971. As noted earlier, the National Commission on Productivity was created in 1970 by action of the President. Of greater immediate importance was the creation in April 1971 of the Joint Project on Productivity Measurement under the direction of the General Accounting Office, the Office of Management and Budget, and the Civil Service Commission. Under informed leadership of career professionals, this project relied heavily on all that had been learned during the 1950s and 1960s about productivity improvement efforts.

Although the project title included measurement, the principal thrust throughout was on effectiveness. As with the productivity measurement effort in the 1960s, the emphasis on measurement in the joint project was designed to focus on necessary disciplines in management. The project resulted in the establishment of a permanent program of productivity measurement and reporting in the federal government which was instituted in August 1972.[29]

A related effectiveness approach in government which is particularly important at high policy levels is the social indicators movement. In March 1966 President Johnson directed the Secretary of Health, Education, and Welfare to develop improved means of charting the nation's social progress. That project resulted in publication in January 1969 of the classic call for development of social indicators, *Toward a Social Report*,[30] prepared by Alice M. Rivlin's Office of Planning and Evaluation in HEW.

Although Congress never responded to that call to support an annual assessment, the Office of Management and Budget published a first report in 1974, *Social Indicators, 1973*.[31] With adoption of the Congressional Budget and Impoundment Control Act of 1974, the need for quantitative descriptions and analyses of general social conditions and trends to facilitate informed policy choices became even more apparent.

Program evaluation in terms of efficiency emerged as an important aspect of performance budgeting in the 1950s. A major phase of evaluation is, of course, effectiveness analysis, since that is where the big payoffs lie. Effectiveness analysis was the principal thrust of PPB. Program evaluation was highlighted in the Legislative Reorganization Act of 1970 in which Congress mandated five-year cost projections for all new programs, provided for standardized data for fiscal control, and directed the General Accounting Office "to review and analyze results of government programs and activities carried on under existing law, including the making of cost-benefit studies."

This requirement resulted in a great expansion of program evaluation efforts in federal, state, and local governments. Among the most important developments was the release in June 1972 of another landmark government publication which was particularly oriented to state and local government needs, *Standards for Audit of Governmental Organizations, Programs, Activities and Functions*.[32]

This publication laid a foundation of practical experience in support of the strong statutory requirements adopted in the Congressional Budget and Impoundment Control Act of 1974. Title VII of that act authorized congressional committees to conduct program testing and analysis activities on their own or to direct agencies to perform evaluations and then report the results to them. The General Accounting Office's program evaluation authority was greatly enlarged by the act.

A final management improvement approach which is intimately related to productivity improvement and program evaluation efforts is management by objectives. The basic concept of this approach and its human dimensions were discussed earlier in this chapter. MBO was instituted in the federal government by a Presidential memorandum of April 18, 1973. The approach was later endorsed by President Gerald Ford for his administration and became an important procedure in the executive branch of the federal government and in federally funded activities of state and local governments.

In sharp contrast to earlier action of the Bureau of the Budget and the Office of Management and Budget under PPB, MBO was initiated in the federal government as a matter of general style, without a prescription of detailed processes. It was promoted not as a new budget system but as a management approach which might come to parallel the budget cycle.

MBO advocates were concerned with the same effectiveness questions which PPB advocates sought to answer: What is government doing? What ought it to do and not do? Under MBO, top federal leaders rejected the earlier PPB orientation toward prescribed and relatively uniform processes for all government. The director of OMB insisted from the beginning on a results-oriented style, preferring not to be tied to a rigid form of MBO or any other narrow framework. However, MBO was soon linked to the budget process, with requirements to submit objectives with budget estimates.

The purposes of MBO as applied in the federal government became quite clear during its first two years: (1) to act as a vehicle for continuous program review, and even high-level analysis, for program policy choices and coordination as under PPB; and (2) to clarify for program managers at every level the expected results and target dates and to provide a framework for evaluation of actual accomplishments as under performance budgeting.

In approach, the most impressive feature of MBO in the federal government was the encouragement of differentiation of application so as to meet situational requirements of various agencies and state and local governments. Because of this relatively open and nonprescriptive approach, MBO as practiced in the federal government became defined by practical experience more than anything else, and the important sources of that experience were performance budgeting, PPB, productivity measures efforts, program evaluation, and social indicators.

The essential connections between these various management improvement approaches may be observed more readily in professionally managed city governments than they can at state or federal levels. Besides the examples cited elsewhere in this chapter, other illustrative examples are the management by objectives program in Charlotte, North Carolina, and the work management program of Riverside, California.[33]

The Charlotte MBO effort was started in 1972 with the preparation of the budget for fiscal year 1973. Before that year Charlotte used a line-item control budget of the sort generally in use before the development of performance budgeting in the 1950s. The city government was able to take ready advantage of the numerous management improvement approaches that had developed gradually during the previous thirty years by adopting an MBO process that was conceptually simple. Since 1972 each city department submits proposed objectives with its related budget request for the coming year. The manager and council review both and adopt approved objectives and budget levels. Then quarterly reviews are held with each department by a budget and evaluation staff, and objectives and budgets for the coming year are related to evaluations of results accomplished.

While conceptually easy, it is clear that this unified management approach as it has evolved in Charlotte requires considerable sophistication in several administrative specialities. And yet it is also clear that the integration of concepts and processes developed since the 1940s has reached such a point of refinement that a professionally managed government can implement them in a reasonably short time.

In Charlotte the payoffs in terms of productivity have met expectations: manpower growth has leveled off; office machines and computer equipment use is more efficient; capital equipment maintenance and use have improved, reducing new purchase requirements; unit cost information on basic services is being developed for further management gains in the future; and the orientation of local administrators and officials is directed increasingly to the accomplishment of objectives and to an understanding of the interrelationships of departmental and program objectives.

The example of Riverside, California, merits note because it employs a "work management program" which at first glance would appear to be only an outgrowth of an industrial engineering technique developed during the scientific management era of the 1920s and 1930s. The program involves micromeasurement of body movements and other work processes for establishment of productivity benchmark criteria. But, in addition to developing work measurement criteria, records, and related processes of production scheduling and control, the city of Riverside has tied its productivity improvement program to a reliance on open communication for direction and feedback. Its program has also built upon professionally developed budget processes responsible for expenditure of a $70 million budget in a city of 161,000 people.

These applications of contemporary management concepts for improving effectiveness, efficiency, and economy in government illustrate the range of important developments with which personnel administration must be familiar if it is to accomplish its objectives. In practice, however, personnel processes too often have remained separate from these important developments, functioning as an isolated staff function, often irrelevant to employee and program management concerns.

For example, as implemented in the federal

government and at other levels, the human factors dimension of MBO which was discussed in the first part of this chapter often has been ignored. The concern of Douglas McGregor with individual employee goal setting and evaluation of results and the even more challenging concepts of Harry Levinson seldom have been raised. When MBO has touched the first-line working levels in governments at all, it has generally been limited to improved communication of established objectives and required evaluation criteria. But that in itself can facilitate greater effectiveness in government, since workers then know what is expected of them and evaluations may be oriented to results rather than to ill-defined personal qualities sometimes associated with employee performance appraisal.

Improved communication may also provide a framework for linking employee perceptions of personal needs and goals to productivity improvement efforts, but that would require major revisions of the performance appraisal approaches usually prevailing in public personnel management. Two exceptions to usual practices are noted below: the appraisal processes of the town of Wellesley, Massachusetts, and of the state of Illinois.

PERFORMANCE APPRAISAL AND ORGANIZATIONAL CHANGE

The term "performance appraisal" in personnel administration traditionally has meant a systematic evaluation of job performance of individual employees to achieve predetermined objectives. Such appraisal programs are widely used at all levels of government, and the approaches employed are the first topic discussed in this last part of this chapter. But actual employee performance appraisal programs which satisfy those who use them or which measure up to current knowledge of human motivation are difficult to find.

Partly for that reason but also because of the more important developments in public management reviewed earlier, there are relatively clear trends from individual to group to organization appraisal. These other aspects of organizational strategies for improved productivity and performance will be discussed in the last section of this chapter. While individual performance appraisal should not be confused with these more recent approaches to organizational improvement, the objectives are related and their success may escalate pressures to minimize the use of the more traditional individual appraisal programs.

Individual Performance Appraisal. An individual performance appraisal program in government usually consists of the following steps:

1. Adoption of a statement (or statements) of policy and objectives;
2. Development of administrative requirements, entailing sets of instructions and procedures and sets of forms for recording appraisals or records of reviews;
3. Implementation by program managers with facilitating support and enforcement by personnel administrators.

Because individual performance appraisal may take many forms, depending on objectives, it is first necessary to decide the purposes and the kinds of employees to be covered. Ordinarily, the objectives are one or more of the following:

1. To provide feedback to employees, supervisors, and other managers on performance —the traditional purpose of individual employee appraisal. When this is the single objective, the assumption is typically made, rightly or wrongly, that individual employees know what is expected of them in their jobs. Discipline, correction, and rewards, including incentive awards, are often associated with this objective.
2. To establish information for employee guidance, development, and training aimed at improved performance. Individual performance review may aim at identifying individual strengths, weaknesses, and development opportunities both for on-the-job learning and for specified formal training.
3. To identify employees with potential for promotion, transfer, or special projects. Use of appraisal of individual performance in a subordinate position as a basis for promo-

tion to a higher-level position can be hazardous, since the required qualities of both positions may be quite different. Also, civil service merit promotion requirements may forbid or limit such use even where factors appear relevant to promotability. Performance appraisal may reveal factors in support of changes in work assignments or transfers to different positions.

4. To establish reference data for personnel decisions, such as compensation and position classification review. Performance "at an acceptable level of competence" is a common requirement for in-grade step increases in step-rate systems of compensation. Pay based on piecework production standards is tied to continuous or short-time output performance. Typically, bonuses or awards also depend on performance ratings. Information derived from appraisals may alert personnel administrators to needs for classification review or other changes in the personnel system.

5. To clarify or to develop mutual goals, objectives, and evaluation criteria. As noted above, performance appraisal in government seldom has moved far in the direction suggested by Douglas McGregor or others who have related it to management by objectives. There are some examples which are oriented to MBO, however.[34] The performance appraisal program adopted in 1973 by the town of Wellesley, Massachusetts, is one instance of this orientation. The performance appraisal form used by the state of Illinois also represents an excellent example of management by objectives and is included here as Figure 12–1.

Related to the identification of performance objectives is the choice of methods. Experimentation with many types has been tried. A listing follows:

1. Production records: Particularly in jobs which are amenable to engineered work standards, records of quantity and quality of production may serve as the principal means of performance evaluation. With the development of improved productivity measures in government during the 1970s (covering 65 to 75 percent of federal production, for example), such methods are becoming increasingly available as substitutes for more subjective approaches.

2. Numerical, alphabetical, or graphic rating scales: These are the typical appraisal approaches used by government. Usually employees are graded on scales from unsatisfactory to outstanding and on such factors as quality and quantity of work, interpersonal relations, and observance of rules.

3. Field reviews or audits: Appraisers are sometimes brought together to review their ratings of employees in an effort to pool experience and information and to reduce bias. Personnel specialists may employ similar methods to audit appraisal processes.

4. Critical incident appraisals: Supervisors may be required to maintain more or less regular records of incidents of positive or negative behavior of employees. Reference may be made to these records for periodic feedback and review.

5. Essay appraisals: Open-ended paragraphs or essays may be required, with or without topical rating guides. Generally, this kind of appraisal calls for some elaboration of the critical incident approach.

6. Self-evaluation: When employees are involved in setting objectives in MBO approaches, it is also common to ask them to evaluate their own performance for review with supervisors, peers, and work groups.

7. Peer review: Appraisals by peers, particularly group appraisal of group output and activities, may be employed where team effort is especially valued. It is necessary, however, to develop group and interpersonal skills as a prerequisite to such review.

8. Subordinate appraisal: As noted earlier in this chapter, Harry Levinson and some other prominent organizational psychologists advocate subordinate appraisal of supervisors and of higher-level organization management. While it is common in government training programs to have participants evaluate their trainers or teachers, such practice is usually restricted to that particular aspect of public personnel administration.

State of Illinois
DEPARTMENT OF PERSONNEL
Springfield, Illinois

INDIVIDUAL DEVELOPMENT AND PERFORMANCE SYSTEM

1. EMPLOYEE'S NAME - LAST, FIRST, MIDDLE	2. DEPARTMENT, BOARD OR COMMISSION	3. DIVISION OR INSTITUTION
4. EMPLOYEE'S SOCIAL SECURITY NUMBER	5. EMPLOYEE'S PAYROLL TITLE	6. TIME IN CURRENT TITLE ______YEARS ______MONTHS

7. PERIOD OF REPORT	8. TYPE OF REPORT
FROM TO	☐ FIRST PROBATIONARY ☐ FINAL PROBATIONARY ☐ ANNUAL ☐ SALARY INCREASE ☐ LAYOFF ☐ DISCHARGE ☐ OTHER (SPECIFY) ________

GENERAL INFORMATION

An objective centered performance evaluation system provides for the collaborative review of employee performance and for the establishment of appropriate work and developmental objectives.

The form itself is a neutral instrument. The value of the system will be determined by the amount of effort individuals are willing to devote to the objective setting and evaluation processes. This evaluation system requires continuous communication between the employee and the supervisor.

The system is an attempt to make the process of evaluation more rational. It helps the employee and supervisor understand more fully what is involved in doing their jobs as well as clarifying the relationship of their work to the work of others around them. This approach helps reduce the problem of misunderstanding by requiring that the employee and supervisor meet and jointly agree to a set of objectives, in order of importance, for the employee's job. The individual gets direct feedback on how he is progressing through the use of the quarterly review sessions. The organization benefits by being better able to plan and coordinate its functions for more effective and economical delivery of services.

The objectives of the organization and the objectives of the individual should be integrated as closely as possible. Those employees who see their own objectives being accomplished, while at the same time achieving the objectives of the organization, are more interested, more motivated and, therefore, more effective in performing their jobs.

The establishment of employee objectives is a five-step process which may be illustrated as follows:

1	2	3	4	5
EMPLOYEE'S ROLE Discuss areas of re-responsibility relating to objectives and self-development needs.	Prepare list of objectives for discussion with supervisor. Discuss and agree on work objectives for this period.	Prepare plans of action to meet objectives for approval of supervisor. Perform the job to be done.	Review progress and discuss any problems with supervisor.	Make self-evaluation and evaluate results for annual appraisal. Prepare list of objectives for next period.
INFORMATION TO BE SHARED Organization objectives; major job responsibilities; self-development needs	OBJECTIVE SETTING	PLANS OF ACTION FOR JOB TO BE DONE	QUARTERLY PROGRESS REVIEW	EVALUATE PERFORMANCE ANNUALLY. RESET OBJECTIVES.
1 **SUPERVISOR'S ROLE** Communicate and discuss appropriate objectives.	2 Prepare a list of objectives with employee. Discuss and agree on work objectives for this period.	3 Approve plans of action for achieving work objectives and review with higher management.	4 Review progress. Make adjustments as required. Provide coaching and assistance.	5 Evaluate performance and results for annual appraisal. Prepare list of objectives for next period.

Each employee will be counseled by his supervisor and a copy of this form filed in the individual's personnel folder not less than once every twelve (12) months. Results of quarterly progress review sessions need be recorded only on copies retained by the employee and the supervisor.

A minimum of three (3) copies of this form will be required--one for the supervisor, one for the employee, and one for the personnel files. Additional copies may be required if needed. If employee position is at a level (unskilled, etc.) that does not lend itself to objective setting, indicate by inserting "N/A" (Not Applicable) wherever necessary.

DP-201R (2-74)   Page 1 of 4

FIGURE 12–1. *Employee evaluation form, state of Illinois. This form stresses a cooperative approach to review of past performance and setting work objectives on a quarterly basis.*

PART I. APPRAISAL OF OBJECTIVES.

Supervisor is to list and evaluate all objectives for which the employee was held accountable during the last reporting period. Mark the appropriate column for each objective.

	Objectives		
	EXCEEDED	MET	NOT MET

PART II. GENERAL APPRAISAL OF EMPLOYEE PERFORMANCE

Complete items 1 through 8 for all employees and items 9 and 10 when applicable. Differences between ratings by employee and by supervisor must be discussed.

	TO BE COMPLETED BY EMPLOYEE			TO BE COMPLETED BY SUPERVISOR			
	EXCEEDS EXPECTATIONS	MEETS EXPECTATIONS	NEEDS IMPROVEMENT	EXCEEDS EXPECTATIONS	MEETS EXPECTATIONS	NEEDS IMPROVEMENT	INSUFFICIENT OPPORTUNITY TO OBSERVE
1. JOB KNOWLEDGE: Consider overall knowledge of duties and responsibilities as required for current job or position	☐	☐	☐	☐	☐	☐	☐
2. PRODUCTIVITY: Evaluate amount of work generated and completed successfully as compared to amount of work expected for this job or position	☐	☐	☐	☐	☐	☐	☐
3. QUALITY: Rate correctness, completeness, accuracy and economy of work - overall quality	☐	☐	☐	☐	☐	☐	☐
4. INITIATIVE: Self motivation - consider amount of direction required - seeks improved methods and techniques - consistence in trying to do better.	☐	☐	☐	☐	☐	☐	☐
5. USE OF TIME: Uses available time wisely - is punctual reporting to work absenteeism - accomplishes required work on or ahead of schedule	☐	☐	☐	☐	☐	☐	☐
6. PLANNING: Sets realistic objectives - anticipates and prepares for future requirements - establishes logical priorities	☐	☐	☐	☐	☐	☐	☐
7. FOLLOW-UP: Maintains control of workloads - allocates resources economically - insures that assignments are completed accurately and timely	☐	☐	☐	☐	☐	☐	☐
8. HUMAN RELATIONS: Establishes and maintains cordial work climate - promotes harmony and enthusiasm - displays sincere interest in assisting other employees	☐	☐	☐	☐	☐	☐	☐
9. LEADERSHIP: Sets high standards - provides good managerial example - encourages subordinates to perform efficiently - communicates effectively	☐	☐	☐	☐	☐	☐	☐
10. SUBORDINATE DEVELOPMENT: Helps subordinates plan career development - grooms potential replacements - gives guidance and counsel	☐	☐	☐	☐	☐	☐	☐

FIGURE 12–1. (*continued.*)

EMPLOYEE'S NAME - LAST, FIRST, MIDDLE

PART III. REMARKS BY SUPERVISOR.

Comment on employee's outstanding achievements. When "not met" is checked in Part I or "needs improvement" is checked in Part II describe the reasons for this rating, and what remedial steps were taken.

PART IV. EMPLOYEE OBJECTIVES FOR NEXT REPORTING PERIOD.

To be established by the employee with input, advice, and agreement of the supervisor. Objectives should be set for each major area of job responsibility, ranked in priority order, and be as measurable as possible. Personal development objectives may be included.

Page 3 of 4

FIGURE 12–1. *(continued.)*

PART V. EMPLOYEE'S COMMENTS.

Employee may comment on all or any part of the information contained in this document, including the evaluation process. If the employee does not concur with the evaluation, check the appropriate box and explain reasons for disagreement.

PART VI. SIGNATURES.

EMPLOYEE'S SIGNATURE	PAYROLL TITLE	DATE

☐ I DO NOT CONCUR (USE PART V FOR COMMENTS)

SUPERVISOR'S SIGNATURE	PAYROLL TITLE	DATE

☐ I HAVE PERSONALLY DISCUSSED THE CONTENTS OF THIS DOCUMENT WITH THE EMPLOYEE AND WE HAVE AGREED TO THE OBJECTIVES SET.

NEXT HIGHER LEVEL SUPERVISOR SIGNATURE (REVIEW)	PAYROLL TITLE	DATE

AGENCY HEAD SIGNATURE (REVIEW)	PAYROLL TITLE	DATE

PART VII. QUARTERLY PROGRESS REVIEW.   (This can be initiated by either the employee or the supervisor.)

The employee and supervisor are to meet quarterly to review progress toward previously agreed upon objectives. If the original objectives need to be adjusted, use the space below to document the change. The employee and supervisor should date and initial the document at the time of each review.

1st quarter
Date _______
Initials:
Emp. _______
Sup. _______

2nd quarter
Date _______
Initials:
Emp. _______
Sup. _______

3rd quarter
Date _______
Initials:
Emp. _______
Sup. _______

(DO NOT WRITE BENEATH THIS LINE)

For use only if third party consultation is required.

FIGURE 12–1. (*continued.*)

9. Assessment centers: As a rule, the above methods are oriented largely to past performance. To appraise future potential, one approach is to bring together a group of employees, engage them in simulated work assignments, and assess their performance there against possible future responsibilities. This is a useful approach when there is no evidence that past performance is related to future success in another position or when little information is known about certain prospective candidates.

Once the objectives and general types of performance appraisal are decided, the administrative requirements must be developed. Affected employees or their union representatives may be involved in this process. It is necessary to determine which persons will make appraisals of others—for example, evaluations of supervisors by subordinates, second-level reviews of appraisals, peer reviews, or appraisal of subordinates by their own supervisors. Frequency of appraisals must be determined and, in the case of annual appraisals, a decision must be made on whether to stagger deadlines throughout the year or to cluster them at one time. Once these programming decisions are determined, instructions and procedural guides must be written and published. Forms must be prepared for recording appraisals.

Two examples of performance appraisal forms are included in this chapter. As noted earlier, Figure 12–1 is from the state of Illinois. The other example is represented in Figure 12–2 and consists of the forms used by the U.S. Civil Service Commission for its own employees: one for those positions at levels of GS–6 and above, and the other for supervisory employees at those levels. The Civil Service Commission forms represent an approach to performance appraisal more traditional than the Illinois example.

The first step in implementing a traditional employee performance appraisal program is to explain it to all involved. The second step is to train those persons responsible for making appraisals. From the review presented at the beginning of this chapter of behavioral science research relative to performance appraisal, it should be clear that no set instructions for all jurisdictions can be prescribed for that training. Rather, performance appraisal must be oriented to the objectives, procedures, and circumstances of particular organizations.

Once those involved are adequately informed and skilled, the next step is to do the appraisals. During this process it is usually the responsibility of personnel administrators to alert program managers to schedules, distribute necessary forms, maintain security of appraisal records, enforce standards, evaluate results, and provide feedback on progress and conclusions. It is also the function of the personnel specialist to formulate and make recommendations for desired changes.

Work Groups and Organizational Change. It should be evident that some of the individual performance appraisal programs just described often conflict with contemporary ideas of human motivation, as reviewed in the first section of this chapter. In fact, some of the programs date back to the scientific management movement and its pessimistic conception of "economic man."

As noted earlier, beginning in the 1950s group methods began to be formulated to accomplish desired organizational outcomes while at the same time individual objectives were met. This was largely a practical effort to cope with dramatic and rapid changes in values, technology, and other forces which challenged the ways in which organizations and individuals had traditionally done things. Also as noted earlier, this development built largely on the conclusions of Kurt Lewin and Carl Rogers: that people are purposeful in their behavior, seeking to achieve objectives which satisfy their needs as they perceive them, and that individuals with developed concepts about themselves change most readily when they share in exploring the reasons and the means for changing.

As early as 1954 the California State Personnel Board, through the leadership of Neely D. Gardner, acted on these ideas and undertook an action training effort which Gardner called organization development.[35] Similar movements in private enterprise, notably in the Esso Standard Oil Company in the late 1950s

U. S. CIVIL SERVICE COMMISSION
MERIT PROMOTION PROGRAM

EVALUATION OF EMPLOYEE PERFORMANCE FOR GS-6 AND HIGHER POSITIONS

DESTROY AFTER

____
DATE

NAME OF EMPLOYEE	TITLE AND GRADE	ORGANIZATIONAL UNIT
PREPARED BY *(Signature)*	TITLE AND GRADE	ORGANIZATIONAL UNIT

WORK RELATIONSHIP TO EMPLOYEE	PERIOD COVERED BY THIS EVALUATION
☐ IMMEDIATE SUPERVISOR ☐ OTHER (EXPLAIN)	MONTH DAY YEAR FROM / / TO / /

TO THE RATER

The information you furnish on this form will be an important element in determining which employees are best qualified for competitive placements. Successful placements depend upon matching employees' abilities to job requirements. You are asked to describe this employee's performance so that his abilities will be clear to evaluation panels and management officials.

Elements of performance are grouped under general headings. First mark each to show its importance in the employee's job. In the appropriate box put:

O if that element is of no importance or of only minor importance.

√ if that element contributes, but is not essential, to good performance.

+ if that element is important in the job.

Then mark each element with the number of the statement that best describes the employee's performance with respect to that element. Mark:

(1) If the employee's performance exceeds expectation to such an extent that it warrants special mention, for placement consideration.

(2) If the employee has demonstrated ability to a degree that is clearly above that expected of a fully competent employee and you would expect him to display the same degree of ability in another position.

(3) If the employee has demonstrated ability to the full extent expected of a thoroughly competent employee and you would recommend him with confidence for another position in which the ability is important.

(4) If the employee's performance is acceptable but you would have some reservations about recommending him for another position in which the ability is important.

(5) If the employee's performance exhibits some definite weakness in this respect.

(X) If the employee does not have the opportunity on the job to show ability in this respect.

It is expected that most elements of performance will be accurately described by a 3. Remember that almost everyone rated in this program has been through careful screening to reach his current position. A "3" describes thoroughly competent performance that is expected of a selected group and a "1" or a "2" goes well beyond this high standard.

All ratings must be supported by facts, with examples if possible.

Use the space under "Comment" to expand on the information about performance conveyed by your element ratings in a manner useful to a panel matching abilities to job demands. Use specific terms and examples and avoid generalities. Do not limit your discussion to the elements given under each heading if the employee has demonstrated other significant job-related capabilities or weaknesses in that area.

After completing the evaluation, write the number and letter of the three elements in which the employee has shown greatest capability, in the space provided. Then give the employee a narrative description of his overall performance in relation to the standards you hold for the job.

Discuss your evaluation with the employee so that he will know how he is measuring up to the standards you are applying to performance on the job. Ask the employee if he believes you have overlooked any of his strong points. Give the employee the opportunity to add any remarks he wishes to make in the spaces provided for that purpose. This discussion can serve as a guide to the employee in realistic career planning.

CSC FORM 1009
November 1970

FIGURE 12–2. *Performance evaluation form, U.S. Civil Service Commission. This form is used for GS-6 and higher pay grades. The first four pages are completed for all employees covered; the last two pages are completed for supervisory employees only.*

IMPORTANCE ON JOB   **PERFORMANCE**

1. JOB KNOWLEDGE

[+]   [ ]   a. Breadth and depth of knowledge of general occupational field.

[+]   [ ]   b. Experience and knowledge needed for specific job.

(In narrative, describe fields of special competence and, as appropriate, comment on developmental progress and needs in current job.)

COMMENT:

2. WORK PRODUCTS

[+]   [ ]   a. Turns out complete, high-quality products.

[ ]   [ ]   b. Produces large quantity of work, or completes projects quickly.

[ ]   [ ]   c. Meets deadlines.

COMMENT:

3. COMMUNICATIONS SKILLS

[ ]   [ ]   a. Displays skill in oral expression: organization of ideas, adapting to the listener and situation, clarity of expression, effective use of language.

[ ]   [ ]   b. Can address groups formally.

[ ]   [ ]   c. Writes well: writing is clear, correct, well-organized, complete, appropriate in style and language. (In narrative, state type of writing: e.g., general, Congressional, or policy correspondence; reports; instructions; research papers.)

COMMENT:

4. WORKING RELATIONSHIPS

[ ]   [ ]   a. Within immediate organization, gets along with co-workers, is good group worker, heeds others' points of view.

[ ]   [ ]   b. Outside immediate organization, wins respect and cooperation of peers, management officials in other parts of Commission or in other agencies or general public. (In narrative, state type or nature of contacts.)

COMMENT:

FIGURE 12–2. (*continued.*)

IMPORTANCE ON JOB	PERFORMANCE	

5. JUDGMENT AND PROBLEM SOLVING

☐ ☐ a. Gets to the root of the problem and makes sound proposals, decisions.

☐ ☐ b. Foresees probable consequences of actions or recommendations.

☐ ☐ c. Can analyze situations, determine issues, gather sufficient facts, weigh alternatives, and arrive at useful conclusions in making studies or in staff-type assignments.

☐ ☐ d. Recognizes situations that supervisor should be consulted on or informed of.

COMMENT:

6. ADAPTABILITY AND CREATIVITY

☐ ☐ a. Recognizes new needs and need for new approaches.

☐ ☐ b. Displays creativity and originality in attaining work objectives.

☐ ☐ c. Adapts readily to changes in program direction or in procedures.

☐ ☐ d. Gives an extra portion when the job requires.

COMMENT:

7. RESPONSIBILITY AND INDEPENDENCE

☐ ☐ a. Carries out assignments on his own; can work with success independently.

☐ ☐ b. Reacts with understanding to opposing views or obstacles to accomplishment.

☐ ☐ c. Sees that necessary things get done.

☐ ☐ d. Can be depended upon, in terms of presence on the job, effective use of time.

☐ ☐ e. Accepts responsibility.

COMMENT:

FIGURE 12–2. *(continued.)*

8. OTHER STRENGTHS deserving special mention

Three greatest capabilities (Give number and letter): _______ _______ _______

EMPLOYEE REVIEW *(Record any comments you have in the space under each numbered rating element, or use the space below, referring to the number and letter of the item you are discussing. If an evaluation was made on CSC Form 1009-A also, check here.* ☐ *)*

I have reviewed this completed evaluation and it has been discussed with me.

____
Date

____
Employee's Signature

My comments on this evaluation are as follows:

SECOND-LEVEL SUPERVISORY REVIEW *(If these comments cover CSC Form 1009-A also, check here.* ☐ *)*
(Where you are able to add significant comments based on your personal knowledge of the employee's performance, you should do so. If you do add any comments, return the evaluation to the employee's immediate supervisor. He will show the form to the employee rated, and give him another opportunity to comment in the space above.)

My comments on this evaluation are as follows:

_______________________ _______________________ _______________________
Date   Signature   Title

I have reviewed the comments of the second level supervisor.

____
Employee's Signature

____
Date

GPO 925-8 58

FIGURE 12–2. *(continued.)*

U. S. CIVIL SERVICE COMMISSION
MERIT PROMOTION PROGRAM

DESTROY AFTER
____
DATE

EVALUATION OF EMPLOYEE PERFORMANCE FOR GS-6 AND HIGHER POSITIONS

COMPLETE FOR SUPERVISORY EMPLOYEES ONLY
(See instructions on CSC Form 1009)

NAME OF EMPLOYEE	TITLE AND GRADE	ORGANIZATION UNIT
PREPARED BY *(signature)*	TITLE AND GRADE	ORGANIZATION UNIT

WORK RELATIONSHIP TO EMPLOYEE	PERIOD COVERED BY THIS EVALUATION
☐ IMMEDIATE SUPERVISOR ☐ OTHER (EXPLAIN)	MONTH / DAY / YEAR FROM / / TO / /

TO THE RATER

This form is used to rate employees in supervisory positions. It is used in conjunction with CSC Form 1009. Follow the instructions on that form.

First mark each element to show its importance in the employee's job. In the appropriate box mark:

o if that element is of no importance or of only minor importance.

√ if that element contributes, but is not essential, to good performance.

+ if that element is important in the job.

Then mark each element with the number of the statement that best describes the employee's performance with respect to that element. Mark:

(3) If the employee has demonstrated ability to the full extent expected of a thoroughly competent employee and you would recommend him with confidence for another position in which the ability is important.

(2) If the employee has demonstrated ability to a degree that is clearly above that expected of a fully competent employee and you would expect him to display the same degree of ability in another position.

(1) If the employee's performance exceeds expectation to such an extent that it warrants special mention for placement consideration.

(4) If the employee's performance is acceptable but you would have some reservations about recommending him for another position in which the ability is important.

(5) If the employee's performance exhibits some definite weakness in this respect.

(x) If the employee does not have the opportunity on the job to show ability in this respect.

The spaces for review by the employee and the second-level supervisor on CSC Form 1009 are used for comment on this form also.

CSC FORM 1009-A
NOVEMBER 1970

FIGURE 12–2. *(continued.)*

IMPORTANCE ON JOB   PERFORMANCE

1. PRODUCTION OF UNIT

a. Quality of work produced by his organization.

b. Quantity of work or length of time to complete projects

c. Meeting deadlines.

COMMENT:

2. DEVELOPMENT OF STAFF

a. Develops employees for competent performance in their current jobs.

b. Provides the maximum opportunity to employees to enhance their skills so they may perform at their highest potential and advance in accordance with their abilities and without regard to race, religion, color, national origin, sex, physical handicap, or any other irrelevant.

c. Arranges for his employees to participate in training and other developmental programs.

COMMENT:

3. MOTIVATION OF EMPLOYEES

a. Develops smooth working relationships with staff and among employees. (Consider turnover because of employee dissatisfaction, number and kinds of employee complaints, patterns of leave taking, and absenteeism.)

b. Employees respond readily to unusual organizational needs, peak workloads.

c. Understands his responsibilities as supervisor. (Consider kinds of problems on which he seeks help and his proposed solutions.)

d. Selects, promotes, disciplines, assigns duties, and evaluates performance of all employees without regard to race, religion, color, national origin, sex, physical handicap, or any other irrelevant factor.

COMMENT:

4. MANAGEMENT SKILLS

a. Makes sound decisions without undue delay.

b. Delegates authority effectively.

c. Sees needs and meets them.

d. Promotes the full realization of equal employment opportunity through affirmative action.

COMMENT:

5. OTHER SUPERVISORY ABILITIES

FIGURE 12–2. (*continued.*)

and in TRW Systems Group in the early 1960s, quickly established organization development (OD) as common procedure.

As noted, OD was formulated as a strategy for managing organizational and personal change and for focusing human energy on accomplishment of desired objectives. It reflected a sharp shift away from the static conception of the "one best way" in administration toward a process view of human behavior and organizational functioning. In this sense, organization development emerged as an approach to "organization becoming."

A definition of OD emerged from action training practices of the 1960s: OD is a managed process of systematic organizational change toward shared goals and their accomplishment through experienced behavior, stressing values of human dignity and organizational justice or reasonableness as well as open, problem-confronting, and participative leadership styles.

Aside from a theoretical definition of OD, as in other applications of behavioral science, approaches to the strategy vary in practice. In earlier discussion in this chapter of applications of motivation theories to general models of management, two quite different approaches were noted: (1) the Blake-Mouton Managerial Grid, based on value judgments as to the most desirable managerial styles proceeding from relatively universal generalizations and prescriptive formulas, and (2) the contrasting contingency model of Lawrence and Lorsch, stressing the different requirements imposed on organizations by different environments.

Despite many important differences in basic OD approaches, it is possible to identify several methods commonly employed in action training and organization development. It must be noted first, however, that the usual practice has been to retain outside expertise to facilitate implementation of these methods. The use of third-party assistance and some common methods of organization development are illustrated in the case of the municipal government of Kansas City, Missouri.

The methods, or "interventions" as they are usually called in OD, employed in Kansas City were the following:

1. Survey feedback: A confidential questionnaire was sent to key city administrators, and individual interviews were conducted with twenty-seven of them. The data gathered were summarized by outside trainers, and meetings were held with all members of the city manager's office and then with the entire top management group of the city. Task force groups were then formed to set key priorities.

2. Task force process: The composition of the temporary task force groups was determined according to motivation and expertise concerning the problems, not according to traditional hierarchical lines. An offsite meeting of half a day was held for reporting task force recommendations.

3. Team building: Several meetings were held of city groups (people who regularly worked together) to focus on their roles, relationships, and responsibilities. Before these meetings a note was sent to participants to explain the term "team building." That note included the following explanation of the method and what was expected of participants:

Method: Members work together to
  a) evaluate their ability to be open and honest with each other;
  b) explore feelings and attitudes in their relationships with each other and the organization;
  c) identify problems and issues which hamper their collaboration;
  d) suggest approaches to solving problems.
Discussion is informal, extended (a half day or more), and usually takes place in an off-site location.
What is expected of participants:
  a) Participants are not pressured to say more than they wish to say: They regulate their own behavior.
  b) Participants are asked to be as open, direct, honest, and objective in their discussion as they feel they can be in the situation.
  c) The content of the discussion is confidential with the group.
  d) To the extent possible, status differences are minimized, and the group operates as a team of equals.
  e) There is a commitment to talk through and resolve person-to-person differences or conflicts that may arise, rather than have them

influence relationships back in the organization.

4. Meetings for organizational work: These meetings focused on substantive matters such as policy questions, internal administrative organization, and relationships with outside forces, such as the Jackson County government. Although the main subject matter of such meetings consisted of actual work which had to be accomplished, some time was devoted to team building "maintenance" and review of how the groups functioned together.
5. Management development: Several activities were employed as parts of a planned strategy of management development. These ranged from individual skills training and assessment of personal roles to interdepartmental "confrontation" meetings aimed at mirroring outside impact and providing feedback.[36]

Kansas City's OD experience illustrates the practical interventions employed in action training to facilitate organizational change. These methods may be stated conceptually to summarize the most common OD activities:

1. Data collection, sensing, and diagnosis of employee, organization, and environmental perceptions, needs, objectives, attitudes, processes, and other factors through surveys, interviews, meetings, and the like.
2. Team building with work groups through intensive problem-identification and problem-solving discussion sessions aimed at developing open and nonthreatening human relationships.
3. Intergroup building to bring different organizational work groups together to explore their relationships and to increase their capacities to relate productively to each other.
4. Organizational mirroring to provide an organizational work unit with feedback on how it is perceived by a full range of other organizational units or to allow an organization as a whole to collect feedback from the key organizations or people in its external environment.

Besides these commonly employed OD methods, there have been and are at any one time many others which may be more or less successful in different situations. For example, sensitivity training was widely practiced in the 1960s and the approach is still used sometimes as a vehicle for personal change and development. Sensitivity training characteristically places a dozen or so people who do not regularly work together into a relatively unstructured group with facilitators who set a climate for interaction but do not lead in the usual sense.

This approach seeks to produce personal and interpersonal data by focusing on the "here-and-now" behavior of participants in the group. Sensitivity training has been controversial from its inception, with critics charging that it often results in psychological damage to some participants who may become objects of severe group pressure and amateurish "therapy." In government particularly, sensitivity training has often been criticized for improper invasion of the personal privacy of employees.

Generally, in contrast to sensitivity training, OD interventions as practiced in the 1970s are relatively structured. Besides the structured interventions noted above, a typical example is force field analysis. This is a simple approach for analyzing a problem which an organization wants to resolve. It presupposes equilibrium at any given time as a result of a balance between forces which restrain change and others which drive or bring about change. To analyze situations where change is desired, the staff members involved are asked to list both the restraining and driving forces. Then they may systematically figure out how to minimize or eliminate the restraining forces and how to maximize the forces of change or even bring new forces to bear on the situation.

As the group processes associated with action training and organization development have developed since the mid-1950s, they have been linked with management approaches such as management by objectives, as illustrated earlier in the example of the city of Barrington, Illinois. With these developments, less attention to traditional practices of individual performance appraisal may be required, with greater energy being devoted to group and organizational setting of objectives, tracking of work methods and progress, and evaluation of results.

Conclusions

Ultimately, evaluation of performance in government must focus on achieved results compared to initial objectives. Too often, however, appraisals have concentrated on the activities of organizations and their employees, determining whether individuals work hard or conform to rules while ignoring whether they produce desired results. But with the growing concern in the 1970s about how to increase government productivity, evaluation has taken on new importance, and with it such achievement-oriented approaches as management by objectives and organization development have taken on greater significance. Consequently, in order to have a constructive impact, personnel administration processes need to be re-oriented to function as integral aspects of general management. At the time of publication, however, most governments had made only slight progress in that direction.

Two actions which go to the heart of the subject of this chapter may serve to help personnel administration move with the mainstream of general management development. First, personnel administrators need to become familiar with general efforts toward government productivity and performance concerns. Second, personnel administrators must realize that employees need to use their work and their work organizations to help them meet their individual needs and goals.

In short, personnel administrators need to evaluate their own performance in terms of their two fundamental objectives: (1) helping their organization accomplish its purposes through full utilization of people, and (2) helping employees achieve their objectives through their organization. The processes for accomplishing these objectives remain secondary so long as they conform to the democratic values of human dignity and rule of law.

[1] Douglas McGregor, THE HUMAN SIDE OF ENTERPRISE (New York: McGraw-Hill Book Company, Inc., 1960), p. 33–44.

[2] Thorstein Veblen, THE THEORY OF THE LEISURE CLASS (New York: Macmillan Inc., 1899), and THE INSTITUTION OF WORKMANSHIP AND THE STATE OF THE INDUSTRIAL ARTS (Macmillan, 1919).

[3] Fritz J. Roethlisberger and William J. Dickson, MANAGEMENT AND THE WORKER (Cambridge, Mass.: Harvard University Press, 1939).

[4] Elton Mayo, THE SOCIAL PROBLEMS OF AN INDUSTRIAL CIVILIZATION (Boston: Harvard University Graduate School of Business Administration, 1946).

[5] Douglas McGregor, "An Uneasy Look at Performance Appraisal," HARVARD BUSINESS REVIEW 35 (May/June 1957): 89–94.

[6] McGregor, THE HUMAN SIDE OF ENTERPRISE, pp. 47–48.

[7] Abraham H. Maslow, TOWARD A PSYCHOLOGY OF BEING (New York: Van Nostrand Reinhold Company, 1962), and THE FARTHER REACHES OF HUMAN NATURE (New York: The Viking Press, Inc., 1971).

[8] Harry Levinson, "On the Motivation of Individuals," in CONTEMPORY MANAGEMENT: ISSUES AND VIEWPOINTS, ed. Joseph W. McGuire (Englewood Cliffs, N. J.: Prentice-Hall, Inc., 1974), pp. 570–574.

[9] Kurt Lewin, FIELD THEORY IN SOCIAL SCIENCE: SELECTED THEORETICAL PAPERS (New York: Harper & Row Publishers, 1951).

[10] Carl B. Rogers, CLIENT-CENTERED THERAPY (Boston: Houghton Mifflin Company, 1951) and ON BECOMING A PERSON (Houghton Mifflin, 1961).

[11] WORK IN AMERICA (Cambridge, Mass.: The MIT Press, 1973). The report's conclusions are summarized here, but they appear in the same order as in the report. See also Richard E. Walton, "Quality of Working Life: What Is It?" SLOAN MANAGEMENT REVIEW 15 (Fall 1973): 11–21.

[12] Frederick Herzberg, WORK AND THE NATURE OF MAN (New York: World Publishing Company, 1966), and Frederick Herzberg, Bernard Mansner, and Barbara Bloch Snyderman, THE MOTIVATION TO WORK (New York: John Wiley & Sons, Inc., 1966).

[13] M. Scott Myers, "Who Are Your Motivated Workers?" HARVARD BUSINESS REVIEW 42 (January/February 1964): 73–88.

[14] The most influential book on TA was by Thomas A. Harris titled I'M OK–YOU'RE OK (New York: Harper & Row Pubishers, 1967). See also Muriel James and Dorothy Jongeward, BORN TO WIN: TRANSACTIONAL ANALYSIS WITH GESTALT EXPERIMENTS (Reading, Mass.: Addison–Wesley Publishing Company, Inc., 1971).

[15] Dean H. Maiben and Charles J. Schwabe, "Management by Objectives," in FIRST TANGO IN BOSTON: A SEMINAR ON ORGANIZATIONAL CHANGE AND DEVELOPMENT (Washington, D.C.: National Training and Development Service, 1973), pp. 83–129.

[16] Chester A. Newland, "MBO Concepts in the Federal Government," THE BUREAUCRAT 2 (Winter 1974): 354–361.

[17] Peter F. Drucker, THE PRACTICE OF MANAGEMENT (New York: Harper & Row Publishers, 1954).

[18] Ibid., p. 94.

[19] Harry Levinson, "Management by Whose Objectives?" HARVARD BUSINESS REVIEW 48 (July/August 1970): 125–134.

[20] Ibid., p. 128.

[21] Robert R. Blake and Jane S. Mouton, MANAGERIAL GRID (Houston: Gulf Publishing Company, 1964).

[22] Paul R. Lawrence and Jay W. Lorsch, ORGANIZATION AND ENVIRONMENT: MANAGING DIFFERENTIATION AND INTEGRATION (Boston: Division of Research, Harvard University Graduate School of Business Administration, 1967); Lorsch and Lawrence, eds., STUDIES IN ORGANIZATION DESIGN (Homewood, Ill.: Richard D. Irwin, Inc., 1970); and Lorsch and Lawrence, eds., DEVELOPING ORGANIZATIONS (Reading, Mass.: Addison–Wesley Publishing Company, Inc., 1969).

[23] U.S., Office of Management and Budget, Civil Service Commission, General Accounting Office, and Bureau of Labor Statistics, PHASE III SUMMARY REPORT: MEASURING AND ENHANCING PRODUCTIVITY IN THE FEDERAL GOVERNMENT (Washington, D.C.: Government Accounting Office, June 1973). For a study of that project and related efforts, see Chester A. Newland, "Symposium on Productivity in Government," PUBLIC ADMINISTRATION REVIEW 32 (November/December 1972).

[24] National Commission on Productivity and Work Quality, EMPLOYEE INCENTIVES TO IMPROVE STATE AND LOCAL GOVERNMENT PRODUCTIVITY (Washington, D.C.: Government Printing Office, 1972), pp. 3–4.

[25] Chester A. Newland, "Productivity and Federal Labor–Management Relations," THE BUREAUCRAT 2, special issue (February 1973): 54–61.

[26] Raymond D. Horton, "Productivity Bargaining in the Public Sector: Caveat Emptor," in MBO AND PRODUCTIVITY BARGAINING IN THE PUBLIC SECTOR, ed. Chester A. Newland (Chicago: International Personnel Management Association, 1974), pp. 37–47.

[27] An informative publication on these processes is by the U.S. Bureau of Labor Statistics titled IMPROVING PRODUCTIVITY: LABOR AND MANAGEMENT APPROACHES (Washington, D.C.: National Commission on Productivity, 1971).

[28] U.S., Bureau of the Budget, MEASURING PRODUCTIVITY (Washington, D.C.: Government Printing Office, 1964).

[29] A comprehensive report resulting from this program was issued by the Joint Financial Management Improvement Program titled REPORT ON FEDERAL PRODUCTIVITY, vol. 1: PRODUCTIVITY TRENDS, FY 1967–1973, and vol. 2: PRODUCTIVITY CASE STUDIES (Washington, D.C.: Joint Financial Management Improvement Program, 1974). The initial Phase III report of this project was cited above in footnote 23.

[30] U.S., Department of Health, Education, and Welfare, TOWARD A SOCIAL REPORT (Washington D.C.: Government Printing Office, 1969).

[31] U.S., Office of Management and Budget, SOCIAL INDICATORS, 1973 (Washington, D.C.: Government Printing Office, 1973).

[32] The International City Management Association devoted the entire February 1974 issue of its journal, PUBLIC MANAGEMENT, to this topic.

[33] David A. Burkholter and Jerry B. Coffman, "Charlotte: Management by Objectives," PUBLIC MANAGEMENT 56 (June 1974): 15–16. The entire issue, focusing on productivity improvement, cites several other examples, including Barrington, Illinois; Dubuque, Iowa; St. Petersburg, Florida; Nashville–Davidson County, Tennessee; and San Diego, California. The Riverside, California, case is reported in another issue: Daniel E. Stone, "Productivity and Performance: Providing the Same Services for No Increased Costs," PUBLIC MANAGEMENT 57 (March 1975): 15–17.

[34] An informative discussion of an MBO-oriented approach to performance appraisal in government is by Robert G. Pajer titled "A Systems Evaluation," PERSONNEL ADMINISTRATION AND PUBLIC PERSONNEL REVIEW 1 (November/December 1972): 42–47.

[35] For an overview of the history and practices of organization development that is focused particularly on public administration, see Larry Kirkhart and Neely D. Gardner, "Symposium on Organization Development," PUBLIC ADMINISTRATION REVIEW 34 (March/April 1974): 97–140. Another publication discussing the applications of action training and organization development in local government is by the National Training and Development Service titled FIRST TANGO IN BOSTON: A SEMINAR ON ORGANIZATIONAL CHANGE AND DEVELOPMENT. Other sources on organization development are much too numerous to cite here, and practices under that label are likewise too varied and widespread to chronicle in a general textbook. Only basic applications in governments can be noted here.

[36] F. Gerald Brown, "Organization Development in Kansas City," in FIRST TANGO IN BOSTON, pp. 287–348.

13

Managing the
Public Personnel Agency

Now here, you see, it takes all the running you can do, to keep in the same place. If you want to get somewhere else, you must run at least twice as fast as that.

Lewis Carroll

Managing a public personnel agency in the 1970s requires the ability to manage change. From the relatively calm waters of the first half of the twentieth century through the increasingly swift currents of the period 1950–1960, the 1970s have seen change burst forth with the force of a Niagara. To try to manage a public personnel agency in the 1970s according to the practices of earlier decades will likely result in management going over the falls in a barrel.

An Overview:
Changes of the 1970s

New roles and new functions have been added to the office of the manager of the public personnel agency, while many traditional functions have been broadened. Actually, this has happened only in those agencies where the capacity to manage change has been demonstrated. In some agencies the role of the personnel manager has been diminished and personnel functions have been assigned elsewhere because the capacity to manage change was lacking. For example, such responsibilities as employer-employee relations, affirmative action, safety, training, and manpower administration have been added or expanded in almost all major cities and in many smaller cities. Have these functions been assigned to the personnel agency, or have they been assigned elsewhere? Does the personnel agency administer a coherent set of functions, or are some of the major personnel functions delegated among other departments?

New Roles

A key change in the role of the public personnel manager is that the manager *must* be part of management. The personnel director acting as a third-party neutral, with management considered as a detached unit, is no longer possible. The personnel manager who is appointed by and responsible to an independent civil service commission must participate in the management of the jurisdiction.

In those jurisdictions where the chief personnel officer is appointed by a personnel board, working with the chief executive as a participating member of management while also serving as a member of an independent civil service board may introduce problems, but they cannot be avoided. Stated simply, it is not possible to manage a personnel department effectively and responsibly and not be part of management.

The position of director of personnel has been established with increasing frequency in jurisdictions throughout the United States during the 1970s. During the 1950s and 1960s a fulltime personnel director usually was not appointed unless a city had 500 or more employees on the payroll. By contrast, many cities now are establishing the position and introducing the concept of a central personnel unit even when there are as few as 100 employees working for the city. Why this change? Because a growing number of cities, towns, and villages find it essential to employ a personnel manager in order to meet the challenges of manpower management which confronts cities of all sizes.

NEW FUNCTIONS

At the same time the 1970s have witnessed both the rapid expansion of existing personnel staffs and the addition of many new kinds of positions to deal with new or modified functions. Such functions have been added at irregular intervals, often because of statutory changes or other forces such as court decisions, federal programs and regulations, and changes in the economy which are beyond the control of local governments. The addition of new functions and the challenge of solving new kinds of problems along with the traditional responsibilities of city personnel departments necessitates continuous organizational change within city personnel departments in order to make the most effective use of available resources.

The advent of formalized employer-employee relations requires the addition of the employee relations function to the management staff. As experience with this function develops and as this function expands, staff is added to perform the duties attendant to the employee relations function.

The inclusion of state and local governments by passage of the 1972 amendments to the Civil Rights Act of 1964 has brought about great changes in recruitment, selection, and placement procedures. The Supreme Court decision in *Griggs* v. *Duke Power* established the legal requirement that all selection activities must be job-related and all selection tests must be validated. The application of the guidelines of the Equal Employment Op-portunity Commission (EEOC) to state and local government in 1972, together with the Griggs decision and an increasing number of other decisions in federal and state courts in the area of selection activities, has had and will continue to have a displacing effect on selection procedures and activities in organizations throughout the United States.

Virtually none of the traditional procedures used by municipal personnel agencies prior to the 1970s meet the standards set forth by the Supreme Court in the Griggs case, by EEOC guidelines (which have the full force of law), or by the decisions of the courts and federal and state agencies. The problems of developing ethical and fair selection procedures in public personnel agencies which meet all legal requirements as well as the commitments of affirmative action for the hiring and promotion of women and members of minority groups have necessitated many changes. Highly trained staff and increased resources are needed to perform recruitment, selection, and placement activities.

NEW PROGRAMS

The federal government has initiated an increasing number of programs that greatly affect local personnel agencies. An almost unending list of programs has issued from Washington since the beginning of the "War on Poverty": Neighborhood Youth Corps, Model Cities, Job Corps, Head Start, and other programs in the mid-1960s, up to the Emergency Employment Act and its successor, the Comprehensive Employment and Training Act (CETA), in the mid-1970s.

Almost all of these federal programs have been devised with little or no input from local agencies and have been laid on the cities and municipalities with little or no lead time to prepare for the newest manpower program. The impact of such federal programs varies from one community to another, but in many cases the amount of staff time required for the new and unexpected programs has been considerable. Existing programs of local personnel agencies often have been disrupted. New staff may need to be hired and trained immediately to implement the new programs. The effect of such programs is especially noticeable in those cities where the personnel agency's staff is small.

At the same time that new federal programs have been created, an increasing number of federal agencies have been given or have assumed varying degrees of regulatory jurisdiction over many municipal personnel functions. In the 1970s there has been a dramatic increase in the total amount of federal funds and in the percentage of federal funds that comprise a city or county's revenue sources. In a number of metropolitan areas, federal revenues account for as much as 25 percent of municipal operating budgets.

As the ability to raise revenues from local sources has diminished, the only major source of additional money available to the cities and counties has become federal revenues. In almost all cases of federal funding, however, strings are attached. Every agency that allocates funds has rules, regulations, guidelines, and statutes to be enforced in the proper expenditure of the money. Many of the federal regulations relate to personnel activities—especially, though not only, selection activities. It is not uncommon for the personnel department of a large jurisdiction to deal concurrently with ten or more federal agencies over the personnel regulations accompanying federal program funding. What is particularly challenging for the personnel manager is that many of the federal regulations conflict: To obey one often is to violate another.

The role of the local government personnel manager as an active participant in intergovernmental relations has emerged in the 1970s in ways which were only dimly perceived in the 1960s and which were undreamed of in the 1950s. The personnel manager and the personnel staff have a great deal of contact with other agencies of government at all levels, not only the federal and state levels but also the new forms of government such as the regional agencies.

The Personnel Manager and the Organization

It is essential that the personnel manager have a holistic view of the city or county's management problems. Personnel management is part and parcel of local government public management. The personnel manager must understand the goals, objectives, and problems of the jurisdiction if he or she is to participate in devising feasible solutions to these problems. It must be understood that personnel administration is a support function to the entire municipal organization. This does not mean it is a "house-keeping" service. It does mean providing the jurisdiction with the needed human resources so that it may be effective.

The management of a local government's manpower and personnel operations necessarily involves managing many areas where conflict and change inevitably occur. Conflicting ideas within a community, together with superimposed and conflicting policies from state and federal agencies, present a formidable challenge to public administrators in meeting that community's needs with a minimum of friction and disruption.

For example, the theory of government as "the employer of last resort" which prevails in many public service employee programs—the objective being the employment of long-term unemployed persons—is contrary to all previous experience of many personnel agencies which traditionally have been concerned with the selection of only those employees who were best qualified according to the merit principle.

Managing a personnel system in the mid-1970s requires the personnel manager to keep up to date with changing theory and practice in organizational systems and with the discoveries of the behavioral sciences. The personnel manager must learn how to translate research and theory into results and action in the real world of day-to-day operations.

The role of the personnel manager involves making decisions and exercising authority (especially in employee relations activities) which may conflict with the policies and practices of individual department heads and line supervisors. It is almost inevitable that, in negotiating a settlement of a contract or agreement, compromises will be made that will be at variance with prior practice or preferences of other local government administrators.

The decision-making authority of the personnel manager when representing the city or county at the bargaining table with recognized employee organizations or with federal or state enforcement agencies presents a new kind of management responsibility. The controller role of the personnel officer still exists with regard to personnel rules and practices, but increasingly the personnel manager is involved in determining the changing rules and practices which are to be enforced.

The role of the personnel manager in employee training and development likewise is growing. The former practice of relying on the private sector to train potential employees is giving way to the practice of creating training programs to meet both short-term and long-term operational needs. Human resources and manpower management require the full exercise of employee training and development programs if the municipal organization is to achieve its goals.

Public personnel administration has sometimes been characterized as "a triumph of technique over purpose." While it is not easy to state what the roles of the public personnel manager should be in the mid-1970s, the statement summarizes very well what the role should not be. The personnel manager's role must be directed toward solving, not compounding, the problems of the municipal organization.

Because it is essential that the personnel manager be part of the municipal organization's management, it is necessary to examine the problems of personnel management which occur because of the personnel manager's placement within the organization's structure. By whom is the personnel manager appointed? To whom does the personnel manager report? For what personnel functions is the personnel manager responsible and accountable? Is the authority of the personnel manager sufficient to carry out the responsibilities assigned? Is there sufficient staff and budget resources to perform the personnel functions assigned?

Who Appoints the Personnel Manager?

In local governments in the United States, the personnel manager may be appointed by several different kinds of appointing authorities: the city or county manager; the chief adminis-

trative officer; the mayor (in strong-mayor cities); the elected council; or an independent civil service commission. Or the personnel manager may be appointed by a combination of the foregoing. For example, he or she may be appointed by the manager or mayor, subject to the approval of the council; or he or she may be appointed by the chief executive, subject to approval of the civil service board. (Since some civil service boards have members either directly or indirectly appointed by employee unions and associations, some personnel officers are appointed, to some degree, with the consent of employee organizations.)

The great majority of appointments are for indefinite terms. However, there are instances of personnel officers appointed for specific terms, with the appointment either related to the term of the elected official making the appointment or specified for a designated number of years.

The identity of the appointing authority affects substantially the kinds of functions, authority, responsibilities, budget, and staff which will be assigned to the personnel manager. The status of the personnel manager within the jurisdiction's organizational structure is much affected by who makes the appointment and to whom the personnel manager will report. This is true for the personnel manager far more than for almost all other department heads. For example, a fire chief's responsibilities and accountability are not much affected by whether he or she is appointed by a manager, mayor, elected council, or fire commission. The responsibilities of the personnel manager concern the entire organization of the jurisdiction; most department heads have responsibility for specific, limited areas of the city's or county's programs.

The effectiveness of the personnel manager in managing the personnel unit and its functions will be greatest when the personnel manager is appointed by and responsible to the chief executive; by the city or county manager, where the council-manager plan exists; and, where the mayor is the chief executive in a strong-mayor city, by the mayor. When the personnel manager is appointed by the chief executive and is accountable to the chief executive, the personnel manager will have the greatest opportunity to plan, oversee, and administer effectively personnel operations on behalf of and as a working part of the organization.

Such is not the case in those instances when the personnel manager is appointed by and responsible to an independent civil service commission. This body does not carry out the executive policy of the government organization. There is an almost automatic exclusion from full participation in city- or county-wide management decisions and activities of a personnel officer who is appointed by and responsible to an independent civil service board. The functions over which such boards have authority may include some but will never include all of the personnel functions which must be administered in a municipal organization in the 1970s. In short, a personnel officer appointed by and responsible to an independent board is severely handicapped in the ability to administer and manage the full range of public personnel activities.

An independent, administrative civil service board in a jurisdiction generally will have responsibility and authority over selection activities, including recruitment, examination, and certification, and generally will have appellate responsibilities, including specified authority to review disciplinary actions taken against civil service employees when an appeal is made to the board. Less frequently a civil service board will have classification responsibilities, with the authority to determine or to recommend to the legislative body proposed changes in classification.

Independent rule-making authority is granted still less often. Most personnel rules are recommended by the independent civil service board, subject to approval by the legislative body. Occasionally, salary-setting or salary-recommending functions are assigned to the board. Almost all other functions in the personnel area— safety, training, salary administration, employee relations, affirmative action, and manpower administration—are performed by other authorities.

In local governments which have independent civil service boards which appoint the personnel officer, it is increasingly common for them to have two or more personnel managers, with each responsible for specific personnel functions. Generally this arrangement greatly complicates the conduct of effective, unified personnel activities. The fracturing and diffusion of personnel responsibilities can result in the following situations: a personnel officer having responsibility for both selection and appeals from discipline; an employee relations officer having responsibility for bargaining negotiations and for grievances; the personnel officer acting as a specialized affirmative action officer; or the personnel officer acting as administrator for employee benefits, including the retirement program.

Managing the personnel unit no longer means administering a few noncontroversial functions within an unchanging staff division. There may be several personnel units within a given municipal organization responsible for differing and overlapping functions and accountable to different appointing authorities, and they may not necessarily work in harmony with one another. This division of the personnel function exists in many federal and state government organizations, but it has not yet developed so pointedly in the smaller, usually more coherent local governments.

To Whom Does
the Personnel Manager Report?

In most cases the personnel manager reports to his or her appointing authority. However, this is not necessarily so in all cases, particularly when more than one appointing authority is involved. Most city personnel managers report to city managers; some report to mayors who serve as chief executives; and some report to independent civil service boards. Other personnel managers have split reporting responsibilities: For some functions they may report to a civil service board; for other functions, to a city manager or mayor.

Some personnel positions, once created, do not appear accountable to anyone and seem to drift about on the jurisdiction's organization chart. This phenomenon is noticeable especially among some of the new, specialized staff positions which may have independent responsibility for certain activities of personnel management, such as affirmative action, manpower project administration, or employee relations.

FOR WHAT PERSONNEL FUNCTIONS IS THE PERSONNEL MANAGER RESPONSIBLE AND ACCOUNTABLE?

In meeting the problems of personnel administration in the 1970s, it is essential that all personnel functions be placed within the same administrative unit and under the charge of one personnel manager. If this has not been done, then one of the major tasks of the personnel manager is to assemble these functions under one administrative roof so that the personnel system might operate most effectively. A personnel officer who supervises only personnel records, selection, and classification is attending to only one part of the total personnel effort. A personnel manager should manage all personnel functions within the organization, and this is facilitated if all functions are in one unit.

There can be substantial barriers to establishing unified personnel departments that administer all or almost all personnel functions for a local government organization. Many such barriers are imposed by state statutes. Some states have passed laws requiring each city to have separate police and fire civil service commissions. In other states, cities are required to use a state administered and controlled civil service system for certain personnel functions.

In some other states, employee relations laws mandated for cities and other local governments require some separation of functions from traditional personnel departments. Such state laws may make impossible the assembling of personnel functions within a single personnel department. Nevertheless, the fullest possible range of personnel activities should be grouped together within one administrative personnel unit. The director of such a department should be delegated authority commensurate with the responsibilities assigned the department.

The traditional view of the personnel officer seen principally as adviser, as well as rule-enforcer, interpreter, and observer, no longer serves. The personnel manager of the 1970s must be active in the management of the personnel activities of the entire organization. A number of cities have recognized the dimensions of this kind of position by creating not simply the title of director of personnel but the title of assistant city manager–personnel, which implies the overall, city-wide dimensions of personnel responsibilities and which also mandates authority sufficient to carry out the expanded work to be done.

Staff and Budget Resources

Although there is no universal formula, a generally reliable staffing ratio for full-service personnel agencies (i.e., those providing all or almost all personnel functions) in the 1970s is retaining about 1 full-time personnel staff member per 100 full-time employees. Therefore, a city with 100 employees will require 1 personnel position; a city with 1,000 employees will require 10. The balance between professional and clerical positions ideally should be about even. Staffing needs of professional positions and clerical positions in most full-service personnel agencies seem equally great.

Most jurisdictions employ fewer than 1,000 employees; most personnel agencies in the United States have fewer than 10 personnel staff members. It is only when a jurisdiction has reached a population over 100,000, and depending upon services provided, that there will be more than 1,000 employees in the organization's work force. It usually is only in these larger organizations that the total number of personnel staff, both professional and clerical, will exceed 10 employees.

The problems of organizing for the personnel function, therefore, differ significantly for the larger cities and counties compared to the medium-sized and smaller ones. Personnel departments of larger jurisdictions have the option of organizing either along generalist lines or by specialized personnel functions. Those which are medium-sized or small usually have no choice: With only one, or at best, a few professional staff members, they almost always must organize along generalist lines.

ORGANIZATION OF STAFF

This book is directed primarily to the personnel administration problems of the medium-sized and smaller local governments. In the larger communities, with employee populations of 1,000 or more, numerous options exist with regard to the organization and utilization of personnel agency staff resources which are not available to personnel departments in the smaller ones. A large city or county's personnel agency may have organizational divisions specializing in position classification, recruitment and selection, benefit administration, labor relations, test validation, and other functions. Figure 13–1 illustrates one of the forms which this divisional organization may take.

In the large jurisdiction there can be a central personnel agency with separate departmental personnel officers. In cases such as this, it is not uncommon to find departmental personnel officers assigned to perform certain departmental personnel functions, such as processing personnel transactions; hiring for special jobs, especially seasonal jobs; handling departmental disciplinary problems; performing departmental training and safety activities, and the like. In any jurisdiction with a department of more than 200 employees, it is very likely that a full-time departmental personnel officer will be needed. In larger cities, departmental personnel officers often are found in departments such as police, fire, public works, recreation and parks, and utilities. In larger

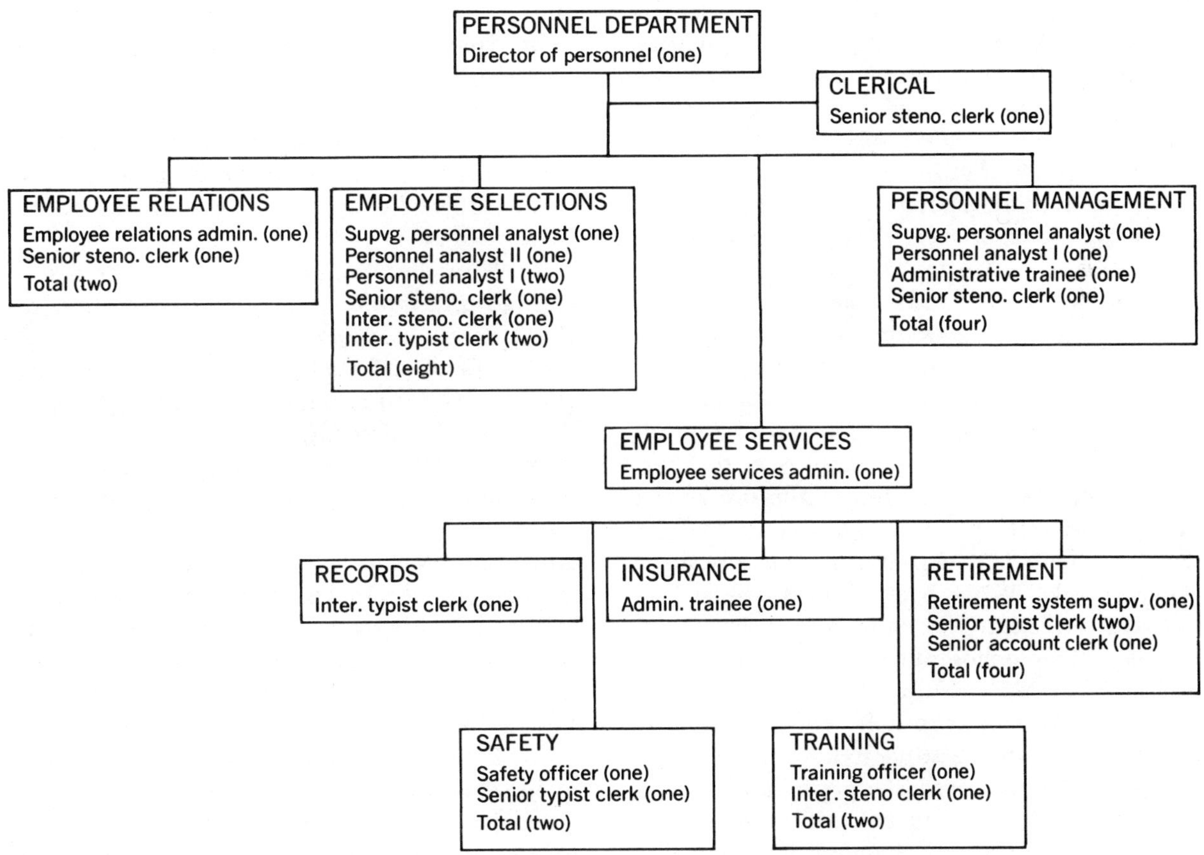

FIGURE 13–1. *Illustrative organization chart for a municipal personnel department. Organization and number of employees in early 1976 in the city of Sacramento, California.*

counties, departmental personnel officers are often found in departments such as sheriff, welfare, health, and public works.

In the medium-sized and smaller jurisdictions, the full-time departmental personnel officer still is uncommon—that is, even in the case of a department with 200 or more employees in a jurisdiction with fewer than 1,000 employees overall, there is not the same need for a full-time personnel specialist within the department that there likely exists in a much larger organization. In the smaller jurisdiction there usually is someone in the larger departments designated with certain personnel responsibilities. This may be the department head or it may be a principal assistant who will be the contact person with the personnel department and who will carry out certain personnel activities at the departmental level. These activities may require a relatively small or a substantial amount of time, but usually they do not demand all the time of the departmental person assigned these activities within a department of a medium-sized or smaller jurisdiction.

In the medium-sized and smaller jurisdictions, the more elaborate personnel service structure that characterizes larger organizations is not needed. Communications are simpler. When everyone knows one another in a smaller agency and where there are relatively fewer work sites and organizational units, there is not the same need for structure that a large agency requires, where it is not possible for all the management staff and employees to know one another simply because of the size of the organization, the many work locations, and the greater number of departments and divisions.

Before the 1970s, being a medium-sized or small jurisdiction was of no particular consequence, because most of the personnel problems were generated within the local organization and therefore could be handled satisfactorily within the existing staff structure. During the 1970s, however, the problem of staffing the personnel agency in the medium-sized and smaller organization changed greatly. The problem stemmed chiefly from the fact that the federal and state laws and the administrative regulations written to cover large employers came to apply with equal force to the medium-sized and small jurisdictions as employers.

A popular foreign small-car manufacturer uses the advertising slogan, "Think small!" A very real problem for the medium-sized and smaller organizations is that most federal and state regulations relating to public personnel activities are written for the large public employer. It is difficult for a medium-sized or smaller jurisdiction's personnel department, for example, to set up a specialized test validation unit when it does not have even one employee specializing in employee selection. (Even if it did have an employee selection specialist, it would not have the necessary numbers of employees or applicants available to perform criterion-related validation studies.)

FEDERAL AND STATE REGULATIONS

The federal and state government agencies which issue personnel regulations affecting the smaller jurisdictions are staffed and served by large, complex personnel operations. There is sufficient staff in personnel offices in the federal and state regulatory agencies to serve their needs. It is generally assumed by these agencies that there is sufficient staff in the local governments subject to the regulations to be able to read, interpret, and carry them out.

The smaller the personnel staff, however, the more devastating the cumulative effect of the federal and state regulations. More and more federal and state laws are being enacted, regulations issued, and court decrees handed down that pertain to personnel activities. Employee relations, until the 1970s a matter for local determination, are now affected by a virtual explosion of new laws, regulations, and practices. Most of these have been issued at the state level. And there may be federal legislation bearing on this personnel area in the years ahead. Employee selection procedures are subject to the regulations of the federal Equal Employment Opportunity Commission, the U.S. Civil Service Commission, the Department of Labor, the Department of Justice, the Commission on Civil Rights, and several other federal bodies and agencies. Safety is regulated by the Occupational Safety and Health Act (OSHA).

The U.S. Supreme Court and the other federal and state courts increasingly are active in the interpretation of Constitutional issues and of numerous statutes and regulations as they apply to personnel problems facing the medium-sized and smaller jurisdictions. Such decisions may affect only one jurisdiction, or all jurisdictions in a given state, or all jurisdictions in the United States. Many court decisions are inconsistent with one another, making difficult the determination of what is legally permissible or enforceable. An increasing number of federal and state court judges are assuming supervision over certain personnel cases that have been litigated, especially in affirmative action matters relating to the employment of women and members of minority groups under the Civil Rights Act of 1964, as amended in 1972.

An increasing proportion of the medium-sized and smaller jurisdiction's personnel department staff time is directed to coping with the thousands of pages of regulations, decisions, and laws which proliferate with such astonishing rapidity. An organization cannot afford to ignore these documents; the consequences of being unaware of or ignoring them can be costly, even catastrophic.

PROBLEMS OF THE 1970s

All jurisdictions, regardless of size, face severe problems in the 1970s. The continuing problems of costs rising faster than municipal revenues is forcing hard decisions on many city councils about which levels of service to reduce or to eliminate. These problems in turn create other problems, such as layoffs of public employees. On this point the seniority system in both the public and private sectors has come under hard questioning. When a reduction in force is necessary, who works and who is laid off? The worker with seniority who may have achieved that seniority in a discriminatory system, or the women and members of minority groups recruited more recently through affirmative action programs? In the mid-1970s management was experimenting with possible solutions such as shared work arrangements and proportional layoffs.

In a jurisdiction with 500 public employees, the personnel department typically will have two or three professional staff persons, plus two or three clerical staff. In jurisdictions with 200 or 300 public employees the personnel department may consist of only one professional staff member with one or two clerical employees. It is in these agencies especially that the capacity of the personnel professional to "think small" is so essential. This is particularly difficult to do when the personnel staff must comply with so many complex regulations. The smaller agencies retain a relatively small number of management personnel to perform all public activities. An increasingly larger share of staff time and energy is required to deal with personnel management problems created by federal and state laws and regulations and by court decisions.

There is no simple answer to the question of how a jurisdiction should staff its personnel department sufficiently in order to cope with this new dimension of public personnel administration. Not all jurisdictions and not all states are affected the same way. Some have felt relatively little impact to date. The small, isolated towns located in rural areas in states with no employee relations legislation on the books have been influenced only to a modest degree by outside regulations, compared to those cities with multiracial populations located in large metropolitan areas in states whose legislatures have shown little restraint in passing laws that greatly affect cities.

It is quite possible that all jurisdictions will be subject in the coming years to even greater regulation by the federal agencies, depending upon the decision of the Supreme Court as to the extent to which Congress can regulate the personnel activities of local governments. The 1974 amendments to the Fair Labor Standards Act brought all governments—federal, state, and local—under coverage of the act.

The coverage of state and local government employees is being challenged in the case of *National League of Cities et al.* v. *Dunlop*. The decision is expected by the winter of 1976. The Supreme Court's decision will determine the extent to which the federal government in the future may regulate local personnel activities, ranging from no regulation at all to partial regulation to complete regulation. The Court's decision in this case also will have an important bearing on the number and kind of personnel staff that jurisdictions will need to carry out their duties and responsibilities while being regulated to a greater or lesser degree.

Some observers have suggested that the application to state and local government of federal laws and regulations now in effect in the private sector will not create significant problems or require additional staff. It must be pointed out, however, that there are substantial differences between the private and the public sectors. Regulations in the private sector have evolved over decades, as have the state and local laws and ordinances which are in effect in the public sector. When federal regulations are suddenly laid on top of the existing state and local laws and regulations, management in the public sector very likely will be confronted with legal uncertainties and administrative confusion.

When federal regulations are promulgated, they of course supersede state and local regulations even if they are in direct conflict. If the federal regulations do not present a conflict, they simply are an overlay to existing state and local legislation. The manager of a public personnel agency in the 1970s must be able to contend with the problems, ambiguities, and the occasional paradoxes caused by these situations.

A case in point: The federal Wage and Hour Amendments of 1974 (amending the Fair Labor Standards Act) together with federal regulation 29 CFR 553, require that employees engaged in fire protection, when the partial overtime exemption under Section 7 (k) of the act is used, must have a work period of not less than 7 days and not more than 28 days. But in Texas a state law requires that larger cities determine the average fire duty week over a period of one year. The federal statute and the state statute are not in direct conflict; therefore, both remain on the books. But a Texas city covered by the state statute cannot compute fire hours within 7 to 28 days, as required by federal law, without violating the state law, and vice versa.

EMPLOYER-EMPLOYEE RELATIONS

The number of bargaining units or "appropriate units" in a jurisdiction also has a direct relationship on the size of the personnel staff responsible for the employer-employee relations function. A possible rule of thumb to follow is that jurisdictions operating under formal or relatively formal employer-employee relations laws (whether they be federal, state, or local laws) will require at least one full-time professional staff member for each five or six bargaining units, especially when the bargaining units are represented by different recognized employee organizations.

Staffing for employee relations still is a relatively new responsibility in most jurisdictions in the United States. Employee relations is a very dynamic concern. The problems of collective bargaining or collective negotiations and the day-to-day administration of the provisions of the resulting agreements and contracts, as well as the problems of handling grievances, preparing for new bargaining, and resolving impasses such as strikes, job actions, and interest arbitration all present new and difficult challenges for many jurisdictions.

Again, there are no easy solutions to the special personnel staffing problem of employee relations for the medium-sized and smaller jurisdictions. Many such jurisdictions, unable to afford full-time specialists to handle employee relations activities, enter into contract arrangements with individuals or firms to carry out negotiations on behalf of the council representatives of recognized employee organizations.

Local jurisdictions increasingly are working together to deal with employee relations. Many exchange information on employee relations. Others have experimented with area-wide bargaining. For example, in California the cities of Livermore and Pleasanton and the Valley Community Services District have conducted joint negotiations with the International Association of Fire Fighters.

The staffing problems involved in conducting employee selection also are difficult. No organization with fewer than 1,000 employees can afford to employ a technical test validation unit which would include an industrial psychologist and other staff members. However, some jurisdictions are working together to provide test validation services which usually only jurisdictions with 50,000 or more employees could provide for themselves. For example, in 1974 twenty-four small California cities formed a consortium to make use of the Selection Consulting Center to validate police and fire entry-level selection procedures.

Resources are made available in some states to assist the medium-sized and smaller jurisdictions in handling many areas of public personnel service. In Oregon the Local Government Personnel Institute (jointly sponsored by the League of Oregon Cities and similar county and school board organizations) provides Oregon cities with technical personnel services, particularly in employer-employee relations. In Michigan the Municipal Personnel Service of the Michigan Municipal League and in California the Cooperative Personnel Service of the California State Personnel Board provide a wide variety of technical personnel services to their cities. Many private consultants offer a variety of services, especially in the area of position classification and pay plans, although few consultants provide testing services.

A partial solution to staffing problems for personnel activities in the medium-sized and smaller jurisdictions may lie in developing cooperative ventures with other local governments or in retaining consultants for specific services. Only rarely, however, are consultants able to address all the personnel staff needs of a jurisdiction in the 1970s.

The decade of the 1970s has seen the computer brought into use by most jurisdictions to serve at least a few purposes. For example, personnel payroll systems increasingly make use of some form of an automated or electronic data processing system. The personnel manager of the 1970s should know the fundamentals and the range of possible uses of data processing. Personnel records systems should be reviewed to see if they can or should be converted to an automated system.

The new and developing areas of affirmative action, employer-employee relations, and intergovernmental relations and regulations have greatly increased the need for the rapid production of various kinds of personnel information. Personnel payroll systems that are programmed for random access use can provide quick and important information for reference in negotiations, impasse proceedings, investigations by regulatory agencies, as well as for planning and operational activities within the local organization itself.

No attempt is made here to identify which personnel records need to be kept or what they should contain. These requirements vary greatly from jurisdiction to jurisdiction. However, the personnel manager should review the records systems to make certain that they serve the purposes of the organization while also facilitating compliance with the various regulatory organizations. For example, federal wage and hour regulations require that certain records be retained for three years and that others, such as departmental time sheets, be retained for two years.

There are many kinds of records which a personnel agency may keep, and the choice depends upon the personnel functions the agency performs. These may include but are not limited to the following: pay records, including overtime and other compensation paid; performance appraisal records; employee personnel files; employment lists and certification records; affirmative action records; competitive examination materials and records; industrial injury and workmen's compensation reports; personnel requisitions; classification records; records of sick leave, vacation leave, and other paid leave; retirement contributions; employee grievances; collective bargaining agreements; arbitration awards; regulatory agency and court decisions, and many others. It goes without saying that sound administration of personnel records is essential.

With the many areas of public personnel management being as dynamic as they are, the personnel department either must have on hand in its own library or must be able to secure through an outside library the technical and professional journals, reporting services, and reference publications that enable the department to keep up with change. It has been observed that the expansion of information is exponential. So much information continually emerges from the "knowledge explosion" that it is nearly impossible to keep fully informed. This being the case, it is more important than ever that the personnel manager and staff make judicious selection and use of the available resources. Professional personnel staff should refer to the continuing flow of information **not** only for the day-to-day administration of personnel activities but for personal and professional development as well.

Professional development should not be limited to reading journals. Active participation in training conferences and professional societies should be encouraged to develop a public personnel staff that is effective and knowledgeable in this fast-changing field.

The manager of a public personnel department should cultivate a wide variety of contacts and relationships. At minimum the personnel manager should know the managers of the other departments of the jurisdiction, especially the operating departments, and understand their goals and problems. The personnel manager should be acquainted with his or her counterparts in other governmental and private industrial organizations within the community. The personnel manager should know the representatives of employee organizations present in the jurisdiction and should be able to identify their problems and objectives. Finally, the personnel manager should be familiar with the various racial and ethnic groups within the community and should be acquainted with the organizations and representatives of these groups.

It should be clear that the problems of fair employment and affirmative action in any jurisdiction cannot be resolved by unilateral action or by the unexamined assumptions held by a personnel executive. To direct successfully the personnel agency, and thereby assist the local organization in achieving its goals, it is vital that the personnel director understand and be sensitive to the needs and aspirations of all the citizens within the community.

Similarly, it is important for the personnel manager to be aware of the goals and objectives of women and members of minority groups. Affirmative action plans for these "affected groups" were emerging as a key area of concern in the mid-1970s.

There are many publics within any jurisdiction. The personnel manager should be aware of them and develop a program which will provide each public with information about the jurisdiction's personnel work and which at the same time will be receptive to information from various groups within the community's publics that is needed by the personnel agency to serve best the needs of the entire community.

The Outlook

There were several major unknown quantities in the mid-1970s as this book went to press that could be expected to have substantial impact on the course of public personnel administration in the remaining years of the 1970s. The Supreme Court's pending decision on the constitutionality of the 1974 amendments to the Fair Labor Standards Act will signal whether there will be significant growth of federal regulation of public personnel activities. The Equal Employment Opportunity Coordinating Council, composed of the departments of Labor and Justice, the U.S. Civil Service Commission, the Equal Employment Opportunity Commission, and the Commission on Civil Rights was expected to issue sweeping regulations in the area of personnel selection. The most serious financial problems that local jurisdictions had experienced for many decades were creating their own great problems. The trend of public employees to organize into unions and employee associations continued. Affirmative action on behalf of women and members of minority groups became an increasingly urgent issue.

As of the mid-1970s the outlook for the future of public personnel administration was unclear because of these unknown and possibly volatile quantities. The best guide that could be recommended for handling the problems of a public personnel agency in the mid-1970s and in the future would be to cultivate the ability to recognize and manage change as it occurs. In this way the public personnel agency can provide in the most effective manner the human resources the local organization required to achieve its goals.

14

The Outlook

In the long run every Government is the exact symbol of its people, with their wisdom and unwisdom.

THOMAS CARLYLE

THE MAJOR ISSUES and approaches to personnel administration in local governments have been described and analyzed in this volume. The discussions have been directed toward the utilization of human resources in local governments that are administered by a strong central administrator who is answerable to an elected council, although it is also recognized that some governments continue to operate either under a semi-independent personnel commission or without full responsibility for personnel management vested in their chief administrative officer. Furthermore, the analyses have been based on the premise that employment and promotion of employees in accordance with demonstrated merit best serves the public interest.

The authors have proceeded from the real-world conditions of the 1970s, and most of them have speculated on the future state of things as well. The outlook for the future is rooted in the facts of the present. The conceptual tools and procedures discussed here could be expected to apply to situations that administrators face in the immediate future. Nevertheless, there is continuing pressure and necessity to reexamine current procedures.

The analysis given in the "Outlook" section of an earlier volume in the ICMA Municipal Management Series, *Management Policies in Local Government Finance*,[1] held that municipalities in the future would have to learn to function in an economy that would no longer experience the strong, steady growth which had occurred in the post-World War II period. The implication was clear and still pertains in the mid-1970s: The outlook for personnel administration is problematic and is not susceptible of easy solutions.

In the first place, local government work forces cannot be expected to expand at the rates they did between 1947 and 1970. Those involved with personnel administration will have to deal with the problems attendant to a "steady state" of financial resources. At the same time, pressures to increase or add services will mount because alternative resources in society are also restricted.

One alternative to this state of affairs is to somehow provide improved service to the public without adding to the jurisdiction's work force. It may even mean operating with fewer employees in some programs. This choice, in turn, suggests a need for job analysis and task enrichment, accompanied by appropriate organizational changes. The conclusions of theory and of experience cited by several contributors to this volume point toward a need for thoughtful planning and handling of employer-employee relationships if these changes are to be accomplished without undue disruption or dysfunction.

The upgrading of positions and classifications will call for careful recruitment and selection of highly qualified candidates as well as the further development of current employees. Both efforts will require reexamination of classification standards. Consequently, policies relating to compensation and other conditions of employment most likely will be modified in some manner.

The continuing trend in the organization of public employees in local, national, and international unions and associations is one of the major facts commanding the attention of public personnel professionals. Concurrent with employees' demands for a bigger role in the determination of personnel policies through negotiation is the growth in political influence exercised by public employee organizations through the electoral and legislative processes. Through political action these organizations have been able to influence state legislation mandating policies relating to employment practices in local governments. Evidence as of this date supports the prediction that this type of political activity is likely to continue and expand.

When state legislatures have not satisfied a sufficient number of these demands, a coalition of public employee organizations has turned to Congress for federal legislation. Intervention by organized public employees in personnel policy making has not been confined to collective bargaining, legislative lobbying, or election activities. Litigation on their behalf in both the federal and state courts has produced a considerable body of judicial rulings that affect salary setting, promotion rights, layoff procedures, and numerous other matters of personnel administration.

Simultaneous with the emergence of public employee organizations as a significant influence in municipal personnel policy making is the growth of legislative and administrative directives from the national and state governments which attempt to define and assure equal opportunity of employment to women and members of minority groups. Legislative standards and judicially stated criteria have been applied in evaluating the local governments' employment behavior as well as their formally stated policies and procedures. As a result, changes have taken place in recruitment and employment, classification standards, and pro-

motion procedures. Moreover, layoff procedures were being questioned in the recessionary economy of the mid-1970s.

Possibly the most difficult aspect of the move toward equal employment opportunity as it relates to local government administrators is the ambiguity and uncertainty arising from differences in interpretation held by those agencies responsible for enforcement. Local governments operating under the merit system have sought for many years to achieve the goal of equal opportunity in public employment. These governments now find themselves subjected to enforcement criteria which, for the most part, have been written to curb abuses committed by those employers who did not accept the basic principles of merit in employment. Their problem is exacerbated by the lack of consensus among federal and state administrators charged with the enforcement of legislative directives from these levels of government. The outlook is that the process of defining standards and clarifying procedures will be protracted over a considerable period of time.

The implication of the numerous developments of the 1960s and 1970s affecting local government personnel policies and procedures is relatively clear: Local government employment policy is neither a solely local affair nor an exclusively administrative matter.

Development of the profession of management and its ancillary profession, personnel administration, since their beginnings in the early years of this century has provided managers and personnel specialists certain analytical tools and concepts to attack problems and reach decisions. At the same time, the professionals have learned that the decision process really is not a search for "the one best way" but is one in which many pressures and influences are weighed and evaluated before proposing a solution or a set of alternatives.

A basic tenet of faith within the managerial profession is that the knowledge and use of the profession's analytical tools will enhance the professional's chances of commanding the course and outcome of decisions. But professional public administrators realize that the field in which they work is a political one, and hence, among the skills necessary in their work is the ability to analyze and cope with the various kinds of political and organizational pressures that seek to influence or control the decision-making process.

Local government management in the early post-World War II era emphasized managerial control of the organization and the personnel comprising it. Grants-in-aid and revenue-sharing programs have since taught city and other local government managers much about the techniques and intricacies of interorganizational and intergovernmental relations. Personnel administrators are now deeply involved with both external as well as internal relationships. Public administrators undoubtedly will be drawn still further into group or associational efforts to achieve consensus of policy and outlook. They must learn to use the resulting cooperative strength to make their perceptions and proposals known at the several levels of government in which decisions on personnel policy are made.

The demands of the job to be done within the individual local government's administrative structure forces the need to participate with colleagues from other jurisdictions as well as with associations of locally elected officers. One of the purposes of this associational activity is to develop new procedures and techniques, but another purpose is to articulate values and goals along with the administrators' perception of the public interest.

---

[1] J. Richard Aronson and Eli Schwartz, "The Outlook," in MANAGEMENT POLICIES IN LOCAL GOVERNMENT FINANCE, eds. J. Richard Aronson and Eli Schwartz, (Washington, D.C.: International City Management Association, 1975), pp. 331–333.

Selected Bibliography

The literature relating to the various aspects of public personnel administration is enormous, and useful items are being added steadily to it. The bibliography included in this book is highly selective and represents informed judgments about basic materials. Books, journal articles, official reports, and other reference sources have been cited in the footnotes of most chapters. To supplement that information, certain materials are recommended in this section for further reference and assistance in keeping up to date on developments. Selected basic sources are given below with brief commentaries. Following that, books and articles pertaining to the subjects of individual chapters are listed.

A very useful publication for following items of current interest in the personnel field is *Personnel Literature,* a monthly prepared by the U.S. Civil Service Commission Library, available from the Government Printing Office. Subject headings aid the selection of items. Its *Annual Index* is a helpful guide to items published.

The Bureau of Labor Statistics of the U.S. Department of Labor publishes the *Monthly Labor Review* which provides data on employment, prices, and wages as well as a survey of current literature on labor subjects.

The American Management Association also provides an information service which deals with subjects related to personnel administration.

The International Personnel Management Association publishes several books and monographs, a current list of which is available on request. Its Public Employee Relations Library series includes monographs on a variety of personnel subjects.

The Industrial Relations Research Association is devoted to the study of employer-employee relations in both the private and public sectors. The proceedings of its annual winter meetings are excellent resources devoting an increasing amount of space to public sector matters.

The New York State School of Industrial and Labor Relations at Cornell University publishes the quarterly *Industrial and Labor Relations Review,* one of the best academic journals treating public sector labor relations. The school also publishes a number of books and monographs.

The Labor-Management Relations Service, associated with the National League of Cities, the U.S. Conference of Mayors, and the National League of Counties publishes a series of pamphlets on labor relations in government. These and the *LMRS Newsletter* are important sources of current information in this field.

Two publishers prepare sets of informational materials in loose-leaf binders. Prentice-Hall, Inc. (Englewood Cliffs, N.J.) publishes *Personnel Management: Policies and Practices.* The Bureau of National Affairs, Inc. (Washington, D.C.) publishes several series in loose-leaf editions. The *Government Employee Relations Report* is devoted mainly to employer-employee relations, contracts, arbitration awards, and court decisions. The *Fair Employment Practices Manual* and *Fair Employment Practices Cases* provide current information regarding legislation, EEOC and state agency directives, and court cases pertaining to employment practices. The *Wage and Hour Manual* covers the Fair Labor Standards Act.

The Municipal Year Book. Annual. International City Management Association. Provides police and fire personnel data among other information on municipal management. In some editions data on unionism, employer-employee relations, and other personnel subjects are given.

Public Personnel Management. Bimonthly. International Personnel Management Association. The major publication in the public personnel field. It is written and edited primarily for those specializing in personnel administration. A book and pamphlet notes section serves as a useful guide to current literature.

Public Management. Monthly. International City Management Association. Written and edited mainly for managers. Frequently an entire issue is devoted to a single personnel management subject, such as employer-employee relations.

Public Administration Review. Bimonthly. American Society for Public Administration. Publishes articles, book reviews, and symposium reports covering the broad spectrum of public administration. Items relating specifically to personnel administration are periodically presented.

Personnel Psychology. Quarterly. Dr. Milton Hakel, Durham, N.C. Journal of applied research which contains articles directly useful to specialists in several subareas of the personnel field. It has an extensive book review section.

Journal of Applied Psychology. Bimonthly. American Psychological Association. Devoted primarily to original investigations in universities, industry, government, police and correctional systems, and health systems. Much of its coverage bears on public personnel administration.

Personnel. Bimonthly. AMACOM, a division of American Management Association. Contains relatively brief practitioner-oriented articles.

Personnel Journal. Monthly. Personnel Journal, Inc. Presents short general articles.

Compensation Review. Quarterly. American Management Association. Contains four or five articles every issue plus regular features such as Compensation Currents section, book reviews, and a digest of articles. Addresses of publications cited are noted.

1. Local Government Personnel Administration: The Setting

ARGYRIS, CHRIS. *Understanding Organizational Behavior.* Homewood, Ill.: Dorsey Press, 1960.

BARNARD, CHESTER I. *The Functions of the Executive.* Cambridge, Mass.: Harvard University Press, 1938.

BLAU, PETER M., and W. RICHARD SCOTT. *Formal Organizations.* San Francisco: Chandler & Sharp Publishers, Inc., 1962.

BLAU, PETER M., and OTIS DUDLEY DUNCAN. *The American Occupational Structure.* New York: John Wiley & Sons, 1967. See chapters 1, 2, 3, 6, and 7.

CAYET, N. JOSEPH. *Public Personnel Administration in the United States.* New York: St. Martin's Press, 1975.

CROUCH, WINSTON W. *Guide for Modern Personnel Commissions.* Chicago: International Personnel Management Association, 1973.

GLASER, BARNEY G., ed. *Organizational Careers: A Sourcebook for Theory.* Chicago: Aldine Publishing Co., 1968.

GOLEMBIEWSKI, ROBERT T. *Perspectives on Public Management: Cases and Learning Designs.* Itasca, Ill.: F. E. Peacock Publishing Co., 1968.

GOLEMBIEWSKI, ROBERT T., and MICHAEL COHEN. *People in Government.* Itasca, Ill.: F. E. Peacock Publishing Co., 1970.

GROSS, BERTRAM M. *The Managing of Organizations,* 2 vols. New York: The Free Press of Glencoe, 1964.

GULICK, LUTHER, and LYNDALL URWICK. *Papers on the Science of Administration.* New York: Institute of Public Administration, 1937.

HAIRE, MASON, ed. *Modern Organization Theory.* New York: John Wiley & Sons, 1959.

KAPLAN, H. ELIOTT. *The Law of Civil Service.* New York: Matthew Bender & Co., 1958.

LAZARSFELD, PAUL F., WILLIAM H. SEWELL, and HAROLD L. WILENSKY, eds. *The Uses of Sociology.* New York: Basic Books, 1967. See Chapter 8.

MARCH, JAMES G., and HERBERT A. SIMON. *Organizations.* New York: John Wiley & Sons, 1958.

MESSICK, CHARLES P. *An Adventure in Public Personnel Administration.* Newark, Del.: University of Delaware Press, 1973.

MOSHER, FREDERICK C. *Democracy and the Pub-*

lic Service. New York: Oxford University Press, 1968.

MUNICIPAL MANPOWER COMMISSION. *Manpower for the Nation's Cities.* New York: McGraw-Hill Book Company, 1962.

NATIONAL CIVIL SERVICE LEAGUE. *A Model Public Personnel Administration Law.* Washington, D.C.: National Civil Service League, 1974.

NIGRO, FELIX A. *Public Personnel Administration.* New York: Henry Holt and Co., 1959.

PFIFFNER, JOHN M., and ROBERT PRESTHUS. *Public Administration.* New York: Ronald Press, 1967. See Part 4.

SIMON, HERBERT A., DONALD W. SMITHBURG, and VICTOR A. THOMPSON. *Public Administration.* New York: Alfred A. Knopf, 1950. See chapters 15–17.

STAHL, O. GLENN. *Public Personnel Administration.* 6th ed. New York: Harper & Row, Publishers, 1971.

STANLEY, DAVID T. *Professional Personnel for the City of New York.* Washington, D.C.: Brookings Institution, 1963.

———. *Managing Local Government under Union Pressure.* Washington, D.C.: Brookings Institution, 1972.

VAN RIPER, PAUL P. *History of the United States Civil Service.* New York: Harper & Row, Publishers, 1958.

2. Administering the Personnel Function

HARVEY, DONALD R. *The Civil Service Commission.* New York: Praeger Publishers, 1970.

MUNICIPAL MANPOWER COMMISSION. *Governmental Manpower for Tomorrow's Cities.* New York: McGraw-Hill Book Company, 1962.

NIGRO, FELIX A. *Public Personnel Administration.* New York: Holt, Rinehart and Winston, 1959.

PAGE, THOMAS, ed. *The Public Personnel Agency and the Chief Executive: A Symposium,* Personnel Report no. 601. Chicago: International Personnel Management Association, 1960.

SAYRE, WALLACE S., ed. *The Federal Government Service.* Englewood Cliffs, N.J.: Prentice-Hall, Inc., 1965.

STAHL, O. GLENN. *Public Personnel Administration.* 6th ed. New York: Harper & Row Publishers, 1971.

———. *The Personnel Job of Public Managers.* Chicago: International Personnel Management Association, 1971.

STAHL, O. GLENN, and RICHARD A. STANFENBERGER. *Police Personnel Administration.* Washington, D.C.: The Police Foundation, 1974.

STRAUSS, GEORGE, and LEONARD R. SAYLES. *Personnel: The Human Problems of Management.* Englewood Cliffs, N.J.: Prentice-Hall, Inc., 1960.

3. Manpower Planning

AZZI, CORRY F. *Equity and Efficiency Effects from Manpower Programs.* Lexington, Mass.: D. C. Heath and Company, 1973.

*BLALOCK, HUBERT M., JR. *Social Statistics.* 2nd ed. New York: McGraw-Hill Book Company, 1972.

COMMITTEE FOR ECONOMIC DEVELOPMENT. *Training and Jobs for the Urban Poor.* New York: Committee for Economic Development, 1970.

*DOWNIE, N. M., and R. W. HEATH. *Basic Statistical Methods.* 3rd ed. New York: Harper & Row Publishers, 1970. Contains explanations of sophisticated statistical techniques, such as regression analysis.

GINZBERG, ELI, ed. *Manpower Strategy for the Metropolis.* New York: Columbia University Press, 1968.

GORDON, ROBERT AARON, ed. *Toward a Manpower Policy.* New York: John Wiley & Sons, 1967.

*HAMMOND, KENNETH R., JAMES E. HOUSEHOLDER, and N. JOHN CASTELLAN, JR. *Introduction to the Statistical Method.* 2nd ed. New York: Alfred A. Knopf, 1970.

KOONTZ, HAROLD. "Making Theory Operational: The Span of Management." *The Journal of Management Studies* 3 (October 1966): 229–243.

LECHT, LEONARD A. *Manpower Needs for Na-*

tional Goals in the 1970's. New York: Frederick A. Praeger, 1969.

LEVITAN, SAR A., GARTH L. MANGUM, and RAY MARSHALL. *Human Resources and Labor Markets.* New York: Harper & Row Publishers, 1972.

LEVITAN, SAR A., and IRVING H. SIEGEL. *Dimensions of Manpower Policy: Programs and Research.* Baltimore: The Johns Hopkins University Press, 1966.

MONAT, WILLIAM R. "The Once and Future Revolution: Manpower Policy in the United States." *Public Administration Review* XX (January/February 1970) : 69–78.

NATIONAL COMMISSION ON PRODUCTIVITY. *So, Mr. Mayor, You Want to Improve Productivity.* . . . Washington, D.C.: Government Printing Office, 1974.

NATIONAL URBAN COALITION. *Counterbudget: A Blueprint for Changing National Priorities, 1971–1976.* New York: Frederick A. Praeger, 1971.

OLYMPUS RESEARCH CORPORATION. *Manpower Planning for Wastewater Treatment Plants,* a manual prepared for the Office of Water Programs, U.S. Environmental Protection Agency, 1972.

PRICE, JAMES L. *Handbook of Organizational Measurement.* Lexington, Mass.: D. C. Heath and Company, 1972.

SELIGMAN, DANIEL. "How 'Equal Opportunity' Turned into Employment Quotas." *Fortune* 87 (March 1973) : 160–168.

SPECIAL TASK FORCE TO THE SECRETARY OF HEALTH, EDUCATION, AND WELFARE. *Work in America.* Cambridge, Mass.: The MIT Press, 1973.

U.S. CIVIL SERVICE COMMISSION. BUREAU OF EXECUTIVE MANPOWER. *Decision Analysis Forecasting for Executive Manpower Planning,* Executive Manpower Management Technical Assistance Paper no. 3. Washington, D.C.: Government Printing Office, 1974.

U.S. CONGRESS. SENATE. COMMITTEE ON LABOR AND PUBLIC WELFARE, SUBCOMMITTEE ON EMPLOYMENT, MANPOWER, AND POVERTY. *The Emergency Employment Act: An Interim Assessment.* Washington, D.C.: Government Printing Office, 1972.

U.S. EQUAL EMPLOYMENT OPPORTUNITY COMMISSION. *Affirmative Action and Equal Employment: A Guidebook for Employers,* vol. 1. Washington, D.C.: U.S. Equal Employment Opportunity Commission, 1974.

* Contains explanations of sophisticated statistical techniques, such as regression analysis.

4. Structuring the Work Force

Organization Concepts, Management Philosophy and Techniques, and Human Behavior

BENNIS, WARREN G. *Changing Organizations.* New York: McGraw-Hill Book Company, 1966.

BOWER, MARVIN. *The Will to Manage.* New York: McGraw-Hill Book Company, 1967.

DRUCKER, PETER F. *The Practice of Management.* New York: Harper and Bros., 1954.

———. *The Effective Executive.* New York: Harper & Row, Publishers, 1967.

ETZIONI, AMITAL, ed., *Readings on Modern Organizations.* Englewood Cliffs, N.J.: Prentice-Hall, Inc., 1969.

GOLEMBIEWSKI, ROBERT T. "Organization Patterns of the Future: What They Mean to Personnel Administration." *Personnel Administration.* (November/December 1969): 8–24.

GULICK, LUTHER, and LYNDALL URICK, eds., *Papers on the Science of Administration.* New York: Institute of Public Administration, 1937. See pages 1–46.

HINRICHS, JOHN R. "Restructuring the Organization for Tomorrow's Needs." *Personnel* 51 (March/April 1974) : 9–19.

KOONTZ, HAROLD, and CYRIL O'DONNELL. *Principles of Management.* 4th ed. New York: McGraw-Hill Book Company, 1968.

KORMAN, ABRAHAM K. *Industrial and Organizational Psychology.* Englewood Cliffs, N.J.: Prentice-Hall, Inc., 1971.

LEVINSON, HARRY. *The Great Jackass Fallacy.* Cambridge, Mass.: Harvard Business School, 1973.

LIKERT, RENSIS. *New Patterns of Organization.* New York: McGraw-Hill Book Company, 1961.

———. *The Human Organization.* New York: McGraw-Hill Book Company, 1967.

MCGREGOR, DOUGLAS. *The Human Side of En-*

terprise. New York: McGraw-Hill Book Company, 1960.

————. *The Professional Manager*. New York: McGraw-Hill Book Company, 1967.

MONCZKA, ROBERT M., and WILLIAM E. REIF. "A Contingency Approach to Job Enrichment Design." *Human Resource Management* 12 (Winter 1973) : 9–17.

ODIORNE, GEORGE S. *Management by Objectives*. New York: Pitman Publishing Company, 1965.

PARKINSON, C. NORTHCOTE. *Parkinson's Law*. Cambridge, Mass.: Riverside Press, 1957.

PETER, LAURENCE J., and RAYMOND HULL. *The Peter Principle*. New York: Bantam Books, 1969.

REIF, WILLIAM E., and ROBERT M. MONCZKA. "Job Redesign: A Contingency Approach to Implementation." *Personnel* 51 (May/June 1974) : 18–28.

SHEPPARD, HAROLD L., and NEAL Q. HERRICK. *Where Have All the Robots Gone? Workers' Dissatisfactions in the '70's*. New York: The Free Press, 1972.

STAHL, O. GLENN. *The Personnel Job of Government Managers*. Chicago: Public Personnel Association, 1971.

————. *Public Personnel Administration*. 6th ed. New York: Harper & Row Publishers, 1962.

TAYLOR, FREDERICK W. *The Principles of Scientific Management*. New York: Harper & Row, 1911.

TOWNSEND, ROBERT. *Up the Organization*. New York: Alfred A. Knopf, Inc., 1970.

WHITE, LEONARD D. *Introduction to the Study of Public Administration*. 4th ed. New York: Macmillan, Inc., 1958.

WOLF, WILLIAM B. *Conversations with Chester I. Barnard*. Ithaca, N.Y.: New York State School of Industrial and Labor Relations, Cornell University, 1973.

Job Analysis and Job Structure

BARUCH, ISMAR, ed. *Position Classification in the Public Service*. Chicago: Public Personnel Association, 1941.

FORD, ROBERT N. *Motivation through the Work Itself*. New York: American Management Association, 1969.

GARNIER, ROBERT C. *The Maintenance of a*

Classification Plan. Chicago: Civil Service Assembly of the United States and Canada, 1953 (out of print) .

SHAFRITZ, JAY M. *Position Classification: A Behavioral Analysis for the Public Service*. New York: Praeger Publishers, Inc., 1973.

U.S. CIVIL SERVICE COMMISSION. *Benchmark Positions Descriptions for the Factor Ranking-Benchmark Approach to the Evaluation of General Schedule Positions, GS-1 through GS-15*. Washington, D.C.: Government Printing Office, 1973.

————. *Classification Principles and Policies*, Personnel Management Series no. 16. Washington, D.C.: Government Printing Office, 1963.

————. *Development of a Framework for a Factor-Ranking Benchmark System of Job Evaluation, TS–73–3*. Washington, D.C.: Government Printing Office, 1973.

————. *Job Analysis: Developing and Documenting Data, BIPP 152–35*. Washington, D.C.: Government Printing Office, 1973.

————. *Models of Evaluation Systems and Pay Structures*, 2 vols. Washington, D.C.: Government Printing Office, 1972.

U.S. DEPARTMENT OF LABOR. *Dictionary of Occupational Titles*, 2 vols. Washington, D.C.: Government Printing Office, 1965.

————. *Handbook for Analyzing Jobs*. 1972.

WASHINGTON. DEPARTMENT OF PERSONNEL. *Task Analysis Handbook* (1973) .

ZOLLITSCH, HERBERT, and ADOLPH LANGSNER. *Wage and Salary Administration*. 2nd ed. Cincinnati: South-Western Publishing Co., 1970.

5. Recruitment and Staffing

ACTION. *Volunteers in ACTION*. Washington, D.C.: Government Printing Office, 1973.

ADVISORY COMMITTEE ON MERIT SYSTEMS STANDARDS. *Progress in Intergovernmental Personnel Relations*. Washington, D.C.: Government Printing Office, 1968.

AREND, FREDERICK H., and J. DAVID PALMER. "HUD's Employee Exchange." *Nation's Cities* 10 (May 1972) : 11, 14–15.

ATLANTA, GEORGIA. COMMUNITY RELATIONS

COMMISSION. "Minority Hiring and Promotion, Update, 1972."

———. "Report on Minority Hiring and Promotion Practices" (31 July 1970) .

———. "Women in City Government" (8 May 1973) .

BADAR, BARRY S. "Opening Public Jobs to the Disadvantaged." In *NCSL Leads the Way in Public Personnel Modernization*. Washington, D.C.: National Civil Service League, 1972, pp. 3–4.

BLUMENFELD, WARREN S. "Application, Application." *Atlanta Economic Review* 23 (May/June 1973) : 8–13.

BOLINO, AUGUST C. *Manpower and the City*. Cambridge, Mass.: Schenkman Publishing Co., 1969.

BROWN, WILLIAM H., III. "Moving Against Job Bias in State and Local Governments." *Good Government* 89 (Winter 1972) : 10, 14–17.

BUBIER, R. H. "Affirmative Action Plan for the City of Fort Lauderdale." Memorandum, 30 October 1974.

———. "Employees Handbook." Fort Lauderdale, Florida, 1974.

CAPLIN, MORTIMER M. "Let's Revamp Merit Systems for Today's Needs." In *NCSL Leads the Way in Public Personnel Modernization*, pp. 17–19.

CHAPMAN, RICHARD L., and FREDERIC N. CLEAVELAND. *Meeting the Needs of Tomorrow's Public Service: Guidelines for Professional Education in Public Administration*. Washington, D.C.: National Academy of Public Administration Foundation, 1973.

CLAGUE, EWAN. "Government Employment and Manpower Planning in the 1970's." *Public Personnel Review* 21 (October 1970) : 279–282.

COLLINS, WILLIAM A. "Summer Employment Programs: A Student's Eye View." *Personnel* 34 (March/April 1958) : 71–75.

COMMITTEE FOR ECONOMIC DEVELOPMENT. *Improving Executive Management in the Federal Government*. New York: Committee for Economic Development, 1964.

COOPER, HARLAN T. "Internships in State and Local Government in the South." Paper presented at the annual meeting of the Southern Political Science Association, New Orleans, La., 7–9 November 1974.

COPPOCK, ROBERT W., and BARBARA BRATTIN COPPOCK. *How to Recruit and Select Policemen and Firemen,* Personnel Report no. 581. Chicago: Public Personnel Association, 1958.

COUTURIER, JEAN J. "Governments Can Be the 'Employers of First Resort'." In *NCSL Leads the Way in Public Personnel Modernization,* pp. 23–26.

DEVINE, EUGENE J. *Analysis of Manpower Shortages in Local Government*. New York: Praeger Publishers, 1970.

DEWALKD, FRANKLIN K. "A Job Hot Line for Recruitment." *Public Personnel Review* 31 (October 1970) : 235–238.

DIAZ DE KROFCHECK, MARIA DOLORES, and CARLOS JACKSON. "The Chicano Experience with Nativism in Public Administration." *Public Administration Review* 34 (November/December 1974) : 534–539.

DINUNZIO, MICHAEL A., ed. "Manning Tomorrow's Cities." Reprinted in *Nation's Cities* 2 (June 1973) .

EYDE, LORRAINE D. "The Status of Women in State and Local Government." *Public Personnel Management* 2 (May/June 1973) : 205–211.

FYE, ANN B. "The Recruitment and Utilization of Women in State and Local Government." Paper prepared for Political Science 845, Georgia State University, 25 May 1974.

GEORGIA. GOVERNOR. *Georgia Intern Program Annual Report 1973*.

GOLEMBIEWSKI, ROBERT T., and MICHAEL COHEN. *People in Public Service*. Itasca, Ill.: F. E. Peacock Publishers, 1970.

GRAVES, HELEN M. "Educational Structuring of Political Internship Experiences." Paper presented at the annual meeting of the Southern Political Science Association, New Orleans, La., 7–9 November 1975.

GROSSMAN, HARRY. "The Equal Employment Opportunity Act of 1972: Its Implications for the State and Local Government Manager." *Public Personnel Management* 2 (September/October 1973) : 370–379.

HARTSFIELD, ANNIE MARY. "The Intergovernmental Personnel Act: Implications for the New Federalism." Paper presented at the annual meeting of the Southern Political Science Association, New Orleans, La., 7–9 November 1975.

HERBERT, ADAM W., ed. "Minorities in Public Administration." *Public Administration Review* 34, symposium issue (November/December 1974.

———. "The Minority Administrator: Problems, Prospects, and Challenges." *Public Administration Review* 34 (November/December 1974) : 556–563.

HOWERTON, ALLAN W. "Recruiters Forum." *Civil Service Journal* 14 (July/September 1973) : 46–47.

INSTITUTE OF URBAN STUDIES. *Executive Manpower for Urban Government.* Vol. 1: *A Regional Manpower Profile.* Vol. 2: *Education for Career Service.* Vol. 3: *Planning and Management Services.* Vol. 4: *Summary and Implementation Procedure.* Arlington, Tex.: Institute of Urban Studies, University of Texas, 1970.

INTERNATIONAL CITY MANAGERS' ASSOCIATION. *Municipal Personnel Administration.* 6th ed. Chicago: International City Managers' Association, 1960.

JACKSON, MATTHEW. *Recruiting, Interviewing, and Selection: A Manual for Line Managers.* London: McGraw-Hill Book Company, 1972.

JAMES, GEORGE. *A Survey of Personnel Practices in Gwinnett County, Georgia, with Recommendations for Establishing a Merit System.* Athens, Ga.: Institute of Government, University of Georgia, 1968.

KRANZ, HARRY. "How Representative is the Public Service?" *Public Personnel Management* 2 (July/August 1973) : 242–255.

———. "Are Merit and Equity Compatible?" *Public Administration Review* 34 (September/October 1974) : 434–440.

LEGLER, JOHN. "Trends in State and Local Government Employment in the Southeast." *Georgia Governmental Review* 6 (Spring 1974) : 1–5.

LIPSETT, LAURENCE, FRANK P. RODGERS, and HAROLD M. KENTNER. *Personnel Selection and Recruitment.* Boston: Allyn & Bacon, Inc., 1964.

U.S. DEPARTMENT OF LABOR. *Manpower Report of the President.* Washington, D.C.: Government Printing Office, 1971.

MCGREGOR, EUGENE B., JR., "Social Equity and the Public Service." *Public Administration Review* 34 (January/February 1974) : 18–28.

MONTAGUE, ROBERT M. "The All-Volunteer Force." *Navy Supply Corps Newsletter* 37 (July 1974) : 21–25.

MOSHER, FREDERICK C. *Democracy and the Public Service.* New York: Oxford University Press, 1968.

MUNICIPAL MANPOWER COMMISSION. *Governmental Manpower for Tomorrow's Cities.* New York: McGraw Hill Book Company, 1962.

NATIONAL CIVIL SERVICE LEAGUE. *A Model Public Personnel Administration Law.* Washington, D.C.: National Civil Service League, 1970.

———. *NCSL Leads the Way in Public Personnel Modernization.* Washington, D.C.: National Civil Service League, 1972.

———. "Survey of Current Personnel Systems in State and Local Governments." *Good Government* 87 (Spring 1971).

NATIONAL LEAGUE OF CITIES–U.S. CONFERENCE OF MAYORS. *An Evaluation of the National Urban Technical Services Research and Demonstration Program.* Washington, D.C.: National League of Cities–U.S. Conference of Mayors, 1973.

———. *Local Government Approaches to Capacity-Building.* Washington, D.C.: National League of Cities–U.S. Conference of Mayors, 1973.

"*Nation's Cities 1974–1975 Annual Directory.*" Compiled by Catherine Satterlee. *Nation's Cities* (July 1974) : 14–42.

NIGRO, FELIX A. *Modern Public Administration.* 2nd ed. New York: Harper & Row Publishers, 1970.

ODIORNE, GEORGE S., and ARTHUR S. HANN. *Effective College Recruiting.* Ann Arbor, Mich.: Bureau of Industrial Relations, University of Michigan, 1961.

PALMER, JOHN D. "Finding the Best Brains:

Recruitment of Quality Personnel for the Public Service in Georgia." *Atlanta Economic Review* 19 (July 1969) : 22–24.

———. "Talent Swap." *Georgia County Government Magazine* 24 (October 1972) : 43–44.

———. "HUD Encourages Stronger Ties with the Academic Community," NASPAA Circular no. 6–72. Washington, D.C.: National Association of Schools of Public Affairs and Administration, 1972.

PELL, ARTHUR R. *Recruiting and Selecting Personnel.* New York: Regents Publishing Co., 1969.

PENNSYLVANIA. CIVIL SERVICE COMMISSION. *SWAP* 12 (July 1974) .

PORTER, WAYNE R., and EDWARD L. LEVINE. "Improving Applicants' Performance in the Completion of Applications." *Public Personnel Management* 3 (July/August 1974) : 314–317.

"Recruiters Forum." *Civil Service Journal* 14 (October/December 1973) : 3–4.

ROSENBLOOM, DAVID H. "A Note on Interminority Group Competition for Federal Positions." *Public Personnel Management* 2 (January/February 1973) : 43–48.

SEALE, CHRISTOPHER P. "Impact of the Georgia Intern Program on Participants' Vocational Goals." Paper presented at the annual meeting of the Southern Political Science Association, New Orleans, La., 7–9 November 1974.

SEIFER, DANIEL M. "Continuing Hard Problems: The 'Hard Core' and Racial Discrimination." *Public Personnel Management* 3 (May/June 1974) : 238–243.

SMART, LYMAN F., and JACK E. McINTOSH. "An Interim Report on the Utah Intergovernmental Personnel Agency." Paper presented at the international conference of the International Personnel Management Association, Miami Beach, Fla., November 1973.

STAATS, ELMER B. "The Public Service: 90 Years Later." Speech presented to the U.S. Department of State, 16 January 1973. Reprinted in *Public Administration Review* 33 (November/December 1973) : 568–572.

STAHL, O. GLENN. *Public Personnel Adminis-*
tration. 6th ed. New York: Harper & Row Publishers, 1971.

STONE, J. L. "The Use of an Applicant Service Questionnaire." *Public Personnel Management* 3 (March/April 1974) : 155–158.

TIMMINS, WILLIAM M. "Intergovernmental Cooperation in Personnel Recruitment and Selection." *State Government Administration* 60 (May 1974) : 8–10.

U.S. CIVIL SERVICE COMMISSION. The scope and number of the commission's publications, available from the Government Printing Office, make them excellent sources of information for personnel administrators. Some titles include *Annual Statistical Report for State and Local Personnel Systems; Equal Employment Opportunity Court Cases; Guide for Affirmative Action and Equal Employment Opportunity in State and Local Governments; Guide to Federal Career Literature; Locating Federal Talent;* and *The Human Equation: Working in Personnel for the Federal Government.*

U.S. DEPARTMENT OF HOUSING AND URBAN DEVELOPMENT. *Personnel Management in Local Model Cities Programs,* Model Cities Management Series bulletin 2. Washington, D.C.: Government Printing Office, 1971.

U.S. DEPARTMENT OF LABOR. WOMEN'S BUREAU. *Calling All Women in Federal Service.* Washington, D.C.: Government Printing Office, 1972.

———. Manpower Administration. *Merchandising Your Job Talents.* Washington, D.C.: Government Printing Office, 1971.

U.S. DEPARTMENT OF LABOR, MANPOWER ADMINISTRATION, AND U.S. CIVIL SERVICE COMMISSION. *Opportunity for All: Changing Personnel Systems under the Emergency Employment Act of 1971,* BIPP 152–17. Washington, D.C.: Bureau of Intergovernmental Personnel Programs, U.S. Civil Service Commission, 1973.

U.S. DEPARTMENT OF LABOR. *Municipal Government Efforts to Provide Career Employment Opportunities for the Disadvantaged,* by Floyd A. Decker, Andrew B. Horgan III, and Lawrence A. Williams.

Research Contract 41–8–001–009, December 1969.

U.S. SENATE. Committee on Governmental Operations. Subcommittee on Intergovernmental Relations. *More Effective Public Service*. S. Rept. 30–854, 93rd Cong., 2d sess., 1974.

VILLANUEVA, A. B. "Public Affairs Internship Programs in Illinois." *Public Personnel Management* 3 (May/June 1974) : 185–192.

VOCINO, THOMAS. "Determining the Need for High Level Personnel in Local Government on a Statewide Basis." *Public Personnel Review* 26 (October 1970) : 239–244.

WILLIAMS, MELBA. *A Guide to the Development and Establishment of an Effective Personnel Management System*. Atlanta, Ga.: Georgia Municipal Association, n.d.

YOUNG, RICHARD A. *Recruiting and Hiring Minority Employees*. New York: American Management Association, 1969.

6. The Selection Process

Books

ADKINS, DOROTHY C. *Construction and Analysis of Achievement Tests*. Washington, D.C.: Government Printing Office, 1947.

ANASTASI, ANNE. *Psychological Testing*. 3rd rev. ed. New York: Macmillan Inc., 1968.

ARGYRIS, CHRIS. *Personality and Organization*. New York: Harper and Brothers, 1957.

BENNIS, WARREN G. *Changing Organizations*. New York: McGraw-Hill Book Company, 1966.

BENNIS, WARREN G., KENNETH D. BENNE, and ROBERT CHIN, eds. *The Planning of Change*. New York: Holt, Rinehart and Winston, 1961.

BERELSON, BARNARD, and GARY A. STEINER. *Human Behavior: An Inventory of Scientific Findings*. New York: Harcourt, Brace and World, 1964.

BERRY, DEAN F. *The Politics of Personnel Research*. Ann Arbor, Mich.: Bureau of Industrial Relations, University of Michigan, 1966.

BLACK, HILLEL. *They Shall Not Pass*. New York: William Morrow & Co., Inc., 1962.

BYHAM, WILLIAM C., and MORTON E. SPITZER. *The Law and Personnel Testing*. New York: American Management Association, 1971.

CAMPBELL, JOHN P., MARVIN D. DUNNETTE, EDWARD E. LAWLER, III, and KARL E. WEICK. *Managerial Behavior, Performance, and Effectiveness*. New York: McGraw-Hill Book Co., 1970.

CRONBACH, LEE J. *Essentials of Psychological Testing*. 3rd rev. ed. New York: Harper & Row Publishers, 1970.

CRONBACH, LEE J., and GOLDINE C. GLESER. *Psychological Tests and Personnel Decisions*. 2nd rev. ed. Urbana, Ill.: University of Illinois Press, 1965.

DONOVAN, J. J., ed. *Recruitment and Selection in the Public Service*. Chicago: Public Personnel Association, 1968.

DUNNETTE, MARVIN D. *Personnel Selection and Placement*. Belmont, Calif.: Brooks/Cole Publishing Co., 1966.

ENGLAND, GEORGE W., and DONALD G. PATERSON. "Selection and Placement: The Past Ten Years." In *Employment Relations Research*. Edited by Herbert G. Heneman et al. New York: Harper and Brothers, 1960.

FREEMAN, FRANK S. *Theory and Practice of Psychological Testing*. 3rd rev. ed. New York: Holt, Rinehart and Winston, Inc., 1962.

GALLAS, NESTA M. *Public Personnel Selection: A Behavioral Analysis of Current Practices*. Ann Arbor, Mich.: University Microfilm, 1968.

GARDNER, JOHN W. *Excellence: Can We Be Equal and Excellent Too?* New York: Harper & Row Publishers, 1961.

GHISELLI, E. E. *The Validity of Occupational Aptitude Tests*. New York: John Wiley & Sons, Inc., 1966.

———. *Theory of Psychological Measurement*. New York: McGraw-Hill Book Company, 1964.

GUION, ROBERT M. *Personnel Testing*. New York: McGraw-Hill Book Company, 1965.

HOFFMAN, BANESH. *The Tyranny of Testing*. New York: Cromwell-Collier Press, 1962.

KILPATRICK, F. P., MILTON C. CUMMINGS, JR., and M. KENT JENNINGS. *The Image of the Federal Service.* Washington, D.C.: Brookings Institution, 1964.

KIRKPATRICK, JAMES J., ROBERT B. EWEN, RICHARD S. BARRETT, and RAYMOND A. KATZELL. *Testing and Fair Employment: Fairness and Validity of Personnel Tests for Different Ethnic Groups.* New York: New York University Press, 1968.

LAWSHE, CHARLES H., and MICHAEL J. BALMA. *Principles of Personnel Testing.* New York: McGraw-Hill Book Company, 1966.

LINDQUIST, EDWARD F., ed. *Educational Measurement.* Washington, D.C.: American Council on Education, 1959.

LIPPITT, RONALD, JEANNE WATSON, and BRUCE WESTLEY. *The Dynamics of Planned Change.* New York: Harcourt, Brace and World, 1958.

MACY, JOHN W., JR. *Public Service: The Human Side of Government.* New York: Harper & Row Publishers, 1971.

MANDELL, MILTON M. *The Selection Process: Choosing the Right Man [sic] for the Job.* New York: American Management Association, 1964.

MARGULIES, NEWTON, and JOHN WALLACE. *Organizational Choice: Techniques and Applications.* Glenview, Ill.: Scott, Foresman and Company, 1973.

MUNICIPAL MANPOWER COMMISSION. *Governmental Manpower for Tomorrow's Cities.* New York: McGraw-Hill Book Company, 1962.

NEWMAN, A. D., and R. W. ROWBOTTOM. *Organization Analysis.* London: Morrison and Gibb, Ltd., 1968.

NIGRO, FELIX A. *Public Personnel Administration.* New York: Henry Holt and Co., 1959.

O'TOOLE, JAMES. *Work and the Quality of Life.* Cambridge, Mass.: MIT Press, 1974.

RITZER, GEORGE, and HARRISON TRICE. *An Occupation in Conflict: A Study of the Personnel Manager.* Ithaca, N.Y.: New York State School of Labor and Industrial Relations, Cornell University, 1969.

ROE, ANNE. *The Psychology of Occupations.* New York: John Wiley & Sons, Inc., 1956.

ROSOW, JEROME M., ed. *The Worker and the Job: Coping with Change.* Englewood Cliffs, N.J.: Prentice-Hall, Inc., 1974.

SCHEIN, EDGAR H. *Organizational Psychology.* Englewood Cliffs, N.J.: Prentice-Hall, Inc., 1965.

SPECIAL TASK FORCE TO THE SECRETARY OF HEALTH, EDUCATION, AND WELFARE. *Work in America.* Cambridge, Mass.: MIT Press, 1973.

STAHL, O. GLENN. *Public Personnel Administration.* 6th rev. ed. New York: Harper & Row Publishers, 1971.

STANLEY, DAVID T. *Professional Personnel for the City of New York.* Washington, D.C.: Brookings Institution, 1963.

STONE, C. HAROLD, and WILLIAM E. KENDALL. *Effective Personnel Selection Procedures.* Englewood Cliffs, N.J.: Prentice-Hall, Inc., 1956.

STRAUSS, GEORGE, and LEONARD SAYLES. *Personnel: The Human Problem of Management.* 3rd ed. Englewood Cliffs, N.J.: Prentice-Hall Inc., 1972.

SUPER, DONALD E., and JOHN D. CRITES. *Appraising Vocational Fitness.* New York: Harper & Row Publishers, 1962.

TYLER, LEONA E. *The Psychology of Human Differences.* 3rd ed. New York: Appleton-Century-Crofts, 1965.

WECHSLER, DAVID. *The Measurement and Appraisal of Adult Intelligence.* 4th rev. ed. Baltimore: The Williams & Wilkins Co., 1958.

WOOD, DOROTHY ADKINS. *Test Construction.* Columbus, Ohio: Charles E. Merrill Publishing Co., 1960.

Reports

ADVISORY COUNCIL ON INTERGOVERNMENTAL PERSONNEL POLICY. *More Effective Public Service: The First Report to the President and the Congress.* Washington, D.C.: Government Printing Office, March 1974.

———. *More Effective Public Service: A Supplementary Report to the President and the Congress.* Washington, D.C.: Government Printing Office, October 1974.

AMERICAN PSYCHOLOGICAL ASSOCIATION. *Standards for Educational and Psychological*

Tests and Measurements. Washington, D.C.: American Psychological Association, 1966.

BIDDLE, RICHARD E. *Discrimination: What Does It Mean?* Chicago: International Personnel Management Association, 1974.

BYHAM, WILLIAM C. *The Uses of Personnel Research.* New York: American Management Association, 1968.

EBEL, ROBERT L., THELMA HUNT, and DONALD R. HARVEY. *Improving Public Personnel Selection,* Personnel Report no. 635. Chicago: Public Personnel Association, n. d.

GALLAS, NESTA M. "Personnel Selection." In *A Fresh Appraisal of Basic Personnel Functions,* Personnel Report no. 654. Chicago: Public Personnel Association, n. d.

GALLAS, NESTA M., and WILLIAM H. T. SMITH. "What It Takes to Make a Professional in the Public Service," monograph 15. Philadelphia: American Academy of Political and Social Science, 1973.

GOODE, CECIL E. *Personnel Research Frontiers.* Chicago: Public Personnel Association, 1958.

GRIFFINHAGEN-KROEGER, INC. *Personnel Concepts and Practices for Modern Urban Government.* Report prepared for the Municipal Manpower Commission. San Francisco: Griffinhagen-Kroeger, Inc. 1961.

INDUSTRIAL RELATIONS COUNSELORS. *Behavioral Science Research in Industrial Relations.* New York: Industrial Relations Counselors, 1962.

MUSSIO, STEPHEN J., and MARY K. SMITH. *Content Validity: A Procedural Manual.* Chicago: International Personnel Management Association, 1973.

NATIONAL CIVIL SERVICE LEAGUE. *A Model Public Personnel Administration Law.* Washington, D.C.: National Civil Service League, 1970.

SAYRE, WALLACE C., and FREDERICK C. MOSHER. *Agenda for Research in Public Personnel Administration.* Washington, D.C.: National Planning Association, 1959.

SEBERHAGEN, LANCE W., MICHAEL D. McCOLLUM, and CONNIE D. CHURCHILL. *Legal Aspects of Personnel Selection in the Public Service.* Chicago: International Personnel Management Association, 1972.

SWEENEY, STEPHEN B., and JAMES C. CHARLESWORTH, eds. *Achieving Excellence in Public Service.* Report of a symposium sponsored by the American Academy of Political and Social Science and the American Society for Public Administration, Philadelphia, August 1963.

TAYLOR, VERNON R. *Test Validity in Personnel Selection,* Public Employment Practices Bulletin no. 2. Chicago: International Personnel Management Association, 1971.

U.S. CIVIL SERVICE COMMISSION. *How People Are Recruited, Examined and Appointed in the Competitive Civil Service.* Washington, D.C.: Government Printing Office, 1959.

7. Employee Development and Training

BENNIS, WARREN G. *Organizational Development: Its Nature, Origin, and Prospects.* Reading, Mass.: Addison-Wesley Publishing Co., 1969.

BENNIS, WARREN G., KENNETH D. BENNE, and ROBERT CHIN, eds. *The Planning of Change.* 2nd ed. New York: Holt, Rinehart and Winston, 1969.

BYERS, KENNETH, ed. *Training and Development in the Public Service.* Chicago: Public Personnel Association, 1970.

CRAIG, ROBERT L., and LESTER BITEL. *Training and Development Handbook.* New York: McGraw-Hill Book Company, 1967.

DRUCKER, PETER. *The Practice of Management.* New York: Harper & Row Publishers, 1954.

GARDNER, NEELY D. *Group Leadership.* Washington, D.C.: National Training and Development Service, 1974.

JUN, JONG S., and WILLIAM B. STORM. *Tomorrow's Organizations: Challenges and Strategies.* Glenview, Ill.: Scott, Foresman and Company, 1973.

HAGUE, HOWDON. *Executive Self-Development.* New York: John Wiley & Sons, Inc., 1974.

LIPPITT, GORDON L., LESLIE E. THIS, and ROBERT G. BIDWELL, JR., eds. *Optimizing Human Resources: Readings in Individual and Organizational Development.* Reading, Mass.: Addison-Wesley Publishing Co., 1971.

McGILL, MICHAEL E. *Action Research: Design for Training and Development.* Washington, D.C.: National Training and Development Service, 1973.

NATIONAL TRAINING AND DEVELOPMENT SERVICE. *Report and Recommendations for the California Municipal Training Service.* Washington, D.C.: National Training and Development Service, 1974.

ODIORNE, GEORGE S. *Training by Objective: An Economic Approach to Management Training.* New York: Macmillan, Inc., 1970.

SAINT, AVICE M. *Learning at Work: Human Resource and Organizational Development.* Chicago: Nelson-Hall Company, 1974.

SOLOMON, LAWRENCE, and BETTY BERZON, eds. *New Perspectives on Encounter Groups.* San Francisco: Jossey-Bass, Inc., Publishers, 1972.

TRACEY, WILLIAM R. *Managing Training and Development Systems.* New York: AMACOM, a division of American Management Association, 1974.

8. Conditions of Employment

Books and Reports

ABOUD, GRACE. *Hiring and Training the Disadvantaged for Public Employment.* Ithaca, N.Y.: New York State School of Industrial and Labor Relations, Cornell University, 1973.

ADLER, JOSEPH, and ROBERT E. DOHERTY, eds. *Employment Security in the Public Sector: A Symposium.* Ithaca, N.Y.: New York State School of Industrial and Labor Relations, Cornell University, 1974.

ADVISORY COUNCIL ON INTERGOVERNMENTAL PERSONNEL POLICY. *More Effective Public Service: The First Report to the President and the Congress.* Washington, D.C.: Government Printing Office, 1973.

CHALMERS, W. ELLISON, and GERALD W. CORMACK. *Racial Conflict and Negotiations: Perspectives and First Case Studies.* Ann Arbor, Mich.: Institute of Labor and Industrial Relations, University of Michigan, 1971.

COMMISSION ON POLITICAL ACTIVITIES OF GOVERNMENT PERSONNEL. *Report of the Commission on Political Activities of Government Personnel,* 3 vols. Washington, D.C.: Government Printing Office, 1968.

FORD, PAMELA S. *Political Activities and the Public Service: A Continuing Problem.* Berkeley, Calif.: Institute of Governmental Studies, University of California, 1963.

GALLOWAY, ROBERT W. *Public Personnel Administration: Critique and Credo.* Chicago: International Personnel Management Association, 1970.

GERHART, PAUL F. *Political Activity by Public Employee Organizations at the Local Level: Threat or Promise,* Public Employee Relations Library no. 44. Chicago: International Personnel Management Association, 1974.

GLICKMAN, ALBERT S., and ZENIA H. BROWN. *Changing Schedules of Work: Patterns and Implications.* Kalamazoo, Mich.: Upjohn Institute for Employment Research, 1974.

GRUENFELD, ELAINE F. *Promotion Practices, Policies, and Affirmative Action.* Ithaca, N.Y.: New York State School of Industrial and Labor Relations, Cornell University, 1975.

INTERNATIONAL PERSONNEL MANAGEMENT ASSOCIATION. *Guidelines for Drafting a Public Personnel Administration Law.* Chicago: International Personnel Management Association, 1973.

MILTON, CATHERINE HIGGS, et al. *Women in Policing.* Washington, D.C.: The Police Foundation, 1974.

NATIONAL CIVIL SERVICE LEAGUE. *The Disadvantaged and Government Jobs: A Bibliography.* Washington, D.C.: Manpower Press, 1973.

———. *Equal Employment Opportunity for Government Employees.* Washington, D.C.: Manpower Press, 1973.

———. National Program Center for Public Personnel Management. *Models for Affirmative Action.* Washington, D.C.: National Civil Service League, 1973.

New Jersey. Department of Civil Service. *A Model Personnel System for New Jersey County and Municipal Governments,* 1974.

Public Personnel Association. *Minority Groups and Merit System Practice,* Personnel Report no. 653. Chicago: Public Personnel Association, n. d.

Stahl, O. Glenn. *Public Personnel Administration.* 6th ed. New York: Harper & Row Publishers, 1971. See chapters 14 and 15.

Stanley, David T. *Managing Local Government under Union Pressure.* Washington, D.C.: Brookings Institution, 1972.

Weiner, Hyman J., Sheila H. Akabas, and John J. Sommer. *Mental Health Care in the World of Work.* New York: Association Press, 1973.

Walker, Nigel. *Morale in the Civil Service.* Edinburgh, Scotland: Edinburgh University Press, 1961.

Weisberger, June. *Job Security and Public Employees.* Ithaca, N.Y.: New York State School of Industrial and Labor Relations, Cornell University, 1973.

Articles

Donahue, Robert J. "Flex Time in New York." *Public Personnel Administration* 38 (July/August 1975) : 212–215.

Guyor, James R. "Spokane Learns from Experience: A Police Officer Physical Fitness Program in which Men and Women Compete Equally." *Public Personnel Administration* 38 (January/February 1974) : 10–18.

Hunt, Thelma. "Critical Issues Facing Personnel Administrators Today." *Public Personnel Management* 3 (November/December 1974) : 464–472.

Talbert, Terry L., et al. "A Study of the Police Officer Height Requirement." *Public Personnel Management* 3 (March/April 1974) : 103–110.

Walker, James, Clive Fletcher, and Donald McLeod. "Flexible Working Hours in Two British Government Offices." *Public Personnel Management* 4 (July/August 1975) : 216–222.

Wisner, Roscoe W. "The Kirkland Case: Its Implications for Personnel Selection." *Public Personnel Management* 4 (July/August 1975) : 263–267.

9. Compensation

Balderston, C. Canby. *Wage Setting Based on Job Analysis and Evaluation.* New York: Industrial Relations Counselors, 1940.

Barbour, A. W. *Principles of Salary and Wage Administration.* Washington, D.C.: National Foremen's Institute, 1949.

Belcher, David. *Wage and Salary Administration.* 2nd ed. Englewood Cliffs, N.J.: Prentice-Hall, Inc., 1962.

Douty, H. M. *Wage Structures and Administration.* Los Angeles: Institute of Industrial Relations, University of California, 1954.

Kroeger, Louis J. *A Fresh Appraisal of Basic Personnel Functions, Pay Policies, and Plans.* Chicago: Public Personnel Association, 1965.

Kroeger, Louis J., et al. *Pricing Jobs Unique to Government.* Chicago: Public Personnel Association, 1964.

Ocheltree, Keith. *How to Prepare a Sound Pay Plan.* Chicago: Public Personnel Association, 1957.

Riegel, John W. *Salary Determination.* Ann Arbor, Mich.: Bureau of Industrial Relations, University of Michigan, 1940.

Warner, Kenneth O., and J. J. Donovan, eds. *Practical Guidelines to Public Pay Administration,* 2 vols. Chicago: Public Personnel Association, 1963, 1965.

10. Labor Relations

Berrodin, Eugene. "Cross-Currents in Public Employee Bargaining." *Public Personnel Review* 29 (October 1968) : 217–220.

Boesel, Andrew W. "APT Personnel-Manpower Shortages and Recruitment Policies." In *Municipal Year Book 1968.* Washington, D.C.: International City Management Association, 1968.

Brookings Institution. Studies of Unionism in Government Series: *The Unions and the Cities,* by Harry H. Wellington and

Ralph K. Winter, Jr. (1971); *Managing Local Government under Union Pressure,* by David T. Stanley (1972); and *Public Employee Unionism: Structure, Growth, Policy,* by Jack Stieber (1973).

CHERNICK, JACK. *Collective Bargaining in New Jersey County Government.* New Brunswick, N.J.: Institute of Management–Labor Relations, Rutgers University, 1973.

DUMIT, THOMAS A. "Labor Problems in Public Employment." *Industrial Relations Law Digest* 8 (October 1966).

GILROY, THOMAS P., and ANTHONY V. SINICROPI, eds. *Collective Negotiations and Public Administration.* Iowa City, Iowa: Center for Labor and Management, University of Iowa, 1970.

HANSLOWE, KURT L. *The Emerging Law of Labor Relations in Public Employment.* Ithaca, N.Y.: New York State School of Industrial and Labor Relations, Cornell University, 1967.

HAZARD, WILLIAM R. "Teachers and Collective Bargaining: A National Dilemma." *Public Personnel Review* 28 (July 1967).

HEISEL, W. D., and J. D. HALLIHAN. *Questions and Answers on Public Employee Negotiation.* Chicago: Public Personnel Association, 1967.

KASSALOW, EVERETT A. "The Prospects for White Collar Union Growth." *Industrial Relations Law Digest* 8 (April 1966).

LEVIN, EDWARD. "A Proposal for an Integrated Labor Relations Program and Policy in Local Government." *Public Personnel Review* 29 (July 1968).

MCKERSIE, ROBERT B. "An Evaluation of Productivity Bargaining in the Public Sector." In *Collective Bargaining and Productivity.* Madison, Wisc.: Industrial Relations Research Association, 1975.

"Municipal Personnel Data." *Municipal Year-Book 1968.* Washington, D.C.: International City Management Association, 1968.

NESVIG, GORDON T. "The New Dimensions of the Strike Question." *Public Administration Review* 28 (March/April 1968).

OSWALD, RUDOLPH A. "Bargaining and Productivity in the Public Sector—A Union View." In *Collective Bargaining and Productivity.*

POSEY, ROLLIN B. "The New Militancy of Public Employees." *Public Administration Review* 28 (March/April 1968).

PRASOW, PAUL. *Scope of Bargaining in the Public Sector—Concepts and Problems.* Washington, D.C.: Government Printing Office, 1972.

Report of the Task Force on State and Local Government Labor Relations. Chicago: National Governors' Conference, 1967.

SASO, CARMEN D. "Massachusetts Local Government Goes to the Bargaining Table." *Public Personnel Review* 28 (July 1967).

SEEGER, MURRAY. "The New Frontier in Unionism." *Agenda* 6 (April 1968).

SMITH, RUSSELL A., HARRY T. EDWARDS, and R. THEODORE CLARK, JR. *Labor Relations Law in the Public Sector.* Indianapolis: Bobbs-Merrill Company, Inc., 1974.

SUTERMEISTER, ROBERT A. *People and Productivity.* New York: McGraw-Hill Book Company, 1963.

THOMPSON, ARTHUR, and IRWIN WEINSTOCK. "White-Collar Employees and the Unions at TVA." *Personnel Journal* 46 (January 1967).

"Unions' New Organizing Targets and Tactics." *Nation's Business* 56 (February 1968).

U.S. DEPARTMENT OF LABOR. BUREAU OF LABOR STATISTICS. *Employment and Earnings,* Bulletin no. 6 (1963) and no. 10 (1967). Washington, D.C.: Government Printing Office.

VOSLOO, WILLEM B. *Collective Bargaining in the United States Federal Civil Service.* Chicago: Public Personnel Association, 1966.

WARNER, KENNETH O., ed. *Collective Bargaining in the Public Service: Theory and Practice.* Chicago: Public Personnel Association, 1967. See especially Frank P. Zeidler, "Impact of Collective Bargaining on Public Administration."

WARNER, KENNETH O., and MARY L. HENNESSY. *Public Management at the Bargaining Table.* Chicago: Public Personnel Association, 1967.

ZAGORIA, SAM. "Bargaining and Productivity in the Public Sector." In *Collective Bargaining and Productivity*.

ZANDER, ARNOLD. "A Union View of Collective Bargaining in the Public Service." In *Management Relations with Organized Public Employees*. Edited by Kenneth O. Warner. Chicago: Public Personnel Association, 1963.

11. Staff Relations

BOWERS, MOLLIE H. *Labor Relations in the Public Safety Services*, Public Employee Relations Library no. 46. Chicago: International Personnel Management Association, 1974.

CIVIL SERVICE ASSEMBLY OF THE UNITED STATES AND CANADA. *Employee Relations in the Public Service*. Chicago: Civil Service Assembly of the United States and Canada, 1942.

FISHER, ROBERT W. "When Workers are Discharged: An Overview." *Monthly Labor Review* 96 (June 1973) : 4–17.

HELMS, ROBERT H., ed. *Handling Employee Grievances*, Public Employee Relations Library no. 2. Chicago: Public Personnel Association, 1968.

KOCHAN, THOMAS A. *Resolving Internal Management Conflicts for Labor Relations*, Public Employee Relations Library no. 41. Chicago: International Personnel Management Association, 1973.

MULCAHY, C. C. "Municipal Personnel Problems and Solutions." *Marquette Law Review* 56 (Spring 1973) : 529.

SASO, CARMEN D., and EARL P. TANIS. *Disciplinary Policies and Practices*, Public Employee Relations Library no. 40. Chicago: International Personnel Management Association, 1973.

SHANE, JOSEPH. "Indirect Functions of the Grievance Procedure." *Public Personnel Management* 2 (May/June 1973) : 171–178.

SPERO, STERLING D., and JOHN M. CAPOZZOLA. *The Urban Community and Its Unionized Bureaucracies: Pressure Politics in Local Government Labor Relations*. New York: Dunellen Publishing Co., 1973.

STAUDAHAR, P. D. "Changing Role of the Injunction in the Public Sector." *Labor Law Journal* 22 (May 1971) : 287.

———. "Public Employee Grievances and Arbitration: Some Unresolved Issues." *Public Personnel Review* 33 (January 1972) : 56–61.

ULLMAN, JOSEPH C., and JAMES P. BEGIN. *Negotiated Grievance Procedures in Public Employment*, Public Employee Relations Library no. 25. Chicago: Public Personnel Association, 1970.

WAUDSCHNEIDER, J. F. "Nip the Grievance in the Gripe." *Supervisory Management* 18 (June 1973) : 33–37.

WERTHER, W. B., JR. "Reducing Grievances through Effective Labor Contract Administration." *Labor Law Journal* 25 (April 1974) : 211–216.

ZEIDLER, FRANK P. *Grievance Arbitration in the Public Sector*, Public Employee Relations Library no. 38. Chicago: Public Personnel Association, 1972.

12. Motivation, Productivity, and Performance Appraisal

BALK, WALTER L. *Managing Scarce Resources in Public Agencies*. Beverly Hills, Calif.: Sage Publishing Co., 1975.

———. "Technological Trends in Productivity Measurement." *Public Personnel Management* 4 (March/April 1975) : 128–133.

———. "Why Don't Public Administrators Take Productivity More Seriously?" *Public Personnel Management* 3 (July/August 1974) : 318–324.

COSTELLO, JOHN M., and SANG M. LEE. "Needs Fulfillment and Job Satisfaction of Professionals." *Public Personnel Management* 3 (September/October 1974) : 454–461.

FIELD, HUBERT S., and WILLIAM H. HALLEY. "Performance Appraisal: An Analysis of State-Wide Practices." *Public Personnel Management* 4 (May/June 1975) : 147–150.

FOURNIES, FERDINAND F. *Management Performance Appraisal: A National Study*. Somerville, N.J.: F. F. Fournies Associates, 1974.

GOMEZ, LUIS R., and STEPHEN J. MUSSIO. "An Application of Job Enrichment in a Civil Service Setting: A Demonstration Study." *Public Personnel Management* 4 (January/February 1975) : 49–54.

HOOPER, KEN, et al. *Improving Employee Productivity: A Case Study,* Public Employee Relations Library no. 39. Chicago: International Personnel Management Association, 1973.

LIBERMAN, AARON, ROGER L. AMIDON, PAUL M. RETICH, BYRON ARBEIT, and EUGENE WILLIAMS. "Personal Evaluation: A Proposal for Employment Standards." *Public Personnel Management* 4 (July/August 1975): 248–258.

LIKERT, RENSIS. *New Patterns of Management.* New York: McGraw-Hill Book Company, 1961.

LOPEZ, FELIX M. *Evaluating Employee Perform-ance.* Chicago: Public Personnel Association, 1968.

MASLOW, ABRAHAM J. *Motivation and Personality.* New York: Harper and Brothers, 1954.

NEWLAND, CHESTER A., et al. *MBO and Productivity Bargaining in the Public Sector,* Public Employee Relations Library no. 45. Chicago: International Personnel Management Association, 1974.

STAHL, O. GLENN. *Public Personnel Administration.* 6th ed. New York: Harper & Row, Publishers, 1971. See chapters 11 and 12.

STONE, THOMAS H. "An Examination of Six Prevalent Assumptions Concerning Performance Appraisal." *Public Personnel Management* 2 (November/December 1973) : 408–414.

WALKER, NIGEL. *Morale in the Civil Service.* Edinburgh, Scotland: Edinburgh University Press, 1961.

List of Contributors

Persons who have contributed to this book are listed below with the editor first and the authors following in alphabetical order. A brief review of experience, training, and major points of interest in each person's background is presented. Since most of the contributors have published extensively, no attempt is made to provide exhaustive lists of books, monographs, articles, or other publications.

WINSTON W. CROUCH (Editor, and Chapters 1, 8, and 14) is a former chairman of the department of political science at the University of California, Los Angeles. He serves as chairman of the Personnel Commission of the Los Angeles Community College District and also served for twelve years as a member of the Los Angeles County Civil Service Commission. He is a former director of the Bureau of Governmental Research. He served as chairman of the ICMA-PPA Task Force on Labor Relations in 1969 and was a consultant to the Advisory Commission on Intergovernmental Relations. He is author of several publications, including *Employer-Employee Relations in Council-Manager Cities* and *A Guide for Modern Personnel Commissions.*

WILLIAM F. DANIELSON (Chapter 13) is personnel director for the city of Sacramento, California, and before this appointment he held a similar position with the city of Berkeley for several years. He served as president of the Municipal Personnel Officers Association for 1975. Long active in writing, speaking, and teaching about public personnel administration, he is also active in professional associations. In 1967 he presented a paper on police compensation to the President's Commission on Law Enforcement and Administration of Justice, and in 1975 he testified before the U.S. Supreme Court on behalf of public interest groups in the case of *National League of Cities*

et al. v *Dunlop,* a landmark action involving the extension of the Fair Labor Standards Act to law enforcement and fire service personnel.

CABOT DOW (Chapter 10) has served as assistant city manager of the city of Bellevue, Washington, since 1972. He also is managing partner of Cabot Dow Associates, a consulting firm specializing in labor-management relations and organization development. Since 1973 the firm has been working with public sector organizations throughout the Pacific Northwest. He has served on state advisory councils and on many occasions has represented management in collective bargaining and in grievance and interest arbitration. Since 1974 he has designed and acted as principal trainer of joint labor-management training sessions focusing on negotiations and impasse resolution. He holds a master's degree in public administration from the University of Washington.

NESTA M. GALLAS (Chapter 6) is dean of graduate studies at the John Jay College of Criminal Justice, the City University of New York. Previous teaching appointments include the New York University Graduate School of Public Administration, the University of Connecticut, the University of Hawaii, and the University of Southern California's School of Public Administration. Her public personnel administration experience has been acquired at both the state and local levels. She was personnel director of the Department of Civil Service for the city and county of Honolulu for five years. Her consulting work has included both public and private agencies, and she has served as public administration adviser in the Public Administration Division of the United Nations. She is 1976 president of the American Society for Public Administration and has been awarded honorary life membership in the International Personnel Management Association. She holds a bachelor's degree in psychology from UCLA and a master's degree and doctorate in public administration from the University of Southern California.

NEELY D. GARDNER (Chapter 7) is professor of public administration at the University of Southern California. Prior to this appointment he was deputy director of the California State Department of Water Resources, and for six years was training officer for the California State Personnel Board. He has been a consultant to several organizations in this country and abroad. He is the author of two textbooks on executive practices and organization. He holds a bachelor's degree from the University of California, Berkeley.

ROBERT C. GARNIER (Chapter 4), currently the personnel director for the city of Milwaukee, has been with the Milwaukee municipal government since 1946, serving as its first classification examiner and in 1964–65 as its first chief labor negotiator. From 1941 to 1946 he was with the Tennessee Valley Authority as personnel staff officer. He has been a member of the executive board of the International Personnel Management Association and has served as president of its Central Region. He also has been president of the Wisconsin chapter of the Industrial Relations Research Association and of the Milwaukee Area Society for Public Administration. He is a member of the administrative management committee of the American Public Works Association and is a life member of that organization. He holds a bachelor's degree from Purdue University in public service engineering.

W. DONALD HEISEL (Chapter 2) is director, Institute of Governmental Research, and adjunct professor in the department of political science, University of Cincinnati. Before joining the University of Cincinnati he served for thirteen years as personnel director for the city of Cincinnati. He has written extensively on personnel organization and public sector labor relations and has served on the task force on labor relations for the National Governors Conference, 1967–70. He is an honorary life member of the International Personnel Management Association.

THOMAS F. LEWINSOHN (Chapter 11) is personnel director for Kansas City, Missouri, and in 1974 was acting director of administration for that municipality. Before coming to Kansas City he served as senior personnel examiner with the State of Kansas Personnel Division. He has written in the fields of recruitment, examinations, and labor relations and has taught modern personnel practices at the University of Missouri at Kansas City for several years. He received a bachelor's degree in personnel and a master's degree in political science and public administration at the University of Kansas.

CHESTER A. NEWLAND (Chapter 12) is director of the Federal Executive Institute, U.S. Civil Service Commission. Prior to this appointment he was a staff member of the Lyndon B. Johnson Library in Austin, Texas, and professor of public administration at both the University of Southern California and the University of Houston. He holds a doctorate in political science from the University of Kansas. His publications have appeared in the fields of city government, public employee unionism, and productivity.

J. DAVID PALMER (Chapter 5) is associate professor of political science at Georgia State University, Atlanta. He has been a member of the faculties of the University of South Carolina and the University of Texas. He was a National Association of Schools of Public Affairs and Administration (NASPAA) fellow and program officer in the Office of Personnel, U.S. Department of Housing and Urban Development, and has been a consultant to the U.S. Civil Service Commission in both the Atlanta regional and Washington, D.C., offices. He has written several articles on personnel and on city and county government. In 1972 he was awarded a special certificate of achievement by HUD for his work in developing and implementing intergovernmental personnel programs for the department. He holds a doctorate from the University of Texas at Austin.

Jerome S. Sanderson (Chapter 9) is personnel director of the Personnel Commission of the Los Angeles Community College District. He has served with the Los Angeles Unified School District Personnel Commission and the federal government. He is a past president of the Southern California Personnel Management Association and is currently a member of the editorial advisory board of *Public Personnel Management*. He holds a master's degree in public administration from the School of Public Administration at the University of Southern California.

William E. Stipek (Chapter 11) is chief of classification and pay in the personnel department of Kansas City, Missouri. His previous experience includes service as director of employee relations for the Ohio Civil Service Employees Association. He holds a bachelor of science degree in business administration from Ohio State University and has done graduate work in industrial relations at Cleveland State University.

Frederick W. Zuercher (Chapter 3) is associate professor of government at the University of South Dakota, where he also directs the Master of Public Administration degree program. He held a fellowship from the National Association of Schools of Public Affairs and Administration (NASPAA) with the U.S. Civil Service Commission in Washington, D.C., and served an additional summer appointment with the commission. He holds a doctorate in political science from the University of California, Los Angeles.

Index

Page numbers in italics refer to illustrations.

N

MUNICIPAL MANAGEMENT SERIES

Local Government
Personnel Administration

TEXT TYPE:
Linotype Baskerville

COMPOSITION, PRINTING, AND BINDING:
Kingsport Press, Kingsport, Tennessee

PAPER:
Allied Publishers Superior Offset

PRODUCTION:
David S. Arnold, Dorothy Caeser, Richard R.
Herbert, and Carla Lofberg Valenta

DESIGN:
Herbert Slobin